Teachers' Roles and Perspectives on AI Integration in Schools

Eriona Çela
University of New York, Tirana, Albania

Narasimha Rao Vajjhala
University of New York, Tirana, Albania

Mathias Mbu Fonkam
Pennsylvania State University, USA

IGI Global
Scientific Publishing
Publishing Tomorrow's Research Today

Vice President of Editorial	Melissa Wagner
Managing Editor of Acquisitions	Mikaela Felty
Managing Editor of Book Development	Jocelynn Hessler
Production Manager	Mike Brehm
Cover Design	Phillip Shickler

Published in the United States of America by
IGI Global Scientific Publishing
701 East Chocolate Avenue
Hershey, PA, 17033, USA
Tel: 717-533-8845
Fax: 717-533-8661
E-mail: cust@igi-global.com
Website: https://www.igi-global.com

Library of Congress Cataloging-in-Publication Data

Names: Çela, Eriona, 1992- editor. | Vajjhala, Narasimha, 1978- editor. | Fonkam, Mathias Mbu, 1964- editor.
Title: Teacher's roles and perspectives on AI integration in schools / edited by Eriona Çela, Narasimha Rao Vajjhala, Mathias Fonkam.
Description: Hershey, PA : IGI Global Scientific Publishing, [2025] | Includes bibliographical references and index. | Summary: "The chapters in this book highlight the diverse ways AI can enhance educational outcomes while emphasizing the critical role teachers play in ensuring its responsible implementation. From empowering educators to leverage AI for personalized learning to fostering inclusivity and addressing infrastructural gaps, this book serves as a vital resource for teachers, policymakers, and researchers seeking to navigate the complexities of AI integration"-- Provided by publisher.
Identifiers: LCCN 2024056993 (print) | LCCN 2024056994 (ebook) | ISBN 9798337310176 (hardcover) | ISBN 9798337310183 (paperback) | ISBN 9798337310190 (ebook)
Subjects: LCSH: Artificial intelligence--Educational innovations. | Teachers--Training of.
Classification: LCC LB1028.43 .T4144 2025 (print) | LCC LB1028.43 (ebook) | DDC 370.78/563--dc23/eng/20241227
LC record available at https://lccn.loc.gov/2024056993
LC ebook record available at https://lccn.loc.gov/2024056994

British Cataloguing in Publication Data
A Cataloguing in Publication record for this book is available from the British Library.

Dr. Eriona Çela

I would like to extend my heartfelt gratitude to my family. Its unwavering support and belief in me have been my guiding light throughout this journey. Thank you for standing by me, for your patience, and for always reminding me of the importance of this work. I am truly fortunate to have you in my life.

Assoc. Prof. Narasimha Rao Vajjhala

I want to thank my family members, particularly my mother, Mrs. Rajeswari Vajjhala, for her blessings and for instilling in me the virtues of perseverance and commitment.

Assoc. Prof. Mathias Fonkam

I would like to express my sincere gratitude to my beloved wife Antonia and our 2 younger ones – my 10-year old princess, Noella, and my 8-year old son, Asobo, for their endless love, patience, understanding and support as I have had to steal time off the dad schedule for this and other work. I also owe much gratitude to the many in this field who have structured and charted the course and on whose shoulders we mostly stand.

Editorial Advisory Board

Table of Contents

Detailed Table of Contents

This chapter examines the transformative role of next-generation artificial intelligence (AI) in education, reshaping traditional learning environments and challenging educators to redefine their professional roles. This chapter discusses how AI enhances educational practices by enabling personalized instruction, supporting data-driven decision-making, and streamlining classroom management, thus improving the efficiency and effectiveness of teaching. The chapter also addresses the pedagogical shifts, ongoing professional development, and ethical considerations necessary for educators to integrate AI into the classroom successfully. By offering strategies for AI integration and highlighting the vital role of teachers in this evolving educational landscape, this chapter seeks to equip educators with the tools and insights to confidently and innovatively embrace the future of teaching.

The COVID-19 crisis disrupted traditional in-school teaching, highlighting both the potential and challenges of distance learning. The abrupt transition exposed the unpreparedness of many teachers and students, emphasizing the need for alternative, technology-supported methodologies. This chapter investigates blended education as an innovative approach integrating classroom and online learning to enhance teaching effectiveness. Through a theoretical examination of blended education and a survey of middle school teachers in Albania, this study evaluates teachers' familiarity with and use of blended learning methods. Data collected from 212 educational stakeholders provide insights into the current state of ICT-supported teaching in Albania. The findings suggest that, while blended learning holds promise for improving educational outcomes, Albanian teachers require further training, and substantial upgrades in ICT infrastructure are necessary to implement this approach in schools fully.

Generative artificial intelligence (AI) is transforming the landscape of educator professional development by offering tools that facilitate personalized learning and efficiency in training. This chapter explores the various applications of AI in professional development, including using AI as a coaching tool, an instructional evaluator, and a content creator. This chapter highlights how AI can streamline tasks like creating lesson plans, analyzing teaching effectiveness, and supporting new teachers. Additionally, the chapter discusses ethical considerations, challenges, and best practices to ensure the responsible integration of AI into professional development, ultimately aiming to enhance teaching effectiveness and student outcomes.

This chapter explores the transformative impact of artificial intelligence (AI) on the roles and responsibilities of school leaders in Morocco, encompassing principals, teachers, and administrators. Drawing on data from 106 schools gathered through interviews and questionnaires, the study evaluates hypotheses concerning AI's influence on school management. Findings indicate that AI tools significantly reduce principals' administrative workload, enabling a stronger focus on pedagogical leadership. Additionally, AI redefines teachers as facilitators of learning, redirects administrators toward strategic tasks, and enhances collaboration between educators and administrators by providing precise insights into student performance. The integration of AI further shifts school leaders' perceptions, encouraging a data-driven approach to management practices. Statistical analysis reveals strong, positive correlations between AI adoption and evolving roles and responsibilities, underscoring the transformative potential of AI in educational leadership.

This chapter explores the transformative impact of artificial intelligence (AI) on curriculum design and course management in education. AI-driven systems enable instructors to tailor learning experiences to students' individual needs, learning styles, and progress, enhancing engagement and support through real-time feedback, intelligent tutoring, and data-driven assessments. By automating administrative tasks like grading and scheduling, AI allows teachers to devote more time to instruction and mentoring. However, integrating AI in education raises ethical considerations, particularly regarding data privacy, security, and algorithmic bias. This chapter emphasizes the importance of transparent data practices to protect student information and ensure fairness in AI applications. While AI enhances educational processes, it cannot replace the guidance, empathy, and critical thinking skills that human educators bring. Ultimately, AI complements human instruction, creating a more inclusive, efficient, and adaptable learning environment for all students.

This chapter explores the use of ChatGPT, an artificial intelligence tool that rapidly processes user inputs, offering valuable support for educational tasks. Given the growing integration of AI in education, it is essential for pre-service teachers—who will be future educators—to understand and utilize ChatGPT effectively, adhering to ethical guidelines for professional development. The study investigates how pre-service chemistry teachers design lesson plans with the aid of ChatGPT and gathers their reflections on these experiences. Six pre-service chemistry teachers participated, each creating a lesson plan by giving specific commands to ChatGPT. These lesson plans focused on chemistry curriculum objectives and aimed to develop a chosen type of intelligence from the theory of multiple intelligences. Following the lesson plan development, semi-structured interviews were conducted to capture participants' insights into their experiences.

This chapter explores the innovative use of digital storytelling as an AI-enhanced teaching strategy to engage learners and foster a deeper willingness to learn. Digital storytelling, the art of creating online narratives for social media, combines visual elements and storytelling techniques to captivate and motivate students. By developing a collection of twenty digitally accessible moral stories, paired with original artwork, the authors demonstrate how AI can be leveraged to create engaging and meaningful educational content. The chapter examines how stories rooted in real-life experiences can teach valuable lessons, integrating AI to adapt content for dynamic learning environments. Furthermore, AI in education aids academic decision-making across course development, pedagogical design, and institutional transformation. Through AI-based digital storytelling, this approach benefits instructors, learners, and administrators alike, presenting new opportunities for growth and innovation in higher education.

The emergence of Artificial Intelligence (AI) offers transformative possibilities for media education, particularly as traditional teaching methods struggle to keep pace with the rapidly evolving digital media landscape. This chapter examines the potential of AI to enrich media education by enabling personalized learning experiences, fostering creativity and innovation, and enhancing critical thinking and media literacy. Using a qualitative research approach that includes a literature review, expert interviews, and case studies, this chapter identifies the primary applications of AI in media education, evaluates its impact on student learning, addresses ethical considerations, and provides practical recommendations for effective AI integration. By understanding both the opportunities and challenges of AI in media education, we can better equip students to meet the complex demands of the digital age.

This chapter examines professors' perspectives on using risk-free artificial intelligence (AI) in higher education classrooms, focusing on the perceived benefits, challenges, and ethical considerations surrounding AI implementation. Researchers gathered insights into professors' experiences and viewpoints on integrating AI into educational settings through a qualitative study using a survey method, semi-structured interviews, and questionnaires. The findings reveal that while AI offers substantial opportunities for enhancing teaching and learning, it also brings notable challenges and ethical concerns. Based on these insights, the chapter recommends best practices to ensure the responsible and effective use of AI tools in higher education.

In today's increasingly diverse educational landscape, culturally responsive literacy practices are not just beneficial—they are essential. This chapter examines strategies for creating literacy ecosystems that honor and reflect learners' cultural, experiential, and linguistic diversity. We argue that adopting a culturally responsive approach strengthens literacy skills, validates students' identities, and promotes social equity. The chapter begins with exploring the theoretical foundations of culturally responsive literacy, emphasizing the importance of recognizing and valuing students' cultural wealth. Following this, a comprehensive framework is provided for building a culturally responsive literacy ecosystem, covering curriculum design, instructional methods, assessment strategies, and classroom management. Ultimately, we demonstrate how these practices foster inclusive environments that empower all learners and encourage active, meaningful engagement with literacy.

Foreword

The rapid advancements in artificial intelligence (AI) are reshaping countless industries, and education is no exception. The integration of AI in schools is not merely a technological innovation but a paradigm shift that challenges traditional teaching practices and redefines the role of educators. This book, *Teachers' Roles and Perspectives on AI Integration in Schools*, is a timely exploration of this transformative moment, providing educators, policymakers, and researchers with an invaluable roadmap for navigating the intersection of AI and education. AI's potential in education is vast, from personalized learning experiences and intelligent tutoring systems to automated administrative tasks that allow educators to focus more on teaching. However, these advancements bring new responsibilities for teachers. They are no longer just subject matter experts; they are facilitators, collaborators with technology, and, most importantly, advocates for ethical and equitable practices in their classrooms. This book recognizes the multifaceted role teachers play in ensuring that AI integration enhances, rather than diminishes, the human connections central to learning.

One of the strengths of this book is its global perspective. The chapters draw from diverse educational contexts, offering insights into how teachers in different regions are embracing AI and addressing its challenges. Whether examining the infrastructural gaps in developing countries or highlighting innovative uses of AI in advanced educational systems, the book provides a comprehensive view of AI's impact on education worldwide. It reminds us that while technology is a global phenomenon, its implementation must consider the local cultural, economic, and social contexts. Another key focus of this book is professional development. Teachers are expected to integrate AI into their classrooms effectively, yet many lack the training and resources to do so. This book emphasizes the importance of continuous professional development to equip educators with the skills and confidence to use AI tools effectively. It advocates for collaborative learning among teachers, administrators, and technologists to create an ecosystem where AI is a tool for empowerment, not a source of intimidation. Ethics and equity are central themes throughout this book. The authors address the ethical dilemmas AI poses, such as data privacy, algorithmic bias, and the potential for widening educational inequalities. By providing frameworks and strategies for ethical AI implementation, the book ensures that teachers can use technology responsibly and advocate for policies that prioritize students' rights and well-being. These discussions are not just theoretical; they are practical and actionable, giving educators the tools to navigate complex ethical landscapes confidently.

The book also explores the evolving relationship between AI and pedagogy. Teachers are learning to harness AI for innovative instructional strategies, from generative AI tools that support lesson planning to AI-driven platforms that facilitate real-time student feedback. The examples in this book illustrate how AI can complement human instruction, enabling educators to focus on higher-order teaching tasks that foster creativity, critical thinking, and collaboration among students. Leadership in AI integration is another critical theme. School leaders and administrators play a pivotal role in setting the vision for how AI is used in education. This book provides valuable insights into the leadership styles and strategies necessary for fostering a culture of innovation and collaboration. By highlighting case studies of successful AI implementation in schools, it inspires leaders to think strategically about the long-term impact of technology on their institutions.

As we stand on the brink of an AI-driven educational future, it is clear that teachers are not just participants in this transformation—they are the architects of it. This book celebrates the creativity, resilience, and dedication of educators who are embracing AI as an opportunity to enhance their teaching practices and better serve their students. It is a testament to the vital role teachers play in shaping the next generation of learners. This book is more than a guide; it is a call to action. It urges educators to engage with AI critically, creatively, and collaboratively. By fostering dialogue among teachers, researchers, and policymakers, it lays the foundation for a future where AI and human ingenuity work in harmony to create more inclusive and effective learning environments. As you embark on this journey through the pages of *Teachers' Roles and Perspectives on AI Integration in Schools*, I invite you to reflect on the transformative potential of AI in education and the pivotal role you, as educators and leaders, play in shaping its trajectory. May this book inspire you to embrace the opportunities and challenges of AI with curiosity, courage, and a commitment to the principles that define quality education.

Vasileios Paliktzoglou

Bahrain Polytechnic, Bahrain

Vasileios Paliktzoglou, an academic and industry professional, holds a Ph.D. in Computer Science from the University of Eastern Finland. He is an active contributor to academia, serving as a guest and associate editor for prestigious journals like the Journal of Information Systems Education (JISE) and IAFOR Journal of Education. He has been a keynote speaker at several academic and industry events, sharing his insights on social computing, collaborative learning, and emerging technologies in higher education. Dr. Paliktzoglou also actively participates in international research projects, highlighting his commitment to advancing knowledge and innovation as the Book Series Editor for the "Emerging Technologies in Education" at Vernon Press and "AI and Education" at STAR Scholars Press. His expertise continues to shape the academic and research landscape at Bahrain Polytechnic

Preface

INTRODUCTION

Artificial intelligence (AI) is rapidly transforming the educational landscape, introducing innovative tools and methodologies that redefine the roles of teachers in modern classrooms. As technology continues to evolve, educators are faced with both unprecedented opportunities and challenges in integrating AI into their teaching practices. This book, Teacher's Roles and Perspectives on AI Integration in Schools, provides a comprehensive exploration of how educators are adapting to and shaping this paradigm shift. This book examines the implications of AI on curriculum design, classroom management, professional development, and the ethical considerations that come with its adoption, offering a nuanced view of the evolving relationship between technology and education.

Through case studies, empirical research, and practical frameworks, the chapters in this book highlight the diverse ways AI can enhance educational outcomes while emphasizing the critical role teachers play in ensuring its responsible implementation. From empowering educators to leverage AI for personalized learning to fostering inclusivity and addressing infrastructural gaps, this book serves as a vital resource for teachers, policymakers, and researchers seeking to navigate the complexities of AI integration. By capturing the voices and experiences of educators from various cultural and educational contexts, it aims to inspire innovative approaches to teaching and learning in an AI-driven era.

Chapter Overview

In Chapter 1 - Empowering Educators in the Era of Next-Generation AI: Redefining the Teacher's Role in an AI-Enhanced Learning Environment, Goh Ying Yingsoon, Suyan Zhang, and Nurul Ain Chua examine the transformative impact of next-generation artificial intelligence (AI) on education and the evolving role of educators. The chapter discusses how AI facilitates personalized instruction, supports data-driven decision-making, streamlines classroom management, enhancing teaching efficiency and effectiveness. It addresses the pedagogical shifts, professional development, and ethical considerations educators need to navigate to integrate AI into classrooms effectively. By providing strategies for AI integration and emphasizing the vital role teachers play, this chapter equips educators with the insights and tools to embrace AI confidently and innovatively, fostering inclusive and engaging learning environments.

In Chapter 2 - Blended Education and the Role of Albanian Teachers in an AI-Enhanced Educational Landscape, Dhurata Lamçja and Salvina Pellumbi investigate the impact of blended education on teaching practices in Albania, particularly how teachers are adapting to a technology-enhanced educational environment post-COVID-19. This chapter analyzes responses from a survey of 212 middle school teachers, examining their familiarity with blended learning methods and the extent of technology integration in classrooms. Findings indicate that while blended learning shows promise for enhancing educational outcomes, Albanian teachers face challenges related to ICT infrastructure and a need for further training. The study underscores the role of Albanian teachers in advancing blended education and highlights the importance of investment in technology and professional development to fully realize the potential of AI in education. This chapter offers insights for policymakers and educators, advocating for a supportive framework that addresses these foundational needs to foster a more adaptive and resilient educational system in Albania.

In Chapter 3 - Harnessing Generative AI for Educator Professional Development, Steven M. Baule and Jordan S. O'Connell examine the transformative impact of generative artificial intelligence (AI) on professional development for educators. This chapter explores various AI applications in enhancing educator training, including using AI as a coaching tool, an instructional evaluator, and a content creator. The authors highlight how AI can streamline tasks like lesson planning, evaluating teaching effectiveness, and supporting new teachers, while also addressing challenges related to ethical considerations, data privacy, and algorithmic bias. This comprehensive discussion offers educators and administrators insights into leveraging AI to foster personalized, efficient, and responsible professional development strategies aimed at improving teaching quality and student outcomes.

In Chapter 4 - The Impact of Artificial Intelligence on Leadership Styles in Schools in Morocco, Ahmed El Hammoumi and Mohamed El Hammoumi explore how artificial intelligence (AI) transforms the roles and responsibilities of school leaders, including principals, teachers, and administrators. Based on data from 106 Moroccan schools collected through interviews and questionnaires, the chapter evaluates AI's influence on school management. Findings reveal that AI significantly reduces principals' administrative workload, enabling a stronger focus on pedagogical leadership. Teachers transition into facilitators of learning, administrators assume more strategic tasks, and data-driven management becomes prevalent. Additionally, AI enhances collaboration by providing precise insights into student performance. This chapter offers valuable insights for decision-makers in Moroccan education on the transformative potential of AI, emphasizing the shift toward efficient, collaborative, and data-informed leadership practices.

In Chapter 5 - Infrastructure and Investment Needs for AI Implementation in Education, Karima Toumi Sayari examines the critical infrastructure and investment frameworks necessary for integrating artificial intelligence (AI) into educational systems. The chapter addresses the physical, technological, and human resources required to implement AI across various educational levels, highlighting disparities in infrastructure between urban and rural areas, as well as between developed and developing regions. Key topics include the scalability of AI solutions, personnel training, technological readiness, and long-term funding. Sayari provides evidence-based recommendations for policymakers, administrators, and investors to optimize resource allocation, aiming to promote equitable and sustainable AI adoption in education. This chapter offers valuable insights into bridging infrastructure gaps and ensuring that AI enhances educational outcomes across diverse settings.

In Chapter 6 - A Framework for the Responsible Integration of Generative AI Tools in Learning, Stephen Ko and Simon C. H. Chan present a comprehensive framework for the ethical and effective use of generative AI (Gen-AI) in educational settings. This chapter discusses the potential of Gen-AI for content creation and personalized learning experiences while addressing challenges such as biases, dependency, and ethical concerns. The proposed framework provides educators, technologists, policymakers, and students with proactive guidelines to navigate these complexities. By prioritizing ethical use and accountability, this chapter equips stakeholders to integrate Gen-AI in ways that enhance student learning outcomes, fostering equitable and responsible AI adoption in education.

In Chapter 7 - AI-Driven Curriculum Design and Course Management, Andi Asrifan, Ashabul Kahfi Susanto, Elpisah Elpisah, Syamsuardi Saodi, and Herlina Herlina explore the transformative impact of artificial intelligence (AI) on curriculum design and course management in education. The chapter emphasizes how AI-driven systems can personalize learning experiences by adapting to individual student needs, enhancing engagement through real-time feedback, intelligent tutoring, and data-driven assessments. AI also automates administrative tasks, freeing educators to focus on teaching and mentoring. Ethical considerations, such as data privacy, security, and algorithmic bias, are also discussed, underscoring the need for transparent data practices to protect student information and promote fairness.

This chapter provides valuable insights into how AI complements human instruction, creating a more inclusive, efficient, and adaptable learning environment.

In Chapter 8 - Investigating Pre-Service Chemistry Teachers' Experiences in Designing Lesson Plans Using ChatGPT, Nagihan Kadıoğlu and Özge Özyalçın Oskay explore how pre-service chemistry teachers utilize ChatGPT as a tool for lesson plan design. This chapter examines the experiences of six pre-service teachers, who, with no prior AI experience, created lesson plans aligned with national chemistry curriculum objectives and targeted specific types of intelligence from the multiple intelligence theory. Through detailed content analysis of their interactions with ChatGPT and subsequent interviews, the authors highlight both the benefits and challenges these future educators encountered. Key factors influencing their experiences include prompt engineering, ethical considerations, and the necessity of informed use. The study provides insights into the potential of AI to support lesson planning, emphasizing the importance of AI literacy in teacher education to effectively integrate such tools into classroom practices while safeguarding educational standards and ethical principles.

In Chapter 9 - Short Digital Storytelling: An AI-Based Innovative Teaching Strategy, Subhasis Sen and Indrani Sen explore the use of AI-enhanced digital storytelling as a method to engage learners and deepen their motivation to learn. This chapter presents digital storytelling as a versatile educational tool that combines visual elements with storytelling techniques to create compelling narratives that resonate with students. Through a collection of twenty digitally accessible moral stories paired with original artwork, the authors illustrate how AI can be leveraged to create immersive and meaningful educational experiences. The chapter addresses how AI-driven storytelling can support academic decision-making in course development, pedagogical design, and institutional transformation. Additionally, it highlights challenges such as data privacy and the ethical implications of using AI in educational content creation. This chapter offers educators, learners, and administrators insights into harnessing AI for enhanced engagement and growth, advocating for the thoughtful integration of AI-based storytelling in modern education.

In Chapter 10 - Integrating Artificial Intelligence in Media Education: Revolutionizing Learning, Creativity, and Critical Thinking, Amaresh Jha and Sanjeev Ratna Singh explore the transformative role of artificial intelligence (AI) in media education. This chapter examines how AI can enrich media education by enabling personalized learning experiences, fostering creativity, and enhancing critical thinking and media literacy. Through a qualitative approach involving literature review, expert interviews, and case studies, the authors identify key applications of AI, such as personalized tutoring, automated content creation, and advanced data analysis. Ethical considerations, including data privacy and bias, are also addressed, alongside practical recommendations for integrating AI responsibly in media programs.

This chapter provides valuable insights for educators and policymakers, advocating for AI-driven innovations that prepare students for the dynamic challenges of the digital media landscape.

In Chapter 11 - Using Risk-Free Artificial Intelligence in the Classroom: Insights from Higher Education Professors, Ankur Nandi, Tapash Das, Tarini Halder, and Santu Karmakar examine professors' perspectives on adopting risk-free AI in higher education. This chapter highlights the benefits and challenges of AI integration in classrooms, alongside ethical considerations such as data privacy and algorithmic bias. Through a qualitative study involving surveys and interviews, the authors capture educators' insights on using AI to enhance teaching and learning, while recommending best practices to ensure responsible AI usage. These recommendations offer a comprehensive framework for educators and institutions aiming to integrate AI in a manner that supports learning outcomes and ethical standards.

In Chapter 12 - Fostering Inclusivity and Empowerment: Crafting Culturally Responsive Literacy Ecosystems, Goh Ying Yingsoon, Suyan Zhang, Nurul Ain Chua, and Yiming Chen examine strategies to create literacy ecosystems that reflect and honor the cultural, linguistic, and experiential diversity of learners. This chapter highlights the theoretical foundations of culturally responsive literacy, underscoring the importance of recognizing students' cultural wealth and promoting social equity. The authors provide a comprehensive framework for designing inclusive literacy ecosystems, focusing on curriculum, instructional methods, assessment strategies, and classroom management. Through practical examples and country-specific insights, particularly from the Malaysian educational context, the chapter demonstrates how culturally responsive practices can enhance student engagement, foster identity validation, and support social justice in education. This approach equips educators with tools to create empowering environments that encourage active, meaningful literacy engagement across diverse student populations.

In Chapter 13 - Integrating Artificial Intelligence to Foster Inclusivity in Social Work and Community Development Education: A Transatlantic Online Collaboration, Jennifer Lanham and Garreth Smith explore how AI can transform social work and community development education by fostering inclusivity. This chapter examines a collaborative project between Campbellsville University in the USA and Technological University Dublin in Ireland, focusing on AI-driven, competency-based educational frameworks that align with the Council on Social Work Education and All-Ireland Standards for Community Work Education. These frameworks emphasize anti-racism, diversity, equity, and inclusion (ADEI), aiming to create nurturing and inclusive learning environments. Through a mix of collaborative platforms and ethical AI integration, this chapter addresses the impact of AI on student engagement and ADEI principles in social work education, offering insights for educators and administrators on effectively using AI to build diverse, inclusive learning communities that prepare students for global social and community work practices.

As education enters an era increasingly defined by artificial intelligence (AI), teachers stand at the forefront of this transformation, navigating new technologies while continuing to nurture the human aspects of learning. This book underscores the indispensable role of educators in ensuring that AI serves as a tool to enhance, rather than replace, the invaluable interpersonal connections central to teaching. By addressing the practical, ethical, and professional dimensions of AI integration, it empowers educators to embrace change confidently and critically, fostering environments that balance technological innovation with empathy and inclusivity. The chapters in this book highlight a critical truth: successful AI integration depends on teachers' ability to adapt and lead with purpose. Whether leveraging AI for personalized instruction, streamlining administrative tasks, or designing culturally responsive curricula, the examples presented emphasize the need for professional development, collaboration, and access to robust infrastructure. These elements are vital for equipping educators to use AI not only as a tool for efficiency but also as a catalyst for creativity and growth in their classrooms.

At the same time, this book calls attention to the ethical considerations surrounding AI in education, including issues of data privacy, algorithmic bias, and equitable access. Teachers must remain vigilant advocates for their students, ensuring that AI implementation upholds principles of fairness, transparency, and inclusivity. By engaging with these challenges thoughtfully, educators can help shape a future where technology enhances learning outcomes while safeguarding the values that define quality education. This preface invites educators, policymakers, and researchers to view AI as an opportunity to reimagine and strengthen educational practices. It encourages a collaborative approach to harness the potential of AI while addressing its limitations. As readers embark on the journey through the chapters that follow, may they find inspiration, insights, and actionable strategies to navigate the exciting yet complex intersection of education and AI with confidence and foresight.

Eriona Çela
University of New York Tirana, Albania

Narasimha Rao Vajjhala
University of New York Tirana, Albania

Mathias Mbu Fonkam
Penn State University, USA

Chapter 1
Empowering Educators in the Era of Next-Generation AI:
Redefining the Teacher's Role in an AI-Enhanced Learning Environment

Goh Ying Yingsoon
https://orcid.org/0000-0002-6654-2887
MARA University of Technology, Malaysia

Suyan Zhang
https://orcid.org/0009-0003-4518-1650
Shandong Jianzhu University, China

Nurul Ain Chua
https://orcid.org/0000-0003-2915-1577
Universiti Malaysia Terengganu, Malaysia

ABSTRACT

This chapter examines the transformative role of next-generation artificial intelligence (AI) in education, reshaping traditional learning environments and challenging educators to redefine their professional roles. This chapter discusses how AI enhances educational practices by enabling personalized instruction, supporting data-driven decision-making, and streamlining classroom management, thus improving the efficiency and effectiveness of teaching. The chapter also addresses the pedagogical shifts, ongoing professional development, and ethical considerations necessary for educators to integrate AI into the classroom successfully. By offering strategies for

DOI: 10.4018/979-8-3373-1017-6.ch001

AI integration and highlighting the vital role of teachers in this evolving educational landscape, this chapter seeks to equip educators with the tools and insights to confidently and innovatively embrace the future of teaching.

INTRODUCTION

The integration of Artificial Intelligence (AI) in education is rapidly accelerating, transforming traditional teaching methods and reshaping the educational landscape. As AI technologies become more sophisticated, they are being leveraged to personalize learning experiences, analyze student data for tailored interventions, and automate administrative tasks, thereby enhancing both the efficiency and effectiveness of educational processes. This shift is driving a paradigm change in how educators interact with students, how content is delivered, and how learning outcomes are assessed, leading to a more dynamic and adaptive educational system that aims to cater to the individual needs of each learner (Zhai, et al, 2021; Zhang, et al, 2021; Williamson, & Eynon, 2020). The integration of AI in education is heralding a revolution that is redefining the very fabric of teaching and learning. This technological leap is not merely an incremental advancement but a fundamental transformation that is challenging the conventions of traditional educational systems. The advent of AI has introduced a wave of innovation, enabling educators to tailor their teaching methods to the unique needs of each student. As the educational landscape evolves, the role of AI is becoming increasingly pivotal in enhancing both the efficiency and the quality of education delivered.

Moreover, the application of AI in educational settings is not limited to personalization; it also extends to the automation of administrative tasks. AI-driven systems can handle routine chores such as grading, scheduling, and record-keeping, thereby liberating educators to focus on more meaningful and impactful activities, such as mentorship and curriculum development. The increasing diversity in educational landscapes is another area where AI is making a profound impact. Educational institutions are now more varied than ever, catering to students from different cultural, linguistic, and socio-economic backgrounds. AI technologies are adept at bridging language barriers, providing real-time translation, and adapting to cultural nuances, thereby creating an inclusive learning environment. This is not merely a matter of convenience but a critical step towards democratizing education and ensuring that every student, regardless of their background, has an equal opportunity to succeed. Furthermore, the assessment of learning outcomes is undergoing a significant shift with the integration of AI. Traditional standardized tests are being complemented, and in some cases replaced, by continuous and formative assessments that AI can perform in real-time. This approach not only provides a more accurate picture of a student's progress but also allows for timely interventions, which can significantly improve learning outcomes.

In Malaysia, the integration of AI in education is gaining momentum as the government recognizes the potential of these technologies to enhance the quality and accessibility of education across the nation. The Ministry of Education has initiated various programs aimed at incorporating AI into the curriculum, starting from primary schools to higher education institutions. Initiatives such as smart classrooms, AI-driven learning platforms, and data analytics for student performance are being piloted in selected schools and universities. Despite the initial challenges of infrastructure and teacher training, Malaysia is committed to developing a workforce that is proficient in AI and its applications. The country is also fostering partnerships with private sector leaders in technology to ensure that the educational system remains competitive and relevant in the global arena. This proactive approach to AI integration is expected to not only improve learning outcomes but also to prepare Malaysian students for the future job market, which is increasingly reliant on digital skills and innovation (Hashim, et al, 2022). The fusion of AI with education is more than a passing trend; it represents a seismic shift in how we conceptualize and deliver learning. As we continue to refine AI technologies and integrate them more deeply into educational systems, we are not only optimizing the processes but also setting the stage for a future where education is universally accessible, deeply personalized, and inherently supportive of each learner's journey.

The advent of AI-enhanced learning environments necessitates a fundamental transformation in the role of educators. As AI assumes a more prominent role in curriculum delivery, assessment, and personalized learning, teachers must adapt their practices to incorporate these technologies effectively. This requires developing new skills in AI integration, data interpretation, and digital pedagogy, as well as fostering a mindset open to innovation and change. Educators must navigate this shift to not only maintain their relevance but also to harness the full potential of AI to enrich the educational experience, support diverse learning styles, and prepare students for a future where AI is an integral part of society (Meng, et al, 2022; Novawan, et al, 2024; Elimadi, et al, 2024).

In AI-enhanced education, the need for educators to adapt is not merely a professional imperative but a critical factor in ensuring the continued success of their students. As AI tools become more sophisticated, educators must serve as the bridge between technology and the human elements of learning, such as motivation, emotional intelligence, and ethical reasoning. This means engaging in continuous professional development to stay ahead of technological advancements and to understand how to integrate AI in ways that complement and enhance their teaching. By embracing this transformation, educators can become architects of learning experiences that blend the best of human interaction with the precision and adaptability of AI, creating a synergistic educational ecosystem that is both supportive and future-focused. This collaborative approach between educators and AI has the potential to redefine the landscape of education, fostering a generation of learners who are not only proficient in technology but also equipped with the skills to navigate and shape a future defined by human-AI collaboration (Meng, et al, 2022).

The primary objective of this chapter is to thoroughly examine the multifaceted impact of AI on contemporary educational practices, with a specific focus on the evolving role of teachers. By delving into how AI is redefining teaching methodologies, classroom dynamics, and the teacher's responsibilities, the chapter aims to provide a comprehensive understanding of the challenges and opportunities that AI presents. It seeks to illuminate the ways in which educators can effectively integrate AI into their teaching to enhance student learning outcomes while also addressing the necessary professional development and ethical considerations that accompany this technological shift.

REVIEW OF LITERATURE

Adaptive Learning Platforms

The impact of AI on educational practices is most pronounced in the realm of personalized instruction, where adaptive learning platforms are revolutionizing the way content is delivered and consumed. These platforms leverage AI algorithms to analyze individual student performance and learning styles, dynamically adjusting the curriculum and pace of instruction to meet each learner's specific needs. This level of customization not only supports students in mastering concepts at their own speed but also identifies and addresses knowledge gaps in real time, thereby enhancing the overall learning experience and outcomes.

The transformative influence of Artificial Intelligence (AI) on educational methodologies is most acutely observed in the domain of personalized instruction. Adaptive learning platforms, powered by sophisticated AI algorithms, are fundamentally altering the landscape of content delivery and consumption. These systems meticulously analyze each student's performance metrics and learning preferences, tailoring the educational curriculum and instructional pace to cater to the unique requirements of every learner. This approach not only empowers students to grasp concepts at a pace that suits them but also proactively identifies and fills knowledge gaps, thereby significantly enhancing the learning experience and educational outcomes. In the context of increasing diversity in educational landscapes, AI-driven personalized instruction plays a pivotal role. It accommodates the varied learning styles, cultural backgrounds, and prior knowledge of students, fostering an inclusive atmosphere where every individual can excel. By adapting to the multifaceted needs of a diverse student body, AI is bridging gaps in educational equity and ensuring that no learner is left behind.

To further underscore the significance of AI in education, it is essential to note that these technologies are not only enhancing student learning but also revolutionizing teacher workflows. By automating routine tasks such as grading and lesson planning, AI is enabling educators to focus more on the qualitative aspects of teaching, such as fostering critical thinking and emotional intelligence. Additionally, the integration of AI in educational settings is poised to prepare students for a future where digital literacy and adaptability to new technologies are paramount. Khan Academy, Knewton Alta, and Smart Sparrow are leading adaptive learning platforms that harness the power of AI to tailor educational experiences to individual students. Khan Academy offers a vast array of free resources, personalizing content through exercises and videos that align with a student's performance. Knewton Alta adapts the difficulty and sequence of its courses to match a student's learning pace and style, while Smart Sparrow empowers educators to design interactive, AI-driven lessons that adjust in real time based on student engagement and understanding. These platforms collectively demonstrate the potential of AI to create more effective and personalized educational journeys (refer Table 1).

Table 1. Adaptive learning platforms

Number	Platform	Elaboration	Supporting literature
1	Khan Academy	Known for its extensive library of free educational resources, Khan Academy's adaptive learning platform personalizes the learning experience by recommending exercises and videos based on a student's progress and performance.	Puri, 2021 Bendou, 2021
2	Knewton Alta	This platform uses adaptive learning technology to provide a customized course experience for students, adjusting the difficulty and sequence of content based on their interactions with the material.	Osipovskaya, & Dmitrieva, 2022
3	Smart Sparrow	An adaptive e-learning platform that allows educators to create interactive, personalized learning experiences. It uses AI to track student engagement and performance, providing real-time feedback and adjusting the learning path accordingly.	Dutta, et al, 2024

Customized Content Delivery

Customized content delivery, facilitated by AI, is revolutionizing the educational landscape by providing students with learning materials that are specifically curated to match their unique learning preferences, strengths, and weaknesses. This approach ensures that each student receives an educational experience that is both relevant and challenging, with content that is delivered at the right difficulty level and in the most effective format, whether that be through videos, interactive simulations, or text-based resources, thereby optimizing the learning process and improving educational outcomes (Kem, 2022; Taylor, et al, 2021).

In an AI-enhanced educational setting, the customization of content delivery is not a one-time adjustment but an ongoing process. AI systems continuously learn from student interactions, adapting the delivery of content in real-time to reflect evolving learning patterns and progress. This dynamic customization not only personalizes the learning journey for each student but also fosters a sense of autonomy and self-direction, as students become active participants in shaping their educational experiences. By integrating AI-driven content delivery, educators can create a more inclusive classroom where diverse learning styles and abilities are accommodated, and where every student can engage with the curriculum in a way that maximizes their understanding and retention. This level of personalization not only enhances the efficiency of teaching but also supports the development of lifelong learning skills that are essential in our rapidly changing world (Bhutoria, 2022).

Data-Driven Decision-Making

Data-driven decision-making in education is empowered by the analysis of student performance, where AI systems collect and interpret a wealth of data points, including grades, engagement levels, and learning patterns. By synthesizing this information, educators can identify trends, pinpoint areas of struggle, and tailor instructional strategies to address individual student needs more effectively. This analytical approach not only enhances the precision of educational interventions but also enables educators to make informed decisions that are grounded in evidence, ultimately leading to improved learning outcomes and a more personalized educational experience (Teng, et al, 2023; Kurilovas, 2020).

In AI-enhanced education, the depth and breadth of student performance analysis are greatly expanded. AI algorithms can process and analyze data at a scale and speed that far surpasses human capabilities, uncovering subtle nuances in learning behaviors that might otherwise go unnoticed. This detailed analysis can inform educators about the effectiveness of different teaching methods, the impact of curriculum changes, and the efficacy of support programs. By providing real-time and historical insights, AI empowers educators to make data-informed adjustments to their teaching practices, curriculum design, and resource allocation. This targeted approach ensures that educational resources are utilized more efficiently, and that students receive the specific support they need to bridge learning gaps, master challenging concepts, and achieve their full potential, thereby creating a more responsive and adaptive educational system (Harry, & Sayudin, 2023). Incorporating discussions on the integration of digital technologies and social justice frameworks within teacher education programs could further illuminate how educators are being equipped to address the diverse literacy needs of culturally and linguistically diverse students. Additionally, examining the role of reflective practices and collaborative learning communities in fostering ongoing cultural competency development among teachers would provide valuable insights into the evolving landscape of literacy instruction.

Predictive analytics plays a pivotal role in early intervention by utilizing AI to forecast potential challenges students may face based on their historical performance data. This proactive approach allows educators to identify at-risk students before they fall behind, enabling timely interventions that can modify learning trajectories and prevent academic difficulties. By leveraging the predictive power of AI, educational institutions can implement targeted support strategies that are both preventative and supportive, thereby enhancing the likelihood of student success and promoting a more equitable learning environment (Shahat Osman, & Elragal, 2021; Buzhardt, et al, 2020). In an AI-enhanced educational setting, the application of predictive analytics is not just a reactive tool but a core component of a proactive educational strategy. AI systems continuously analyze a wide array of data points, including academic performance, attendance records, behavioral patterns, and even social media interactions, to generate nuanced predictions about each student's future academic path. This enables educators to implement preventive measures that are highly individualized, addressing the unique needs of each student. Moreover, AI can help in designing personalized learning plans that mitigate identified risks, ensuring that students receive the right kind of support at the right time. By integrating predictive analytics into the fabric of AI-enhanced education, schools can create a safety net that promotes a culture of continuous improvement and student well-being, ultimately leading to higher retention rates, improved academic outcomes, and a more supportive educational ecosystem (Adnan, et al, 2021).

Augmented Classroom Management

To enhance the educational experience, modern classrooms are increasingly adopting augmented classroom management systems that streamline administrative tasks and promote personalized learning. These systems integrate automated grading and feedback mechanisms, which not only save teachers valuable time but also provide students with immediate, constructive insights into their performance, fostering a more efficient and engaging academic environment (Deeva, et al, 2021; Erickson, et al, 2020; Wilson, et al, 2021). In AI-enhanced education, the integration of automated grading and feedback systems goes beyond mere time-saving convenience; it represents a significant advancement in the way students receive and process educational feedback. AI can analyze complex assignments, such as essays and problem-solving exercises, with a level of detail that would be impractical for teachers to manage individually. This allows for consistent and objective evaluation of student work, while also offering personalized feedback that highlights specific areas for improvement. By leveraging natural language processing and machine learning, AI can even provide guidance on writing style, argumentation, and conceptual understanding. As a result, students benefit from a learning experience that is both personalized and scalable, empowering them to take charge of their educational journey with the support of instant, actionable feedback designed to enhance their learning outcomes and develop their self-assessment skills (Hooda, et al, 2022).

Incorporating additional examples, such as using culturally relevant project-based assignments that allow students to explore their own heritage or providing multiple-choice questions that draw from a wide range of cultural perspectives, can further enhance the inclusivity of assessment methods. Moreover, offering language support and translation services for assessments can ensure that students from non-English speaking backgrounds are not disadvantaged, thereby fostering a more equitable and culturally sensitive learning environment.

Monitoring Student Engagement

Augmented classroom management systems are revolutionizing the educational landscape by incorporating advanced tools for monitoring student engagement in real-time. These innovative platforms track various metrics such as attendance, participation, attention spans, and interaction with course materials, enabling educators to identify disengaged students promptly and tailor their teaching methods to re-engage them, ultimately creating a dynamic and inclusive learning atmosphere that caters to the diverse needs of the classroom (Soltis, et al, 2020; Pabba, & Kumar, 2022). In an AI-enhanced education setting, these monitoring systems not only provide teachers with immediate insights into student engagement but also leverage machine learning algorithms to predict engagement patterns and suggest personalized interventions. By analyzing a wealth of data points, AI can help identify the underlying causes of disengagement, whether they are related to the curriculum, teaching methods, or individual student challenges. This proactive approach allows educators to address issues before they escalate, ensuring that each student receives the support they need to succeed. Furthermore, AI can facilitate the creation of adaptive learning experiences that respond to students' engagement levels, adjusting the difficulty and pace of content to maintain optimal challenge and interest, thereby enhancing the overall educational experience and promoting a culture of continuous improvement in the classroom (Almusaed, et al, 2023).

Evolving Responsibilities and Opportunities for Teachers

As educational landscapes evolve, teachers are experiencing a significant shift in their responsibilities, moving away from traditional content delivery to a more dynamic role as facilitators of learning. This transition allows educators to focus on nurturing critical thinking, problem-solving skills, and fostering a collaborative environment, thereby empowering students to take ownership of their education and preparing them for the complexities of the modern world (Fitria, & Suminah, 2020). In an AI-driven education system, this shift from content delivery to facilitation is both facilitated and necessitated by the capabilities of artificial intelligence. AI can assume the role of content provider, offering personalized learning experiences and adaptive instruction that cater to each student's pace and style of learning. This approach allows teachers to concentrate on higher-level tasks such as guiding discussions, challenging students' thinking, and encouraging the application of knowledge in creative ways. By leveraging AI to handle the dissemination of information, educators can transform their classrooms into hubs of exploration and discovery, where students are encouraged to interact with the material, ask questions, and engage in peer-to-peer learning, thus preparing them to be lifelong learners capable of navigating a world where AI is an integral part of everyday life (Saaida, 2023).

In the evolving educational landscape, teachers are increasingly prioritizing the development of higher-order thinking skills and critical thinking over rote memorization. This shift in focus allows educators to challenge students to analyze, evaluate, and create, rather than simply recalling information, thereby equipping them with the intellectual tools necessary to navigate complex problems and make informed decisions in an ever-changing world (Miterianifa, et al, 2021; Venkatraman, et al, 2022). To effectively cultivate these skills, educators must design lessons that require deep engagement and active participation from students. This involves posing open-ended questions, encouraging debate and discussion, and providing opportunities for project-based learning that mirrors real-world challenges. By doing so, students are not only taught content but also how to apply their knowledge in novel situations, think critically about information, and develop solutions that are both innovative and ethically sound. Additionally, teachers should model critical thinking themselves, demonstrating the thought processes and strategies involved in complex problem-solving, and providing constructive feedback that guides students toward higher levels of cognitive development and self-reflection (Kimmel, 2024).

In the age of digital transformation, teachers are embracing the opportunity to collaborate with artificial intelligence to create innovative teaching methods that enhance the learning experience. By integrating AI tools, educators can personalize instruction, identify individual student needs, and develop adaptive learning pathways, thus leveraging technology to augment their teaching practices and foster a more effective and engaging educational environment (Kim, 2024; Kim, et al, 2022). This collaboration also entails a reevaluation of the teacher's role, transforming it from a sole provider of knowledge to a facilitator of learning who leverages AI to amplify their impact. Teachers can use AI to analyze data on student performance, identify patterns, and tailor their instruction to address specific gaps in understanding. Furthermore, AI can support teachers in creating immersive learning experiences through simulations, gamification, and virtual reality, which can make abstract concepts more tangible and stimulate student curiosity. By continuously exploring and experimenting with these AI-powered methods, educators can push the boundaries of traditional teaching, inspiring students to become active participants in their education and preparing them for a future where human-AI collaboration is the norm (Guan, et al, 2020).

AI tools are revolutionizing professional development for teachers by providing personalized learning experiences, analyzing teaching practices, and offering tailored feedback, enabling educators to refine their skills, experiment with new methodologies, and stay abreast of the latest educational trends, thereby enhancing their overall effectiveness and job satisfaction (Celik, 2023). To support ongoing professional development, educators can leverage three AI-driven tools: an AI-Powered Observation and Feedback System that offers detailed insights into teaching practices and student engagement through video analysis, Adaptive Learning Platforms that tailor professional development content to individual needs and learning styles, and Virtual Reality Training Simulations that provide immersive practice environments with AI-generated real-time feedback to refine classroom management and instructional skills (refer table 2).

Table 2. AI tools

Number	Tool	Elaboration	Supporting literature
1	AI-Powered Observation and Feedback System	This tool uses AI to analyze classroom videos, providing teachers with insights on their teaching methods, student engagement, and areas for improvement, all while maintaining privacy and confidentiality.	Alyammahi, 2020
2	Adaptive Learning Platforms	These platforms use AI to adapt the content and pace of professional development courses to match the individual needs and learning styles of educators, ensuring a more effective and personalized training experience.	Muñoz, et al, 2022 Kabudi, et al, 2021
3	Virtual Reality (VR) Training Simulations	VR simulations create immersive environments where teachers can practice and refine their classroom management, instructional techniques, and student interaction skills in a risk-free setting, with AI providing real-time feedback and guidance.	Xie, et al, 2021

ADDRESSING CONCERNS ABOUT AI IN EDUCATION

Addressing concerns about the potential automation of educational tasks by AI, it's crucial to emphasize that while AI can streamline administrative and grading processes, its primary role should be to complement, not replace, the nuanced and empathetic approach that human educators bring to the classroom, ensuring that the essence of teaching—fostering critical thinking, emotional intelligence, and personal growth—remains central to the educational experience (Akgun, & Greenhow, 2022). To address concerns about the potential automation of educational tasks by AI, it's vital to position AI as a support tool that relieves teachers of administrative burdens, adopt a human-centered approach to its implementation that preserves the relational aspects of teaching, and maintain transparency and open communication with stakeholders about AI's role and limitations, ensuring that the core of educational experience remains centered on human connection and the development of critical thinking and emotional intelligence (refer table 3).

Table 3. Concerns about the potential automation of educational tasks by AI

Number	Focus	Elaboration	Supporting literature
1	AI as a Support Tool	AI should be positioned as a support tool that aids educators in handling repetitive tasks, allowing them more time to focus on the creative and relational aspects of teaching that require human insight and empathy.	Kim, et al, 2022
2	Human-Centered AI Implementation	Educational institutions should adopt a human-centered approach to AI implementation, ensuring that the technology is used to enhance the teacher's ability to connect with students and facilitate deeper learning experiences.	Wilkens, et al, 2021
3	Transparency and communication	To alleviate concerns, it's essential to maintain transparency about AI's role in education and communicate clearly with all stakeholders about how AI is being used, its limitations, and the ongoing importance of human educators in the process.	Bogina, et al, 2022

Maintaining a Human Touch in Teaching

In the face of AI's growing presence in education, addressing concerns about maintaining a human touch in teaching involves reassuring stakeholders that the irreplaceable elements of human interaction—such as empathy, emotional support, and the ability to inspire—will continue to be at the heart of educational practice, with AI serving as a tool to enhance, rather than diminish, the personal and transformative impact of teachers on their students (Yang, et al, 2021). To uphold this human touch, educators must intentionally design learning experiences that integrate the strengths of both human teachers and AI technologies. This means identifying areas where AI can streamline administrative tasks or provide personalized learning paths, thereby freeing up teachers to focus on the relational aspects of education. By fostering a classroom culture that values personal connections and encourages open dialogue, teachers can create a supportive learning environment where students feel seen and heard. Additionally, professional development programs should emphasize the importance of teacher-student relationships and provide strategies for educators to deepen these connections, ensuring that the essence of teaching remains centered on the unique and compassionate engagement that only a human teacher can provide (Renz, & Vladova, 2021).

Ensuring Equity and Accessibility in AI-Enhanced Learning

To ensure equity and accessibility in AI-enhanced learning, it is essential to design and implement these technologies with inclusivity in mind, addressing potential biases, providing equal access to resources, and accommodating diverse learning needs, thereby democratizing educational opportunities and empowering all students, regardless of their background or circumstances, to benefit from the advancements in educational technology (Patil, 2024). Moreover, ongoing assessment and feedback mechanisms should be established to monitor and address any emerging disparities in AI-enhanced education. This includes evaluating the impact of AI tools on different student populations and making necessary adjustments to ensure that no student is left behind. By prioritizing universal design principles and culturally responsive teaching, educators can create learning environments that are not only technologically advanced but also welcoming and supportive for all students. This commitment to equity extends beyond the classroom to policy-making and resource allocation, where decision-makers must prioritize funding and support for under-resourced schools and communities to bridge the digital divide and foster a truly inclusive educational landscape (Edeni, et al, 2024).

The role of policy in supporting culturally responsive ecosystems is critical, as national and local guidelines can shape the development of inclusive education strategies that honor and respect the cultural backgrounds of all students. Furthermore, involving communities and families in the policy-making process ensures that educational initiatives are not only culturally sensitive but also reflective of the values and needs of the populations they serve.

NECESSARY PEDAGOGICAL SHIFTS FOR EDUCATORS

Adopting a Growth Mindset Towards AI Integration

Educators must adopt a growth mindset towards AI integration, viewing it as an opportunity to enhance their teaching practices rather than a threat, which involves continually learning about new technologies, being open to change, and embracing the potential of AI to create more personalized and dynamic learning experiences for their students (Shah, 2023). This shift in mindset also requires a commitment to professional development and lifelong learning. Educators should seek out opportunities for training and collaboration that focus on AI integration, such as workshops, online courses, and peer learning communities. By doing so, they can stay informed about the latest AI tools and pedagogical approaches, and they can share their experiences and insights with colleagues. This collaborative approach not only empowers educators to innovate within their classrooms but also contributes to a collective effort to transform education through the thoughtful and effective use of AI, ultimately leading to more engaging and effective teaching strategies that cater to the diverse needs of all students (Wang, et al, 2021).

Developing Digital Literacy and AI Proficiency

In response to the digital age, educators are tasked with developing digital literacy and AI proficiency, not only to effectively utilize these tools in their teaching but also to guide students in becoming informed and capable users of technology, thereby equipping the next generation with the skills necessary to navigate and thrive in an increasingly AI-driven world (Ng, et al, 2023). To accomplish this, educational programs must be thoughtfully designed to integrate digital literacy and AI education across all disciplines. This means offering hands-on, project-based learning that allows students to explore, experiment, and create with digital tools and AI systems. By doing so, students can develop a practical understanding of how AI works, its potential applications, and its limitations. Additionally, educators should encourage critical thinking about the societal impacts of AI, including its ethical implications and the potential for bias. By nurturing a generation that is not only tech-savvy but also ethically conscious and critical of the digital world, we can ensure that students are prepared to be active participants and responsible creators in our evolving digital society (Kateryna, et al, 2020). Digital literacy hence plays a pivotal role in culturally responsive ecosystems by enabling educators to tailor digital tools and e-learning platforms to meet the diverse needs of various cultural groups, thereby enhancing inclusivity and promoting literacy. Ensuring that digital content is culturally relevant and accessible helps bridge the gap in educational equity, allowing all students to thrive in the digital age.

Balancing Traditional Teaching Methods with AI-Enhanced Approaches

Balancing traditional teaching methods with AI-enhanced approaches requires educators to thoughtfully integrate new technologies while preserving the timeless value of established pedagogies, ensuring that the human element of teaching is retained and enriched by the precision and adaptability that AI offers, ultimately creating a harmonious blend that maximizes learning outcomes for all students (Toksha, et al, 2022). To achieve a harmonious blend of traditional and AI-enhanced teaching methods, educators can develop blended learning models that harness AI for personalized instruction and feedback while maintaining direct teaching and Socratic dialogue. They can also employ AI to refine their pedagogical techniques, using data to customize lesson plans, and schools should prioritize professional development that equips teachers with the knowledge to integrate AI in a way that enhances their teaching without compromising the personal connection they cultivate with students (refer Table 4).

Table 4. Harmonious blend of traditional and AI-enhanced teaching methods

Number	Focus	Elaboration	Supporting literature
1	Blended Learning Models	Teachers can create blended learning models that combine the best of both worlds, using AI to personalize learning and provide instant feedback, while still engaging in direct instruction and Socratic dialogue to foster deep understanding.	Kumar, et al, 2021
2	AI-Enhanced Pedagogical Techniques	Educators can use AI to enhance traditional pedagogical techniques, such as leveraging AI-generated data to tailor their lesson plans to meet the specific needs and learning styles of their students.	Kakhkharova, & Tuychieva, 2024
3	Professional Development on AI Integration	Schools should offer professional development focused on how to integrate AI effectively, helping teachers to understand the strengths of AI and how it can complement their existing teaching strategies without undermining the personal touch they provide.	Celik, 2023

PROFESSIONAL DEVELOPMENT AND ETHICAL CONSIDERATIONS

Updating Teacher Training Programs to Include AI Integration

Professional development programs must be updated to include comprehensive training on AI integration, equipping teachers with the knowledge and skills to ethically and effectively incorporate AI tools into their classrooms, while also addressing the broader implications of these technologies on educational equity, privacy, and the future of teaching (Celik, 2023). Furthermore, it is imperative that these professional development programs emphasize the importance of fostering a growth mindset among educators. By encouraging teachers to embrace lifelong learning and adapt to the evolving landscape of AI in education, we can ensure that they remain at the forefront of innovation. This approach will not only enhance their ability to integrate AI tools but also empower them to become advocates for responsible AI use, promoting inclusive practices that cater to diverse student needs and bridging the digital divide that may exist within their communities (Celik, 2023; Celik, et al, 2022).

Navigating Ethical Issues Related to Data Privacy and Student Consent

Navigating ethical issues related to data privacy and student consent in AI-enhanced education necessitates a proactive approach, where educators are trained to understand and adhere to legal standards, transparently communicate with students and parents about data usage, and implement robust security measures to protect sensitive information, thereby upholding the trust and rights of all stakeholders in the educational process (Tzimas, & Demetriadis, 2021). Furthermore, it is imperative that educational institutions foster a culture of accountability and continuous improvement in their handling of student data. This involves not only the establishment of clear data governance policies but also the regular review and update of these policies to align with evolving technologies and regulatory landscapes. By engaging in ongoing professional development and staying abreast of best practices, educators can ensure that AI applications are used responsibly and that the rights of students to privacy and informed consent are preserved. This comprehensive approach to ethical data management not only mitigates risks but also models digital citizenship for students, preparing them to navigate their own digital futures with awareness and confidence (Sharma & Kumar, 2024).

Promoting Ethical AI Use in Education

Promoting ethical AI use in education involves fostering a culture of responsibility and accountability among educators, administrators, and technologists, where AI applications are developed and deployed with a commitment to fairness, transparency, and the well-being of students, ensuring that the benefits of AI are balanced with the protection of individual rights and the integrity of the educational experience (Nguyen, et al, 2023). To achieve this, educational institutions must integrate ethical considerations into the very fabric of their AI adoption strategies. This means embedding ethical AI principles into curriculum development, teacher training programs, and procurement processes for AI tools. It also requires the establishment of multi-stakeholder forums where educators, students, parents, and AI developers can openly discuss the implications of AI in the classroom, exchange perspectives, and collaboratively develop guidelines for its ethical deployment. By doing so, educational communities can cultivate an environment where AI is not just a tool for efficiency, but a force for equity and empowerment, enhancing the educational journey while safeguarding the dignity and privacy of every learner (Holmes, et al, 2022).

ROLE OF TEACHERS IN THE NEW EDUCATIONAL PARADIGM

Guiding Students in Navigating AI Tools and Resources

In the new educational paradigm, teachers play an essential role in guiding students through the complexities of AI tools and resources, serving as mentors who not only facilitate access to technology but also impart critical judgment, digital literacy, and the ethical considerations necessary for responsible engagement with AI in both academic and real-world contexts (Fitria, & Suminah, 2020). In the evolving educational landscape, teachers are pivotal in preparing students for the AI era by fostering digital literacy and critical thinking skills, enabling students to discern the credibility of AI-generated content and understand algorithmic biases. They are also instrumental in embedding ethical discussions within the curriculum, using case studies to explore AI's societal impacts and readying students to make ethical decisions. Moreover, educators facilitate hands-on AI projects and collaborative opportunities, providing students with practical experience that bridges the gap between theory and the real-world application of AI tools and resources (refer Table 5).

Table 5. Guiding students in navigating AI tools and resources

Number	Focus	Elaboration	Supporting literature
1	Fostering Digital Literacy and Critical Thinking Skills	Teachers can help students develop the necessary digital literacy skills to evaluate and discern the credibility and reliability of AI-generated content. By fostering critical thinking, educators can empower students to question assumptions, understand biases inherent in AI algorithms, and make informed decisions when utilizing AI tools.	Jia, et al, 2024
2	Integrating Ethical Discussions into Curriculum	As AI becomes more prevalent, teachers have the responsibility to integrate discussions on the ethical implications of AI into the curriculum. By examining case studies and real-world scenarios, educators can guide students in understanding the potential consequences of AI on society, privacy, employment, and more, thus cultivating a generation equipped to make ethical choices in an AI-driven world.	Zhang, et al, 2023
3	Facilitating Hands-On AI Projects and Collaborations	Teachers can organize hands-on projects that allow students to engage directly with AI tools and resources, fostering a deeper understanding of AI capabilities and limitations. By encouraging collaboration with AI developers and other stakeholders, educators can provide students with practical experience in developing AI solutions, thereby bridging the gap between theoretical knowledge and practical application.	Hamza, et al, 2024

Fostering Human Connection and Social Skills

As AI becomes more prevalent in education, teachers remain vital in fostering human connection and social skills, providing the personal touch and relational context that algorithms cannot replicate, and ensuring that students develop the emotional intelligence and collaborative abilities needed to succeed in a world where interpersonal communication is still paramount (Markauskaite, et al, 2022). In conjunction with leveraging AI to enhance learning, educators must prioritize activities that promote face-to-face interaction and team-based projects. By designing lessons that require students to engage in dialogue, debate, and creative problem-solving, teachers can create opportunities for students to practice empathy, active listening, and consensus-building. These experiences are not just supplementary to the curriculum but are fundamental to the holistic development of students, equipping them with the skills to navigate complex social dynamics and to build meaningful relationships in both their personal and professional lives. In this way, educators can complement the efficiencies of AI with the irreplaceable value of human interaction (Rusmiyanto, et al, 2023).

Advocating for the Ethical and Responsible Use of AI in Education

Teachers are pivotal advocates for the ethical and responsible use of AI in education, championing policies and practices that prioritize student well-being, data privacy, and equitable access, while also educating their peers, students, and the broader community about the potential benefits and risks associated with AI, thereby shaping a future where technology serves to enhance, not undermine, the fundamental principles of education (Adams, et al, 2023). Furthermore, teachers serve as crucial intermediaries in the discourse on AI's role in education by actively participating in the development of guidelines and standards for AI implementation. They ensure that AI tools are used to augment learning experiences without compromising the integrity of educational outcomes. By advocating for transparency in AI systems and for the protection of students' digital rights, teachers help to maintain a balance between innovation and the preservation of the human element in teaching, which is essential for nurturing the unique talents and needs of each student. Their advocacy also extends to addressing potential biases and inequalities that AI might perpetuate, thereby striving for a more inclusive and just educational system (Khreisat, et al, 2024).

AI in Education with Cultural Responsiveness in Malaysia

In Malaysia, the integration of AI in education is being thoughtfully approached with cultural responsiveness at its core, ensuring that advanced technologies are aligned with the nation's diverse ethnic and religious tapestry. By incorporating elements that respect and reflect the unique cultural backgrounds of Malaysian students, AI systems are designed not only to enhance personalized learning experiences but also to foster inclusivity and understanding, thereby empowering learners to navigate a globalized world while preserving their cultural identities (Amdan, et al, 2024b). The efficiency of AI tools in STEM education in Malaysia has been remarkable, significantly enhancing the learning experience by providing personalized curricula, interactive simulations, and real-time feedback, which has not only improved students' understanding and application of complex scientific and mathematical concepts but also fostered a culture of innovation and critical thinking (Amdan, et al, 2024b). As these AI tools expand into non-STEM education, they are poised to revolutionize the teaching of humanities and social sciences by offering immersive historical recreations, language learning through adaptive platforms, and data-driven insights into human behavior, thereby bridging the gap between traditional and modern educational methodologies.

Additionally, the advancement of AI-tools in Technical Vocational Education and Training (TVET) in Malaysia has significantly empowered both students and tutors by enhancing the learning experience through personalized curricula, immersive simulations, and real-time feedback, thereby bridging the gap between theoretical knowledge and practical skills, and ultimately equipping learners with the competencies needed to thrive in a rapidly evolving job market (Amdan, et al, 2024a). In Malaysia, the adoption of AI-based chatbots in higher-education institutions is being advanced through a novel hybrid PLS-SEM-neural network modelling approach, which synergistically combines Partial Least Squares Structural Equation Modelling (PLS-SEM) for theoretical framework validation with neural network analysis for predictive accuracy, thereby providing a comprehensive understanding of the factors influencing chatbot integration and enabling institutions to optimize their deployment strategies for enhanced student support and operational efficiency as studied by Mohd Rahim, et al, (2022).

The implementation of culturally responsive pedagogy in Asia presents a multifaceted challenge for Malaysia, where educators strive to integrate indigenous knowledge and cultural practices into the curriculum to make learning more meaningful and relatable for students. Despite the potential to foster greater engagement and academic success among diverse learners, Malaysia faces hurdles such as limited resources, teacher training gaps, and resistance to change within the traditional education framework, necessitating a collaborative and innovative approach to overcome these barriers and create a science education system that truly resonates with the cultural fabric of the nation (Halim, et al, 2022).

CONCLUSION

The chapter highlights the transformative impact of AI on education, emphasizing the need for teachers to adapt to new roles and responsibilities. Key insights include the potential for AI to personalize learning, support data-driven education, and improve classroom management. The chapter also addresses concerns about AI automation and underscores the importance of human interaction in teaching. It identifies essential pedagogical shifts, such as developing digital literacy and balancing traditional methods with AI-enhanced approaches and outlines the professional development and ethical considerations necessary for educators. Ultimately, the chapter empowers teachers to integrate AI effectively and ethically, ensuring they remain central to the educational process. To encourage educators to embrace the future of teaching with confidence and innovation, it is crucial to provide ongoing support, resources, and opportunities for growth that empower them to explore and integrate new technologies, fostering a mindset of continuous learning and adaptability that will enable them to lead the way in creating dynamic, AI-enhanced educational experiences (Wang, et al, 2023).

Exploring the implications of intersectionality within literacy ecosystems is essential, as it illuminates how the overlapping identities of race, gender, and socio-economic status compound to shape unique educational experiences and challenges for students. Understanding these intersecting dynamics allows for the creation of more nuanced and effective educational interventions that address the complex needs of diverse learners. This is to encourage educators to embrace the future of teaching with confidence and innovation by considering the implications of intersectionality within literacy ecosystems. The strategic integration of AI in education is of paramount importance as it allows for the optimization of learning processes, the personalization of educational content, and the enhancement of teacher efficiency, ultimately leading to more inclusive and effective educational outcomes that prepare students for the challenges of a technology-driven society (Schiff, 2022). By harnessing the transformative power of AI in education, we are not only equipping students with the skills to navigate the digital future but also fostering a learning environment that celebrates diversity, empowers individual potential, and ushers in a new era of equitable and enriching educational experiences.

REFERENCES

Adams, C., Pente, P., Lemermeyer, G., & Rockwell, G. (2023). Ethical principles for artificial intelligence in K-12 education. *Computers and Education: Artificial Intelligence*, 4, 100131. DOI: 10.1016/j.caeai.2023.100131

Adnan, M., Habib, A., Ashraf, J., Mussadiq, S., Raza, A. A., Abid, M., Bashir, M., & Khan, S. U. (2021). Predicting at-risk students at different percentages of course length for early intervention using machine learning models. *IEEE Access : Practical Innovations, Open Solutions*, 9, 7519–7539. DOI: 10.1109/ACCESS.2021.3049446

Akgun, S., & Greenhow, C. (2022). Artificial intelligence in education: Addressing ethical challenges in K-12 settings. *AI and Ethics*, 2(3), 431–440. DOI: 10.1007/s43681-021-00096-7 PMID: 34790956

Almusaed, A., Almssad, A., Yitmen, I., & Homod, R. Z. (2023). Enhancing student engagement: Harnessing "AIED"'s power in hybrid education—A review analysis. *Education Sciences*, 13(7), 632. DOI: 10.3390/educsci13070632

Alyammahi, A. (2020). *Investigating the Impact of AI-Powered Digital Educational Platforms on Students' Learning and Teachers' Practice in Abu Dhabi Schools* (Doctoral dissertation, The British University in Dubai).

Amdan, M. A. B., Janius, N., Jasman, M. N. B., & Kasdiah, M. A. H. B. (2024a). Advancement of ai-tools in learning for technical vocational education and training (TVET) in Malaysia (empowering students and tutor). *International Journal of Science and Research Archive*, 12(1), 2061–2068. DOI: 10.30574/ijsra.2024.12.1.0971

Amdan, M. A. B., Janius, N., & Kasdiah, M. A. H. B. (2024b). Concept paper: Efficiency of Artificial Intelligence (AI) tools For STEM Education In Malaysia. *International Journal of Science and Research Archive*, 12(2), 553–559. DOI: 10.30574/ijsra.2024.12.2.1273

Bendou, I. (2021). *Automatic Arabic Translation of English Educational Content Online using Neural Machine Translation: the Case of Khan Academy.*

Bhutoria, A. (2022). Personalized education and artificial intelligence in the United States, China, and India: A systematic review using a human-in-the-loop model. *Computers and Education: Artificial Intelligence*, 3, 100068. DOI: 10.1016/j.caeai.2022.100068

Bogina, V., Hartman, A., Kuflik, T., & Shulner-Tal, A. (2022). Educating software and AI stakeholders about algorithmic fairness, accountability, transparency and ethics. *International Journal of Artificial Intelligence in Education*, 32(3), 1–26. DOI: 10.1007/s40593-021-00248-0

Buzhardt, J., Greenwood, C. R., Jia, F., Walker, D., Schneider, N., Larson, A. L., Valdovinos, M., & McConnell, S. R. (2020). Technology to guide data-driven intervention decisions: Effects on language growth of young children at risk for language delay. *Exceptional Children*, 87(1), 74–91. DOI: 10.1177/0014402920938003

Celik, I. (2023). Towards Intelligent-TPACK: An empirical study on teachers' professional knowledge to ethically integrate artificial intelligence (AI)-based tools into education. *Computers in Human Behavior*, 138, 107468. DOI: 10.1016/j.chb.2022.107468

Celik, I., Dindar, M., Muukkonen, H., & Järvelä, S. (2022). The promises and challenges of artificial intelligence for teachers: A systematic review of research. *TechTrends*, 66(4), 616–630. DOI: 10.1007/s11528-022-00715-y

Deeva, G., Bogdanova, D., Serral, E., Snoeck, M., & De Weerdt, J. (2021). A review of automated feedback systems for learners: Classification framework, challenges and opportunities. *Computers & Education*, 162, 104094. DOI: 10.1016/j.compedu.2020.104094

Dutta, S., Ranjan, S., Mishra, S., Sharma, V., Hewage, P., & Iwendi, C. (2024, February). Enhancing Educational Adaptability: A Review and Analysis of AI-Driven Adaptive Learning Platforms. In *2024 4th International Conference on Innovative Practices in Technology and Management (ICIPTM)* (pp. 1-5). IEEE. DOI: 10.1109/ICIPTM59628.2024.10563448

Edeni, C. A., Adeleye, O. O., & Adeniyi, I. S.Chima Abimbola EdeniOlabisi Oluwakemi AdeleyeIdowu Sulaimon Adeniyi. (2024). The role of AI-enhanced tools in overcoming socioeconomic barriers in education: A conceptual analysis. *World Journal of Advanced Research and Reviews*, 21(3), 944–951. DOI: 10.30574/wjarr.2024.21.3.0780

Elimadi, I., Chafiq, N., & Ghazouani, M. (2024). Artificial Intelligence in the Context of Digital Learning Environments (DLEs): Towards Adaptive Learning. In *Engineering Applications of Artificial Intelligence* (pp. 95–111). Springer Nature Switzerland. DOI: 10.1007/978-3-031-50300-9_6

Erickson, J. A., Botelho, A. F., McAteer, S., Varatharaj, A., & Heffernan, N. T. (2020, March). The automated grading of student open responses in mathematics. In *Proceedings of the tenth international conference on learning analytics & knowledge* (pp. 615-624). DOI: 10.1145/3375462.3375523

Fitria, H., & Suminah, S. (2020). Role of teachers in digital instructional era. *Journal of social work and science education, 1*(1), 70-77.

Guan, C., Mou, J., & Jiang, Z. (2020). Artificial intelligence innovation in education: A twenty-year data-driven historical analysis. *International Journal of Innovation Studies*, 4(4), 134–147. DOI: 10.1016/j.ijis.2020.09.001

Halim, L., Ramli, M., & Ali, M. N. (Eds.). (2022). *Culturally Responsive Science Pedagogy in Asia: Status and Challenges for Malaysia, Indonesia and Japan.* DOI: 10.4324/9781003168706

Hamza, M., Siemon, D., Akbar, M. A., & Rahman, T. (2024, April). Human-AI Collaboration in Software Engineering: Lessons Learned from a Hands-On Workshop. In *Proceedings of the 7th ACM/IEEE International Workshop on Software-intensive Business* (pp. 7-14).

Harry, A., & Sayudin, S. (2023). Role of AI in Education. [INJURITY]. *Interdiciplinary Journal and Hummanity*, 2(3), 260–268.

Hashim, S., Omar, M. K., Ab Jalil, H., & Sharef, N. M. (2022). Trends on technologies and artificial intelligence in education for personalized learning: Systematic literature. *Journal of Academic Research in Progressive Education and Development*, 12(1), 884–903. DOI: 10.6007/IJARPED/v11-i1/12230

Holmes, W., Porayska-Pomsta, K., Holstein, K., Sutherland, E., Baker, T., Shum, S. B., Santos, O. C., Rodrigo, M. T., Cukurova, M., Bittencourt, I. I., & Koedinger, K. R. (2022). Ethics of AI in education: Towards a community-wide framework. *International Journal of Artificial Intelligence in Education*, 32(3), 1–23. DOI: 10.1007/s40593-021-00239-1

Hooda, M., Rana, C., Dahiya, O., Rizwan, A., & Hossain, M. S. (2022). Artificial intelligence for assessment and feedback to enhance student success in higher education. *Mathematical Problems in Engineering*, 2022(1), 5215722. DOI: 10.1155/2022/5215722

Jia, X. H., & Tu, J. C. (2024). Towards a New Conceptual Model of AI-Enhanced Learning for College Students: The Roles of Artificial Intelligence Capabilities, General Self-Efficacy, Learning Motivation, and Critical Thinking Awareness. *Systems*, 12(3), 74. DOI: 10.3390/systems12030074

Kabudi, T., Pappas, I., & Olsen, D. H. (2021). AI-enabled adaptive learning systems: A systematic mapping of the literature. *Computers and Education: Artificial Intelligence*, 2, 100017. DOI: 10.1016/j.caeai.2021.100017

Kakhkharova, M., & Tuychieva, S. (2024, April). AI-Enhanced Pedagogy in Higher Education: Redefining Teaching-Learning Paradigms. In 2024 *International Conference on Knowledge Engineering and Communication Systems (ICKECS) (Vol. 1*, pp. 1-6). IEEE.

Kateryna, A., Oleksandr, R., Mariia, T., Iryna, S., Evgen, K., & Anastasiia, L. (2020). Digital literacy development trends in the professional environment. *International Journal of Learning. Teaching and Educational Research*, 19(7), 55–79.

Kem, D. (2022). Personalised and adaptive learning: Emerging learning platforms in the era of digital and smart learning. *International Journal of Social Science and Human Research*, 5(2), 385–391. DOI: 10.47191/ijsshr/v5-i2-02

Khreisat, M. N., Khilani, D., Rusho, M. A., Karkkulainen, E. A., Tabuena, A. C., & Uberas, A. D. (2024). Ethical Implications Of AI Integration In Educational Decision Making: Systematic Review. *Educational Administration: Theory and Practice*, 30(5), 8521–8527.

Kim, J. (2024). Leading teachers' perspective on teacher-AI collaboration in education. *Education and Information Technologies*, 29(7), 8693–8724. DOI: 10.1007/s10639-023-12109-5

Kim, J., Lee, H., & Cho, Y. H. (2022). Learning design to support student-AI collaboration: Perspectives of leading teachers for AI in education. *Education and Information Technologies*, 27(5), 6069–6104. DOI: 10.1007/s10639-021-10831-6

Kimmel, S. (2024). AI Facilitated Critical Thinking in an Undergraduate Project Based Service-Learning Course. *Journal of Behavioral and Applied Management*, 24(2), 123–130. DOI: 10.21818/001c.122149

Kumar, A., Krishnamurthi, R., Bhatia, S., Kaushik, K., Ahuja, N. J., Nayyar, A., & Masud, M. (2021). Blended learning tools and practices: A comprehensive analysis. *IEEE Access : Practical Innovations, Open Solutions*, 9, 85151–85197. DOI: 10.1109/ACCESS.2021.3085844

Kurilovas, E. (2020). On data-driven decision-making for quality education. *Computers in Human Behavior*, 107, 105774. DOI: 10.1016/j.chb.2018.11.003

Markauskaite, L., Marrone, R., Poquet, O., Knight, S., Martinez-Maldonado, R., Howard, S., Tondeur, J., De Laat, M., Buckingham Shum, S., Gašević, D., & Siemens, G. (2022). Rethinking the entwinement between artificial intelligence and human learning: What capabilities do learners need for a world with AI? *Computers and Education: Artificial Intelligence*, 3, 100056. DOI: 10.1016/j.caeai.2022.100056

Meng, N., Dhimolea, T. K., & Ali, Z. (2022). AI-enhanced education: Teaching and learning reimagined. In *Bridging human intelligence and artificial intelligence* (pp. 107–124). Springer International Publishing. DOI: 10.1007/978-3-030-84729-6_7

Miterianifa, M., Ashadi, A., Saputro, S., & Suciati, S. (2021, January). Higher order thinking skills in the 21st century: Critical thinking. In *Proceedings of the 1st International Conference on Social Science, Humanities, Education and Society Development*, ICONS 2020, 30 November, Tegal, Indonesia. DOI: 10.4108/eai.30-11-2020.2303766

Mohd Rahim, N. I., & Iahad, A., N., Yusof, A. F., & A. Al-Sharafi, M. (. (2022). AI-based chatbots adoption model for higher-education institutions: A hybrid PLS-SEM-neural network modelling approach. *Sustainability*, 14(19), 12726. DOI: 10.3390/su141912726

Muñoz, J. L. R., Ojeda, F. M., Jurado, D. L. A., Peña, P. F. P., Carranza, C. P. M., Berríos, H. Q., & Vasquez-Pauca, M. J. (2022). Systematic review of adaptive learning technology for learning in higher education. *Eurasian Journal of Educational Research*, 98(98), 221–233.

Ng, D. T. K., Leung, J. K. L., Su, J., Ng, R. C. W., & Chu, S. K. W. (2023). Teachers' AI digital competencies and twenty-first century skills in the post-pandemic world. *Educational Technology Research and Development*, 71(1), 137–161. DOI: 10.1007/s11423-023-10203-6 PMID: 36844361

Nguyen, A., Ngo, H. N., Hong, Y., Dang, B., & Nguyen, B. P. T. (2023). Ethical principles for artificial intelligence in education. *Education and Information Technologies*, 28(4), 4221–4241. DOI: 10.1007/s10639-022-11316-w PMID: 36254344

Novawan, A., Walker, S. A., & Ikeda, O. (2024). The new face of technology-enhanced language learning (TELL) with artificial intelligence (AI): Teacher perspectives, practices, and challenges. *Journal of English in Academic and Professional Communication*, 10(1), 1–18. DOI: 10.25047/jeapco.v9i1.3754

Osipovskaya, E., & Dmitrieva, S. (2022). The Issue of Adaptive Learning as Educational Innovation. In *Technology, Innovation and Creativity in Digital Society: XXI Professional Culture of the Specialist of the Future* (pp. 606-617). Springer International Publishing. DOI: 10.1007/978-3-030-89708-6_50

Pabba, C., & Kumar, P. (2022). An intelligent system for monitoring students' engagement in large classroom teaching through facial expression recognition. *Expert Systems: International Journal of Knowledge Engineering and Neural Networks*, 39(1), e12839. DOI: 10.1111/exsy.12839

Patil, V. (2024). *The Potential of AI in Enhancing Education Access and Quality.*

Putri, A. A. (2021). The effectiveness of khan academy as a science learning support to improve student's mastery of skills: Literature review. *Journal of Environmental and Science Education*, 1(2), 52–56. DOI: 10.15294/jese.v1i2.50370

Renz, A., & Vladova, G. (2021). Reinvigorating the discourse on human-centered artificial intelligence in educational technologies. *Technology Innovation Management Review*, 11(5), 5–16. DOI: 10.22215/timreview/1438

Rusmiyanto, R., Huriati, N., Fitriani, N., Tyas, N. K., Rofi'I, A., & Sari, M. N. (2023). The role of artificial intelligence (AI) in developing English language learner's communication skills. *Journal of Education*, 6(1), 750–757.

Saaida, M. B. (2023). AI-Driven transformations in higher education: Opportunities and challenges. *International Journal of Educational Research and Studies*, 5(1), 29–36.

Schiff, D. (2022). Education for AI, not AI for education: The role of education and ethics in national AI policy strategies. *International Journal of Artificial Intelligence in Education*, 32(3), 527–563. DOI: 10.1007/s40593-021-00270-2

Shah, P. (2023). *AI and the Future of Education: Teaching in the Age of Artificial Intelligence*. John Wiley & Sons.

Shahat Osman, A. M., & Elragal, A. (2021). Smart cities and big data analytics: A data-driven decision-making use case. *Smart Cities*, 4(1), 286–313. DOI: 10.3390/smartcities4010018

Sharma, S., & Kumar, N. (2024). NAVIGATING THE ETHICAL LANDSCAPE OF AI-BASED RESOURCES IN EDUCATION: IMPLICATIONS FOR LEARNING, PROPER USAGE, AND COURSE DESIGN ENHANCEMENT. *The Online Journal of Distance Education and e-Learning : TOJDEL*, 12(2), 92.

Soltis, N. A., McNeal, K. S., Atkins, R. M., & Maudlin, L. C. (2020). A novel approach to measuring student engagement while using an augmented reality sandbox. *Journal of Geography in Higher Education*, 44(4), 512–531. DOI: 10.1080/03098265.2020.1771547

Taylor, D. L., Yeung, M., & Bashet, A. Z. (2021). Personalized and adaptive learning. *Innovative learning environments in STEM higher education: Opportunities, Challenges, and Looking Forward*, 17-34.

Teng, Y., Zhang, J., & Sun, T. (2023). Data-driven decision-making model based on artificial intelligence in higher education system of colleges and universities. *Expert Systems: International Journal of Knowledge Engineering and Neural Networks*, 40(4), e12820. DOI: 10.1111/exsy.12820

Toksha, B., Kulkarni, T., & Gupta, P. (2022). Impact of AI on teaching pedagogy and its integration for enhancing teaching-learning. In *Artificial Intelligence in Higher Education* (pp. 137–152). CRC Press. DOI: 10.1201/9781003184157-7

Tzimas, D., & Demetriadis, S. (2021). Ethical issues in learning analytics: A review of the field. *Educational Technology Research and Development*, 69(2), 1101–1133. DOI: 10.1007/s11423-021-09977-4

Venkatraman, S., Benli, F., Wei, Y., & Wahr, F. (2022). Smart classroom teaching strategy to enhance higher order thinking skills (HOTS)—An agile approach for education 4.0. *Future Internet*, 14(9), 255. DOI: 10.3390/fi14090255

Wang, X., Li, L., Tan, S. C., Yang, L., & Lei, J. (2023). Preparing for AI-enhanced education: Conceptualizing and empirically examining teachers' AI readiness. *Computers in Human Behavior*, 146, 107798. DOI: 10.1016/j.chb.2023.107798

Wang, Y., Liu, C., & Tu, Y. F. (2021). Factors affecting the adoption of AI-based applications in higher education. *Journal of Educational Technology & Society*, 24(3), 116–129.

Wilkens, U., Langholf, V., Ontrup, G., & Kluge, A. (2021). Towards a maturity model of human-centered AI–A reference for AI implementation at the workplace. *Competence development and learning assistance systems for the data-driven future*, 179-197.

Williamson, B., & Eynon, R. (2020). Historical threads, missing links, and future directions in AI in education. *Learning, Media and Technology*, 45(3), 223–235. DOI: 10.1080/17439884.2020.1798995

Wilson, J., Huang, Y., Palermo, C., Beard, G., & MacArthur, C. A. (2021). Automated feedback and automated scoring in the elementary grades: Usage, attitudes, and associations with writing outcomes in a districtwide implementation of MI Write. *International Journal of Artificial Intelligence in Education*, 31(2), 234–276. DOI: 10.1007/s40593-020-00236-w

Xie, B., Liu, H., Alghofaili, R., Zhang, Y., Jiang, Y., Lobo, F. D., Li, C., Li, W., Huang, H., Akdere, M., Mousas, C., & Yu, L. F. (2021). A review on virtual reality skill training applications. *Frontiers in Virtual Reality*, 2, 645153. DOI: 10.3389/frvir.2021.645153

Yang, S. J., Ogata, H., Matsui, T., & Chen, N. S. (2021). Human-centered artificial intelligence in education: Seeing the invisible through the visible. *Computers and Education: Artificial Intelligence*, 2, 100008. DOI: 10.1016/j.caeai.2021.100008

Zhai, X., Chu, X., Chai, C. S., Jong, M. S. Y., Istenic, A., Spector, M., Liu, J.-B., Yuan, J., & Li, Y. (2021). A Review of Artificial Intelligence (AI) in Education from 2010 to 2020. *Complexity*, 2021(1), 8812542. DOI: 10.1155/2021/8812542

Zhang, H., Lee, I., Ali, S., DiPaola, D., Cheng, Y., & Breazeal, C. (2023). Integrating ethics and career futures with technical learning to promote AI literacy for middle school students: An exploratory study. *International Journal of Artificial Intelligence in Education*, 33(2), 290–324. DOI: 10.1007/s40593-022-00293-3 PMID: 35573722

Zhang, K., & Aslan, A. B. (2021). AI technologies for education: Recent research & future directions. *Computers and Education: Artificial Intelligence*, 2, 100025. DOI: 10.1016/j.caeai.2021.100025

ADDITIONAL READING

Abulibdeh, A., Zaidan, E., & Abulibdeh, R. (2024). Navigating the confluence of artificial intelligence and education for sustainable development in the era of industry 4.0: Challenges, opportunities, and ethical dimensions. *Journal of Cleaner Production*, 437, 140527. DOI: 10.1016/j.jclepro.2023.140527

Baskara, F. R. (2023, September). Navigating pedagogical evolution: The implication of generative AI on the reinvention of teacher education. In *Prosiding Seminar Nasional Universitas Jabal Ghafur (Vol. 2*, pp. 409-421).

Ivković, J., & Stanković, V. (2024). Revolutionizing Educational Paradigms: Integrating Precision-Engineered AI into Next-Generation. *Wearable Technologies*.

Kim, J. (2024). Leading teachers' perspective on teacher-AI collaboration in education. *Education and Information Technologies*, 29(7), 8693–8724. DOI: 10.1007/s10639-023-12109-5

LIU, C. C., & GU, X. Q. (2024). Developing Frames for Change: The Impact Of Generative AI on the Broad Practices of Teacher Educators. *Exploring New Horizons: Generative Artificial Intelligence and Teacher Education*, 225.

Nguyen, N. D. (2023). Exploring the role of AI in education. *London Journal of Social Sciences*, (6), 84–95. DOI: 10.31039/ljss.2023.6.108

Rudolph, J., Ismail, M. F. B. M., & Popenici, S. (2024). Higher education's generative artificial intelligence paradox: The meaning of chatbot mania. *Journal of University Teaching & Learning Practice*, 21(6), 1–35. DOI: 10.53761/54fs5e77

Shi, L. (2023). *Exploring the Emerging Roles of Artificial Intelligence in Teaching Practices and Its Relationships with Teachers* (Doctoral dissertation, University of Georgia).

Singh, R. J. (2023). Transforming higher education: The power of artificial intelligence. *International Journal of Multidisciplinary Research in Arts. Science and Technology*, 1(3), 13–18.

KEY TERMS AND DEFINITIONS

Adaptive Learning: A teaching approach powered by AI that customizes educational content based on each student's progress, learning style, and needs.

Artificial Intelligence (AI): The simulation of human intelligence in machines designed to think, learn, and solve problems autonomously, often used to enhance educational processes.

Blended Learning: A teaching method combining traditional in-person instruction with online learning, allowing for a flexible, personalized educational experience.

Data-Driven Decision-Making: The process of using data insights to guide instructional practices and improve student learning outcomes in education.

Digital Literacy: The ability to effectively use digital tools and platforms, including AI applications, to access, evaluate, and communicate information in educational settings.

Ethical AI Use: Responsible integration of AI in education, ensuring transparency, privacy, and fairness while avoiding biases in automated systems.

Personalized Instruction: Tailoring teaching strategies and materials to meet the unique needs of each student, often enhanced through AI-driven adaptive learning tools.

Professional Development: Ongoing education and training for educators to keep up with new teaching strategies, technology, and AI tools in the educational field.

Teacher Facilitation: The evolving role of educators from content delivery to guiding and mentoring students, especially important in AI-enhanced classrooms.

Technology Acceptance Model (TAM): A framework for understanding individuals' acceptance of new technologies based on perceived usefulness and ease of use, applicable to AI in education.

Chapter 2
Blended Education and the Role of Albanian Teachers in an AI-Enhanced Educational Landscape

Dhurata Lamçja
https://orcid.org/0009-0000-1744-9507
Albanian University, Albania

Salvina Pellumbi
University of Elbasan, Albania

ABSTRACT

The COVID-19 crisis disrupted traditional in-school teaching, highlighting both the potential and challenges of distance learning. The abrupt transition exposed the unpreparedness of many teachers and students, emphasizing the need for alternative, technology-supported methodologies. This chapter investigates blended education as an innovative approach integrating classroom and online learning to enhance teaching effectiveness. Through a theoretical examination of blended education and a survey of middle school teachers in Albania, this study evaluates teachers' familiarity with and use of blended learning methods. Data collected from 212 educational stakeholders provide insights into the current state of ICT-supported teaching in Albania. The findings suggest that, while blended learning holds promise for improving educational outcomes, Albanian teachers require further training, and substantial upgrades in ICT infrastructure are necessary to implement this approach in schools fully.

DOI: 10.4018/979-8-3373-1017-6.ch002

INTRODUCTION

The world is characterized by many rapid changes, some of which have come and from the rapid development of information and communication technology. In modern times, the influence of information technology and communication increasingly it becomes more inclusive in many social spheres. This implementation does not bypass it nor education. The educational system at present is in a transition stage. Education must adapt to continuous changes in technology, and use them extensively in the learning process. Education must respond to these changes, at a fast rate, with internal quantitative and qualitative developments to transmit systematic knowledge and skills, coherent and stable in students, then reflecting these in society for creating a more positive future for everyone. Technology has the power and potential to transform professional teaching environment. It affects successful teaching and creates opportunities for teachers to learn and collaborate with each other, through exchanging ideas and experiences and solving common pedagogical problems (Lalima, 2017).

In today's rapidly evolving world, the role of information and communication technology (ICT) has become increasingly pervasive, impacting various sectors including education. The swift advancements in ICT have created an urgent need for educational systems to adapt in order to equip students with the necessary skills and knowledge to thrive in a future dominated by technology. Educational institutions must now integrate these technologies into their teaching methods, transitioning from traditional models to a more dynamic and flexible framework. This integration facilitates collaboration among teachers and enhances the learning experience for students. Blended education, which combines the advantages of traditional face-to-face learning with technology-mediated instruction, offers a promising solution to bridge the gap between traditional and modern educational methodologies. While face-to-face learning is essential for social interaction, emotional development, and the cultivation of critical thinking skills, technology-based learning enhances accessibility and provides opportunities for personalized, self-paced education. The aim of this chapter is to explore how blended education, supported by the use of artificial intelligence (AI), can address the evolving needs of education in Albania. It will examine the role of Albanian teachers in this digital transition and how AI can enhance blended learning environments to foster student engagement and learning outcomes. The aim of this chapter is to evaluate the role of blended education in the context of Albania's evolving educational landscape, particularly how teachers are adapting to the integration of ICT and AI to improve instructional practices and student outcomes.

EVOLUTION OF BLENDED LEARNING

Definitions and Frameworks of Blended Learning

Blended learning, as commonly defined by Graham (2021), combines face-to-face instruction with computer-mediated instruction. This hybrid approach includes various methods and technologies designed to enhance the learning experience. This framework aligns with Driscoll's (2020) categorization, which includes models such as the blended presentation and interaction model and the blended block model. In their approach, Cleveland-Innes and Wilton (2018) stress the importance of designing blended learning experiences that are cohesive, ensuring that the different modalities complement one another in achieving the learning outcomes. Moreover, Driscoll (2020) expands on this by identifying multiple blended learning models: the blended presentation and interaction model, the blended block model, and the fully online model. Each of these models integrates varying degrees of in-person and digital learning experiences, offering flexibility to adapt to diverse educational contexts.

Blended learning has also been studied through Wenger's Community of Practice (CoP) framework. Smith, Hayes, and Shea (2017) conducted a critical review of CoP's use in online and blended learning research, identifying 41 studies that explicitly referenced Wenger's theory. While CoP is useful for understanding social learning in blended environments, the review found that many studies only focused on verifying known elements, such as joint enterprise, without exploring more complex aspects like professional identity development or epistemic engagement. This gap highlights the need for future research that delves deeper into CoP's potential for blended learning environments. Blended learning frameworks are essential for understanding how digital and in-person elements can be cohesively integrated. Aparicio, Bacao, and Oliveira (2016) provide an in-depth e-learning theoretical framework that emphasizes the interplay of technology, pedagogy, and learning outcomes. Their framework highlights the importance of aligning technological tools with pedagogical goals to create a more effective blended learning environment. This theoretical approach underscores the need for carefully selected digital tools that enhance both student engagement and the learning process, reinforcing the core principles of blended learning.

Activity Theory has also been applied to blended learning research. Karasavvidis (2009) used it to examine how students engaged with online resources, discovering that students often only used materials essential for course survival, rather than fully utilizing all available learning tools. This suggests that the success of blended learning depends on how well digital resources are integrated into the curriculum. When students see online resources as critical to their success, they are more likely to engage with them deeply, supporting the overall learning process. In addition to these theories, Rajkoomar and Raju (2016) emphasized the importance of a structured framework for blended learning in higher education. Their work, focusing on South African universities, underlined that blended learning should be purposefully designed to combine delivery methods, teaching styles, and student competencies. This framework provided a roadmap for incorporating both pedagogical and technological elements into the learning process, ensuring that blended learning maximizes its potential for enhancing student outcomes.

Blended learning integrates digital technologies with traditional face-to-face teaching methods, allowing for flexible and varied learning experiences. Ting (2014) explores podcasting as a tool within a blended learning framework, particularly in language learning. Ting argues that podcasting enhances student engagement and supports language acquisition by offering multimodal learning opportunities, such as audio and video content. This approach allows learners to access and interact with the material outside the classroom, reinforcing the flexibility and accessibility that blended learning promotes.

Student Engagement and Outcomes in Blended Learning

Student engagement is a critical factor in the success of blended learning environments. Halverson and Graham (2019) developed a conceptual framework for understanding engagement in blended learning, identifying both cognitive and emotional indicators. Their work underscored the importance of monitoring engagement levels through real-time and minimally intrusive measures, which help educators assess the effectiveness of instructional changes. However, research also suggests that student engagement with digital resources in blended learning can be inconsistent. Karasavvidis (2009) found that students often limit their use of online resources to what they perceive as necessary for passing the course, neglecting additional materials that could enhance their learning experience. This minimal engagement with online tools can undermine the full benefits of blended learning, particularly when students do not perceive the digital components as integral to their success.

Moreover, Ting (2014) explored the use of podcasting as a blended learning tool in language education. The study found that podcasts provide an effective way for students to learn vocabulary and language use, particularly when integrated into a broader blended learning framework. This suggests that multimodal learning tools, such as podcasts, can enhance the engagement and learning outcomes of students in blended environments. Blended learning models have been proven to enhance student engagement by incorporating digital tools with traditional classroom experiences. Several studies emphasize the importance of different engagement dimensions—cognitive, emotional, and behavioral—within blended learning environments. Emmanuel, Bhandigadi, and Ch'ng (2019) analyzed how Wawasan Open University

(WOU) aimed to increase student engagement through multiple channels such as Learning Management Systems (LMS), tutorial classes, and communication tools like WhatsApp and emails. The study, involving 600 students, found that participation in tutorial classes, LMS, and student motivation were closely associated with improved academic outcomes. It was noted that students who engaged more deeply in tutorial activities and LMS interactions had better retention and success rates. This underscores the importance of blended learning as a mechanism for sustained student engagement in open and distance learning environments.

Adams et al. (2020) expanded on this by investigating how demographic factors (age, gender, field of study) influence student engagement within blended learning models in Malaysian higher education. Their study used the Blended Learning Readiness Engagement Questionnaire and found that cognitive, emotional, and behavioral engagement processes are influenced by these demographic variables. Students in private and public institutions showed different levels of engagement depending on their backgrounds, but overall, high levels of engagement were observed across the board. This suggests that while blended learning promotes engagement, institutions must consider demographic differences to optimize its effectiveness. Lecturers should use this insight to reflect on their own teaching methods and how they can better adapt to technological advancements and the needs of diverse student populations. Vermare (2023) demonstrated that student-centered blended learning approaches, such as flipped classrooms, further enhance engagement. By allowing students to access materials at their own pace and engaging them in interactive in-class activities, this flipped classroom model significantly improved student participation and learning outcomes. Vermare's study, conducted within a pre-university masterclass, showed that combining independent online learning with interactive face-to-face activities led to a more engaging educational experience, filling a gap in secondary education research on flipped classrooms. The findings emphasize that blended learning environments need to be structured to support both independent and collaborative learning, offering flexibility while ensuring active participation.

Similarly, Oprescu (2020) investigated the impact of blended learning in Romania's pre-university system. By integrating Web 2.0 technologies like blogs, wikis, and podcasts, the study found that the blended learning method encourages a more student-centered approach, significantly enhancing interpersonal communication and student engagement. The research also highlighted the redefined roles of teachers and students in blended learning environments, where teachers adopt more facilitative roles, and students take on more responsibility for their own learning. This shift contributes to higher engagement levels as students become more active participants in their education, compared to traditional methods. In the realm of distance learning, Frank, Kurtz, and Levin (2002) explored the integration of blended learning in pre-university refresher courses in Israel, particularly in mathematics and physics.

Their study followed the use of synchronous and asynchronous learning tools in distance education, finding that blended learning facilitated more regular student-teacher interactions and sustained engagement over time. By blending face-to-face sessions with digital tools, the courses allowed remote students to stay connected and engaged with course materials, demonstrating the effectiveness of blended learning in distance education settings. Ramachandra and Heng (2018) conducted a study on a blended learning introductory programming course in Singapore, finding that male students and those with prior exposure to programming performed better in a blended learning environment.

This study also revealed that blended learning pedagogy provided an accessible framework for students with varying levels of prior experience, offering a balance of in-person and online resources that helped bridge knowledge gaps. The results suggest that blended learning can accommodate diverse student backgrounds, but pre-existing knowledge can still influence the level of engagement and academic performance. Loots, Strydom, and Posthumus (2023) provide a comprehensive analysis of factors that support student engagement in blended learning environments within and beyond the classroom. Their study, grounded in qualitative data from the South African Survey of Student Engagement, highlights the importance of relational engagement and social interaction in both curricular and extracurricular spaces. The authors emphasize that while technology facilitates learning, it cannot replace the value of face-to-face interaction. The research calls for blended learning designs that integrate technology while maintaining relational engagement to foster holistic student development.

Bazelais (2022) examines the relationship between blended learning and academic performance in higher education, particularly within STEM disciplines. Conducted with pre-university CEGEP science students, the study comprises three empirical investigations into the effects of blended learning on academic outcomes. The research explores various blended learning strategies, such as two-stage quizzes, peer formative feedback, asynchronous video instructions, and online assessments, in enhancing students' engagement and performance. Bazelais concludes that blended learning can positively impact academic achievement but underscores the need for further research to clarify its effects across contexts. Lastly, Basogain et al. (2018) explored the use of blended learning in teaching computational thinking through courses in the USA and Latin America. Their research found that integrating visual programming tools such as Scratch and Alice in blended learning environments significantly improved students' engagement and understanding of computational concepts. The courses were supported by learning platforms that facilitated innovative pedagogical strategies, further demonstrating the power of blended learning to enhance both engagement and learning outcomes in technical subjects.

Across these studies, it becomes clear that blended learning has the potential to significantly enhance student engagement through its ability to integrate multiple modes of instruction. Whether in open distance learning or traditional classroom settings, blended learning creates opportunities for increased participation, motivation, and academic performance. The studies demonstrate that blended learning is most effective when it takes into account the diverse needs of students, including their backgrounds, prior knowledge, and engagement preferences, while offering flexible learning environments that support both independent and collaborative work.

The Role of Teachers in Blended Learning

Blended learning significantly transforms the role of teachers from traditional lecturers to facilitators and guides. Teachers are now responsible for motivating students to engage in critical thinking and ensuring their digital safety. According to Shivam and Singh (2015), blended learning merges classroom and online education, helping students stay motivated while encouraging a deeper understanding of the subject. Similarly, Jokinen and Mikkonen (2013) highlight that blended learning in nursing programs presents challenges but offers opportunities for practical, technology-supported education, which motivates students through real-life applications. Teachers must adopt various pedagogical approaches to create an effective blended learning environment. Hubackova and Semradova (2016) emphasize the teacher's role in organizing blended learning and ensuring students' successful navigation of both online and offline resources. As teachers take on a guiding role, students gain independence in managing their learning processes, facilitated by Learning Management Systems (LMS). Bliuc et al. (2012) add that the success of blended learning hinges on how teachers design the course and manage their dual role in the blended environment. These studies suggest that while the role of teachers has shifted to facilitating and mentoring, their engagement is key to ensuring that students remain active participants in their learning journeys.

In language learning, the teacher's role remains critical, especially in conversation-driven subjects. Neumeier (2005) explains that in blended learning, teachers must determine the optimal balance between in-person instruction and technology to maintain interaction and ensure language skills development. Similarly, Kaur (2013) argues that effective blended learning requires teachers to navigate both technical and pedagogical challenges to foster meaningful learning experiences. Dangwal (2017) explores the concept of blended learning as an innovative educational approach, emphasizing the integration of traditional classroom teaching with online learning. The study outlines the advantages of blended learning, such as increased flexibility, collaborative learning, and better student engagement. However, it also highlights challenges, including the need for sufficient technological infrastructure and motivated teachers and students. Dangwal concludes that while blended learning is an effective educational method, its successful implementation requires careful planning, teacher training, and the right blend of online and offline resources.

The importance of teachers in blended learning is further emphasized in studies focusing on self-regulated learning. Kharb and Samanta (2016) found that blended learning increases students' motivation for independent study and enhances their cognitive skills. Teachers, in this context, act as motivators and facilitators, guiding students in managing their learning processes while ensuring they have access to appropriate resources. However, transitioning to blended learning environments comes with challenges for teachers. Comas-Quinn (2011) highlights that teachers often struggle with their evolving identity in blended settings. Moving from traditional teaching to blended learning requires more than just technical skills; it requires a pedagogical shift where teachers embrace their new roles and responsibilities. The study found that teachers faced challenges in adjusting to the complexities of online teaching, further suggesting that professional development and pedagogical training are essential for a successful transition. The role of teachers in blended learning is multifaceted, requiring them to be facilitators, guides, motivators, and digital safety enforcers. Teachers must adapt to new technologies and pedagogical frameworks to ensure that students are engaged and successful in blended learning environments. As research demonstrates, the effectiveness of blended learning depends largely on the teacher's ability to navigate these changes and create a supportive, interactive learning environment.

Challenges in Implementing Blended Learning

The challenges of implementing blended learning are well-documented. Wong, Tatnall, and Burgess (2014) developed a framework to assess the readiness, intensity, and impact of blended learning. Their study of a blended accounting course in Australia revealed that while students appreciated the flexibility of online learning, they still valued face-to-face instruction. The study also highlighted the importance of student readiness and the need for institutions to assess whether students are prepared to engage with blended learning models before fully implementing them. For example, in education institutions in Saudi Arabia, Alebaikan (2011) found that while blended learning had significant potential, its implementation required careful consideration of pedagogical strategies and infrastructure. This is particularly true in contexts where technological resources are limited or where students and faculty may lack familiarity with digital tools. Ramakrisnan et al. (2012) echoed these concerns, noting that small, private institutions often face additional hurdles in adopting blended learning due to space and resource constraints.

A key factor influencing the success of blended learning is student and instructor attitudes toward technology. Bervell, Nyagorme, and Arkorful (2020) identified performance expectancy, effort expectancy, and facilitating conditions as key determinants of student attitudes toward Learning Management Systems (LMS). Their study revealed that when students have positive attitudes toward LMS, they are more likely to engage fully with the blended learning components of their courses. Conversely, negative attitudes can create barriers to effective learning. Another challenge highlighted by Cronje (2020) is that many definitions of blended learning focus on the blend of instructional methods without adequately addressing the learning itself. Cronje argues that blended learning definitions should be grounded in learning theory, specifically integrating both behavioral and constructivist approaches. This ensures that blended learning not only mixes instructional modalities but also supports deeper learning processes through hands-on activities and engagement.

Blended Education in an AI-Enhanced Educational Landscape

Generative AI refers to systems designed to create new content based on patterns found in existing data, utilizing techniques such as neural networks. Aydın & Karaarslan (2023) explain that Generative Adversarial Networks (GANs) are a popular method in which a generator creates data and a discriminator evaluates it, leading to improved outputs over time. Applications of generative AI span various domains, including image and text generation, music composition, drug discovery, and data augmentation. These innovations hold transformative potential in education, particularly in personalized learning and creative tools (Kayyali, 2024).

The future of blended learning lies in its ability to adapt to the changing needs of students and educational institutions. Becher Araujo Moraes (2023) emphasized the need for continuous evaluation of blended learning models, particularly in the post-pandemic context. As institutions recalibrate their teaching methods, blended learning offers a flexible and scalable solution to meet the demands of diverse student populations. Ali, Joyes, and Ellison (2015) proposed the third generation of an aligned activity system as a theoretical framework for blended learning research. This framework integrates both online and classroom activities and emphasizes constructive alignment, ensuring that course objectives, assessments, and learning activities are coherently linked. This approach can help institutions develop more effective blended learning environments that cater to different learning styles and needs. Heinze and Procter (2004) argued that communication is key to the success of blended learning courses. Their research, based on action research cycles at the University of Salford, highlighted the importance of transparency and clear communication between students and instructors in blended learning environments. This ensures that students understand the expectations and are able to navigate the blend of online and face-to-face components effectively.

Wong (2024) emphasizes the growing importance of AI-enhanced blended learning in creating more flexible, personalized, and engaging educational environments. AI tools allow real-time feedback and customized learning, contributing to more dynamic and student-centered teaching approaches. Meng, Dhimolea, & Ali (2022) review how AI applications like learning analytics and machine learning shape the educational landscape. They highlight how AI enhances decision-making processes for teachers, administrators, and students, supporting better student outcomes through personalized learning plans and smart learning environments. Sharma & Kumar (2024) delve into the ethical implications of AI use in education, focusing on issues such as fairness, privacy, and the need for transparency in AI-driven platforms. They highlight that AI's role in education should be balanced with human oversight to ensure that ethical standards are upheld in teaching and learning environments. Yang et al. (2024) investigates the role of AI in STEM education. Through an extensive bibliometric analysis of AI-related studies, they identify that AI enhances student motivation and performance in STEM subjects by allowing for more tailored and exploratory learning experiences. This finding underlines the transformative potential of AI for fostering engagement and improving educational outcomes.

Sargiotis (2024) explores how AI and Big Data analytics are used to create virtual learning infrastructures. These technologies allow institutions to optimize resources and provide scalable, flexible learning systems. AI-driven learning environments enable a more personalized approach, increasing inclusivity and adaptability in education. Wang & Rao (2024) propose an AI-based blended teaching framework aimed at enhancing digital learning capacities. They focus on the integration of smart classrooms and AI-powered knowledge graphs to better connect offline and online instruction. Their model illustrates how AI can drive precise, interactive, and personalized blended learning experiences. Alshahrani & Qureshi (2024) discuss the multifaceted roles of generative AI in enhancing various educational processes, including programming proficiency, writing, and student engagement. They propose that AI tools like ChatGPT can personalize and augment learning, although they also caution about the need for ethical guidelines to avoid over-reliance on automation. Sanders & Mukhari (2024) focus on AI's impact on blended learning in South African higher education. They emphasize the necessity of professional development, technological infrastructure, and strong institutional support to ensure effective AI integration in educational practices. Mutambik (2024) highlights how AI-powered automation can streamline educational processes, particularly in Saudi Arabian universities, providing an alternative pathway for sustainable education. AI's role in learning management systems (LMS) allows for more efficient administrative processes and improved educational outcomes.

All these studies demonstrate how AI-enhanced blended learning improves student engagement and personalization. While AI can facilitate learning through real-time feedback, data-driven insights, and customized content, the success of these tools depends on ethical implementation, robust infrastructure, and professional development for educators. The integration of AI into blended learning also offers opportunities to create more inclusive and scalable educational environments, addressing the diverse needs of learners. Dziuban & Picciano (2021) predict that blended learning, combining online and in-person methods, will continue to shape education. The complexity introduced by emerging technologies, along with the challenges caused by events like the COVID-19 pandemic, demands a reassessment of traditional educational models, with AI expected to play a key role in reshaping these. Baig (n/a) highlights the transformative power of AI in higher education, including personalized learning and predictive analytics. AI's capability to identify at-risk students and offer tailored interventions is seen as revolutionary, especially in regions where access to quality education is a challenge, like Pakistan. However, ethical concerns, such as data privacy and bias, require careful attention to ensure fair and transparent use of these tools. Islam et al. (2024) propose a collaborative learning platform that uses AI-driven recommendation systems to connect learners based on complementary skills. By balancing AI-generated content and human interaction, the platform promotes peer learning while fostering inclusivity and community engagement.

Zhang & Aslan (2021) review empirical studies on AI in education, highlighting the proven benefits of AI technologies in enhancing learning outcomes. They point to the need for ethical frameworks and interdisciplinary collaboration to optimize AI's educational impact. Syahrizal, Yasmi & Mary (2024) explore AI's role in Islamic education, utilizing the ADDIE model for creating multimedia-based learning materials. The study shows how AI-enhanced content can transform teaching, offering a personalized and interactive approach to learning religious education. Sundari, Penthala & Nayyar (n/a) emphasize the symbiotic relationship between AI tools and pedagogical practices, where AI-driven adaptive learning platforms personalize educational content to better fit the needs of individual learners. Sarnovska, Rybinska & Mykhailichenko (2024) focus on AI's role in language learning through personalized paths and intelligent tutoring, revolutionizing foreign language instruction by tailoring lessons to individual student needs.

The AI-enhanced program at St. Paul University Philippines (SPUP) aligns with the university's mission of values-oriented, Christ-centered education. It aims to prepare students for an AI-driven world, fostering global citizens through an internationalized curriculum that promotes sustainability, community, and charity.

By combining advanced AI knowledge with the spiritual and ethical dimensions of Paulinian education, the program is designed to leave a positive legacy and impact both locally and globally. The program's development model is shaped collaboratively by key stakeholders to ensure effective implementation (Ang & Aragon, 2020). The latest research on the field suggests that integration of AI in education brings personalized, data-driven learning experiences and redefines both teaching methods and student engagement. While AI enhances learning through customized educational content and automated systems, the ethical and social implications, such as data privacy and bias, remain significant challenges that require attention.

BLENDED EDUCATION: THE ALBANIAN CASE

Implementing blended learning requires full commitment the part of educational authorities and managements educational institutes. It needs a well-planned design that include all individuals from the top to the bottom of education hierarchy. This teaching methodology requires not only expertise to increase the capacities of teachers in schools, but also improved technology infrastructure in schools. Therefore, the implementation of blended education requires an additional budget in the budget of the Ministry of Education.

The studies provided offer a broad spectrum of insights into blended learning's evolving role in higher education, especially in Albania. Prifti (2020) emphasizes that satisfaction with online elements significantly enhances students' learning experiences compared to traditional methods. Babameto & Pano (2024) present an evolving perspective, especially post-COVID, on how Albanian higher education is adopting blended learning, with lessons learned during the pandemic. Kraja (2023) discusses the ongoing digital transformation in Albania's education system, underscoring that while progress has been made, significant challenges remain in smart education's development (Qafzezi, 2023). Several other studies stress the critical importance of internationalization in Albanian higher education institutions through online collaborative learning, fostering engagement beyond national boundaries (Qafzezi, 2023). Vrenozi et al. (2020) highlight professors' perceptions of online teaching, pointing to a preference for blended learning, which is deemed safer and more adaptable to future challenges. Digital competence remains a key challenge in Albania. Miço & Cungu (2022) emphasize the lack of infrastructure and training for teachers, while Zekaj (2023) outlines the opportunities AI integration presents in supporting educators. Additionally, Thanasi & Mema (2024) focus on AI's role in mathematics education, illustrating how AI tools improve individual learning experiences and teacher effectiveness. Moreover, studies like those by Tseng & Lin (2024) explore the potential of AI technologies like GPT-3.5 in augmenting students' academic writing skills, demonstrating how AI enhances learning without compromising individuality. Collectively, these studies provide valuable insights into the evolving digital and AI-enhanced landscape of higher education in Albania and the broader Balkans.

The Albanian education system is in a transitional phase, seeking to adapt to modern teaching methodologies that incorporate ICT. According to constructivist learning theories, students build knowledge through social interaction and engagement with their environment. Educational institutions in Albania are beginning to adopt blended education to help develop critical thinking and digital skills among students. The Agency for Quality Assurance in Pre-University Education (ASCAP) in Albania has been promoting blended education by providing schools and teachers with guidelines and tools to integrate technology into their classrooms. Blended education in Albania combines traditional teaching methods with online learning. Schools have implemented different models of blended education, including rotation models, flexible models, self-blend models, and improved virtual models. These models offer teachers flexibility in adapting their lessons to suit the needs of their students. Most of the combined education programs include four models which are also presented in the Albanian curriculum by ASCAP are 1. Rotation models; 2. Flexible model; 3. The Self-Blend model; and 4. Improved virtual model. The models provide guidance on how to organize and implement them; school and teachers have the flexibility to adapt and apply them depending on the conditions and opportunities and needs, enriching them with other elements. It is important to bring to attention. Teachers can start implementing certain models in a multi-step manner. This guide presents the application methodology, as well as the advantages and disadvantages of each model. The teachers of some pilot schools have been trained to implement these models (ASCAP, n.d).

METHODOLOGY

This study employed a mixed-methods approach to evaluate the implementation of blended education in Albania. The methodology incorporated both quantitative and qualitative data collection through a survey distributed to teachers in pilot and non-pilot schools. The survey aimed to assess teachers' familiarity with blended learning models, the extent of technology use in classrooms, and the challenges faced in the adoption of these methods. The research further examined how teachers perceive blended education in an AI-enhanced context, capturing nuanced differences between pilot and non-pilot schools. The quantitative component consisted of structured, closed-ended questions, while the qualitative component involved open-ended questions that allowed teachers to elaborate on their experiences, use of technology, and support needs. This mixed-methods approach provided a comprehensive view of the readiness and challenges faced by teachers in Albania, reflecting the broader dynamics of AI-enhanced education and the unique experiences of educators in both pilot and non-pilot schools.

Survey Design

A survey was designed to assess the perceptions and experiences of teachers in Albania regarding the implementation of blended education. The survey targeted two groups: teachers from schools that had participated in a pilot blended learning project and teachers from non-pilot schools. The survey consisted of 16 questions, combining closed-ended and open-ended formats, aimed at understanding teachers' familiarity with blended learning models, their use of technology in the classroom, the challenges they face, and their perceived effectiveness of the blended approach. Quantitative data was gathered through structured questions, while qualitative insights were collected via open-ended responses that encouraged teachers to elaborate on their blended education practices, the tools they use, and the types of support they need. The closed-ended questions aimed to measure the frequency of specific technologies used in classrooms and the extent of training teachers had received on blended learning methodologies. The open-ended questions provided a platform for teachers to describe their personal experiences, understanding of blended education, and the challenges they face with technological integration.

Sampling

The sampling for this study involved teachers from various educational institutions across Albania, including primary and secondary schools, both public and private. The aim was to capture diverse perspectives on the implementation of blended learning in both environments, as well as to explore any significant differences in the adoption and understanding of blended education. The study aimed to gather a representative sample of educators with different teaching backgrounds, experiences, and familiarity with blended learning and AI-enhanced education. A total of 212 teachers participated in the survey, which included educators from primary, middle, and high schools, both public and private. The participants represented schools and institutions across Albania, including but not limited to: "Luigj Gurakuqi" in Elbasan, "Mahir Domi" high school, "Vasil Kamami" high school, "Qamil Guranjaku" school, "Mark Dashi" school in Fier, and various others. This sample provided a broad spectrum of educational environments, ensuring that the findings reflect a variety of school contexts.

Data Analysis

The data collected from the survey was analyzed using both quantitative and qualitative methods. Quantitative data, including responses to closed-ended questions, were analyzed using frequency and percentage distribution to understand the extent of blended learning usage, the types of technologies employed, and the challenges teachers face. The qualitative data, derived from open-ended questions, were analyzed using thematic analysis, which identified common themes related to teachers' experiences with technology, their perceptions of AI in education, and the challenges of integrating blended learning models. The results were categorized based on key themes, including technology usage frequency, familiarity with blended learning, perceptions of AI, and infrastructural challenges. This combination of qualitative and quantitative analysis allowed for a comprehensive understanding of the current state of blended education in Albania.

FINDINGS

The demographic data from the study provide key insights into the teaching workforce in Albania, particularly in the context of blended education. Most participants (43%) fall within the age range of 41-50 years, followed by 29% who are over 50 years old. This suggests that a significant proportion of educators in the sample are at a more advanced stage in their careers, likely with a wealth of experience. The smaller representation of younger teachers, especially those aged 30 or younger (6%), indicates that blended learning practices may be adopted primarily by mid-career and veteran educators. This age distribution is relevant when considering the adoption of new teaching models, such as blended learning, and the integration of AI into education. Teachers in the middle or late stages of their careers may face different challenges and have different perspectives on technology adoption compared to younger, more tech-savvy teachers.

Figure 1. Demographics - Age

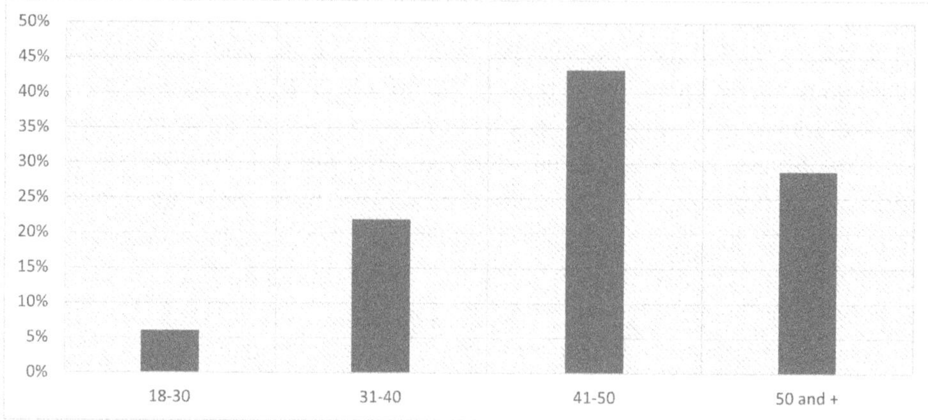

The gender distribution as shown in Figure-1, further enriches this demographic analysis, with 87% of participants being female and only 11% male. This is reflective of the broader trends in Albania's education sector, where teaching is predominantly a female-dominated profession. The high percentage of female teachers suggests that gender considerations should be considered when developing training and professional development programs for blended education and AI-enhanced teaching. Female educators may face different challenges in adopting new technologies, such as balancing professional development with other responsibilities. Therefore, support systems should be tailored to address these gender-specific dynamics.

Figure 2. Demographics - Years of Experience

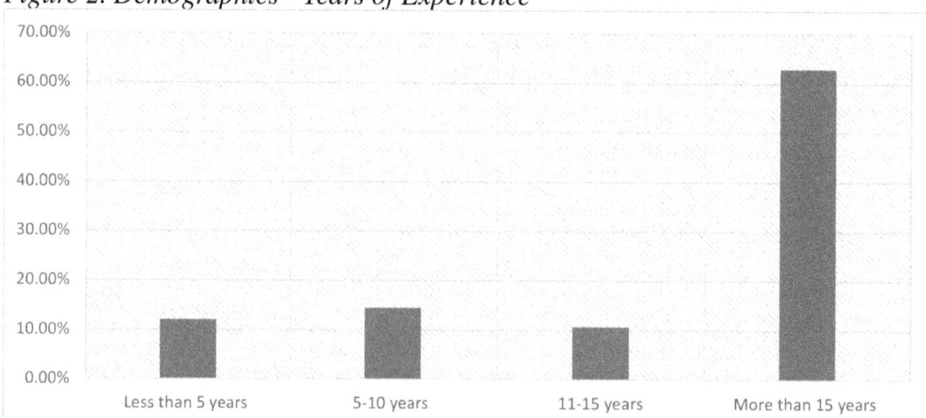

When considering teaching experience, the data shows that a substantial majority of participants (63%) have more than 15 years of experience in education as shown in Figure-2. This suggests that the teaching workforce represented in this study has a deep-rooted understanding of traditional education methods but may require targeted professional development to fully integrate new models such as blended learning and AI-enhanced teaching. Meanwhile, 14% of respondents have 5-10 years of experience, and 12% have less than 5 years. This range of experience highlights the diverse teaching backgrounds of the participants and points to the potential for a multi-generational approach to adopting blended education practices.

Figure 3. Demographics - Gender

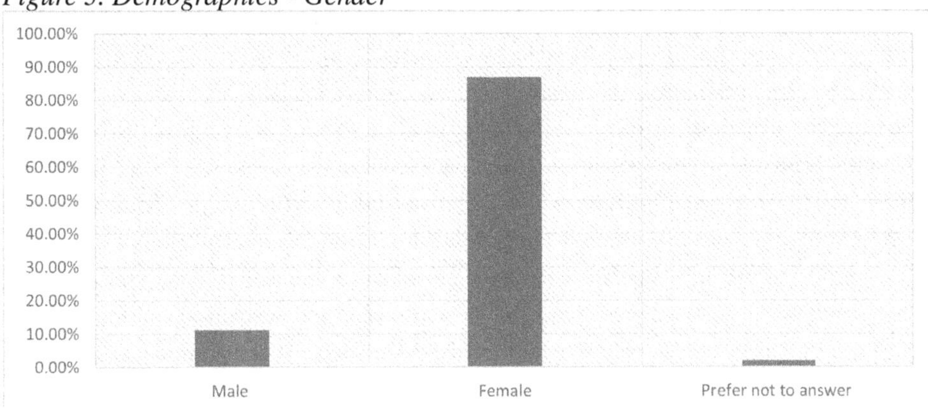

The data on age, experience, and gender (see Figure 3) provide a foundation for understanding the context within which blended education is being implemented in Albania. These demographic factors could influence how teachers perceive and adopt new educational technologies and models. Teachers in the older age groups and with more experience may benefit from targeted training to enhance their familiarity with blended learning and AI, while younger teachers might bring a fresh perspective but may need to adapt traditional methods to these new tools. Gender-based dynamics also play a role in shaping how teachers approach these evolving educational models.

The study reflected a broad and diverse representation of educational institutions across Albania, encompassing a variety of school types and administrative offices, which underscores the comprehensive nature of the data collected. Participants included educators from primary schools, secondary schools, high schools, and both public and private institutions, ensuring that perspectives from a wide range of educational environments were captured. Participants were from educational institutions such us Private school, "Mahir Domi" high school; "Vasil Kamami" high school;

“Qamil Guranjaku” school; “Mark Dashi “school, Fier; “Avni Rustemi” primary school Vlore; “Rrapo Hasimi” primary school Kanine; primary schools in Durrës; “Luigj Gurakuqi” Elbasan, DRAP institution in Korça, Fadil Gurmani educationa insitutions, “Ibrahim Ceka”, “Qamil Guranjaku”, Local educational office in Maliq, “Petro Sota” high school, “Servete Maci”, “Naim Frashëri”, “Avni Rustemi” “Liri Gero” “11 Dhesmoret” Labinot, “Kusarth&J.Dilo”, “V. Predushi”, “Gjocaj”, “Haxhi Qira” Burizane, “Sulë Harri” Elbasan, “Jusuf Puka: Durrës, “Mark Trokthi” Lac, “Green” school, “QG” Elbasan, “Abdyql Paralloi, School sin Kuqan, Prrenjas and in Belsh, “Kostantin Shpatara”, Vasil Karamani”, “Jorgji Dilo”, “Europa”, “Rilindja”, “Xhafer Hakani”, “Andon Zako Cajupi”, “MIsto Mame”, “Aleks Buda”, “Jeronim de Rada”, Local educational office in Elbasan, “Mahmud Ali Cungu”, “Mahmud dhe Ali Cungu”, “Onufri”, “Hekuran Maneku”, Local educationl office in Pogradec, “Halit Uruci”, “Bardhyl Popa”, “Lili Gero”, “Qemal Haxhihasani”, “Leke Gjiknuri”, “Liri Gero”, local educational office in Berat, and “Kico Blushi”.

Institutions from different cities and regions of Albania were part of the study, including prominent urban centers such as Elbasan, Fier, Durrës, and Vlore, as well as smaller regions like Kanine, Belsh, and Maliq. Schools like “Mahir Domi” High School and “Vasil Kamami” High School, along with institutions like “Qamil Guranjaku” and “Rrapo Hasimi” Primary Schools, represented the primary and secondary education sectors, providing insights into blended learning practices across different education levels. The inclusion of educational offices, such as DRAP in Korça and local education offices in Elbasan, Maliq, and Berat, adds a critical administrative perspective to the study, offering a more holistic view of how blended learning and AI-enhanced education are being perceived at both the classroom and institutional levels.

This wide representation of institutions helps to ensure that the findings reflect the educational diversity present in Albania, from rural to urban settings, and from highly resourced private schools to under-resourced public ones. The inclusion of multiple types of schools and administrative offices also enables the study to draw conclusions that are broadly applicable to the Albanian education system as a whole. By capturing the experiences of teachers and administrators across this range of educational contexts, the study provides a comprehensive look at the challenges and opportunities of implementing blended education within the Albanian educational landscape. This diversity will also help in identifying region-specific challenges or disparities that may require targeted interventions or policies to promote the effective adoption of blended learning and AI tools across the country.

Figure 4. Does the school where you work use blended learning methods?

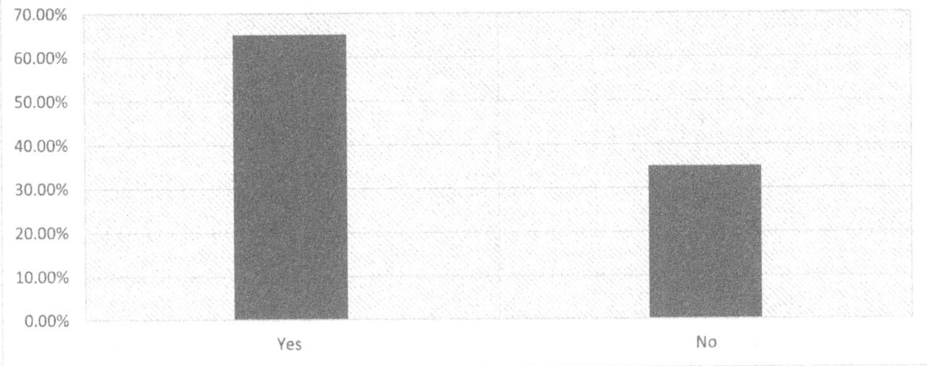

The data reveals that 65% of the participants (see Figure-4) confirmed the use of blended learning methods, indicating a notable level of integration of this educational approach across various schools in Albania. This suggests that a significant portion of schools are already embracing blended learning, combining traditional face-to-face instruction with digital or online methods to enhance teaching and learning experiences.

However, the remaining 35% of respondents indicated that they do not currently utilize blended learning methods, reflecting a gap in the adoption of such approaches. This divide points to the need for further exploration of the barriers preventing the full implementation of blended education in some schools. Factors such as lack of resources, infrastructure, or professional development could be influencing this disparity. The fact that a majority of educators are utilizing blended learning highlights a positive trend towards modernizing the educational environment. However, the data also underscores the need for targeted efforts to support the 35% of schools that have not yet adopted these methods, ensuring that blended learning is accessible and feasible for all educational institutions across the country. This could involve increased investment in technology, infrastructure, and teacher training programs aimed at facilitating the integration of blended education, especially in under-resourced schools or regions.

Figure 5. How often do you use technology (e.g., computers, tablets, software) in your teaching practices?

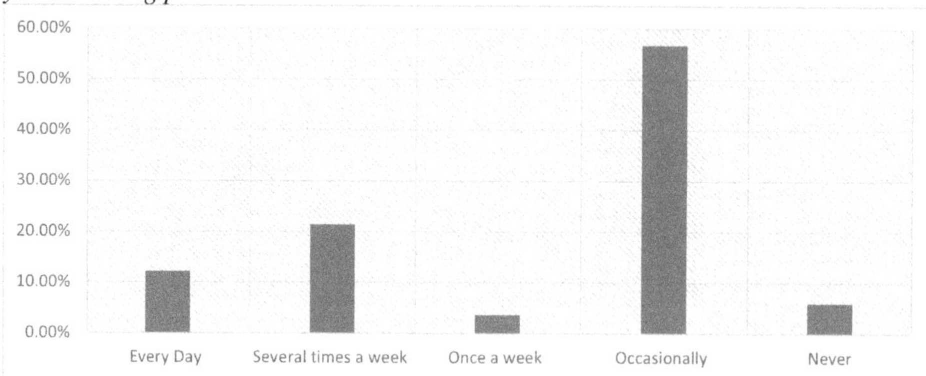

The responses regarding the frequency of technology (see Figure-5) use in teaching practices highlight a diverse range of approaches among educators in Albania. The data shows that while 12% of respondents use technology daily, indicating a strong integration of digital tools in their teaching, a larger portion of respondents, 21%, use technology several times a week. This suggests that regular but not necessarily consistent use of technology is more common. Additionally, a smaller group, 4%, use technology once a week, which may indicate a more limited or structured approach to technology integration in their lessons. Notably, 6% of respondents reported that they "never" use technology in their teaching practices, revealing that there is still a portion of educators who do not incorporate any digital tools into their instruction. This might be due to a lack of resources, training, or familiarity with technology, particularly in less technologically developed areas. The majority of the responses, approximately 57%, fell under the "occasionally" category, suggesting that while many educators are open to using technology, it is not yet a fully integrated or consistent part of their teaching routine. This distribution reflects a general inclination toward utilizing technology in the classroom, but also emphasizes that the frequency of use varies widely among educators. The variation in technology use highlights potential disparities in access to technological resources and professional development. Schools with more frequent technology use may benefit from better infrastructure or more proactive teacher training programs, while those using technology less often could face barriers such as limited access to equipment or insufficient technical support. This data suggests a need for targeted initiatives to support teachers in effectively integrating technology into their teaching practices on a more consistent basis. By addressing challenges such as access to resources, ongoing professional development, and technical support, educators can be better equipped to incorporate technology into their daily instruction, enhancing the learning experience for students across the board.

Figure 6. Which of the following tools do you use most often in class?

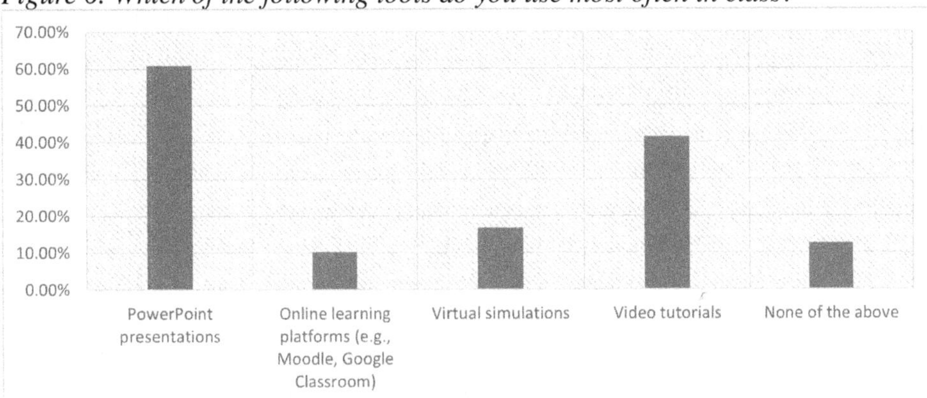

The data indicates that PowerPoint presentations are the most used tool among educators, with 60% of respondents (see Figure-6) employing them in their teaching practices. This highlights the widespread acceptance of PowerPoint as an effective tool for structuring lessons, delivering content, and enhancing student engagement through visual aids. Its popularity suggests that educators find it both accessible and useful for organizing and presenting information in a clear, structured way that helps students grasp complex concepts. In addition to PowerPoint, 41.4% of respondents use video tutorials, which offer dynamic content delivery that can cater to different learning styles, especially visual and auditory learners. Video tutorials can also help in reinforcing content outside the classroom, as students can watch and review materials at their own pace. The use of videos reflects a shift towards incorporating multimedia into lessons, making learning more interactive and engaging. However, only 16.7% of respondents are using virtual simulations, a tool known for providing interactive, hands-on experiences that can enhance students' understanding of complex subjects. The relatively low adoption of virtual simulations suggests that either these tools are not as readily available in all educational contexts or that teachers require more training and support to incorporate them effectively into their teaching practices. Virtual simulations offer significant potential for deeper learning, particularly in subjects like science, mathematics, and vocational studies, where experiential learning can enhance comprehension.

Interestingly, only 10.2% of educators are using online learning platforms to foster collaborative learning environments. These platforms, which include tools such as Moodle, Google Classroom, and other Learning Management Systems (LMS), can greatly enhance the blended learning experience by facilitating communication, resource sharing, and interactive learning opportunities. The limited use of these platforms points to a potential area for growth, as online platforms are key to fostering ongoing collaboration, feedback, and personalized learning paths. On the other hand, 12.6% of educators reported that they do not use any of these tools, which highlights an opportunity for greater integration of technology in the classroom. This could be due to a variety of factors, such as lack of access to necessary resources, insufficient training, or hesitation to adopt new technologies. This group represents a critical area for intervention, where professional development and infrastructure improvements could encourage wider adoption of educational technologies.

While a significant portion of educators are incorporating digital tools like PowerPoint and video tutorials, there is room for further integration of more advanced and collaborative tools like virtual simulations and online learning platforms. Increasing access to and training on these tools could not only enhance the teaching experience but also provide students with more interactive and engaging learning environments.

Figure 7. How familiar are you with blended learning models that integrate face-to-face and online learning?

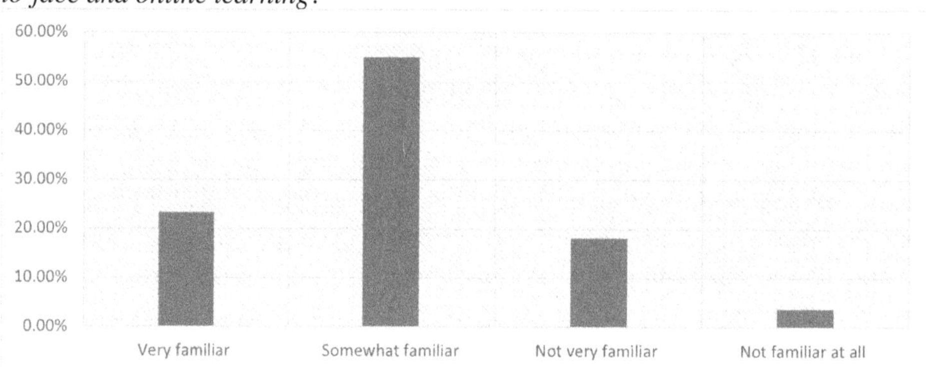

The responses regarding familiarity with blended learning models indicate a varied understanding of this educational approach among teachers. With approximately 55% of respondents (see Figure-7) indicating they are somewhat familiar with blended learning, it suggests that a large portion of educators have a foundational grasp of the concept but may not be fully versed in all the intricacies or best practices associated with it. This moderate level of familiarity indicates that while blended learning is not entirely new to many teachers, they might still require additional support to deepen their understanding and apply the model more effectively in their classrooms.

The 23% of respondents who reported being very familiar with blended learning models reflect a smaller, but significant group of educators who have a strong understanding of the concept. These educators are likely more equipped to implement blended learning effectively, integrating both face-to-face and online learning seamlessly. Their familiarity suggests they may already be utilizing advanced strategies for combining digital and in-person instruction, which could serve as examples or mentors for their peers who are less experienced.

On the other hand, 18% of teachers who are not very familiar with blended learning models, and the 4% who are not familiar at all, underscore a notable gap in knowledge that requires attention. These groups highlight the need for professional development initiatives that specifically focus on introducing blended learning methodologies and providing hands-on training to help teachers build confidence and competence in integrating digital tools with traditional classroom instruction. The presence of these knowledge gaps also suggests that while blended learning may be gaining traction, it has not yet reached universal adoption or understanding, particularly in schools or regions where access to training and resources may be limited.

The diverse range of familiarity with blended learning presents both a challenge and an opportunity. There is a clear need for targeted professional development, particularly for those who are unfamiliar or only somewhat familiar with blended learning models. Enhancing educators' knowledge and providing them with the necessary resources and support can help close these gaps and lead to more consistent and effective implementation of blended learning across different educational contexts. Additionally, schools can leverage the expertise of the 23% of very familiar educators to mentor and guide their colleagues, fostering a culture of shared learning and innovation in the use of blended learning strategies.

Figure 8. Are you familiar with the potential of artificial intelligence (AI) in education (e.g., adaptive learning systems, chatbots)?

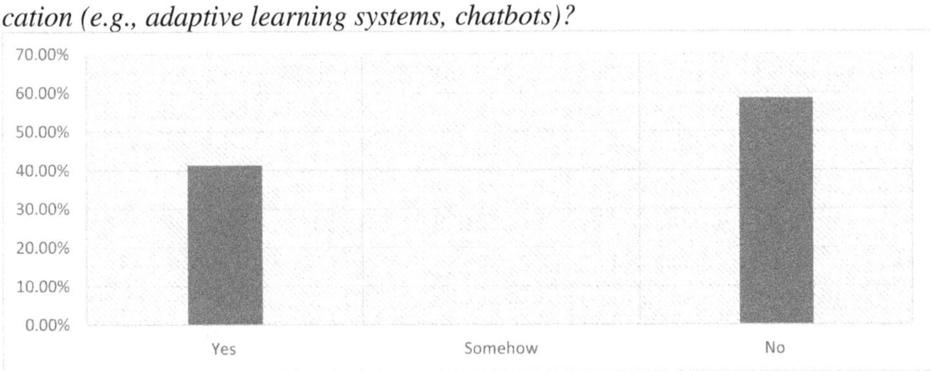

The responses regarding familiarity with the potential of artificial intelligence (AI) in education reveal a significant knowledge gap among educators (see Figure-8). A striking 60% of respondents indicated that they have limited or no awareness of AI applications in education, such as adaptive learning systems and chatbots. This lack of familiarity points to a broader issue: while AI is rapidly gaining attention and application in various sectors, including education, many teachers have yet to fully explore or understand its capabilities and potential benefits. This could be due to a combination of factors, such as limited access to training on AI tools, the novelty of AI in educational contexts, or a hesitancy to adopt unfamiliar technologies in the classroom.

Conversely, the 40% of respondents who expressed familiarity with AI in education represent a growing contingent of educators who recognize the transformative potential of AI tools. These individuals likely understand how AI can personalize learning, automate administrative tasks, and support adaptive learning environments that respond to individual student needs in real-time. Their knowledge suggests that some schools or regions may be more advanced in integrating AI into their teaching practices, offering a glimpse into the future possibilities of education that is enhanced by AI-driven tools.

The contrast between the two groups—those familiar with AI and those who are not—underscores the pressing need for professional development initiatives that focus on introducing AI technologies to educators in a practical and accessible way. The high percentage of teachers unfamiliar with AI suggests that many schools may not yet be investing in or promoting AI tools, possibly due to limited resources, lack of infrastructure, or a focus on more traditional educational technologies. However, the growing awareness among the 40% of respondents suggests that there is interest and potential for growth in this area.

Addressing this gap through targeted training programs could help bridge the divide between those who are familiar with AI and those who are not. Schools and educational policymakers should prioritize creating opportunities for educators to explore AI's potential and learn how to integrate it into their teaching practices effectively. Additionally, the responses indicate that schools and education systems that are already utilizing AI could serve as case studies or models for others, demonstrating the benefits and practical applications of AI in education.

The findings highlight a critical juncture in the evolution of technology-enhanced education. While some educators are beginning to embrace AI, a significant majority still require support and guidance to leverage its full potential. By addressing this knowledge gap, schools can ensure that all educators are equipped to harness the power of AI, leading to more personalized, efficient, and effective teaching and learning experiences.

Figure 9. How confident do you feel about integrating AI tools into your teaching practices?

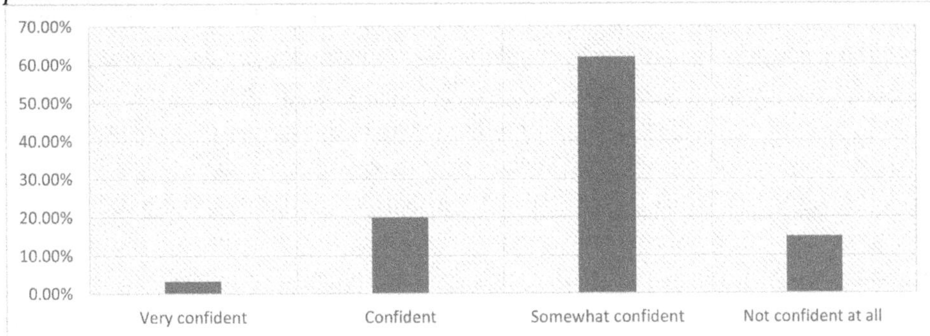

The responses regarding confidence in integrating AI tools into teaching practices reveal a nuanced perspective on educators' readiness to embrace this emerging technology (see Figure-9). A significant portion of respondents, 62%, reported feeling “Somewhat confident,” indicating that while many teachers are open to incorporating AI into their classrooms, they still lack full certainty about its application. This moderate level of assurance suggests that while educators see potential in AI tools, they may require further guidance, support, or training to feel fully comfortable using them effectively. These educators are likely aware of AI’s potential benefits but may not have had sufficient hands-on experience with these tools, or they may be unsure of how to best integrate AI in a way that enhances learning outcomes.

In contrast, the 20% of respondents who expressed being “Confident” demonstrate a higher level of proficiency and comfort in integrating AI tools. These teachers likely have more experience or exposure to AI technologies and have successfully implemented AI-driven systems such as adaptive learning platforms, chatbots, or AI-based assessment tools. Their confidence reflects a growing trend among some educators to embrace cutting-edge technologies that can automate tasks, personalize learning experiences, and improve efficiency in educational settings. These educators can serve as early adopters and potentially lead efforts to integrate AI more broadly within their institutions, offering mentorship to less experienced colleagues.

However, the 15% of respondents who reported feeling “Not confident at all” present a clear challenge for the broader implementation of AI in education. This group likely represents teachers who have had limited exposure to AI, or who may be resistant to adopting new technologies due to a lack of training, fear of change, or concerns about the complexity of AI tools. Their lack of confidence underscores the importance of providing targeted professional development programs that not only introduce AI but also build educators' skills and comfort levels in a practical, hands-on manner. For this group, more comprehensive training and ongoing support will be critical to ensure that AI can be seamlessly integrated into their teaching practices.

The distribution of confidence levels also highlights a broader trend in educational technology adoption, where early adopters and moderately confident educators can pave the way for wider usage, but success will depend on addressing the concerns and limitations experienced by less confident teachers. Schools and education systems must prioritize support structures, such as peer mentoring, technical assistance, and accessible resources, to bridge the gap between confident and less confident educators.

These findings emphasize the need for a strategic, inclusive approach to AI integration in education. While many teachers are open to using AI and some are already doing so effectively, a significant proportion of educators still need more resources and training to build their confidence. By addressing these needs, education systems can ensure that all teachers are prepared to use AI tools to enhance their teaching and improve student outcomes.

Figure 10. What kind of support would you seek to integrate AI tools in the classroom?

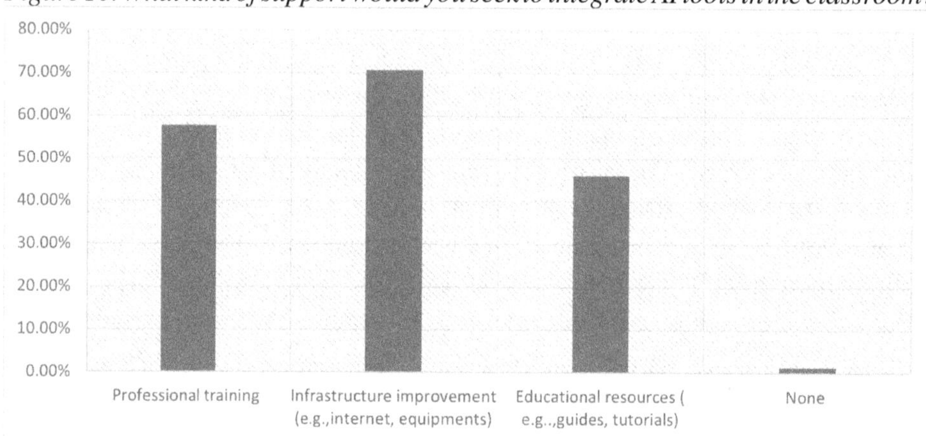

The responses regarding the type of support needed to integrate AI tools in the classroom reveal a clear demand for a multifaceted approach to building capacity among educators (see Figure-10). The most common response, selected by 70.7% of participants, emphasized the need for infrastructure improvement, highlighting that without adequate resources such as reliable internet access and appropriate technological devices, the integration of AI will remain a significant challenge. This finding suggests that even if educators are open to incorporating AI tools into their teaching practices, the lack of necessary infrastructure could act as a significant barrier, particularly in schools or regions where digital resources are limited. Improving infrastructure is a foundational requirement for AI integration, and without addressing this issue, the benefits of AI in education may remain unrealized for many teachers and students.

Professional training, selected by 57.7% of respondents, underscores the importance of continuous professional development for educators. While many teachers may be familiar with basic technologies, integrating AI tools—such as adaptive learning platforms or chatbots—requires specialized knowledge and skills. The fact that over half of the respondents indicated a need for professional training highlights that simply having access to AI technologies is not enough; teachers must also understand how to effectively use these tools to enhance learning outcomes. This finding suggests that comprehensive, ongoing training initiatives are essential for building educators' confidence and competence in AI. Professional training programs could cover areas such as how to use AI for personalized learning, automating administrative tasks, or fostering collaboration in virtual learning environments.

The need for educational resources, cited by 46% of respondents, further reinforces the importance of providing teachers with practical tools to aid in the integration of AI. Guides, tutorials, and step-by-step instructions can help bridge the gap between theoretical knowledge and practical application. These resources are particularly valuable for teachers who may not have the opportunity to attend formal training sessions but still wish to enhance their teaching with AI tools. Providing accessible, user-friendly resources ensures that educators at all levels of familiarity with AI can find support when needed.

The fact that respondents were able to select more than one option indicates that teachers recognize that multiple forms of support are necessary to successfully integrate AI into the classroom. The combination of infrastructure improvement, professional training, and educational resources points to a holistic approach, where both the technological and human factors are addressed. For AI to become a transformative force in education, schools and policymakers need to prioritize investments in infrastructure, alongside robust support systems for educators.

This analysis suggests that while there is enthusiasm for the use of AI in education, the successful integration of these tools will depend on providing comprehensive support to teachers. Without adequate infrastructure, even the most well-trained educators will face difficulties. Conversely, without training and resources, even well-equipped schools may not fully realize the benefits of AI. As such, a coordinated effort that includes upgrading infrastructure, offering targeted professional development, and providing accessible resources is essential for fostering the effective use of AI in Albanian schools.

Figure 11. How much do you agree with the statement: Combined education increases student engagement and improves learning outcomes.

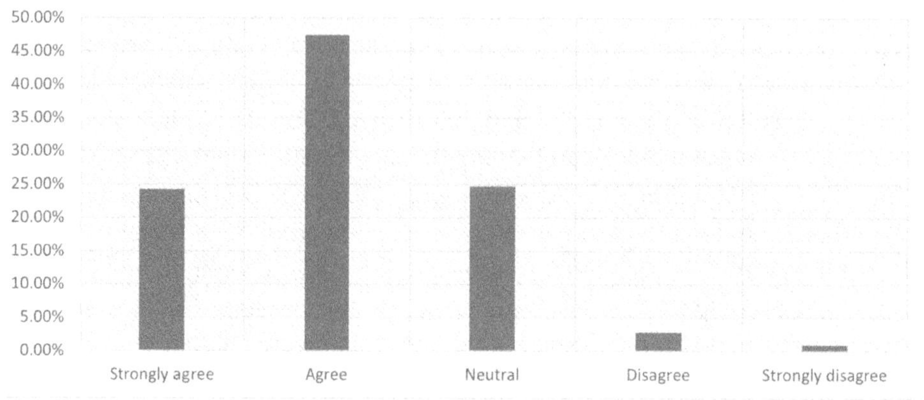

The responses to the statement about the effectiveness of combined education in increasing student engagement and improving learning outcomes show a generally positive attitude among the respondents (see Figure-11). A significant portion—47% of respondents—agreed, suggesting that a large number of educators see clear benefits in blending face-to-face and online learning approaches. This support is reinforced by the 24% who strongly agree, indicating that nearly three-quarters of respondents (71%) acknowledge the advantages of combined education in enhancing the learning experience. This demonstrates a general consensus on the value of blended education models, as they appear to engage students more effectively by combining traditional and digital methods. However, the 25% who remain neutral could reflect either uncertainty or a lack of sufficient experience with blended education to form a definitive opinion. This group represents a significant portion of respondents, and their neutral stance suggests that they may require further exposure to the practical benefits of blended education or more structured support to integrate these models effectively in their teaching. Their responses indicate potential for increased buy-in through targeted interventions like additional training or showcasing best practices of successful blended learning implementation.

Interestingly, a small but notable minority expressed skepticism about combined education. 3% of respondents disagreed, and a larger 24% strongly disagreed, indicating that a quarter of the participants hold reservations about the effectiveness of blended learning in improving student engagement and outcomes. This opposition could be attributed to various factors, such as challenges related to the implementation of blended models, difficulties in managing technology, or a preference for traditional teaching methods. The presence of such a sizable group opposed to blended learning underscores the need for further exploration into the specific concerns these educators have. These could range from technological barriers to doubts about the pedagogical value of blended education in certain subjects or settings. While the majority of educators support blended education, there is a clear need to address the concerns of those who remain skeptical. Additional training, demonstrations of successful blended learning models, and addressing logistical challenges (such as infrastructure and access to technology) could help shift neutral or opposing views toward a more favorable perception. The findings suggest that while blended learning has been positively received by many, the path to universal acceptance and confidence in its benefits requires ongoing support, professional development, and perhaps re-evaluating the tools and methods used to implement these models.

Figure 12. How often do your students show enthusiasm or increased participation when technology is integrated into lessons?

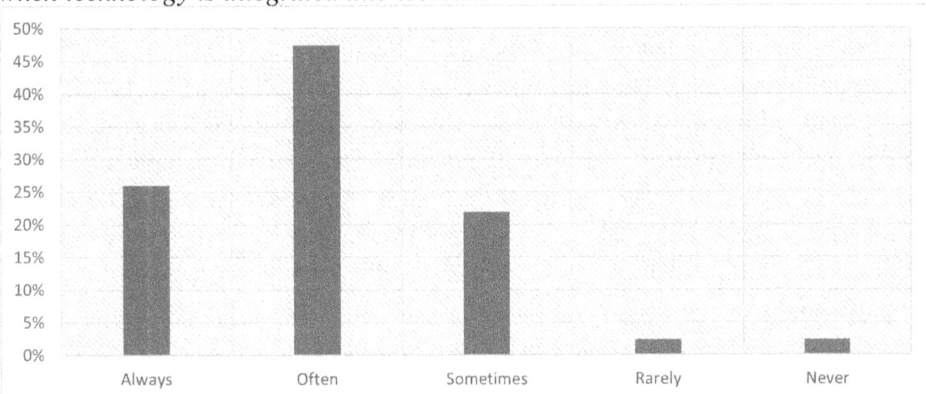

The results regarding student enthusiasm when technology is integrated into lessons reveal a largely positive impact of digital tools on student engagement. 26% of respondents indicated that their students always show enthusiasm when technology is used, reflecting strong and consistent engagement from this group of students (see Figure-12). This finding suggests that for some educators, technology integration has become a key factor in stimulating interest and active participation in the learning process.

Additionally, 48% of respondents reported that students often demonstrate increased participation when technology is included in the classroom. This majority response indicates that for most teachers, the introduction of technological tools—whether through presentations, online platforms, or other digital resources—contributes to a significant improvement in student involvement. This frequent positive response suggests that while not all students are always highly engaged, technology still plays an important role in enhancing the classroom experience for a substantial portion of learners.

The remaining 22% of respondents noted that students sometimes engage positively, signaling a more moderate response. This group suggests that while technology does foster engagement in certain instances, it may not be consistently effective across all students or contexts. This variability could depend on factors such as the type of technology used, the students' familiarity with the tools, or the relevance of the technology to the subject matter.

At the lower end of the spectrum, 2% of respondents expressed that their students rarely show enthusiasm when technology is integrated, and another 2% reported that their students never respond positively to its use. Although these percentages are small, they highlight that for a minority of educators, technology does not seem to significantly enhance engagement. This could be due to a lack of sufficient infrastructure, limited access to digital tools, or perhaps resistance from students who prefer more traditional learning methods.

These findings suggest that technology has a generally positive effect on student engagement, with the majority of educators seeing improvements in participation when digital tools are used. However, the moderate response from some educators and the negative experience reported by a small percentage suggest that the impact of technology is not universally effective and that further exploration is needed to understand the factors influencing its success in different educational environments. Supporting educators in selecting the right tools and offering professional development opportunities could help maximize the benefits of technology integration for all students.

Figure 13. What is the biggest challenge you face when integrating technology or blended learning models in teaching?

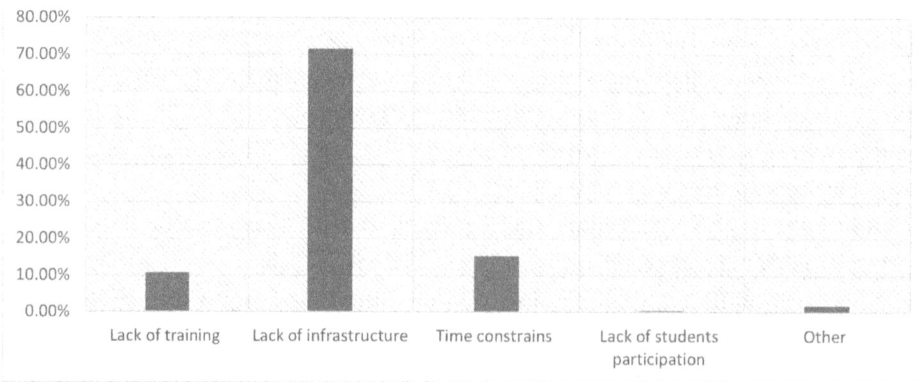

The data reveals that the lack of infrastructure is the most significant barrier to effectively integrating technology into teaching practices, as 72% of respondents identified this as a major issue (see Figure-13). This overwhelming response suggests that many educators are facing challenges related to the availability and quality of technological resources, such as reliable internet access, modern hardware (computers, tablets), and adequate classroom equipment like projectors. Without these basic tools, teachers are limited in their ability to implement blended learning and other technology-driven methods, which hampers their efforts to modernize and improve educational outcomes. In addition to infrastructure limitations, time constraints were noted by 15% of respondents. This indicates that while teachers may have the desire and understanding to integrate technology into their lessons, they often struggle to find the time to plan, prepare, and execute tech-based lessons effectively. The rapid pace of classroom schedules, combined with the added effort required to incorporate technology, can create significant hurdles for teachers, preventing the consistent use of digital tools. Finally, 11% of participants pointed to the lack of training as a critical challenge. This suggests that many educators feel underprepared to utilize the available technology effectively, even if the infrastructure is in place. Without proper training on how to use digital tools and integrate them into pedagogical strategies, the benefits of technology in education remain untapped. This finding emphasizes the need for more targeted professional development programs focused on digital literacy and pedagogical techniques that align with technology use. The data highlights a clear need for investment in both infrastructure and professional development to support teachers in overcoming these challenges. The widespread recognition of these barriers suggests that addressing them could lead to significant improvements in the adoption and effectiveness of technology in Albanian classrooms, thereby enhancing the overall quality of education.

The responses to the question about the impact of blended learning on teachers' roles reveal a strong consensus on its positive effects. Many educators expressed that blended learning significantly enhances both lesson planning and student interaction. They noted that incorporating technology into lessons makes them more engaging and attractive, fostering a stronger connection between teachers and students. This engagement encourages active participation from students, creating a more dynamic and interactive learning environment. Additionally, several respondents emphasized that this approach facilitates easier communication, both in and out of the classroom, which ultimately improves the overall quality of education. One educator mentioned, "*Blended learning is very effective in enhancing the learning process*," highlighting how it can enrich traditional teaching methods. The ability to deliver content in diverse formats allows teachers to cater to different learning styles, thus creating more personalized instruction. This customization helps address the diverse needs of students, especially those who may benefit from alternative learning materials such as video tutorials or interactive simulations.

The flexibility of blended learning also enables students to work at their own pace, promoting independent learning and critical thinking skills. At the same time, some teachers acknowledged that blended learning requires more preparation time and a solid understanding of technology. As one respondent noted, "*It requires more preparation time but is effective as we move towards the future.*" This reflects an awareness of the demands that blended learning places on educators, but also recognition of its long-term benefits. Another teacher highlighted how blended learning connects theoretical knowledge with practical applications: "*It has a significant impact because it connects theory with practice.*" This shows how technology can enhance the relevance of lessons, making learning more meaningful for students. However, concerns regarding infrastructure and training were also present. Some educators pointed out that inadequate resources and insufficient training can impede the successful implementation of blended learning. Despite these challenges, the overall sentiment remains highly positive, with educators believing that the benefits of blended learning outweigh the difficulties. Blended learning is seen as a valuable tool that enhances the teaching process, increases student engagement, and fosters a more interactive and effective learning environment.

The responses regarding the additional support needed for teachers in Albania to effectively implement blended learning and AI in education highlight several key areas of concern, primarily focusing on infrastructure, training, and resources. A significant number of educators emphasized the critical need for improved infrastructure, with many expressing frustration over the lack of necessary technological tools and reliable internet access. Phrases such as "Infrastructure remains the main problem" and "*We need the necessary tools*" were frequently mentioned, signaling that without sufficient infrastructure, it becomes nearly impossible for teachers to integrate technology into their lessons effectively. One teacher succinctly captured this concern by stating, "*Every class should have a smart board and internet access.*" This sentiment reflects the broader need for equitable access to modern technology in schools, which is seen as a fundamental component for fostering an AI-enhanced educational landscape. In addition to infrastructure, the need for effective and specialized training programs was another recurring theme.

Many teachers expressed dissatisfaction with the current training available, noting that it often lacks practical application. As one teacher remarked, "*Effective training is essential because most training sessions provide little benefit.*" This highlights a clear gap between the theoretical nature of existing professional development programs and the hands-on, actionable training that educators need. Teachers are asking for more relevant, ongoing training that keeps them up to date with the latest technological advancements and equips them with the skills to apply these tools in the classroom effectively. Another respondent echoed this sentiment, stating, "*Continuous training is necessary to keep up with technological advancements.*" Furthermore, the need for adequate teaching materials and resources was a consistent concern among educators. Many pointed to the lack of digital resources, laptops, and projectors as significant barriers to effectively delivering blended education. One teacher encapsulated this concern by stating, "*We need to ensure that every classroom is equipped with the necessary tools for effective teaching.*" This comment underscores the broader issue of resource allocation, which remains a key challenge in many Albanian schools. Teachers believe that having access to adequate digital resources would not only enhance the learning experience but also facilitate smoother integration of AI and other technological tools in their teaching practices. The responses indicate that while teachers in Albania are generally optimistic about the potential of blended learning and AI in education, the successful implementation of these tools requires a strong foundation in terms of infrastructure, continuous and practical training, and access to essential teaching materials. Addressing these areas will be crucial for advancing the role of AI in Albania's educational system and supporting teachers in adopting innovative methods to enhance student learning outcomes.

The responses regarding experiences with blended learning in the classroom reveal a mix of successes and challenges faced by educators in Albania, highlighting both the potential and the obstacles that accompany this educational approach. On the positive side, many teachers pointed out the engaging and dynamic nature of blended learning. One educator remarked, "*Students feel satisfied, and the lesson passes without them realizing,*" emphasizing how integrating technology can create a more interactive and immersive learning experience. This aligns with broader research that indicates the effectiveness of blended learning in fostering student engagement and participation. Teachers found that incorporating digital tools, such as multimedia content and interactive platforms, helped keep students interested and attentive throughout the lesson. The successful engagement of students suggests that blended learning can facilitate a more enjoyable and impactful learning environment. However, some educators noted challenges related to maintaining student motivation. As one teacher mentioned, "*Routine does not spark motivation,*" pointing to the difficulty of sustaining student interest if the use of technology becomes repetitive or lacks innovation.

This comment underscores the importance of continually evolving blended learning practices to keep the content fresh and engaging for students. Without proper variety and creative use of digital tools, the effectiveness of blended learning may diminish over time. A particularly compelling success story involved a teacher who worked with a student with special needs, sharing that the student was able to partially understand fractions through blended learning methods. This demonstrates the flexibility and inclusivity of blended learning, which can be tailored to accommodate diverse learning needs and abilities. The use of visual aids, interactive exercises, and self-paced learning tools in a blended format can offer more personalized support, allowing students with different learning styles or challenges to grasp complex concepts at their own pace. Several educators also reflected on their experiences during the COVID-19 pandemic, a period that required a swift transition to online teaching. One teacher recalled, "*We managed to continue teaching virtually despite our unpreparedness,*" showcasing the resilience and adaptability of teachers in the face of a sudden and unprecedented shift to remote learning. This adaptability highlights the potential of blended learning to provide continuity in education during crises, even when educators have limited prior experience with technology. While many teachers acknowledged their initial lack of preparation, they also recognized that the forced shift to online teaching accelerated their learning curve, leading to a broader acceptance of blended education models. The experiences shared by educators in Albania illustrate both the successes and challenges of blended learning. While the approach has proven effective in engaging students and catering to diverse learning needs, sustaining motivation and ensuring adequate preparation and resources remain key challenges. Nonetheless, the adaptability of educators and the positive outcomes in specific cases, such as with students who have special needs, demonstrate the promising potential of blended learning when applied thoughtfully and with the right support.

DISCUSSION

Teacher Training and Familiarity with Blended Learning

The findings revealed that Albanian teachers demonstrated varying degrees of familiarity with blended learning methodologies, significantly influenced by the availability of structured training. Teachers who had received formal training in blended learning methodologies, whether through pilot projects or professional development programs, demonstrated a deeper understanding of how to implement these models effectively. These teachers were better equipped to engage students using AI-enhanced tools such as online quizzes, learning platforms, and adaptive learning systems. They also reported that students were more responsive and engaged when technology was seamlessly integrated into lessons. In contrast, a considerable number of teachers, particularly those from schools without formal exposure to blended learning models, had a more superficial understanding of the concept. Many equated the use of technology with simpler tasks such as PowerPoint presentations or basic communication tools like WhatsApp. This mirrors findings from Emmanuel et al. (2019) at Wawasan Open University, where limited exposure to structured blended methodologies similarly affected technology integration in classrooms. Without formal training, these teachers could not fully leverage the potential of blended learning to transform teaching practices.

Infrastructure and Access to Technology

Infrastructure emerged as one of the most significant challenges in the implementation of blended education in Albania. Teachers from various schools, particularly in non-pilot institutions, reported severe limitations in terms of access to the necessary technology. Only a small percentage (3%) of teachers had invested in personal projectors, while many others relied on their own laptops due to a lack of sufficient ICT resources in schools. This disparity was most evident in rural areas, where educational facilities often lacked basic technological infrastructure, such as internet access or interactive boards, to support effective blended learning.

These findings parallel challenges noted in Oprescu (2020), who documented similar infrastructure deficits in Romania's education system. Teachers faced difficulties engaging students due to the lack of proper ICT resources. Likewise, in Albania, these deficits have hindered the potential of blended learning to make a meaningful impact in non-pilot schools. Dangwal (2017) emphasized the need for substantial investments in infrastructure and teacher motivation to realize the full benefits of blended learning, a sentiment echoed in the current study. The study also highlighted a critical need for ongoing technical support. Teachers reported challenges with basic ICT operations, such as connecting projectors and navigating educational software. This finding is consistent with Miço & Cungu (2022), who pointed to similar gaps in digital competence among Albanian educators. The current study underscores the urgent need for professional development programs that align with European and international standards to close these gaps and support the sustainable implementation of blended learning models.

The Role of AI in Blended Education

The use of AI-enhanced tools was another crucial aspect examined in this study. Teachers in schools that had access to AI-driven platforms, such as adaptive learning systems and automated assessments, reported higher levels of student engagement and improved academic performance. These tools allowed educators to provide more personalized feedback, adapt lessons to individual learning needs, and create a more interactive and engaging learning environment. However, the study also revealed that a majority of teachers, particularly in non-pilot schools, had limited familiarity with AI technologies. Their technology use remained basic, involving presentations or simple online searches, without taking full advantage of AI's capabilities to personalize learning and improve outcomes. This gap highlights a need for broader professional development focused on AI integration in education, as noted by Sanders & Mukhari (2024) and Zhang & Aslan (2021). Both studies emphasized that the barriers to AI adoption in education, including infrastructure and digital literacy, must be addressed for AI to fully enhance educational experiences.

Teacher Perspectives and the Need for Capacity Building Programs

Despite challenges related to infrastructure and training, teachers across all schools expressed enthusiasm for integrating technology and AI into their classrooms. The majority of educators recognized the potential benefits of blended learning in enhancing lesson planning, improving student interaction, and fostering engagement. However, the study revealed a significant need for capacity-building programs, particularly in non-pilot schools, where teachers had limited exposure to advanced blended learning models. The findings align with Rajkoomar and Raju's (2016) argument that successful blended learning depends on pedagogical skills that must be nurtured through continuous training and support. Teachers in pilot schools, who benefitted from formal training, demonstrated higher engagement with blended learning strategies, while their counterparts in non-pilot schools expressed frustration with their lack of preparation and confidence in using these tools. Jokinen and Mikkonen (2013) similarly emphasized the importance of ongoing professional development to transition effectively to blended learning environments. The current study highlights the critical need for structured, continuous teacher support in Albania.

Student Engagement and Learning Outcomes

The findings of the study consistently indicated that students responded positively to the integration of technology in their learning. Teachers in pilot schools reported particularly high levels of student engagement when AI-driven platforms were used to personalize instruction and create interactive experiences. In these settings, students were more motivated to participate in lessons, and overall learning outcomes improved. While teachers in non-pilot schools also noted positive reactions from students when using basic technology, the lack of access to advanced AI-enhanced tools limited the depth of student engagement. This is consistent with Basogain et al. (2018), who found that AI-powered tools such as Scratch and Alice fostered creativity and increased student participation in higher education. Loots, Strydom, and Posthumus (2023) also demonstrated how digital tools could increase relational engagement, improving student-teacher interactions and participation.

CONCLUSION

Blended learning has evolved into a flexible and dynamic approach to education, integrating digital tools with traditional teaching methods. The literature suggests that while blended learning offers significant benefits—such as increased engagement, flexibility, and improved learning outcomes—its success depends on thoughtful design, adequate infrastructure, and positive attitudes toward technology. Theoretical frameworks such as Wenger's CoP, Activity Theory, and the third-generation activity system offer valuable insights into how blended learning environments can be optimized. Future research should focus on refining these models and exploring new ways to support student engagement and learning in diverse educational contexts. Blended education represents a powerful teaching methodology that can bridge the gap between traditional and online learning. While Albanian schools have made strides in implementing this approach, there are still significant barriers to overcome, particularly in terms of infrastructure and teacher training. By addressing these challenges, Albania can ensure that its education system is equipped to meet the demands of the future and provide students with the skills they need to succeed in a technology-driven world.

The findings of this study emphasize the importance of teacher training, adequate infrastructure, and the integration of AI tools in successfully implementing blended education in Albania. Teachers in schools that received formal training and had access to the necessary technology reported higher levels of student engagement, enhanced lesson planning, and improved learning outcomes. In contrast, educators in schools with limited resources struggled to implement blended learning effectively, primarily due to infrastructural deficiencies and insufficient professional development. The study demonstrates that while enthusiasm for blended learning is high, the Albanian education system still faces significant hurdles in realizing its full potential. To overcome these challenges, a strategic, multi-level approach is required, focusing on teacher capacity-building, increased investment in ICT infrastructure, and the creation of national policies that align with international standards for AI in education. By addressing these issues, Albania can ensure that its educational landscape is better equipped to meet the demands of a technology-driven future.

One of the major barriers identified in the study is the lack of sufficient ICT infrastructure, particularly in non-pilot schools. The need for teachers to provide their own laptops, along with limited access to projectors and other essential technology tools, hinders the effective implementation of blended learning. Even in schools where blended learning is partially implemented, a significant portion of teachers struggles with basic ICT tasks, such as connecting devices and using educational software. Without proper infrastructure and ongoing technical support, the adoption of AI-enhanced education will remain limited. Furthermore, the study demonstrates that when properly supported by technology, blended learning significantly enhances student engagement. This aligns with global findings on the positive impacts of AI and digital tools on student engagement and personalized learning. However, for Albania to fully benefit from AI-enhanced learning, investments in technology infrastructure and teacher training must be prioritized. As education continues to evolve in the context of AI, the study highlights both the potential and the challenges in integrating AI into blended learning environments. While the promise of personalized learning and more efficient educational practices is evident, many teachers remain unfamiliar with AI technologies and lack the tools to fully integrate AI into their teaching practices. The findings suggest that successful AI integration in Albanian schools will require not only investments in technology but also ethical guidelines, digital literacy, and the development of AI-specific pedagogical frameworks. While the enthusiasm for blended learning is high among Albanian educators and students, significant hurdles remain in terms of infrastructure, teacher readiness, and the integration of AI tools. Addressing these challenges is essential to fully realizing the benefits of blended education and AI-enhanced learning in Albania's educational landscape.

REFERENCES

Adams, D., Joo, M. T. H., Sumintono, B., & Oh, S. P. (2020). Blended Learning Engagement in Higher Education Institutions: A Differential Item Functioning Analysis of Students' Backgrounds. *Malaysian Journal of Learning and Instruction*, 17(1), 133–158. DOI: 10.32890/mjli2020.17.1.6

Agjencia e Sigurimit të Cilësisë së Arsimit Parauniversitar. (n.d.). Udhëzues. https://www.ascap.edu.al/category/udhezues/

Alebaikan, R. (2011, February). A blended learning framework for Saudi higher education. In *A paper Presented at the Second International Conference of E-Learning and Distance Learning, Riyadh: National Center for E-Learning and Distance Learning*.

Ali, M. F., Joyes, G., & Ellison, L. (2015). Proposing the third generation of an aligned activity system as a theoretical framework in blended learning research. *Jurnal Teknologi, 75*(3). Alshahrani, K., & Qureshi, R. J. Review the Prospects and Obstacles of AI-Enhanced Learning Environments: The Role of ChatGPT in Education.

Ang, S. M. O., & Aragon, M. J. D. (2020). *Development of AI-Enhanced Information Technology Program: Preparing Today's Students in AI Era* (No. 4049). EasyChair.

Ang, S. M. O., & Aragon, M. J. D. (2020). *Development of AI-Enhanced Information Technology Program: Preparing Today's Students in AI Era* (No. 4049). EasyChair.

Aparicio, M., Bacao, F., & Oliveira, T. (2016). An e-learning theoretical framework. *An e-learning theoretical framework*, (1), 292-307.

Babameto, E., & Pano, D.Dr. Etleva Babameto, Dr. Doriana Pano. (2024). The Future Higher Education in Albania in the Digital Era–Challenges and Opportunities. [Baig, M. A. A. The Future of AI in Higher Education: Opportunities & Challenges Ahead: AI and Higher Education.]. *Journal of Electrical Systems*, 20(4s), 1809–1820. DOI: 10.52783/jes.2244

Basogain, X., Olabe, M. Á., Olabe, J. C., & Rico, M. J. (2018). Computational thinking in pre-university blended learning classrooms. *Computers in Human Behavior*, 80, 412–419. DOI: 10.1016/j.chb.2017.04.058

Bazelais, P. (2022). *Investigating the Impact of Blended Learning on Academic Performance in Higher Education*. McGill University.

Becher Araujo Moraes, S. (2023). Blended learning in higher education: an approach, a model, and two theoretical frameworks. In *Journal of Teaching and Learning in Higher Education* (Vol. 4, No. 1). Malmö universitet. DOI: 10.24834/jotl.4.1.820

Bervell, B., Nyagorme, P., & Arkorful, V. (2020). LMS-enabled blended learning use intentions among distance education tutors: Examining the mediation role of attitude based on technology-related stimulus-response theoretical framework. *Contemporary Educational Technology*, 12(2), ep273. DOI: 10.30935/cedtech/8317

Bliuc, A. M., Casey, G., Bachfischer, A., Goodyear, P., & Ellis, R. A. (2012). Blended learning in vocational education: Teachers' conceptions of blended learning and their approaches to teaching and design. *Australian Educational Researcher*, 39(2), 237–257. DOI: 10.1007/s13384-012-0053-0

Cekrezi, A. (2021, June). How Fair is Education Policy in Albania? In *London International Conference, June 2021: PROCEEDINGS 2021-3* (Vol. 3). UKEY Publishing. DOI: 10.31039/ljss.2021.1.42

Cleveland-Innes, M., & Wilton, D. (2018). Guide to blended learning.

Comas-Quinn, A. (2011). Learning to teach online or learning to become an online teacher: An exploration of teachers' experiences in a blended learning course. *Re-CALL*, 23(3), 218–232. DOI: 10.1017/S0958344011000152

Cronje, J. (2020). Towards a new definition of blended learning. *Electronic Journal of e-Learning*, 18(2), 114–121. DOI: 10.34190/EJEL.20.18.2.001

Dangwal, K. L. (2017). Blended learning: An innovative approach. *Universal Journal of Educational Research*, 5(1), 129–136. DOI: 10.13189/ujer.2017.050116

Dziuban, C. D., & Picciano, A. G. (2021). Education and Blended Learning: Some Possible Futures. In *Blended Learning* (pp. 365-402). Routledge.

Emmanuel, J. S., Bhandigadi, P., & Ch'ng, L. K. (2019). Student Engagement and Its Impact on Achievement in a Blended Learning Environment in Malaysia. *Asian Journal of Distance Education*, 14(1), 56–67.

Frank, M., Kurtz, G., & Levin, N. (2002). Implications of presenting pre-university courses using the blended e-learning approach. *Journal of Educational Technology & Society*, 5(4), 137–147.

Graham, C. R. (2021). Exploring definitions, models, frameworks, and theory for blended learning research. In *Blended Learning* (pp. 10–29). Routledge. DOI: 10.4324/9781003037736-3

Graham, C. R., Henrie, C. R., & Gibbons, A. S. (2013). Developing models and theory for blended learning research. In *Blended learning* (pp. 13–33). Routledge.

Halverson, L. R., & Graham, C. R. (2019). Learner engagement in blended learning environments: A conceptual framework. *Online Learning : the Official Journal of the Online Learning Consortium*, 23(2), 145–178. DOI: 10.24059/olj.v23i2.1481

Heinze, A., & Procter, C. T. (2004). Reflections on the use of blended learning.

Hubackova, S., & Semradova, I. (2016). Evaluation of blended learning. *Procedia: Social and Behavioral Sciences*, 217, 551–557. DOI: 10.1016/j.sbspro.2016.02.044

Islam, A., Ali, R., Singh, G., Islam, B., Islam, A., & Hossain, S. (2024, May). An Evaluation of AI-Enhanced Collaborative Learning Platforms. In *2024 International Conference on Communication, Computer Sciences and Engineering (IC3SE)* (pp. 207-211). IEEE. DOI: 10.1109/IC3SE62002.2024.10593320

Jokinen, P., & Mikkonen, I. (2013). Teachers' experiences of teaching in a blended learning environment. *Nurse Education in Practice*, 13(6), 524–528. DOI: 10.1016/j.nepr.2013.03.014 PMID: 23608218

Karasavvidis, I. (2009, January). Activity Theory as a theoretical framework for the study of blended learning: a case study. In *Proceedings of the 6th International Conference on Networked Learning* (pp. 195-202).

Kaur, M. (2013). Blended learning-its challenges and future. *Procedia: Social and Behavioral Sciences*, 93, 612–617. DOI: 10.1016/j.sbspro.2013.09.248

Kayyali, M. (2024). Future possibilities and challenges of AI in education. In *Transforming education with generative AI: Prompt engineering and synthetic content creation* (pp. 118–137). IGI Global. DOI: 10.4018/979-8-3693-1351-0.ch006

Kharb, P., & Samanta, P. P. (2016). Blended learning approach for teaching and learning anatomy: Students' and teachers' perspective. *Journal of the Anatomical Society of India*, 65(1), 43–47. DOI: 10.1016/j.jasi.2016.06.001

Kraja, P. (2023). Report on Smart Education in Albania. In *Smart Education in China and Central & Eastern European Countries* (pp. 51–79). Springer Nature Singapore. DOI: 10.1007/978-981-19-7319-2_3

Lalima, K. L. D., & Lata Dangwal, K. (2017). Blended Learning: An Innovative Approach. Universal. *The Journal of Educational Research*, 5(1), 129–136. DOI: 10.13189/ujer.2017.050116

Loots, S., Strydom, F., & Posthumus, H. (2023). Learning from students: Factors that support student engagement in blended learning environments within and beyond classrooms. *Journal of Student Affairs in Africa*, 11(2), 73–88. DOI: 10.24085/jsaa.v11i2.4897

Meng, N., Dhimolea, T. K., & Ali, Z. (2022). AI-enhanced education: Teaching and learning reimagined. In *Bridging human intelligence and artificial intelligence* (pp. 107–124). Springer International Publishing. DOI: 10.1007/978-3-030-84729-6_7

Miço, H., & Cungu, J. (2022). The Need for Digital Education in the Teaching Profession: A Path toward Using the European Digital Competence Framework in Albania. *IAFOR Journal of Education*, 10(2), 29–50. DOI: 10.22492/ije.10.2.02

Mutambik, I. (2024). The Use of AI-Driven Automation to Enhance Student Learning Experiences in the KSA: An Alternative Pathway to Sustainable Education. *Sustainability (Basel)*, 16(14), 5970. DOI: 10.3390/su16145970

Neumeier, P. (2005). A closer look at blended learning—Parameters for designing a blended learning environment for language teaching and learning. *ReCALL*, 17(2), 163–178. DOI: 10.1017/S0958344005000224

Open Society Foundation for Albania. (n.d.). Home. https://www.osfa.al/

Oprescu, C. M. (2020). Exploring the potential of the blended learning method in the romanian pre-university educational system. In *Conference proceedings of» eLearning and Software for Education «(eLSE)* (Vol. 16, No. 02, pp. 610-619). Carol I National Defence University Publishing House. DOI: 10.12753/2066-026X-20-166

Pfoertsch, W., & Sulaj, K. (2023, December). Integrating Artificial Intelligence with Customer Experience in Banking: An Empirical Study on how Chatbots and Virtual Assistants Enhance Empathy. In *2023 International Conference on Computing, Networking, Telecommunications & Engineering Sciences Applications (CoNTESA)* (pp. 69-74). IEEE. DOI: 10.1109/CoNTESA61248.2023.10384979

Prifti, R. (2020). Implementation of blended learning in a higher education institution in Albania: An analysis of factors that affect students' learning experience. *International Journal of Innovation and Learning*, 27(3), 233–253. DOI: 10.1504/IJIL.2020.106809

Qafzezi, E. (2023). Online Collaborative Learning in Higher Education in Albania: Some Necessary Innovations. *International Journal of Management. Knowledge and Learning*, 12(1), 2–11.

Rajkoomar, M., & Raju, J. (2016). A framework using blended learning for innovative teaching and learning. *Res Rev J Educ Stud*, 2, 1–9.

Ramachandra Rao, V., & Heng, N. M. (2018). Teaching basic programming to pre-university students through blended learning pedagogy: A descriptive study.

Ramakrisnan, P., Yahya, Y. B., Hasrol, M. N. H., & Aziz, A. A. (2012). Blended learning: A suitable framework for e-learning in higher education. *Procedia: Social and Behavioral Sciences*, 67, 513–526. DOI: 10.1016/j.sbspro.2012.11.356

Sanders, D. A., & Mukhari, S. S. (2024). Lecturers' perceptions of the influence of AI on a blended learning approach in a South African higher education institution. *Discover Education*, 3(1), 135. DOI: 10.1007/s44217-024-00235-2

Sargiotis, D. (2024). Integrating AI and Big Data in Virtual Infrastructures: Transforming Educational Landscapes for the Future. *Available atSSRN* 4789850. DOI: 10.2139/ssrn.4789850

Sarnovska, N., Rybinska, J., & Mykhailichenko, Y. (2024). Enhancing university remote language learning through innovative applications of artificial intelligence technologies amidst global challenges. *Teaching Languages at Higher Educational Establishments at the Present Stage.Intersubject Relations*, (44), 151–165.

Sharma, S., & Kumar, N. (2024). Navigating the ethical landscape of ai-based resources in education: Implications for learning, proper usage, and course design enhancement. *The Online Journal of Distance Education and e-Learning : TOJDEL*, 12(2), 92.

Shivam, R., & Singh, S. (2015). Implementation of Blended Learning in Classroom: A review paper. *International Journal of Scientific and Research Publications*, 5(11), 369–372.

Smith, S. U., Hayes, S., & Shea, P. (2017). A Critical Review of the Use of Wenger's Community of Practice (CoP) Theoretical Framework in Online and Blended Learning Research, 2000-2014. *Online Learning : the Official Journal of the Online Learning Consortium*, 21(1), 209–237. DOI: 10.24059/olj.v21i1.963

Sundari, M. S., Penthala, H. R., & Nayyar, A. Transforming Education through AI-Enhanced Content Creation and Personalized Learning Experiences. In *Impact of Artificial Intelligence on Society* (pp. 98–118). Chapman and Hall/CRC.

Syahrizal, S., Yasmi, F., & Mary, T. (2024). AI-enhanced teaching materials for education: A shift towards digitalization. *International Journal of Religion*, 5(1), 203–217. DOI: 10.61707/j6sa1w36

Thanasi, T., & Mema, O. (2024). Enhancing Mathematics Education with Artificial Intelligence. *EIRP Proceedings, 19*(1), 518-523.

Ting, K. Y. (2014). Blended Learning as a Theoretical Framework for the Application of Podcasting. *English Language Teaching*, 7(5), 128–135. DOI: 10.5539/elt.v7n5p128

Tseng, Y. C., & Lin, Y. H. (2024). Enhancing English as a Foreign Language (EFL) Learners' Writing with ChatGPT: A University-Level Course Design. *Electronic Journal of e-Learning*, 22(2), 78–97. DOI: 10.34190/ejel.21.5.3329

Vermare, E. G. (2023). *Student-Centred Blended Learning in a Flipped Classroom for a Pre-University Masterclass* (Master's thesis, University of Twente).

Vrenozi, B., Harasani, K., Memeti, A., & Dukaj, E. (2020). Evaluation of the online learning process during the Covid-19 pandemic period towards better future approaches of higher education perspectives on the Balkans.

Wang, Q., & Rao, Y. (2024, May). Research on the Enhancement of Digital Capabilities in AI-based Blended Teaching Processes. In *Proceedings of the 2024 International Conference on Computer and Multimedia Technology* (pp. 330-336). DOI: 10.1145/3675249.3675308

Wong, K. K. (2024, June). Blended Learning and AI: Enhancing Teaching and Learning in Higher Education. In *International Conference on Blended Learning* (pp. 39-61). Singapore: Springer Nature Singapore. DOI: 10.1007/978-981-97-4442-8_4

Wong, L., Tatnall, A., & Burgess, S. (2014). A framework for investigating blended learning effectiveness. *Education + Training*, 56(2/3), 233–251. DOI: 10.1108/ET-04-2013-0049

Yang, Y., Sun, W., Sun, D., & Salas-Pilco, S. Z. (2024). Navigating the AI-Enhanced STEM education landscape: A decade of insights, trends, and opportunities. *Research in Science & Technological Education*, •••, 1–25. DOI: 10.1080/02635143.2024.2370764

Zekaj, R. (2023). AI language models as educational allies: Enhancing instructional support in higher education. *International Journal of Learning. Teaching and Educational Research*, 22(8), 120–134.

Zhang, K., & Aslan, A. B. (2021). AI technologies for education: Recent research & future directions. *Computers and Education: Artificial Intelligence*, 2, 100025. DOI: 10.1016/j.caeai.2021.100025

ADDITIONAL READING

Gligorea, I., Cioca, M., Oancea, R., Gorski, A. T., Gorski, H., & Tudorache, P. (2023). Adaptive learning using artificial intelligence in e-learning: A literature review. *Education Sciences*, 13(12), 1216. DOI: 10.3390/educsci13121216

Hamadneh, N. N., Atawneh, S., Khan, W. A., Almejalli, K. A., & Alhomoud, A. (2022). Using artificial intelligence to predict students' academic performance in blended learning. *Sustainability (Basel)*, 14(18), 11642. DOI: 10.3390/su141811642

Liu, X., & Bai, H. (2024, May). Application of Artificial Intelligence Technologies in Blended E-Learning Platforms. In *2024 5th International Conference on Big Data and Informatization Education (ICBDIE 2024)* (pp. 251-262). Atlantis Press. DOI: 10.2991/978-94-6463-417-4_23

Miyaji, I. (2011). Comparison between Effects in Two Blended Classes Which E-Learning Is Used inside and outside Classroom. *Online Submission*, 8(4), 468–481.

KEY TERMS AND DEFINITIONS

Adaptive Learning Systems: AI-driven platforms that adjust the difficulty and type of content in real-time to match the learning pace and style of each student.

AI-Enhanced Learning: The use of artificial intelligence tools in education to personalize learning experiences, automate assessments, and support adaptive learning based on individual student needs.

Blended Education: An educational approach combining traditional face-to-face instruction with online learning to create a flexible and engaging learning experience.

Digital Literacy: The ability to effectively use digital tools and platforms, essential for both students and educators in blended and technology-enhanced education environments.

Ethical AI in Education: The consideration of privacy, fairness, and transparency in the use of AI technologies within educational settings to ensure responsible and equitable application.

ICT Infrastructure: The technological resources, including internet access, computers, and interactive boards, required to support digital and AI-based learning environments.

Learning Management Systems (LMS): Software platforms like Moodle or Google Classroom that facilitate online learning, communication, and resource sharing in blended education.

Personalized Learning: An instructional approach that tailors educational content to each learner's strengths, needs, and interests, often facilitated by AI technologies.

Professional Development: Training programs aimed at equipping teachers with the skills needed to effectively use technology and AI in the classroom.

Student Engagement: The level of interest, motivation, and active participation that students demonstrate in a learning environment, essential for successful blended education.

Chapter 3
Harnessing Generative AI for Educator Professional Development

Steven M. Baule
https://orcid.org/0000-0002-6954-7499
Winona State University, USA

Jordan S. O'Connell
https://orcid.org/0009-0006-1740-138X
NICC, USA

ABSTRACT

Generative artificial intelligence (AI) is transforming the landscape of educator professional development by offering tools that facilitate personalized learning and efficiency in training. This chapter explores the various applications of AI in professional development, including using AI as a coaching tool, an instructional evaluator, and a content creator. This chapter highlights how AI can streamline tasks like creating lesson plans, analyzing teaching effectiveness, and supporting new teachers. Additionally, the chapter discusses ethical considerations, challenges, and best practices to ensure the responsible integration of AI into professional development, ultimately aiming to enhance teaching effectiveness and student outcomes.

INTRODUCTION

Generative artificial intelligence (AI) is opening new possibilities in such widely disparate disciplines from data analysis to poetry. Educators are having to address how to transform their instructional practices within the scope of a landscape rich

DOI: 10.4018/979-8-3373-1017-6.ch003

with generative AI tools. As educators wrestle with the realities of an AI inclusive instructional world, there is a significant need for early and ongoing professional development (PD) for educators to be able to fully prepared to address the new instructional realities brought forth by an AI-rich environment (Ferikoğlu & Akgün, 2022). Traditionally, time for professional development has been a critical concern for many educators. Therefore, though generative AI does have the potential to make significant shifts in the instructional environment, AI tools can also be harnessed to help educators manage their professional development in the fluid times ahead.

This chapter will explore the ways educators can use AI tools to empower their professional development. This exploration delves into the various ways generative AI can be applied to enhance the professional growth of educators and offers a fresh perspective on traditional educator training methods as well as addressing potential concerns about AI use in professional development. By providing practical strategies, educators and administrators can use this chapter to effectively implement AI-powered tools in their professional development programs. This chapter will discuss the potential benefits and challenges that come with integrating AI tools into educator training and support systems, ensuring that these innovations contribute positively to the educational ecosystem. Furthermore, this narrative will also explore the ethical considerations and best practices that must be adhered to when incorporating AI tools into professional development, ensuring that the use of those resources is both responsible and impactful.

AI tools may be used to change the landscape of professional development by offering versatile tools that cater to the diverse needs of educators. As a training planner, AI can efficiently design personalized learning pathways and ensure that professional development is tailored to individual needs. Acting as a professional development coach, AI provides real-time feedback and support, helping educators refine their skills continuously. In its role as an instructional evaluator, AI tools can analyze teaching methods and outcomes, offering data-driven insights for improvement. For course review, AI can automate the assessment process, ensuring that courses meet high standards of quality and relevance. Generative AI tools can serve as valuable resources for new teacher orientation offering onboarding support that acclimates educators to their roles quickly. As an instructional designer, AI tools assist in creating engaging and effective learning experiences. In grading, AI tools can streamline the assessment process and assist educators in ensuring they are grading equitably. Finally, as an automated research assistant, AI tools can gather and synthesize information, allowing them to stay informed while still focused on their teaching goals. Together, these AI-driven applications create a comprehensive support system that can enhance nearly every facet of professional development.

PROFESSIONAL DEVELOPMENT COACHING

At the frontier of AI in education, professional development coaching integrates AI tools capable of providing customized support that directly addresses educators' unique pedagogical challenges. AI can serve as a personal development coach, delivering real-time feedback and tailored resources to help teachers refine their skills and adapt to changing scholastic dynamics. AI can now enable educators to focus on specific areas of improvement, whether it's enhancing instructional materials or strategies, developing deeper content knowledge, or even burnishing a curriculum vitae (CV). By utilizing AI as a coaching tool, teachers can streamline and track their professional growth, ensuring their development stays on-track and remains aligned with their immediate teaching goals (Ding, et al., 2024)

An extremely simple use of generative AI coaching is to ask ChatGPT to create and improve an educator's professional biography. Such bios are often requested of educators for a range of reasons. It is often included in learning management systems (LMS) introductory course materials. Bios are requested when presenting, speaking, or writing as well. The following prompt was used to generate both a short 100 word and a longer 250 word biography. Some conferences may ask for an abbreviated 50 word biography.

Can you use the attached CV and draft a short (100 word) bio for {insert name] as well as a 250 word version? Please focus on academic appointments and academic degrees as well as the type and topics of publications and presentations?

The result for the 100 word bio is below from ChatGPT 4o:

Steven M. Baule is an Associate Professor of Leadership Education at Winona State University, where he also serves as Director of the Education Doctorate Program. He holds a Ph.D. in Leadership and Educational Policy Studies from Loyola University Chicago and an Ed.D. in Instructional Technology from Northern Illinois University. Dr. Baule's extensive academic career includes numerous publications and presentations focusing on educational leadership, instructional technology, and school library development. He has authored several books and articles that delve into topics such as technology planning, leadership, and historical military research.

Here is an example of an AI generated 250 word biography from Gemini:

Jordan O'Connell is an experienced educator with a passion for using technology to enhance learning experiences. He has over 13 years of experience in higher education, serving in various roles including instructional designer, adjunct instructor, and student success coach. O'Connell is currently pursuing a Doctor of Education in Education at Winona State University. He holds a Master of Arts in History from the University of Wisconsin-Eau Claire and has completed coursework towards a Master of Arts in Political Science. His teaching experi-

ence spans online, hybrid, and face-to-face formats, encompassing courses in American history, government, and strategies for success. He is adept at utilizing technology to create engaging and effective learning environments. O'Connell is a frequent presenter at educational conferences, with recent presentations at the Effordability Summit 2024 and upcoming presentations at the Council for Adult and Experiential Learning (CAEL). He is also a published author, with recent articles appearing in eCampus News and Essays in Education.
Here are some highlights of O'Connell's recent work:

- *Publications:*
  - *"Reimagining Oral Assessment in the Age of AI" (eCampus News, January 2024)*
  - *"Book Review: Robot-Proof: Higher Education in the Age of Artificial Intelligence" (Essays in Education, April 2024)*
  - *"Student Recordings: A New Element in the Online Classroom" (eCampus News, September 2024)*
- *Presentations:*
  - *Effordability Summit 2024*
  - *Council for Adult and Experiential Learning (CAEL) (upcoming)*

O'Connell is committed to continuous improvement in teaching and learning. He holds certifications from the Online Learning Consortium in curating resources for faculty, collaborating for course development, and designing with accessibility in mind. He is also a Quality Matters Online Course Evaluator and an AVID for Higher Education Campus Trainer.

EasyPeasy (https://easy-peasy.ai/) actually includes a professional bio generator for educators. It will take up to 1000 characters of personal information in the form of bullets or key words. It can be generated in first, second, or third person. The tool allows the user to request a specific tone of voice as well. It can be generated in a range of languages and in three lengths.

Creating a Professional Development Plan

A simple entirely off the shelf use of generative AI could be to assist educators in planning their required annual professional development. First, at the most basic level, using a generative AI tool such as ChatGPT to help draft professional development goals for a school year or other academic span is a viable option. Dellarocas (2023) identified that developing personalized learning paths for employees will be a major impact for training and development in all types of organizations. For instance, an extremely simple prompt *Can you please draft a set of professional development goals for me as an assistant professor covering instruction, student support, research, and university service?* generated twelve draft goals, three for each enumerated area. Though they were generic, they were usable frames to build a specific set of goals from. One instructional example was:

Curriculum Development: Review and update course materials to align with current industry standards and research trends. Aim to revise at least one course syllabus each semester, incorporating new research findings and technology where applicable.

Less generalized drafts would be easy to obtain by uploading a copy of the specific professional development or evaluative requirements for the chatbot to consider in developing its responses. An elementary teacher could use a prompt to *Can you please identify a set of annual development goals for me as a third grade teacher covering culturally relevant instruction, classroom management for students with autism, and parent interactions?* One response for creating an inclusive environment was:

Action Plan: Incorporate student identities into classroom discussions and materials. Use diverse role models, books, and case studies to reflect various cultures and backgrounds.

A generative AI chatbot could similarly be used to help an educator develop an individualized learning plan for themselves. One example would be to ask the bot: *Can you outline a 30 day (or fewer) plan for me to become proficient with mermaid code?* It responded with the following plan broken down by days within weekly units:

Here's a 30-day plan to become proficient with Mermaid code:

Week 1: Introduction and Basics

Day 1-2: Introduction to Mermaid

Read the [official Mermaid documentation] (https://mermaid-js.github.io/mermaid/#/).

Understand what Mermaid is, its use cases, and how it integrates with Markdown.

Day 3-4: Basic Diagrams

Learn the syntax for creating flowcharts.

Practice creating simple flowcharts using basic shapes like rectangles, circles, and arrows.

Create a flowchart representing a simple process (e.g., a morning routine).

Day 5-6: Sequence Diagrams

Study the syntax for sequence diagrams.
Practice creating sequence diagrams to model interactions (e.g., a login process).
Focus on understanding lifelines, messages, and activation bars.

Day 7: Recap and Practice

Review what you've learned so far.
Create one or two complex diagrams combining flowcharts and sequence diagrams.
… [abbreviated to show the first week] …

A second example was generated using Microsoft Co-Pilot. Co-Pilot was asked to put the plan into graphical form, but AI tools still struggle with integrating text and graphics. In this case, none of the graphics came out as usable.

Prompt for Co-Pilot: *Can you draft a professional development plan for learning how to use Co-Pilot with PowerPoint in two weeks. Please build out the learning plan as a graphic, table or chart.* A second prompt was necessary asking *Can you add three to four concrete points under each bullet point?*

Table 1. Here is a more detailed professional development plan for learning how to use co-pilot with PowerPoint in two weeks:

Week 1	Week 2
Day 1-2 Introduction to Co-pilot and PowerPoint basics. · Understand the purpose and benefits of using Co-pilot with PowerPoint. · Familiarize yourself with the PowerPoint interface and basic functionalities. · Set up Co-pilot and integrate it with PowerPoint.	**Day 8-9:** Advanced Co-pilot techniques in PowerPoint. · Learn how to use Co-pilot for data visualization and charts. · Explore advanced design and formatting options. · Practice creating interactive presentations with Co-pilot.
Day 3-4 Exploring Co-pilot features and functionalities. · Learn how to use Co-pilot to create and edit slides. · Explore Co-pilot's capabilities for generating content and design suggestions. · Practice using Co-pilot to enhance presentations with multimedia elements.	**Day 10-11:** Creating a project using Co-pilot and PowerPoint. · Plan and outline a comprehensive presentation project. · Use Co-pilot to develop and refine the content. · Incorporate feedback and make necessary revisions.
Day 5-6: Hands-on practice with Co-pilot in PowerPoint. · Create a sample presentation using Co-pilot's features. · Experiment with different design templates and layouts. · Use Co-pilot to add animations and transitions to your slides.	**Day 12-13:** Peer review and feedback on the project. · Present your project to peers for review. · Gather constructive feedback and suggestions. · Make improvements based on the feedback received.
Day 7: Review and Q&A session. · Review the key concepts and features learned during the week. · Address any questions or challenges encountered. · Discuss best practices for using Co-pilot effectively.	**Day 14:** Final assessment and certification. · Complete a final assessment to demonstrate your proficiency. · Receive a certification of completion. · Reflect on your learning journey and set goals for future development.

Some bots can create reading lists for PD topics of interest. Generally, the bots are better at book-heavy reading lists and are less effective at identifying narrower articles or online resources of value to the educator. However, bots will get better at identifying current resources in the next few iterations of AI engine development. The current bots are good at providing lists of foundational texts on a topic, normally identifying ten to fifteen texts when asked for a reading list, ranging from the seminal to the contemporaneously popular. Entered into Google Gemini and ChatGPT 4o separately, the prompt, *Can you please draft a reading list of recommended books for me as an assistant professor covering instruction, student support, research, and university service?* generated lists of fifteen and sixteen titles, respectively. Only one book (Kelsky's *The Professor Is In)* overlapped. When also provided with the100 word bio for Dr. Baule, above, both Gemini and GPT 4o generated shorter lists, tallying fourteen and twelve works. The only text that overlapped on these more focused lists was *Research Design: Qualitative, Quantitative, and Mixed Methods Approaches* by John W. Creswell and J. David Creswell, a text Dr. Baule routinely incorporates into his graduate-level instruction.

Orientation Timelines

A chatbot, or a similar tool, can be an effective way for developing an orientation timeline for a new employee by using a job description as a guide. Once the chatbot is given the key tasks, responsibilities, and skills outlined in the job description, it can generate a customized onboarding schedule. This schedule could include orientation sessions, training modules, shadowing opportunities, and check-ins aligned with the specific role requirements. By breaking down the job description into phases, such as understanding organizational culture, mastering technical skills, and achieving performance milestones, the chatbot can create a step-by-step timeline to ensure a smooth and structured onboarding process. The chatbot could be programmed to send reminders, track progress, and provide resources for the new hire, ensuring consistent communication and support throughout their orientation. It could be instructed to help new employees quickly in areas of policy that they just covered or run through skill-based scenarios with new orientees.

Overall PD Plans

Each educator has a unique set of strengths, areas for growth, and career aspirations. Traditional professional development often follows a one-size-fits-all approach, which may not address the specific needs of each educator. AI tools can revolutionize this process by analyzing an educator's past experiences, current skills, and professional goals to create a personalized learning path and promote greater instructional self-efficacy (Lee et al., 2024). An AI-powered platform like LinkedIn Learning can assess an educator's current skills and interests by analyzing their job role, past assignments, and self-assessment data. The platform might notice that a teacher is proficient in classroom management but has limited experience with integrating technology into instruction. Based on this analysis, the AI tool generates a personalized learning path that includes courses on digital tools for education, blended learning strategies, and advanced classroom technology integration. These paths can be tailored to an educator's needs while remaining flexible. This can allow for adjustments as an educator progresses or as new needs arise. The educator can receive recommendations for specific workshops, online courses, and relevant articles, ensuring that their professional development is both targeted and efficient.

A corollary of overall development plans would be creating a chatbot to quiz educators on the key areas of focus for the year and then identify areas of strength and focused areas for growth to recommend development priorities aligned to the institution's strategic priorities. For instance, with new teachers, it would be reasonable to build out a dedicated chatbot to answer questions based only on institutional manuals, handbooks, and policies using a tool like NotebookLM. This would allow new teachers to have a reliable tool to gather information and ask questions without having to rely on peers or supervisors. A teacher might ask such a bot to review emergency procedures the night before the first scheduled fire drill for instance to refresh their memory or to provide a summary for their use during the drill. This could be ongoing support and guidance throughout the first year of teaching. Such bots would be much quicker for faculty to use instead of the current traditional or digital resources as searching through a single bot would streamline the process. This would be especially helpful when a newer staff member is unsure of where to look for the information. A single source for rules and potentially even curricular information would streamline searching and data access for most educators. MagicSchool now includes a professional development planner (https://app.magicschool.ai/tools/pd-planner) among its tools for educators.

Generating Differentiated Professional Development Materials

At a basic level, most institutions require all staff to participate in certain professional development workshops or statutorily required training. Instead of providing all staff with the same training materials, AI tools can generate situational discussion questions that are appropriate to various job alike workgroups. The office staff, custodial workers, admissions staff, instructors, and instructional coaches could all receive materials appropriate to their needs and based upon their work environments (al-Zyoud, 2020). This could lead to less frustration with such required training where employees often do not see an immediate application to their role in the organization.

At a deeper level, AI tools can assist in developing materials for a range of knowledge or skill levels. Stephen Haines (1998) spoke about five levels of professional development towards personal mastery from unconscious incompetence through a high-level of consistence performance. Building that high-level of performance generally requires training at three levels; familiarization, skill development and then mastery or expertise development (Polaris, 2018). One common complaint for institutional workshops is they are often one size fits all or a one and done approach. Generative AI can assist presenters and trainers in developing differentiated materials. Based on either self-selection or a quick assessment, faculty members could then be grouped by their experience levels. Those who were new to a topic would receive familiarization materials to learn the basics concepts and vocabulary of the topic. Those who already have a basic understanding could move forward to the skill building phase of training. For those who already have the necessary skills, opportunities to fully implement those skills in practical applications to innovate further and master the topic. This last piece is often lost in institutional training as the focus must rightly be on the more basic levels. The ability to use generative AI to build out scenarios or even serve as a chatbot peer can allow an instructor to provide higher level training and potential extension for educators with less time than traditional instructional development might take.

Automated Tracking of Continuing Education Units (CEUs)

Educators are often required to earn a certain number of continuing education units (CEUs) or professional development hours to maintain their licenses. Manually tracking these hours can be time-consuming and prone to error, especially when educators attend multiple events across different platforms. AI can potentially streamline this process by automating the tracking and documentation of CEUs. Imagine an AI-powered system integrated into an institution's human resources portal. As the educator participates in webinars, workshops, and courses, the system automatically logs the time spent on each activity and converts it into the appropriate number of CEUs. For instance, after completing a two-hour online course on differentiated instruction, the platform automatically updates the educator's profile with the earned CEUs, without requiring any manual input. The system could send reminders when the educator is nearing a deadline for required CEUs, ensuring that they remain compliant with certification requirements. At the end of the year, an educator can easily generate a report summarizing all the CEUs earned, ready to submit for recertification.

AI AS AN INSTRUCTIONAL COACH

In current classrooms, technology has become an invaluable ally in enhancing the educational experience. Learning management systems already use word count, sentence complexity, and peer-to-peer engagement to help faculty monitor participation and engagement in online courses. One of the most innovative tools at the disposal of educators is the use of AI to analyze video recordings of actual classroom instruction. This technology assesses student engagement and participation by tracking various indicators such as eye contact, facial expressions, and body language that can provide insights about learners' behaviors (Akgun & Greenhow, 2022). For instance, during a math lesson, the AI might notice that students frequently look away or show signs of confusion when a particular concept is being explained. This insight allows teachers to identify which parts of their lesson need more clarity or a different approach. Guskey and Link (2022) identify the need for consistent non-judgmental feedback for educators to improve. Similarly, principals and instructional coaches often refrain from providing constructive feedback to avoid potentially damaging personal relationships with educators. AI offers a non-judgmental approach without the potential to damage interpersonal relationships. Three current tools that can be used for this type of analysis include:

- M-Powering Teachers (https://www.mpoweringteachers.com/): developed by Stanford, this tool uses natural language processing to analyze classroom interactions and provide feedback on teaching practices
- TeachFX (https://teachfx.com/): is one of the first commercial products aimed directly at teachers to provide AI-driven instructional feedback.
- Amazon Rekognition (https://aws.amazon.com/rekognition/): can analyze video content to detect objects, activities, and even facial expressions, which can be used to assess student engagement and participation.

TeachFX (2024a), for instance, measures the amount of time students talk compared to students within a classroom setting, the use of teacher's questioning techniques and the use of standards-aligned vocabulary within the lesson. TeachFX (2024b) articulates that it works to boost student engagement where an analysis classroom video archives showed that the average student only spoke approximately 27 seconds an hour. Using the insights from the AI generated feedback, teachers were able to improve student in-class participation by 13%. Similar improvements may be observed as teachers, supervisors, and instructional coaches are able to utilize these analytic tools to provide constructive non-evaluative feedback going forward.

Generation and Evaluation of Teaching Strategies

Some LMSs have already developed simple AI tools that will generate assessment ideas for instructors. D2L's Lumi allows instructors to select a specific level of Bloom's taxonomy that the instructor wishes to target. The tool will then provide three to five ideas for modifying and uplifting an extant assignment or discussion (Chapman, 2024). Similarly, Lumi can pull from selected course files, video, presentation, and/or OER content to generate competency-aligned quiz question groups. The Campus Technology Insider Podcast highlighted an illustrative example from a community college after a course developer unexpectedly took leave during a time-sensitive Certified Nursing Aid course build. During the developer's absence, instructional designers were able to use D2L Lumi to create hundreds of quiz questions and dozens of assignments and discussions, aligned with the state nurse aide curriculum, the college's institutional course objectives, the developer's curriculum mapping, and the required publisher materials. The course developer was able to quickly review the AI-generated work upon return and pilot the course in short order (Campus Technology, 2024).

There are four core principles in building assignments that are more likely to resist the successful use of generative AI tools. The first is to require students to incorporate personal experiences or include local content within their responses. The second is to ask for multi-modal products. Most generative AI tools provide mono-modal text-based, audio, or graphical creations. Asking for a combination of media will deter the misuse of the current generation of generative AI tools. Instructors should consider more process-oriented assessments that focus on evaluating students at multiple stages of their work rather than just the final product. This can provide the instructor with more insights into the student's learning process. Even making the change to allow the student to generate the outline for a paper via a generative tool and then ask the student to critique that same outline pushes the assignment up Bloom's Taxonomy as the student must critically assess the output in comparison to simply creating one. Real-time assessments such as live presentations, debates, or recorded video responses to prompts represent a fourth way to defy the misuse of generative AI (Baule & Carter, 2024).

Table 2. There are several tools that can assist instructors in the revision of assignments. A simple prompt for MS Co-Pilot: Can you please provide three recommendations to improve this assignment and make it resistant to being completed by generative AI tools? [Attach the assignment].

Criterion	Exceeds Expectations	Meets Expectations	Does Not Meet Expectations	Did Not Complete
Organization	The response is accurate, well-defended, and addresses all facets of the question(s).	The response is sufficiently accurate, adequately defended, and addresses the central question(s).	The response is insufficiently accurate, poorly defended, and/or fails to address the central question(s).	The response is inaccurate and/or plagiarized.
Voice	The response is unscripted and effectively communicates the student's original ideas and perspective.	The response is mostly unscripted and adequately communicates the student's perspective.	The response is scripted and/ or generally fails to communicate the student's perspective.	The student's voice is absent or incoherent.
Reference	The response directly references and cites supportive evidence from the text, lectures, and/or course materials and demonstrates a complete understanding of the disciplinary context.	The response directly references supportive evidence from the text, lectures, or course materials and exhibits a satisfactory awareness of disciplinary context.	The response indirectly references text, lectures, or course materials and exhibits a partial awareness of the disciplinary context.	The response is stated without reference to the text, lectures, or course materials and exhibits limited awareness of disciplinary context.

One of the responses to this prompt was to require a peer review and revision prior to submission. This aligns with the point above that suggests process oriented iterative assignments. It would foster peer interaction and critical thinking as well as potentially defeating the wholesale use of generative AI tools. A number of education focused tools provide tools specifically created for providing feedback on making current assignments AI-resistant. One such tool is Magicschool.AI's aptly named AI-Resistant Assignments tool (https://app.magicschool.ai/tools/ai-resistant-assignment). Magicschool's tool allows the instructor to submit an assignment, and it will generate three to four suggestions for improving the assignment to make it more challenging for AI chatbots to complete. Other tools can be used to achieve similar aims. ChatGPT recommended the addition of a "student voice" criterion to an existing assignment rubric when asked how to incentivize more authentic contributions on an online discussion board. The addition of the criterion has served as a highly useful framework for centering important conversations around "AI-giarism" with students (Ka Yuk Chan, 2023) Student Learning Assessment Rubric

Analysis of Student and LMS Data

One of the three facets of instructional coaching is data analysis. Generative AI can be used to identify successful teaching strategies based on student performance data. By analyzing data from assessments, quizzes, and other sources, AI algorithms can identify correlations between specific teaching methods and student outcomes. Teachers can identify effective and ineffective instructional strategies and make data-driven decisions about their teaching practices after reviewing such data. AI platforms can provide teachers with real-time feedback and suggestions for improving their instructional techniques.

For example, if AI algorithms detect that students are struggling with a particular concept through the analysis of quiz scores or other student data, they can suggest alternative teaching methods or provide additional resources for students needing additional support to master a concept. This could be as simple as an item analysis of test results or a more in-depth review of how often and for how long students accessed which LMS materials and how that resource utilization correlated to test results. This can help teachers to address student needs more effectively and improve overall learning outcomes. AI tools can integrate data from multiple sources, including instructional data warehouses, to provide a comprehensive evaluation of teaching performance. For example, AI algorithms can combine data from classroom observations, student surveys, classroom assessments, and standardized testing results to identify areas where teachers could improve. This can help teachers to develop a more holistic understanding of their teaching effectiveness and make informed decisions about their professional development.

AI-Powered Course Review and Improvement

Reflective practice is an essential element for successful educators (Woodward, et al, 2023). Generative AI can support reflective practice among educators by conducting analysis of curricular and student data for course improvement. Like the potential analysis of classroom activities, AI could also be used for analyzing recorded lectures and providing insights for improving presentations. Simple AI tools like Zoom's AI Companion meeting summaries generate a record of what occurred during class sessions, small group tutoring, or even advising sessions for easy review and reflection. While AI generated class sessions can help an instructor review what was covered and ensure the instructor addressed everything the day's lesson included. Summaries of small group tutoring sessions could help identify those items students had the most questions about from a given unit or lesson. This could help the instructor determine if there was a need for reteaching during the next regular class session.

Identifying areas for improvement and suggesting specific strategies to enhance course effectiveness can be done by asking AI tools to go through the curriculum materials. A review of instructional materials can potentially identify any learning objectives that are not adequately covered. For instance, an AI tool could analyze a unit on climate change and identify that while the unit covers the causes and effects of climate change, it may not adequately address the potential solutions or mitigation strategies. By identifying these gaps, teachers can adjust instructional materials to better ensure that students are fully prepared to successfully meet the learning objectives.

Institutional teams can create searchable datasets of best practices and successful teaching strategies could be managed through generative tools as well. Development of a depository of such exemplary instructional materials for various subjects and learning styles can be utilized by educators. Educators could query the dataset for suggestions on improving their own instructional practices. For instance, a teacher struggling to engage students in a geometry lesson could explore the database for examples of effective hands-on activities or innovative assessment strategies used by other teachers in similar contexts. A second example could be a teacher who is looking for ways to differentiate instruction for students with different learning needs. They could pinpoint within the database examples of lesson plans that incorporate targeted instructional approaches, such as visual aids, hands-on activities, and cooperative learning. By analyzing these examples, the teacher can identify strategies that are likely to be effective for their students and adapt them for their own classroom context and student needs.

Artificial intelligence can be used to review lesson plans. This is another potential tool for individual professional improvement. A range of prompts are available for instructors at all levels to develop robust lessons. For example, teachers can use AI tools to receive feedback on their lesson plans, identifying areas where they can incorporate more interactive elements or differentiate instruction to meet diverse student needs. Additionally, AI can help educators stay updated with the latest educational research and best practices by providing summaries of recent studies and suggesting ways to integrate new findings into their teaching strategies. These tools can enhance the quality of lesson plans as well as support continuous professional growth by offering personalized, actionable insights for instructors at all points in their career development.

The Texas Computing Educators Association (TCEA) provides some excellent resources for teachers and other educators wishing to improve or expand their use of generative AI tools. Included among those resources is an excellent prompt template to create a draft lesson plan.

Generate a [INSERT TOTAL LESSON TIME], [INSERT GRADE LEVEL] *lesson plan as a table. The table should have columns for "Objectives," "Standards," "Pre-Assessment," "Activities," "Post-Assessment," "Accommodations," and "Time".*

Here are the standards for the lesson:

[COPY AND PASTE SPECIFIC STANDARDS HERE]

I would like for you to generate the objectives, pre-assessment, activities, post-assessment, and accommodations for the lesson plan which should be about [INSERT SPECIFIC LESSON TOPIC HERE].

In the standards column, include the full standards for each corresponding aspect of the lesson.

In the time column, include the amount of time that should be spent on that aspect of the lesson.

Provide a pre-assessment activity to complete at the beginning of the lesson and a post-assessment activity to complete at the end of the full lesson. (Horn, 2023).

There are several additional prompt libraries for lesson plan development freely available online. Thinkific's Colin Burton provides a list of the 25+ Best Prompts for Instructional Designers (Burton, 2023). Burton provides an expansion of lesson plan generation aligning them to a variety of instructional design models, focusing on Bloom, and embracing the TPACK model. More Useful Things, which is an offshoot of Ethan and Lilach Mollick's One More Thing (https://www.oneusefulthing.org/) blog. Some of the more useful prompt libraries are listed below:

- AI for Education https://www.aiforeducation.io/prompt-library-lesson-planning
- Inside SEL https://insidesel.com/prompt-library-for-educators/
- More Useful Things https://www.moreusefulthings.com/instructor-prompts
- Teacher's Buddy https://www.teachersbuddy.com/region/us
- Teaching Channel https://www.teachingchannel.com/k12-hub/blog/65-ai-prompts-for-lesson-planning/
- Thinkific: https://www.thinkific.com/blog/best-chatgpt-prompts-for-instructional-designers/

Existing lesson plans can be reviewed to provide additional suggestions for differentiating instruction based on student needs and learning styles. In many cases, particularly in skills courses like math or language arts, AI tools can provide examples related to specific student interest areas or related to the time of year. For instance, with a group of students who are particularly interested in music, AI can generate music-related word problems. Similarly, baseball related examples could be generated around the World Series to improve student engagement. Generative AI can be used to translate lesson plans and assignments into other languages to share with parents, ESL students, or other support staff.

Review and Revision of Syllabi

Beyond lesson planning and assignment review, AI tools can assist educators with review and revision of syllabi. Generative AI tools can significantly enhance the quality and effectiveness of instructor syllabi by providing personalized, data-driven insights and recommendations. Balancing AI recommendations with their own expertise allows instructors to leverage the strengths of both human judgment and advanced technology.

An effective approach is to use AI tools as a supplementary tool rather than a primary decision-maker. For instance, an instructor might use AI to draft a revision of the syllabus, then apply their experience (and potentially that of their instructional coach, etc.) to determine which if any revisions to make. A note here that is valid in the case of syllabi and all other instructional materials throughout, the educator needs to ensure that they ensure human review and ultimately agency over all uses of artificial intelligence. The educator should never feel obligated to follow the results of generative AI. The results of all such tools require human review before moving forward. This ensures that the final product benefits from AI's data-driven insights while still reflecting the instructor's unique teaching style and understanding of their students' needs.

If AI tools recommend incorporating more multimedia resources into a course, for example, the instructor can evaluate whether these resources align with the course objectives and are accessible to all students. By critically assessing AI-generated recommendations and integrating them with their own expertise, instructors can create more effective and personalized educational experiences. This collaborative approach will enhance the quality of instruction while allowing educators to retain human agency over pedagogical innovation.

An excellent way AI tools can be used as a supplementary tool is for instructors to ask AI to analyze syllabi for accessibility and bias issues. AI tools can review the language and structure of a syllabus to identify and suggest improvements for clarity and inclusivity. For example, the AI might recommend using more plain language, providing alternative formats for key materials, or including statements that explicitly support diverse learning needs. Additionally, AI can help instructors stay compliant with institutional policies and accreditation requirements by cross-referencing the syllabus content with relevant guidelines and standards. By leveraging these capabilities, instructors can create syllabi that are not only comprehensive and well-organized but also supportive of all students' learning journeys. Tools can potentially make recommendations for improving digital accessibility as well.

Review of End of Course Evaluations

Student feedback as received via end of course evaluations or other student feedback loops provides instructors with another opportunity to use AI. AI can analyze past course evaluations and feedback to identify common areas where students struggled or expressed dissatisfaction. Based on such an analysis, the AI tool can suggest adjustments to the course, such as incorporating more review sessions, adding supplementary materials, or adjusting the pacing of the course. Instructors may find the need to expand the time used to cover topics students find difficulty with. This ensures that the next syllabus is tailored to address the specific needs and preferences of the student cohort, ultimately leading to a more engaging and effective learning experience. If instructors provide a beginning of course survey asking students about what they expect in a course and what an instructor can do to assist students in being successful, AI can be asked to evaluate those responses and make suggestions for instructor action, additional materials, or other supports to be added to the course. These insights can potentially further add to student success.

The integration of AI in educational settings has the potential to revolutionize assessment practices and provide deep insights into student performance. By leveraging AI's ability to quickly and reliably analyze large datasets, educators can enhance the accuracy, efficiency, and personalization of classroom assessments. This section explores four key areas where AI can make a significant impact: AI-powered analysis of trends in course and student assessment data, automated grading assistance and consistency checks, early identification of students at risk of falling behind, and the generation of personalized intervention strategies based on individual student data.

AI-Powered Analysis of Trends in Course and Student Assessment Data

AI's capacity to process and analyze vast amounts of data enables educators to identify trends and patterns that might otherwise go unnoticed. For example, AI can analyze historical assessment data to uncover trends in student performance over time. This analysis can reveal which topics or concepts students consistently struggle with, allowing instructors to adjust their teaching strategies accordingly. In a mathematics course, AI tools might identify that students consistently perform poorly on questions related to algebraic expressions. With this insight, the instructor can allocate more time to teaching and reinforcing this topic, perhaps by incorporating additional practice problems or interactive activities. Supplemental instructional materials could be recommended for those students based upon the specific issues identified for each. AI could analyze data across multiple courses to identify broader trends. If students in a particular program consistently underperform in courses requiring critical thinking skills, the instructor might consider revising the curriculum to include more opportunities for developing these skills. By providing a comprehensive view of student performance, AI-powered analysis can assist educators to make data-driven decisions that enhance the overall effectiveness of their teaching in much less time than traditional analysis processes would take.

Automated Grading Assistance and Consistency Checks

Grading can be a time-consuming and subjective process. AI-powered grading tools can assist educators by automating the grading of objective assessments and providing consistency checks for subjective evaluations. These tools can grade multiple-choice, true/false, and short-answer questions quickly and accurately, freeing up instructors to focus on more complex tasks. In a large introductory biology course, AI can grade hundreds of multiple-choice exams in a matter of minutes, providing immediate feedback to students. However, this is only a precursor to the real advantage of rapid AI grading, which will allow for instructors to modify instruction in response to student performance on the assessment in real-time. This ability to conduct item level analytics and then potentially make the necessary adjustments in instructional practices and materials to better support student success is exponentially more efficient than without generative AI tools.

AI tools can be used for subjective assignments such as essays as well. Particularly with difficult to grade essays, an AI tool can assess student work in relationship to a rubric. The instructor can use the AI generated points as a place to start writing their own assessment. Often, the most difficult part of providing feedback is translating the instructor's thoughts into constructive feedback. AI can draft those initial points of feedback which the instructor can then choose to use or discard or to potentially ignite their own thoughts. Utilization of the automated (pre-written) feedback field within online rubric tools spiked, for instance, once faculty began to use AI chatbots in the design and writing of their rubrics. Generic criteria and levels were joined by new, standard-specific feedback that offered suggestions to the student immediately after scoring. This will be a more powerful feature as learning management systems gradually integrate AI tools designed to complement the instructor role, and when the feedback can be automatically personalized to the student. Working smarter, not harder, will result in better student feedback with the help of AI.

Automated grading tools offer the potential for more detailed feedback. Today, students can easily upload assignment instructions and their instructor's grading rubric alongside a draft of their own work prior to course submission. Their AI tool of choice can highlight specific areas where they are likely to lose points and provide suggestions for improvement, increasing the odds that the instructor feedback ultimately delivered is personalized and simpler to implement. Chatbots are increasingly relied on to serve "instructor-like functions" by students and teachers alike (Chen et al., 2020, p. 75277). Instructors are already building and sharing no-code chatbots using tools such as Dante.AI, tuned to their personal curriculum, lectures, syllabi, and course goals, accessible to their students 24/7 and on campus holidays. Automated grading tools will continue to augment and expedite evaluation and feedback for students and faculty alike and help more students achieve mastery by the end of the course term.

AI can provide consistency checks by analyzing the grading patterns of different instructors or even peer reviewers. If the AI detects significant discrepancies in grading, it can flag these for review, ensuring that all students are assessed fairly and consistently. It could be used as a prompt for professional development in a Professional Learning Community (PLC), team or department meeting. This could be a productive way for instructors to discuss how each view particular common assessments and if there needs to be further discussion about the importance of various aspects of the rubric or standards. If necessary, the group could decide to make revisions or to work to align their collective grading practices.

Early Identification of Students at Risk of Falling Behind

Identifying and engaging at-risk students is an underrepresented professional development topic that directly impacts student learning and achievement. One of the most powerful applications of AI in education is its ability to identify students who are at risk of falling behind by analyzing a variety of data points, such as attendance records, participation in online discussions, and performance on assessments. Using AI tools to determine the leading indicators of potential struggle, teachers can improve their strategies for successfully intervening. In an online learning environment, AI can monitor student engagement by tracking metrics such as login frequency, time spent on course materials, and participation in discussion forums. If a student shows signs of disengagement, such as infrequent logins or low participation, the AI can notify the instructor, who can then reach out to the student to offer support. Automated grading tools offer the potential for more detailed feedback. A second example would allow AI to highlight specific areas where many students lost points and provide suggestions for improvement, making the feedback process more informative and actionable. Instructional coaches and supervisors can use these points for professional development with new staff and refresher training for more experienced staff. By using AI analyzed data, educators can identify the leading indicators of student struggle and intervene before the student falls too far behind, improving retention rates and overall student success. Identifying leading indicators and providing enough time for educators to act on those indicators has been a long-term struggle in education. AI has the potential to provide more accurate, robust, and quickly actionable points of intervention for at risk students, even before the risk noticeably presents.

Generation of Personalized Intervention Strategies

AI's ability to analyze individual student data allows for the creation of personalized intervention strategies tailored to each student's unique needs. These strategies can address specific areas where a student is struggling and provide targeted support to help them improve. However, when working with educators, those personalized learning plans can be de-identified and used in helping educators, particularly those new to a particular assignment on how to identify students at potential risk. They can use the previously created intervention plans as learning tools to determine the effectiveness of those plans. In a Spanish course, AI tools can analyze a student's performance on various language skills, such as reading, writing, listening, and speaking. If the AI tool identifies that a student is struggling with listening comprehension, it can recommend specific exercises and resources to help the student improve in this area. The instructor can then gauge the effectiveness of the intervention and determine whether or not to recommend or revise it in the future. AI can generate personalized study plans based on a student's identified learning styles and preferences. For instance, if a student learns best through visual aids, the AI can suggest videos, infographics, and other visual resources to supplement their learning. Personalized intervention strategies can help students improve in specific areas while enhancing their overall learning experience by catering to their individual needs and preferences. Instructors can have AI track the effectiveness of the various plans over time so instructors can see which of these strategies are most effective over time.

By harnessing the power of AI to analyze large datasets, educators can make data-driven decisions that enhance the effectiveness of their teaching and improve student outcomes. Automated grading tools and consistency checks streamline the assessment process, while early identification of at-risk students and personalized intervention strategies ensure that all students receive the support they need to succeed. As AI continues to evolve, its potential to transform assessment practices will only grow, offering new opportunities for improving educator understanding of how to most effectively improve student learning.

AI-Powered Literature Review and Summarization

For educators engaged in research or seeking to stay current in their field, generative AI tools can serve as valuable assistants in keeping up to date with best practices in education and reducing the amount of time necessary to focus on those tasks. Generative AI can significantly streamline the process of conducting literature reviews, which is often a time-consuming task for educators. By leveraging AI, educators can quickly sift through vast amounts of academic papers, articles, and journals to identify relevant studies and summarize key findings. An educator researching the impact of remote learning on student performance can use AI tools to scan thousands of articles and extract summaries of studies that focus on remote learning outcomes. This allows the educator to quickly gather a comprehensive overview of existing research without having to manually read each paper. In low incident special education fields, an AI-powered literature review tool can help a teacher identify the latest advancements in working with a specific learning disability by summarizing the most recent articles on the disability in question. This enables the researcher to stay updated with cutting-edge developments and incorporate them into their practice. There are a number of excellent summary tools currently available including the AI assistant built into Adobe Acrobat (https://www.adobe.com/acrobat/generative-ai-pdf.html). Some of the currently best rated summarizing tools include:

- AI Summarizer https://www.summarizer.org/ ($6.99/month)
- Editpad https://www.editpad.org/tool/text-summarizer (Free)
- Paraphraser https://www.paraphraser.io/text-summarizer ($23/month +)
- Scite https://scite.ai/ ($20/month)
- Semrush https://www.semrush.com/goodcontent/summary-generator/ (Free)
- Writesonic https://writesonic.com/text-summarizer ($16/month)

Automated Notetaking

Attending conferences and workshops are crucial for educators to stay informed about the latest research and best practices in education. Taking detailed notes during presentations can be challenging. AI can assist by automatically transcribing and summarizing conference proceedings or meetings allowing educators to focus on engaging with the content. For example, during an educational technology conference, an AI tool can transcribe keynote speeches and panel discussions in real time. After the conference, the tool can generate concise summaries of each session, highlighting the main points and presenting key takeaways. This provides educators with a valuable resource to refer to and share with colleagues. At a STEM workshop, an AI-powered note-taking tool can capture detailed notes each session. Researchers can later review the summarized notes to identify important insights and trends discussed during the event, facilitating knowledge sharing and collaboration beyond the attendees. The AI tool could even look for trends among the various sessions and identify those trends specifically for the educators in attendance.

Assistance in Drafting Research Papers and Grant Proposals

Writing research papers and grant proposals requires meticulous attention to detail and adherence to specific guidelines. Generative AI can assist educators by providing suggestions for structuring their documents, improving language and clarity, and ensuring compliance with formatting requirements. An educator preparing a grant proposal for a new educational program can use AI to generate a well-structured outline based on the proposal's objectives and requirements. The AI tool can suggest relevant literature to review and help refine the language to make the proposal more compelling. The educator can consider the sources recommended and ensure journal citations are accurate. AI tools can assist in editing the paper for grammar, style, and coherence, ensuring that the final manuscript is polished and ready for submission. It seems to become common in many areas, such a public relations, (need a cite here) for professionals to use AI to generate a rough draft. It would be simple enough for educators to use AI to generate a first draft of a grant or other research proposal. If the educator can provide the tool a successful example to work with, the strength of a first draft would increase significantly.

Compilation and Analysis of Research Data

Data compilation and analysis are critical components of the research process. AI can automate data collection from various sources, organize the data into meaningful formats, and perform complex analyses to uncover patterns and offer insights. Many online survey tools such as Qualtrics and SurveyMonkey already have AI enabled features. Microsoft Forms will likely soon have Co-Pilot integrated into its interface and Google's Gemini will be integrating into Google Forms. An educator studying student engagement can use AI to collect data from online learning platforms, surveys, and classroom observations. The AI tool can then draft an initial analysis of the data to identify trends in student participation and performance, providing valuable insights to inform instructional strategies. Additionally, the AI tool can perform initial statistical analyses to determine the effectiveness of a new instructional strategy aiding in the development of evidence-based conclusions. The ability of AI tools to conduct a range of analytics in a short time span can give researchers a head start on data analysis.

Keeping Up to Date

Staying current with developments in multiple fields can be challenging for educators who teach interdisciplinary courses or have diverse research interests. AI tools can help by curating personalized updates and summaries of the latest research and trends across various disciplines. For example, an educator teaching a course on environmental science and policy can harness AI to receive regular updates on new research findings, policy changes, and technological advancements in both fields. This ensures the educator can provide students with the most current and relevant information, integrated directly into an existing lesson plan. AI tools can curate articles, conference proceedings, and news updates, allowing the educator to stay informed about the latest trends and integrate interdisciplinary perspectives into their work. By leveraging generative AI, educators can enhance their research capabilities, streamline administrative tasks, and stay informed about the latest developments in their field. This saves time and enables educators to focus on their primary goal: advancing knowledge and improving educational outcomes.

AI AS A TOOL FOR PROFESSIONAL LEARNING COMMUNITIES (PLCs)

Professional Learning Communities (PLCs) are a common method for fostering collaboration and continuous improvement among educators. By bringing educators together to engage in reflective dialogue, examine student data, and develop instructional strategies, PLCs promote a culture of collective efficacy. However, managing the logistics of PLCs, ensuring sustained engagement, and differentiating professional development can be challenging. This is where artificial intelligence can play a transformative role, enabling PLCs to operate more efficiently, provide tailored support, and ensure deeper learning and collaboration.

One of the main challenges in PLCs is organizing meetings, collecting data, and ensuring follow-through on action plans. AI can automate many of these logistical tasks. For instance, AI-driven platforms can schedule meetings based on participants' availability, send reminders, and automatically generate agendas based on previous meeting outcomes. AI can also help organize and analyze data, such as student performance, classroom observations, or surveys, allowing teachers to focus on meaningful discussions rather than administrative work.

Generative AI tools can be used to personalize professional development within PLCs. Using data on teachers' areas of expertise and development needs, AI systems can recommend relevant articles, videos, or online courses that align with both individual and group goals. For instance, if a PLC is focused on improving literacy instruction, the AI could highlight resources tailored to the needs of each member, whether they are novice teachers needing foundational strategies or experienced educators looking for advanced techniques. This differentiation ensures that all members of the PLC engage in targeted learning promoting more effective and impactful collaboration. Generative AI tools such as Harvard's BlockTalk (https://

blocktalk.gse.harvard.edu/), which was developed to support K-12 educators using Scratch to teach computer programming. BlockTalk is intended to allow teachers to work through a set of simulation scenarios to support coding work in elementary and secondary schools (Ross, 2024).

AI's ability to process and analyze large datasets can enhance data-driven decision making in PLCs. Traditionally, teachers analyze student data manually to identify patterns or gaps in learning. AI tools can streamline this process by providing instant insights from multiple data sources, such as standardized test scores, formative assessments, or student behavior reports. For example, an AI system could highlight trends in student performance across various demographic groups, flagging areas where certain students are falling behind. This data can then guide the PLC's focus, ensuring that teachers are addressing the most critical issues in their classrooms. Additionally, AI tools can offer predictive analytics, helping PLCs identify potential future challenges. If student data suggests that certain students are at risk of falling behind based on current trends, AI tools can alert teachers for early intervention with targeted strategies. By providing a clear, data-informed comprehensive picture of student learning, AI can assist PLCs to engage in more informed and focused discussions.

Feedback and reflection are essential elements of effective PLCs, and generative tools can enhance these processes in meaningful ways. AI-powered tools can facilitate real-time feedback loops within PLCs, offering suggestions for improving instructional strategies based on teacher input and student outcomes. For instance, if a PLC is experimenting with a new teaching technique, AI tools can track its impact on student performance and suggest adjustments based on patterns observed in the data. AI tools can support individual reflection by offering personalized feedback on teachers' instructional practices. As mentioned earlier, AI tools could analyze videos of classroom instruction, providing insights on areas such as student engagement, time spent on different activities, or even tone and language used during lessons. This kind of reflective data allows teachers to engage in deeper self-assessments and more meaningful discussions with their PLC peers about how to improve their practice. Incorporating emerging AI tools into PLCs offers a pathway to more efficient, personalized, and impactful professional development. By automating logistical tasks, enhancing data-driven decision making, and supporting continuous feedback and reflection, AI tools may empower teachers to focus on collaborating to improve student outcomes. In doing so, AI tools can help PLCs live up to their full potential as engines of growth and innovation within schools.

CHALLENGES AND LIMITATIONS OF IMPLEMENTING AI-POWERED PROFESSIONAL DEVELOPMENT FOR EDUCATORS

As the integration of artificial intelligence into education grows, AI-powered professional development tools present exciting opportunities to enhance teacher learning and collaboration. Implementing these tools comes with several challenges and limitations that must be carefully navigated to ensure success. These challenges include resistance to change among educators, technical infrastructure requirements, cost considerations, the potential for over-reliance on AI-generated recommendations, addressing biases in AI algorithms, maintaining the human element in professional development, and balancing AI-driven insights with educator autonomy and creativity.

Resistance to Change Among Educators

Educators' resistance to incorporating AI into their professional development and teaching practices stems from several factors, lack of familiarity and technical skills, fear of job displacement, skepticism about the effectiveness of AI, and the loss of human connections. Many teachers feel apprehensive about incorporating AI into their practice, particularly if they are accustomed to traditional forms of professional development, such as face-to-face workshops and peer discussions (Wu, et al., 2023). This discomfort can lead to reluctance in adopting AI-powered tools (Prabhakar, 2024). The rapid pace of technological advancement often outstrips educators' ability to keep up, creating a skills gap that fuels resistance. Concerns about being replaced by technology is not unfounded. As AI capabilities expand, some educators worry that their roles might become obsolete. This fear echoes historical precedents, such as the Luddite movement during the Industrial Revolution (Correlation One, 2023). More recently, the 2024 longshoremen's strike highlighted similar concerns in another industry, underscoring the pervasive nature of this fear across various sectors. Some educators question whether AI can truly enhance their teaching or professional development. This skepticism often stems from a lack of evidence demonstrating AI's effectiveness in educational contexts or from negative experiences with poorly implemented technology initiatives (Poth, 2023). Many teachers value the interpersonal aspects of their profession, including collaboration with peers and mentorship. There's a concern that AI-driven professional development might diminish these important relational elements (Prabhakar, 2024). To address these concerns, leaders, coaches, and institutions need to provide comprehensive training and ongoing support to build educators' confidence in using AI tools. Educators must see demonstrations of how AI can augment rather than replace human expertise, emphasizing its role as a supportive tool. Organizations must ensure transparent communication about the implementation and use of AI in professional development (Poth, 2023).

Educators must make sure that they do not become over reliant on AI generated recommendations. While AI offers valuable insights, overreliance on AI recommendations can lead to several issues including diminished critical thinking where educators might be tempted to accept AI-generated recommendations without scrutiny, potentially compromising their professional judgment. Passive acceptance can lead to a decline in critical thinking skills crucial for effective teaching and instructional reflection. Generative AI tools, despite their sophistication, may not fully capture the nuanced contexts of individual classrooms or students. Blindly following AI recommendations without considering these contextual factors can lead to inappropriate or ineffective interventions. Overreliance on AI in decision-making processes raises ethical questions as well. Particularly regarding data privacy and the potential for algorithmic bias. Educators must remain vigilant about these issues to ensure fair and equitable treatment of all students (Nguygen, n.d.). While AI holds significant promises for enhancing professional development in education, its successful integration requires careful consideration of these barriers. By addressing resistance to change and promoting a balanced approach to AI utilization, educational institutions can harness the benefits of AI while maintaining human agency over all aspects of teaching and learning.

It requires that the school or district ensures that there are clear brakes on machine decision making and human agency retains ultimate decision making. There is the potential for overreliance on machine decisions and following AI generated courses of action. There is a risk that educators may come to rely too heavily on AI-generated recommendations, potentially stifling critical thinking and professional judgment. AI systems can analyze data and suggest targeted professional development, but they are not infallible. Like students misapplying an exciting academic source, an over-reliance on AI could lead educators to follow recommendations without considering their unique student or classroom contexts or questioning the validity of the suggestions. For example, an AI system might recommend a particular instructional strategy based on data patterns, but that strategy may not be appropriate for a specific group of students with unique needs. Educators must remain critical and reflective, using AI as a tool to inform their practice rather than as a directive to follow unquestioningly. Encouraging educators to view AI recommendations as starting points for discussion rather than definitive solutions is crucial for maintaining trust and integrity in a classroom. Overcoming this challenge requires providing educators with ongoing professional development and demonstrating how AI can complement their expertise rather than replace it (Aghaziarati et al., 2023).

Infrastructure Requirements and Cost

AI-powered professional development tools require robust technical infrastructure, including reliable internet access, up to date hardware, and software support. Schools with limited resources may struggle to implement some AI tools effectively, particularly in rural or underfunded areas where technology infrastructure may be outdated or inadequate. While AI-powered tools can enhance professional development, the initial investment and ongoing costs may be prohibitive for some schools and districts. These costs, particularly the cost of training staff, can be burdensome to many districts. For under-resourced schools, allocating funds for AI-based professional development tools may compete with other needs, such as teacher raises, building maintenance, or other programs. To mitigate this challenge, schools might explore partnerships with technology companies, higher education institutions, or apply for grants to help cover the costs. Districts may wish to conduct a cost-benefit analysis to determine whether the long-term advantages of AI-powered professional development justify the initial investment. Increasing competition and rapid advances in space will likely continue to drive down costs, enabling more and more school districts to experiment with AI-powered tools that save time and reduce instructor workload (Davis & Lee, 2023). The integration challenges include the need to consider the way in which generative AI tools can integrate within the organization's current digital learning environment (DLE) (Aghaziarati et al., 2023). One cannot build or utilize these systems without integration into the existing DLE and consider the integration costs in both time and capital. Additionally, generative systems need to be integrated into the extant cybersecurity milieu within an organization.

Addressing Potential Biases in AI Algorithms

AI systems are as unbiased as the data and algorithms that power them. If the data used to train an AI model is biased, the resulting recommendations can perpetuate inequalities, particularly for marginalized student populations. For example, if an AI system is trained on data that predominantly reflects the performance of students from higher-income areas, the recommendations it provides might be less effective for educators working in low-income communities. Addressing this challenge requires ongoing vigilance in the development and refinement of AI algorithms. Schools and districts must ensure that the data used to train AI systems is representative and that AI models are regularly audited to identify and mitigate biases. Aghaziarati, et al. (2023) outlined the need to consider algorithmic bias as well as inequity in access and cultural relevance. Selecting AI tools that prioritize ethical considerations and transparency in their algorithms is essential to ensuring that AI-powered professional development tools promote equity rather than perpetuate these biases "at scale" (Gillani et al., 2023, p. 101). Though ethical questions remain, the use of AI-powered tools could counter inherent human biases among teachers, a prospect that should excite educational practitioners.

Maintaining the Human Element and Balance in Professional Development

As mentioned earlier in this section, generative AI tools are intended to assist in human decision making and educational decisions should be data-informed, but not data-driven. AI can provide valuable insights and automate certain aspects of professional development. However, it cannot replace, nor should it be considered a replacement for, the human connections that are central to effective teaching. The Consortium of School Networking (CoSN) and TeachAI (2023) identified seven principles for working with AI and those apply to professional development as well as instructional use of AI tools. Ongoing use of AI tools to support professional development needs to be regularly evaluated, balanced, confirm academic integrity, and maintain human agency as well as compliance with policies and statues. Users need to ensure they are using AI to support institutional PD and instructional goals. AI tools should be adopted in ways that promote growing AI literacy among educators.

Educators benefit when collaborating with peers, receiving personalized feedback from mentors, and engaging in reflective dialogue, elements that no AI tool, no matter how advanced, can fully replicate. While AI can generate personalized learning resources for a teacher struggling with classroom management, that teacher may need emotional support and practical advice that can only come from a trusted colleague or instructional coach. To maintain the human element, AI-powered professional development should be used to strengthen, not replace, peer interactions, coaching, and collaborative learning communities. Nazaretsky, et al. (2022) articulated the need to retain teacher agency as a key method in gaining teacher trust and ensuing teachers understand that they can modify the recommendations provided by AI tools.

One of the greatest values of AI tools in professional development is its ability to provide data-driven insights, but it is equally important to balance these insights with educator autonomy and creativity. Teachers are professionals with deep knowledge of their students and classroom environments, and they should retain the flexibility to make instructional decisions based on their unique contexts. If an AI system might suggest a particular reading intervention based on student data, a teacher may choose to modify or reject the recommendation based on their understanding of the classroom dynamics or the interests of individual students. Encouraging teachers to use AI tools to augment their expertise, rather than replace it, ensures that professional development remains a dynamic process that fosters both innovation and professional growth no matter what developments come next in deep learning and artificial intelligence.

EMERGING TRENDS AND FUTURE POSSIBILITIES FOR AI IN EDUCATOR PROFESSIONAL DEVELOPMENT

The role of educators is already evolving in response to rapid AI advances. Teachers are becoming facilitators of learning, guiding students in navigating AI-enhanced educational environments. This shift necessitates ongoing professional development that focuses on building AI competencies (AI knowledge, AI skills, and AI attitudes) among educators as well (Kitcharoen, et al., 2024). This chapter concludes by exploring several emerging trends and future possibilities that hold promise for transforming how educators learn and grow in their profession. As emerging AI technologies continue to improve and move towards the conceptual breakthrough of AGI, educators will be able to more fully integrate extended realities, such as augmented reality and virtual realities into professional development. Currently the Mayo Clinic (Morreale, 2024) is building virtual anatomical models that can assist physicians and other health care professionals to better understand anatomy and health care options. How long until this technology moves into education?

Integration of Virtual and Augmented Reality in AI-Powered Training Simulations

One of the most exciting developments is the integration of virtual and augmented reality (VR/AR) in AI-powered training simulations. Digital twin technology, which creates virtual replicas of physical environments, can be used to develop immersive virtual classrooms. For instance, educators can practice classroom management and instructional strategies in a risk-free, simulated environment that mirrors real-world scenarios (Smith, 2023). This approach can enhance the realism of pre-service training and allow for personalized feedback and iterative practice, leading to more effective professional development. Mixed-reality headsets from companies like Meta can enable realistic opportunities for novice educators to deal with parental situations or student scenarios more realistically than traditional roleplaying. Among administrative professional development needs are the ability to fully interact with parents and interact with school boards. Fully interacting with school boards is one of the most articulated needs for aspiring district-level administrators. A digital twin of a school board could provide significant professional development for those aspiring leaders. Such a twin environment could be used by leadership development institutions to provide interview coaching.

Advanced Natural Language Processing for More Sophisticated AI Mentoring

Advancements in natural language processing (NLP) are enabling more sophisticated AI mentoring systems. These systems can understand and respond to complex queries, provide nuanced feedback, and engage in meaningful dialogue with educators. Future AI mentors may be able to understand and respond to complex queries, provide nuanced feedback, and engage in meaningful dialogue with educators. This level of interaction will deepen professional growth and support continuous learning in several ways. For instance, AI systems can analyze teachers' lesson plans and offer targeted suggestions for improvement. For instance, an AI mentor might identify areas where a lesson could be more engaging, suggest additional resources to support learning objectives, or recommend differentiation strategies for diverse learners (Mentoring Complete, 2024). During or after a lesson, AI mentors can provide immediate feedback on teaching techniques, classroom management, and student engagement. This timely input allows educators to make rapid adjustments to their practice. The concept of pairing AI mentors with digital twin simulations of classrooms represents a significant leap forward in teacher preparation and development. This will allow teachers to experiment with new methods of instruction and classroom management in a risk-free environment before introducing them into an actual classroom. Digital twin technology will allow teachers to explore various "what-if" scenarios, such as how different teaching methods might impact student outcomes or how to handle challenging classroom situations. Consider a high school science teacher preparing to introduce a complex topic like genetic engineering. The AI mentor, after analyzing the teacher's lesson plan, might suggest incorporating more interactive elements to enhance student engagement. The teacher could then use the digital twin simulation to practice a new inquiry-based learning activity. The AI mentor could observe and provide feedback on aspects of instruction allowing the teacher to refine their approach before delivering the lesson to their actual students. This iterative process, combining AI mentorship with realistic simulations, allows for rapid skill development and increased confidence in implementing new teaching strategies.

Predictive Analytics for Proactive Professional Development Planning

Predictive analytics has the potential to impact educator professional development. By analyzing data on educators' performance, learning preferences, and career trajectories, AI can predict future professional development needs and recommend targeted PD programs. For instance, an AI system might identify a teacher's need for additional support in integrating technology into the classroom and suggest relevant workshops or courses (Kurni, et al., 2023). This approach could support novice and other struggling educators with professional development is timely, relevant, and aligned to support both educators' goals and student success.

Envision the following example. The fictional Evergreen School District implemented an AI-powered predictive analytics system to enhance its professional development program. analyzed various data points for each educator, including: student performance data, classroom observation reports, student behavior data, professional development history and career goals and aspirations for each educator. After six months of data collection and analysis, the AI system could identify several trends and made targeted recommendations to improve new teacher support through a series of workshops on effective classroom management strategies, specifically tailored for math instruction, to be offered proactively at the beginning of the second quarter. The system identified a group of veteran English teachers who showed interest in using technology but had low confidence scores in this area. The system suggested a mentorship program pairing these teachers with tech-savvy colleagues and recommended specific online courses on digital literacy and educational technology tools for both the English teachers and their mentors. Noticing a district-wide trend of underutilization of student data in instructional decision-making, the system recommended a comprehensive data literacy program. This included workshops on data interpretation, using data to inform instruction, and ethical considerations in educational data use.

Cross-Institutional Collaboration Facilitated by AI-Powered Networks

AI-powered networks have the potential to develop cross-institutional collaboration, breaking down silos and fostering a culture of shared learning. These networks connect educators from different schools, districts, and may cross national boundaries, enabling the sharing of resources, best practices, and support. One example could be an AI-driven platform that matches teachers with similar interests or challenges, creating opportunities for peer mentoring and collaborative problem-solving. A study of scientific collaborative networks in Europe showed that collaboration tends to continue where early collaborations had occurred and that funding can help to erase the barriers posted by geographical and national barriers (Resce, et al., 2022). Educators should be able to harness AI tools to assist in building collaborative networks which should then encourage more demographically diverse collaborations across institutions and areas. This collaborative approach can enhance individual professional development and encourage educators to broaden the scope of their research and reporting.

CONCLUSION

The power of generative AI can be used to support educators' professional development and growth. These personalized, data-informed professional development opportunities that were previously unimaginable are now available with minimal initial investments. This chapter aimed to provide a comprehensive summary for educational institutions and individual educators looking to leverage AI tools to enhance their personal and collective professional growth and, ultimately, improve student outcomes. While AI-supported professional development tools offer significant potential for improving teaching and learning, they must be implemented thoughtfully to address the challenges and limitations outlined above. By balancing the benefits of AI with the need for human interaction, critical reflection, and professional autonomy, educators can leverage these tools to enhance their practice while maintaining the creativity and judgment that define effective teaching.

REFERENCES

Aghaziarati, A., Nejatifar, S., & Abedi, A. (2023). Artificial intelligence in education: Investigating teacher attitudes. *AI and Tech in Behavioral and Social Sciences*, 1(1), 35–42. DOI: 10.61838/kman.aitech.1.1.6

Akgun, S., & Greenhow, C. (2022). Artificial intelligence in education: Addressing ethical challenges in K-12 settings. *AI and Ethics*, 2(3), 431–440. DOI: 10.1007/s43681-021-00096-7 PMID: 34790956

al-Zyoud, H. M. M. (2020). The role of artificial intelligence in teacher professional development. *Universal Journal of Educational Research*, 8(11B), 6263–6272. DOI: 10.13189/ujer.2020.082265

Baule. S. M. & Carter, E. (2024, September 24). Four tips for designing AI-resistant assessments. *Tech & Learning*.

Burton, C. (2023, June 26). 25+ best ChatGPT prompts for instructional designers. https://www.thinkific.com/blog/best-chatgpt-prompts-for-instructional-designers/

Campus Technology. (2024, August). *Streamlining instructional design with generative AI* [Podcast]. https://campustechnology.com/Podcasts/2024/08/Streamlining-Instructional-Design-with-Generative-AI.aspx?admgarea=podcast

Chapman, J. (2024, August 1). Lumi Pro for Brightspace idea generation for assignments overview. https://community.d2l.com/brightspace/kb/articles/26143

Chen, L., Chen, P., & Lin, Z. (2020). Artificial intelligence in education: A review. *IEEE Access : Practical Innovations, Open Solutions*, 8, 75264–75278. DOI: 10.1109/ACCESS.2020.2988510

Correlation One. (2023, June 23). Five barriers to AI readiness. https://www.correlation-one.com/blog/5-barriers-to-ai-readiness

CoSN and Teach AI. (2023). AI guidance for schools toolkit: Principles for AI in education. https://www.teachai.org/toolkit-principles

Creswell, J. W., & Creswell, J. D. (2018). *Research design: Qualitative, quantitative, and mixed methods approaches* (5th ed.). SAGE Publications.

Davis, R. O., & Lee, Y. J. (2023). Prompt: ChatGPT, create my course, please! *Education Sciences*, 14(1), 24. DOI: 10.3390/educsci14010024

Dellarocas, C. (2023, December 8). How genAI could accelerate employee learning and development. *Harvard Business Review,* https://hbr.org/2023/12/how-genai-could-accelerate-employee-learning-and-development

Ding, A. E., Shie, L., Yang, H., & Choi, I. (2024, June). Enhancing teacher AI literacy and integration through different types of cases in teacher professional development. *Computers and Education Open*, 6, 100178–1000191. DOI: 10.1016/j.caeo.2024.100178

Ferikoğlu, D., & Akgün, E. (2022). An investigation of teachers' artificial intelligence awareness: A scale development study. *Malaysian Online Journal of Educational Technology*, 10(3), 215–231. DOI: 10.52380/mojet.2022.10.3.407

Gillani, N., Eynon, R., Chiabaut, C., & Finkel, K. (2023). Unpacking the "Black Box" of AI. *Education.Journal of Educational Technology & Society*, 26(1), 99–111. DOI: 10.30191/ETS.202301_26(1).0008

Guskey, T. R., & Link, L. J. (2022). Feedback for teachers: What evidence do teachers find most useful? *AASA Journal of Scholarship & Practice*, 4(4), 9–20.

Gutiérrez-Caneda, B., Vázquez-Herrero, J., & López-García, X. (2023). AI application in journalism: ChatGPT and the uses and risks of an emergent technology. *El Profesional de la Información*, 32(5), e320514. Advance online publication. DOI: 10.3145/epi.2023.sep.14

Haines, S. G. (1998). *The managers guide to systems thinking & learning*. HRD Press.

Horn, E. (2023, July 27). Prompts for lesson planning with ChatGPT. https://blog.tcea.org/prompts-for-lesson-planning-with-chatgpt/

Ka Yuk Chan, C. (2023). Is AI changing the rules of academic misconduct? An in-depth look at students' perceptions of 'AI-giarism.' The University of Hong Kong. https://www.researchgate.net/publication/371347082_Is_AI_Changing_the_Rules_of_Academic_Misconduct_An_In-depth_Look_at_Students'_Perceptions_of_'AI-giarism'

Kelsky, K. (2015). *The professor is in: The essential guide to turning your Ph.D. into a job*. Three Rivers Press.

Kitcharoen, P., Howimanporn, S., & Chookaew, S. (2024). Enhancing teachers' AI competencies through artificial intelligence of things professional development training. *International Journal of Interactive Mobile Technologies*, 18(2), 4–15. DOI: 10.3991/ijim.v18i02.46613

Kurni, M., Mohammed, M. S., & Srinivasa, K. S. (2023). *A beginner's guide to introduce artificial intelligence in teaching and learning*. Springer.

Lee, Y.-J., Davis, R. O., & Ryu, J. (2024). Korean in-service teachers' perceptions of implementing artificial intelligence (AI) education for teaching in schools and their AI teacher training programs. *International Journal of Information and Education Technology (IJIET)*, 14(2), 214–219. Advance online publication. DOI: 10.18178/ijiet.2024.14.2.2042

M-powering teachers (2024). About. https://www.mpoweringteachers.com/

Mentoring Complete. (2024, January 29). The future of AI in mentorship. https://www.mentoringcomplete.com/the-future-of-ai-in-mentorship/

Moreale, R. (2024, September 27). NextGen Med and data at scale. Presentation to Rochester (MN) Chamber of Commerce. The Mayo Clinic.

Nazaretsky, T., Ariely, M., Cukurova, M., & Alexandron, G. (2022). Teachers' trust in AI-powered educational technology and a professional development program to improve it. *British Journal of Educational Technology*, 53(4), 914–931. DOI: 10.1111/bjet.13232

Nguyen, T. (n.d.) Generative AI in education: Benefits, barriers, and use cases. Neurond. https://www.neurond.com/blog/generative-ai-in-education

Polaris Learning. (2018, April 3). The three stages of training, development and competence. https://polaris-learning.com/three-stages-training-development-competence/

Poth, R. D. (2023, November 9). Effective professional development on AI. Edutopia. https://www.edutopia.org/article/ai-professional-development-helps-teachers-tech-integration/

Prabhakar, R. R. C. (2024). Barriers to AI adoption for non-technical educators in the digital age. *Journal of Scientific and Engineering Research*, 11(8), 211–214.

Resce, G., Zinilli, A., & Cerulli, G. (2022). Machine learning prediction of academic collaboration networks. *Scientific Reports*, 12(1), 1–16. DOI: 10.1038/s41598-022-26531-1 PMID: 36539469

Ross, E. M. (2024, October 2). How generative AI can support professional learning for teachers. Harvard Graduate School of Education. https://www.gse.harvard.edu/ideas/usable-knowledge/24/10/how-generative-ai-can-support-professional-learning-teachers

Teach, F. X. (2024a). About TeachFX. https://teachfx.com/

Teach, F. X. (2024b). Research. https://teachfx.com/research

Woodward, D., Booth, S., Allen, E., Forbes, A., & Morton, C. (2023, November). Reflective practice for educators and learners, and the benefits of being a reflective practitioner. *Scope: Contemporary Research Topics (Learning & Teaching)*, 12, 96–103.

Wu, W., Burdina, G., & Gura, A. (2023). Use of Artificial Intelligence in Teacher Training. *International Journal of Web-Based Learning and Teaching Technologies*, 18(1), 1–15. DOI: 10.4018/IJWLTT.331692

ADDITIONAL READING

Brandão, A., Pedro, L., & Zagalo, N. (2024). Teacher professional development for a future with generative artificial intelligence–an integrative literature review. *Digital Education Review*, (45), 151–157. DOI: 10.1344/der.2024.45.151-157

Moorhouse, B. L., Wan, Y., Wu, C., Kohnke, L., Ho, T. Y., & Kwong, T. (2024). Developing language teachers' professional generative AI competence: An intervention study in an initial language teacher education course. *System*, 125, 103399. DOI: 10.1016/j.system.2024.103399

Nikolopoulou, K. (2024). Generative Artificial Intelligence in Higher Education: Exploring ways of harnessing pedagogical Practices with the assistance of ChatGPT. *International Journal of Changes in Education*, 1(2), 103–111. DOI: 10.47852/bonviewIJCE42022489

Nyaaba, M., & Zhai, X. (2024). Generative AI professional development needs for teacher educators. *Journal of AI*, 8(1), 1–13. DOI: 10.61969/jai.1385915

KEY TERMS AND DEFINITIONS

Artificial Intelligence (AI): The simulation of human intelligence processes by machines, especially computer systems, involving learning, reasoning, and self-correction.

Content Creation: The process of generating educational materials, resources, and activities tailored to learning objectives, often automated or enhanced by AI to save time and improve quality.

Data-Driven Decision-Making: Using data analysis and interpretation to inform and guide educational strategies, improving learning outcomes and professional practices.

Ethical Considerations: The principles of fairness, transparency, and responsibility that guide the appropriate use of AI in educational contexts, ensuring decisions and practices respect all stakeholders.

Generative AI: A subset of artificial intelligence that creates new content, such as text, images, or sound, based on input data, often used for lesson planning and personalized learning.

Instructional Evaluation: The process of assessing teaching methods and effectiveness, where AI can offer insights based on data analytics to enhance educational practices.

Lesson Planning: The structured design of instructional content and activities to meet learning objectives, increasingly supported by AI to streamline development and tailor plans to individual needs.

Personalized Learning: An educational approach that tailors instruction to meet individual students' needs, often enabled by AI through adaptive learning technologies.

Professional Development: Continuous education and training for educators to improve their teaching skills and stay current with educational advancements, with AI now aiding in personalization and efficiency.

Teaching Effectiveness: A measure of how well educational objectives are achieved, where AI tools can help analyze and improve teacher performance and student engagement.

Chapter 4
The Impact of Artificial Intelligence on Leadership Styles in Schools in Morocco

Ahmed El Hammoumi
Polydisciplinary Faculty of Taza, Morocco

Mohamed El Hammoumi
Faculté des Sciences et Techniques de Fès, Morocco

ABSTRACT

This chapter explores the transformative impact of artificial intelligence (AI) on the roles and responsibilities of school leaders in Morocco, encompassing principals, teachers, and administrators. Drawing on data from 106 schools gathered through interviews and questionnaires, the study evaluates hypotheses concerning AI's influence on school management. Findings indicate that AI tools significantly reduce principals' administrative workload, enabling a stronger focus on pedagogical leadership. Additionally, AI redefines teachers as facilitators of learning, redirects administrators toward strategic tasks, and enhances collaboration between educators and administrators by providing precise insights into student performance. The integration of AI further shifts school leaders' perceptions, encouraging a data-driven approach to management practices. Statistical analysis reveals strong, positive correlations between AI adoption and evolving roles and responsibilities, underscoring the transformative potential of AI in educational leadership.

DOI: 10.4018/979-8-3373-1017-6.ch004

INTRODUCTION

The integration of artificial intelligence (AI) in schools has become an unavoidable reality, bringing significant changes in school management and teaching practices. This study aims to explore how the introduction of AI is changing the roles and responsibilities of school leaders, such as principals, teachers, and administrators. We are interested in understanding the impacts of this technology on the distribution of time and responsibilities, as well as on the dynamics of collaboration and decision-making within schools. AI tools, ranging from the automation of administrative tasks to the personalization of teaching, are designed to transform educational and administrative practices. AI offers possibilities such as improving the management of administrative tasks (Chen et al., 2023) and adapting educational content to the individual needs of students (Li and Zhang, 2022). However, the specific implications of these technologies for the roles of school leaders, especially in the Moroccan context, have not yet been widely explored.

This study adopts a quantitative approach to analyze the effects of AI on the roles and responsibilities of school leaders in Moroccan institutions. By using a structured questionnaire based on a Likert scale, we aim to collect precise data on the perceptions of school principals, teachers, and administrators. Our field of research focuses on the school context in Morocco, a context that is often less studied in the international literature on AI in education. The main objective of this chapter is to determine how the introduction of AI influences the roles of school leaders in Morocco. We are looking at four key aspects: the reduction of time spent on administrative tasks, the improvement of pedagogical leadership, the transformation of the roles of teachers, and the evolution of the responsibilities of administrators. We will also seek to assess whether AI promotes better collaboration between teachers and administrators and whether it encourages more data-driven management practices (Miller et al., 2024; Peterson and Smith, 2023). This study aims to provide valuable insights for decision-makers and practitioners in education in Morocco, highlighting the specific effects of AI on school leadership practices in a local context. By contributing to the understanding of local dynamics influenced by AI, we hope to inform future developments and adaptations of educational and administrative practices in Morocco.

LITERATURE REVIEW

The impact of AI on leadership styles in schools is a relatively recent but rapidly expanding field of research. This literature review examines the key contributions in this field, focusing on three main areas: the AI tools used in schools through empirical studies, specific applications in school management and teaching, the evolution of leadership roles, and the challenges associated with the integration of AI. The integration of artificial intelligence (AI) in schools takes various forms, ranging from the automation of administrative tasks to the personalization of teaching. This section examines the types of AI tools used, their specific applications in school management and teaching, as well as exemplary case studies illustrating their implementation.

Types of AI Tools Used

The AI tools used in schools generally fall into several main categories:

- **Intelligent Tutorial Systems (ITS)**: These systems use machine learning algorithms to provide personalized instruction to students. They adapt the educational content according to the performance and individual needs of the students, offering real-time support and personalized feedback (VanLehn, 2011).
- **Learning Analytics**: Learning analytics tools collect and analyze data on student behavior and performance to identify trends and patterns. This information can help educators adapt their teaching strategies and intervene proactively to support students in difficulty (Siemens, 2013).
- **Administrative Management**: AI can automate administrative tasks such as scheduling, registration management, and communication with parents. These tools reduce the workload of administrators and improve operational efficiency (Luckin et al., 2016).

Several empirical studies have been carried out in this context. Indeed, Holmes, Bialik, and Fadel (2019) describe how AI can personalize learning by analyzing student data to adapt educational content to their specific needs. Intelligent tutoring systems, for example, can offer individualized support, improve student engagement, and increase academic performance (VanLehn, 2011). In terms of administrative management, Luckin et al. (2016) point out that AI can automate repetitive tasks, such as scheduling and managing student records, allowing school leaders to focus on more strategic aspects of their role. Brynjolfsson and McAfee (2014) add that AI can provide real-time analytics to support decision-making, making processes more efficient and based on concrete data.

The introduction of AI is transforming the roles and responsibilities of school leaders. According to Avolio, Walumbwa, and Weber (2009), leaders must now adopt a more adaptive and innovation-oriented leadership style. Transformational leadership, which inspires and motivates the members of the organization to achieve high goals, is particularly relevant in this context (Bass, 1985). School leaders must also develop skills in information technology management and data analysis. This implies continuous training and professional development to stay up to date with technological advances (Cator & Adams, 2013). Leaders who can master these skills can use AI to improve the quality of teaching and organizational effectiveness. To better understand the impact of artificial intelligence (AI) in schools, several studies have been conducted. These studies examine various applications of AI, ranging from improving academic performance to optimizing school management. Here are some exemplary studies, including the authors, the methods used, and the results obtained.

Pane et al. (2014) have done a study on the effect of Intelligent Tutorial Systems on Student Performance. This study is carried out on students from 147 secondary schools spread over several school districts. The data are collected through standardized test scores in mathematics before and after using the smart tutorial. and the results obtained show that the students using the Cognitive Tutor showed significantly higher performance gains in mathematics compared to those following a traditional education. However, the performance gains were particularly pronounced among students who were initially weak in mathematics, suggesting that AI can help fill learning gaps (Pane et al., 2014). Another study was carried out by Michael Bienkowski, Mingyu Feng, and Barbara Means (2012) on the use of Learning Analysis to Identify Students at Risk. On a sample of Students from several grade levels in the Los Angeles School District, this learning analysis made it possible to accurately identify students at risk of dropping out of school. The data is collected from demographic data, student grades, absenteeism rates, and educational interventions, and the results obtained have shown that the learning analysis has made it possible to accurately identify students at risk of dropping out of school, that targeted interventions based on data have led to an improvement in student retention and success rates, and that teachers have been able to customize educational interventions according to the specific needs of students, which has improved academic performance.

Another study on the impact of chatbots on university enrollment management was done by Lindsay C. Page and Hunter Gehlbach in 2017. On a sample of first-year students at several universities, the data is collected by the enrollment rate, interactions with the chatbot, and student satisfaction, and the results show that the use of the AdmitHub chatbot increased the enrollment rate of first-year students. However, students reported high satisfaction with the support provided by the chatbot, noting that it was useful for answering common administrative questions and that the chatbot has reduced the workload of administrators and improved the overall efficiency of the registration processes.

Fryer et al. (2019) carried out a study on the Impact of AI on Student Motivation and Engagement. This study was done on a sample of Students from different grade levels using an intelligent tutorial. the data are collected from Measures of motivation, commitment and academic performance before and after using the tutorial, and the results obtained show that the students using the smart tutorial showed a significant increase in motivation and commitment compared to a control group following a traditional teaching, that the gamified components of the smart tutorial have helped to maintain students' interest and improve their participation and that the academic performance of students using the smart tutorial has also improved, showing the positive impact of AI on learning. Luckin et al. (2016) have carried out a study on the Use of AI for the Personalization of Teaching in Colleges. On a sample of middle school students using different intelligent tutoring systems, they collected data by Academic performance, student and teacher satisfaction, and qualitative feedback, and the results obtained showed that ITS allowed an effective personalization of teaching, adapting lessons and exercises to the individual needs of students, that teachers reported an improvement in the engagement and results of students using ITS, and that the study also noted a high satisfaction of students and teachers regarding the use of ITS, indicating a positive acceptance of AI in the educational context.

Other studies have been conducted in different countries around the world. For example, a study titled Leadership Transformation Through AI in Finnish Schools by Sahlberg & Hargreaves (2020) examines the role of AI in Finnish schools, which are known for their strong focus on innovation. The researchers found that the introduction of AI systems in schools allowed school leaders to focus more on developing educational strategies and innovation. Administrative tasks were automated, thus improving time management. Leadership in the context of AI required strong technological skills and the ability to adopt an adaptive and collaborative management style. Another study on AI in Educational Leadership in Singapore was conducted by Tan & Gopinathan (2019). This case study focused on the use of AI in Singaporean schools, where the education system has integrated AI to improve operational efficiency and decision-making. The results showed that the integration of AI allowed school leaders in Singapore to access real-time data dashboards, facilitating decisions based on precise and rapid analyses. The study also highlights the importance for educational leaders to possess data management skills to maximize the benefits of AI technologies. AI has optimized resource allocation and improved human resource management in educational institutions.

In a similar vein, a study titled Artificial Intelligence and Educational Leadership in the UK was conducted by Harris & Jones (2020), through a survey of British school leaders using AI platforms for administrative and educational management. This study revealed that AI frees up time for leaders, allowing them to focus on vision and educational innovation. However, the study also highlighted challenges, particularly regarding technology acceptance among teachers and students, as well as the need to rethink leadership skills to include technological management. Eacott (2021) conducted a study on AI and Decision-Making in Australian Educational Leadership. According to a qualitative study of school leaders in Australia, focused on the impact of AI on strategic decision-making, he concluded that AI has strengthened the accuracy and speed of decisions in Australian schools. Educational leaders were able to use AI tools to anticipate student learning trends, thereby improving educational planning. The study recommends that future leaders receive training in AI to better understand how to utilize it in an educational context.

Zhang & Liu (2020) addressed the same topic with their study on AI in Leadership Development in Chinese Higher Education, examining the effects of AI technologies in Chinese universities on leadership development. In Chinese higher education institutions, AI is used to analyze data on academic and administrative performance. The results indicate that rectors and administrators who integrate AI into their decision-making processes adopt a more innovation-oriented leadership style. The study emphasizes the importance of ongoing training in AI for university leaders. Finally, a study titled Global Perspective on AI-Driven Educational Leadership was conducted by UNESCO (2021). The report, based on surveys and case studies in various countries, including contributions from institutions in Europe, Latin America, and Africa, showed that both developed and developing countries are gradually integrating AI to improve educational management. However, technological infrastructure and access to training remain major challenges for developing countries. Educational leadership in these countries is transforming, but greater training in digital skills is needed for leaders to fully exploit AI tools. These global studies demonstrate that AI offers significant potential to transform educational leadership in various contexts, enhancing administrative efficiency and enabling more strategic decision-making. However, challenges remain, particularly regarding ongoing training for leaders, acceptance by staff, and access to technological infrastructure, especially in developing countries.

Applications in School Management and Teaching and the Evolution of Leadership Roles with AI

The application of AI tools in schools encompasses a variety of administrative activities, such as the automation of student management and financial tasks, which makes it possible to reduce the workload of administrators and free up time for strategic tasks. At the same time, these tools facilitate the personalization of teaching by adapting educational content to the individual needs of students, which can improve the effectiveness of learning. In addition, AI contributes to the analysis of student performance and the management of school data, thus allowing more informed decision-making based on accurate data. Intelligent tutoring systems, such as those developed by Carnegie Learning, offer personalized learning in mathematics by adapting the exercises and lessons to the specific needs of each student. These systems have shown a significant improvement in student performance (Pane et al., 2014). Learning analysis tools, such as those used by the Los Angeles School District, allow educators to track student progress, identify students at risk and customize interventions. These tools provide data visualizations and reports that help school leaders make informed decisions (Bienkowski, Feng, & Means, 2012).

The use of virtual assistants and automated systems, such as chatbots developed by AdmitHub, helps schools and universities manage registration processes, answer student questions and provide continuous administrative support. This frees up time for educational and strategic tasks (Page & Gehlbach, 2017). The integration of artificial intelligence (AI) in schools has led to a significant transformation of the roles and responsibilities of school leaders. This change has modified traditional leadership practices and has favored the emergence of new management styles.

This section examines how the roles of school leaders have evolved with AI, compares traditional and modern leadership styles, and presents examples of leaders who have successfully integrated AI into their institutions. -Transformation of the Roles and Responsibilities of School Leaders The introduction of AI has had a profound impact on the roles of school principals, teachers and administrators. School principals, for example, have seen their responsibilities evolve from day-to-day management to a more strategic and vision-oriented role. AI allows for increased automation of administrative tasks such as absence management, schedule planning and financial data management (Bennett et al., 2022). This automation reduces the administrative burden and allows directors to focus more on strategic and pedagogical aspects of their role (Johnson and Davis, 2023).

For teachers, AI has facilitated the personalization of teaching and the management of student performance, thus changing their traditional role from a simple provider of knowledge to that of facilitator of individualized learning. Teachers can now use AI tools to create lesson plans that are more tailored to students' specific needs and to track their progress in real time (Li and Zhang, 2022). As a result, they are led to adopt more data-centric and results-based approaches to improve the effectiveness of their teaching (Green et al., 2023).

Comparison of Traditional and Modern Leadership Styles Traditional leadership styles in schools were often focused on centralized and hierarchical management, with a strong emphasis on direct control and supervision of educational and administrative processes. The principals made decisions based mainly on their experience and direct observations of school practices (Smith & Jones, 2020). With the advent of AI, modern leadership styles are characterized by a more collaborative and data-driven approach. Modern school leaders use AI tools to obtain accurate and real-time information about student performance and the effectiveness of teaching practices. They adopt a more participatory leadership style, relying on data to guide decisions and promoting collaboration between teachers and administrators (Dawson & Archer, 2022). This shift towards a more data- and results-oriented management reflects a transformation towards more agile and adaptive leadership approaches (Miller & Davis, 2024).

In the United States, a school principal in Seattle has implemented an AI system for monitoring student performance, allowing increased personalization of teaching and better identification of individual student needs. This approach has not only improved students' academic performance but has also strengthened collaboration between teachers and parents (Peterson & Smith, 2023). These examples illustrate how a strategic use of AI can transform school leadership practices, by allowing more effective management, personalization of teaching and improvement of academic results.

The training of school leaders is essential to guarantee an effective and ethical use of AI (Buchanan & McMenemy, 2010). It is crucial to ensure that leaders understand not only the technical aspects of AI, but also its ethical and legal implications, especially in terms of data privacy. Another challenge is the unequal access to technology. Schools located in disadvantaged areas may not have the necessary resources to implement AI tools, thus exacerbating existing inequalities (Zawacki-Richter et al., 2019).

ETHICAL CONCERNS AND EQUITY ISSUES IN THE ADOPTION OF ARTIFICIAL INTELLIGENCE (AI) IN SCHOOLS

AI systems can be biased due to the data on which they are trained. If this data reflects historical or social prejudices, AI may reproduce and amplify these biases. For example, recommendation systems may favor certain groups of students over others, creating inequalities in access to educational resources (O'Neil, 2016; Holstein et al., 2019). The use of AI requires the collection of large amounts of data on students, raising privacy concerns. It is crucial to ensure that students' personal data is protected and that its use complies with data protection regulations. Parents and students should be informed about how their data is used and can provide informed consent (Regan & Jesse, 2019). AI can exacerbate existing inequalities if certain schools or communities do not have access to the necessary technologies. Schools in underprivileged areas may find themselves disadvantaged compared to those with sufficient resources to adopt AI tools. It is important to ensure equitable access to these technologies so that all schools benefit from the same opportunities for innovation (Zawacki-Richter et al., 2019).

The integration of AI may change the role of teachers and raise concerns about the dehumanization of education. Teachers may be perceived as less necessary, which can affect their professional status and morale. It is crucial to maintain a balance between using AI to enhance teaching and preserving the importance of human contact in the educational process (Wang et al., 2019). It is essential to establish clear standards regarding accountability in cases of issues related to AI. Who is responsible for AI errors or biases that affect students' academic outcomes? Schools must be transparent about the algorithms used and how decisions are made to gain the trust of students, parents, and teachers (Binns, 2018).

Students should have a voice in how AI is integrated into their education. This includes the right to be informed and to give informed consent before AI systems are deployed. Students should also be able to express their concerns regarding the use of AIin their learning (Shadbolt, 2020). The ethical concerns and equity issues related to the adoption of AI in schools are complex and require thorough consideration. For AI to have a positive impact on education, it is essential to address these concerns proactively by promoting transparency, accessibility, and respect for students' rights. Schools, educators, policymakers, and technologists must collaborate to ensure that AI is used ethically and equitably, supporting an inclusive and fair learning environment for all students. It is therefore imperative to develop policies and strategies to ensure that all students, regardless of their socio-economic background, can benefit from the benefits of AI. Based on the underlying hypothesis, the conceptual model presented in **Figure 1,** offers a visual representation that illustrates the relationships and key elements involved in the context under study.

Figure 1. Conceptual model

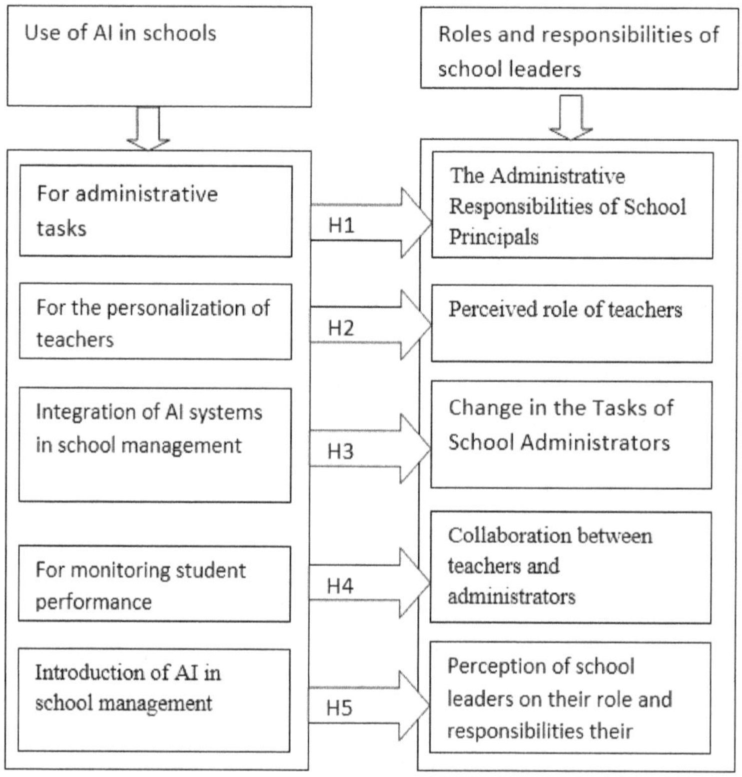

Throughout this work, this article explores the research on the impact of Artificial Intelligence on Leadership Styles by taking Schools in Morocco as a field of study. However, this conceptual model aims to illustrate how the introduction of artificial intelligence (AI) in schools affects the roles and responsibilities of school principals, teachers, and administrators.

HYPOTHESES OF THE STUDY

The study aims to identify how the introduction of AI modifies the roles and responsibilities of school leaders, such as principals, teachers, and administrators. This impact is expressed by the Administrative Responsibilities of School Principals, the Role of Teachers in the Personalization of Teaching, the Change in the Tasks of School Administrators with AI, the Collaboration between Teachers and Administrators, and the perception of school leaders on their roles and responsibilities. The research hypotheses tested, using regression analysis, on a sample are the following:

Hypothesis 1: The use of AI tools reduces the time that school principals devote to administrative tasks, allowing them to focus more on pedagogical leadership.

Hypothesis 2: The use of AI technologies for the personalization of teaching modifies the role of teachers, transforming them from knowledge providers to learning facilitators.

Hypothesis 3: The integration of AI systems in schools changes the daily tasks of school administrators, allowing them to focus more on strategic tasks and less on repetitive tasks.

Hypothesis 4: The introduction of AI improves collaboration between teachers and administrators by providing accurate and real-time data on student performance.

Hypothesis 5: The introduction of AI changes the perception of school leaders about their roles and responsibilities, encouraging them to adopt more data-driven management practices.

METHODS

This section of the study describes the analytical techniques used to examine the models, variables, research hypotheses, and the interdependence between the use of AI and its impact on Leadership Styles in schools in Morocco. The data used in the empirical research described in this article were obtained through face-to-face interviews with school leaders, teachers, and administrators in Morocco. These data concern the use of AI and its impact on leadership style. It is important to note the absence of an exhaustively documented database on the leadership styles adopted using AI. In addition, this research places particular emphasis on the use of primary data. Thus, we distributed a questionnaire addressing various topics, in addition to the one examined in this article, to various actors such as secondary school leaders (44.11%), general teachers (38.23%), and administrators (17.66%). It should be noted that personal relationships played a decisive role in our research, facilitating the scheduling of appointments with the targeted respondents. Thanks to the questionnaire tool, we examined 106 geographically dispersed schools.

After the data collection, a processing phase was carried out using two multivariate statistical tests, with the assistance of the SPSS 25 software. The first test includes a factor analysis, specifically the principal component analysis (PCA), as well as Cronbach's alpha, in order to refine the scales of measurement of the dependent variable in the conceptual model (impact of AI on the leadership styles adopted in schools in Morocco). At this stage, a clear factorial structure has been recorded for both modalities of this variable, exceeding the thresholds recommended by Hair et al. (2006) in terms of reliability and validity of the measurement scales.

Table 1. Results of the validity and reliability of the measurement scales

Components	Alpha de Cronbach	items	Variance explained in %	Number of items
Use of AI tools for administrative tasks	0,720	-the automation of repetitive administrative tasks. -improving the efficiency of administrative communication.	76%	02
Use of AI technologies for the personalization of teaching	0,746	-the adaptation of teaching programs to the individual needs of students. -the implementation of individualized learning paths. -track the progress of each student.	78%	03
Integration of AI systems in school management	0,753	-Collaboration with teachers -optimization of the allocation of school resources. -the improvement of the strategic planning of the school.	68,26%	03
Use of AI for monitoring student performance	0,736	-the analysis of student performance data in real time. -quick identification of students in difficulty. -monitoring the evolution of student performance over time. -the ease of communicating student results to parents and teachers.	72,24%	04
the Administrative Responsibilities of School Principals	0,742	-Time spent on administrative tasks -Time devoted to pedagogical leadership	71,55%	02
the Role of Teachers in the Personalization of Teaching	0,750	-Perceived role of teachers -Time devoted to the personalization of the teaching -Self-evaluations of teachers)	68,78%	03
Distribution of tasks for school administrators	0,722	-Distribution of daily tasks - the job description - Change in the Tasks of School Administrators.	72,23%	03

continued on following page

Table 1. Continued

Components	Alpha de Cronbach	items	Variance explained in %	Number of items
collaboration between Teachers and Administrators	0,702	-open and transparent communication between teachers and administrators. -the level of trust between teachers and administrators. -The objectives of the school are developed in collaboration between teachers and administrators. -the joint effort to find solutions to school challenges.	69,09%	04
the perception of school leaders on their role and responsibilities	0,724	-the impression of having a positive influence on teachers and students. -the ability to effectively lead the teaching team. -Effective management of the human and material resources of the school. -the ability to develop and communicate a clear vision for the school. -conflict resolution skills.	74,45%	05

Hypothesis Testing by Regression Analysis

The multiple linear regression is the regression chosen to simultaneously analyze the link between various explanatory variables (more than two) and a variable to be explained. "The principle consists in examining the relationship between the variable to be explained and the other explanatory variables that best account for the reality of the observations. This relationship is expressed by the regression equation which presents the variable to be explained as the sum of each of the explanatory variables affected by their coefficients to which a constant term is added" (Crauser et al. 1989). This explanatory method is used to test the hypothesis of our model. This offers us the opportunity to test our research model in a global context and thus determine the importance and significance of each explanatory variable in the variation of the roles and responsibilities of school leadership following an introduction of artificial intelligence in school management. This allows us to translate our conceptual model under the following two equations:

- The introduction of AI in school management= $\beta1$ Administrative Responsibilities+ $\beta2$ Perceived role of teachers + $\beta3$ Change in the Tasks of Administrators + $\beta4$ Collaboration between teachers and administrators + $\beta5$ Perception of school leaders on their role and responsibilities + ϵ The testing of the hypothesis in this work according to this method requires the use of certain indicators such as: -Verification of the variance inflation factor (VIF) and tolerance criteria to ensure that the model does not contain unnecessary explanatory variables. The VIF must be less than 10 and the tolerance criteria less than 1.

- The Fischer-Snedecor test allows the interpretation of the statistical significance of the results obtained and the contribution of each explanatory variable. Its value denoted by significance "Signif F" designates that the observed value of the Fischer-Snedecor statistic must be less than 0.05 for the threshold of 5% or 0.01 for a threshold value of 1% for the null hypothesis, stipulating the non-existence of a linear relationship between the explanatory variables and the variable to be explained, to be rejected.
- The student t-test makes it possible to verify if the estimate obtained for the non-standardized regression coefficient or the non-standardized lambda (B) is significantly far from zero. Its value must be less than 0.05 for a threshold value of 5% or less than 0.01 for a threshold value of 1%. We carried out a verification of the VIF and the tolerance to verify the absence of multicollinearity, that the model does not contain unnecessary explanatory variables. The VIF must be less than 10 and the tolerance criteria less than 1. In our case, the absence of multicollinearity problems is obvious, as shown in Table 2, where the tolerance levels vary between 0.5 and 0.9, and the VIF remains less than 10.

Table 2. Coefficients of collinearity of variables in the research model

Model		**Collinearity Statistics**
		Tolerance
1	(Constant)	
	The use of AI For administrative tasks	**,555**
	The use of AI for the personalization of teachers	**,903**
	Integration of AI systems in school management	**,537**
	The use of AI For monitoring student performance	**,748**
	Introduction of AI in the school	**,925**

Testing the Theoretical Model

The validation of the hypothesis of the theoretical model leads us to proceed to the significance test of the model. This analysis will take place in two stages: an analysis of its overall meaning, then of its individual meaning.

We examined the overall significance of the model, all the explanatory variables that have an influence on the dependent variable. This test could be formulated as follows: is there at least one significant explanatory variable? The determination of the overall significance of the model was carried out using the Fischer statistic, which indicates whether the explanatory variables have an influence on the variable to be explained. The arbitration was carried out using a comparison of the value of the estimated F statistic as tabulated by Fischer. The SPSS 25 program automatically provided the probability associated with the calculated F statistic, which greatly facilitated the analysis. Thus, comparing the probability associated with the F statistic to a threshold of 5% retained should suffice. In the case where a probability linked to the statistic F is less than a threshold of 5%, then the hypothesis H0 can be rejected in favor of the alternative hypothesis according to which the regression is globally significant. In our case, for the explanatory variables of the change in the roles and responsibilities of school leadership, the Fischer statistic found by the SPSS 25 program is F = 21.4593 and the associated probability is less than 5% (0.00 < 0.05), then the null hypothesis is rejected and the model is globally significant (see Table 3).

Table 3. ANOVA Model Regression Index

ANOVA[a]					
Model		**Sum of Squares**	**ddl**	**Mean Square**	**F**
1	Regression	15,837	5	3,1674	21,4593
	Residuals	14,907	101	,1476	
	Total	30,744	106		

a. Predictors: (Constant), introduction of AI in administrative tasks, For the personalization of teachers, Integration of AI systems in school management, For monitoring student performance and Introduction of AI in the school.
b. Dependent Variable: Roles and responsibilities of school leaders.

Individual Significance Test

To address the individual significance of the variables, we used the Student statistic directly provided by the SPSS 25 program. The assumption of significance of the variable is retained when the threshold considered as the value of the estimated Student statistic is higher than that tabulated by Student. In this research, the rejected probability provided by SPSS 25 at the selected threshold level will be used. The estimation results indicated in Table N°4 show that four variables are statistically significant given the probability assigned to them:

- The variable "The use of AI For administrative tasks" is significant at a threshold of 1% since the statistical rules of the Student test are respected ($t > 2$, $p = 0.008 < 0.01$).
- The variable "The use of AI For the personalization of teachers" is significant at 5% ($t > 2$, $p = 0.013 < 0.05$).
- The variable "Integration of AI systems in school management" is significant at 1% ($t > 2$, $p = 0.007 < 0.01$).
- The variable "The use of AI To monitor student performance" is significant at 1% ($t > 2$, $p = 0.007 < 0.01$).
- The variable "Introduction of AI in the school" is significant at 5% ($t > 2$, $p = 0.021 < 0.05$).

In addition, the results of this regression show that the significant relationships between the introduction of AI in the management of schools and the change in the roles and responsibilities of school leadership are strongly positive.

Table 4. Coefficients of individual significance

Coefficients [a]							
Model		Non-standardized Coefficients		Standardized Coefficients	t	Sig.	Collinearity Statistics
		B	Error standard	Beta			Tolerance
1	(Constant)	-,135	,481		-,281	,779	
	The use of AI For administrative tasks	,753	,069	,214	2,227	,008	,555
	The use of AI for the personalization of teachers	,324	,128	,246	2,527	,013	,537
	Integration of AI systems in school management	,287	,104	,336	2,76	,007	,903
	The use of AI For monitoring student performance	0,255	0,127	0,293	2,038	0,003	0,748
	Introduction of AI in the school	0,049	,138	0,327	2,358	0,021	,925
a. Dependent Variable: Roles and responsibilities of school leaders							

RESULTS AND DISCUSSION

Regarding the results of the conceptual model test (Table 3), the probability associated with the Fisher test in the ANOVA model has a value below the error threshold of 5% (Sig = 0.000 < 0.05), thus indicating that the null hypothesis is rejected and that the model is globally significant. In particular, the portion explained by the model (regression = 15,837) significantly exceeds the unexplained portion (residuals =14,907). This observation is consistent with the value of the adjusted R-squared statistic (0.742), which also provides indications concerning the quality of the econometric model (Table 6). Thus, it demonstrates that the variables representing the quality of the construction of the relations of introduction of AI in the management of schools 74.2% of the variance of change in the roles and responsibilities of school leadership. Regarding the evaluation of the significance of the variables (Table 4), the values and probabilities associated with the student t-test generated by SPSS 25 indicate that two variables are statistically significant (t > 2 and sig < 5%). These variables are the introduction of AI in administrative tasks, in the personalization of teachers, the integration of AI systems in school management, the use of AI for monitoring student performance and introduction of AI in the school. This result is in accordance with the five hypotheses of our research. Table 5 presents a summary of the results obtained.

Table 5. Summary of the results of the hypotheses

Hypotheses	E Explanatory variables	Variables to explain	Coefficient β	Significance	t Student	Validation
H1	Use of AI for administrative tasks	Administrative Responsibilities	,214	,008	2,227	confirmed
H2	Using AI for teacher personalization	Perceived role of teachers	,246	,013	2,527	confirmed
H3	Integration of AI systems in school management	Change in the Tasks of Administrators	,336	,007	2,76	confirmed
H4	The use of AI for monitoring student performance	Collaboration between teachers and administrators	,293	,003	2,038	confirmed
H5	Introduction of AI in schools	Perception of school leaders on their role and responsibilities	,327	,021	2,358	confirmed

Indeed, based on these statistical results, this research summarizes the relationship between the significant variables and the explained variable of our conceptual model through the following equation: Change in the roles and responsibilities of school leaders = 0.214 Use of AI for administrative tasks + 0.246 Use of AI for teacher customization+ 0.336 Integration of AI systems in school management+ 0.293 Use of AI to monitor student performance+0.327 Introduction of AI in schools-0.135

Table 6. Summary of the models

					Edit statistics					
Modele	R	R-two	R-two adjusted	Standard error of estimate	Variation of R-two	Variation of F	ddl1	ddl2	Sig. Variation of F	Durbin-Watson
1	,736[a]	,742	,654	,39598	,742	21,4593	5	101	,000	1,653

- Predictors: (Constant), introduction of AI in administrative tasks, For the personalization of teachers, Integration of AI systems in school management, For monitoring student performance and Introduction of AI in the school.

- Dependent Variable: Roles and responsibilities of school leadership.

The results of your conceptual model test reveal significant positive relationships between the introduction of AI in school management and the change in the roles and responsibilities of school leadership. Specifically, the significant variables AI for administrative tasks, teacher personalization, school management integration, and student performance monitoring highlight the transformational impact AI can have in schools. These findings align with your research hypotheses. To contextualize these results within the Moroccan educational system, examples from schools like Lycée Mohammed V and Groupe Scolaire La Résidence can be insightful. These institutions have explored AI-driven administrative tools, such as automating student attendance tracking and performance analytics. AI's role in optimizing teacher customization has been noted in some international school setups in Morocco, where AI tools assist in personalizing learning modules based on individual student needs. Furthermore, Moroccan private schools adopting AI-based platforms for administrative management have reported streamlined operations, allowing leadership teams to focus more on strategic development and innovation.

In public schools, where resources are often constrained, the adoption of AI remains nascent but promising. Pilot projects supported by initiatives like Moroccan Ministry of National Education's Digital Transformation Plan aim to explore the use of AI in monitoring student performance and improving teacher training programs. These examples provide real-world applications of the statistical results from your model, showing how AI can enhance school leadership roles and responsibilities, especially in administrative efficiency and educational personalization.

CONCLUSION

This chapter aimed to examine how the introduction of artificial intelligence (AI) is changing the roles and responsibilities of school leaders, including principals, teachers and administrators. The results obtained thanks to the regression analysis on a sample of 106 schools in Morocco have confirmed the research hypotheses formulated. However, the introduction of AI in the management of schools has for effects:

- The reduction of administrative tasks for school principals: The use of AI tools reduces the time spent on administrative tasks, allowing principals to focus more on pedagogical leadership.

- The transformation of the role of teachers: The use of AI technologies for the personalization of teaching modifies the role of teachers, transforming them from knowledge providers to learning facilitators.
- the change in administrators' tasks: The integration of AI systems in schools is changing the daily tasks of school administrators, allowing them to focus more on strategic tasks and less on repetitive tasks.
- improving collaboration between teachers and administrators: The introduction of AI improves collaboration by providing accurate and real-time data on student performance. -changing the perception of school leaders: The introduction of AI is changing the perception of school leaders about their role and responsibilities, encouraging them to adopt more data-driven management practices

The statistical analyses revealed significant and positive results for each of these hypotheses. The Fischer and Student tests demonstrated that the explanatory variables selected had a significant influence on the variable to be explained, namely the change in the roles and responsibilities of school leaders. The multiple regression made it possible to model this relationship and to translate the conceptual model into a clear economic equation. In summary, the study confirms that the introduction of AI in Moroccan schools has a significant impact on the roles and responsibilities of school leaders. AI not only improves administrative efficiency, but it also redefines educational and collaborative functions within schools. These results suggest a need for adaptation and continuous training for school leaders to maximize the benefits of AI in the educational environment.

REFERENCES

Alavi, M., & Leidner, D. E. (2021). Knowledge management and knowledge management systems: Conceptual foundations and research issues. *Management Information Systems Quarterly*, 25(1), 107–136. DOI: 10.2307/3250961

Argyris, C., & Schön, D. A. (1978). *Organizational learning: A theory of action perspective*. Addison-Wesley.

Binns, R. (2018). Fairness in Machine Learning: Lessons from Political Philosophy. *Proceedings of the 2018 Conference on Fairness, Accountability, and Transparency*.

Chesbrough, H. (2003). *Open innovation: The new imperative for creating and profiting from technology*. Harvard Business School Press.

Davenport, T. H. (2005). *Thinking for a living: How to get better performances and results from knowledge workers*. Harvard Business School Press.

Davenport, T. H., & Prusak, L. (1998). *Working knowledge: How organizations manage what they know*. Harvard Business Press.

Drucker, P. F. (2019). *The effective executive: The definitive guide to getting the right things done*. Routledge., DOI: 10.4324/9780367330752

Eacott, S. (2021). AI and Decision-Making in Australian Educational Leadership. *Educational Management Administration & Leadership*, 49(3), 399–415.

Getz, I., & Carney, B. (2009). *Freedom, Inc.: Free your employees and let them lead your business to higher productivity, profits, and growth*. Crown Business.

Giraud, L., & Autissier, D. (2020). *Nouveaux modes de management organisationnel: Enjeux et pratiques*. Dunod.

Haider, S. (2022). *Digital transformation and innovation: Leveraging digital technologies for business success*. Springer.

Hamel, G. (2007). *The future of management*. Harvard Business School Press.

Harris, A., & Jones, M. (2020). Artificial Intelligence and Educational Leadership in the UK. *Educational Management Administration & Leadership*, 48(4), 578–598.

Holstein, K., Wortman, J., Daumé, H.III, & Dudik, M. (2019). Improving Fairness in Machine Learning Systems: What Do Industry Practitioners Need? *Proceedings of the 2019 CHI Conference on Human Factors in Computing Systems*. DOI: 10.1145/3290605.3300830

Laloux, F. (2014). *Reinventing organizations: A guide to creating organizations inspired by the next stage in human consciousness*. Nelson Parker.

Lee, M. Y., & Edmondson, A. C. (2017). Self-managing organizations: Exploring the limits of less-hierarchical organizing. *Research in Organizational Behavior*, 37, 35–58. DOI: 10.1016/j.riob.2017.10.002

Liebowitz, J. (2016). *Knowledge management handbook: Collaboration and social networking*. CRC Press., DOI: 10.1201/9781315279740

McAfee, A. (2009). *Enterprise 2.0: New collaborative tools for your organization's toughest challenges*. Harvard Business Press.

Mintzberg, H. (2009). *Managing*. Berrett-Koehler Publishers.

Nonaka, I. (1994). A dynamic theory of organizational knowledge creation. *Organization Science*, 5(1), 14–37. DOI: 10.1287/orsc.5.1.14

Nonaka, I., & Takeuchi, H. (1995). *The knowledge-creating company: How Japanese companies create the dynamics of innovation*. Oxford University Press., DOI: 10.1093/oso/9780195092691.001.0001

Nonaka, I., & Takeuchi, H. (2019). *The wise company: How companies create continuous innovation*. Oxford University Press.

Nonaka, I., & von Krogh, G. (2009). Tacit knowledge and knowledge conversion: Controversy and advancement in organizational knowledge creation theory. *Organization Science*, 20(3), 635–652. DOI: 10.1287/orsc.1080.0412

O'Neil, C. (2016). *Weapons of Math Destruction: How Big Data Increases Inequality and Threatens Democracy*. Crown Publishing Group.

Paquet, G., Schooten, V., & Simon, S. (2020). *Digital governance: Navigating the new technological epoch*. Routledge.

Polanyi, M. (1966). *The tacit dimension*. University of Chicago Press.

Quivy, R., & Van Campenhoudt, L. (1995). *Manuel de recherche en sciences sociales*. Dunod.

Regan, P. M., & Jesse, J. (2019). *Data Privacy Law: A Practical Guide to the GDPR and Other International Regulations*. Routledge.

Rigby, D. K., Sutherland, J., & Takeuchi, H. (2016). Embracing agile. *Harvard Business Review*. Advance online publication. DOI: 10.1177/0008125616635597

Robertson, B. J. (2015). *Holacracy: The new management system for a rapidly changing world.* Henry Holt and Company.

Sahlberg, P., & Hargreaves, A. (2020). Leadership transformation through AI in Finnish schools. *International Journal of Leadership in Education*, 23(5), 594–610.

Shadbolt, N. (2020). Ethics and AI: The Issues. *AI & Society*, 35(4), 767–776.

Tan, C., & Gopinathan, S. (2019). AI in Educational Leadership in Singapore. *Educational Management Administration & Leadership*, 47(1), 87–104.

Teece, D. J. (2018). Dynamic capabilities: Routines versus entrepreneurial action. *Journal of Management Studies*, 55(7), 1248–1260. DOI: 10.1111/joms.12311

Teece, D. J., Pisano, G., & Shuen, A. (1997). Dynamic capabilities and strategic management. *Strategic Management Journal*, 18(7), 509–533. DOI: 10.1002/(SICI)1097-0266(199708)18:7<509::AID-SMJ882>3.0.CO;2-Z

Tidd, J., & Bessant, J. (2021). *Managing innovation: Integrating technological, market and organizational change* (7th ed.). John Wiley & Sons., DOI: 10.1002/9781119741686

UNESCO. (2021). *Global perspective on AI-driven educational leadership.* United Nations Educational, Scientific and Cultural Organization.

Wang, F., Wang, Z., & Hwang, G. J. (2019). Integrating AI into Education: The Role of Teachers. *Journal of Educational Technology & Society*, 22(1), 80–92.

Wenger, E. (2000). Communities of practice and social learning systems. *Organization*, 7(2), 225–246. DOI: 10.1177/135050840072002

Zahra, S. A., & George, G. (2002). Absorptive capacity: A review, reconceptualization, and extension. *Academy of Management Review*, 27(2), 185–203. DOI: 10.2307/4134351

Zawacki-Richter, O., Marín, V. I., Bond, M., & Gouverneur, F. (2019). Systematic Review of Research on Artificial Intelligence in Higher Education – Where Are the Educators? *International Journal of Educational Technology in Higher Education*, 16(1), 39. DOI: 10.1186/s41239-019-0171-0

Zhang, W., & Liu, J. (2020). AI in Leadership Development in Chinese Higher Education. *Journal of Higher Education Policy and Management*, 42(2), 131–144.

ADDITIONAL READING

Avurakoghene, O. P., & Oredein, A. (2023). Educational leadership and artificial intelligence for sustainable development. *OP Avurakoghene & AO Oredein, Educational Leadership and Artificial Intelligence for Sustainable Development, Shodh Sari-An International Multidisciplinary Journal, 2*(3).

Jaja, M. D., Osuji, C. U., & Wey-Amaewhule, B. (2023). Principals' Leadership Styles and Job Productivity Among Teachers in Secondary Schools in Rivers State. *African Journal of Information, Economics and Management Research, 1*(2).

Shal, T., Ghamrawi, N., & Naccache, H. (2024). Leadership styles and AI acceptance in academic libraries in higher education. *Journal of Academic Librarianship*, 50(2), 102849. DOI: 10.1016/j.acalib.2024.102849

Sharma, R. K., & Sharma, K. K. The Role of Leadership Style towards Digital Transformation of Educational Institutes in Era of Industrial Revolution 4.0. *Indian Economy*, 57.

KEY TERMS AND DEFINITIONS

Artificial Intelligence (AI): A branch of computer science focused on creating systems that can perform tasks typically requiring human intelligence, such as learning, reasoning, and problem-solving.

Data-Driven Management: A management approach that utilizes data analysis to inform and guide decision-making, often enhancing efficiency and accuracy.

Educational Leadership: The process of guiding and managing educational institutions, focusing on improving educational outcomes, supporting teachers, and fostering a positive school environment.

Intelligent Tutoring Systems (ITS): AI-based tools that offer personalized instruction to students by adapting lessons to their individual learning needs and progress.

Learning Analytics: The collection and analysis of data on student learning behaviors and outcomes to optimize educational strategies and interventions.

Pedagogical Leadership: A leadership style that emphasizes supporting and enhancing teaching and learning practices, often focusing on curriculum and instructional quality.

Role Transformation: The process of changing or evolving job roles, often in response to new technologies, to better meet organizational or educational goals.

School Administration: The management and coordination of school operations, including student services, staffing, scheduling, and compliance with educational policies.

Student Performance Monitoring: The use of tools and data analysis to track students' academic progress, identify learning challenges, and provide timely support.

Chapter 5
Infrastructure and Investment Needs for AI Implementation in Education

Karima Toumi Sayari
Al-Zahra College for Women, Oman

ABSTRACT

This chapter explores the critical infrastructure and investment frameworks required for successfully integrating artificial intelligence (AI) in educational settings. This chapter explores the investment patterns and financial considerations essential for establishing the physical, human, and technological infrastructure across various educational levels. The analysis reveals notable infrastructure gaps and identifies the investment needed to support digital education through AI. Key areas discussed include the scalability of AI solutions, personnel training requirements, technological readiness, and long-term funding needs. Additionally, the chapter highlights disparities in infrastructural preparedness between urban and rural schools and across developed and developing countries. To promote equitable access and sustainable AI adoption, this chapter offers evidence-based recommendations for investors, educational administrators, and policymakers on optimizing resource allocation.

INTRODUCTION

As AI becomes more prominent in several industries, it is also finding its way into education. Artificial intelligence (AI) is quickly becoming an integral part of many educational programs in an effort to improve students' academic performance.

DOI: 10.4018/979-8-3373-1017-6.ch005

Innovative solutions provided by AI such as intelligent tutoring systems and customized learning tools have the potential to improve educational experiences and results. While we are excited about these new developments, we must not lose sight of the potential dangers and challenges that may accompany them. This chapter explores the possible uses of AI in education and highlights key aspects to ensure the appropriate and ethical use of technology in classrooms

Artificial intelligence goes beyond technical terms; it signifies a major shift in the approach to teaching and learning. This change is being driven by the need for educational experiences that are more efficient, personalized, and interesting. A bright future for education seems to be ahead of us as educational institutions investigate various AI uses, ranging from administrative assistance to individualized teaching (Alwabel, 2024). Intelligent tutoring systems, automated grading systems, and individualized learning platforms are some of the uses in education. These tools provide individualized learning experiences by responding to the demands of each individual learner. Learning becomes more dynamic and captivating with the use of virtual reality and AI-powered content production tools, which are revolutionizing educational material. Moreover, AI streamlines administrative duties, allowing teachers to concentrate on creative instruction (UNESCO, 2019).

Developing countries have underfunded public education systems that lack the resources needed for improvement. The introduction of AI into education can help to mitigate these concerns, providing cost-effective alternatives to reduce administrative burdens and costs, e.g., marking, and unlocking new learning experiences for disadvantaged groups. AI can facilitate better instructional design, predictive analytics, and adaptive navigation interfaces. AI can help ease the introduction of innovative teaching practices and learner-active environments. AI can improve the learning experience of students, providing immersive and interactive interfaces that can foster community interactions and social skill building. AI can help increase access to education, with e-learning systems that can be used via online platforms and smartphones. Education institutions that adopt AI will become faster, better, and cheaper. In sum, AI has the potential to provide not only a continued welfare gain but a higher real income to the majority of the working population, who are members of the global middle class (Imchen & Ndem, 2020; Kayode-Ajala, 2023). Aderibigbe et al. (2023) examined the role of Artificial Intelligence (AI) in developing countries, focusing on bridging the gap between its vast potential and effective implementation. The study investigated the current landscape of AI adoption in developing countries, by analyzing the potential benefits, challenges, and ethical considerations. Through a comprehensive review of literature and case studies, the paper explored strategies and solutions for harnessing AI's transformative power in diverse sectors. The findings emphasize the importance of capacity building, public-private partnerships, and tailored policy frameworks to address infrastructure limitations and skill gaps.

The main idea of this chapter is to analyze the concept of artificial intelligence (AI) in education and suggest the classification of artificial intelligence and its application in education. This analysis goes along with the examination of the mechanisms and infrastructure needed for AI usage in the educational process while presenting the current challenges and risk. The chapter aims to answer the following questions:

- What does AI mean for education?
- How can we specify the types of AI? What do AI applications look like in education from the perspective of process support and process improvement?
- Why do education parallel AI concentrate on physical infrastructure, digital libraries, and open culture?

The analysis of opportunities provided by AI could contribute to the strategy items aimed at promoting AI-education cooperation, optimize collaboration within universities and between universities, and accelerate the global academic community to enhance AI by establishing economic, social, and ethical guidelines.

SCOPE OF AI IN EDUCATION AND THE NEED FOR AI LITERACY

Since AI literacy is a new topic in the twenty-first century, there isn't much literature accessible. "AI literacy" is the term used to describe the capacity to comprehend, apply, monitor, and critically evaluate AI applications without necessarily having the ability to create AI models themselves (Ng et al., 2021). According to Laupichler et al.(2022), "AI literacy" focuses mostly on students who lack a background in computer science, or "non-experts," and includes AI competences that the general public should have. Long and Magerko (2020) reasoned that AI literacy is connected to other previously established literacy in relevant domains. These connections show themselves in a variety of ways. Since people must be able to utilize computers in order to comprehend AI, digital literacy is a requirement for AI literacy. However, AI literacy does not always need computational literacy. A definition of AI literacy was developed by Long and Magerko (2020, p. 2), who define it as "a set of competencies that enables individuals to critically evaluate AI technologies, communicate and collaborate effectively with AI, and use AI as a tool online, at home, and in the workplace"

AI is widely considered as an irreplaceable tool for education. First, it can create learning partnerships, providing an opportunity for students to access a set of diversified learning tools and tutors. Secondly, AI enables universities to stage innovative curricula, facilitating hands-on learning opportunities. Such personalized learning simplifies complex problems by building and testing algorithms on large datasets. Nevertheless, AI in education has a parallel face consisting of supporting infrastructure and open culture. This enables the development of university AI services and sharing the development to facilitate comparative data analysis (Yu, 2023). Ng et al. (2021) seeks to address identified deficiencies in understanding the effective methods for incorporating AI literacy into educational curriculum and the role of educators in facilitating learners' development of AI literacy. The components identified in their investigation of the Technological, Pedagogical, and Content Knowledge (TPACK) framework are classified according to learning artefacts, pedagogical strategies, and topic areas. They adopt the TPACK model because it is extensively utilized in research to determine how educators can integrate technology into their pedagogical approaches and content knowledge, while conceptualizing the requisite skills and understanding necessary for incorporating pertinent technologies in AI literacy education.

BENEFITS AND CHALLENGES OF AI IN EDUCATION

The landscape of technological innovation is changing at a rate never seen before in the twenty-first century. Looi (2024) argued that AI, a synthesis of human creativity, computational power, and technological expertise, is at the forefront of this transformation. Artificial intelligence has evolved from a theoretical concept of enabling computers to think of a realistic reality with many uses. Its revolution signifies a paradigm shift in human connection, cognition, and learning, beyond mere technology enhancement. The potential for revolutionary change in education via AI is substantial, offering promising opportunities to reinvent teaching and learning.

The study of Hashem et al. (2024) investigates the effectiveness of AI generative ChatGPT as a teaching assistant to reduce effort and relieve fatigue in secondary school. Preparation of lessons and creation of material were significant contributors to teacher fatigue. ChatGPT was assessed via targeted inquiries in English, science, and mathematics, using an explanatory research technique to analyze its capabilities in tailored planning and content generation, because to the little current literature on this topic. The study highlights the benefits of ChatGPT in customized planning via task-specific recommendations and collaboration between artificial intelligence and humans. The findings support the fact that the incorporation of AI technologies enhances teacher preparation, improves instructional support, and streamlines resource allocation, hence amplifying AI's educational efficacy while underscoring the need of alleviating the burnout for academic advancement.

One educational practice which offers potential and maybe a revolutionary role in language teaching and learning was proposed by Looi et al. as an opportunity for mobile language learning, often considered in the practice of "out-of-school learning," but with the help of some new and exciting "in-school possibilities." After the literature review, examining the existing state of the art in m-learning, some of the present challenges in m-learning development in the teaching/learning context are discussed. This body of educational practice technology serves well in understanding the actual needs of the field, highlights several of those, prompts quite many questions on educated practice, technology development, and implementation in the educational context, and positions the field and establishes a foundation for future research in m-learning (Kimsesiz, 2023, Huang & Looi, 2021).

Wang et al. (2024) conducted a systematic review on Artificial intelligence's impact on education. This research investigates how AI applications impact academic performance, emotional perception, learning behavior, and cognitive ability, among other aspects of learning. Several studies have shown the significant positive impact of AI technology on students' academic performance. Evaluation-centered e-learning systems significantly improved students' academic performance and cleared up misconceptions, especially for those with little prior knowledge, according to Wang's (2014) study. Additionally, students have expressed positive opinions about the use of AI in the classroom. They have also shown improved attentiveness (Rong et al., 2022) and increased engagement in the learning process (Liu et al., 2022).

Real-world examples help frame the needs and actions around such products. Furthermore, in the work towards innovative utilizations of AI in education, acceptance remains key. People in charge of K-12 and initial post-secondary schools and programs must see and understand the monetary and other infrastructure requirements and must understand how the AI-derived product, no matter how sophisticated, will be implemented at the school or program level. Given a world of differing AI products, with different methodologies behind them, different theoretical learning or personalized instruction drivers, and different infrastructure, monetary, and other investment needs for implementation, how can successful artificial intelligence in educational case studies teach us about what is necessary to develop and put into practice such products at the school and program level? (Carvalho et al., 2022; Yang, 2022)

INFRASTRUCTURE REQUIREMENTS FOR AI IMPLEMENTATION

According to the United Nations Educational, Scientific, and Cultural Organization (UNESCO) ICSU (2017), current education programs are not preparing people well enough to meet growing demands for digitally skilled professionals. The demand to harness AI for economic growth and societal benefit also drives a continuous need to develop the workforce of future AI-skilled professionals. Most of the required investment in supporting the technology workforce is related to AI expert solutions in these front-running sectors, although significant investment will be required in developing access to AI expert solutions for inclusive development, education, health, security, and justice.

This section discusses and provides an analysis of infrastructure and investment needs required upfront for AI Generic technologies and future AI Education and Learning Platforms the major expectations and infrastructure requirements to successfully implement AI interventions in education. In particular, we review challenges relating to AI-enabled teaching and learning in the field. The section covers major challenges for implementing AI in education in the context of primary, secondary, and tertiary education locations. The section outlines demands for digital infrastructure in education required to harness the transformative potential of AI. Based on an overview of current digital infrastructure and ICT investment trends, by focusing on selected challenges concerning infrastructure requirements in the education sector. Also, it outlines the main gaps that exist for investments in education related to frontier technologies, in general (such as broadband and mobile technologies) and AI expert solutions and AI education platforms (Mhlanga, 2021). Two Dimension dictate the need of different infrastructure for the AI incorporation in education. The Pedagogical dimension is on using AI to improve teaching and learning outcomes, while the Governance component tackles issues related to privacy, security, and accountability. The operational component handles infrastructural and training-related problems. By encouraging a thorough understanding of the implications of AI integration in academic settings, the framework ensures that stakeholders are aware of their responsibilities and can act accordingly.

Professional Development and Training for Educators

Human factors are crucial, and maybe the most important infrastructure need is the professional development needed for educators to use AI efficiently and advance their AI skills. Regardless of the field to which they have belonged, this is necessary, particularly in the digital economy. The foundation for using AI in education is training and support for educators, who will be the main users of these technologies in the classroom. The emphasis of digital literacy on teachers is found in the literature under various names that are comparable, such as digital teaching literacy or digital teaching competency. In recent years, the educational literature has prioritized the definition of digital literacy, particularly about training and assessing teachers globally (Marín and Castaneda, 2023).

It is important to offer professional learning for teachers to facilitate the implementation of AI in classrooms. A key challenge is that many students are already more comfortable with the technology than their teachers, which means teachers often need to rely on visual language (VL) support for classroom management. Therefore, educators require specialized training not only in how to use AI in the classroom but also in the ethical issues surrounding the use of these tools (Nazaretsky et al., 2022; Ayanwale et al., 2022). AI education should give the framing needed to help learners critically consider the creation and consumption of these tools. Educators should develop a deep understanding of the social, cultural, ethical, and legal aspects of AI, addressing issues such as bias, privacy, algorithmic accountability and transparency, and the potential impacts on jobs and education (Chiu et al., 2023; Joshi et al., 2021).

As mentioned previously, teachers are central to the implementation of AI in classrooms, and they have several concerns and needs. The AI community has recognized that teacher professional development is one of the most significant factors influencing the implementation of educational AI programs. Increasing support for educators in this area is essential; teachers need to acquire a thorough understanding of the technology in order to use it effectively and appropriately. However, a survey of teachers' attitudes towards AI and the skills needed to manage AI in the classroom, together with the professional skills of educators to apply AI systems, was not found in the existing literature. Therefore, further well-designed research on the application of AI systems in real educational settings is required (Bragg et al., 2021).

What are the new skills and competencies needed for AI technologies? The list is quite extensive here and is influenced by the type of employment or demand considered. The list is also wide, in part because it varies among experts who are interviewed. Researchers who are focusing on the implications for society, economic development, and labor markets from the implementation of AI at the local, national, and international levels address this issue. Coding skills, problem-solving skills, teamwork competencies, critical thinking, data literacy, commitment competency, interpersonal or emotional intelligence, creativity, innovative competency, and understanding or knowledge about the use of AI are important. At the level of technical education, skills in the development and use of models, data, and algorithms are relevant.

Skills and competence development are intrinsically important dimensions of our ability to cope with challenges, and increasingly they form the core of our efforts to prepare for an uncertain future. Education, as the main institution tasked with developing the needed skills and competencies, needs to now, more than ever, rely on technology to support those efforts. This requires not only the digital and technical expertise to use the tools in schools and educational systems, but an awareness and understanding of the capabilities and limitations of tools, including AI applications. In short, to us, AI should also have a proper meaning of 'augmented intelligence' in the classroom and across the education chain.

Hadjerrouit (2010) highlights the importance of teachers and offers a theoretical framework for promoting Digital literacy in the classroom by teaching educators how to create and assess digital learning materials. Cultural usability (the chosen learning styles and choices of students) and pedagogical usability are the two primary elements influencing this activity. In order to have a significant impact on teachers' pedagogy and cause them to adopt constructivist or learner-centered approaches, the curriculum must include DL in all areas in a goal-oriented manner (Hadjerrouit, 2010). Additionally, compared to traditional materials, digital learning tools need to enhance the learning process, and educators need to be made aware that ICT is not value-neutral.

Hardware and Software Needs

Artificial intelligence products are quite strong, and several AI products on the market may be obtained when the problem is biological. Systems such as web pages with different difficulties expressed and 24-hour behavior patterns can serve the interests of individuals in addressing different questions or solving issues. AI may assess questions about the amount of interest and which tasks are feasible within given limits. Individual aid using AI may become a reality with a strong global economy and the future. Many software vendors such as IBM, which promotes smart AI options for big businesses, both Microsoft and Google, which deliver goods either by free access to artificial information or by public commercial products, and allow mentors and teachers to make intelligent recommendations, introduce students to real AI solutions. Yet these technologies are not like a learning process networking. We noticed a tiny number of technology projects aimed at pre-university education while validating prospective AI solutions. Finally, hostel testing practitioners are less involved in requesting and responding to a big public company's strategies about the use of the tool for a high quantity of trainees (Renz and Hilbig, 2020).

There are many foreign companies such as IBM, Google, Microsoft that produce high quality AI products to handle various tasks. Nevertheless, the use of AI implementation products in the educational system is still low. When going through the studies about the use of AI within educational institutions, the authors noticed that most of them aimed to discover the effectiveness of individual tools, but they had mostly implementable programs and were running the systems less often due to the lack of response to the huge quantities of use by foreign big software sellers (Renz and Hilbig2020). Nowadays, no provincial organization is considering the development of a consistent AI hardware and software solution aimed entirely at the training system. It is important to clarify the needs for implementing AI in educational systems from a technical point of view (Luan et al.2020; Bogina et al.2022; Alahmari et al.2023).

Data Management and Security

There are two main arguments made for better transparency: firstly, the correlation argument; and secondly, to maintain public trust in AI. Concerns about privacy are compounded in education settings; they are especially acute when schoolchildren are being monitored and assessed, as they do not have the legal capacity to agree to any form of data harvest. Incidents undermine public trust in AI, and hence the pace of regulations. To some extent, perceptions are created by the narratives provided on AI in news media coverage. When privacy or security concerns get played out in the public sphere, the reaction is often quite intense. This leads to a quicker response from politicians in the form of laws or regulations. This is what is likely to happen with respect to data privacy (Woo et al.2021; Jones et al., 2020).

One major concern about AI is its potential use/misuse of the vast amounts of behavioral and personal data it collects. To improve the data integration and interoperability process, many recommendations have referred to establishing a unified UK data management governmental and AI research framework. In AI, public perception undoubtedly influences its impact and, hence, the pace and shape of AI regulations. It is essential to have secure AI data platforms and to alleviate and manage privacy risks.

INVESTMENT OPPORTUNITIES IN AI FOR EDUCATION

Despite the rich opportunities for AI to fundamentally change education and the strong demand in the market, and the resultant industry growth, there are constraints acting as a deterrent for AI companies to realize their full growth potential. AI startups, even with great potential in schools, colleges, and universities, struggle with a long sales cycle, limited resource capacity, the expense of hiring a K–12 or higher education-focused sales team, and the varied implementation and procurement challenges in the educational market that differ from the enterprise space. Serving the educational market has proven particularly difficult for companies because the challenges of meeting the unique needs and expectations of administrators, teachers, and learners are wildly divergent. In addition, cloud systems in schools and universities are weak, and software applications conflict with MDM. However, given the largely untapped revenue potential in the education space, many companies continue to pursue the market (Kuleto et al., 2021).

The use of AI technology in educational institutions is mostly limited to face recognition in schools and colleges. However, educators are increasingly understanding that AI-enabled adaptive learning is essential to increase productivity and learner outcomes. In K–12 and higher education, AI applications can assist learners in acquiring knowledge, enhancing their cognitive functions, and supporting complex activities such as understanding speech or recognizing objects. These applications are expected to bring significant benefits to learners in both traditional and online education. For the first time in history, AI can radically expand and optimize education opportunities for a billion or more people around the world. The AI market for education is expected to grow at a rapid pace within the next few years. The B2B market, comprised of schools, colleges, universities, governments, and other training and development organizations, is expected to outgrow the consumer market through 2026. The demand for AI-based enterprise educational solutions is expected to have constant growth owing to the increasing deployment of such solutions globally (Ahmad et al., 2021).

Public and Private Funding Sources

In investment infrastructure in developing countries, macroeconomic stability and political stability are considered. The government of the day must proactively participate in collaborating with the private sector to gain from and contribute to the rapid transformation of technology and AI tools and platforms for education. Public education institutions (including relevant ministries) should keep abreast of the evolution of AI technology to ensure it is leveraged for effective and equitable outcomes in education. Ministries of finance have a significant role to play in developing public-private partnerships, particularly given the shift away from the traditional content provider role of the education industry towards the adoption of educational technology solutions.

Even in advanced economies, the public component in AI investment overshadows the private one. This asymmetry is likely to be even more pronounced in developing countries and emerging markets. While the necessity and perceived impact of public sector investment in education are well established, the role of the private sector, until recently, was typically limited to vocational education, training and re-skilling, utilizing proprietary technology. With AI, however, there is a growing recognition that private sector investments in more foundational formal education outcomes like proficiency in math, literacy, and science, for example, can yield substantial future benefits. Public-private funding strategies can come in various forms. From technology companies focusing more on tools and platforms, investing in content producers and educational software providers, or supporting complementary policies to aid traditional education systems.

POLICY AND REGULATORY FRAMEWORKS FOR AI IN EDUCATION

In an era of rapid change, AI in education should be developed and delivered by private parties with a strong sense of industry stewardship including digital responsibility and long-term societal interests, rather than fully-fledged high-profit commercial industries. The trilateral relationship of government, industry and societal or public interest should be further developed to a more sophisticated multi-stakeholder model. This alignment of economic and social purpose has been developed within the not-for-profit industries through governance and ownership structures that reflect values and mission of the activity. Such mechanisms provide substantial scope for development in a fast-moving digital industry provided there is political and social demand. Although the online provision of early learning could be seen as a "brave new world" incursion into the domain of work traditionally performed by adults, exceptional attention should also be given to the key role of human teachers in the provision of educational guidance (Williamson, 2024; Park & Lim, 2022).

Within a multi-level governance system and policy frameworks supporting AI implementation in education, regulations and oversight processes should be carefully crafted, balancing necessary safeguards with entrepreneurship and dynamism in the market. The complexity and diversity of tasks that may be performed by AI used in educational activities and services do not lend themselves to a simple "one-size-fits-all" regulatory or oversight regime (Holmes & Porayska-Pomsta, 2022). Governments should be especially cautious about imposing overly prescriptive regulations that stifle innovation or learning. Policy and regulatory frameworks should follow broad-risk responsive strategies that are open to learning and adaptive as the technology develops. A risk framework provides practical direction to a self-reflective stakeholder partnership that is focused on the future of the education technology system rather than an overly mechanical horizon scan of current issues. This will require infrastructure – in terms of legal and regulatory foundations, education resources, and investment incentives – that enable and drive a culture of digital stewardship, including responsible blended assessment (Chen & Esmaeilzadeh, 2024; Familoni, 2024).

Ethical Considerations

In the context of AI in education, significant ethical concerns arise with regard to the data collected and processed by the AI system, the potential personalization used within the system, the privacy and security of the stakeholder groups, and the responsibility for decision-making. It is important to ensure the ethical development and use of AI in education and to ensure that stakeholders are able to critically understand and fairly use AI in education. From the beginning, AI makes ethical questions more mainstream, compelling us to confront them and make choices about the values that we embed within AI systems. If left untreated, the existing inequality of capabilities and opportunities to use AI will widen and result in a series of concerns about fairness, privacy, and security, with long-term effects on democratic society. Such questions should not be ignored and should be addressed at every stage of AI design, development, and application.

Data Privacy and Protection

When using AI in developing countries, ethical and legal frameworks need to be properly taken into account. User permission, algorithmic accountability, and data protection all need stringent legislation. These regulations must be tailored to particular local circumstances while still adhering to international ethical standards. Ensuring the ethical use of AI guards against potential misuse and promotes its responsible and beneficial usage in developing countries (Aderibigbe et al., 2023). To ensure the proper use of these technologies and to build trust, it is essential to negotiate ethical challenges while utilizing AI. By vigorously opposing discrimination, promoting justice, and giving privacy and security a priority, stakeholders can contribute to the development of AI systems that respect moral values and benefit society.

The study of Quin et al. (2020), on technology trust and AI ethics in education examined Users' perceptions of trust in AI-based educational systems using interviews and Netnography. They determined which elements of technology, environment, and individuality affected people's confidence in AI-based educational systems. The study revealed that Functionality, helpfulness, interpretability, reliability, and interface are all aspects of technology. The kindness of educational institutions, data management, instructor competency, official norms, and knowledge attributes are all examples of context-related variables. Individual-related aspects include how one views learning, how one is inclined to engage with instructors, how one views artificial intelligence, and how one is inclined toward autonomy.

SUSTAINABILITY OF AI INVESTMENTS

Artificial intelligence is a rapidly developing field of technology that has the potential to completely transform human social relationships. AI has started to create new teaching and learning tools in the field of education, which are now being tested in various settings. To ensure its sustainability, AI requires sophisticated infrastructures and enormous initial installation expenses, and ongoing operational costs associated with system maintenance, updates, and teacher training, to guarantee success and continuity. AI implementation in education varies considerably between countries, like its implementation in other different sectors. As discussed in previous sections, the available infrastructure determines and impacts this implementation. Effective long-term implementation necessitates comprehensive teacher training programs, balancing immediate requirements with future scalability, and defining explicit success metrics while ensuring system adaptability to evolving educational demands and emerging technologies.

The government's goal in almost all developing nations is to raise the standard of education, and one way to do this is by introducing modern technologies like artificial intelligence. Most governments are increasing their investments in AI-based technologies in order to broaden the scope of higher education. AI courses with applied processes covering key concepts like machine learning, planning, and data structures have immediately affected decision-makers in academics. Before implementing the mechanisms of AI-driven systems, educational institutions must thoroughly examine their value system. Higher education institutions in poor nations have yet to embrace artificial intelligence (AI), despite technology's growing popularity (Rana et al., 2024).

Emerging being defined as trends within the next two years. As with previous concepts, these timings are highly uncertain and widely debated, and the listed trends operate along qualitative dimensions rather than strict chronologies. It is also important to observe that more immediate trends of innovation or change may reflect longer-term trends in how the general context of education is evolving. With the elements classified, the chapter then concludes with a discussion of challenges that these trends pose to AI for educational systems currently and in the future. According to the findings of a study given to international students in July 2024, the most prevalent use of artificial intelligence technologies among college students is assistance with drafting cover letters and resumes. Additionally, according to two thirds of respondents, they utilized AI to help with research, writing, and tailored content suggestions. Globally, 86% of students acknowledge using artificial intelligence (AI) in their academic work. One of the first nations in the world to fully integrate artificial intelligence (AI) into everyday life is China. The graph displays, by segment, the percentage of AI investment transactions value in China's education sector as of May 2019. At that time, almost 45% of AI investment transactions in China's education sector were related to self-adaptive learning (Statista, 2024).

Personalized Learning Platforms

Student outcomes data allow for the predictive modeling of which learning trajectory and content are likely to benefit each student, or to potentially identify barriers and develop programming to support their progress. AI can enable non-expert support staff, extensions for volunteers in a classroom, nurses, or technology coaches to be able to provide mentorship to this large and growing set of learners. Another set of data being generated and collected is from tools such as eBooks, audiobooks, and other interactive instructional materials, which are available on many apps and software suites that are designed to support readers with different needs and levels. Educational technology designed to support language learners with reading, writing, speaking, and listening generates a valuable stream of linguistic data that can be analyzed with AI techniques to inform programming and refining classroom material (Bilkis et al., 2024; Deiana et al., 2023; Sriwastwa et al., 2023).

Personalized learning platforms, particularly adaptive educational technology, are the most downstream area of AI adoption in education. Here, AI is increasing student engagement and understanding by providing more individualized and customized resources and assistance. Personalized learning platforms require robust prior knowledge of all users, integration of tutoring technologies, and significant pre-existing knowledge banks and database architecture. Using AI in a personalized learning format requires many kinds of data, which may include assessment data about students' knowledge and skills, students' social and emotional inputs for building richer models of how humans learn, and long-term data to measure outcomes.

CONCLUSION

The value of having a solid foundation in artificial intelligence skills is already high and will only grow in the years to come. This has become an urgent need for everyone: students of all disciplines, educators and professionals, as we are living in a world that is at least partially influenced by artificial intelligence. Education is one area where artificial intelligence (AI) has made inroads. The adoption of AI in Education results in several benefits. The creation of novel assessment techniques, upskilling, and assessment technologies that may provide teachers and students with more accurate and fast feedback are some of these advantages and enhance learning outcomes. It has long been believed that trust influences people's adoption of technology. The need for a higher education system is fueled by a variety of factors, including acceptance of change, resource availability, adaptability, and prospective rewards. As a result, there is an increasing need for an appropriate infrastructure varying from educators training and digital skills to physical infrastructure like software, systems, financial resources. Therefore, this study provides an initial summary of efforts in the subject of AI literacy in adult and higher education and should be seen as a request for further research in this area. It is also necessary to recognize and confront the growing digital gap and its exacerbation of already existing inequities. Moreover, it is critical to create ethical standards that regulate the usage of AI technologies as they are further included into educational settings. Robust stakeholder engagement, meticulous infrastructure planning, and transparent governance structures—supported by diverse funding sources and risk mitigation strategies—are critical components of success.

REFERENCES

Ahmad, S. F., Rahmat, M. K., Mubarik, M. S., Alam, M. M., & Hyder, S. I. (2021). Artificial intelligence and its role in education. *Sustainability (Basel)*, 13(22), 12902. DOI: 10.3390/su132212902

Akgun, S., & Greenhow, C. (2022). Artificial intelligence in education: Addressing ethical challenges in K-12 settings. *AI and Ethics*, 2(3), 431–440. Advance online publication. DOI: 10.1007/s43681-021-00096-7 PMID: 34790956

Alahmari, F., Naim, A., & Alqahtani, H. (2023). E-learning modeling technique and convolution neural networks in online education. In *IoT-Enabled Convolutional Neural Networks: Techniques and Applications* (pp. 261-295). River Publishers. DOI: 10.1201/9781003393030-10

Alenezi, M. (2023). Digital learning and digital institution in higher education. *Education Sciences*, 13(1), 88. Advance online publication. DOI: 10.3390/educsci13010088

Alwabel, R. (2024). *The Future of AI in Education: Important Cautions to Consider.*

Andrejevic, M., & Selwyn, N. (n.d.). *Facial recognition technology in schools: Critical questions and concerns.* Learning., DOI: 10.1080/1469662121

7. Ayanwale, M. A., Sanusi, I. T., Adelana, O. P., Aruleba, K. D., & Oyelere, S. S. (2022). Teachers' readiness and intention to teach artificial intelligence in schools. *Computers and Education: Artificial Intelligence*, 3, 100099. DOI: 10.1016/j.caeai.2022.100099

Bhise, A., Munshi, A., Rodrigues, A., & Sawant, V. (2022). Overview of AI in education. In *Artificial Intelligence in Higher Education* (pp. 31–62). CRC Press. DOI: 10.1201/9781003184157-2

Bilkis, M., Kohler, J. M., & Vilariño, F. (2024). Challenge-device-synthesis: A multi-disciplinary approach for the development of social innovation competences for students of artificial intelligence. *arXiv preprint arXiv:2405.19243.* DOI: 10.21125/edulearn.2024.1501

Bogina, V., Hartman, A., Kuflik, T., & Shulner-Tal, A. (2022). Educating software and AI stakeholders about algorithmic fairness, accountability, transparency and ethics. *International Journal of Artificial Intelligence in Education*, 32(3), 1–26. DOI: 10.1007/s40593-021-00248-0

Bragg, L. A., Walsh, C., & Heyeres, M. (2021). Successful design and delivery of online professional development for teachers: A systematic review of the literature. *Computers & Education*, 166, 104158. Advance online publication. DOI: 10.1016/j.compedu.2021.104158

Byrd, D., & Polychroniadou, A. (2020, October). Differentially private secure multi-party computation for federated learning in financial applications. In *Proceedings of the First ACM International Conference on AI in Finance* (pp. 1-9). DOI: 10.1145/3383455.3422562

Carvalho, L., Martinez-Maldonado, R., Tsai, Y. S., Markauskaite, L., & De Laat, M. (2022). How can we design for learning in an AI world? *Computers and Education: Artificial Intelligence*, 3, 100053. DOI: 10.1016/j.caeai.2022.100053

Celik, I., Dindar, M., Muukkonen, H., & Järvelä, S. (2022). The promises and challenges of artificial intelligence for teachers: A systematic review of research. *TechTrends*, 66(4), 616–630. Advance online publication. DOI: 10.1007/s11528-022-00715-y

Chen, Y., & Esmaeilzadeh, P. (2024). Generative AI in medical practice: In-depth exploration of privacy and security challenges. *Journal of Medical Internet Research*, 26, e53008. Advance online publication. DOI: 10.2196/53008 PMID: 38457208

Chiu, T. K., Moorhouse, B. L., Chai, C. S., & Ismailov, M. (2023). Teacher support and student motivation to learn with artificial intelligence (AI) based chatbot. *Interactive Learning Environments*, •••, 1–17. DOI: 10.1080/10494820.2023.2172044

Crisostomo, M., Bernarte, P., & Ambag, S. (2022). Cross-cultural translation studies in the context of artificial intelligence: Challenges and response. *European Online Journal of Natural and Social Sciences: Proceedings*, 11(4 (s)), 187–199. DOI: 10.18690/978-961-286-555-8.7

Deiana, G., Dettori, M., Arghittu, A., Azara, A., Gabutti, G., & Castiglia, P. (2023). Artificial intelligence and public health: Evaluating ChatGPT responses to vaccination myths and misconceptions. *Vaccines*, 11(7), 1217. DOI: 10.3390/vaccines11071217 PMID: 37515033

Familoni, B. T. (2024). *Cybersecurity challenges in the age of AI: Theoretical approaches and practical solutions*. Computer Science & IT Research Journal., DOI: 10.1007/s40593-021-00147-2

Fernández-Batanero, J. M., Montenegro-Rueda, M., Fernández-Cerero, J., & García-Martínez, I. (2022). Digital competences for teacher professional development: Systematic review. *European Journal of Teacher Education*, 45(4), 513–531. DOI: 10.1080/02619768.2020.1827389

Hadjerrouit, S. (2010). A theoretical framework to Foster digital literacy: The case of digital learning resources. In Reynolds, N., & Turcsányi-Szabó, M. (Eds.), *Key competencies in the knowledge society* (pp. 144–154). Springer., DOI: 10.1007/978-3-642-15378-5_14

Hashem, R., Ali, N., El Zein, F., Fidalgo, P., & Khurma, O. A. (2024). AI to the rescue: Exploring the potential of ChatGPT as a teacher ally for workload relief and burnout prevention. *Research and Practice in Technology Enhanced Learning*, 19, 104701. Advance online publication. DOI: 10.1186/s41039-023-00180-8

Hemachandran, K., Verma, P., Pareek, P., Arora, N., Kumar, K. V. R., Ahanger, T. A., & Ratna, R. (2022). Artificial intelligence: A universal virtual tool to augment tutoring in higher education. *Computational Intelligence and Neuroscience*, 2022, 1–8. Advance online publication. DOI: 10.1155/2022/1410448 PMID: 35586099

Holmes, W., & Porayska-Pomsta, K. (2022). The ethics of artificial intelligence in education: Practices, challenges, and debates. *srce.hr*. https://doi.org/DOI: 10.1007/s11528-022-00660-5

Huang, W., & Looi, C. K. (2021). A critical review of literature on "unplugged" pedagogies in K-12 computer science and computational thinking education. *Computer Science Education*, 31(1), 83–111. Advance online publication. DOI: 10.1080/08993408.2020.1789411

Imchen, A., & Ndem, F. (2020). Addressing the learning crisis: An urgent need to better finance education for the poorest children. *UNICEF*. https://ed.gov

Jones, K. M., Asher, A., Goben, A., Perry, M. R., Salo, D., Briney, K. A., & Robertshaw, M. B. (2020). "We're being tracked at all times": Student perspectives of their privacy in relation to learning analytics in higher education. *Journal of the Association for Information Science and Technology*, 71(9), 1044–1059. DOI: 10.1002/asi.24358

Joshi, S., Rambola, R. K., & Churi, P. (2021). Evaluating artificial intelligence in education for next generation. *Journal of Physics: Conference Series*, 1714(1), 012039. DOI: 10.1088/1742-6596/1714/1/012039

Kayode-Ajala, O. (2023). Establishing cyber resilience in developing countries: An exploratory investigation into institutional, legal, financial, and social challenges. *International Journal of Sustainable Infrastructure for Cities and Societies*, 8(9), 1–10. https://vectoral.org

Kimsesiz, F. (2023). An examination of digitalized self-directed language learning practices of tertiary level EFL learners in Türkiye. *Journal of Educational Technology and Online Learning*, 6(3), 683–701. DOI: 10.31681/jetol.1276105

Kuleto, V., Ilić, M., Dumangiu, M., Ranković, M., Martins, O. M., Păun, D., & Mihoreanu, L. (2021). Exploring opportunities and challenges of artificial intelligence and machine learning in higher education institutions. *Sustainability (Basel)*, 13(18), 10424. DOI: 10.3390/su131810424

Laupichler, M. C., Aster, A., Schirch, J., & Raupach, T. (2022). Artificial intelligence literacy in higher and adult education: A scoping literature review. *Computers and Education: Artificial Intelligence*, 3, 100101. DOI: 10.1016/j.caeai.2022.100101

Littlejohn, A., Beetham, H., & McGill, L. (2012). Learning at the digital frontier: A review of digital literacies in theory and practice. *Journal of Computer Assisted Learning*, 28(6), 547–556. DOI: 10.1111/j.1365-2729.2011.00474.x

Liu, C.-C., Liao, M.-G., Chang, C.-H., & Lin, H.-M. (2022). An analysis of children's interaction with an AI chatbot and its impact on their interest in reading. *Computers & Education*, 189, 104576. Advance online publication. DOI: 10.1016/j.compedu.2022.104576

Long, D., & Magerko, B. (2020). What is AI Literacy? Competencies and Design Considerations. *Proceedings of the 2020 CHI Conference on Human Factors in Computing Systems*, 1–16. https://doi.org/DOI: 10.1145/3313831.3376727

Luan, H., Geczy, P., Lai, H., Gobert, J., Yang, S. J., Ogata, H., & Tsai, C. C. (2020). Challenges and future directions of big data and artificial intelligence in education. *Frontiers in Psychology*, 11, 580820. DOI: 10.3389/fpsyg.2020.580820 PMID: 33192896

Marín, V., & Castañeda, L. (2023). Developing Digital. *Literacy, Teaching and Learning*, •••, 1089–1108. DOI: 10.1007/978-981-19-2080-6_64

Mhlanga, D. (2021). Artificial intelligence in the industry 4.0, and its impact on poverty, innovation, infrastructure development, and the sustainable development goals: Lessons from Africa. *Sustainability (Basel)*, 13(18), 10424. DOI: 10.3390/su13115788

Nazaretsky, T., Ariely, M., Cukurova, M., & Alexandron, G. (2022). Teachers' trust in AI-powered educational technology and a professional development program to improve it. *British Journal of Educational Technology*, 53(4), 914–931. DOI: 10.1111/bjet.13232

Ng, D. T. K., Leung, J. K. L., Chu, S. K. W., & Qiao, M. S. (2021). Conceptualizing AI literacy: An exploratory review. *Computers and Education: Artificial Intelligence*, 2, 100041. DOI: 10.1016/j.caeai.2021.100041

Park, J., & Lim, H. (2022). Privacy-preserving federated learning using homomorphic encryption. *Applied Sciences (Basel, Switzerland)*, 12(9), 1240. DOI: 10.3390/app12091240

Renz, A., & Hilbig, R. (2020). Prerequisites for artificial intelligence in further education: Identification of drivers, barriers, and business models of educational technology companies. *International Journal of Educational Technology in Higher Education*, 17(1), 14. DOI: 10.1186/s41239-020-00193-3

Rong, Q., Lian, Q., & Tang, T. (2022). Research on the influence of AI and VR technology for students' concentration and creativity. *Frontiers in Psychology*, 13, 767689. Advance online publication. DOI: 10.3389/fpsyg.2022.767689 PMID: 35401322

Sriwastwa, A., Ravi, P., Emmert, A., Chokshi, S., Kondor, S., Dhal, K., ... & Gupta, R. (2023). Generative AI for medical 3D printing: A comparison of ChatGPT outputs to reference standard education. *3D Printing in Medicine, 9*(1), 21. https://doi.org/DOI: 10.1186/s41205-023-00152-6

Su, J., Zhong, Y., & Ng, D. T. K. (2022). A meta-review of literature on educational approaches for teaching AI at the K-12 levels in the Asia-Pacific region. *Computers and Education: Artificial Intelligence*, 3, 100053. DOI: 10.1016/j.caeai.2022.100065

Van de Cruys, S., Bervoets, J., & Moors, A. (2022). Preferences need inferences: Learning, valuation, and curiosity in aesthetic experience. In *The Routledge international handbook of neuroaesthetics* (pp. 475-506). Routledge. 45- Wang, T., & Park, J. (2021). Design and implementation of intelligent sports training system for college students' mental health education. *Frontiers in Psychology, 12*, Article 634978. https://doi.org/DOI: 10.3389/fpsyg.2021.634978

Williamson, B. (2024). The social life of AI in education. *International Journal of Artificial Intelligence in Education*, 34(1), 97–104. DOI: 10.1007/s40593-023-00342-5

Woo, H., LeTendre, G. K., Pham-Shouse, T., & Xiong, Y. (2021). The use of social robots in classrooms: A review of field-based studies. *Educational Research Review*, 33, 100388. DOI: 10.1016/j.edurev.2021.100388

Yang, W. (2022). Artificial intelligence education for young children: Why, what, and how in curriculum design and implementation. *Computers and Education: Artificial Intelligence*. DOI: 10.1016/j.caeai.2022.100068

Yu, H. (2023). Reflection on whether Chat GPT should be banned by academia from the perspective of education and teaching. *Frontiers in Psychology*, 14, 1181712. Advance online publication. DOI: 10.3389/fpsyg.2023.1181712 PMID: 37325766

ADDITIONAL READING

Aithal, P. S., & Aithal, S. (2023). How to increase emotional infrastructure of higher education institutions. [IJMTS]. *International Journal of Management, Technology, and Social Sciences*, 8(3), 356–394. DOI: 10.47992/IJMTS.2581.6012.0307

Mhlanga, D. (2021). Artificial intelligence in the industry 4.0, and its impact on poverty, innovation, infrastructure development, and the sustainable development goals: Lessons from emerging economies? *Sustainability (Basel)*, 13(11), 5788. DOI: 10.3390/su13115788

Prasad, K. R., Karanam, S. R., Ganesh, D., Liyakat, K. K. S., Talasila, V., & Purushotham, P. (2024). AI in public-private partnership for IT infrastructure development. *The Journal of High Technology Management Research*, 35(1), 100496. DOI: 10.1016/j.hitech.2024.100496

Williamson, B. (2019). Policy networks, performance metrics and platform markets: Charting the expanding data infrastructure of higher education. *British Journal of Educational Technology*, 50(6), 2794–2809. DOI: 10.1111/bjet.12849

KEY TERMS AND DEFINITIONS

AI Literacy: The ability to understand, apply, monitor, and critically assess artificial intelligence applications, enabling users to interact with AI effectively in various settings.

Digital Infrastructure: The foundational physical and technological assets, such as hardware, software, and networks, necessary to support digital education and AI integration.

Equitable Access: The principle of providing fair and equal opportunities for all students, regardless of geographic, socioeconomic, or other barriers, to access AI-enhanced educational resources.

Human Resource Development: The process of training and equipping educators and staff with skills and knowledge required for effective AI implementation in educational environments.

Investment Frameworks: Structured financial models and strategies used to allocate resources efficiently for AI infrastructure, training, and technological upgrades in education.

Personalized Learning Platforms: AI-driven educational tools that adapt to individual learning needs, providing customized instructional content and resources.

Scalability: The capacity of AI systems and infrastructure to expand and handle increasing demands within educational environments without losing efficiency.

Technological Readiness: The degree to which an educational institution is prepared, in terms of technology and resources, to implement AI solutions effectively.

Training Requirements: The specific skills and knowledge educators and administrators must acquire to implement and manage AI tools in educational settings.

Urban-Rural Disparities: The differences in access to AI and educational resources between urban and rural areas, often due to variations in infrastructure and funding.

Chapter 6
A Framework for the Responsible Integration of Generative AI Tools in Learning

Stephen Ko
The Hong Kong Polytechnic University, Hong Kong

Simon C. H. Chan
https://orcid.org/0000-0001-5871-3837
The Hong Kong Polytechnic University, Hong Kong

ABSTRACT

Generative artificial intelligence (Gen-AI) tools are increasingly utilized in educational settings for tasks ranging from content creation to personalizing learning experiences. While these tools offer considerable potential to transform education, their integration brings challenges, including biases, dependency, and ethical dilemmas. Addressing these challenges and ethical concerns is essential to fully leveraging Gen-AI to promote equitable and effective learning. This chapter presents a framework for the responsible use of Gen-AI tools in learning environments, offering guidance to educators, technologists, policymakers, students, and other stakeholders. The framework provides proactive guidelines to navigate the complexities of Gen-AI, ensuring these tools are employed ethically and effectively to enhance student learning outcomes.

DOI: 10.4018/979-8-3373-1017-6.ch006

INTRODUCTION

Artificial intelligence (AI) has become an integral part of our daily lives, impacting every aspect of the world. From healthcare and business to transportation and education, AI has revolutionized the way we work, communicate, and interact. As AI continues to advance and permeate various industries, its impact on education is becoming increasingly significant. McKinsey (2023) predicted that AI is likely to have the most impact on knowledge-oriented work, especially in education. In schools, students not only learn with AI-powered tools and resources, but they are also being prepared for a future work where AI will play a crucial role. AI has the potential to profoundly impact learning in various ways; it can be used to create personalized learning experiences, generate individualized educational content, and provide real-time feedback to students. While its advancement is promising, it presents challenges concerning biases and ethical considerations associated with the use of AI in the realm of education (Sedkaoui & Benaichouba, 2024).

In light of the opportunities and challenges of using Gen-AI in education, it is imperative to prioritize responsible development of Gen-AI in fostering equitable and effective learning experiences. As Gen-AI continues to develop at lightning speed, this chapter aims to provide a guidance framework for the responsible use of Gen-AI tools in learning. This framework is intended to provide guidelines to help educators address the challenges proactively, ensuring that Gen-AI tools are used ethically and effectively to enhance student learning. The remainder of this chapter is organized as follows: the first section is an overview of Gen-AI . Section 2 explores the various ways in which Gen-AI impacts every part of the world, and how Gen-AI continues to shape the future of our society. Section 3 delves into the opportunities and challenges of AI/Gen-AI in education, highlighting its role in transforming student learning. Section 4 offers a guidance framework for the responsible use of Gen-AI tools in learning. The chapter concludes with future research directions and a summary.

BACKGROUND

Gen-AI, short for generative artificial intelligence, refers to a subset of AI that focuses on creating new content, such as images, text, or audio, that is indistinguishable from content created by humans (Routley, 2023). It can create human-like text and content, and answer questions in a conversational manner. This technology uses machine learning algorithms to analyse and learn from existing data in order to generate new content (Routley, 2023). One of the key techniques used in Gen-AI is generative adversarial networks (GANs), which consist of a generator and a discriminator that work together to create realistic content (Goodfellow et al., 2020). The generator creates new content, while the discriminator evaluates the content to determine if it is real or generated, through which the generator learns to create increasingly realistic content, while the discriminator becomes better at distinguishing between real and generated content. A GAN is a deep learning architecture. It trains two neural networks to compete against each other to generate more authentic new data from a given training dataset (Routley, 2023).

Gen-AI can generate content through neural networks (Routley, 2023). A neural network consists of tremendous amounts of data, images, text, sounds, etc., which form the basis of AI. Users input a prompt with a description. Prompts can be in the form of words, numbers, or photos. And AI uses its neural network to generate new content that is similar to the ones from which it has trained. For example, Gen-AI can generate news articles, poetry, scripts, and creating new images based on existing ones, such as crafting a new portrait from a person's face or a scenery. It can also produce new music tracks and sound effects. In educational settings, AI can perform tasks that typically require human intelligence or intervention, including content creation and the personalization of learning experiences (Acar, 2024). For instance, educators can utilize AI-driven content generators to develop customized textbooks and teaching materials that adapt to students' learning pace and comprehension (Horn & Staker, 2016). Gen-AI can efficiently summarize large volumes of text, enabling users to quickly extract key information and gain insights from articles, research papers, or meeting notes (Pranathi Software, 2023). AI tutors and chatbots can offer real-time feedback to students, fostering a more interactive learning experience (Walkington & Bernacki, 2019). Additionally, Gen-AI can assist in writing code snippets, explaining programming concepts, and generating documentation based on code comments (Witts, 2024). Gen-AI tools can also automate repetitive tasks like content generation and grading, allowing educators to focus more on innovative pedagogical activities (Tong et al., 2019).

The OpenAI GPT (Generative Pre-trained Transformer) models, and in particular, the transformer architecture that OpenAI uses, represent a significant Gen-AI research breakthrough. GPT-4 is the latest iteration in the series of GPT models developed by OpenAI. It builds on the success of its predecessor, GPT-3, introducing several key improvements in model architecture, training methodology, and performance (Idrees, 2024). GPT-4 continues to use the transformer architecture, which relies on self-attention mechanism. Self-attention mechanism enables the model to compute attention scores for each word in relation to all other words in the input sequence, capturing contextual information (Sengupta, 2023). GPT-4 employs a multi-layered self-attention mechanism, allowing it to process text inputs with remarkable contextual understanding simultaneously (Idrees, 2024). The training process of GPT-4 consists of two main stages: pre-training and fine-tuning (Ordax,

2024; Sengupta, 2023). During pre-training, the model learns from a vast corpus of publicly available text from the Internet, learning to predict the next word in a sentence and thereby understanding the statistical patterns and linguistic nuances in the data. The objective is to maximize the likelihood of predicting the correct next word given the previous context. Fine-tuning is the subsequent stage where GPT-4 undergoes additional training on specific tasks. This involves using labeled data for tasks such as question answering, summarization, translation, and more. This process enables the model to specialize in these tasks and refine its language generation capabilities accordingly.

In addition to OpenAI GPT-4, other popular Gen-AI tools include but are not limited to the following: Google Gemini for writing, planning, learning, and more, seamlessly integrated with other Google services; Microsoft Copilot for content generation, summarization, multilingual content translation, optimization, seamlessly integrated with other Microsoft services; IBM watsonx: for enterprise applications choosing from multi-model varieties to scale up the impact of AI with trusted data, integrated with IBM various services; Jasper AI for businesses scaling up marketing content like blog articles, social media posts, sales emails, website copy, and more; Copy.ai for content, prospecting at scale, enriching customer relationship management, and much more; Writesonic for content generation for blogs, ads, and social media, with real-time data that drive traffic; Midjourney for Generates AI images, artistic and photorealistic images; and some others.

APPLICATIONS OF GEN-AI

AI impacts every part of the world by driving innovation, improving efficiency, and transforming various industries and aspects of our daily lives. As AI continues to advance, its impact is expected to grow and reshape the world in profound ways. In a recent study, Sedkaoui and Benaichouba (2024) reviewed existing literature on Gen-AI and examined how it impacts different industries and sectors as follows:

Healthcare

Gen-AI models can significantly accelerate drug development by generating new compounds with specific functionalities and predicting their interactions with biological systems (Patronov et al., 2022; Stokes et al., 2023). By creating innovative pharmacological compounds and estimating their interactions with the human body, Gen-AI holds immense potential for customized medicine and targeted therapeutics (Stokes et al., 2023). By analyzing individual genetic and health data, Gen-AI can develop personalized treatment plans, enhancing patient care through predictive analytics and remote monitoring (Ghaffar Nia et al., 2023). This technology has reduced the workload of physicians, minimized human errors, and shortened diagnosis times, while improving the prediction and detection of numerous diseases such as cancers, heart, lung, skin, genetic, and neural disorders; consequently, it leads to better health outcomes and reduced healthcare costs (Ghaffar Nia et al., 2023; Shen et al., 2023).

Business

Gen-AI is set to revolutionize marketing by enhancing capabilities in campaign personalization, unstructured customer data analysis, process automation, idea generation and opportunity identification (Harkness et al., 2023). According to a recent Everest Group report, more than 75% of enterprises are deploying or planning to deploy Gen-AI in various functions, including operations and customer services. These investments often take the form of Gen-AI pilot programs to enhance agent-assist capabilities, improve content creation, enrich knowledge bases, analyse customer feedback, and manage the agent lifecycle (Sharma et al., 2024).

For instance, crafts retailer Michaels Stores is leveraging Gen-AI to deepen customer engagement through more personalized and frequent interactions (Harkness et al., 2023). The company has developed a content generation and decision-making platform to assist with copy development and to better understand how different customer segments respond to various messages. Similarly, personal-clothing service Stitch Fix uses Gen-AI to help stylists interpret customer feedback and provide tailored product recommendations (Harkness et al., 2023).

A direct-to-consumer retailer is employing Gen-AI to resolve customer tickets, such as order-taking or repair requests (Harkness et al., 2023). By automating process steps—retrieving information from the back end, making necessary changes, and replying to customers in the brand's voice—the company has achieved an over 80 percent reduction in time to first response and a four-minute decrease in average ticket resolution time. Additionally, Gen-AI models can also develop creative product designs that are not only functional but also optimal for production efficiency and resource use (Chen et al., 2023b). Mattel is using AI in Hot Wheels product development to generate four times as many product concept images as before, inspiring new features and designs (Harkness et al., 2023).

Gen-AI models can be used for risk assessment, fraud detection, and algorithmic trading in the financial industry (Chen et al., 2023a). It can detect unusual patterns and anomalies in financial transactions, such as credit card usage, helping financial institutions to identify and block potentially fraudulent activities. In addition, Gen-AI can be used to automate repetitive and time-consuming tasks such as recruiting candidates, responding to customer service requests, assessing the creditworthiness of borrowers and processing insurance claims. It is also being used to develop personalized financial services and elevate customer experience through chatbots and virtual assistants.

In the manufacturing sector, Gen-AI can be leveraged to optimize processes and simulate potential scenarios (Boles, 2024). This technology offers manufacturers greater opportunities to tailor operations to their specific needs. While current large language models (LLMs) are trained on extensive datasets, Gen-AI enables the customization of smaller language models using data from a manufacturer's specific industrial IoT devices. Gen-AI enhances digital twins—virtual replicas of physical systems—by introducing "what if" scenarios. These dynamic digital twins can accurately mirror real-world systems, allowing for tests on how individual reconfigurations or changes might impact system operations. They can simulate a wide range of alternative scenarios to assess how more efficient process paths, varying energy levels, safety improvements, and other factors might influence daily operations.

Transportation

Gen-AI has the capability to streamline and enhance various tasks throughout the transportation life cycle, from reducing the time needed to onboard new carriers to simplifying the freight audit process (Riemann et al., 2024). By allowing users to query unstructured datasets and receive organized responses, Gen-AI can transform the carrier onboarding process by automating credential verification, compliance checks, and performance evaluations. Additionally, AI-powered communication platforms can enable real-time collaboration between carriers and shippers. As Gen-AI becomes more adept at understanding a specific system, it can learn the type of information carriers require during a load life cycle, for example, how weather and traffic impact route changes, the preferred communication channels of carriers, and the optimal timing for communications (Riemann et al., 2024). This AI-driven aggregation of behavior and content will lead to improvements in service levels and route optimization, as well as enhanced overall supply chain visibility, without necessitating significant increases in operations staff or software development resources.

AI-driven algorithms are highly effective at processing large datasets, making them ideal for comprehensive freight audits (Riemann et al., 2024). Such a system can autonomously verify invoices, identify discrepancies, and ensure compliance with contractual agreements. In essence, AI can facilitate real-time root-cause analysis, expedite resolutions, and improve compliance with payment terms, enabling operations teams to minimize errors, reduce manual workload, and enhance accuracy in financial transactions. From predictive analytics for demand forecasting to route optimization based on historical performance, Gen-AI provides valuable, customized, and real-time data.

IMPACT OF GEN-AI ON LEARNING

Gen-AI has the potential to profoundly impact learning in various ways. It can be used to create personalized learning experiences, generate individualized educational content, and provide real-time feedback to students. Gen-AI can analyse students' learning styles, preferences, and performance data to craft personalized, engaging and interactive learning experiences. For example, Gen-AI can tailor learning experiences by developing personalized textbooks, video lectures, quizzes, exercises, and immersive simulations, leading to improved knowledge acquisition and retention (Gilardi et al., 2023; Ratten & Jones, 2023).

AI-powered adaptive learning platforms could elevate student performance and engagement (Luo & Hsiao-Chin, 2023; Zhang & Aslan, 2021). By acting as a digital tutor, conversation partner, and writing assistant, Gen-AI enables learners to practice and improve their language skills according to their own pace and individual needs (Li et al., 2024). Take Khanmigo, Khan Academy's AI-powered assistant, as an example. It offers a conversational platform where learners can ask questions and receive personalized explanations across various subjects like math, science, and humanities (Acar, 2024). This helps students identify areas for improvement and track their progress, keeping them motivated and engaged in their learning journey. Additionally, chatbots can function as virtual mentors and coaches by analysing individual requirements and offering suitable learning materials, providing students with personalized advice and assistance throughout the learning process (Abbas et al., 2022; Chen et al., 2023a; Guo & Wang, 2024).

Gen-AI tools can offer valuable learning support for vulnerable groups and disadvantaged students (Athanassopoulos et al., 2023; Chan & Hu, 2023). Gen-AI tools can offer speech-to-text and text-to-speech features, helping students with visual or hearing impairments. Students can also utilize Gen-AI for a variety of tasks, including brainstorming ideas, outlining, synthesizing information, summarizing large volumes of text, preparing literature review, striking the right tone for specific purposes, transforming text for different writing needs (e.g., emails, job descriptions, business plans, business reports, executive summaries, etc.) and proofreading such as grammatical correction, sentence structure improvement, vocabulary suggestions, paraphrasing, and overall polishing (Atlas, 2023; Crawford et al., 2023). Additionally, Gen-AI can assist with writing full essays, solving problem sets, translating written assignments from one language into another, and generating code, aiding students who are non-native speakers or have reading difficulties (García-Peñalvo, 2023).

KEY CHALLENGES OF GEN-AI IN LEARNING

While Gen-AI has the potential to transform student learning and educators can leverage Gen-AI to create more effective and engaging learning environments that cater to the needs of individual students, it presents several challenges that need to be addressed as follows:

Bias and Fairness

Gen-AI is not neutral; its design and use have ethical implications (Coeckelbergh, 2023). Gen-AI systems can inherit or reinforce biases present in the training data, leading to unfair or discriminatory outcomes if the systems are not developed with a conscious effort to include diverse and representative training datasets (Iskender, 2023; Noble, 2018; Sanderson, 2023; Zharovskikh, 2024). According to a UNESCO study, it revealed worrying tendencies in LLMs to produce gender bias, as well as homophobia and racial stereotyping. Women were described as working in domestic roles far more often than men, four times as often by one model, and were frequently associated with words like "home", "family" and "children", while male names were linked to "business", "executive", "salary", and "career" (UNESCO & IRCAI, 2024).

In educational settings, Gen-AI can create personalized content that may reinforce existing biases or fail to offer equitable learning opportunities, thereby widening the digital divide due to a lack of inclusion (Nguyen et al., 2023). Sha et al. (2022) note that bias is common in most real-world datasets. These biased datasets can introduce unfairness into algorithms, perpetuating historical prejudices and demographic disparities (Idowu et al., 2024). A study on the fairness of institutional data in predicting student success found that while such data provides insights into students' demographic and academic backgrounds, it can increase bias against historically disadvantaged students (Yu et al., 2020). This exacerbates the discriminatory tendencies of language models (Idowu et al., 2024).

Although non-native speakers, refugees, and individuals with disabilities could benefit from Gen-AI in learning, they are often underserved due to socioeconomic barriers and a lack of tailored educational resources in schools (Li et al., 2024). For instance, standardized curricula may not address the diverse needs of students, particularly those with learning disabilities, language barriers, or different cultural backgrounds. Schools in low-income areas often receive less funding, leading to fewer resources for students and teacher training, as well as inadequate facilities.

Ethical Considerations

The use of Gen-AI in educational settings raises ethical concerns about its responsible application (Adiguzel et al., 2023; Sullivan et al., 2023). AI's role in surveillance and data collection can infringe on individual privacy rights. User inputs, including prompts and responses, may be used for training LLMs, leading to concerns that sensitive information could be inadvertently accessed by others (Kajiwara & Kawabata, 2024). There have been reports of Samsung employees accidentally inputting confidential company information into ChatGPT, highlighting the risk of information leakage (Gupta et al., 2023).

Another ethical question is: Who is accountable for the outputs of Gen-AI? If outputs from LLMs plagiarize content and users (students) incorporate this into their learning and assessments, either intentionally or unintentionally, who is held accountable? Should the responsibility lie solely with the users (students), or should developers, educators, and other stakeholders also share the accountability? According to Moorhouse et al. (2023), plagiarism can take three forms: copying and pasting AI-generated responses, using multiple AI paraphrasing tools such as Quillbot to avoid detection, and failing to properly document the use of AI in assessment tasks.

Who should take the lead in making technology safer and more ethically acceptable? For instance, should developers incorporate hidden prompts to ensure ethical responses without compromising freedom of expression and the right to information? Should educators set ground rules for the responsible use of Gen-AI in educational settings? Should students make every effort to use the information responsibly and ethically? Additionally, could an overreliance on Gen-AI tools undermine students' genuine efforts to develop writing competence (Warschauer et al., 2023)? These questions emphasize the need for ethical guidelines and governance to ensure that Gen-AI systems are used transparently and responsibly.

Quality and Accuracy

The effectiveness of Gen-AI tools is greatly influenced by the quality of the prompts provided. Users' ability to craft well-thought and specific questions is crucial for obtaining accurate and relevant answers (Henrickson & Meroño-Peñuela, 2023). Crafting effective prompts is essential to harnessing the full power and potential of Gen-AI. For example, providing detailed information in prompts is particularly important when dealing with images (Siegel, n. d.). Additionally, the quality of responses can vary significantly depending on the specific LLM in use. If a model's training data lacks sufficient depth or breadth, the Gen-AI responses may not meet expectations (Nazir & Wang, 2023).

Some fundamental questions arise: Can educators and students trust the outputs of Gen-AI applications? If not, how can trust be established? One of the risks associated with these natural language applications is their tendency to "hallucinate," producing inaccurate outputs with complete confidence (Thorp, 2023). They can even fabricate references and sources that do not exist (Deloitte, 2023). When Gen-AI generates confident-sounding outputs that are inaccurate and lack grounding in verifiable facts, data, or algorithmic patterns, ensuring the quality and accuracy of the content becomes essential but challenging. For instance, if human fact-checking of Gen-AI outputs becomes overly laborious, it could negatively impact the learning experience by leveraging the power and potential of Gen-AI. Striking the right balance between the trustworthiness of information produced by Gen-AI and human oversight is an ongoing challenge (Deloitte, 2023).

Lack of Human Touch

While Gen-AI has the potential to personalize learning experiences, concerns arise about its lack of the human touch and empathy essential for effective teaching and learning (Choi et al., 2023). Although Gen-AI can process and generate text based on data patterns, it often struggles with nuanced understanding of context, cultural differences, and subtleties (Gison, 2024). Human creativity and intuition are driven by personal experiences, emotions, person-to-person interactions, and a deep contextual understanding of the world. In contrast, Gen-AI relies on pre-existing data and algorithms, limiting its ability to think outside the box or generate truly original ideas (Gison, 2024). Overreliance on Gen-AI could diminish students' critical thinking skills and creativity (Warschauer et al., 2023). Therefore, it is crucial to balance the use of Gen-AI with human interaction, creativity, curiosity, and compassion to maintain a supportive and nurturing learning environment (Stackpole, 2023).

SOLUTIONS AND RECOMMENDATIONS

Addressing the above-mentioned challenges requires a multidisciplinary approach that involves educators, technologists, policymakers, and students working together to develop guidelines, standards, and best practices for the responsible use of Gen-AI in learning environments. They should all actively engage in discussions about the responsible and effective deployment of Gen-AI tools, promoting awareness and cultivating a responsible use of Gen-AI as part of a culture in learning environments. As Gen-AI tools are evolving quickly and new ways of using them are emerging, these guidelines should set out common directions for the responsible use of Gen-AI in learning. They should be living guidance, providing flexibility for users of these guidelines to adapt to their own specific contexts.

Different institutions have issued guidance on how to use Gen-AI tools appropriately to ensure that benefits of those tools are fully utilized while mitigating the risks (Moorhouse et al., 2023; UNESCO, 2021). However, the proliferation of guidelines and recommendations has resulted in a complex landscape that makes it difficult to decide which guidelines should be followed in a particular context. Considering the current state of technological development and the commonalities of the existing guidelines from various institutions (Moorhouse et al., 2023), a framework for the responsible use of Gen-AI in learning environments should encompass ethical, technical, and pedagogical considerations but they are not binding. Below is a framework for the responsible use of Gen-AI tools in learning (see Figure 1):

Figure 1. A framework for the responsible use of Gen-AI tools in learning

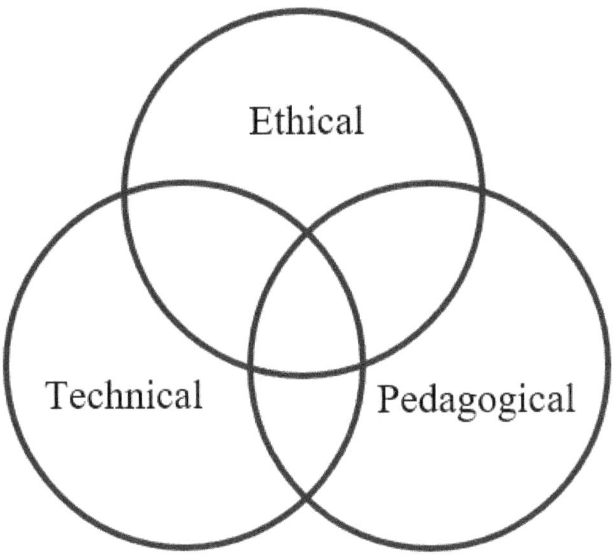

Framework for the Responsible Use of Gen-AI in Learning

Ethical aspects

Declaration of the Use of Gen-AI: For Gen-AI to be used in a responsible manner, it is imperative to prioritize ethical considerations. Transparency and consent should be central to this aspect. Perkins et al. (2024) provided an Artificial Intelligence Assessment Scale for educators to communicate with students as to the extent of Gen-AI usage in assessments (see Table 1). Instructors may consider incorporating it into their syllabi, reflecting their own perspective and specific approach to using Gen-AI in their courses.

Table 1. The artificial intelligence assessment scale

1	**No AI**	**AI must not be used at any point during the assessment. The assessment is completed entirely without AI assistance. This level ensures that students rely solely on their knowledge, understanding, and skills.**
2	AI-assisted idea generation and structuring	AI can be used in the assessment for brainstorming, creating structures, and generating ideas for improving work. No AI content is allowed in the final submission.
3	AI-assisted editing	AI can be used, but your original work with no AI content must be provided in an appendix. AI can be used to make improvements to the clarity or quality of student created work to improve the final output, but no new content can be created using AI.
4	AI task completion, human evaluation	AI is used to complete certain elements of the task, with students providing discussion or commentary on the AI-generated content. This level requires critical engagement with AI generated content and evaluating its output. Any AI created content must be cited.
5	Full AI	AI should be used as a 'co-pilot' in order to meet the requirements of the assessment, allowing for a collaborative approach with AI and enhancing creativity. Students may use AI throughout their assessment to support their own work and do not have to specify which content is AI generated.

The use of Gen-AI in learning should align with ethical guidelines and regulations in specific contexts. Institutions should provide and facilitate up-to-date training on verifying output, addressing biases and protecting intellectual property rights. To be transparent, students are required to indicate which Gen-AI tools have been used substantially in their learning processes (Moorhouse et al., 2023). Reference to the tool(s) could include the name, version, date, etc. and how it was used and affected the learning process. Students are also required to make the input (prompts) and output available. For example, if students are allowed to employ AI-enabled tools in their course assessments, they should declare their use and reflect on the processes as indicated below:

- I declare that Gen-AI tools have been/not been used to prepare and produce the submitted work.

Then students should indicate which Generative AI tools they utilised and explain how the generated materials have been incorporated into their submitted work.

- I acknowledge the use of [1. insert AI system(s) and link] to [2. specific use of generative artificial intelligence].
- I entered the following prompts: [3. list of prompts].
- The output from the generative artificial intelligence was [4. Explanation of use].

Students should also be held accountable for the integrity of the content generated by or with the support of Gen-AI tools. They should adopt a critical approach to using the output produced by Gen-AI tools and be aware of the tools' limitations, such as biases, hallucinations and inaccuracies. Thus, students should confirm the followings:

- I have read, understood and followed the requirements of the subject and, in particular, the requirements related to using Gen-AI in this assessment/assignment;
- the work in this assessment/assignment is my own work;
- no part of this assessment/assignment is taken from other people's work and/or other sources, including Gen-AI output, without giving them credit through proper referencing;
- all references have been clearly cited in the convention and format appropriate for this assessment/assignment;
- I acknowledge that I am aware of the limitations of Gen-AI tool(s), including but not limited to biases, hallucinations, and inaccuracies; any unauthorised or unacknowledged use of Gen-AI in assessments is considered an act of academic dishonesty, subject to disciplinary actions.

Technical Aspects

Addressing the technical challenges of Gen-AI involves a multi-faceted approach that includes human oversight, enhancing model robustness, improving data quality, ensuring ethical considerations and accountability. The Ethics Guidelines for Trustworthy Artificial Intelligence outline seven essential requirements that AI systems must meet to be deemed trustworthy (European Commission, 2019). An assessment list is provided to help assess the implementation of each requirement:

Human Agency and Oversight: AI systems should empower individuals, enabling them to make informed decisions and uphold their fundamental rights. Proper oversight mechanisms, such as human-in-the-loop, human-on-the-loop, and human-in-command approaches, must be ensured. This necessitates ongoing research and evaluation of the impact of Gen-AI on learning outcomes, which include monitoring the effectiveness of AI systems, gathering feedback from students and educators, and using data-driven insights to refine the use of Gen-AI (Hagiu & Wright, 2023). A good example of human-in-the-loop integration is Grammarly, an AI-powered writing assistant that aids users in improving grammar, spelling, punctuation, and style. Grammarly offers real-time suggestions as users write in various applications or websites. Users can choose to accept or reject these suggestions, which helps refine the algorithm and creates a data feedback loop. Additionally, Grammarly employs human reviewers to evaluate the AI-generated suggestions and address ambiguous cases (e.g., when a user rejects a suggestion without a clear reason), rather than solely relying on user feedback. At the same time, it is essential to provide ongoing professional development for educators to familiarize them with the latest development of Gen-AI tools and effective integration and refinement of Gen-AI into their pedagogies (Moorhouse et al., 2023).

Technical Robustness and Safety: AI systems must be resilient and secure. They should incorporate fallback plans to address potential failures and ensure accuracy, reliability, and reproducibility to minimize and prevent unintentional harm. Leveraging the strengths of different LLMs can enhance accuracy and robustness (Praveen et al., 2024). These measures ensure that AI systems used in learning environments are secure, reliable, and resilient to potential vulnerabilities or malfunctions, thereby enhancing quality and accuracy.

Privacy and Data Governance: AI systems must fully respect privacy and data protection. The geographical location of servers can complicate compliance with specific data privacy regulations, such as the General Data Protection Regulation in the European Union (Alier et al., 2021). Effective data governance mechanisms should be in place to ensure data quality and integrity, as well as to legitimize access to data.

Transparency: The data, system, and AI business models should be transparent. Traceability mechanisms can aid in achieving this (Zharovskikh, 2024). For example, making the algorithms used in AI content generation transparent allows for better scrutiny. AI systems and their decisions should be explained in a manner suitable for the concerned stakeholders. Users must be aware that they are interacting with an AI system and be informed of its capabilities and limitations.

Diversity, Non-Discrimination, and Fairness: It is important to be mindful of potential biases in the training data. Unfair bias must be avoided to prevent negative implications such as the marginalization of vulnerable groups and the exacerbation of prejudice and discrimination. This can be achieved by diversifying data sources for representation and balance, and through continuous monitoring and refining of the models' outputs (Idowu et al., 2024; Zharovskikh, 2024). Efforts can also be made to understand unique challenges faced by the vulnerable groups and how AI can be tailored to address them. AI systems therefore should be accessible to all, regardless of disability or diverse background, and involve relevant stakeholders throughout their lifecycle to ensure that the content generated by AI is fair, inclusive, and representative of diverse perspectives.

Societal and Environmental Well-being: AI systems should benefit all human beings, including future generations. They must be sustainable and environmentally friendly, considering the impact on the environment and other living beings. Their social and societal impacts should be carefully evaluated.

Accountability: Mechanisms must be established to ensure responsibility and accountability for AI systems and their outcomes (Zharovskikh, 2024). Auditability, which allows for the assessment of algorithms, data, and design processes, is crucial, especially in critical applications. Additionally, adequate and accessible redress should be provided. Quality assurance mechanisms must be in place to ensure that content generated by Gen-AI meets educational requirements and standards while regularly reviewing and evaluating the accuracy, relevance, and appropriateness of AI-generated materials.

Pedagogical Aspects

The rapid advancement of Gen-AI has sparked growing interest among educators in using AI to transform educational practices (Cai et al., 2023). Beyond ethical and technical considerations, it is crucial to implement strategies for effectively integrating AI/Gen-AI into pedagogy. The key principles are to incorporate AI/Gen-AI tools into the curricula in a manner that aligns with learning objectives and enhances educational experience. AI challenges the role of educators and the essence of teaching (Bearman et al., 2023; Bozkurt, 2023). A recent study revealed their mixed feelings of optimism and pessimism about AI's impact on future education (Lee et al., 2024). While recognizing that AI holds promise in teaching and learning, some educators feel overwhelmed and uncertain about how to effectively leverage it, especially regarding its applications and initial steps. They worry that AI-powered individualized learning paths or adaptive feedback will add to their administrative workload (Conway, 2024). They also feel the need to master complex programming skills or data analytics to use AI-based systems effectively. They are therefore slow to adapt to new technologies due to resistance to changing their teaching practices (McGrath et al., 2023). Their perceptions and readiness to adopt AI tools are crucial for successful integration of AI into pedagogies (Mohamed, 2024).

Redesign of Pedagogies: Conway (2024) highlights the benefits of AI-powered adaptive systems compared to traditional teaching practices—fixed syllabi, rigid exams, and identical pacing for all students. The syllabus becomes dynamic, with

AI creating personalized learning maps based on each student's understanding and progress. Students advance at their own pace, receiving extra support when needed. Adaptive learning platforms generally come with features like authoring tools, e-learning templates, gamification elements, and analytics suites (SafetyCulture.com). Educators can use AI course creation features to quickly generate lessons by entering the course topic, with the platform automatically including subtopics, text, images, and quizzes. Gamification elements like games and quizzes enhance learners' motivation. Reporting and analytics identify learning gaps for individuals and teams. Learners can access lessons on the go if platforms are compatible with Android and Apple devices.

Adaptive learning tailors content delivery to match a learner's knowledge level, preferences, and needs (Schulze, 2024). Personalization can be applied in several ways:

1. **Initial Level Assessment:** Understanding each learner's knowledge and abilities through questionnaires, quizzes, or self-assessments. Educators can use Learning Management Systems or AI tools to analyze performance and identify struggling topics (Conway, 2024).
2. **Personalized Learning Paths:** Creating individualized and flexible paths based on initial assessments, allowing students to progress at their own pace. Students move to the next topic after demonstrating competency, with additional support for those who need it such as review guides and practice prompts, and enrichment activities for advanced learners (Conway, 2024).
3. **Flexible Learning Content:** Combining learning elements to ensure skill development at each learner's pace. AI-powered platforms update course material with fresh content, allowing educators to curate or automatically integrate AI-driven recommendations (Conway, 2024). Learning objectives remain consistent, but pathways can be flexible.
4. **Real-Time Support:** Providing immediate feedback and assistance to enhance learning effectiveness. Continuous assessment replaces high-stakes exams, with frequent quizzes and interactive exercises offering AI-generated feedback (Conway, 2024).
5. **Progress Analysis:** Continuously collecting data on learning progress to inform strategies. Continuous assessment provides early warnings of struggles, enabling timely intervention (Conway, 2024).
6. **Motivation Through Interaction:** Engaging learners with content aligned to their interests and gamification elements like points and interactive quizzes (Schulze, 2024).
7. **Technology Utilization:** Leveraging algorithms, AI, and machine learning to enhance the learner's experience with minimal effort. Tools like LLMs and AI-enabled feedback platforms provide personalized feedback and differentiated

learning paths automatically, reducing manual input and allowing educators to focus on core teaching (Conway, 2024).

To address concerns about how to get started, Conway (2024) offers a practical guide to adopting AI-powered adaptive learning with the principle: Start Small, Scale Gradually. Educators can begin with incremental automation, such as feedback generation, practice questions, or real-time assessments, using a platform's onboarding guide to create personalized quizzes or deliver automated feedback. Tools that require no technical expertise and offer plug-and-play functionality can be utilized. Finally, adaptive learning can be scaled in larger classrooms by allowing AI to handle feedback loops and performance tracking.

To monitor and evaluate learners' performance across adaptive learning platforms, Salman and Alexandron (2024) suggest using digital fingerprints to quantify learning effectiveness. As learners engage with content, their digital fingerprints are reflected in trace data. Big data enables computational modeling of learner's behavior to adapt to individual needs. The learning analytics are categorized into seven types:

1. **Temporal Engagement Metrics (TEM):** These metrics quantify time-related learner activities, such as total time spent on a course, frequency of visits, session duration and distribution, and regularity of study patterns. TEM provides insights into learning behavior, aligning with foundational research on the temporal nature of learning and its impact on outcomes (Knight et al., 2017).
2. **User Interaction Metrics (UIM):** These capture engagement aspects like total logins, session counts, event records, average clicks per second, device usage, and navigational actions within the course (Li et al., 2022; Salman & Alexandron, 2024).
3. **Video Interaction Metrics (VIM):** These include metrics like the number of unique videos watched, time spent on videos, portions viewed, and interaction actions such as play, pause, and speed changes (Jin, 2023; Salman & Alexandron, 2024).
4. **Forum Interaction Metrics (FIM):** These focus on social learning activities in forums, including threads viewed, posts read, and questions asked. Natural Language Processing methods can extract meaningful features from forum activity (Li et al., 2022; Salman & Alexandron, 2024).
5. **Problem Interaction Metrics (PIM):** These capture problem-solving activities, including attempts, success rates, response times, and hint usage (Alexandron et al., 2023; Salman & Alexandron, 2024).

6. **Resource Engagement Metrics (REM):** These metrics measure engagement with supplementary materials, such as pages read in digital textbooks, frequency and duration, downloads, and clicks on external references (Jin, 2023; Salman & Alexandron, 2024).
7. **N-gram:** N-grams model sequences of learning actions by enumerating combinations of length N, such as a trigram representing [watching a video]→[visiting the forum]→[solving a problem] (Jin, 2023; Salman & Alexandron, 2024).

Redesign of Assessments: It is essential to design activities that foster the development of critical thinking, creativity, problem-solving, and digital literacy skills, with an emphasis on the importance of using AI/Gen-AI as a tool to support learning, rather than as a replacement for critical thinking and creative problem-solving. For instance, students may be required to connect course content, class discussions, and lived experience in preparing their assignments. Instructors may encourage collaborative projects where students can work together to apply course concepts in real world situations or problems (Moorhouse et al., 2023). It is also advisable for students to reference their learning experiences in the context of a project, making it more personal and relevant to real-world situations and issues, as well as to the examples and topics covered in class. This reflective practice ensures a fair assessment of students' understanding and abilities, especially if they generate or select material they do not fully comprehend or cannot contextualize within their work (Coulton et al., 2023).

Students can be asked to keep a progress log detailing how they have used Gen-AI and reflect on the use of Gen-AI using a template provided. The guiding questions for reflection include but are not limited to the following: what were the roles and purposes of using Gen-AI tools in your work; how did the use of Gen-AI help you achieve the intended learning outcomes of the assessment: how did the use of Gen-AI influence your work progress and outcomes; which aspects of Gen-AI were particularly beneficial to your work; what were the limitations and challenges you encountered in using Gen-AI tools; if so, how did you overcome them and mitigate the risks; and how would have you used Gen-AI differently in future work.

Acknowledgement of Using Gen-AI tools: To date, concerns remain regarding the effectiveness of detection tools like iThenticate and Turnitin, which are designed to identify plagiarism but may produce false positives and negatives (Alier et al., 2024; Moorhouse et al., 2023; Topinka, 2024). Consequently, institutions can incorporate lessons on the mechanisms and infrastructure of AI, along with its ethical implications and limitations. These lessons should include discussions about bias, fairness, privacy, accuracy, and the academic integrity of using AI tools (Moorhouse et al., 2023). To this end, instructors may require students to declare their use of AI tools in assessments, specifying which tools were used and how they were utilized.

Additionally, instructors can remind students to critically evaluate, verify, and refine AI-generated outputs in their work. To encourage this practice, instructors can incorporate AI-related competencies into assessment rubrics, such as critical thinking, creativity, problem-solving, and digital literacy skills.

Use of Process and Staged Assessment Design: Instructors can design various methods for students to demonstrate their knowledge beyond written text. These methods include traditional forms of assessment such as verbal presentations, paper-based examinations, physical practices, and viva voce, which cannot be directly produced by AI tools (Cassidy, 2023; Coulton et al., 2023; Moorhouse et al., 2023). Breaking larger assignments into smaller pieces is another possible way. Staged assignments can provide information for instructors on student performance, and the opportunity for students to receive formative feedback and/or peer feedback during the learning process (Moorhouse et al., 2023).

Training and Development: To harness the potential of AI/Gen-AI in education, it is crucial to understand its capabilities and limitations, the specific needs of learners and educators, and best practices for integrating AI tools into teaching (Kohnke et al., 2023; Liu & Ma, 2023; Warschauer et al., 2023). AI literacy frameworks have evolved from focusing solely on technical aspects within computer science and engineering to embracing interdisciplinary collaboration. Biagini et al. (2024) advocate for expanding beyond computer science and engineering to include knowledge-based (understanding the principles behind AI algorithms and AI systems), operational (applying AI concepts), critical (enhancing critical thinking), and ethical dimensions (considering justice, responsibility, ethics, and safety). This approach suggests that AI education should not be confined to computer science and engineering alone but integrated across all curricula. This can prepare students for future career challenges (Bao & Li, 2023; Jeon & Lee, 2023; Yim, 2024).

In a critical review of teaching and learning AI literacy, Yim's (2024) study highlights that AI literacy intersects with digital literacy, data literacy, computational thinking, and AI ethics, emphasizing a transdisciplinary approach that considers both technological and societal impacts. Given the interdisciplinary and multi-dimensional nature of AI literacy, it underscores the importance of training and development for educators. Regular workshops can keep them updated on emerging trends and applications. For example, seminars on the forces shaping university education can focus on how technologies like AI/Gen-AI, extended reality, and hybrid campus solutions impact higher education and pedagogical design globally. Teacher-sharing sessions can feature redesigning Gen-AI expected assessments and integrating AI into pedagogies. Involving student AI ambassadors and educators in AI Communities of Practice can help co-design and validate processes for integrating AI into teaching (Lee et al., 2024). As a matter of fact, a good understanding of the challenges and opportunities of adopting AI/Gen-AI can guide the development of support systems and resource allocation (Kohnke et al., 2023; Ulla et al., 2023), while considering institutional contexts, educational goals, strategic priorities, and the diverse needs of learners and educators.

FUTURE RESEARCH DIRECTIONS

This study contributes to existing research by proposing a holistic, interdisciplinary approach to unlocking the power of AI/Gen-AI in the educational sector. By adopting this framework, institutions and educators can ensure the responsible and effective use of AI/Gen-AI tools in learning environments, addressing ethical, technical, and pedagogical considerations. Ultimately, it is expected to lay the groundwork for a more comprehensive and inclusive approach to integrating AI/Gen-AI into pedagogies. These guidelines are based on the current state of AI technology and the surrounding policy landscapes. Given the dynamic nature of both, these guidelines must continuously adapt and evolve. Regular updates are necessary to ensure they remain a valuable resource for institutions, instructors, students, and other stakeholders. In this AI era, humans and machines collaborate to achieve outcomes that neither could accomplish independently (Deloitte, 2023). Human-AI collaboration emphasizes that AI should complement, rather than replace, human educators and students. It is crucial to encourage educators to work proactively and closely with AI systems to provide students with personalized support and guidance, thereby enhancing their learning experience. Ongoing evaluation and research should be conducted to measure the impact of the framework and guidelines on learning effectiveness, and to explore educators' readiness, their adoption and challenges, and professional development requirements within the context of human-AI collaboration. Expanding research effort to focus on interdisciplinary studies and emerging technologies, platforms and tools could further yield a broader range of insights.

CONCLUSION

This chapter provides a guidance framework for the responsible use of Gen-AI tools in learning. By adopting a three-pronged approach, it aims to equip institutions, educators, developers, students, and other stakeholders with guidelines to proactively address challenges from ethical, technical, and pedagogical perspectives, ensuring that Gen-AI tools are used ethically and effectively to enhance student learning. For Gen-AI to be used responsibly, it is crucial to prioritize ethical considerations during implementation. Transparency and consent should be central to the use of Gen-AI in education. Addressing the technical challenges of AI requires a multi-faceted approach that involves human oversight, model robustness, data governance, ethical considerations and accountability. Beyond ethical and technical aspects, it is essential to implement strategies for effectively integrating AI/Gen-AI into pedagogies. Such integration involves ensuring that AI/Gen-AI tools are incorporated into the curricula in ways that align with learning objectives and enhance the educational experience. It is also important to design activities that foster the development of critical thinking, creativity, problem-solving, and digital literacy skills, emphasizing the use of AI/Gen-AI as a tool to support learning rather than as a replacement for critical thinking and creative problem-solving. Ultimately, leveraging both human and artificial intelligence marks a paradigm shift from a traditional knowledge and skills acquisition approach to a more dynamic, intelligence-based framework.

REFERENCES

Abbas, N., Whitfield, J., Atwell, E., Bowman, H., Pickard, T., & Walker, A. (2022). Online chat and chatbots to enhance mature student engagement in higher education. *International Journal of Lifelong Education*, 41(3), 308–326. DOI: 10.1080/02601370.2022.2066213

Acar, O. A. (2024). Commentary: Reimagining marketing education in the age of generative AI. *International Journal of Research in Marketing*, 41(3), 489–495. DOI: 10.1016/j.ijresmar.2024.06.004

Adiguzel, T., Kaya, M. H., & Cansu, F. K. (2023). Revolutionizing education with AI: Exploring the transformative potential of ChatGPT. *Contemporary Educational Technology*, 15(3), ep429. DOI: 10.30935/cedtech/13152

Alexandron, G., Wiltrout, M. E., Berg, A., Gershon, S. K., & Ruipérez-Valiente, J. A. (2023). The effects of assessment design on academic dishonesty, learner engagement, and certification rates in MOOCs. *Journal of Computer Assisted Learning*, 39(1), 141–153. DOI: 10.1111/jcal.12733

Alier, M., Casañ Guerrero, M. J., Amo, D., Severance, C., & Fonseca, D. (2021). Privacy and e-learning: A pending task. *Sustainability (Basel)*, 13(16), 9206. DOI: 10.3390/su13169206

Athanassopoulos, S., Manoli, P., Gouvi, M., Lavidas, K., & Komis, V. (2023). The use of ChatGPT as a learning tool to improve foreign language writing in a multilingual and multicultural classroom. *Advances in Mobile Learning Educational Research*, 3(2), 818–824. DOI: 10.25082/AMLER.2023.02.009

Atlas, S. (2023). ChatGPT for higher education and professional development: A guide to conversational AI. https://digitalcommons.uri.edu/cba_facpubs/548

Bao, Y., & Li, B. (2023). A preliminary study on graduate student instructors' exploration, perception, and use of ChatGPT. *International Journal of Computer-Assisted Language Learning and Teaching*, 13(1), 1–23. DOI: 10.4018/IJCALLT.332873

Bearman, M., Ryan, J., & Ajjawi, R. (2023). Discourses of artificial intelligence in higher education: A critical literature review. *Higher Education*, 86(2), 369–385. DOI: 10.1007/s10734-022-00937-2

Biagini, G., Cuomo, S., & Ranieri, M. (2024). Developing and validating a multidimensional AI literacy questionnaire: Operationalizing AI literacy for higher education. In Schicchi, D., Taibi, D., & Temperini, M. (Eds.), *Proceedings of the first international workshop on high-performance artificial intelligence systems in education* (p. 1), 0.

Boles, C. (2024, April 17). The impact of Generative AI In manufacturing. *Forbes.* https://www.forbes.com/councils/forbestechcouncil/2024/04/17/the-impact-of-generative-ai-in-manufacturing/

Bozkurt, A. (2023). Generative artificial intelligence (AI) powered conversational educational agents: The inevitable paradigm shift. *Asian Journal of Distance Education*, 18(1), 198–204.

Cai, Q., Lin, Y., & Yu, Z. (2023). Factors influencing learner attitudes towards ChatGPT-assisted language learning in higher education. *International Journal of Human-Computer Interaction*, •••, 1–15. DOI: 10.1080/10447318.2023.2291616

Cassidy, C. (2023, January 10). Australian universities to return to 'pen and paper' exams after students caught using AI to write essays. *The Guardian.* https://www.theguardian.com/australianews/2023/jan/10/universities-to-return-to-pen-and-paper-exams-after-students-caught-using-ai-to-write-essays

Chan, C. K. Y., & Hu, W. (2023). Students' voices on generative AI: Perceptions, benefits, and challenges in higher education. *International Journal of Educational Technology in Higher Education*, 20(43), 1–18. DOI: 10.1186/s41239-023-00411-8

Chen, B., Wu, Z., & Zhao, R. (2023a). From fiction to fact: The growing role of generative AI in business and finance. *Journal of Chinese Economic and Business Studies*, 21(4), 471–496. DOI: 10.1080/14765284.2023.2245279

Chen, Y., Xu, Z., & Gong, B. (2023b). Generative design for product innovation: A comprehensive review. *Artificial Intelligence for Engineering Design, Analysis and Manufacturing*, 37(1), 1–35.

Choi, E. P. H., Lee, J. J., Ho, M. H., Kwok, J. Y. Y., & Lok, K. Y. W. (2023). Chatting or cheating? The impacts of ChatGPT and other artificial intelligence language models on nurse education. *Nurse Education Today*, 125, 105796. DOI: 10.1016/j.nedt.2023.105796 PMID: 36934624

Coeckelbergh, M. (2023, March 29). Chatbots can kill. *Medium.* https://coeckelbergh.medium.com/chatbots-can-kill-d82fde5cf6ca

Conway, T. (2024, September 13). Adaptive learning: A practical guide to personalized paths and future-ready teaching. *Linkedin*. https://www.linkedin.com/pulse/adaptive-learning-practical-guide-personalized-paths-conway-ph-d--ixqce

Coulton, P., Jacobs, N., Lindley, J., Richards, D., Stockton, G., & Whitham, R. (2023). Design pedagogy and generative AI. DPxGenAI Working Group, Lancaster University School of Design.

Crawford, J., Cowling, M., & Allen, K. A. (2023). Leadership is needed for ethical ChatGPT: Character, assessment, and learning using artificial intelligence (AI). *Journal of University Teaching & Learning Practice*, 20(3). Advance online publication. DOI: 10.53761/1.20.3.02

Deloitte. (2023). *Proactive risk management in generative AI*. Deloitte AI Institute.

European Commission. (2019). *Ethics guidelines for trustworthy AI*. European Commission.

García-Peñalvo, F. J. (2023). The perception of artificial intelligence in educational contexts after the launch of ChatGPT: Disruption or Panic? *Education in the Knowledge Society*, 24, e31279.

Ghaffar Nia, N., Kaplanoglu, E., & Nasab, A. (2023). Evaluation of artificial intelligence techniques in disease diagnosis and prediction. *Discover Artificial Intelligence*, 3(1), 5. DOI: 10.1007/s44163-023-00049-5

Gilardi, F., Alizadeh, M., & Kubli, M. (2023). ChatGPT outperforms crowd workers for text-annotation tasks. *Proceedings of the National Academy of Sciences of the United States of America*, 120(30), E2305016120. DOI: 10.1073/pnas.2305016120 PMID: 37463210

Gison, C. (2024, April 7). Overcoming the limitations of AI in creative content generation. *Medium*. https://medium.com/@chasegison/overcoming-the-limitations-of-ai-in-creative-content-generation-7e0e08f31207

Goodfellow, I., Pouget-Abadie, J., Mirza, M., Xu, B., Warde-Farley, D., Ozair, S., Courville, A., & Bengio, Y. (2020). Generative adversarial networks. *Communications of the ACM*, 63(11), 139–144. DOI: 10.1145/3422622

Guo, K., & Wang, D. (2024). To resist it or to embrace it? Examining ChatGPT's potential to support teacher feedback in EFL writing. *Education and Information Technologies*, 29(7), 8435–8463. DOI: 10.1007/s10639-023-12146-0

Gupta, M., Akiri, C., Aryal, K., Parker, E., & Praharaj, L. (2023). From ChatGPT to threatGPT: Impact of generative AI in cybersecurity and privacy. *IEEE Access : Practical Innovations, Open Solutions*, 11, 80218–80245. DOI: 10.1109/ACCESS.2023.3300381

Hagiu, A., & Wright, J. (2023). To get better customer data, build feedback loops into your products. *Harvard Business Review*. https://hbr.org/2023/07/to-get-better-customer-data-build-feedback-loops-into-your-products

Harkness, L., Robinson, K., Stein, E., & Wu, W. (2023). *How generative AI can boost consumer marketing*. McKinsey & Company.

Henrickson, L., & Meroño-Peñuela, A. (2023). Prompting meaning: A hermeneutic approach to optimising prompt engineering with ChatGPT. *AI & Society*. https://link.springer.com/article/10.1007/s00146-023-01752-8

Horn, M. B., & Staker, H. (2016). *Blended leaning: 21st century learning revolution*.

Idowu, J. A., Koshiyama, A. S., & Treleaven, P. (2024). Investigating algorithmic bias in student progress monitoring. *Computers and Education: Artificial Intelligence*, 7, 100267. Advance online publication. DOI: 10.1016/j.caeai.2024.100267

Idrees, H. (2024, July 10). The evolution of transformers: From 'attention is all you need' to GPT-4. *Medium*.https://medium.com/@hassaanidrees7/the-evolution-of-transformers-from-attention-is-all-you-need-to-gpt-4-1baac3c038cd

Iskender, A. (2023). Holy or unholy? Interview with Open AI's ChatGPT. *European Journal of Tourism Research*, 34, 3414. DOI: 10.54055/ejtr.v34i.3169

Jeon, J., & Lee, S. (2023). Large language models in education: A focus on the complementary relationship between human teachers and ChatGPT. *Education and Information Technologies*, 28(12), 15873–15892. DOI: 10.1007/s10639-023-11834-1

Jin, C. (2023). MOOC student dropout prediction model based on learning behavior features and parameter optimization. *Interactive Learning Environments*, 31(2), 714–732. DOI: 10.1080/10494820.2020.1802300

Kajiwara, Y., & Kawabata, K. (2024). AI literacy for ethical use of chatbot: Will students accept AI ethics? *Computers and Education: Artificial Intelligence*, 6, 100251. DOI: 10.1016/j.caeai.2024.100251

Knight, S., Wise, A. F., & Chen, B. (2017). Time for change: Why learning analytics needs temporal analysis. *Journal of Learning Analytics*, 4(3), 7–17. DOI: 10.18608/jla.2017.43.2

Kohnke, L., Moorhouse, B. L., & Zou, D. (2023). Exploring generative artificial intelligence preparedness among university language instructors: A case study. *Computers and Education: Artificial Intelligence*, 5, 100156. DOI: 10.1016/j.caeai.2023.100156

Lee, D., Arnold, M., Srivastava, A., Plastow, K., Strelan, P., Ploeckl, F., Lekkas, D., & Palmer, E. (2024). The impact of generative AI on higher education learning and teaching: A study of educators' perspectives. *Computers and Education: Artificial Intelligence*, 6, 100221. DOI: 10.1016/j.caeai.2024.100221

Li, B., Lowell, V. L., Wang, C., & Li, X. N. (2024). A systematic review of the first year of publications on ChatGPT and language education: Examining research on ChatGPT's use in language learning and teaching. *Computers and Education: Artificial Intelligence*, 7, 100266. DOI: 10.1016/j.caeai.2024.100266

Li, S., Du, J., & Sun, J. (2022). Unfolding the learning behaviour patterns of MOOC learners with different levels of achievement. *International Journal of Educational Technology in Higher Education*, 19(1), 22. DOI: 10.1186/s41239-022-00328-8

Liu, G., & Ma, C. (2023). Measuring EFL learners' use of ChatGPT in informal digital learning of English based on the technology acceptance model. *Innovation in Language Learning and Teaching*, •••, 1–14.

Luo, Q. Z., & Hsiao-Chin, L. Y. (2023). The influence of AI-powered adaptive learning platforms on student performance in Chinese classrooms. *Journal of Education*, 6(3), 1–12. DOI: 10.53819/81018102t4181

McGrath, C., Pargman, T. C., Juth, N., & Palmgren, P. J. (2023). University teachers' perceptions of responsibility and artificial intelligence in higher education: An experimental philosophical study. *Computers and Education: Artificial Intelligence*, 4, 100139. DOI: 10.1016/j.caeai.2023.100139

McKinsey. (2023). *What's the future of generative AI? An early view in 15 charts.* McKinsey & Company.

Mohamed, A. M. (2024). Exploring the potential of an AI-based Chatbot (ChatGPT) in enhancing English as a Foreign Language (EFL) teaching: Perceptions of EFL Faculty Members. *Education and Information Technologies*, 29(3), 3195–3217. DOI: 10.1007/s10639-023-11917-z

Moorhouse, B. L., Yeo, M. A., & Wan, Y. W. (2023). Generative AI tools and assessment: Guidelines of the world's top-ranking universities. *Computers & Education*, 5, 100151.

Nazir, A., & Wang, Z. (2023). A comprehensive survey of ChatGPT: Advancements, applications, prospects, and challenges. *Meta-Radiology*, 1(2), 100022. DOI: 10.1016/j.metrad.2023.100022 PMID: 37901715

Nguyen, A., Ngo, H. N., Hong, Y., Dang, B., & Nguyen, B. T. (2023). Ethical principles for artificial intelligence in education. *Education and Information Technologies*, 28(4), 4221–4241. DOI: 10.1007/s10639-022-11316-w PMID: 36254344

Noble, S. U. (2018). *Algorithms of oppression: How search engines reinforce racism.* New York University Press. DOI: 10.18574/nyu/9781479833641.001.0001

Ordax, E. (2024, January 16). Fine tuning vs. pre-training. *Medium.* https://medium.com/@eordaxd/fine-tuning-vs-pre-training-651d05186faf

Patronov, A., Papadopoulos, K., & Engkvist, O. (2022). Has artificial intelligence impacted drug discovery? *Methods in Molecular Biology (Clifton, N.J.)*, 2390, 153–176. DOI: 10.1007/978-1-0716-1787-8_6 PMID: 34731468

Perkins, M., Furze, L., Roe, J., & MacVaugh, J. (2024). The Artificial Intelligence Assessment Scale (AIAS): A framework for ethical integration of generative AI in educational assessment. *Journal of University Teaching & Learning Practice*, 21(6). Advance online publication. DOI: 10.53761/q3azde36

Pranathi Software. (2023, December 6). NLP text summarization for 5 best APIs, AI models. *Medium.* https://medium.com/@pranathisoftwareservices/nlp-text-summarization-for-5-best-apis-ai-models-5b61534483a2

Praveen, S. V., Gajjar, P., Ray, R. K., & Dutt, A. (2024). Crafting clarity: Leveraging large language models to decode consumer reviews. *Journal of Retailing and Consumer Services*, 81, 103975. DOI: 10.1016/j.jretconser.2024.103975

Ratten, V., & Jones, F. (2023). Generative artificial intelligence (ChatGPT): Implications for management educators. *International Journal of Management Education*, 21(3), 100857. DOI: 10.1016/j.ijme.2023.100857

Riemann, C., Ostendorf, S., & Umphres, B. (2024). *Generative AI in transportation management: AI's impact on supply chain logistics*. Deloitte.

Routley, N. (2023). *What is generative AI? An AI explains.* World Economic Forum.

Salman, A., & Alexandron, G. (2024). The digital fingerprint of learner behavior: Empirical evidence for individuality in learning using deep learning. *Computers and Education: Artificial Intelligence*, 100322.

Sanderson, K. (2023, March 16). GPT-4 is here: what scientists think. *Nature.* https://www.nature.com/articles/d41586-023-00816-5

Schulze, S. (2024, April 2). Adaptive learning: What it is & how AI supports it. *Medium.*https://masterplan.com/en-blog/adaptive-learning

Sedkaoui, S., & Benaichouba, R. (2024). Generative AI as a transformative force for innovation: A review of opportunities, applications and challenges. *European Journal of Innovation Management*. Advance online publication. DOI: 10.1108/EJIM-02-2024-0129

Sengupta, S. (2023, April 1). A deep dive into GPT's transformer architecture: Understanding self-attention mechanisms. *GPTFrontier*. https://www.gptfrontier.com/a-deep-dive-into-gpts-transformer-architecture-understanding-self-attention-mechanisms/

Sha, L., Raković, M., Das, A., Gašević, D., & Chen, G. (2022). Leveraging class balancing techniques to alleviate algorithmic bias for predictive tasks in education. *IEEE Transactions on Learning Technologies*, 15(4), 481–492. DOI: 10.1109/TLT.2022.3196278

Sharma, S., Das, A., Birari, A., & Agrawal, S. (2024). *Customer experience unleashed: Harnessing Gen AI and tech innovations for next-level customer engagement*. Everest Group.

Shen, Y. Q., Heacock, L., Elias, J., Hentel, K. D., Reig, B., Shih, G., & Moy, L. (2023). ChatGPT and other large language models are double-edged swords. *Radiology*, 307(2), e230163. DOI: 10.1148/radiol.230163 PMID: 36700838

Siegel, J. (n.d.). *The art of the prompt: How to get the best out of generative AI.* Microsoft. https://news.microsoft.com/source/features/ai/the-art-of-the-prompt-how-to-get-the-best-out-of-generative-ai/

Stackpole, B. (2023). *Why generative AI needs a creative human touch*. MIT Sloan School of Management.

Stokes, J. M., Yang, K., & Adams, J. H. (2023). Generative AI for drug discovery. *Science*, 382(6642), 1001–1010.

Sullivan, M., Kelly, A., & McLaughlan, P. (2023). ChatGPT in higher education: Considerations for academic integrity and student learning. *Journal of Applied Learning and Teaching*, 6(1), 31–40.

Thorp, H. H. (2023). ChatGPT is fun, but not an author. *Science*, 379(6630), 313. DOI: 10.1126/science.adg7879 PMID: 36701446

Tong, M. S., Zheng, H. Q., & Wan, G. C. (2019). Improvement of education method by using artificial intelligence technology. In *2019 IEEE international conference on engineering, technology and education* (TALE) (pp. 1–5). IEEE. DOI: 10.1109/TALE48000.2019.9225891

Topinka, R. (2024, February 13). The software says my student cheated using AI. They say they're innocent. Who do I believe? *The Guardian*. https://www.theguardian.com/commentisfree/2024/feb/13/software-student-cheated-combat-ai

Ulla, M. B., Perales, W. F., & Busbus, S. O. (2023). To generate or stop generating response: Exploring EFL teachers' perspectives on ChatGPT in English language teaching in Thailand. *Learning: Research and Practice*, 9(2), 168–182. DOI: 10.1080/23735082.2023.2257252

UNESCO. (2021). *AI and education: Guidance for policymakers*. United Nations Educational, Scientific and Cultural Organization. https://unesdoc.unesco.org/ark:/48223/pf0000376709

UNESCO, & IRCAI (2024). *Challenging systematic prejudices: An investigation into gender bias in large language models*. The United Nations Educational, Scientific and Cultural Organization (UNESCO) and International Research Centre on Artificial Intelligence (IRCAI). https://www.unesco.org/en/articles/generative-ai-unesco-study-reveals-alarming-evidence-regressive-gender-stereotypes

Walkington, C., & Bernacki, M. L. (2019). Personalizing algebra to students' individual interests in an intelligent tutoring system: Moderators of impact. *International Journal of Artificial Intelligence in Education*, 29(1), 58–88. DOI: 10.1007/s40593-018-0168-1

Warschauer, M., Tseng, W., Yim, S., Webster, T., Jacob, S., Du, Q., & Tate, T. (2023). The affordances and contradictions of AI-generated text for writers of English as a second or foreign language. *Journal of Second Language Writing*, 62, 101071. DOI: 10.1016/j.jslw.2023.101071

Witts, J. (2024, August 20). [AI code generation solutions for developers. *Expert Insights*. https://expertinsights.com/insights/the-top-ai-code-generation-solutions-for-programmers/]. *Top (Madrid)*, 5, •••.

Yim, I. H. Y. (2024). A critical review of teaching and learning artificial intelligence (AI) literacy: Developing an intelligence-based AI literacy framework for primary school education. *Computers and Education: Artificial Intelligence*, 7, 100319. DOI: 10.1016/j.caeai.2024.100319

Yu, R., Li, Q., Fischer, C., Doroudi, S., & Xu, D. (2020). Towards accurate and fair prediction of college success: Evaluating different sources of student data. *Proceedings of the 13th international conference on educational data mining,* 292-301.

Zhang, K., & Aslan, A. B. (2021). AI technologies for education: Recent research and future directions. *Computers & Education*, 2, 100025.

Zharovskikh, A. (2024, April 23). Bias in generative AI: Types, examples, solutions. *InData Labs.* https://indatalabs.com/blog/generative-ai-bias

ADDITIONAL READING

Bowen, J. A., & Watson, C. E. (2024). *Teaching with AI: A practical guide to a new era of human learning*. Johns Hopkins University Press. DOI: 10.56021/9781421449227

Clark, H. (2023). *The AI infused classroom.* Elevate Books EDU.

Douglas, A. (2024). *The AI-powered classroom: A practical guide to enhancing teaching and learning with artificial intelligence.* Graffham Consulting Ltd.

Khan, S. (2024). *Brave new words: How AI will revolutionize education (and why that's a good thing).* Penguin Random House.

Miller, M. (2023). *AI for educators: Learning strategies, teacher efficiencies, and a vision for an artificial intelligence future.* Dave Burgess Consulting, Inc.

Poth, R. D. (2024). *How to teach AI: Weaving strategies and activities into any content area.* International Society for Technology in Education.

Pratschke, B. M. (2024). *Generative AI and education: Digital pedagogies, teaching innovation and learning design.* Springer. DOI: 10.1007/978-3-031-67991-9

Summers, V. R. (2024). *The power of AI for educators: Revolutionize teaching to stay competitive, dramatically reduce workload, and personalize learning to increase student engagement and motivation.* Kindle Edition.

KEY TERMS AND DEFINITIONS

Artificial Intelligence Assessment Scale: A 5-point scale for educators to communicate with students as to the extent of Gen-AI usage in assessments.

Chatbot: A computer program that simulates and processes human conversation with an end user, either written or spoken. Modern chatbots increasingly use conversational AI techniques such as natural language processing to understand user questions and automate responses to them.

Generative AI: A subset of AI that focuses on creating new content, such as images, text, or audio, that is indistinguishable from content created by humans.

GPT-4: The latest iteration in the series of Generative Pre-trained Transformer models developed by OpenAI. It builds on the success of its predecessor, GPT-3, introducing several key improvements in model architecture, training methodology, and performance.

Hallucination: Producing inaccurate outputs with complete confidence.

Large Language Models: A category of foundation models trained on immense amounts of data, enabling them to understand and generate natural language and other types of content to perform a wide range of tasks.

Prompt: Instructions given to an artificial intelligence system, guiding it to generate a specific output or perform a particular task. Prompts can include questions, instructions, contextual information, and partial input for the model to complete or continue. Once the model receives a prompt, depending on its type, it can generate text, embeddings, code, images, videos, music, and more.

Chapter 7
AI-Driven Curriculum Design and Course Management

Andi Asrifan
https://orcid.org/0000-0002-9934-6129
Universitas Negeri Makassar, Indonesia

Ashabul Kahfi Susanto
https://orcid.org/0009-0000-3765-4655
Universitas Negeri Makassar, Indonesia

Elpisah Elpisah
Universitas Patompo, Indonesia

Syamsuardi Saodi
https://orcid.org/0000-0001-8551-9300
Universitas Negeri Makassar, Indonesia

Herlina Herlina
Universitas Negeri Makassar, Indonesia

ABSTRACT

This chapter explores the transformative impact of artificial intelligence (AI) on curriculum design and course management in education. AI-driven systems enable instructors to tailor learning experiences to students' individual needs, learning styles, and progress, enhancing engagement and support through real-time feedback, intelligent tutoring, and data-driven assessments. By automating administrative tasks like grading and scheduling, AI allows teachers to devote more time to instruction and mentoring. However, integrating AI in education raises ethical considerations,

DOI: 10.4018/979-8-3373-1017-6.ch007

particularly regarding data privacy, security, and algorithmic bias. This chapter emphasizes the importance of transparent data practices to protect student information and ensure fairness in AI applications. While AI enhances educational processes, it cannot replace the guidance, empathy, and critical thinking skills that human educators bring. Ultimately, AI complements human instruction, creating a more inclusive, efficient, and adaptable learning environment for all students.

INTRODUCTION

AI is changing curriculum design and course management in education (Mallik & Gangopadhyay, 2023) (Aliabadi et al., 2023) (Johnson et al., 2022). AI is making education more efficient, accessible, and adaptable at all levels, from personalized learning routes to administrative automation. It transforms education delivery, assessment, and optimization beyond technological help. AI-driven curriculum design uses massive data sets to personalize instruction. These systems can recommend learning resources or change course pace based on a learner's skills, weaknesses, progress, and preferences. This individualized approach ensures that each student receives a customized education, enhancing engagement and outcomes. AI also lets teachers evaluate teaching methods and materials in real-time to improve curricula. AI also deeply affects course management. Automating grading, scheduling, and student feedback lets teachers focus on teaching and coaching (Núñez et al., 2023) (Chaudhry & Kazim, 2021). Predictive analytics from AI-powered systems help universities identify underperforming students and suggest early remedies. These systems streamline course management while maintaining excellent education standards. AI helps create dynamic, adaptable learning environments. Gamification, virtual labs, and intelligent tutoring technologies boost student engagement and deliver real-time feedback using AI. These advances make learning more dynamic, immersive, appealing, and successful for various learners.

As AI evolves, its importance in education will grow. Future innovations like AI tutors and virtual classrooms will make learning more accessible and personalized (Kamalov et al., 2023) (Yang, 2021) (Zhang & Aslan, 2021). AI integration requires addressing equality, data privacy, and algorithmic biases. AI can transform education by tackling these difficulties and creating a more inclusive, efficient, and adaptive learning environment. Georgia State University uses AI-driven tutoring (Strielkowski et al., 2024) (Yadav & Shrawankar, 2025). The institution used "Pounce," an AI-based chatbot, to help students with administrative questions, engagement, and dropout rates. Pounce answers enrollment, financial aid, and campus resource issues 24/7 to help students navigate difficult processes and stay on track. Arizona State University uses adaptive learning technologies to personalize student learning (Strielkowski et al., 2024) (Moskal, 2023). These platforms change content and tempo based on each student's progress and needs in real time. If a student struggles with a concept, the platform provides extra resources or practice problems to fill the gap. Both examples show how AI improves operational efficiency by automating administrative duties, facilitates personalized learning, and retains students by giving timely, targeted assistance. These examples highlight how AI can make education more accessible, interesting, and responsive to diverse student requirements, transforming learning in many educational contexts.

Historical Context: From Traditional to AI-Driven Education

The evolution of education has been marked by significant shifts, from traditional models to the current integration of artificial intelligence (AI)(Mallik & Gangopadhyay, 2023) (Aliabadi et al., 2023) (Yao, 2021). Historically, education was based on teacher-centered approaches where knowledge was delivered through lectures, textbooks, and standardized assessments. This model, widely used for centuries, emphasized rote learning and uniformity, with little room for personalization or flexibility in addressing individual student needs. In the early stages of formal education, the focus was primarily on the transmission of information from teacher to student, with limited feedback loops. The curriculum was designed to be one-size-fits-all, if all students learned at the same pace and in the same way. The industrial revolution further reinforced this model, as education systems were structured similarly to factories, aiming to produce a standardized workforce (Abele et al., 2017) (Edgley, 2006). The traditional approach, while effective for its time, often failed to accommodate different learning styles and individual needs, leaving gaps in student engagement and achievement.

The shift towards more learner-centered approaches began in the mid-20th century, with the emergence of theories that emphasized active learning, critical thinking, and student autonomy. Educational reformers like John Dewey and Maria Montessori advocated for more interactive and experiential forms of learning. The introduction of computers into classrooms in the latter half of the 20th century also paved the way for technology-enhanced education, although these early tools were primarily used to supplement traditional teaching methods rather than transform them (Shaji & Nagaraj, 2020) (Chen et al., 2020) (Aflalo, 2014). The advent of the internet and digital learning platforms in the late 1990s and early 2000s marked a pivotal point in education. With the rise of e-learning, students were no longer bound to physical classrooms or fixed schedules. However, while online learning offered flexibility, it still lacked the capacity to fully personalize the learning experience, and challenges in engagement and retention remained.

The integration of AI into education has introduced a new paradigm shift. Unlike previous technological advancements, AI has the ability to fundamentally change how education is delivered. AI-enhanced methodologies offer personalized learning experiences, adapting content and pace to suit individual students' needs. It can analyze vast amounts of data to continuously optimize curricula, making real-time adjustments that were previously impossible. AI-driven education systems enable automated assessments, intelligent tutoring, and predictive analytics to support student success, moving away from one-size-fits-all models to more adaptive and inclusive frameworks (Artificial Intelligence and the Future of Teaching and Learning, 2023) (Núñez et al., 2023).

The Need for AI in Curriculum and Course Management

The demand for personalized, adaptive, and data-driven education models has grown significantly in recent years, driven by the increasing diversity of learners and the rapid pace of technological change. Traditional education systems, which often rely on rigid curricula and standardized instruction, struggle to address the individual needs of students in today's dynamic learning environments (Ogwu et al., 2022). This is where AI steps in, offering innovative solutions that allow for more personalized and flexible approaches to both curriculum design and course management. One of the primary reasons for the need for AI in education is the shift towards personalized learning. Every student has unique learning styles, strengths, and challenges, yet conventional educational methods are not equipped to cater to such diversity. AI-driven tools can analyze a student's performance, preferences, and learning patterns in real-time, adapting the curriculum to ensure that each learner progresses at their own pace. This adaptive learning approach ensures that students receive the right level of challenge, keeping them engaged and preventing them from falling behind or becoming disengaged due to material that is too easy or too difficult (Ray & Pani, 2021) (Taylor et al., 2021).

AI also plays a crucial role in managing the increasing volume of data generated in modern educational environments. Instructors and administrators need to analyze vast amounts of information related to student performance, course effectiveness, and curriculum outcomes. Traditional data analysis methods are time-consuming and often lack the depth needed for actionable insights. AI, however, can process large datasets quickly and accurately, providing educators with real-time analytics that help optimize learning outcomes. This data-driven approach allows for continuous improvement of course content and structure, ensuring that it remains relevant, effective, and aligned with industry demands. In addition to personalization and data analytics, AI is instrumental in streamlining course management tasks (Kabudi et al., 2021) (Magomadov, 2020). By automating administrative duties like grading, scheduling, and feedback, AI reduces the workload on educators, enabling them to focus more on teaching and mentoring. Automated systems can assess student work, provide instant feedback, and even predict which students are at risk of underperforming, allowing for timely interventions. This enhances the overall learning experience and boosts student success rates.

AI-DRIVEN CURRICULUM DESIGN: FOUNDATIONS AND KEY CONCEPTS

AI and Adaptive Learning Systems

AI-powered adaptive learning systems are changing education by adapting content to students' needs and learning styles (Graf & Kinshuk, 2013) (Colchester et al., 2016). These techniques are much better than one-size-fits-all teaching methods that ignore students' different skills, interests, and learning paces. Adaptive learning platforms use AI to tailor information to each student's ability level, learning speed, and preferences. AI-driven adaptive learning systems evaluate and interpret student performance data continually. These systems analyze student behavior with learning materials to determine strengths, shortcomings, and progress. The system can adapt the curriculum to provide more resources, explanations, or practice for a student who repeatedly has difficulties with a topic. If a student masters a subject, the platform can challenge them with more challenging content, boosting engagement and motivation (Joksimovíc et al., 2017). Real-time feedback makes AI-based adaptive learning beneficial (Martin et al., 2020). Adaptive learning platforms can update the curriculum based on student performance, unlike traditional teaching approaches that wait until after an exam or term. This personalization reduces the risk of students falling behind or disengaging by providing support when they need it. These systems consider multiple learning styles. Some students learn visually, others hands-on or auditorily. AI can accommodate these preferences by delivering content via films, interactive simulations, or written explanations (Yannier et al., 2020) (Lowry, 1951). Diverse content distribution improves student engagement and retention because students are more likely to acquire material in their learning style.

AI-driven adaptive learning solutions personalize learning and give educators insights. By evaluating student performance data, teachers might find trends like prevalent problems or effective teaching tactics. This helps instructors make data-driven decisions to improve the curriculum and better serve students. Recent adaptive learning technology research show advances in AI-driven individualized curriculum for individual learning demands. According to García-Martínez et al. (2023), adaptive systems can use real-time data to change course tempo, complexity, and topic concentration based on student performance. AI identifies student weaknesses and provides additional guidance or resources to improve knowledge, making learning more personalized. Kamalov et al. (2023) underline how adaptive learning platforms use cognitive and behavioral data like quiz scores and task time to change instructional pathways. Adjustments keep students engaged without overwhelming them with ideal learning challenges. If a student excels in a topic, the system may expedite the lesson flow, but if they struggle, it slows down or provides extra practice. AI systems that adapt to diverse learning speeds and styles create an inclusive educational environment, according to these findings. Including this research would demonstrate the chapter's relevance to current trends in personalized, data-driven learning and validate AI's revolutionary role in student-centered education.

Personalized Learning Paths

AI is leading the way in personalized learning paths, turning standardized courses into a student-centered experience (Bhutoria, 2022) (Mohammed & Watson, 2019). AI can assess massive volumes of student performance, preference, and progress data to create personalized learning routes that meet individual needs and learning styles. AI-driven systems analyze student learning habits and outcomes to uncover trends for personalized learning (Xie et al., 2019). AI can real-time assess a student's strengths and shortcomings, changing the curriculum to focus on areas that need work and allowing the learner to proceed faster through topics they already know. Instead of a one-size-fits-all approach, students can learn at their own pace and level, keeping them involved and motivated.

Student learning preferences—visual, auditory, or kinesthetic—are also considered in personalized learning paths. AI can present content in each learner's preferred format (Xie et al., 2019). For example, visual learners may receive more diagrams, films, and infographics, while hands-on learners may receive interactive simulations or practical tasks. This customized method improves student engagement and retention by making content more relatable. AI-powered platforms can also track a student's progress and adapt their learning path. This dynamic personalization lets students receive targeted treatments when they struggle and advanced material when they flourish. AI constantly refines the learning path to keep pupils from being overwhelmed or under-stimulated, making learning more efficient and effective (Belfer et al., 2022) (Srinivasan & Murthy, 2021).

AI-driven tailored learning paths provide a learner-centric approach that gives students more control over their education, which is highly beneficial. AI provides continuous feedback and coaching, allowing students to customize their learning journey and focus on areas for improvement (García-Martínez et al., 2023). This motivates and gives them ownership over their education. Personalized learning routes let educators assess student success. AI can identify student struggles, allowing teachers to alter their methods or provide more support. AI can also recommend learning resources to assist teachers choose the best ones for each student.

Curriculum Optimization Through Data Analytics

Optimization of curriculum to meet learning goals and industry demands is more important than ever in today's fast-changing educational scene (Agus et al., 2023) (Li et al., 2008). AI, big data, and learning analytics can help achieve this goal. AI helps educational institutions adjust course content in real time to meet the changing needs of students and the job market by using massive volumes of student data. AI-driven curriculum optimization relies on huge data from learning activities. All student interactions with learning materials—completing an assignment, participating in a discussion, or taking an exam—create data points (Magomadov, 2020). AI systems can examine this data to find student knowledge gaps, trends, and patterns. These insights help educators and curriculum designers identify course strengths and weaknesses. AI can identify areas where many students struggle with a concept and provide extra resources, explanations, or teaching styles.

Beyond reacting to student performance, AI-driven insights enable proactive curriculum modification (Chaudhry & Kazim, 2021). AI can guarantee course content meets goals by comparing student outcomes to learning objectives. AI optimizes continuously, not just after term or semester ends. It updates the curriculum in real time as data suggests improvements. This dynamic strategy keeps students on track to meet learning outcomes and gives teachers quick feedback on their strategies. A key part of AI-based curriculum optimization is aligning educational content with industry needs (Núñez et al., 2023) (Wang & Lester, 2023). Skills and knowledge needed by companies change with the work market. AI can monitor labor market data and job trends to keep courses updated with industry needs. Technology, healthcare, and business require continuously changing abilities; thus, this is crucial. AI helps schools' close skills gaps and improve graduates' employability by integrating real-time industry data into curriculum design. Additionally, AI-driven curriculum optimization incorporates various student demographics. As adult learners, part-time students, and individuals with varied educational backgrounds increase, curriculum must be adaptable enough to fit their learning paces and preferences (Nguyen, 2014). AI can track student progress and adapt content to provide individualized pathways and meet course goals.

ENHANCING COURSE MANAGEMENT WITH AI

AI in Automating Administrative Tasks

AI automates scheduling, grading, student feedback, and performance tracking, revolutionizing course management (Chaudhry & Kazim, 2021). These laborious tasks take up a lot of time and effort for instructors, taking away from teaching and student engagement. With AI-powered tools, educators can focus more on teaching and mentoring and less on administrative tasks. Automatic scheduling is a major way AI is changing course management. Course timelines, meetings, and assignments are time-consuming and demand careful planning. AI systems can automate these processes by assessing classroom availability, instructor scheduling, and student preferences (Meccawy, 2018) (Gunasena et al., 1989). AI can create ideal schedules that avoid conflicts and enhance productivity by digesting this data in real time. Additionally, AI systems may dynamically adapt schedules to accommodate instructor availability and room allocations with minimal disturbance. AI is crucial for automating grading, especially in big classrooms or courses with several evaluations (Núñez et al., 2023). Traditional grading can be time-consuming and biassed. However, AI-driven grading systems can accurately and consistently grade assignments, tests, and essays. Due to NLP improvements, these systems can rapidly grade multiple-choice exams and short answer and essay-style responses. AI can also find patterns in student answers, revealing areas where they require more education.

AI can automate student feedback, another course administration benefit. Timely and constructive feedback is essential for student progress, but it can be difficult for teachers, especially in big classes. AI tools may identify student strengths and weaknesses and provide individualized feedback. AI can analyze student submissions, participation, and evaluations to provide deep insights into student progress, allowing instructors to intervene early if a student is suffering (Zhang et al., 2024). Automated feedback systems give pupils regular, real-time input to grow and learn. AI-powered chatbots and virtual assistants improve educator-student communication (Wollny et al., 2021). These AI-powered applications can answer student questions about course schedules, assignments, and grades, decreasing instructor workload. Automation saves time and ensures students get timely responses. AI-powered administrative systems generate data for long-term course planning in addition to these direct benefits. AI can help teachers change curriculum and teaching methods by monitoring student performance, engagement, and feedback (Zhang & Aslan, 2021). Data-driven course administration and instructional design improve student and educator experiences by streamlining and improving them.

AI-Driven Assessment and Feedback

AI-driven assessment and feedback systems automate grading and give students real-time, individualized feedback, changing education (Lowry et al., 1951) (Swiecki et al., 2022). Advanced algorithms in these systems help educators evaluate student work more efficiently and precisely. AI is changing assessments and student learning by decreasing manual grading and providing immediate, constructive feedback. One of the biggest benefits of AI-driven assessment systems is quick feedback. Traditional grading techniques postpone student feedback (Bayerlein, 2014). By the time they get their results, students may not remember their thoughts or mistakes, which might impair learning. AI-powered grading tools can immediately examine student submissions and provide feedback. Students may immediately learn from their mistakes and change their approach, improving the learning experience. AI-driven grading systems can grade everything from multiple-choice quizzes to essays and coding exercises (Swiecki et al., 2022). AI can now assess written responses for coherence, relevance, and depth thanks to NLP. AI techniques may identify common grammar, structural, and logic errors and recommend improvements. This detailed feedback helps students comprehend their mistakes and improve, deepening their understanding.

In addition, AI systems grade objectively and consistently. Human grading is valuable, but weariness, bias, and subjective interpretation can cause errors. Swiecki et al. (2022) and Lowry et al. (1951) found that AI eliminates these influences and assesses students fairly using preset criteria. In big classes, when grading multiple individuals and tasks might be difficult, this consistency is helpful. AI-driven systems can analyze student performance patterns across time as well as assignments. These systems show a student's learning trajectory by recording several assignments or exams. This data can help teachers target interventions by identifying student strengths and weaknesses (Ysseldyke & Tardrew, 2007) (Du, 2022). If a student frequently does poorly in a certain area, an AI system can notify the educator or recommend extra resources to assist the student improve. AI improves formative assessment, which monitors student development and provides feedback rather than a final mark. AI tools can generate quizzes, assignments, and practice problems that adjust in difficulty based on a student's performance (Tomasik et al., 2018) (Mozer et al., 2019). This dynamic method engages students and challenges and supports them throughout their education.

Intelligent Tutoring Systems (ITS)

Intelligent Tutoring Systems (ITS) powered by artificial intelligence are revolutionizing how students receive tailored educational support (Yuce et al., 2019) (Walker et al., 2013). AI-driven tutoring systems customize curriculum and feedback for each student. ITS tracks student progress in real time and targets problem areas, making learning more engaging and effective. ITS's main benefit is personalized education like a tutor. Time and financial constraints make it hard for traditional classrooms to meet each student's needs (Nye, 2014). ITS can tailor assistance based on a student's learning pace, skills, and limitations. A learner struggling with a math idea can use the system to get more practice problems, step-by-step explanations, and relevant resources. This tailored approach ensures each student receives support regardless of class size or resource limitations. ITS tracks student progress on every encounter in addition to tailored education. The algorithm can identify trends like repeated errors or topics that need more review (Xhakaj et al., 2016) (Yuce, 2019). ITS finds trends in student progress that educators may miss. This provides early interventions for failing students, averting further decline. If a student repeatedly does poorly in a subject, the system might inform the educator or recommend more materials, tutoring, or alternate teaching methods to aid the student.

Targeted interventions are key to ITS. AI-powered technologies estimate student obstacles based on learning trends. ITS can change difficulty, provide extra workouts, and provide hints (Bhagat et al., 2018). This keeps pupils from being overwhelmed by difficult subjects or bored by easy material. ITS keeps students engaged and motivated by maintaining an ideal level of difficulty, fostering consistent learning progress. ITS works across many subjects and learning methods. The system may tailor teaching to science, language, and history students' inclinations. ITS is useful in elementary, higher, and corporate learning environments due of its adaptability. Intelligent Tutoring Systems also aid educators by offering detailed insights into student performance (Yuce et al., 2019) (Bhagat et al., 2018). Teachers can obtain complete data provided by ITS, which shows areas where students are excelling or suffering. This data allows teachers to adjust their lessons to class issues or specific students who need more help.

Educational settings with limited resources have many problems when implementing AI. First, underfunded schools struggle to afford AI infrastructure, including modern gear, software, and upkeep. Many organizations cannot afford expensive AI technology, preventing them from embracing these transformative tools. Rural and low-income areas lack reliable internet, up-to-date computers, and enough storage for AI adoption, compounding this challenge. Professional training is another obstacle. AI tools generally demand specialized understanding for educators and administrators. In low-resource schools, AI training can be expensive and time-consuming, hindering curriculum integration. Partnerships with technology companies can help solve these problems. Scalable, low-cost AI solutions for resource-constrained situations allow schools to use fundamental AI functions without breaking the bank. By using external servers, open-source AI tools and cloud platforms cut infrastructure expenses. Accessible professional development programs, possibly financed by AI vendors or educational funding, can help educators use AI effectively. These solutions can help underfunded schools integrate AI and reap its educational benefits.

THE ROLE OF AI IN ENHANCING LEARNING ENGAGEMENT

Gamification and AI-Enhanced Learning Environments

Tenório et al. (2018) and Hakak et al. (2019) show how AI-powered gamification is changing education by developing dynamic, interactive learning environments that engage students. AI-driven educational platforms may customize and motivate learning by adding goals, challenges, and leaderboards. This method makes learning fun and keeps students focused on their goals. AI-enhanced gamification adapts to student preferences, learning styles, and motivations. AI lets learners customize gamified aspects to meet their needs, unlike traditional learning environments (Bhutoria, 2022). Some students enjoy competition and earning badges, while others prefer collaboration or exploration-driven challenges. AI systems alter gamified aspects in real time based on student behavior, engagement, and performance to keep the experience challenging and rewarding.

AI-powered gamification improves learning by delivering instant feedback and prizes, which keep students engaged (Alsawaier, 2017). When students finish a task or reach a milestone, AI systems can provide quick feedback on their progress and areas for development. Like famous games' feedback loops, this immediate reinforcement informs players of their achievements and next actions. This gives students a sense of accomplishment and progress, encouraging them to learn. AI can also dynamically modify task and challenge level based on student achievement (Holstein et al., 2020). To push high-achieving students, the system can present increasingly difficult problems. The AI can also help struggling students with simpler tasks or more resources. For long-term engagement, AI-driven gamification adapts to keep learning challenging but not too easy.

AI enriches gamified environments by boosting collaboration and peer engagement and personalizing learning. AI systems can group students by ability level, learning choice, or interest, encouraging teamwork and competition to engage and deepen learning. Students may work together to complete a group challenge or compete in a friendly problem-solving contest, with AI balancing teams and assigning tasks based on ability. Moreover, AI-enhanced gamification goes beyond traditional classrooms and may be used to virtual learning settings, making it particularly effective in online education. AI-powered platforms can replicate immersive environments where students solve challenges in real-world scenarios, participate in role-playing exercises, or engage in interactive simulations that make abstract concepts more tangible (Johnson & Levine, 2008) (Zhang & Aslan, 2021). These engaging environments allow students to experiment, fail safely, and learn via trial and error, which is rare in traditional education.

AI-Driven Interactive Simulations and Virtual Labs

AI-powered interactive simulations and virtual labs are giving students safe, controlled hands-on learning experiences (Yannier et al., 2020). These AI-powered tools let students apply theoretical knowledge to real-world situations, improving their comprehension and memory of complex concepts. AI simulates real-life scenarios and locations to provide immersive learning experiences that are hard to recreate in regular classrooms. An important benefit of AI-driven simulations and virtual labs is that they give students practical, hands-on experience without the hazards or costs (Sánchez-Caballé et al., 2020). In medicine, engineering, and science, labs and resources are scarce or expensive. AI-powered virtual labs can accurately imitate these environments, allowing students to conduct experiments, run diagnostics, and control virtual equipment like in real life. Virtual labs allow medical students to practice surgery without risk before working on patients. Engineering students can design and test buildings virtually, learning from triumphs and failures without purchasing resources.

AI improves simulations by delivering real-time feedback and adaptive learning (Swiecki et al., 2022) (Kleinheksel, 2014). AI can track students' actions, assess their judgments, and provide quick feedback in virtual environments. In a chemistry virtual lab, a student who mixes chemicals wrongly may receive a warning or corrective feedback to assist them learn the correct process. Real-time feedback helps students understand the topic and learn via trial and error, which is essential to experiential learning. AI can also change assignment complexity based on student achievement to keep students engaged without overwhelming them. AI-powered simulations and virtual labs can construct complex, dynamic situations that meet diverse learning objectives (Wieman et al., 2008) (Sánchez-Caballé et al., 2020). In a business simulation, students operate a virtual company and make marketing, finance, and HR decisions. Students must modify their plans in real time to change market conditions, unanticipated hurdles, and competitive pressures from the AI system. This comprehensive, interactive learning experience develops critical thinking and problem-solving abilities and prepares students for real-world uncertainty.

Additionally, AI-driven virtual labs offer scalable and accessible learning. Virtual simulations can provide high-quality, hands-on learning for students in distant or impoverished places without access to modern labs (Brinson, 2015). This democratizes education, giving more students access to advanced tools and resources regardless of location or income. Flexible simulations allow students to practice and experiment at their own speed, revisiting concepts or experiments as needed to enhance learning. AI-driven simulations and virtual labs improve individual and group learning. Student teams can solve problems or compete in virtual environments. AI can pair students with comparable ability levels or complement talents to create a collaborative learning environment that mimics real-world teamwork.

AI-Generated Adaptive Learning Materials

Personalized, dynamic AI-generated learning materials like quizzes, assignments, and simulations are revolutionizing education by adapting to individual learners' needs in real-time (Núñez et al., 2023) (Taylor et al., 2021). These materials use artificial intelligence to monitor student performance and present content that challenges or supports them, making learning more entertaining and effective. AI motivates students and optimizes learning speed by adapting difficulty, tempo, and content type to their abilities. AI-generated adaptive learning materials can rapidly adjust to student performance. AI systems monitor student replies, assess their understanding, and adjust the content (Kamalov et al., 2023). To challenge students, the AI system may ask more difficult questions if they master a concept in a quiz. If the learner struggles with certain areas, the AI can provide more practice problems, shorter explanations, or a new format (e.g., video or interactive simulation) to help them understand. This ongoing adjustment offers a personalized learning route that helps pupils improve their weakest skills.

By aligning information with student learning, AI-generated adaptive materials help preserve student interest (Phillips et al., 2020). Static texts and pre-designed exams generally ignore student learning speeds. Some students quickly comprehend topics and get bored with repeating exercises, while others may feel overwhelmed if the material moves too fast. AI solves this problem by customizing learning, so the level of difficulty matches the student's ability. This keeps pupils challenging but not overworked, boosting engagement and lowering dissatisfaction. Additionally, AI-generated learning materials improve formative assessment. AI systems can guide students through learning by monitoring student interactions in real time (Liang et al., 2023). An AI-generated quiz may flag incorrect answers and provide explanations or recommendations, allowing students to correct mistakes quickly. By correcting mistakes immediately, this feedback enhances retention and understanding.

In addition to quizzes and assignments, AI-driven simulations can aid adaptive learning. These simulations offer hands-on, interactive learning that adapts to student input. In a virtual lab, a student's solution may activate different scenarios, making learning more personalized and immersive. These adaptive simulations promote deeper engagement by tailoring tasks to learners' ability levels, encouraging critical thinking and problem-solving. AI-generated adaptable materials are useful for varied learning contexts due to their scalability and accessibility (Kadaruddin, 2023) (Holstein et al., 2020). AI can personalize curriculum for students in huge university classes, online courses, and corporate training programs, assuring success for all. AI can offer material in text, video, simulations, or interactive activities based on the student's learning style.

CHALLENGES AND ETHICAL CONSIDERATIONS IN AI-DRIVEN EDUCATION

Privacy and Data Security in AI-Enhanced Learning

Privacy and data security concerns are growing as AI-driven education collects and uses student data. AI-powered educational systems collect massive amounts of personal and academic data to tailor learning (Luan et al., 2020) (Boddington, 2017). However, this data dependence makes sensitive data vulnerable to misuse, breaches, and unauthorized access. Student data volume is a major issue in AI-enhanced learning (Ma & Jiang, 2023). AI systems track learning patterns, assessment outcomes, age, location, and behavioral features. This data is useful for personalizing education, but improper handling can be dangerous. Data breaches, unlawful access, or malicious use of personal information can lead to identity theft or student profiling. To preserve this sensitive data, educational institutions must establish strong data protection procedures.

AI system utilization of student data raises ethical and security concerns. AI platforms use algorithms to analyze and forecast student performance, which can affect interventions, course placements, and grading. If not managed properly, data-driven decision-making could result in skewed outcomes or unfair treatment of specific student groups. Educational institutions must ensure that AI systems use data transparently and that students and parents are aware of this (Akgün & Greenhow, 2021). Preventing data misuse that harms or disadvantages students requires clear guidelines. AI-enhanced learning privacy and data security also depend on consent. The extent of data collection and analysis may be unclear to students, especially younger ones. Students and their guardians must give informed consent to data collection, use, and access. Transparency increases student-institution trust, which is essential for AI-driven learning settings.

Educational institutions must implement strict data security measures to reduce privacy threats (Tsai et al., 2020) (Huang, 2023). To safeguard student data, use encryption, access limitations, and security audits. When possible, anonymize data to lessen breach identification risk. The European General Data Protection Regulation (GDPR) and the US Family Educational Rights and Privacy Act (FERPA) require institutions to handle student data in accordance with tight criteria. Student data privacy raises ethical considerations in AI-driven education (Berendt et al., 2020). For personalized learning, AI systems collect academic performance, learning habits, and sometimes behavioral data. AI systems' richness of data makes them ideal targets for data breaches, putting students' personal data at danger. To preserve student data and sustain AI system confidence, strong security and data anonymization are necessary.

Algorithmic bias, when AI models trained on unrepresentative data favor particular groups, is another major issue. AI grading systems educated on data from high-performing institutions may underestimate the potential of underprivileged children. Biases can limit chances and perpetuate inequities for pupils of different socioeconomic origins. This requires developers and instructors to employ varied, balanced datasets and routinely verify AI algorithms for fairness. Human oversight of AI decision-making can also discover and reduce biases. We must address these ethical issues to guarantee that AI improves educational equity and does not perpetuate disparities (Kunjumuhammed, 2024).

Bias and Fairness in AI Algorithms

As AI becomes more incorporated into education, prejudice in AI algorithms is a major ethical issue. AI systems, which personalize learning, assess student performance, and anticipate outcomes, make decisions using massive information. If these databases contain biased information, AI algorithms may perpetuate or worsen inequities, unfairly treating specific student groups. AI-driven education must prioritize fairness and prejudice prevention to ensure equitable learning chances for all students (Feuerriegel et al., 2020; Çelik, 2022). Historical data used to train AI systems may reveal societal biases such as race, gender, socioeconomic class, and others (Çelik, 2022; Yargar et al., 2019; Allam et al., 2023). When trained on data that overrepresents wealthier students, an algorithm designed to predict student success may favor them and underestimate those from underprivileged backgrounds. If the training data misrepresents student writing styles or learning patterns, AI systems employed in automated grading may disadvantage non-native speakers and minority students.

An example of bias is biased learning suggestions. Based on biased data, AI systems that monitor student performance may offer more difficult courses or resources to some students and less difficult content to others. This can reinforce inequality by limiting opportunities for some children to succeed. Promoting equity in AI-driven education requires fair access to learning materials and support for all students (Çelik, 2022). Educational institutions and AI developers must construct transparent, bias-tested algorithms to address these problems (Akgün & Greenhow, 2021). Making sure AI model datasets are varied and reflective of all students is crucial. To avoid bias, include data from different demographic groups, learning styles, and educational situations. It's also important to audit AI systems regularly to find and fix bias. Developers should evaluate fairness from data gathering to algorithm design and implementation in AI. AI openness is essential. Students, educators, and parents should understand how AI algorithms make judgments, what data they use, and how biases are minimized. Transparency builds trust and allows for closer inspection, identifying and addressing biases early. Diverse teams of educators, data scientists, and ethicists can design and create AI systems to assure varied perspectives and reduce bias (Chen et al., 2023). Adding human oversight to AI decision-making reduces bias. AI can analyze data faster and more efficiently than humans, but educators should verify AI-generated recommendations, especially when they affect high-stakes decisions like course placements or exams. Human-AI collaboration can find and fix biases that automated systems miss.

The Role of Teachers in AI-Driven Classrooms

Teachers' roles are changing as AI becomes increasingly common in education. AI can personalize learning, automate administrative processes, and provide real-time feedback, but it cannot replace human teachers (Guilherme, 2017). AI-driven classrooms require instructors to combine technology's benefits with human-centered learning. Teachers guide students, encourage critical thinking, and provide emotional support that AI cannot. One of the biggest changes AI makes to the classroom is its ability to grade, track student progress, and organize course materials. Teachers may focus on instructional design, mentorship, and student interaction without administrative constraints thanks to automation. AI can give statistics on student performance and recommend individualized learning paths, but teachers must evaluate this data to fulfill individual needs and emotional well-being (Holstein et al., 2019; Rožman et al., 2023). Teachers can employ AI-generated insights to better understand each student's strengths and challenges, but they must also engage with kids personally because learning is about human growth as well as academic progress.

AI systems can adjust information to kids' learning styles, but teachers foster critical thinking and creativity. AI is good at providing factual information and responding to student performance, but it can't inspire intellectual curiosity, deeper debates, or thinking beyond formulaic answers. Teachers must foster learning environments where students ask questions, explore ideas, and solve problems (Roeper et al., 2014) (Fahri, 2022). This combination between AI's efficiency and human-centered instruction makes pupils active learners. AI affects teachers' mentoring and emotional support. Student learning is social and emotional, and AI cannot replace encouragement, inspiration, and understanding. Teachers must form relationships with pupils, recognize emotional and social issues, and provide holistic support. AI can personalize curriculum, but only teachers can offer empathy and support to help children overcome obstacles and build resilience (Lei et al., 2023). Teachers in AI-driven classrooms must also adjust to new tech. To use AI tools in teaching, teachers need professional development and continuing learning. AI should complement instructors' job by helping them interact with students and personalize learning.

CONCLUSION

Finally, AI is making curriculum creation and course management more tailored, efficient, and accessible. This move from one-size-fits-all to adaptive, data-driven methods is changing how students learn and how educators accommodate various needs. From automating administrative duties to delivering real-time feedback and producing adaptive learning routes, AI makes education more responsive to student and industry needs. AI-driven adaptive learning systems, intelligent tutoring systems, and automated assessments serve students in real time and improve instruction. However, AI in education raises serious ethical and practical issues. Data privacy, algorithmic bias, and teacher roles in AI-enhanced schools must be considered. To preserve student data and ensure fairness, educators and legislators must implement strong safeguards and transparent policies. AI can improve education, but it cannot replace empathy, mentorship, and critical thinking. Teachers are vital for deeper learning and adopting AI-driven insights for holistic growth. As technology advances, AI in education may deliver more personalized, inclusive, and engaging learning experiences. Education systems globally may become more equal and successful by tackling present obstacles and embracing AI's potential, empowering students to attain their full potential through creative, AI-driven learning environments.

REFERENCES

Abele, E., Chryssolouris, G., Sihn, W., Metternich, J., ElMaraghy, H., Seliger, G., Sivard, G., ElMaraghy, W., Hummel, V., Tisch, M., & Seifermann, S. (2017, January 1). Learning factories for future oriented research and education in manufacturing. Elsevier BV, 66(2), 803-826. DOI: 10.1016/j.cirp.2017.05.005

Aflalo, E. (2014, May 14). The Invisible Barrier to Integrating Computer Technology in Education. *Canadian Center of Science and Education*, 3(2). Advance online publication. DOI: 10.5539/jel.v3n2p120

Agus, M., Purnomo, W., Fatkhurohman, A., Marifah, M., Mardliyah, S., & Supratikta, H. (2023, July 13). The Impact of Implementation of the 2013 Curriculum Transition to the Independent Learning Curriculum on Learning Interests of SMA Negeri 9 Students in South Tangerang., 06(07). DOI: 10.47191/jefms/v6-i7-16

Akgün, S., & Greenhow, C. (2021, September 22). Artificial intelligence in education: Addressing ethical challenges in K-12 settings. *AI and Ethics*, 2(3), 431–440. DOI: 10.1007/s43681-021-00096-7 PMID: 34790956

Akgün, S., & Greenhow, C. (2021, September 22). Artificial intelligence in education: Addressing ethical challenges in K-12 settings. *AI and Ethics*, 2(3), 431–440. DOI: 10.1007/s43681-021-00096-7 PMID: 34790956

Aliabadi, R., Singh, A., & Wilson, J E. (2023, January 1). Transdisciplinary AI Education: The Confluence of Curricular and Community Needs in the Instruction of Artificial Intelligence. Springer International Publishing, 137-151. DOI: 10.1007/978-981-99-7947-9_11

Allam, H., Dempere, J., Akre, V., & Flores, P. (2023, January 1). Artificial Intelligence in Education (AIED): Implications and Challenges. Atlantis Press, 126-140. DOI: 10.2991/978-94-6463-286-6_10

Alsawaier, R S. (2017, November 14). The effect of gamification on motivation and engagement. Emerald Publishing Limited, 35(1), 56-79. DOI: 10.1108/IJILT-02-2017-0009

Artificial Intelligence and the Future of Teaching and Learning. (2023, December 4). https://tech.ed.gov/files/2023/05/ai-future-of-teaching-and-learning-report.pdf

Bayerlein, L. (2014, January 9). Students' feedback preferences: how do students react to timely and automatically generated assessment feedback?. Taylor & Francis, 39(8), 916-931. DOI: 10.1080/02602938.2013.870531

Belfer, R., Kochmar, E., & Serban, I V. (2022, January 1). Raising Student Completion Rates with Adaptive Curriculum and Contextual Bandits. Springer Science+Business Media, 724-730. DOI: 10.1007/978-3-031-11644-5_74

Berendt, B., Littlejohn, A., & Blakemore, M. (2020). AI in education: Learner choice and fundamental rights. *Learning, Media and Technology*, 45(3), 312–324. ucl.ac.uk. DOI: 10.1080/17439884.2020.1786399

Bhagat, K K., Rodrigo, M M T., & Chang, C. (2018, May 11). Current status, challenges, and opportunities of the Intelligent Tutoring System (ITS) in developing countries in Asia. Informa, 382-395. DOI: 10.4324/9781315694382-36

Bhutoria, A. (2022, January 1). Personalized education and Artificial Intelligence in the United States, China, and India: A systematic review using a Human-In-The-Loop model. Elsevier BV, 3, 100068-100068. DOI: 10.1016/j.caeai.2022.100068

Boddington, P. (2017, January 1). Towards a Code of Ethics for Artificial Intelligence. Springer International Publishing. DOI: 10.1007/978-3-319-60648-4

Brinson, J R. (2015, July 10). Learning outcome achievement in non-traditional (virtual and remote) versus traditional (hands-on) laboratories: A review of the empirical research. Elsevier BV, 87, 218-237. DOI: 10.1016/j.compedu.2015.07.003

Çelik, İ. (2022, August 29). Towards Intelligent-TPACK: An empirical study on teachers' professional knowledge to ethically integrate artificial intelligence (AI)-based tools into education. Elsevier BV, 138, 107468-107468. DOI: 10.1016/j.chb.2022.107468

Chaudhry, M. A., & Kazim, E. (2021, July 7). Artificial Intelligence in Education (AIEd): A high-level academic and industry note 2021. *SSRN*, 2(1), 157–165. DOI: 10.2139/ssrn.3833583 PMID: 34790953

Chen, X., Xie, H., & Hwang, G. (2020, January 1). A multi-perspective study on Artificial Intelligence in Education: grants, conferences, journals, software tools, institutions, and researchers. Elsevier BV, 1, 100005-100005. DOI: 10.1016/j.caeai.2020.100005

Chen, Y., Clayton, E. W., Novak, L. L., Anders, S., & Malin, B. (2023, March 24). Human-Centered Design to Address Biases in Artificial Intelligence. *Journal of Medical Internet Research*, 25, e43251–e43251. DOI: 10.2196/43251 PMID: 36961506

Colchester, K., Hagras, H., Alghazzawi, D., & Aldabbagh, G. (2016, December 17). A Survey of Artificial Intelligence Techniques Employed for Adaptive Educational Systems within E-Learning Platforms. Polish Neural Network Society, the University of Social Sciences in Lodz & Czestochowa University of Technology, 7(1), 47-64. DOI: 10.1515/jaiscr-2017-0004

Du, Y. (2022, January 4). Application of the Data-Driven Educational Decision-Making System to Curriculum Optimization of Higher Education. Wiley, 2022, 1-8. DOI: 10.1155/2022/5823515

Edgley, R. (2006, July 9). Education for Industry. https://www.tandfonline.com/doi/full/10.1080/0013188770200104

Fahri, L M. (2022, August 31). The Effect of Problem-Based Learning Strategies and Direct Learning Strategies on Students' Fiqh Learning Outcomes. Altezoro s.r.o. (Slovak Republic) and Publishing Center "Dialog" (Ukraine), 8(8), 2025-2031. DOI: 10.22178/pos.84-5

Feuerriegel, S., Dolata, M., & Schwabe, G. (2020, May 11). Fair AI. *Business & Information Systems Engineering*, 62(4), 379–384. DOI: 10.1007/s12599-020-00650-3

García-Martínez, I., Batanero, J. M. F., Cerero, J. F., & León, S. P. (2023, January 1). Analysing the Impact of Artificial Intelligence and Computational Sciences on Student Performance: Systematic Review and Meta-analysis. *University of Alicante*, 12(1), 171–171. DOI: 10.7821/naer.2023.1.1240

Graf, S., & Kinshuk, K. (2013, May 22). Adaptive Technologies. Springer Nature, 771-779. DOI: 10.1007/978-1-4614-3185-5_62

Guilherme, A. (2017, February 4). AI and education: The importance of teacher and student relations. *AI & Society*, 34(1), 47–54. DOI: 10.1007/s00146-017-0693-8

Gunasena, U., Kumara, S., & Soyster, A L. (1989, January 1). A KNOWLEDGE-BASED SYSTEM FOR COURSE SCHEDULING. Taylor & Francis, 3(4), 463-482. DOI: 10.1080/08839518908949938

Hakak, S., Noor, N F M., Ayub, M. N., Affal, H., Hussin, N., Ahmed, E., & Imran, M. (2019, March 5). Cloud-assisted gamification for education and learning. https://www.sciencedirect.com/science/article/pii/S0045790618304968

Holstein, K., Aleven, V., & Rummel, N. (2020, January 1). A Conceptual Framework for Human–AI Hybrid Adaptivity in Education. Springer Science+Business Media, 240-254. DOI: 10.1007/978-3-030-52237-7_20

Holstein, K., Aleven, V., & Rummel, N. (2020, January 1). A Conceptual Framework for Human–AI Hybrid Adaptivity in Education. Springer Science+Business Media, 240-254. DOI: 10.1007/978-3-030-52237-7_20

Holstein, K., Aleven, V., & Rummel, N. (2020, January 1). A Conceptual Framework for Human–AI Hybrid Adaptivity in Education. Springer Science+Business Media, 240-254. DOI: 10.1007/978-3-030-52237-7_20

Holstein, K., McLaren, B M., & Aleven, V. (2019, January 1). Designing for Complementarity: Teacher and Student Needs for Orchestration Support in AI-Enhanced Classrooms. Springer Science+Business Media, 157-171. DOI: 10.1007/978-3-030-23204-7_14

Huang, L. (2023, June 30). Ethics of Artificial Intelligence in Education. *Student Privacy and Data Protection.*, 16(2), 2577–2587. DOI: 10.15354/sief.23.re202

Johnson, D., Alsharid, M., El-Bouri, R., Mehdi, N., Shamout, F. E., Szenicer, A., Toman, D., & Binghalib, S. (2022, June 28). An Experience Report of Executive-Level Artificial Intelligence Education in the United Arab Emirates. *Association for the Advancement of Artificial Intelligence*, 36(11), 12766–12773. DOI: 10.1609/aaai.v36i11.21555

Johnson, L. F., & Levine, A. H. (2008, April 16). Virtual Worlds: Inherently Immersive. *Theory into Practice*, 47(2), 161–170. DOI: 10.1080/00405840801992397

Joksimovíc, S., Poquet, O., Kovanović, V., Dowell, N., Mills, C., Gašević, D., Dawson, S., Graesser, A. C., & Brooks, C. (2017, November 14). How Do We Model Learning at Scale? A Systematic Review of Research on MOOCs. *Review of Educational Research*, 88(1), 43–86. DOI: 10.3102/0034654317740335

Kabudi, T., Pappas, I O., & Olsen, D H. (2021, January 1). AI-enabled adaptive learning systems: A systematic mapping of the literature. Elsevier BV, 2, 100017-100017. DOI: 10.1016/j.caeai.2021.100017

Kadaruddin, K. (2023, August 2). Empowering Education through Generative AI. *Innovative Instructional Strategies for Tomorrow's Learners.*, 4(2), 618–625. DOI: 10.56442/ijble.v4i2.215

Kamalov, F., Calonge, D. S., & Gurrib, I. (2023, August 16). New Era of Artificial Intelligence in Education: Towards a Sustainable Multifaceted Revolution. *Sustainability (Basel)*, 15(16), 12451–12451. DOI: 10.3390/su151612451

Kamalov, F., Calonge, D. S., & Gurrib, I. (2023, August 16). New Era of Artificial Intelligence in Education: Towards a Sustainable Multifaceted Revolution. *Sustainability (Basel)*, 15(16), 12451–12451. DOI: 10.3390/su151612451

Kleinheksel, A. (2014, May 17). Transformative Learning through Virtual Patient Simulations. *Clinical Simulation in Nursing*, 10(6), e301–e308. DOI: 10.1016/j.ecns.2014.02.001

Kunjumuhammed, S. K. (2024). Artificial Intelligence in Addressing Educational Inequality Dimensions in Higher Education Institutions (HEIs): A Critical Review. Risks and Challenges of AI-Driven Finance: Bias, Ethics, and Security, 146-164. [HTML]

Lean, J., Moizer, J., Derham, C., Strachan, L., & Bhuiyan, Z. (2020, November 5). Real World Learning: Simulation and Gaming. Springer Nature, 187-214. DOI: 10.1007/978-3-030-46951-1_9

Lei, L., Li, J., & Li, W. (2023, April 4). Assessing the role of artificial intelligence in the mental healthcare of teachers and students. Springer Science+Business Media. DOI: 10.1007/s00500-023-08072-5

Li, E Y., Yen, H J R., & Cheng, C J. (2008, January 9). A fit-gap analysis of e-business curricula and job demand in Taiwan and the US. Elsevier BV, 51(3), 969-987. DOI: 10.1016/j.compedu.2007.09.013

Liang, J., Wang, L., Luo, J., Yan, Y., & Fan, C. (2023, December 22). The relationship between student interaction with generative artificial intelligence and learning achievement: Serial mediating roles of self-efficacy and cognitive engagement. *Frontiers of Medicine*, 14, 1285392. Advance online publication. DOI: 10.3389/fpsyg.2023.1285392 PMID: 38187430

Lowry, O., Rosebrough, N., Farr, A., & Randall, R. (1951, November 1). PROTEIN MEASUREMENT WITH THE FOLIN PHENOL REAGENT. Elsevier BV, 193(1), 265-275. DOI: 10.1016/S0021-9258(19)52451-6

Luan, H., Géczy, P., Lai, H., Gobert, J. D., Yang, S. J., Ogata, H., Baltes, J., Guerra, R. D. S., Li, P., & Tsai, C. (2020, October 19). Challenges and Future Directions of Big Data and Artificial Intelligence in Education. *Frontiers of Medicine*, 11, 580820. Advance online publication. DOI: 10.3389/fpsyg.2020.580820 PMID: 33192896

Ma, X., & Jiang, C. (2023, May 30). On the Ethical Risks of Artificial Intelligence Applications in Education and Its Avoidance Strategies., 14, 354-359. DOI: 10.54097/ehss.v14i.8868

Magomadov, V. S. (2020, November 1). The application of artificial intelligence and Big Data analytics in personalized learning. *Journal of Physics: Conference Series*, 1691(1), 012169–012169. DOI: 10.1088/1742-6596/1691/1/012169

Mallik, S., & Gangopadhyay, A. (2023, May 5). Proactive and reactive engagement of artificial intelligence methods for education: A review. *Frontiers of Medicine*, 6, 1151391. Advance online publication. DOI: 10.3389/frai.2023.1151391 PMID: 37215064

Martin, F., Chen, Y., Moore, R L., & Westine, C D. (2020, June 15). Systematic review of adaptive learning research designs, context, strategies, and technologies from 2009 to 2018. Springer Science+Business Media, 68(4), 1903-1929. DOI: 10.1007/s11423-020-09793-2

Meccawy, M. (2018, July 29). The Brilliant Scheduler: Automated Scheduling System for Video Conferencing Courses. *Canadian Center of Science and Education*, 11(3), 82–82. DOI: 10.5539/cis.v11n3p82

Mohammed, P., & Watson, E. (2019, January 1). Towards Inclusive Education in the Age of Artificial Intelligence: Perspectives, Challenges, and Opportunities. Springer Nature, 17-37. DOI: 10.1007/978-981-13-8161-4_2

Moskal, P. D., Dziuban, C. D., & Picciano, A. G. (2023). Data Analytics and Adaptive Learning: Research Perspectives. [HTML]

Mozer, M C., Wiseheart, M., & Novikoff, T P. (2019, February 19). Artificial intelligence to support human instruction. National Academy of Sciences, 116(10), 3953-3955. DOI: 10.1073/pnas.1900370116

Nguyen, H. (2014, November 29). Grounded in Practice: Designing & Implementing Relevant and Student-Centered Curriculum. Emerald Publishing Limited, 161-181. DOI: 10.1108/S1479-366020140000021019

Núñez, J L M., Harris, P., Fernández, R P., Abbas, A., & Radovanović, D. (2023, January 1). Does intrinsic motivation mediate perceived artificial intelligence (AI) learning and computational thinking of students during the COVID-19 pandemic?. Elsevier BV, 4, 100128-100128. DOI: 10.1016/j.caeai.2023.100128

Nye, B D. (2014, October 7). Intelligent Tutoring Systems by and for the Developing World: A Review of Trends and Approaches for Educational Technology in a Global Context. Springer Science+Business Media, 25(2), 177-203. DOI: 10.1007/s40593-014-0028-6

Ogwu, E N., Emelogu, N U., Azor, R O., & Okwo, F A. (2022, July 16). Educational Technology Adoption in Instructional Delivery in the New Global reality. Springer Science+Business Media, 28(1), 1065-1080. DOI: 10.1007/s10639-022-11203-4

Phillips, A., Pane, J F., Reumann-Moore, R., & Shenbanjo, O. (2020, February 27). Implementing an adaptive intelligent tutoring system as an instructional supplement. Springer Science+Business Media, 68(3), 1409-1437. DOI: 10.1007/s11423-020-09745-w

Ray, A., & Pani, P. (2021, January 1). Learning Continuum in a Blended Mode: A Case of a Skill-based Course. DOI: 10.2991/assehr.k.211224.020

Roeper., Pace, S., & Marshall, S P. (2014, October 5). Re-Imagining Specialized STEM Academies: Igniting and Nurturing Decidedly Different Minds, by Design. https://www.tandfonline.com/doi/abs/10.1080/02783190903386884

Rožman, M., Tominc, P., & Vrečko, I. (2023, August 29). Building skills for the future of work: Students' perspectives on emerging jobs in the Data and AI Cluster through artificial intelligence in education., 8(2). DOI: 10.54517/esp.v8i2.1670

Sánchez-Caballé, A., Esteve-Mon, F. M., & González-Martínez, J. (2020, January 5). What to Expect When You Are Simulating?: About Digital Simulation Potentialities in Teacher Training. https://www.igi-global.com/gateway/article/241256

Shaji, S., & Nagaraj, P. (2020, December 22). Integration of Technology in English Language Classrooms: A Research Review., 9(S1-Dec2020), 26-29. DOI: 10.34293/english.v9iS1-Dec2020.3608

Srinivasan, V., & Murthy, H. (2021, January 1). Improving reading and comprehension in K-12: Evidence from a large-scale AI technology intervention in India. Elsevier BV, 2, 100019-100019. DOI: 10.1016/j.caeai.2021.100019

Strielkowski, W., Grebennikova, V., Lisovskiy, A., Rakhimova, G., & Vasileva, T. (2024). AI-driven adaptive learning for sustainable educational transformation. Sustainable Development. wiley.com

Swiecki, Z., Khosravi, H., Chen, G., Martínez-Maldonado, R., Lodge, J M., Milligan, S., Selwyn, N., & Gašević, D. (2022, January 1). Assessment in the age of artificial intelligence. Elsevier BV, 3, 100075-100075. DOI: 10.1016/j.caeai.2022.100075

Taylor, D., Yeung, M., & Bashet, A Z. (2021, January 1). Personalized and Adaptive Learning. Springer International Publishing, 17-34. DOI: 10.1007/978-3-030-58948-6_2

Tenório, M M., Reinaldo, F., Góis, L A D., Lopes, R P., & Santos, G D. (2018, January 1). Elements of Gamification in Virtual Learning Environments. Springer Nature, 86-96. DOI: 10.1007/978-3-319-73204-6_12

Tomasik, M. J., Berger, S., & Moser, U. (2018, November 20). On the Development of a Computer-Based Tool for Formative Student Assessment: Epistemological, Methodological, and Practical Issues. *Frontiers of Medicine*, 9, 2245. Advance online publication. DOI: 10.3389/fpsyg.2018.02245 PMID: 30515119

Tsai, Y., Whitelock-Wainwright, A., & Gašević, D. (2020, March 13). The privacy paradox and its implications for learning analytics. DOI: 10.1145/3375462.3375536

Walker, E., Rummel, N., & Koedinger, K R. (2013, October 17). Adaptive Intelligent Support to Improve Peer Tutoring in Algebra. Springer Science+Business Media, 24(1), 33-61. DOI: 10.1007/s40593-013-0001-9

Wang, N., & Lester, J C. (2023, June 1). K-12 Education in the Age of AI: A Call to Action for K-12 AI Literacy. Springer Science+Business Media, 33(2), 228-232. DOI: 10.1007/s40593-023-00358-x

Wieman, C., Adams, W. K., & Perkins, K. K. (2008, October 30). PhET: Simulations That Enhance Learning. *Science*, 322(5902), 682–683. DOI: 10.1126/science.1161948 PMID: 18974334

Wollny, S., Schneider, J., Mitri, D. D., Weidlich, J., Rittberger, M., & Drachsler, H. (2021, July 15). Are We There Yet? - A Systematic Literature Review on Chatbots in Education. *Frontiers of Medicine*, 4, 654924. Advance online publication. DOI: 10.3389/frai.2021.654924 PMID: 34337392

Xhakaj, F., Aleven, V., & McLaren, B M. (2016, January 1). How Teachers Use Data to Help Students Learn: Contextual Inquiry for the Design of a Dashboard. Springer Science+Business Media, 340-354. https://doi.org/DOI: 10.1007/978-3-319-45153-4_26

Xie, H., Chu, H., Hwang, G., & Wang, C. (2019, June 6). Trends and development in technology-enhanced adaptive/personalized learning: A systematic review of journal publications from 2007 to 2017. Elsevier BV, 140, 103599-103599. https://doi.org/DOI: 10.1016/j.compedu.2019.103599

Yadav, U., & Shrawankar, U. (2025). Artificial Intelligence Across Industries: A Comprehensive Review With a Focus on Education. AI Applications and Strategies in Teacher Education, 275-320. [HTML]

Yang, H. (2021, February 1). Explore How Artificial Intelligence and VR Technology will Change the Development of Future Education. *Journal of Physics: Conference Series*, 1744(4), 042146–042146. DOI: 10.1088/1742-6596/1744/4/042146

Yannier, N., Hudson, S E., & Koedinger, K R. (2020, February 3). Active Learning is About More Than Hands-On: A Mixed-Reality AI System to Support STEM Education. Springer Science+Business Media, 30(1), 74-96. https://doi.org/DOI: 10.1007/s40593-020-00194-3

Yannier, N., Hudson, S E., & Koedinger, K R. (2020, February 3). Active Learning is About More Than Hands-On: A Mixed-Reality AI System to Support STEM Education. Springer Science+Business Media, 30(1), 74-96. https://doi.org/DOI: 10.1007/s40593-020-00194-3

Yao, Y. (2021, November 2). Deep Integration of AI and TPACK: Reconstruction of Teachers'. *Knowledge Structure in the Post-pandemic Era.*, 3, 150–154. DOI: 10.54691/bcpep.v3i.28

Yarger, L., Payton, F C., & Neupane, B. (2019, December 17). Algorithmic equity in the hiring of underrepresented IT job candidates. Emerald Publishing Limited, 44(2), 383-395. https://doi.org/DOI: 10.1108/OIR-10-2018-0334

Ysseldyke, J., & Tardrew, S. (2007, September 25). Use of a Progress Monitoring System to Enable Teachers to Differentiate Mathematics Instruction. Taylor & Francis, 24(1), 1-28. https://doi.org/DOI: 10.1300/J370v24n01_01

Yuce, A., Abubakar, A M., & İlkan, M. (2019, July 25). Intelligent tutoring systems and learning performance. Emerald Publishing Limited, 43(4), 600-616. https://doi.org/DOI: 10.1108/OIR-11-2017-0340

Zhang, K., & Aslan, A. B. (2021, January 1). AI technologies for education: Recent research & future directions. https://www.sciencedirect.com/science/article/pii/S2666920X21000199

Zhang, X., Li, H., Liu, Z., Chen, Z., Zhou, H., Rong, W., & Ouyang, Y. (2024, March 1). A Review of Data Mining in Personalized Education. *Current Trends and Future Prospects.*, 1(1), 26–50. DOI: 10.1007/s44366-024-0019-6

ADDITIONAL READING

Abbasi, B. N., Wu, Y., & Luo, Z. (2024). Exploring the impact of artificial intelligence on curriculum development in global higher education institutions. *Education and Information Technologies*, •••, 1–35. DOI: 10.1007/s10639-024-13113-z

Admane, R., Sawale, P. S., Jayasree, R., Kurup, S. J., & Thomas, S. A. (2024). Artificial Intelligence in Education: Tailoring Curriculum to Individual Student Needs through AI-Based Systems. *Library Progress International*, 44(3), 8922–8930.

Ahmed, J. (2024). Integrating Artificial Intelligence into Curriculum Design. *Multidisciplinary Journal of Emerging Needs of Curriculum*, 1(2), 10–19.

George, A. S. (2023). Preparing students for an AI-driven world: Rethinking curriculum and pedagogy in the age of artificial intelligence. *Partners Universal Innovative Research Publication*, 1(2), 112–136.

Karataş, F., Eriçok, B., & Tanrikulu, L. (2024). Reshaping curriculum adaptation in the age of artificial intelligence: Mapping teachers' AI-driven curriculum adaptation patterns. *British Educational Research Journal*, berj.4068. DOI: 10.1002/berj.4068

KEY TERMS AND DEFINITIONS

Adaptive Learning: A technology-driven educational approach that customizes learning materials to individual students' needs, preferences, and learning speeds, enhancing engagement and comprehension.

Algorithmic Bias: Systematic and repeatable errors in AI algorithms that result in unfair treatment of certain groups or individuals, often stemming from biased data inputs or flawed algorithm design.

Artificial Intelligence (AI): A branch of computer science focused on creating machines capable of simulating human intelligence, including problem-solving, decision-making, and adapting to new information.

Curriculum Optimization: The process of using data analytics to continually improve and adjust educational content, ensuring alignment with student needs and current industry requirements.

Data Privacy: The protection of students' personal information from unauthorized access, ensuring that sensitive data collected by AI systems is used responsibly and securely.

Intelligent Tutoring Systems (ITS): AI-driven platforms that provide personalized guidance and feedback to students, mimicking the support of a human tutor to enhance learning outcomes.

Personalized Learning: An educational approach that tailors the content, pace, and style of instruction to individual learner profiles, promoting effective and engaging experiences.

Real-Time Feedback: Immediate responses provided to students on their performance, enabled by AI, allowing them to correct mistakes and enhance their understanding as they learn.

Student Engagement: The level of interest, motivation, and involvement a student has in their learning, which AI can support by making learning experiences more interactive and tailored.

Virtual Labs: Simulated environments that allow students to perform experiments and apply theoretical knowledge without the physical resources, fostering hands-on learning experiences in a digital space.

Chapter 8
Investigating Pre-Service Chemistry Teachers' Experiences in Designing Lesson Plans Using ChatGPT

Nagihan Kadıoğlu
https://orcid.org/0000-0003-4911-8985
Hacettepe University, Turkey

Özge Özyalçın Oskay
https://orcid.org/0000-0002-9368-5381
Hacettepe University, Turkey

ABSTRACT

This chapter explores the use of ChatGPT, an artificial intelligence tool that rapidly processes user inputs, offering valuable support for educational tasks. Given the growing integration of AI in education, it is essential for pre-service teachers—who will be future educators—to understand and utilize ChatGPT effectively, adhering to ethical guidelines for professional development. The study investigates how pre-service chemistry teachers design lesson plans with the aid of ChatGPT and gathers their reflections on these experiences. Six pre-service chemistry teachers participated, each creating a lesson plan by giving specific commands to ChatGPT. These lesson plans focused on chemistry curriculum objectives and aimed to develop a chosen type of intelligence from the theory of multiple intelligences. Following the lesson plan development, semi-structured interviews were conducted to capture participants' insights into their experiences.

DOI: 10.4018/979-8-3373-1017-6.ch008

INTRODUCTION

Artificial Intelligence

Nowadays, also called the age of digitalization, technological developments have also affected the 21st century business world. It has become very difficult for individuals who cannot follow technological developments in their field and keep up with change to find a place in the business world (Ng et al., 2021). The rapid development of technology has profoundly affected every aspect of life in today's world. Artificial intelligence (AI) is one of the latest advances in technology, and although it emerged in the first half of this century, it is now considered to be the driving force of technology. AI is a field of study that is based on human intelligence and can imitate it through computers and produce products in different areas of daily life (Çam et al., 2021; Hu, 2023).

There are different definitions for artificial intelligence. But basically, the common view in all of them is divided into two. These two views can be expressed as "intelligent programming" and "humanoid reactions". The fact that a machine shows human-like behaviors such as problem solving, reasoning, generalization and inference can be defined as artificial intelligence in a sense that machines use high-level cognitive skills (Arslan, 2020).

McCarthy et. al (1955) defined artificial intelligence as "the ability of machines to show human-like behaviors". Kurzweil (2005), another person well-known for his work on artificial intelligence, has defined artificial intelligence as the art of solving problems by machines by placing artificial intelligence on the basis of imitating humans and characterizing the problems solved by humans as jobs that require intelligence. Axe, on the other hand, defined artificial intelligence as "intelligent programs that solve complex problems, not only predetermined problems but also create responses to a new situation" (cited in Nabiyev, 2012).

Akyürek (2013) created a definition for artificial intelligence by utilizing the similarity between computer and human. In this definition, human neural networks are likened to artificial neural networks. He stated that by using artificial neural networks, machines create information processing systems by imitating human beings based on the working state of the human brain. Artificial intelligence studies that emerge as a result of imitating human intelligence can be stated as the modeling of human learning by machines. Considering that learning processes in humans occur in the brain, it is possible to create machines by examining the structure of the brain. Based on the fact that learning in humans occurs through the interaction in brain cells called neurons, artificial neural networks were created on computers and learning was simulated (Yılmaz & Kaya, 2021).

Historical Development of Artificial Intelligence

The philosophical foundations and first concrete steps of artificial intelligence can be traced back to the 17th century. In the 17th century, the race to create automata that mimic human and animal behavior began in all segments of society, especially the ruling and aristocratic class. This race was also reflected in the philosophical perspective of the period. Descartes (1596-1650), one of the famous philosophers of the period, likened human beings to machines working with a clock-like mechanism. After this period, when many human behaviors began to be imitated, the British mathematician Charles Babbage (1792-1871) aimed to imitate the mental characteristics of human beings instead of their physical characteristics and developed the first calculator called "Difference Engine" (Coşkun & Gülleroğlu, 2021).

In the modern sense, artificial intelligence studies gained importance during and after the World War II. During the World War II, Alan Mathison Turing changed the fate of the war by inventing the first fully automatic code-breaking machine called "Bombe", which could be considered important in the conditions of that day (Acar, 2020). The term "artificial intelligence" was first used in a workshop on artificial intelligence organized by John McCarthy at Dartmouth College in 1956 (Coşkun & Gülleroğlu, 2021). The first human-like intelligent robot was built in Japan in 1972 under the name WABOT-I (Acar, 2020). In 1997, the program called "Deep Blue", produced by IBM, defeated the world chess champion Garry Kasparov in a chess match. In this match, Garry Kasparov competed against a program that could process 200 million chess moves per second and lost. With this event, it was seen that computers could be better than humans in some areas (Schultz and Ellen-Schultz, 2007). In the early 2000s, artificial intelligence started to enter homes for the first time with the vacuum cleaner named "Roomba". By 2006, large companies such as Facebook, Netflix and Twitter started to use artificial intelligence (Acar, 2020).

Today, when we live in the era of Big Data, artificial intelligence has easily found many different application areas. Especially in the fields of banking, technology and entertainment, artificial intelligence applications are used effectively (Elmas, 2018). Many applications such as Siri-like personal assistants, driverless cars, instant language translations, intelligent education management systems, virtual classrooms, patient tracking systems, game theory and strategic planning, hand, speech, face and pattern recognition, automation, robotics, etc. have turned into artificial intelligence applications that are constantly developed and updated to make our lives easier in some way. In order to see this process as a whole, the development of some of the most important milestones in artificial intelligence over the years is shown below (Arslan, 2020).

Use of Artificial Intelligence in Education

The education system is a system that interacts with people and is affected by all kinds of changes and developments in society. One of the biggest challenges in the education system is that people learn at different rates and in different ways. Although each student develops differently, they can exhibit different levels of learning abilities. Some students have more developed analytical thinking skills, while others have more developed constructivist, communicative or literary skills. In this case, artificial intelligence is needed in education as individualized education according to the skills of students (Çolak, 2022).

Developing education systems aim to raise individuals with high imagination and creativity instead of monotonous and robotized individuals by taking advantage of the advantages brought by artificial intelligence technology. Research conducted in this direction shows that education systems focus on improving the intellectual abilities of individuals and aim to equip people with creative thinking and imagination to become individuals who can solve different problems (Kaya, 2024). Artificial intelligence technologies can offer personalized learning experiences according to students' individual needs and learning styles. By analyzing data such as students' interests, strengths, weaknesses and previous performances, appropriate content, materials and learning methods can be provided. This can increase students' motivation and help them progress more effectively in the learning process.

Artificial intelligence can track students' learning pace and progress and provide them with appropriate levels of challenge. Adaptive learning systems can help students build on their strengths and support their weaknesses. Customized learning plans can be created based on students' individual learning needs, so that it is possible to maximize the potential of each student. Artificial intelligence can quickly assess students' performance and provide feedback through automated assessment systems. Students' performance on tasks such as exams, assignments or project work can be analyzed and evaluated by AI algorithms. Artificial intelligence can continuously track student progress and achievements. By analyzing data such as which subjects students have difficulties in, which subjects they understand better, and in which areas they need more support, targeted interventions can be made to students. In this way, students can complete their deficiencies and progress.

Artificial intelligence technologies have the potential to improve distance education processes. It can offer students more interactive experiences in live or online courses. Also, the ability to automatically translate or audio-deliver learning materials can make learning more accessible and make it easier to deal with challenges such as language or disabilities. Ethical issues and data privacy concerns related to the use of AI should also be considered. Students' personal data can be collected and analyzed through the use of AI systems. It is important to protect this data properly, ensure confidentiality and obtain students' consent. While AI offers many opportunities to students in the field of education, it can also bring ethical and social issues that need to be considered. Therefore, it is important to use AI carefully in education, to protect data privacy, and to protect the interests of students (Aşık et.al, 2023).

Teachers should take a central role in the effective use of artificial intelligence in the classroom. Teachers should be the determinant of when and how to use artificial intelligence tools. In addition, artificial intelligence tools and the results obtained as a result of the data provided by these tools will help teachers to decide how to use various resources in the best way. The increasing impact of artificial intelligence-based tools is an indication that the role of the teacher in the classroom will also change. With the introduction of these applications into the classroom, different skills are expected from teachers. These skills can be listed as follows:

- Develop a comprehensive understanding of what AI systems can do and make evaluations and appropriate judgments about new AI products.
- They need to develop research skills to properly evaluate the data provided by AI technologies, interpret the data in the most useful way and guide students in the right direction by understanding what the data analysis tells them.
- Since teachers will now have AI assistants in addition to the natural learning process, they need to have the skills to manage it effectively (İşler & Kılıç, 2021).

ChatGPT

ChatGPT is one of the most popular AI tools and has the potential to offer great opportunities for the development of these skills, also called 21st century skills. ChatGPT (Chat Generative Pre-Trained Transform) is an AI-powered chatbot specializing in dialogue building, also classified as Big Language Model (OpenAI, 2022). Various researches in artificial intelligence (AI) fields such as machine learning, computer vision and natural language processing were developed by OpenAI on November 30, 2022. These models, which process thousands of gb of data, understand the patterns and structure of language, generate relevant and meaningful responses to user prompts, and provide meaningful content (Cooper, 2023).

ChatGPT, a cutting-edge language generation model, offers the user many opportunities such as “Content Generation”, “Education and Research”, Write Documentation”, “Generate Regular Expressions”, “Virtual Assistants” (Adeshola & Adepoju, 2023). ChatGPT is frequently used in many fields due to its accessible and user-friendly interface (Jeon & Lee, 2023), its ability to create impressive texts in seconds (Rudolph et al., 2023), to produce human-like texts and to establish more realistic dialogues with the user (Tlili et al., 2023), unlike other generative artificial intelligence models (Geerling et al., 2024; Kung et al., 2023; Pavlik, 2023; Schwendicke et al, 2020).

ChatGPT in Education

When we look at the use of AI such as ChatGPT in the field of education in general, AI tools are a tool used by students to get support in tasks such as preparing their homework, creating content, and preparing texts. Teachers use AI for teaching activities such as creating course materials, translating languages, creating assessment tasks and evaluating students' performance (Chassignol et al, 2018; Lo, 2023). One of the major reasons why the potential of AI has not yet been fully utilized in education is that the role of teachers in the educational integration of AI-based tools has so far been overlooked (Seufert et al., 2021). It is not right to expect any AI tool, including ChatGPT, to completely replace teachers. Rather than being a competitor to teachers, AI is thought to act as an assistant to help them work more efficiently and reduce the workload in educational activities (Labadze et al., 2021).

ChatGPT is an effective tool for education as in other fields, but it is very important to use it safely and in accordance with ethical principles in education. It is necessary for both teachers and students to be familiar with ChatGPT and to have knowledge about its use in order to use ChatGPT effectively. Since ChatGPT is a new technology that is only 2 years old, it may not be easily adopted by teachers and their experience may be limited (Halaweh, 2023). Therefore, at this point, it is very important that pre-service teachers, who are prone to the use of technology, digital natives and students of today and teachers of the future, are introduced to ChatGPT in their pre-service education. If pre-service teachers gain experience in the use of ChatGPT while they are still students, it is very likely that they will use ChatGPT more effectively and consciously in designing instructional environments etc. when they become teachers. At the same time, it is thought that teachers who can use ChatGPT well will be able to guide their students in the right way.

Ways to Use ChatGPT

Student Support and Assistance: ChatGPT can be used to provide support and assistance to students in their learning process. Students can submit their questions to ChatGPT to ask for help in understanding topics or for guidance on their assignments.

Educator Support and Guidance: ChatGPT can be used to provide pedagogical support and teaching materials to educators. Educators can direct questions about curriculum planning, lesson content or teaching strategies to ChatGPT and get suggestions or resources.

Assignment and Project Guidance: ChatGPT can guide students with assignments and projects. Students can consult ChatGPT and get advice on topics such as topic selection, research methods or content organization.

Language Learning: ChatGPT can provide language learners with support to improve their language skills. Whether it is grammar, word meanings, pronunciation or practical speaking, ChatGPT can guide learners and provide opportunities to practice.

Learner Feedback: ChatGPT can help students to provide feedback. Students can submit their written work to ChatGPT and receive feedback on grammar mistakes, spelling mistakes or content editing.

Student Evaluation: ChatGPT can be used to assess student performance. By providing students with test questions, quizzes or tasks, it can evaluate their responses and provide feedback. This can help students identify their strengths and identify areas where they need to improve.

Learning Materials and Resources: ChatGPT can be used to provide students with learning materials and resources. Students can inquire about book recommendations, articles, videos or online resources on the topic. This can enable students to do in-depth research and benefit from the diversity of resources.

Teacher Training and Professional Development: ChatGPT can be used as a tool for teacher training and professional development. Teachers can interact with ChatGPT to get information and advice on topics such as pedagogy, classroom management or teaching strategies.

Communication and Collaboration: ChatGPT can enable students to interact with each other and with their teachers. It can guide students for group projects, discussions or collaborative tasks and help them improve their communication skills (Sevli, 2023).

Advantages of ChatGPT in Education

One of the big advantages of using ChatGPT in education is the ability to deliver personalized learning experiences. ChatGPT can be used to provide personalized tutoring and feedback to students based on their individual learning needs and progress. In their study, Chen et al. (2020) showed that a conversational agent based on a generative model like ChatGPT can provide personalized mathematics instruction to students, which can lead to better learning outcomes. The study showed that the conversational agent can provide explanations tailored to students' misconceptions and adapt to students' level of understanding. A study by Johnson et al. (2016) showed that a generative model (ChatGPT) trained on a data set of bilingual sentence pairs can accurately translate between languages by achieving state-of-the-art results on various translation criteria. Liu et al. (2022) conducted a study to examine the effects of an artificial intelligence chatbot on children's interest in reading. The research focused on analyzing the interaction between children and the chatbot and its impact on children's reading engagement. The findings revealed that the AI chatbot had a positive impact on children's reading experiences, leading to increased interest and engagement in reading activities. Another study was conducted by Obari and Lambacher (2019) on the use of artificial intelligence to improve the English language skills of Japanese native speakers. The aim of the study was to find out the effect of artificial intelligence combined with 21st century skills on improving native speakers' English language skills. The results of the study showed that both groups improved their English language skills. The researchers found that artificial intelligence combined with 21st century skills improved English language skills.

ChatGPT's ability to adapt to students' individual needs, preferences and learning styles, providing tailored responses and guidance that address their unique needs, increases student engagement and motivation and leads to improved learning outcomes. ChatGPT facilitates interactive and engaging learning experiences. Unlike traditional online learning tools, chatbots provide dynamic and responsive interactions. Students can ask questions, receive immediate feedback and engage in active dialog with the virtual assistant. This interactive structure develops deeper understanding, encourages critical thinking and engages students throughout the learning process.

ChatGPT contributes to making education more accessible and inclusive. Students with learning disabilities can benefit from the personalized and adaptive nature of the chatbot. In addition, ChatGPT democratizes education and promotes lifelong learning opportunities by providing access to education for individuals who do not have the resources or time to attend traditional classes. ChatGPT is available around the clock, giving students immediate access to information and support. This continuous availability ensures that students can get help whenever they need it, enhancing their learning experience and minimizing delays in accessing resources.

While ChatGPT cannot replace human trainers, it supports their efforts in the training process. Trainers can use ChatGPT as a tool to provide additional resources, reinforce concepts, and support individualized learning. The chatbot can help answer frequently asked questions, offer explanations, and provide supplementary materials, freeing up time for trainers to focus on higher-level instruction and personalized guidance. ChatGPT enables students to engage in continuous learning and receive constant feedback. Through regular interactions with the chatbot, students can consolidate their knowledge, practice their skills and receive immediate feedback on their performance. This iterative feedback loop contributes to continuous improvement and allows students to effectively track their progress. ChatGPT reduces reliance on physical resources and streamlines the learning process. Students can access information, materials and guidance through the chatbot without the need to conduct extensive research or access multiple resources. This efficiency in resource use and time management allows students to focus on key concepts and maximize learning outcomes (Sevli, 2023).

Limitations in the Use of ChatGPT

A number of challenges can be encountered in the use of ChatGPT in education. Language models like ChatGPT generate responses based on the data it is trained on. However, their responses cannot always be guaranteed to be accurate and reliable. The model can sometimes produce results that contain misleading information. Therefore, human oversight and supervision is important to verify the accuracy of ChatGPT's responses in the training context and correct them when necessary.

When asked about possible ethical issues related to the use of ChatGPT in education, the following possibilities can be listed:

- the reliability and accuracy of the information it provides
- potential biases in the data leading to discriminatory or misleading responses
- privacy issues as it may collect and store personal information about students
- lack of human interaction, which reduces the quality of the educational experience for students
- overreliance and dependence on technology
- transparency and accountability (Adıgüzel et al., 2023) as it can be difficult to determine how decisions are made by the chatbot.

Data Privacy and Security: Language models like ChatGPT can access personal and sensitive information when interacting with users. This raises concerns about data privacy and security. Appropriate measures should be taken to ensure the protection and privacy of learners' or trainers' data.

Algorithmic Bias: ChatGPT generates responses using the grammatical and semantic relationships it has learned based on training data. However, because training data is collected from a variety of sources and is subject to personal context, it may contain algorithmic biases. This can result in the generation of inaccurate or discriminatory responses towards students or instructors belonging to different cultural, ethnic or linguistic groups. It is important to diversify training data and implement algorithmic controls to reduce bias.

Human Interaction and Dependency: ChatGPT has the potential to provide personalized support to students and instructors. However, an education or training experience based entirely on ChatGPT cannot completely replace human interaction. Opportunities should be provided for students to interact with real teachers and other students, develop social skills and collaborate.

Suitability Issues for Educational Purposes: Due to the nature of ChatGPT, as a generic language model, it uses general language structures learned from educational data. However, when used in the educational domain, customized responses may be required for a specific curriculum or learning objectives. In this case, special training and adjustments may be required for ChatGPT to produce responses that are appropriate for the educational content and curriculum objectives.

Scalability and Accessibility: Language models such as ChatGPT require large amounts of computational power and resources. This can raise scalability and accessibility issues. Educational institutions and teachers should have the necessary infrastructure and resources to use this technology. Otherwise, it may be difficult for this technology to be equally accessible and benefit all students.

Technical Skills and Training Process: The use of ChatGPT in education means that teachers and students may need some technical skills to be able to use this technology effectively. Training process and support are important for teachers and students to learn how to interact with this technology and how to guide it in the right way (Sevli, 2023).

ChatGPT in Chemistry Education

In the light of the above-mentioned information, as in all areas of education, all artificial intelligence tools and ChatGPT, one of the most widely used, provide great convenience and benefits to teachers and students in the field of chemistry education. In addition to its general advantages, ChatGPT can create interactive simulations and animations that help students visualize and understand complex chemical concepts and reactions. This can be done in a sequence from simple to complex. Reactions with software such as Unity, Unreal Engine and Blender, synthesis steps shown with moving arrows, three-dimensional designed experimental setups can be used.

Artificial intelligence can provide a more engaging and effective learning experience by adjusting the difficulty and pace of lessons based on student performance. Applications that can analyze content according to the learning speed and capacity of the student can also create a knowledge pool accordingly (Cheung et al., 2021). Artificial intelligence can predict students' future achievement by using mathematical modeling to provide personalized study recommendations and data-driven predictions about their future performance. This can keep the student's motivation high in the process and enable them to create a rational study pattern for the future (Chavez et al., 2023; Ouyang et al., 2023). By using artificial intelligence to analyze student data and provide personalized and interactive learning experiences, chemistry education can be made more effective, engaging and accessible for all students.

When teachers determine the outcomes of the subject they will teach, the characteristics of their students, and the levels of the lessons they want to prepare, artificial intelligence can prepare lesson plans, activities, and assessment and evaluation tools for teachers. Chatbots have been used in educational settings, including Science, Technology, Engineering and Mathematics (STEM) disciplines, as they have the potential to help students learn core content in a responsive, interactive and confidential way (Chen et al., 2022). Although ChatGPT is a language-based model that has the potential to organize complex concepts of chemistry such as structural properties, formulas, and mathematical aspects, investigating ChatGPT as a potential learning tool in an AI-driven environment is an important research gap, especially in the field of chemistry education (Leon & Widhani, 2023). Chemistry is an experimental science and hands-on activities play an important role in understanding abstract concepts. Although there are few studies in the literature, there are some studies in which ChatGPT is used in chemistry lab education. For example, Humphry and Fuller (2023) investigated the potential use of ChatGPT in university-level chemistry laboratories, focusing on ChatGPT's ability to write specific sections of laboratory reports. As an experiment, the researchers used a prompt asking ChatGPT to write a concluding sentence for an undergraduate chemistry lab experiment on density and evaluated ChatGPT's response. Similarly, Araújo and Saúde (2024) investigated the use of ChatGPT in a chemistry lab. The researchers analyzed the prompts given to ChatGPT for five compulsory chemistry lab activities in the 11th grade curriculum and evaluated the performance of ChatGPT. Problems are as important as hands on activities in understanding chemistry.

Therefore, evaluating the performance of AI tools such as ChatGPT in solving chemistry problems is one of the interesting topics. For example, Yalçın Çelik and Çoban (2023) analyzed the responses of two chatbots (ChatGPT and Bard) to open-ended questions about surface tension and determined their performances. According to the findings of the study, it was determined that the chatbots scored 35 and 38 points out of 60 points, they had the same average scores in the same questions, they answered the question at the analyzing level incorrectly, they got the highest score from the question at the creating level, and there were inaccuracies/deficiencies in their answers. There are also studies comparing the performance of ChatGPT with student performances. Clark (2023) examined the use of ChatGPT in solving the final questions of a general chemistry course and evaluated ChatGPT's performance in terms of the accuracy of its answers and the quality of its explanations. As a result of the study, it was found that although ChatGPT was very skilled in defining the concept, ChatGPT's problem solving success was well below the class average. Kharchenko & Babenko (2024) investigated the potentials and limitations of large language models (LLMs) such as ChatGPT, Gemini, and Copilot. In the study, the researchers used a self-created questionnaire to identify the most popular AI-based services among the participants' pre-service teachers. Then, they compared the performance of these LLMs with the performance of pre-service teachers. At the end of the study, it was found that all three LLMs gave mostly correct answers to low-level questions, but gave incomplete or incorrect answers to questions requiring comparison and logical inference. The results show that while LLMs are promising mainly for tasks that do not require deep logical reasoning, the performance of LLMs is generally lower than that of students

The use of AI-based technology in education is inevitable as it is an attractive and low-cost alternative. However, it is not possible to completely replace teachers (Felix, 2020). This is because chatbots lack human characteristics such as empathy, judgment and common sense (Murtarellia et al., 2021). AI cannot undertake various academic tasks, including creative activities such as developing new teaching methods, interpersonal interaction such as solving student problems, complex reasoning and problem solving such as evaluating the effects of decisions made (Dempere et al., 2023). Moreover, since it is essential for students to know how to prompt the ChatGPT, to analyze the output, and especially to understand the chemical principles for which they are seeking an answer in order to use the ChatGPT effectively, each of these skills needs to be developed during the chemistry course in order for the ChatGPT to successfully replace the student response (Humphry & Fuller, 2023). Thus, although AI has a strong potential to transform teaching and learning processes, the role of Chemistry teachers and their expertise in the field is crucial for the sustainability of the quality of Chemistry lessons, especially from a scientific and pedagogical point of view (Araújo & Saúde, 2024).

Ethics and AI

Integrating ChatGPT into education can produce various conflicts of interest crises, especially with regard to research ethics, authorship, rights and ownership, raising important ethical considerations and potential challenges that need to be addressed to ensure responsible and fair use (Nam & Bai, 2023; Nguyen & Sirichokcharoenkun, 2023). Nguyen and Sirichokcharoenkun (2023) highlighted important ethical considerations and potential challenges for ethical and inclusive implementation of ChatGPT in educational settings and listed them as; "Bias and Fairness," "Privacy and Data Security," "Responsible AI Use," "Equity and Accessibility," "Dependence on AI and Human Role," "Ethical Guidelines and Policies," "Transparency and Explainability," "Continuous Evaluation and Improvement." The researchers identified these ethical considerations and potential challenges for users to organize the integration of ChatGPT into education in a responsible and ethical way. As a result, it is very important to adopt an ethical and inclusive approach to the integration of AI in order to strike a balance between harnessing the power of AI and addressing the challenges it poses (Alasadi & Baiz, 2023).

Use of Artificial Intelligence and Prospective Chemistry Teachers

This rapid development in technology and AI technology requires prospective teachers, who will be the teachers of the future, to be aware of technological developments and to be individuals who can use technology correctly and effectively. Teachers' competencies in using AI technologies directly affect their ability to integrate these technologies into educational processes (Zhou et al., 2021). Increasing teachers' awareness of AI and developing positive attitudes towards these technologies are critical for the successful implementation of AI-based educational practices (Chen et al., 2020). In order to use artificial intelligence technologies effectively in education, teachers' awareness and attitudes towards these technologies should be improved. AI and natural language processing technologies have the potential to reduce teachers' workload, increase student achievement, and optimize teaching methods. However, teachers need to have sufficient knowledge and skills to use these technologies effectively.In this context, it is of great importance that teacher education programs include comprehensive training on how artificial intelligence and other digital tools can be used in education. Especially in courses such as chemistry, which are defined as abstract by students, pre-service teachers have a great need to use educational technologies in order to teach the subject to students effectively and permanently.

In the light of this information, it is thought that it will be valuable for pre-service teachers who are trained to guide the education process in the future to be aware of the applications that can be made with ChatGPT and to use this tool effectively in accordance with ethical principles in terms of their professional development. In addition, it is thought that investigating pre-service teachers' first experiences with ChatGPT and their opinions about it will contribute to future studies based on the use of artificial intelligence in education and its effect on educational activities. For all these reasons, the aim of this study is to examine the lesson plans created by pre-service chemistry teachers using ChatGPT and to determine the opinions of pre-service teachers about these experiences. For this purpose, the following questions were sought to be answered in this study:

1. How are the experiences of pre-service chemistry teachers who have no previous experience with AI in designing lesson plans with ChatGPT?

2. What are the opinions of pre-service chemistry teachers who have no previous experience with AI about their experiences of designing lesson plans with ChatGPT?

METHOD

In this study, the lesson plans prepared by pre-service chemistry teachers using ChatGPT in accordance with the subject outcomes in the national chemistry curriculum for the development of a type of intelligence they chose from the theory of multiple intelligences and the prompts they gave to ChatGPT while preparing these lesson plans were examined. In addition, individual interviews were conducted with pre-service teachers and their opinions about their experiences in creating lesson plans using ChatGPT were determined. In the study conducted for this purpose, case study design, one of the qualitative research methods, was used. The results of case studies cannot be generalized to a single population, but the existing situation is evaluated with a detailed approach within its own conditions (Yıldırım & Şimşek, 2013; Yin, 2009).

Participants

The participants of this study consisted of 6 pre-service teachers who were attending the 3rd year of Chemistry Teaching Department and had no experience in artificial intelligence. All of the participants had taken courses such as Instructional Technologies and Material Design, Chemistry Curricula, Chemistry Teaching Curricula, Chemistry Teaching Theories and Approaches in previous years and were successful. Before the study started, interviews were conducted with the participants and pre-service teachers who had not used any artificial intelligence tools such as ChatGPT were included in the study.

Data Collection Process

Since the participants had no previous experience in using ChatGPT, an informational meeting about artificial intelligence and ChatGPT was held with the participants at the beginning of the study. In this meeting, first of all, the participants were provided with the free version of ChatGPT, ChatGPT-3.5. Then, the participants were informed about the purposes for which ChatGPT can be used in the field of education and how to prompt ChatGPT. Afterwards, the participants were given a trial application. Since ChatGPT has Turkish language support, the participants carried out all conversations with ChatGPT in their native language,

Turkish. Although it is a common idea that AI tools such as ChatGPT respond better to prompts in English, the application was conducted in Turkish since the participants' English skills were not sufficient.

Participants first prepared the questions they would ask in this trial application. It is possible to open multiple chat tabs in ChatGPT and all of them are automatically saved. Participants also used multiple chat tabs to create the same content and experimented by creating prompts with different wording in each chat section. In this way, participants could ask the same question in different ways and compare the response performance of the chatbot. After the trial implementation, the actual implementation was started. Throughout the process (refer to Figure-1), the researchers allowed the participants to benefit from resources such as internet, books, etc. The participants were able to evaluate the accuracy of the answers given by the ChatGPT because they were familiar with the national chemistry curriculum and lesson plan preparation processes thanks to the courses they had successfully completed in previous semesters. In order to make their prompts more understandable and effective, the participants supported the conversation with statements such as "Pretend to be an experienced chemistry teacher", "You are a chemistry teacher who teaches 9th graders...". According to the answers given by the chatbot, sometimes the participants asked the same question in different ways and asked the chatbot to answer a second time. No time limit was imposed on the participants for the main application.

Figure 1. Data collection process

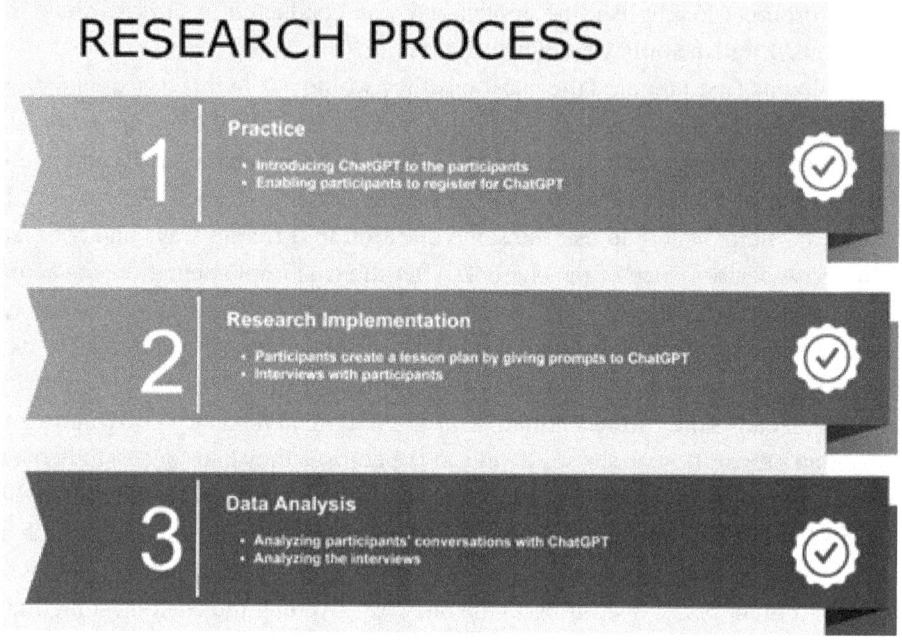

2.3 Data analysis

The data of this study consisted of screenshots of the participants' conversations with ChatGPT-3.5 during the lesson plan preparation process and interviews with the participants. Content analysis method was used to analyze all the data collected in the study.

Findings

In this study, the experiences of pre-service chemistry teachers who have never used artificial intelligence in any field before in preparing lesson plans using ChatGPT-3.5 were examined. In this section, the findings of the participants' conversations with ChatGPT-3,5 and the interviews with the participants analyzed by content analysis are explained respectively. The pre-service teachers were numbered as PST1, PST2... to protect anonymity for confidentiality.

Pre-service Chemistry Teachers' Experiences with ChatGPT

Each of the pre-service teachers participating in the study chose a type of intelligence from the theory of multiple intelligences and a subject from the national curriculum, and designed a lesson plan using the teaching model/method/technique etc. of their preference. Table 1 shows the preferences of the pre-service teachers.

Table 1. Pre-service Teachers' Lesson Plan Preferences

Pre-Service Teacher	Intelligence Type	Subject / Outcome / Grade Level Preference	Teaching Model / Method / Technique ... etc. Preference
PST1	Visual-Spatial	Subject: Environmental Chemistry Outcome: "Suggests solutions to reduce the effects of chemical pollutants that harm the environment." Grade Level: Grade 9	5E Learning Model
PST2	Visual-Spatial & Physical	Topic: Atomic Models Objective: "Explains Dalton, Thomson, Rutherford and Bohr atomic models." Grade Level: 9th Grade	Not specified
PST3	Visual-Spatial	Topic: Mixtures Acquisition: "Classifies mixtures according to their properties." Grade Level: Grade 10	POE (Predict- Observe-Explain)
PST4	Social	Topic: Chemical and Physical Changes Outcome: "Distinguish physical and chemical change on the basis of the amount of bond energy formed and broken." Grade Level: Grade 9	Story, game
PST5	Mathematical & Visual-Spatial	Topic: Gases Outcome: "Explains the properties used in the description of gases." Grade Level: Grade 11	5E Learning Model
PST6	Musical	Topic: Periodic System Outcome: "Classifies the elements according to their place in the periodic system." Grade Level: 9th Grade	5E Learning Model

When Table 1 is examined, it is seen that the participants predominantly preferred visual-spatial intelligence as the type of intelligence and the 9th grade level as the grade level. Some of the participants started their conversations with ChatGPT by first asking questions about the type of intelligence and subject they chose in order to determine the responsiveness of ChatGPT. During the interviews, the pre-service teachers stated that they got more efficiency by starting the conversation in this way.

Some participants started the conversation directly by giving information themselves. Figure 2 and Figure 3 show sample conversation starters.

Figure 2. Example of a conversation started by asking ChatGPT a question (PST2)

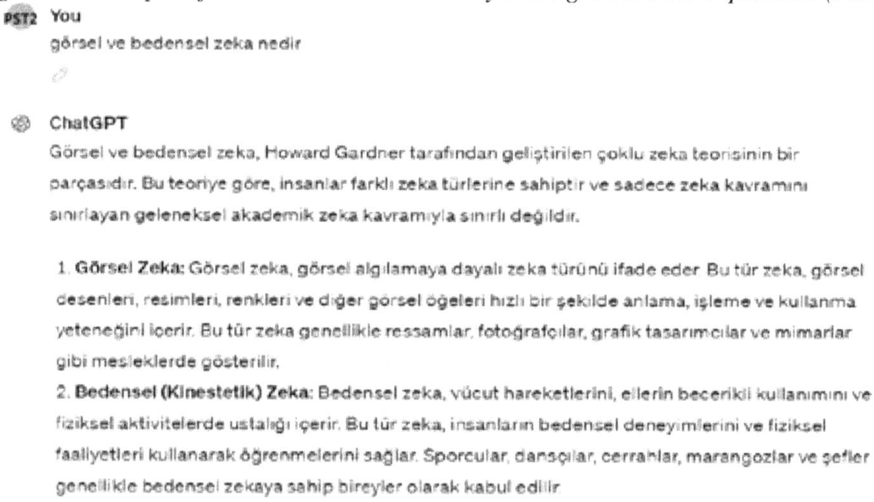

PST2 You

görsel ve bedensel zeka nedir

ChatGPT

Görsel ve bedensel zeka, Howard Gardner tarafından geliştirilen çoklu zeka teorisinin bir parçasıdır. Bu teoriye göre, insanlar farklı zeka türlerine sahiptir ve sadece zeka kavramını sınırlayan geleneksel akademik zeka kavramıyla sınırlı değildir.

1. **Görsel Zeka:** Görsel zeka, görsel algılamaya dayalı zeka türünü ifade eder. Bu tür zeka, görsel desenleri, resimleri, renkleri ve diğer görsel öğeleri hızlı bir şekilde anlama, işleme ve kullanma yeteneğini içerir. Bu tür zeka genellikle ressamlar, fotoğrafçılar, grafik tasarımcılar ve mimarlar gibi mesleklerde gösterilir.
2. **Bedensel (Kinestetik) Zeka:** Bedensel zeka, vücut hareketlerini, ellerin becerikli kullanımını ve fiziksel aktivitelerde ustalığı içerir. Bu tür zeka, insanların bedensel deneyimlerini ve fiziksel faaliyetleri kullanarak öğrenmelerini sağlar. Sporcular, dansçılar, cerrahlar, marangozlar ve şefler genellikle bedensel zekaya sahip bireyler olarak kabul edilir.

[Translation of the conversation from the Turkish language:

PST2: What are visual and bodily intelligence? |

ChatGPT: 1. Visual Intelligence: Visual intelligence refers to a type of intelligence based on visual perception. This type of intelligence involves the ability to quickly understand, process, and use visual patterns, images, colors, and other visual elements. It is often displayed in professions such as painters, photographers, graphic designers, and architects.

2. Bodily (Kinesthetic) Intelligence: Bodily intelligence involves mastery of body movements, skillful use of hands, and proficiency in physical activities. This type of intelligence enables individuals to learn through bodily experiences and physical actions. Athletes, dancers, surgeons, carpenters, and chefs are often considered individuals with bodily intelligence.]

Figure 2 shows the screenshot of the conversation initiated by PST2 by asking a question. In the rest of the conversation, PST2 gave the targeted grade level and outcome information to ChatGPT and asked it to design a lesson plan.

Figure 3. Example of a conversation that starts by providing information to ChatGPT (PST1)

PST1 You

Çoklu zeka gruplarından görsel zeka türüne sahip öğrencilerin gelişimlerini destekleyebilecek Türk Ortaöğretim Kimya Öğretim Programında yer alan 9. sınıf Çevre Kimyası konusunda Çevreye zarar veren kimyasal kirleticilerin etkilerinin azaltılması konusunda çözüm önerilerinde bulunur kazanımına yönelik deneyimli bir kimya öğretmeni olarak 5e öğrenme modeline göre; giriş aşamasını konuya ilişkin görsellerle desteklenebilecek bir dijital hikaye senaryosunun, keşfetme aşamasını konuya ve dijital hikayeye bağlı olarak öğrencileri araştırmaya yönlendirebilecek 5 adet problem durumunun, açıklama aşamasını görsel zekaya hitap edebilecek keşfetme aşamasında öğrencilere verilen problem durumuyla ilişkili olarak öğretmenin yapabileceği farklı bir etkinliğin, derinleştirme aşamasını öğrencilerin süreç boyunca elde ettiği bilgileri yeni durumlar üzerinde kullanabilecek etkinliklerin, değerlendirme aşamasını ise yine görsel zekaya hitap eden bir panoda yer alabilecek öğrenci projelerin oluşturduğu bir ders planı oluştur.

ChatGPT

Tabii, işte 5E öğrenme modeline göre hazırlanmış bir ders planı:

Ders Planı: Çevre Kimyası - Çevreye Zarar Veren Kimyasal Kirleticilerin Etkilerinin Azaltılması

Ders Konusu: Çevreye Zarar Veren Kimyasal Kirleticilerin Etkilerinin Azaltılması

Sınıf Seviyesi: 9. Sınıf

Zeka Türü: Görsel Zeka

1. Giriş Aşaması (Keşfetme):

- Öğrencilere çevreye zarar veren kimyasal kirleticilerin etkileri hakkında kısa bir giriş yapılır.
- Dijital bir hikaye senaryosu gösterilerek öğrencilerin ilgisini çekilir. Senaryoda çevreye zarar veren bir kimyasal kirleticiye bağlı bir sorun vurgulanır.
- Öğrencilere sorular sorularak konuyla ilgili önceki bilgileri hatırlamaları sağlanır ve konuya merak uyandırılır.

[Translation of the conversation from the Turkish language: PST1: As an experienced chemistry teacher, create a lesson plan based on the 5E learning model for the 9th-grade *Environmental Chemistry* topic in the Turkish Secondary Education Chemistry Curriculum, targeting the objective of proposing solutions to reduce the effects of chemical pollutants harmful to the environment, to support the development of students with visual intelligence from the multiple intelligence groups.

Engage phase: A digital story scenario that can be supported with visuals related to the topic.

Explore phase: Five problem situations that, depending on the topic and the digital story, can guide students to research.

Explain phase: A different activity the teacher can conduct related to the problem situation given to students during the explore phase, appealing to visual intelligence.

Elaborate phase: Activities in which students can use the information they obtained throughout the process in new situations.

Evaluate phase: Student projects that can be displayed on a board appealing to visual intelligence.

ChatGPT: Of course, here is a lesson plan prepared according to the 5E learning model:

Lesson Plan: Environmental Chemistry - Reducing the Effects of Harmful Chemical Pollutants on the Environment

Topic: Reducing the Effects of Harmful Chemical Pollutants on the Environment
Grade Level: 9th Grade
Intelligence Type: Visual Intelligence
1. Engage Phase (Explore):
- A brief introduction is given to students about the effects of harmful chemical pollutants on the environment.
- A digital story scenario is shown to capture students' interest. In the scenario, a problem related to a harmful chemical pollutant is highlighted.
- Questions are asked to help students recall their previous knowledge on the topic and to spark curiosity about the subject.]

Figure 3 shows that PST1, unlike PST2, starts the conversation with detailed information. PST1 included detailed information in this way throughout the entire conversation with ChatGPT.

After the initial conversations, the pre-service teachers gave various prompts to ChatGPT to design their imagined lesson plans. The participants' preferences for continuing the conversation also differed from each other. While some of the participants instructed ChatGPT to design the whole lesson plan in detail, others gave section-by-section prompts according to the steps of the lesson plan. These preferences of the candidates in directing the conversation were also reflected in their views on designing lesson plans with ChatGPT.

Figure 4. Example of a step-by-step prompt to ChatGPT (PST4)

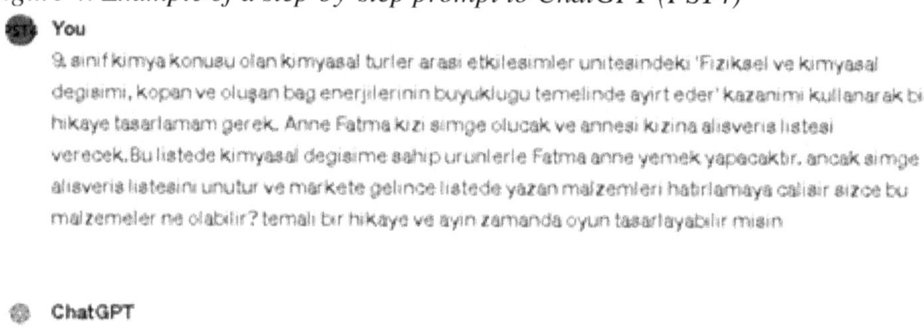

[Translation of the conversation from the Turkish language: PST4: I need to design a story using the learning objective "Distinguish between physical and chemical changes based on the magnitude of bond energies broken and formed" from the 9th-grade chemistry unit on interactions between chemical species. The characters will be a mother, Fatma, and her daughter, Simge. The mother will give a shopping list to her daughter. Fatma will cook using products that involve chemical changes.

However, Simge forgets the shopping list and tries to remember the ingredients once she reaches the store. Could you design a story and a game with the theme, "What do you think these ingredients might be?"?

ChatGPT: Of course! Here's your story and game:]

After determining what to use in the lesson plan, PST4 gave step-by-step prompts. Figure 4 shows the story creation prompt s/he gave to ChatGPT to use in a part of the lesson plan. In the interview, PST4 stated that she made better progress by giving prompts in stages in this way. Although she divided the lesson plan into sections, PST4 thought that she still needed to give detailed prompts and evaluated this situation positively. PST4 stated that in this way, s/he thought that s/he had improved herself/himself in terms of how s/he should give prompts to ChatGPT. Figure 5 shows PST3's conversation with ChatGPT with a single prompt.

Figure 5. Example of a single prompt to ChatGPT (PST3)

You

ŞİMDİ SENDEN Türkiye 2018 öğretim programında yer alan ' Karışımları niteliklerine göre sınıflandırır.

a. Homojen ve heterojen karışımların ayırt edilmesinde belirleyici olan özellikler açıklanır.

b. Homojen karışımların çözelti olarak adlandırıldığı vurgulanır ve günlük hayattan çözelti örnekleri verilir.

c. Heterojen karışımlar, dağılan maddenin ve dağılma ortamının fiziksel hâline göre sınıflandırılır.

ç. Karışımlar çözünenin ve/veya dağılanın tanecik boyutu esas alınarak sınıflandırılır. ' kazanımı kapsamında TGA kuramına göre görsel uzamsal zekayı kullanarak 2 ders saati yani 80 dakikalık bir ders planı hazırla

You

unutmaki sen deneyimli bir öğretmensin ona göre hazırla

[Translation of the conversation from the Turkish language: **You**: Now, I want you to prepare a lesson plan for 80 minutes (2 lesson hours) using the *Predict-Observe-Explain* (POE) model and incorporating visual-spatial intelligence, based on the learning objective from the 2018 Turkish Curriculum, which is "Classify mixtures according to their properties."

a. The determining characteristics in distinguishing between homogeneous and heterogeneous mixtures are explained.
b. It is emphasized that homogeneous mixtures are referred to as solutions, and examples of solutions from daily life are given.
c. Heterogeneous mixtures are classified according to the physical properties of the dispersed substance and the dispersing medium.

d. Mixtures are classified based on the particle size of the dissolved or dispersed substance.

You: Don't forget, you are an experienced teacher, so prepare it accordingly.]

Figure 5 shows the prompts given by PST3 to ChatGPT. Since PST3 did not get the response s/he expected from her/his first prompt, s/h tried to strengthen her/his prompt by saying "you are an experienced chemistry teacher". In the interview with PST3, said that he had to explain too much to ChatGPT to make her/his make the plan s/he thought of and this caused her/him to waste time. While preparing a lesson plan in which POE theory was included, s/he stated that he tried very hard while giving prompts to ChatGPT and that ChatGPT moved away from the target with each explanation he made. However, PST3 stated that it understood ChatGPT's concepts in the later stages of the chat and gave suggestions according to what he wanted, and that he added the experiment activity and evaluation questions suggested by ChatGPT to the lesson plan without changing them. However, since s/he did not receive the material support s/he expected from ChatGPT, she evaluated this process negatively in general.

PST6, who, like PST 3, thought that ChatGPT was inadequate in designing a new material, asked ChatGPT to create a concept map to be used in the lesson plan. Figure 6 shows the concept map created by ChatGPT.

Figure 6. Example of a concept map generated by ChatGPT (With the prompt of PST6)

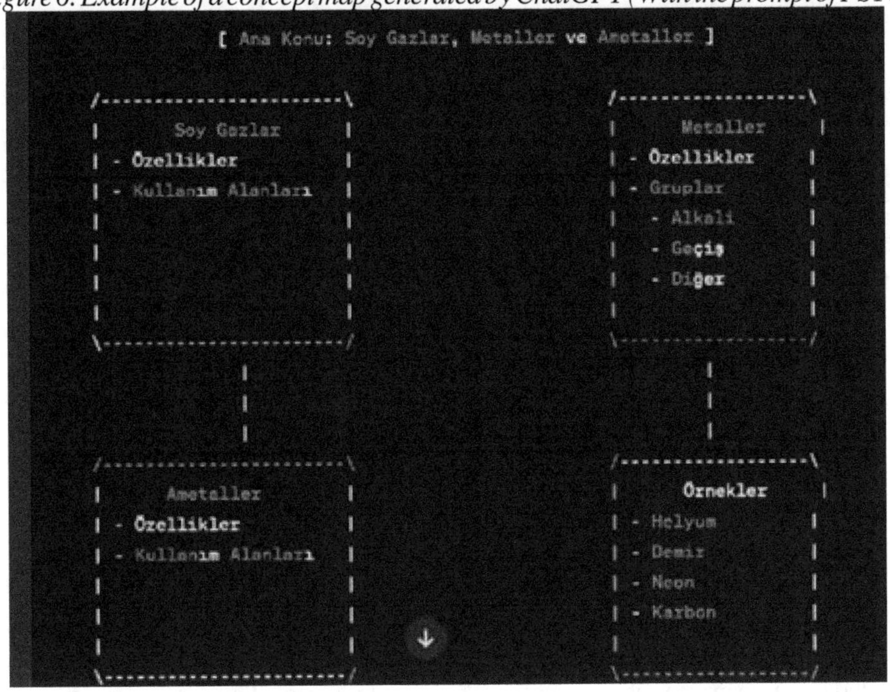

Table 2. Translation of the conversation from the Turkish language Main Topic: Noble Gases, Metals, and Nonmetals

Noble Gases **- Properties**	**Metals** **- Properties** **- Groups** **Alkali** **Transition** **Other**
- Uses	
Nonmetals - Properties - Uses	Examples - Helium - Iron - Neon - Carbon

PST6 stated that s/he did not include the concept map shown in Figure 6 in the lesson plan on the grounds that it did not include concept map features such as connecting sentences and concept hierarchy.

Pre-service Chemistry Teachers' Opinions on ChatGPT

In order to determine the opinions of pre-service teachers about ChatGPT, individual interviews were conducted with each pre-service teacher for an average of 10 minutes. Audio recordings were taken during the interviews with the pre-service teachers. The audio recordings were analyzed with Microsoft Office Word program/typewriter. At the beginning of the study, the participants were informed through the voluntary participation form that they would be audio-recorded and that their names would remain confidential.

In these interviews, pre-service teachers were asked,

1. "How would you evaluate the process of preparing a lesson plan using ChatGPT? What were your favorite and most difficult aspects?"
2. "Would you use ChatGPT for preparing lesson plans etc. in the future?" questions were asked.

Pre-service Teachers' Opinions on the Process of Preparing Lesson Plans with ChatGPT. When the pre-service teachers' answers to the first question of the study were analyzed, it was seen that they found it interesting to use ChatGPT and were divided into two groups about whether they liked it or not. The pre-service teachers who said that they were a little nervous at the beginning because they had never used an AI tool before, stated that they got used to it as they practiced. For example, PST5 expressed this situation as follows: "I had difficulty when I first started using it, I got used to it as I used it. There were places to be careful in its use... When it did not give a detailed prompt, it included other subjects." The fact that pre-service teachers have never used ChatGPT before constitutes the basis of their negative opinions. It was determined that the most difficult aspect of the participants was that they had no experience in this subject. There are pre-service teachers who characterize the use of ChatGPT as completely difficult. For example, PST3's view that "In my opinion, this application requires too much attention and too much detail... it makes it very difficult to use" is an example of this situation. All pre-service teachers who participated in the study said that they could use ChatGPT effectively only when they gave detailed prompts and characterized this situation as negative. On the other hand, when the opinions of the pre-service teachers were analyzed, all pre-service teachers stated that in order to benefit from ChatGPT, it is necessary to use it consciously, but some of the candidates evaluated this situation negatively while others evaluated it positively. The pre-service teachers who evaluated this situation negatively argued that using ChatGPT is usually time-consuming. Table 2 shows the codes and categories of pre-service teachers' opinions.

Table 3. General Opinions on the Experience of Using ChatGPT

Category	Code	Pre-service Teacher
Negative	● Boring	PST6
	● It takes time	PST3, PST6
	● The need for detailed commands	PST1, PST2, PST3, PST4, PST5, PST6
	● Misdirection	PST3, PST5
	● Inadequate material support	PST3
	● *The necessity of being an informed user	PST3, PST6
	● Completely difficult	PST3, PST6
Positive	● Difficult at first, easier as you get used to it	PST1, PST2, PST4, PST5
	● Creative	PST1, PST2, PST4, PST5
	● Practical/Facilitating	PST1, PST4, PST5
	● Adequate Material Support	PST2, PST4
	● The necessity of being an informed user	PST1, PST2, PST4, PST5,
	● Assistant to the teacher	PST1, PST2, PST3, PST4, PST5, PST6

*The code for the necessity of being a conscious user was evaluated in both positive and negative categories as it differed according to the inferences of the participants.

*The code for the necessity of being a conscious user was evaluated in both positive and negative categories as it differed according to the inferences of the participants.

As seen in Table 2, all participants consider ChatGPT as an auxiliary tool for the teacher rather than a substitute for the teacher. Pre-service teachers think that in order to use ChatGPT effectively, it is necessary to have domain knowledge as well as the tendency to use AI tools. PST1 stated that "I think one important point that I think should not be overlooked here is that you should not start this business with completely zero knowledge. Otherwise, there may be problems with guidance and an inefficient experience." Her/his statement also supports this situation.

Pre-service Teachers' Opinions on Whether They Will Use ChatGPT in the Future. The second question asked to the pre-service teachers in the interviews was whether they would use ChatGPT again after this study. Of the 6 pre-service teachers who participated in the study, 4 said that they would continue to use ChatGPT. 2 pre-service teachers (PST3 and PST6) stated that they were not very interested in using ChatGPT again. PST3 answered this question as follows: "Instead of having a lesson plan prepared by this application, it is an application that I will use only to get your opinion or to have different ideas where I get stuck. Because giving detailed prompts is very time consuming." Similarly, PST6, who had a generally negative opinion about the use of ChatGPT, said, "The application may be good in terms of giving ideas... but I don't like working with such a program. That's why it seemed a bit boring to me, I don't think I would use it much... I chose what I would use from some of the things he suggested... what it suggested didn't make sense."

LIMITATIONS OF THE STUDY

This study is limited to pre-service chemistry teachers who have no experience with any AI tool such as ChatGPT and their views on their experiences in preparing lesson plans using ChatGPT. Although the participants have successfully completed courses such as Instructional Technologies and Material Design, Chemistry Curricula, Chemistry Teaching Curricula, Chemistry Teaching Theories and Approaches, they do not have enough experience in both lesson plan preparation and using AI. In addition, the ethical dimensions of using AI in the lesson plan design task such as plagiarism and data privacy were not examined in the study.

AI is becoming an integral part of our lives day by day. It is thought that further studies on the use of AI tools in education with a larger and more experienced group of participants will provide more comprehensive results about the place of AI in education.

DISCUSSION AND RECOMMENDATIONS

In this study, the experiences of pre-service teachers who have never used ChatGPT before in preparing lesson plans using ChatGPT and their opinions about these experiences were analysed. Preparing lesson plans is very important for pre-service teachers and teachers who want to provide an effective learning environment for their students. ChatGPT has the potential to be an effective tool for pre-service teachers and teachers who want to enrich their lesson plans with different activities. ChatGPT has attracted a great deal of attention since the first day it was released, and easy-to-implement suggestions have been presented by different researchers for its use in the field of education, which will help educators to create course curricula (Watkins, 2022). However, the experience of creating lesson plans with ChatGPT, which we encounter in every field in our lives day by day, is an important and current issue with a limited number of studies. van den Berg & du Plessis (2023) sought an answer to the question 'How can ChatGPT and generative AI potentially contribute to lesson planning, foster critical thinking and promote openness in teacher education?' in their study. In the study conducted according to exploratory case study research design, they investigated in detail how ChatGPT can help lesson planning. The texts created by ChatGPT were used for document analysis. In order to determine the extent to which ChatGPT can create a lesson on a specific topic at a specific level, the researchers gave an initial command with the question 'Can you design an English second language lesson on prepositions for Grade 6 learners?' and proceeded with this command. The results of the study show that generative language models such as ChatGPT can be useful in providing teachers and pre-service teachers with materials and support mechanisms such as lesson plans.

The pre-service teachers who were the participants of this study had no previous experience with ChatGPT. When the findings of the study were analysed, it was seen that the pre-service teachers had different experiences from each other. The individual differences of the pre-service teachers were also reflected in their opinions. Firstly, the screenshots of the pre-service teachers' conversations with ChatGPT were analysed. It was observed that the commands of each of the pre-service teachers to start a conversation with ChatGPT were directly related to the lesson plan they wanted to make. None of the pre-service teachers started their conversations with ChatGPT with the expression of greeting. However, ChatGPT is not only an AI tool but also a chatbot. While they were told that they could use greetings in the ChatGPT usage meeting held with pre-service teachers, none of the pre-service teachers preferred this. The responses of the pre-service teachers to the commands they gave and their views on the use of ChatGPT were generally parallel to each other. While pre-service teachers who had difficulty in giving prompts to ChatGPT described ChatGPT as time-consuming and challenging, pre-service teachers who did not have much difficulty in giving commands had more positive opinions. This is a remarkable result and shows that individual differences are effective in evaluations regarding the use of ChatGPT.

The participants' negative opinions about the prompts they gave to ChatGPT once again emphasize the importance of using appropriate prompts. Chatbots that can be used as teaching assistants such as ChatGPT are likely to make mistakes, and the use of an appropriate prompt can help improve the quality of ChatGPT's output (Araújo & Saúde, 2024). With the popularization of artificial intelligence, prompt engineering has become a widely used method to improve the effectiveness of Big Language Models such as ChatGPT through the creation of well-crafted instructions (Araújo & Saúde, 2024). Prompt engineering is becoming increasingly important as it enables the optimization of AI capabilities through the input provided to it. In this sense, an effective structured prompt should cover four key elements: Clarity and Precision, Contextual Information, Desired Format, and Verbosity Control (Lo, 2023). In investigating the effectiveness of ChatGPT, working with participants who have knowledge about the use of appropriate prompts may lead to different results. Students with positive views reported that ChatGPT helped them to develop their creativity. ChatGPT provides pre-service teachers with a variety of teaching strategies and activities, which encourages creative thinking. Pre-service teachers get new and innovative ideas that they can implement in their lessons (Holmes et al., 2019).

On the other hand, it was observed that even the pre-service teachers with negative views were not completely against the use of ChatGPT. These pre-service teachers stated that ChatGPT could be used to get ideas or to design a simpler activity. These pre-service teachers stated that if they used ChatGPT more than necessary, their creativity could be negatively affected. For this reason, they stated that they preferred to use it in more 'simple' tasks. This is a remarkable result. Although ChatGPT provides convenience to users in many areas, this situation also brings some disadvantages. For example, individuals frequently using ChatGPT in every subject may make them overly dependent on ChatGPT. These conveniences offered by technology may cause pre-service teachers not to develop their pedagogical knowledge and skills sufficiently, and may cause pre-service teachers to feel inadequate in this regard. Pre-service teachers may worry that they may be inadequate in developing their own lesson planning skills if they use ChatGPT too much (Luckin et al., 2016).

On the other hand, ChatGPT helps pre-service teachers to create their lesson plans quickly, thus saving more time and enabling them to focus on the course content. The pre-service teachers mostly stated that ChatGPT does not dull ideas, on the contrary, it can improve creativity. It was also observed that the pre-service teachers' preferences for continuing their conversations with ChatGPT were different from each other. While pre-service teachers who asked for more than one task in a command in the progression of the conversation could not get efficiency from the conversation, pre-service teachers who gave only one command in each conversation benefited from ChatGPT more effectively. The expectations of pre-service teachers from ChatGPT brought along ethical problems such as plagiarism. Since the pre-service teachers had no experience and knowledge about ChatGPT or other AI tools, situations such as the candidates' use of all the lesson plans, materials, etc. created by ChatGPT as they are, and their lack of testing the information provided by ChatGPT reveal the danger of plagiarism. Cases of cheating and plagiarism with misinformation and prejudices found in ChatGPT's responses have worried educational experts (Trust et al., 2023).

The content produced by ChatGPT may not always be compatible with the curriculum and may sometimes contain erroneous information. For this reason, pre-service teachers should carefully examine the lesson plans produced and make adjustments (Zawacki-Richter et al., 2019). For this reason, it is thought that it is important to address the information produced by ChatGPT in the context of accuracy and reliability in the studies to be conducted on the use of ChatGPT, and to include the issue of ethics in this context. When the opinions and experiences of pre-service teachers were analysed, it was seen that the individual differences of pre-service teachers greatly affected their opinions and experiences. Similarly, Turmuzi et al. (2024), in a study conducted with pre-service teachers who had experience with ChatGPT, found that individual differences affected the views on the use of ChatGPT. Turmuzi et al. (2024) used both quantitative and qualitative methodologies together in their study in which they examined the views of students who used ChatGPT in classroom learning on the use of ChatGPT. In order to collect quantitative data, a 5-point Likert-type 16-item questionnaire was distributed to the participants via Google Forms. A total of 45 students participated in the study, and the selected participants were 5th semester students who were able to use and familiar with the ChatGPT application. The qualitative data of the study consisted of interviews with the participants who completed the questionnaire and were willing to be interviewed. The interviews were conducted to learn more about the students' perceptions about the use of ChatGPT in the learning process. According to the survey results, ChatGPT identified different degrees of effectiveness among students using it. Some students use the technology less, while others actively use it as an important component of their education. Another noteworthy result is that students' purposes for using ChatGPT vary. Some students use it to increase their productivity or learning skills, while others are motivated by the ease of access to information.

Studies on the future of using artificial intelligence in education reveal that pre-service teachers' use of these technologies as an assistive tool has the potential to make them more pedagogically confident (Holmes et al., 2019). The use of artificial intelligence tools such as ChatGPT, especially to guide pre-service teachers and support their pedagogical development, is considered to be very important for the future of the teaching profession. Reflecting on the activities generated by ChatGPT can help broaden teachers' perspectives and inspire creativity by offering many different activities and approaches to teach a particular subject (van den Berg & du Plessis, 2023). Therefore, further studies on how individual differences such as technology usage level, teaching content knowledge, teaching professional knowledge, TPACK level, use of technological tools such as computers, etc. affect teachers' perspectives on ChatGPT may provide more comprehensive information. At the same time, the fact that they have no experience with AI tools is also a factor. In future studies, it is recommended to conduct research with participants who have different levels of experience with its use.

CONCLUSION

This chapter underscores the transformative potential of ChatGPT in lesson planning, particularly for pre-service chemistry teachers. The experiences of participants reveal both the opportunities and challenges of integrating AI tools in educational contexts. While ChatGPT facilitates the creation of lesson plans and supports the development of instructional materials, it also highlights the importance of effective prompt engineering to maximize AI's potential in delivering relevant and customized content. These experiences underscore the necessity for pre-service teachers to acquire a foundational understanding of AI, as it plays a growing role in modern education. The study findings indicate that while ChatGPT can enhance creativity and efficiency in lesson planning, its limitations—such as occasional inaccuracies and the need for ethical considerations—demand cautious and informed use. Additionally, individual differences in adaptability to AI tools suggest that teacher education programs should include AI literacy training to prepare future educators for effective technology integration. Overall, this chapter contributes valuable insights into the evolving role of AI in education, offering practical recommendations for balancing AI's benefits with the essential human elements of teaching and ethical practices in educational settings.

REFERENCES

Acar, O. (2020). *Yapay zeka fırsat mı yoksa tehdit mi?* Kriter Yayınevi.

Adeshola, I., & Adepoju, A. P. (2023). The opportunities and challenges of ChatGPT in education. *Interactive Learning Environments*, •••, 1–14. DOI: 10.1080/10494820.2023.2253858

Adiguzel, T., Kaya, M. H., & Cansu, F. K. (2023). Revolutionizing education with AI: Exploring the transformative potential of ChatGPT. *Contemporary Educational Technology*, 15(3), ep429. DOI: 10.30935/cedtech/13152

Akyürek, H. A. (2013). *Yapay zekâ teknikleri kullanarak akıllı iş gücü yönetimi (Yayımlanmamış yüksek lisans tezi)*. Mevlana Üniversitesi.

Alasadi, E. A., & Baiz, C. R. (2023). Generative AI in Education and Research: Opportunities, concerns, and solutions. *Journal of Chemical Education*, 100(8), 2965–2971. DOI: 10.1021/acs.jchemed.3c00323

Araújo, J. L., & Saúde, I. (2024). Can ChatGPT enhance chemistry laboratory teaching? Using prompt engineering to enable AI in generating laboratory activities. *Journal of Chemical Education*, 101(5), 1858–1864. DOI: 10.1021/acs.jchemed.3c00745

Arslan, K. (2020). Eğitimde yapay zeka ve uygulamaları. [Derleme Makale Western Anatolia Journal of Educational Sciences.]. *Batı Anadolu Eğitim Bilimleri Dergisi*, 11(1), 71–88.

Aşık, F., Yıldız, A., Kılınç, S., Aytekin, N., Adalı, R., & Kurnaz, K. (2023). Yapay Zekânın Eğitime Etkileri. [JSHSR]. *International Journal of Social and Humanities Sciences Research*, 10(98), 2100–2107. DOI: 10.5281/zenodo.8307107

Çam, M. B., Çelik, N. C., Turan Güntepe, E., & Durukan, Ü. G. (2021). Öğretmen adaylarının yapay zekâ teknolojileri ile ilgili farkındalıklarının belirlenmesi. *Hatay Mustafa Kemal Üniversitesi Sosyal Bilimler Enstitüsü Dergisi*, 18(48), 263–285.

Chassignol, M., Khoroshavin, A., Klimova, A., & Bilyatdinova, A. (2018). Artificial Intelligence trends in education: A narrative overview. *Procedia Computer Science*, 136, 16–24. DOI: 10.1016/j.procs.2018.08.233

Chavez, H., Chavez-Arias, B., Contreras-Rosas, S., Alvarez-Rodríguez, J. M., & Raymundo, C. (2023). Artificial neural network model to predict student performance using nonpersonal information. *Frontiers in Education*, 8, 1106679. DOI: 10.3389/feduc.2023.1106679

Chen, X., Xie, H., Zou, D., & Hwang, G.-J. (2020). Application and theory gaps during the rise of artificial intelligence in education. *Computers and Education: Artificial Intelligence*, 1, 100002. DOI: 10.1016/j.caeai.2020.100002

Chen, Y., Chen, Y., & Heffernan, N. (2020). Personalized math tutoring with a conversational agent. arXiv preprint arXiv:2012.12121.

Chen, Y., Jensen, S., Albert, L. J., Gupta, S., & Lee, T. (2022). Artificial intelligence (AI) student assistants in the classroom: Designing chatbots to support student success. *Information Systems Frontiers*, 25(1), 161–182. DOI: 10.1007/s10796-022-10291-4

Cheung, S. K. S., Kwok, L. F., Phusavat, K., & Yang, H. H. (2021). Shaping the future learning environments with smart elements: Challenges and opportunities. *International Journal of Educational Technology in Higher Education, 18*(1), 16, s41239-021-00254-1. DOI: 10.1186/s41239-021-00254-1

Clark, T. M. (2023). Investigating the use of an artificial intelligence chatbot with general chemistry exam questions. *Journal of Chemical Education*, 100(5), 1905–1916. DOI: 10.1021/acs.jchemed.3c00027

Çolak, A. F. (2022). Okullarda yapay zeka öğretimi için geliştirilen kurs planı ve içeriklerin öğrencilerin üstbilişsel davranışlarına etkisi / The effect of course plan and contents developed for artificial intelligence teaching in secondary schools on students' metacognitive behaviors, Trabzon Üniversitesi / Lisansüstü Eğitim Enstitüsü, Yüksek lisans tezi

Cooper, G. (2023). Examining science education in ChatGPT: An exploratory study of generative artificial intelligence. *Journal of Science Education and Technology*, 32(3), 444–452. DOI: 10.1007/s10956-023-10039-y

Coşkun, F., & Gülleroğlu, H. D. (2021). Yapay zekanın tarih içindeki gelişimi ve eğitimde kullanılması. *Ankara Üniversitesi Eğitim Bilimleri Fakültesi Dergisi, 54*(3), 947-966. DOI: , E-ISSN: 2458-8342, P-ISSN: 1301-3718.DOI: 10.30964/auebfd.916220

Dempere, J., Modugu, K., Hesham, A., & Ramasamy, L. K. (2023). The impact of ChatGPT on higher education. *Frontiers in Education*, 8, 1206936. Advance online publication. DOI: 10.3389/feduc.2023.1206936

Elmas, Ç. (2018). *Yapay zeka uygulamaları*. Seçkin Yayıncılık.

Felix, C. (2020). In Sengupta, E., Blessinger, P., & Makhanya, M. S. (Eds.), *"The role of the teacher and AI in education" in International perspectives on the role of Technology in Humanizing Higher Education Innovations in higher education teaching and learning* (Vol. 33, pp. 33–48). Emerald Publishing Limited.

Geerling, W., Mateer, G. D., Wooten, J., & Damodaran, N. (2023). Is ChatGPT smarter than a student in principles of economics? SSRN *Electronic Journal,* 1-24. https://doi.org/DOI: 10.2139/ssrn.4356034

Halaweh, M. (2023). ChatGPT in education: Strategies for responsible implementation. *Contemporary Educational Technology*, 15(2), ep421. DOI: 10.30935/cedtech/13036

Holmes, W., Bialik, M., & Fadel, C. (2019). *Artificial Intelligence in Education: Promises and Implications for Teaching and Learning*. Center for Curriculum Redesign.

Hu, L. (2023). Generative AI and future. Last accessed 2024/05/01 from https://pub.towardsai.net/generative-ai-and-future-c3b1695876f2

Humphry, T., & Fuller, A. L. (2023). Potential ChatGPT use in undergraduate chemistry laboratories. *Journal of Chemical Education*, 100(4), 1434–1436. DOI: 10.1021/acs.jchemed.3c00006

İşler, B., & Kılıç, M. (2021). Eğitimde yapay zekâ kullanimi ve gelişimi. *Yeni Medya Elektronik Dergisi*, 5(1), 1–11.

Jeon, J., & Lee, S. (2023). Large language models in education: A focus on the complementary relationship between human teachers and ChatGPT. *Education and Information Technologies*, 28(12), 15873–15892. DOI: 10.1007/s10639-023-11834-1

Johnson, M., Schuster, M., Le, Q., Krikun, M., Wu, Y., Chen, Z., ... & Chen, Y. (2016). Google's neural machine translation system: Bridging the gap between human and machine translation. arXiv pre.

Kaya, İ. (2024). *Eğitim yönetiminde yapay zekâ kullanımına ilişkin okul yöneticileri ve öğretmenlerin görüşleri / School administrators and teachers' views on the use of artificial intelligence in education administration. İstanbul Aydın Üniversitesi / Lisansüstü Eğitim Enstitüsü / Eğitim Bilimleri Ana Bilim Dalı*. Yüksek Lisans Tezi.

Kharchenko, Y. V., & Babenko, O. M. (2024). Advantages and limitations of large language models in chemistry education: A comparative analysis of ChatGPT, Gemini and Copilot. *IX International Workshop on Professional Retraining and Life-Long Learning using ICT: Person-oriented Approach, co-located with the 19th International Conference on ICT in Education, Research, and Industrial Applications (ICTERI 2024) September 23, 2024, Lviv, Ukraine*

Kung, T. H., Cheatham, M., Medenilla, A., Sillos, C., De Leon, L., Elepaño, C., Madriaga, M., Aggabao, R., Diaz-Candido, G., Maningo, J., & Tseng, V. (2023). Performance of ChatGPT on USMLE: Potential for AI-assisted medical education using large language models. *PLOS Digital Health*, 2(2), e0000198. DOI: 10.1371/journal.pdig.0000198 PMID: 36812645

Kurzweil, R. (2005). *The Singularity Is Near: When Humans Transcend Biology*. Penguin Books.

Labadze, L., Grigolia, M., & Machaidze, L. (2023). Role of AI chatbots in education: Systematic literature review. *International Journal of Educational Technology in Higher Education*, 20(1), 1–17. DOI: 10.1186/s41239-023-00426-1

Leon, A. J., & Vidhani, D. (2023). ChatGPT needs a chemistry tutor too. *Journal of Chemical Education*, 100(10), 3859–3865. DOI: 10.1021/acs.jchemed.3c00288

Liu, C., Liao, M., Chang, C., & Lin, H. M. (2022). An analysis of children' interaction with an AI chatbot and its impact on their interest in reading. *Computers & Education*, 189, 104576. DOI: 10.1016/j.compedu.2022.104576

Lo, C. K. (2023). What is the impact of ChatGPT on education? A rapid review of the literature. *Education Sciences*, 13(4), 410–455. DOI: 10.3390/educsci13040410

Lo, L. S. (2023). The art and science of prompt engineering: A new literacy in the Information Age. *Internet Reference Services Quarterly*, 27(4), 203–210. DOI: 10.1080/10875301.2023.2227621

McCarthy, J., Minsky, M. L., Rochester, N., & Shannon, C. E. (1955). A proposal for the Dartmouth summer research project on artificial intelligence. *AI Magazine*, 27(4), 12–14.

Murtarellia, G., Gregory, A., & Romentia, S. (2021). A conversation-based perspective for shaping ethical human–machine interactions: The particular challenge of chatbots. *Journal of Business Research*, 129, 927–935. DOI: 10.1016/j.jbusres.2020.09.018

Nabiyev, V. V. (2012). Yapay Zekâ: İnsan-Bilgisayar Etkileşimi. Baski Yeri: Seçkin Yayıncılık.

Nam, B. H., & Bai, Q. (2023). ChatGPT and its ethical implications for STEM research and higher education: A media discourse analysis. *International Journal of STEM Education*, 10(1), 66. Advance online publication. DOI: 10.1186/s40594-023-00452-5

Ng, D. T. K., Leung, J. K. L., Chu, S. K. W., & Qiao, M. S. (2021). Conceptualizing AI literacy: An exploratory review. *Computers and Education: Artificial Intelligence*, 2, 100041100051. DOI: 10.1016/j.caeai.2021.100041

Nguyen, T., & Sirichokcharoenkun. (2023). The limitations and potential of chatgpt in chemistry education. Available online: https://www.researchgate.net/publication/374087925_The_Limitations_and_Potential_of_ChatGPT_in_Chemistry_Education

Obari, H., & Lambacher, S. (2019). Improving the English Skills of Native Japanese Using Artificial Intelligence in a Blended Learning Program. Retrieved from: https://files.eric.ed.gov/fulltext/ED600973.pdf

Open, A. I. (2022, November 30). Introducing ChatGPT. OpenAI. https://openai.com/blog/chatgpt

Ouyang, F., Wu, M., Zheng, L., Zhang, L., & Jiao, P. (2023). Integration of artificial intelligence performance prediction and learning analytics to improve student learning in online engineering course. *International Journal of Educational Technology in Higher Education*, 20(1), 4. DOI: 10.1186/s41239-022-00372-4 PMID: 36683653

Pavlik, J. V. (2023). Collaborating With ChatGPT: Considering the Implications of Generative Artificial Intelligence for Journalism and Media Education. *Journalism & Mass Communication Educator*, 78(1), 84–93. DOI: 10.1177/10776958221149577

Rudolph, J., Tan, S., & Tan, S. (2023). ChatGPT: Bullshit Spewer or the end of traditional assessments in higher education? *Journal of Applied Learning and Teaching*, 6(1), 342–363. DOI: 10.37074/jalt.2023.6.1.9

Schultz, D. P. ve Ellen-Schultz, S. (2007). *Modern psikoloji tarihi* (Y. Aslay, çev.). İstanbul: Kaknüs Yayınları.

Schwendicke, F. A., Samek, W., & Krois, J. (2020). Artificial intelligence in dentistry: Chances and challenges. *Journal of Dental Research*, 99(7), 769–774. DOI: 10.1177/0022034520915714 PMID: 32315260

Seufert, S., Guggemos, J., & Sailer, M. (2021). Technology-related knowledge, skills, and attitudes of pre-and in-service teachers: The current situation and emerging trends. *Computers in Human Behavior,* 115, Article 106552. https://doi.org/.chb.2020.106552DOI: 10.1016/j

Sevli, O. (2023). ChatGPT'nin Eğitim Alanında Kullanımı (Using ChatGPT in Education). Conference: 4th International Black Sea Modern Scientific Research Congress (4. Uluslararası Karadeniz Modern Bilimsel Araştırmalar Kongresi) June 2023 At: Rize, Turkey

Tlili, A., Shehata, B., Adarkwah, M. A., Bozkurt, A., Hickey, D. T., Huang, R., & Agyemang, B. (2023). What if the devil is my guardian angel: ChatGPT as a case study of using Chatbots in education. *Smart Learning Environments*, 10(1), 15. DOI: 10.1186/s40561-023-00237-x

Trust, T., Whalen, J., & Mouza, C. (2023). Editorial: ChatGPT: Challenges, opportunities, and implications for teacher education. *Contemporary Issues in Technology & Teacher Education*, 23(1), 1–23.

Turmuzi, M. (2024). Perceptions of primary school teacher education students to the use of ChatGPT to support learning in the Digital Era. *International Journal of Information and Education Technology (IJIET)*, 14(5), 721–732. DOI: 10.18178/ijiet.2024.14.5.2097

van den Berg, G., & du Plessis, E. (2023). ChatGPT and Generative AI: Possibilities for İts contribution to lesson planning, critical thinking and openness in teacher education. *Education Sciences*, 13(10), 998. DOI: 10.3390/educsci13100998

Watkins, R. (2022, December 19). Update your course syllabus for chatGPT. *Medium.* https://medium.com/@rwatkins_7167/updating-your-course-syllabus-for-chatgpt-965f4b57b003

Yalçın-Çelik, A. & K.Çoban, Ö. (2023). Kimya sorularının cevaplanmasında yapay zekâ tabanlı sohbet robotlarının performansının incelenmesi. *TEBD, 21*(3), 1540-1561. https://doi.org/DOI: 10.37217/tebd.1361401

Yıldırım, A., & Şimşek, H. (2013). *Sosyal bilimlerde nitel araştırma yöntemleri.* Seçkin Yayıncılık.

Yılmaz, A. ve Kaya, U. (2021). *Derin öğrenme* (3. Baskı). İstanbul: Kodlab.

Yin, R. K. (2009). *Case study research design and methods* (4th ed.). Sage.

Zawacki-Richter, O., Marín, V. I., Bond, M., & Gouverneur, F. (2019). Systematic review of research on artificial intelligence applications in higher education–Where are the educators? *International Journal of Educational Technology in Higher Education*, 16(1), 1–27. DOI: 10.1186/s41239-019-0171-0

Zhou, Y., & Chen, L. ve Xu, Y. (2021). Impact of AI-based language learning tools on students' motivation and engagement. *Educational Technology Research and Development*, 69(5), 1201–1219.

ADDITIONAL READING

Araújo, J. L., & Saúde, I. (2024). Can ChatGPT Enhance Chemistry Laboratory Teaching? Using Prompt Engineering to Enable AI in Generating Laboratory Activities. *Journal of Chemical Education*, 101(5), 1858–1864. DOI: 10.1021/acs.jchemed.3c00745

Markos, A., Prentzas, J., & Sidiropoulou, M. (2024). Pre-Service Teachers' Assessment of ChatGPT's Utility in Higher Education: SWOT and Content Analysis. *Electronics (Basel)*, 13(10), 1985. DOI: 10.3390/electronics13101985

Powell, W., & Courchesne, S. (2024). Opportunities and risks involved in using ChatGPT to create first grade science lesson plans. *PLoS One*, 19(6), e0305337. DOI: 10.1371/journal.pone.0305337 PMID: 38885244

Ramnarain, U., Ogegbo, A. A., Penn, M., Ojetunde, S., & Mdlalose, N. (2024). Pre-Service Science Teachers' Intention to use Generative Artificial Intelligence in Inquiry-Based Teaching. *Journal of Science Education and Technology*, •••, 1–14. DOI: 10.1007/s10956-024-10159-z

Tekin, N. (2025). Using Artificial Intelligence to Evaluate the Nature of Science Myths: A Comparison of Pre-Service Science Teachers and ChatGPT. In *AI Applications and Strategies in Teacher Education* (pp. 253-274). IGI Global.

KEY TERMS AND DEFINITIONS

Artificial Intelligence (AI): A field of technology focused on creating systems that can perform tasks requiring human intelligence, such as problem-solving, learning, and language processing.

ChatGPT: A language-based AI tool developed by OpenAI, specializing in generating text-based responses that simulate human conversation and assist with various tasks, including educational content creation.

Educational Technology: The use of digital tools and resources to enhance learning, teaching, and assessment processes in educational settings.

Ethical AI Use: The responsible application of artificial intelligence, ensuring that usage aligns with principles of transparency, fairness, and privacy.

Flipped Learning Model: An instructional approach where traditional in-class learning and homework activities are reversed, often incorporating technology for pre-class learning.

Lesson Planning: The process of outlining instructional activities, objectives, and assessments to guide a structured learning experience.

Multiple Intelligences: A theory that suggests individuals have different types of intelligences, such as logical, linguistic, or visual-spatial, which influence their learning preferences and strengths.

Pre-Service Teacher: An individual in training who is preparing to become a certified teacher, often through hands-on experience and professional development in teaching methods.

Prompt Engineering: The art of crafting effective input prompts to optimize the responses generated by AI models like ChatGPT.

Student Engagement: The level of interest, motivation, and active participation demonstrated by students in their learning activities.

Chapter 9
Short Digital Storytelling:
An AI-Based Innovative Teaching Strategy

Subhasis Sen
BITM, Sri Balaji University, Pune, India

Indrani Sen
https://orcid.org/0009-0007-4367-3239
Independent Researcher, India

ABSTRACT

This chapter explores the innovative use of digital storytelling as an AI-enhanced teaching strategy to engage learners and foster a deeper willingness to learn. Digital storytelling, the art of creating online narratives for social media, combines visual elements and storytelling techniques to captivate and motivate students. By developing a collection of twenty digitally accessible moral stories, paired with original artwork, the authors demonstrate how AI can be leveraged to create engaging and meaningful educational content. The chapter examines how stories rooted in real-life experiences can teach valuable lessons, integrating AI to adapt content for dynamic learning environments. Furthermore, AI in education aids academic decision-making across course development, pedagogical design, and institutional transformation. Through AI-based digital storytelling, this approach benefits instructors, learners, and administrators alike, presenting new opportunities for growth and innovation in higher education.

DOI: 10.4018/979-8-3373-1017-6.ch009

INTRODUCTION

Digital storytelling is an art of creating online stories in social media. It enhances willingness to learn by engaging students (Chena et al., 2023). Digital stories are short and pertaining to an individual (Meadows, 2003). It has been widely used as a mechanism to enable networking between student community (Alismail, 2015; Karakoyun and Kuzu, 2016; Niemi et al., 2018). Alismail (2015) seconded that communication between peers improve while working as a team in digital storytelling. Niemi et al. (2014) stated that digital storytelling leads to collaborative learning while sharing each other perspective. Digital storytelling contributes towards personality development of children by finding the meaning of life through interactions and experiences leading to social and psychological well-being (Bruner, 2003; Pahl, 2011; Sen and Banerjee, 2022). The significance of storytelling has led to emergence of collaborative communication tools and techniques for production of short stories (G¨ottel, 2011) and termed as Digital Storytelling Technologies (DST). Simonton (2013) developed a model which includes the formation of scientific creativity requiring communication between three entities viz. domain, field, and individual. Sak and Ayas (2013) stated that scientific creativity is association among different "abilities, skills, and knowledge".

A disruptive innovation is termed as "An innovation process in which technologies, products or services are initially inferior to those provided by incumbents in the attributes that mainstream consumers value, but these technologies, products or services can attract and satisfy the consumers in low-end or new markets with advantages in performance attributes (such as being cheap, simple, or convenient) that these consumers value but which at the same time are neglected by mainstream markets. Over time, through the incremental improvement of technology or process, a disruptive innovation gradually satisfies the needs of mainstream consumers, to attain certain market share from or even replace incumbents in mainstream markets. Disruptive Innovation theory was proposed in 1997 by Christensen and focuses on how a new product or service enters the marketplace and disrupts existing competitors with specific emphasis on the eventual overturning of dominant market players." (Si and Chen, 2020; Keiper et al., 2023). We are experiencing digital storytelling as a disruptive innovation to under-graduate and post-graduate education.

AI IN EDUCATION (AIEd)

AIEd is usage of AI technologies in teaching and learning of students (Hwang et al., 2020). In online higher education, AI has the capability to provide automated student learning system (Christudas et al., 2018) with automatic evaluation (Aluthman, 2016) for judging learning outcomes (Almeda et al., 2018; Moreno-Marcos et al., 2019). AIEd can aid academic administrators in designing course curriculum, pedagogical approach, and digital transformation. Sen and Banerjee (2023) stated in a research study - "The education system should help in assistance and adaptability of faculty members in virtual academic delivery. Online teaching strategies should ensure emotional, cognitive, and social engagement among student managers leading to ideal teacher-student and student-student interactive environment."

MORAL STORY 1 – A PERFECTIONIST IN LOVE

Jeremy was a nice and intelligent guy with a good physique and belonging to a lower middle-class family. His aim was to become the best in whatever he wanted to do and reach perfection. He was not being liked by many as he always used to deep dive to find the truth of everything which can be many times a harsh reality. Whenever he was in love with something he tried his level best to fulfil the requirements to reach perfection. But one day he was rejected by a girl whom he loved while doing post-graduation despite doing his best to impress her. The reason for rejection was not known to him but later he came to know that the girl was already engaged by going through her social media. From then onwards, he realized that he will never love a human being as it is a two-way traffic and started working hard in his profession, hobbies and got so much involved so that he can reach perfection. Other than parental love, he fell in love with profession and hobbies and made up his mind to not get married. His relatives and friends tried many times to convince him to get married. But the shock of rejection in love from a woman haunted him throughout his life and decided to make love with something which he enjoyed doing.

Lesson:

Moral of the story is when someone gets hurt in love it becomes a turning point for an individual while understanding meaning of life (refer to Figure-1).

Figure 1. A Perfectionist in Love

MORAL STORY 2 – THE RARITY OF TRUE FRIENDSHIP

Siddharth and Sumedh were good friends since their college days. They did their graduation together. Both visited the same coaching centres and did joint study to score well in the examinations. But after their graduation both had to lead their own lives away from each other owing to higher studies and choosing different streams. But the strength of their friendship was strong and stayed connected over phone. One coincidence happened that they got married on the same day and year and both invited each other. Post marriage they could not maintain the same kind of friendship as distance reduces the strength of association. But even today they smile and at times cry in their own remembering the deeds, fun, struggles, and acts done together. There was a mental wavelength match as well as likings when they used to discuss on different issues which they noticed and knew. But they never got time to meet each other post marriage owing to family and job commitments.

Lesson:

Moral of the story is when you meet a friend every day for many years and suddenly leave each other, it does not matter much initially. But it gives a lot of pain as day passes by remembering the time spent together (refer to Figure-2).

Figure 2. The Rarity of True Friendship

MORAL STORY 3 - TWO FRIENDS WITH A COMMON GOAL

Javed and Jasmine were two friends and authors and had a similar thought process and writing acumen who occasionally used to meet and discuss about their existing work and future goals. They helped each other in fulfilling professional commitments. Jasmine had to relocate with a copyediting job offer but despite that they kept their professional tie up. But one day an incident happened, Javed was observed by his parents talking over phone to a woman of different community. Javed's family was conservative and told him to stop communicating with the woman belonging to another religion. This was a big issue and mentally it affected Javed more than Jasmine. As time passes, we slowly adapt to the situation and accept the reality. So, both Javed and Jasmine stopped communicating with each other. The hidden agenda was both liked each other but could not express their feelings for each other as the opportunity never came. After sometimes both of them got settled and lived the rest of life happily without forgetting memories of meeting each other till the end.

Lesson:

Moral of the story is journey of life takes us to a point where we are indecisive owing to commitments and leaves us helpless (refer to Figure-3).

Figure 3. Two friends with a common goal

MORAL STORY 4 - A FRIEND IN NEED MAY NOT BE A FRIEND INDEED

Ravi and Chetak were colleagues and always fond of walking and working together whenever any task was given to any one of them. Ravi was polite in nature, meticulous, greedy, and shrewd. But Chetak was an honest, loyal, and hardworking guy. Ravi was eager to take any assignment outside the office because of daily allowance and stay in a luxurious hotel. But Chetak never used to say "No" to any initiative which Ravi wanted to do collaboratively. Being friends, Chetak was to overlook the bad things in Ravi and supported as a partner to any task undertaken. They both were sincere and hardworking and enjoyed the stay and allowance offered by the company. One day suddenly, Chetak was called and asked to leave the organization because of the lack of performance. Chetak was shell shocked as he was one of the high performers. Ravi also knew that but did not speak a single word in his favour. Ravi told Chetak that he will take him wherever he will work in future and will be leaving the organization soon. But Chetak kept trying during the notice period and landed up with five offers and he left to join another organization. After a few months Ravi also left and joined a much better organization than Chetak was associated. But Ravi did not even bother to call Chetak since they left each other.

Lesson:

Moral of the story is title itself as sudden friendship dies with time since there is no purpose of meeting (refer to Figure-4).

Figure 4. A Friend in need may not be a Friend indeed

MORAL STORY 5 - FOX AND THE MONKEY COMMUNITY

Once upon a time there was a clever fox who wanted to become the king of the jungle. He used to collect information about other animals and report to the Lion King for becoming a close associate. Monkeys were very friendly, helpful, self-sufficient, and playful. They were happy with their cute family. But the fox did not like this attitude and became jealous. He informed the King that monkeys were becoming popular, powerful, and forming a team to compete against the King. So, without putting any thought the Lion slowly started killing baby monkeys through his subordinates to restrict their population. This was really concerning the mother monkeys, and they went to the King requesting to safeguard their babies. The Lion King ordered the monkeys to stay away from each other instead of forming a community of monkeys and live a peaceful life forever. The monkeys agreed to the King's order and divided their friends and family members into different corners of the jungle to survive.

Lesson:

Moral of the story is jealousy and competition have become so harsh that it can break the bonding between friends and family members (refer to Figure-5).

Figure 5. Fox and the Monkey Community

MORAL STORY 6 - A STRONG BIRD AND CARING BOY

There was a small sparrow who used to visit a boy everyday searching for food. The boy used to offer breadcrumbs, biscuits with a small pot filled with water. But there was danger of pigeons who were equally interested to have the food offered to the sparrow. But the boy was alert, and he immediately threw water to get rid of pigeons. One day the sparrow fell ill so the boy was concerned and bought a nest to treat the sparrow. The sparrow was treated inside the nest with medicines and care and after a few days he started flying again. The sweet relationship between sparrow and the boy went on for almost 3 years and then the day came the boy had to bid goodbye to the sparrow. The sparrow was offered food that day but denied it and looked after the boy with a sorrowful face. Then he flew away and never looked back. The boy kept thinking and puzzled that the sparrow whom he was feeding for years used to visit him not for food but there was something greater than that.

Lesson:

Moral of the story is even birds have feelings and emotions and understand relationships better than human beings (refer to Figure-6).

Figure 6. A Strong Bird and Caring Boy

MORAL STORY 7 - WIMBLEDON! A DISTANT DREAM

Pulok is born in a lower middle-class family. He is playful, friendly, and never used to miss any chance of visiting the sports arena to watch his favourite sports personalities. His favourite Sports is Lawn Tennis. But also used to play Gully Cricket and Football at College Level. His passion for attending sporting events has grown while he watched live international cricket events. But the desire to watch the grand slam became more intense when he started playing the game. But incidentally there has been no Grand Slam in India and only four tournaments in lawn tennis are Australian Open, USA Open, French Open and Wimbledon considered as Grand Slam. Out of these the most prestigious one is Wimbledon and played on grass court with discipline, dress code and an opportunity to meet all-time greats in tennis. Pulok's next destination is to watch Wimbledon. But the ticket prices to Wimbledon is so high that he started sending emails to tennis authorities requesting to give an opportunity to watch Wimbledon live. One day he got a reply that Wimbledon is meant for people who can only afford or else viewing from home on TV is the only other option. So, Pulok started saving money keeping in mind that one day his dream of visiting Wimbledon will be fulfilled.

Lesson:

Moral of the story is willingness to achieve backed by purchasing power can only bring you a dream world (Refer to Figure-7).

Figure 7. Wimbledon! A Distant Dream

MORAL STORY 8 - A FRIEND FROM KALIMPONG

It was during the monsoon season 30 years back we took admission in the same college and used to walk back home not just to save money but to spend time talking about each other and studies. The Kalimpong friend was staying with a family and doing their household work away from his parents and attending the evening college. But the students who used to study in that college were coming from an ordinary to rich background which includes me too, but Kalimpong Friend used to feel comfortable talking to me. Usually, he was a quiet chap and never used to get angry. This is just a common sense that people from mountains are peace loving, tolerant, friendly but get angry if someone takes advantage of their goodness. I asked him one day why he is studying commerce and doing graduation. He replied there is not much growth from the place he belongs and wants to join the Indian Army after studies. My schedule during graduation days was tough managing both work, studies and attending evening college. But I used to get a lot of positive vibes after meeting him. Sometimes I feel that because of those days gained the strength to work harder for survival. The story ended abruptly when the friend I used to return Home regularly suddenly stopped coming to college. But the biggest suspense was that nobody knew about his whereabouts other than me. There was no communication from his end as during those days the mobile phone was just being launched and it was a costly device. I pray to God that he is settled today, might have joined the Indian Army. But till date his departure from our graduation days is vague. He might be reading this story one day and connect.

Lesson:

True Friendship is immortal (refer to Figure-8).

Figure 8. A Friend from Kalimpong

MORAL STORY 9 - A HAPPY MAN

Once upon a time there lived a man with a high degree of helping attitude. He never used to say no to anyone while seeing the sorrow of people in spite of richness at one pole and poverty at the other pole. He was observant about people and tried to understand their stories of life. But every time he felt that none of the people were completely happy. So, he used to put triggers to check whether the person who is sharing or discussing something might be influenced by his advice or suggestion. What he found out is that the rich have the fear of not getting the price of their investment and loves to discuss their prosperity whereas the poor people like to convey that if their financial condition improves, they can fulfil their needs. But the happiest person with whom he interacted are those who do not have anything especially the fear of losing anything and usually they enjoy when others are happy.

Lesson:

Moral of the story is wealth and poverty are relative and states of mind. But the person who lives in the present without any expectation makes others happy (Refer to Figure-9).

Figure 9. A Happy Man

MORAL STORY 10 – JOB OF A HOMEMAKER

Parvati was married to Shiv. Both were happily married couple. But whenever Parvati used to socialize or meet new people, she was asked one question especially from working women "are you working somewhere?". Her answer was always "NO". Answering the same question even from people who do not know her one day she went into depression. Shiv asked her one day "why are you looking depressed?". Parvati said bluntly that she wants to do something to earn a livelihood. Then Shiv asked her one more question "Is that you want to do a job to prove that you can also be a working woman or wish to pursue a career?". Parvati replied that she wants to be a working woman. Shiv and Parvati kept quiet for some time and then Shiv stood up and stated working women can never do what you are doing that is managing a home and maintaining a family bond. If one can manage a home, she can manage anything in the world - the most challenging task. So, Shiv said to her whenever anyone asks you "what are you doing?" please reply boldly and proudly that you are a homemaker and doing the most difficult job in the world.

Lesson:

Moral of the story is - never get bog down by criticism and lead a life of your own (Refer to Figure-10).

Figure 10. Job of a Homemaker

MORAL STORY 11 - A GIRL WHO WANTS TO RETURN HOME TO STAY WITH FAMILY & FRIENDS

A young girl who left home at an early age while seeing starvation in family always wanted to return Home whenever possible. But the situation was such whenever there was an opportunity to return, she was strongly opposed by the people of his village since there was not much growth. In this way years went by, and the girl turned into woman developed a trauma of not returning home until unless required. Then one day she got a call from one of his old friends for an alumni meet. She made up her mind to leave but again there was something or the other kept on coming which stopped her to meet the friends.

Lesson:

Usually, people never forget the soil where they are born but the acquaintances make the difference while making the decision to settle down in place of comfort (Refer to Figur-11).

Figure 11. A Girl who wants to return Home to stay with Family & Friends

MORAL STORY 12 - BOBBY'S STRUGGLE

At an early age of 24 years just after appearing for graduation, Bobby left his hometown for a job abroad thinking to earn for livelihood since his parents could not afford him. He wanted to stay in home with his parents. He was exploited abroad working 7 days a week and his passport was confiscated so that he cannot leave. After tolerating for almost one and half years, he called his parents one day saying that his passport was taken by his boss where he was working. Somehow Bobby's family using influence rescued him from the alien country and he returned home. He was happy but there was a huge burden on his shoulders to earn money. Bobby decided to join a private firm where he was paid very less and had to work from 9 am to 6 pm. Bobby was now a little experienced and mature and decided to go for higher education so that he could earn more money.

His parents used to indirectly make him realize that home was like a hotel where Bobby can pay and stay. When Bobby's batchmates were either enjoying or going for higher education, he was doing a 9 am to 6 pm job. That was one thing annoying Bobby, so he cracked the entrance test to do post-graduation and join a prestigious University in his hometown after 3 years of working. His family was happy to hear that and decided to pay the educational expenses which really was a surprise for Bobby, and he thanked his parents. That was the turning point in Bobby's life. But the struggle continued as he was working from 9 am to 6 pm but the college timing was 6:20 pm to 9:20 pm. Bobby requested his boss to allow him to leave the office at 5:30 pm so that he could pursue higher studies. It was accepted. The University where he joined was extremely strict and he had to maintain 75 percent attendance. But after 1 year of working along with higher studies, suddenly one of his subordinates used abusive words against Bobby stating that he was leaving office early although Bobby got the permission from his boss to leave the office early. But Bobby was shocked after hearing his subordinate and decided to leave the job. Bobby was diligent, hardworking, and honest in his work. Over and above, his salary was much less compared to his subordinates since lesser qualified and experienced. But the pressure of earning money on Bobby continued as parents paid for his education, so they wanted return on investment. So, Bobby convinced his parents saying that he would complete his post-graduation and earn more money with higher qualifications.

Lesson:

Moral of the story is our entire life goes in earning money without even realising the struggles that shape our career (Refer to Figure-12).

Figure 12. Bobby's Struggle

MORAL STORY 13 – THE ILLUSION

There is a village name Jugaad where people suffer from scarcity of water. But every time a person in Jugaad is asked when your water problem will be resolved they use to respond by saying next week. They are so positive that in their minds water is always flowing and everyone is happy having fresh water. One day a monk visits & asks for a glass of water in one of the households. The woman in the home has offered him an empty glass thinking the glass is filled with water. The monk smiles & says "water water everywhere but not a drop to drink".

Lesson:

Moral of the story is the gap between thinking and doing which people fail to understand and passionately believe in their ability to resolve a problem without understanding the reality (Refer to Figure-13).

Figure 13. The Illusion

MORAL STORY 14 - PECULIAR BEHAVIOUR SYNDROME (PBS) IN A NON-EGALITARIAN SOCIETY

There was a group of people who used to enjoy everything in a society viz. putting the sound system in full volume by disturbing children who were appearing for examinations especially during festivals, Adults and Senior Citizens playing outdoor games every day and organizing tournaments, celebrating their community festival by ignoring other community festivals and quite surprising setting rules for the children who were motivated by their behaviour wanted to play outdoor games, playing music and a huge discrimination between communities. Children (5 to 18 years old) are like clay which can be moulded to make the idol of Lord Ganesha. They are pristine and want to have fun by playing, enjoying which they learn from Adults and Senior Citizens. The biggest problem of non-egalitarian society is that the earning members think this is their right to do anything and cannot compromise on fun by spoiling the young buds. These children started misbehaving and doing things against the society as in adolescent stage if anyone is punished can take a toll in child psychology.

Lesson:

Moral of the story is we are living in a society where adults are behaving rudely with children without any maturity and children after observing peculiar behaviour syndrome (PBS) of adults and senior citizens becoming matured individuals. This is one of the major reasons why young people are getting obsessed with mobile phones and online gaming when they face restrictions and discrimination in their surroundings (Refer to Figure-14).

Figure 14. Peculiar Behaviour Syndrome (PBS) in a Non-Egalitarian Society

MORAL STORY 15 - TWO FRIENDS WHO PARTED BUT CANNOT FORGET EACH OTHER

One boy and One girl used to spend time together playing outdoor games, enjoying their childhood days together in celebrating festivals, imagining things as childhood acts, and used to visit each other's home occasionally either for lunch or dinner invitations. Their parents were liberal minded and happy to see them spent time together. But the Society where they stayed started thinking they were lovers. One day they decided to stop meeting each other and focused on doing their mundane tasks. This brought extreme mental agony and experience of facing non-egalitarian people who used to throw comments. Now both are grown up, achieved success in their respective career and got married to the person whom they love each other. But the feelings of lost friendship still there in one corner of their minds. The issue was both of their nature resembles, food habits similar and thought process same. The occasional meetings also bring them memories of childhood but thinking about inequality they remain calm and only look to each other without a word.

Lesson:

Moral of the story is our intentions are pristine, but surroundings pose a barrier to our psychological development which changes the character of a person (Refer to Figure-15).

Figure 15. Two friends who parted but cannot forget each other

MORAL STORY 16 - A GIRL WHO LOVES TO FLY

A girl was born in a poor family. Her parents - Father was a Carpenter and Mother was a Maid. She was having a peculiar attraction towards aeroplane flying in the sky especially those who were going abroad. She was staying in one room terrace flat rented by her parents, airy and full of light. She always used to run seeing an aeroplane in the sky. Her parents could not afford luxury living but her willingness to fly in an aeroplane always haunted her. She kept trying and studied hard to go abroad. But when she realised her merit, intelligence and capacity was not like others who were flying abroad, it was a big shock and difficult to digest. But she kept on trying. She grew up, became an adult, and kept trying to fly abroad with an assignment professionally. But her circumstances, family commitments and job did not allow her to fly abroad.

Lesson:

Moral of the story is a person must forgo the most precious desire to survive in a ruthless competitive world (Refer to Figure-16).

Figure 16. A Girl who loves to fly

MORAL STORY 17 - A BOY WHO LOVED MUSIC

A boy, the first grandchild, was born in a joint family, healthy and at the same time busy continuously with mischievous acts as he was growing. The childhood days spent with parents and grandparents were golden hours. The only music lover in the family was the grandfather with whom he used to spend his leisure time knowing the nuances of Indian Classical Music. As he became adolescent started learning a musical instrument and became passionate about music. Slowly the joint family was broken into nuclear families due to personal reasons that caused a break in learning music. When the boy turned into a man, he was so fond of music that he imitated the great musicians and developed his own style of composing and performing in the auditorium. But there was a monetary crisis in the family, so he had to leave all that he learnt in vain and accept a job in an alien country. The career path changed as he became a working professional from a musician. Life changed suddenly and the boy turned into a man eventually started earning handsomely to run his family. The man was happy but had to forgo something precious to earn a livelihood.

Lesson:

Moral of the story is we have never realised the value until losing something that we are passionately pursuing (Refer to Figure-17).

Figure 17. A Boy who loved Music

MORAL STORY 18 - THE LOST SMILE

Two birds were friends and flying high together. One day a hunter came and injured one of the birds. But luckily the injured bird was captured by a bird lover in a different country and treated with medicines and care till the injury was healed. But after recovery the injured flyer started looking for the bird as they were flying together and greeting others with a natural smile from top of the sky. Then he got one more bird friend with whom he started flying again. It was difficult initially to adjust with the new friend but somehow, they got the rhythm to move together. But no one ever thought about the bird who lost his injured friend, and the peers wanted him to smile always as it was an entertainment and treat to see someone smile. When the bird realised for survival smiling is important, he kept on smiling with tears in the eyes just to make others happy. But one day the old friends met again while flying but it was never the same situation and smile, they enjoyed together and parted after seeing each other.

Lesson:

Moral of the story is a sensitive living being can never be treated in a similar fashion as for a mentally strong living being. When we realise that two individuals are not the same, it is too late (Refer to Figure 18).

Figure 18. The Lost Smile

MORAL STORY 19 - A SENSITIVE PERSON TURNING RUDE

Harry was born and brought up in a joint family at Mexico where everyone was treated equally and even the food was distributed equally. Discrimination of individuals started when family members started thinking about how to earn more for a better living. Harry faced extremely good behaviour till one day he was told not to use his uncle's computer blaming him for screwing the device although he never did anything wrong. Then he grew up and faced extremely hot summers and so again he used to rest a few hours in the comfort of air condition during afternoon which was again installed by his uncle and was offered to him. He was slowly able to realise a family which was once accepted for unity breaking down into parts due to inequality of income among family members. So, the joint family dispersed into nuclear families having different tastes and preferences. But till today there is cohesiveness among family members although having differences in opinion and income.

In the second stage of life which Harry went through made him stronger as one day while watering a few plants planted by him in front of his balcony he was opposed and later the president, secretary and treasurer of the society came shouting to his home stating that he was not allowed to plant trees in the Society. He was shell shocked as since childhood it was taught planting a tree was equivalent to saving a life. But the society was against the same. The biggest learning of Harry was when he started earning. Every organization he was employed used to be happy with his work. But whenever a company pays remuneration, it also ensured to dominate individuals by raising the voice in other words verbal abuse of the boss. He tolerated the same and kept working and changed organizations for growth. Even he served outside the comfort zone in other nations to experience a different work culture but discrimination of individuals in terms of religion, language, caste, and creed was quite transparent which was bothering Harry. All these experiences turned Harry from a soft-hearted sensitive individual to a rude person which affected his personal life. But at the same time, he was apologetic to people after realization.

Lesson:

Moral of the story is human nature is the outcome of circumstances and experiences that they go through in life (Refer to Figure-19).

Figure 19. A Sensitive Person turning Rude

MORAL STORY 20 - A GENERATION UNABLE TO COPE WITH INDIAN CLASSICAL MUSIC

Vedant, a boy who was born and brought up in a musical family with grandfather organizing a classical musical conference for 40 years and mother, an accomplished classical dancer, and a teacher. His listening skills were sharp and used to pick up ragas in Sarod (musical instrument) after observing the greatest of the Indian Classical Artists. But due to higher education Vedant had to compromise in learning music. But he never lost hope and tried to hold on to it as he grew up and got busy in professional life. One thing he realized while playing tunes that the artists whom he used to respect and follow slowly getting aged and next generation musicians are not keen to inherit classical Indian music. Music is like the sound of an ocean flowing in such a way that viewers are waiting to hear and be natural. When Vedant was asked by his friends what is music according to him. He replied by saying "music is subtle, sweet, and sublime. Just keep enjoying either by playing or listening till you are alive."

Lesson:

Moral of the story is if you put strong effort without knowing the basics it will sound like an empty vessel (Refer to Figure-20).

Figure 20. A Generation unable to cope with Indian Classical Music

MORAL STORY 21 - THE MASTER AND HIS DISCIPLE

Kedar was an artistic and cultured person and enjoyed all forms of art and music. One day he visited a musical concert where he was mesmerized by a musical instrument named Santoor played by Pandit Harish. He was fond of music and connected Pandit Harish for learning the instrument. Initially he used to visit Panditji's home for learning and practice since the instrument was a little costly for him to afford. Pandit Harish offered him an old instrument at a reasonable price which he bought after a few months and started practising at home. Slowly Kedar became one of the favourite students of Pandit Harish and Panditji wanted him to accompany in all concerts as a support for playing the Tanpura (instrument for maintaining the scale). Kedar grabbed the opportunity to learn by sitting on the dais along with his Music Guru. This was a game changer and groomed Kedar to overcome stage fear, perform in front of audience and public speaking. Later on, Kedar had to relocate for official commitments and his partnership with Pandit Harish was no more. But

Panditji remembered Kedar despite so many disciples during his lifetime. After 25 years Panditji received an invitation to play Santoor in the city where Kedar was residing and working with an IT company. Panditji was not aware of Kedar's whereabouts after he left him. Kedar went for the musical concert after knowing that his Guru was performing. But incidentally could not hear him because of the change of schedule in the cultural programme. But Kedar waited outside the auditorium to meet Pandit Harish. After waiting for almost one hour, he saw his Guru with his wife coming out of the auditorium to board the vehicle and going back to the hotel organized by the Cultural Committee. For a moment, it seemed like time stopped when both Kedar and Pandit Harish looked at each other. Kedar was so happy that tears came to his eyes by meeting his Guru and they took a few photographs. Pandit Harish told Kedar if he knew that Kedar was in the city where he performed then a VIP ticket which was quite expensive was available for him. Kedar shared his contact and told his Guru that whenever he would visit here to let him know for meeting again.

Lesson:

Moral of the story is relationship between Master and Disciple always stays despite distance and lessons learnt once cannot be forgotten (Refer to Figure-21).

Figure 21.The Master and his Disciple

CONCLUSION

This chapter demonstrates how digital storytelling, powered by AI, serves as an innovative and effective teaching strategy, enhancing engagement and learning in educational environments. By presenting a collection of short, digitally accessible moral stories accompanied by original artwork, the chapter highlights AI's ability to make educational content both compelling and adaptable to diverse learning needs. Through this approach, digital storytelling not only fosters student interest but also encourages reflection and moral development, creating a more holistic learning experience. The potential of AI-driven digital storytelling extends beyond student engagement, supporting educators and administrators in refining pedagogical strategies, designing curriculum, and fostering institutional transformation. However, the chapter also emphasizes the importance of a balanced approach in the integration of AI, mindful of ethical concerns such as data privacy and technology's impact on learning dynamics. As education continues to evolve, AI-based storytelling promises to be a valuable tool in cultivating an interactive, inclusive, and adaptable educational landscape.

ACKNOWLEDGEMENT

The chapter portrays the society we live in, and all the stories written out of the experience authors have observed. None of them are true stories and hopefully your comments, appreciations, and shares for the content in the book will encourage us to write more in future about moral stories. As authors, we would like to extend our heartfelt gratitude to Sri Balaji University, Pune (India) for providing the platform to think, act and motivation to publish.

REFERENCES

Alismail, H. A. (2015). Integrate digital storytelling in education. *Journal of Education and Practice*, 6(9), 126–129.

Almeda, M. V., Zuech, J., Utz, C., Higgins, G., Reynolds, R., & Baker, R. S. (2018). Comparing the factors that predict completion and grades among for-credit and open/MOOC students in online learning. *Online Learning : the Official Journal of the Online Learning Consortium*, 22(1), 1–18. DOI: 10.24059/olj.v22i1.1060

Aluthman, E. S. (2016). The effect of using automated essay evaluation on ESL undergraduate students' writing skill. *International Journal of English Linguistics*, 6(5), 54. DOI: 10.5539/ijel.v6n5p54

Bruner, J. (2003). *Making stories: Law, literature, life*. Harvard University Press.

Chena, Y., Liub, M., & Cheng, Y. (2023). Discovering Scientific Creativity with Digital Storytelling. *Journal of Creativity*, ISSN: 2713-3745, 33 (1), 100041, DOI: 10.1016/j.yjoc.2022.100041

Christudas, B. C. L., Kirubakaran, E., & Thangaiah, P. R. J. (2018). An evolutionary approach for personalization of content delivery in e-learning systems based on learner behavior forcing compatibility of learning materials. *Telematics and Informatics*, 35(3), 520–533. DOI: 10.1016/j.tele.2017.02.004

G¨ottel, T. (2011). Reviewing children's collaboration practices in storytelling environments. In *Proceedings of the 10th international conference on interaction design and children* (Vol. 11, pp. 153–156). IDC. https://doi.org/DOI: 10.1145/1999030.1999049

Haenlein, M., & Kaplan, A. (2021). Artificial intelligence and robotics: Shaking up the business world and society at large. *Journal of Business Research*, 124, 405–407. DOI: 10.1016/j.jbusres.2020.10.042

Hwang, G. J., Xie, H., Wah, B. W., & Gašević, D. (2020). Vision, challenges, roles and research issues of artificial intelligence in education. *Computers and Education: Artificial Intelligence*, 1, 100001. DOI: 10.1016/j.caeai.2020.100001

Kalantari, S., Rubegni, E., Benton, L., & Vasalou, A. (2023). "When I'm writing a story, I am really good" Exploring the use of digital storytelling technology at home. *International Journal of Child-Computer Interaction*, 38, 100613, ISSN 2212-8689, DOI: 10.1016/j.ijcci.2023.100613

Karakoyun, F., & Kuzu, A. (2016). The investigation of preservice teachers' and primary school students' views about online digital storytelling. *European Journal of Contemporary Education*, 15(1), 51–64.

Keiper, M. C., Fried, G., Lupinek, J., & Nordstrom, H. (2023). Artificial intelligence in sport management education: Playing the AI game with ChatGPT. Journal of Hospitality, Leisure, Sport & Tourism Education, 33, 100456, ISSN 1473-8376, https://doi.org/DOI: 10.1016/j.jhlste.2023.100456

Meadows, D. (2003). Digital storytelling: Research-based practice in new media. *Visual Communication*, 2(2), 189–193. DOI: 10.1177/1470357203002002004

Moreno-Marcos, P. M., Alario-Hoyos, C., Munoz-Merino, P. J., & Kloos, C. D. (2019). Prediction in MOOCs: A Review and Future Research Directions. *IEEE Transactions on Learning Technologies*, 12(3), 384–401. DOI: 10.1109/TLT.2018.2856808

Niemi, H., Niu, S., Vivitsou, M., & Li, B. (2018). Digital storytelling for twenty-first-century competencies with math literacy and student engagement in China and Finland. *Contemporary Educational Technology*, 9(4), 331–353. DOI: 10.30935/cet.470999

Ouyang, F., Zheng, L., & Jiao, P. (2022). Artificial intelligence in online higher education: A systematic review of empirical research from 2011 to 2020. *Education and Information Technologies*, 27(6), 7893–7925. DOI: 10.1007/s10639-022-10925-9

Pahl, K. (2011). My family, my story: Representing identities in time and space through digital storytelling. *Teachers College Record*, 113(13), 17–39. DOI: 10.1177/016146811111301302

Sak, U., & Ayas, M. (2013). Creative scientific ability test (C-SAT): A new measure of scientific creativity. *Psychological Test and Assessment Modeling*, 55, 316–329.

Sen, S., & Banerjee, S. (2022). How Sport-for-Development Initiatives Influence Quality of Life in Post Pandemic Era? *Jharkhand Journal of Development and Management Studies*, 20 (4). 9535-9548, https://www.xiss.ac.in/JJDMS/archives

Sen, S., & Banerjee, S. (2023). Adverse Effects of Online Education on Student Engagement during Covid-19: Review, Synthesis and Research Agenda. CARDIOMETRY. 293-301. https://doi.org/DOI: 10.18137/cardiometry.2023.26.293301

Si, S., & Chen, H. (2020). A literature review of disruptive innovation: What it is, how it works and where it goes. *Journal of Engineering and Technology Management*, 56, 101568, ISSN 0923-4748, https://doi.org/DOI: 10.1016/j.jengtecman.2020.101568

Simonton, D. K. (2013). Scientific creativity as combinatorial process. In Carayannis, E. G. (Ed.), *Encyclopedia of creativity, invention, innovation and entrepreneurship* (pp. 1592–1595). Springer., DOI: 10.1007/978-1-4614-3858-8_388

Stahl, B. C., Andreou, A., Brey, P., Hatzakis, T., Kirichenko, A., Macnish, K., Laulh'e Shaelou, S., Patel, A., Ryan, M., & Wright, D. (2021). Artificial intelligence for human flourishing – Beyond principles for machine learning. *Journal of Business Research*, 124, 374–388. DOI: 10.1016/j.jbusres.2020.11.030

ADDITIONAL READING

Belda-Medina, J., & Goddard, M. B. (2024). AI-Driven Digital Storytelling: A Strategy for Creating English as a Foreign Language (EFL) Materials. *International Journal of Linguistics Studies*, 4(1), 40–49. DOI: 10.32996/ijls.2024.4.1.4

Fan, M., Cui, X., Hao, J., Ye, R., Ma, W., Tong, X., & Li, M. (2024, May). StoryPrompt: Exploring the Design Space of an AI-Empowered Creative Storytelling System for Elementary Children. In *Extended Abstracts of the CHI Conference on Human Factors in Computing Systems* (pp. 1-8).

Vigna-Taglianti, J. (2024). AI-Generated Images as a Teaching Tool in Foreign Language Acquisition. *«Technology and language»(Технологии в инфосфере), 5*(3), 85-105.

Woo, D. J., Guo, K., & Salas-Pilco, S. Z. (2024). Writing creative stories with AI: Learning designs for secondary school students. *Innovation in Language Learning and Teaching*, •••, 1–13. DOI: 10.1080/17501229.2024.2384884

KEY TERMS AND DEFINITIONS

AI-Enhanced Learning: The integration of artificial intelligence to support and enhance learning processes, personalizing content, feedback, and instructional methods.

Collaborative Learning: An educational approach where learners work together to solve problems or complete tasks, often enhanced by AI-supported platforms that facilitate communication and teamwork.

Critical Thinking: The process of analyzing information objectively to make reasoned judgments, which AI-driven storytelling can stimulate by presenting complex, thought-provoking narratives.

Digital Storytelling: The practice of using digital tools to create and share stories online, often combining visuals and narrative to engage learners in interactive ways.

Engagement: The level of interest and active participation in learning activities, which digital storytelling can boost by offering immersive and relatable content.

Ethical AI: The responsible use of artificial intelligence in ways that respect privacy, transparency, and fairness, crucial for its implementation in educational settings.

Learner-Centric Design: An instructional approach focused on meeting the unique needs and preferences of learners, often enhanced by AI tools that adapt content for individuals.

Moral Storytelling: The use of narratives that convey ethical lessons or values, aimed at fostering personal and social development in learners.

Personalized Learning: Tailoring educational content to fit individual learner needs and preferences, made possible by AI algorithms that analyze user data.

Virtual Classroom: An online learning environment where students and instructors interact in real time, often enhanced by AI to create a collaborative and adaptive space for learning.

Chapter 10
Integrating Artificial Intelligence in Media Education:
Revolutionizing Learning, Creativity, and Critical Thinking

Amaresh Jha
https://orcid.org/0000-0002-6083-1610
University of Petroleum and Energy Studies, India

Sanjeev Ratna Singh
https://orcid.org/0000-0002-5899-2749
Bennett University, India

ABSTRACT

The emergence of Artificial Intelligence (AI) offers transformative possibilities for media education, particularly as traditional teaching methods struggle to keep pace with the rapidly evolving digital media landscape. This chapter examines the potential of AI to enrich media education by enabling personalized learning experiences, fostering creativity and innovation, and enhancing critical thinking and media literacy. Using a qualitative research approach that includes a literature review, expert interviews, and case studies, this chapter identifies the primary applications of AI in media education, evaluates its impact on student learning, addresses ethical considerations, and provides practical recommendations for effective AI integration. By understanding both the opportunities and challenges of AI in media education, we can better equip students to meet the complex demands of the digital age.

DOI: 10.4018/979-8-3373-1017-6.ch010

INTRODUCTION

Emerging technologies are slowly playing an integral part in our daily lives. This integration of artificial intelligence (AI) is the latest iteration in the development, and with it comes a new frontier of both opportunity and challenge for students as well as educators. This chapter will investigate the history as well evolution of AI in media and also explores its integrated application in media education, giving an all-inclusive review through which these technologies are bringing change to the field. Now the development of media education is a part and parcel with the progressive development of technology and changes in the media environment. These developments are reflected in the more recent integration of AI into media education, which seems to be a game changing evolution in the way media knowledge or skills are shared.

While a distinct, formal program in media education originated in the early 20th century with the coming of the newspaper, radio and later television, media education is also regulated teaching professionals how to teach critical or other aspects of media literacy in schools. Initially, the emphasis was on media literacy with the aim of helping students to think critically about and understand what they consumed in the media. One of the early objectives of media education was to appreciate the power that the media can wield on public opinion and culture. For instance, the "media effects" model began in the 1920s and 1930s; it assumed an audience that simply received media messages passively. To educate the public about this, one of the pioneers (McLuhan, 1964) gave structure to critical media studies in his groundbreaking book. Formal media education, as a distinct entity from media studies, is seen mainly in the northern hemisphere such as the United States, Canada, Europe and Australia at this point in time. This was common in primary and secondary schools up until about 1969-1970 when larger cities established programs for gifted students who were removed from their regular schools and taken to special centralised sites on an half-day basis; it has ebbed considerably. At first, media literacy was targeted at teaching students how to see something critically, teaching students how to analyse media content in a methodical way. Television is the single most important medium today that has eventually come to be "a faculty" of American education beginning with its rise during the 1950s and again in the 1960s when educators forged efforts to educate young viewers about valuable methods for analysing television content critically.

Interest in media education rose over the course of the 1970s and 1980s as a response to renewed recognition of the power of mass media and concerns about how it could be used. The emphasis broadened from the study of media content to media creation, reflecting new trends in video and film production at that time. The work of educators like Len Masterman, who argued for a pedagogy which prioritised critical thinking and active media engagement (Masterman, 1985), was influential at this time. Although the roots of media education can be traced back to the post-World War II era, significant traction came during the 1970s and 1980s. During this time media education grew beyond the study of propagandistic content alone, to also include much more production themselves, spurred on by various video and film movements in particular. Digital technology started to define media education in the new ways that we know during the 1990s. This changed as the internet and digital tools were introduced, greatly shifting traditional media practices that schools then needed to fold into their programs. Media education integrated multimedia production, digital journalism and online content creation (Jenkins, 2006).

The last 30 years have witnessed significant change in both the context and content of media education and now we are living through an information revolution. With the internet and digital media in the late 20th century, we began to move away from traditional media literacy towards digital literacy. Among them, scholars like Davide Buckingham (2003) pointed out the need for education systems to open towards new digital culture and prepare students for a possibilist social environment of using or producing virtual artefacts. Participatory media literacy was a concept that burgeoned in the 2000s with the rise of social media platforms. Later, participatory culture was introduced, defining the state where people are no longer consuming media, but also becoming producers and supporters of media which they enjoy and are passionate about (Jenkins et al. 2009). This transition necessitated competition to evolve and introduce fresh pedagogies and curricula that would enable dissenters as a way of student exploring a critical citizenship in social media, the digital zeitgeist. In general, media education has expanded to include concepts ranging from critical thinking and the evaluation of media, to ideas concerning how we should use media in a way that is ethically considerate. Media education is an interdisciplinary enterprise which converges on such fields as communication studies, journalism, visual arts and information technology (Livingstone 2004).

The rapid advancement of technology has irrevocably altered our daily lives. AI stands as the most recent iteration of this technological evolution, presenting both unprecedented opportunities and formidable challenges for students and educators alike. This chapter delves into the historical context and evolution of AI in media, exploring its integrated application within media education. Through a comprehensive review, we aim to understand how these technologies are reshaping the field. This chapter aims to:

1. **Delineate the historical trajectory of AI in the media landscape.**
    - Identify pivotal milestones and advancements in AI technology that have shaped its role in media.
    - Analyze the evolution of AI integration across various media sectors.

2. **Investigate the integration of AI within media education.**
    - o Examine specific applications of AI in media education programs and courses.
    - o Evaluate the influence of AI on curriculum design, teaching methods, and student learning outcomes.
3. **Assess the transformative potential of AI in media education.**
    - o Identify the potential advantages and challenges associated with AI integration.
    - o Explore how AI can enhance student learning, foster creativity, and prepare students for future media careers.
    - o Consider the ethical implications of AI in media education, such as bias, privacy, and job displacement.

The Advent of AI

Once relegated to science fiction, AI is now part of our everyday lives. The words "artificial intelligence" and AI were first used by John McCarthy in 1956 during the Dartmouth Conference which brought together researchers from a range of fields to discuss whether machines could be designed to think and learn (McCarthy et al., 2006). There have been many different milestones in the development of AI over the years. It was in the 90s that we started to see some of the first exciting results from machine learning, especially using neural networks.

The emergence of algorithms, such as backpropagation facilitated the training of neural networks (Rumelhart et al., 1986), which provided computational systems advanced enough to rise 'beyond intelligence', affecting speech recognition, image processing and natural language processing among other tasks. Big data and computational power, both became increasingly important in the early 21st century, also played a bigger and bigger role in AI research. Companies reaching accomplishments hailed as milestones, like IBM's Watson's Jeopardy and IBM's Deep Blue supercomputer which famously beat chess champion Garyy Kasparov in 1997 (Ferrucci et al. 2013). Today, AI touches almost every industry, in healthcare and finance to entertainment and education. Its applications in natural language processing, computer vision and predictive analytics have brought into play a brand new way to interact with technology and information (Goodfellow et al. 2016). In modern media education, AI is making in-roads to build capacities of curriculum and pedagogy. The personalised learning experience, with AI helps give feedback in real-time and also aids in creation of content. Some examples of this are AI-aided analytics to ascertain the strengths and weaknesses of students to facilitate personalised tutoring and adaptive learning paths (Kulkarni, 2020). AI also acts as a key in automating repetitive tasks to help teachers concentrate more on critical thinking and creative aspects of teaching. New administrative processes and education quality are being streamlined thanks to tools such as automated grading systems, plagiarism detection software and AI-drive content curation platforms (Luckin et al., 2016).

AI has made a deep impact on the two pillars of media education, namely Content Writing and Journalism. Proponents can also train AI-powered devices, such as using natural language processing (NLP) tools or machine learning algorithms to automate news generation, composite media, and process large arrays of curated data. As such, AI-driven technologies in film and video production are reimagining a swath of areas within the creative process (Table 1). AI tools are in full action from pre to post-production like script analysis, scene prediction, video editing etc. Scripts can be analysed by machine learning algorithms and based on parameters like plot construction, character building, and dialogues it can predict if a film is likely to succeed (Eliashberg et al. 2014). AI-powered video editing tools, such as Adobe Sensei and many others automate a lot of the post-production process from colour correction all the way through to scene detection and effects enhancement (Adobe, 2020). Because of such tools, media students can experiment with more advanced editing styles and easily create professional video projects. Modern media education should also include social media and digital marketing strategies. AI is being used to pick up on social media trends, craft markets that target their audience with precision, and to adapt the content for the various platforms (Leeflang et al., 2014). Now, AI algorithms have the power to process huge volumes of social media data which can provide an insight into trend topics and sentiment analysis and audience engagement. Such and similar insights are extremely valuable to media students, who study digital marketing campaigns, audience behaviour etc. They also develop hands-on digital marketing experience with AI-powered platforms, such as Hootsuite and Buffer, which help them manage and automate social media content.

Table 1. Impact of AI on Journalism and Mass Communication Studies

Feature	Impact on Journalism and Mass Communication Education
Personalized Learning	Tailored curriculum based on student's strengths, weaknesses, and learning style; AI-powered tutoring and feedback
Automated Content Creation	AI can generate news articles, scripts, and social media content, freeing up students to focus on critical thinking and analysis
Data Analysis and Visualization	AI tools can help students analyze large datasets, identify trends, and create compelling visualizations
Ethical Considerations	AI raises ethical questions about bias, misinformation, and job displacement; students need to learn how to use AI responsibly
Skill Development	AI is driving demand for skills like data journalism, natural language processing, and machine learning

continued on following page

Table 1. Continued

Feature	Impact on Journalism and Mass Communication Education
New Teaching Methods	AI-powered simulations and virtual reality can provide immersive learning experiences
Accessibility	AI can help break down barriers to education by providing personalized support and adaptive learning tools
Cost-Effectiveness	AI-powered tools can reduce costs associated with traditional education, such as textbooks and physical infrastructure

LITERATURE REVIEW

Media education has evolved and shifted dramatically over the past three decades as AI entered into the new age of media literacy. The purpose of this literature review is to explore the reported history of media education, its pedagogical approaches, and how AI integration changes the landscape of learning extension as well as creativity, critical thinking. Instead, thorough citation of the extant academic literature shows a dynamic feedback loop between them historically conditioned as well as via contemporary advances in AI. In fact, one of the reasons media education rose to prominence in the latter half of the 20th century was due to concerns around society evolving from a print-based culture to a mass-media informed one. The emphasis initially has been upon media literacy: that is on equipping students with the skills needed to engage critically with mediatised material (Buckingham, 2003). The National Association for Media Literacy Education defines media literacy as the "the ability to access, analyze, evaluate, create, and act using all forms of communication" (NAMLE, 2007).

During the last thirty years or so, pedagogical orientations of media education transformed from a primarily teacher-led to an increasingly learner-centred one. Curriculum embracing a constructivist perspective, informed by Freire and others, is attentive to developing critical thinking and active learning (Freire, 1970). In many ways, this is much like the concept of students constructing knowledge by interacting with media (media => peers => faculty). The introduction of the digital media has changed the pedagogical side of the digital face among media educators in the late 20th and early 21st century. But in addition, new media created platforms for producing and interpreting content that fostered a pedagogy of active, experiential learning (Hobbs, 2010). The internet has made thousands of media outlets instantly accessible and increased the scope of what can be included (or excluded) in media literacy education.

AI for instance has already become an innovation in education where it calls human intelligence to be checked by computers of other sorts. One of the major contributing factors from AI in the field of education is personalised learning. Online learning experiences using AI personalise the learning process for each student with their custom requirements according to their unique needs, speed, and variations in the ways of learning (Chen et al., 2020). That personalisation translates to more engagement and potentially better learning outcomes. AI-powered systems tailored to individual learners in media education lets them explore at their own pace and get prompt feedback from teachers. Knewton is one of the platforms that does this using AI to dynamically alter learning materials, and thereby offer a personalised educational experience to every student in real time (Knewton, 2014).

On the other hand, AI makes it possible for human beings to scale one-to-one instruction and support, intelligent tutoring systems (ITS) is one example of this. These systems simulate individualised human tutoring by adjusting to the students performance and also providing tailored feedback and scaffolding (Graesser et al., 2001). Those that provide an opportunity for interactive simulating and practice exercises in media production and analysis can achieve significant resonance across media studies education. AI promotes creativity explicitly and implicitly by providing a practical creative tool and an imaginative inspiration for creative thinking as well. Students are able to create media with AI-powered tools in unique ways. For instance, AI is used to edit video clips, mimic music, and create visual art, which provides different expression modes for students to explore (Elgammal et al. 2017). Other tools use AI to streamline the time students spend on tedious technical tasks related to media production, like Adobe's Sensei, an AI and machine learning platform that can automatically edit photos or crop videos intelligently (Adobe, 2018).

AI is also aiding creativity when it collaborates with humans. In many cases, this collaboration sparks new imaginations and directions which are unlikely to be attained by human labour alone (Ahuja, 2019). AI-based content can be used as a baseline, where students would be required to innovate ideas on top of them while developing media projects. That is what the role of AI looks like when it comes to promoting critical media education. In general, critical thinking is the ability to recognize and evaluate assumptions/arguments, and synthesise information in order to logically arrange it into premises (Paul et al. 2005). An interrogation into the applications of AI is relevant in order to support the continual processes of critique and re-edge in media education. AI for analytics and visualisation of data to help students grasp complex media landscapes. An example can be to allow students to utilise tools like IBM Watsons for getting insights on media trends and audience responses which will enable them to critically analyse the impact and aftermath of a media content.

If more scalable, AI algorithms could even be used to process a mass of media content to identify trends, biases and misinformation. This function helps students become critically informed readers of the assumptions and implied narratives in media text (Diakopoulos et al., 2019). We also leveraged the work of existing AI-enabled systems being used for fact-checking, such as Factmata who is working with school students to identify credible sources and distinguish between real and fake news (Factmata 2017), in order to demonstrate that an educational implementation of AI can have a positive impact. As much as AI is instrumental for media education, it also has a few ethical dilemmas and problems in some cases. If not designed and monitored correctly, AI systems may also reinforce or exacerbate pre-existing biases (Bolukbasi et al., 2016). Finally, we need to adopt the mantra of: not teaching AI media stereotypes or discriminated content. Educators have to be diligent about evaluating the fairness of an AI tool and being more inclusive.

As AI powers every aspect of online education, it gathers and processes readings on student behaviours; however; as much use as data has been put to, privacy issues are a constant debate. The concern for protecting student information and using it responsibly is essential (West, 2019). Institutions relate RDP for better sensing which enhance protections around data and digital rights literacy among the students must be followed to bring transparency. Supported by AI, production of video content creation gets more affordable than ever, which leads to the turn tool Wibbitz in media production education. The tools enabled students to concentrate on storytelling and creativity, with AI managing the more technical aspects (Wibbitz, 2019). Integration such as this is critical to student readiness in a digital media landscape that is continually changing. The application of AI in media education is as yet developing, and there are a lot of conceivable bearings. Future research could examine how AI converges with wider disciplinary paths, such as sociology and psychology or cultural studies within media education. Thus, considering the perspectives of media consumption and production reminded us of a larger picture of the influence or impact of AI on education.

It would also be of interest to see how AI-powered applications perform in longitudinal studies over time on learner achievements. If conducted, such studies could help determine the long-term advantages and disadvantages of using AI in media education. It is important to develop an ethical framework for using AI in media education as a whole. Most of all, the frameworks should establish comprehensive bias-aware AI for social good for education with drift-as-a-service as a framework pillar. Teaching AI in media education has evolved over the last three decades (from teacher centred method to progressively active and technology facilitated). AI allows students to learn independently, and create a unique creative and critical literacy experience. However, this in turn compiles some ethical dilemmas also which need to be addressed. However, with AI becoming more complex and far-reaching in its applications, there is a tantalising opportunity for it to help revolutionise media education even further by preparing students for 21st-century challenges.

AI and Media Education Landscape

AI technology has dramatically reshaped the media education landscape. Numerous fields have directly benefited from the remarkable advancements in modern artificial intelligence. A new era of innovation in education is one such area. Beyond this shift in focus, there has also been a growing emphasis on individualized student learning, particularly within media education programs. Such a learning environment, characterized by its dynamic, responsive, and effective nature, is made possible by personalized experiences created by AI. This is a revolutionary shift given the limitations of traditional education. This chapter delves into the implications of personalized AI-driven learning, exploring how it can be adapted to media education and the potential outcomes of this endeavor.

Intelligent Tutoring Systems and Adaptive Personalization

One aspect of AI in education that has garnered particular attention is the development of intelligent tutoring systems (ITS) for real time feedback using AI algorithms. These systems deal with processing of data on the students' interactions and on the basis of them identify student strength or weakness to provide them a better support model (Nkambou et al., 2010). It includes changing the lesson plans, material level and added resources according to the ability level and way of learning of each student. For example, an ITS in a media education program would keep track of the number of video edits that have been made by a student. If it recognised that a student struggled with colour grading, it could construct exercises or tutorials to suit, and place them in one-on-one virtual environments to iron out where the difficulties lay. The AI-powered systems are understanding more and more from media production, giving way to focus on the learning needs of each individual.

Adaptive Learning for Increased Enhancing Learning

The dynamic adjustment of content by AI is one of the highlights in providing learners with engaging and useful learning experiences. As students work through a curriculum, the nature of content, and its complexity, is constantly modified by AI systems to fit individual learning paces (Woolf, 2009). This adaptivity prevents students from being bored by work that is too easy or intimidated by material that is too difficult. Studies and Statistics show adaptive learning platforms increase student retention and satisfaction. According to Knewton (2015), student retention rates saw a 30% increase with the help of adaptive learning technologies in higher education. As per EdSurge (2019), the pass rates of students using adaptive learning tools were 50 percent higher than those who continued to use traditional means. These numbers demonstrate the power of AI-guided personalization in improving media learning outcomes.

Ethical Considerations and Challenges of AI in Media Education

AI in media education presents a complex landscape with ethical considerations and challenges that must be carefully addressed. One major concern is data privacy, as AI systems often rely on large datasets of student information. Ensuring the secure and ethical handling of this data is crucial to protect student privacy and maintain trust. Additionally, algorithmic bias poses a significant challenge. AI algorithms can perpetuate existing biases present in the data they are trained on, leading to unfair or discriminatory outcomes for students. It is essential to develop and implement bias mitigation techniques to ensure that AI systems are fair and equitable. Another important consideration is the potential impact of AI on social inequalities. AI-powered tools may not be accessible to all students, exacerbating existing disparities. Ensuring equitable access to AI-enhanced education is crucial to prevent further marginalization. Furthermore, the increasing commercialization of AI in education raises concerns about corporate influence over curriculum and content. It is essential to maintain educational autonomy and prioritize student interests over commercial gains.

AI for Real-Time Feedback Mechanisms

The second place AI has a big impact on media education is the area of delivering real-time feedback. This provides real-time feedback to correct errors and reinforce the rewarding actions that improve learning outcomes (Xu, 2024). For more advanced types of tasks, like multimedia project assessments where grade-matching might not be feasible both due to subjectivity and sheer intricacies of the task, AI systems can offer alternative feedback. For instance, in a media studies course where students are making a short documentary. An AI can break down many aspects of their work, from narrative structure to audio and visual cohesiveness, and return detailed feedback. This is not only beneficial to students as they continue to develop their projects, but it also helps them understand more about important processes and principles of media production.

They assist a lot in keeping the motivation and involvement of the students alive, which is a vital aspect of successful learning. These platforms personalise education and make the learning journey more interactive and therefore more relevant to a person's interests. Even more elements of gamification (badges, leaderboards, progress indicators) will spur students even further with physical targets and rewards (Hamari el al., 2014). Statistical analysis by Gallup (2018) indicated an active relation in performance with 2.5 times better academic achievement levels than disengaged students. When gamification was integrated into the educational platforms, adoption rates increased by nearly 20%, learner performance improved almost 15% (Bui, et al.)

AI in assessment is about more than testing. This allows methods of formative and summative assessments that are more indicative of the true learning and proficiency of a student (Baker et al. 2014). These assessments may be in the form of multiple choice, simulations or project-based evaluations, all of which offer something quite different when compared to a pen and paper test. They can evolve continuously calibrated with respect to an unique learning path and for higher education offer a very complete view of student performances. For instance, in a media production course, you could use AI assessments to give students opportunities to experience simulated real-world situations where they have to choose what content to present in a news article on a tight deadline. These simulations are a better indicator of capabilities than exams as they need to be pursued in real-like environments which require the application of knowledge and skills. With these complex tasks, AI excels at analysing performance for more accurate and meaningful reviews.

AI in media education will pave the way for individually tailored learning experiences, redefining how educators teach and students learn. AI can provide a solution by using intelligent tutoring systems, adaptive content, real-time feedback and creative assessment methodologies which are driven towards improving learning outcomes along with engagement.However, unlocking these capabilities entails addressing concerns around privacy; reducing algorithmic bias; and developing the capacity of those working with these technologies. So, as AI-enabled platforms can advance in and combine learning together with the next steps towards even greater personalisation and effectiveness in media education, it means not just enhancement of the students' understanding but also how well they are prepared to handle what is an ever-evolving and complex tricky world out there.

AI for Meaningful Creativity and Innovation

The significance of AI to media education is that it has put us at a threshold of a bloom-like period which is transitory yet an epochal frontier for creativity and innovation as well. According to Smith (2022), the incorporation of generative AI models along with other AI tools into the media curriculum does not just improve creative capabilities among students, but also raise content production success rates. This chapter reviews the various resources and datasets available and elaborates on how artificial intelli-gence can complement creativity and in-no-vation by offering endless solutions through media education.

Generative AI models, like Generative Adversarial Networks (GANs) are the main driving force creating Creative Atmosphere within media education, one such model (Table 2). The second use case, the high-fidelity, visual-audio modelling (Brown et al. 2017), represents the first instance where students were mobilised to innovate new and rich creative outputs that were previously unimaginable. Sheerman (2020) reported a 30% increase in originality and diversity, when students produced AI-augmented solutions for their projects compared to conventional methods. This is an example of how the AI platform can surface the creativity in learners by helping them with their ideas, and then allowing the kids to innovate on implementation.

Table 2. AI and Content Creation

Feature	Impact on Creativity
Idea Generation	AI can generate a vast number of ideas, sparking new creative directions and helping overcome creative blocks
Content Creation	AI can assist in creating various types of content, such as writing, music, art, and code, freeing up creators to focus on higher-level concepts
Experimentation and Exploration	AI can help creators explore new styles, techniques, and mediums, pushing the boundaries of their creativity
Collaboration	AI can collaborate with humans, providing complementary skills and perspectives that can lead to innovative outcomes
Personalized Learning	AI can provide tailored feedback and recommendations, helping creators develop their unique creative voice
Accessibility	AI can democratize creativity by providing tools and resources that were previously inaccessible to many
Inspiration	AI-generated content can inspire new ideas and approaches, stimulating the creative process
Automation of Routine Tasks	AI can automate repetitive tasks, allowing creators to focus on more creative aspects of their work

Inspiring a New Generation of Stories

Incorporating AI into the creative process is a student being able to explore storytelling practices in ways that were impossible before. AI systems are implemented for the writing of concepts, scripts and graphic design so that students have even lesser effort producing original perspective (Jones et al 2020). What AI can do is sift through terabytes of data to figure out patterns and create story arcs that this generation will jive with, more than any other. For example, a 2021 survey carried out by the National Association of Media Educators (NAME) has found educators using AI tools with their pupils had the narrative framework and thematic coherence were stronger where narrative structures and thematic coherence showed a 72 percent increase in quality.

Improving the Production of Visual and Auditory Content

Apart from ideation and scripting, AI has a great impact on the production of both visual as well as audio files in Media education. AI enabled graphic generation using DeepArt, Adobe Sensei, and other similar applications that require no expertise in the field of technology (Liu et al., 2018). These platforms support the generation and manipulation of intricate visual content which can further aid a transparent and collaborative education system. AI use in graphic design classes can increase student engagement and the technical quality. The results of another study have presented that students used AI resources and wanted to use them as a leg in their graphic design courses along with bloom's digital taxonomy, contributing to student learning experiences (Muji et al. 2024).

Democratising Content Creation

The democratisation of content creation by AI is among the greatest promises it holds for media education. AI tools, however, are becoming more accessible and user-friendly to overcome traditional barriers of restricted software or technical expertise (Chen et al., 2021). This makes media production more inclusive by allowing a wider variety of students to take part. Designed with intuitive interfaces, AI tools allow everyone from non-technical students to hobbyists to carry out difficult content creation tasks. For example, Canva is a machine learning–driven online platform that allows users to easily produce professional-quality graphics (Green et al. 2020).

Also, the availability of AI certainly reduces the slipped space between various education backgrounds. Free or low-cost AI tools can help level the playing field for students from schools with limited resources or underfunded art programs, so their work is also competitive compared to that coming out of more privileged institutions (Rodriguez et al. 2022). This flattening of the game possibility is vital to provide equal instructional chances. One can see the role of AI (UNESCO report, 2022) for global education equity where AI tools in media literacy have reduced the difference between rich and poor students by 15% over the last five years.

AI and Human Synergy

AI and human creativity can go together perfectly; for both developing classes, it is the synergy of collaboration between them that lies at the heart of what a modern media education looks like. Because AI has created tools to manage the iterative and technical elements of creativity, students can focus more directly on the conceptual and interpretive aspects of their domain; areas like ideation or even meta levels of critical thinking (Anderson et al. 2021). This approach is consistent with the feedback structure, another manner in which AI can countervail false beliefs by providing real time, evidence-based feedback on more accurate alternatives to incorrect (Ford et al. 2020).

It is an excellent tool which can deliver real-time feedback to students so that they constantly keep committing efforts towards the technical and creative aspects of their submitted projects. For example, before a video is published AI could check and correct the technical quality (lighting, sound levels), aesthetic interchangeable-ness (visual order; emotional synchronicity), themes, overlaps themes or even respond to one author) as of precise word phrasing, plot symmetry (Wright et al. 2019). Studies conducted in Media Education Research Journal (2021) also found that students who received both human and AI-generated feedback wrote projects with scores 20% higher than those who only received human-based feedback. This showed that artificial intelligence is involved in both the production and also complements how ideas are executed creatively.

The development and expression dynamic in media education with AI have become complete. AI has the potential to engage in hybrid experimental art, media practices incorporating procedural computational methods. AI has transformed every industry, bringing such virtual reality experience ever delightful with live-action mixed CGI impossible to support in any traditional media format. Media education with AI is a new level in creativity and innovations. The students are given the opportunity to use generative AI models in order to experiment with more time-intensive content creation, one of these great ideas that brings forth new forms of storytelling. By offering a merged human creativity and AI, the next era of media production is opened up to new possibilities where automating the process for all formats encourages students to produce more while breaking them out of frames. Additionally, as AI removes the restrictions of more complex methodologies to produce and curate content, it means that no student should be left behind due to simply not being skilled in the right tools. Given all of these fundamental changes to how the world works it feels like we should all embrace AI into our home as a welcome 4th child. It is officially established that AI has become one of us, we all know AI-defined future media academic space possibly opens a huge room to endless creativity and innovation and without doubt shaping it significantly.

A Catalyst for Strengthening Critical Thinking and Media Literacy

The advent of AI technology has marked a strong impact on different sectors, and this counts for media education. For the first time ever in the last year, AI has shown us how to break old rules of media nutrition — and what that opens up (and brings with it). Artificial Intelligence tools deliver existing content to consumers more efficiently, but with the risk of encouraging fake news and stereotypes. However, there is no framework guiding how to teach media literacy; the critical thinking skills students will need in this kind of environment. Critical thinking is a tool with which to examine information and come to sensible decisions, or formulate logical solutions, in any environment where you are well enough. Media Literacy and Critical Thinking For example, critical thinking within a media literacy framework might involve considering the content, identifying bias, and evaluating sources (Kahne et al. 2017). For nearly a decade, AI-powered tools have proven to be powerful means for delivering these skills. This part looks at the potential of AI-assistive tools to teach students how to identify media, sifting through bias and detecting misinformation.

Algorithmic bias is a key concern surrounding AI in the media. Social media and streaming websites are also using algorithms for their content recommendation service, which introduces a persistent issue of algorithmic bias in recommendations, because such recommendations are more aimed for user engagement, than for user knowledge (O'Neil 2016). Algorithms on social media for instance rank content that results in these more clicks and views from AI over Facebook or YouTube (Pariser, 2011), possibly encouraging echo chambers and filter bubbles. Research suggests that these biased algorithms can deepen political polarisation with users being shown content based on their preconceived beliefs, creating an echo chamber (Bakshy et al. 2015). Learning tools based on AI can help students discover these biases. For instance, AI operating on these platforms can imitate different user roles to demonstrate the differences in algorithmic recommendations between types of users' preferences and behaviours. Therein lies the role such tools could play to nudge students towards a more nuanced understanding that content curation profoundly affects how they consume media and yet equally significant is the opportunity in seeking alternative sources of information (Diakopoulos, 2016).

Misinformation and Fake News

Another major challenge brought about by the digital age is the spread of misleading and fake news. Unfortunately, with the prevalence of AI technologies being used to disseminate these false narratives, it makes it even harder for ourselves and our communities to distinguish between truth and lies (Vosoughi et al. 2018). Empirical research shows that false news spreads much farther, faster, deeper, and more broadly on social media than in the case of true news . One should emphasise on why accurate AI tools in schools and education getaways are so important. They can also be employed with AI-based tools to train students in spotting, and analysing misinformation. For instance, AI-driven fact-checking applications can assess the accuracy of news articles and social-media feeds (Graves 2018). Using natural language processing (NLP) and machine learning algorithms, the apps will crosscheck various data points against confirmed sources to deliver a crowdsourced authentication of whether or not the facts are valid. If we train students in the use of these tools in finishing schools, media education or elsewhere, this makes them more discerning subjects for any information or knowledge imparted to them.

Already many educational bodies and organisations are using AI tools in their media literacy programmes. One curriculum developed by the Stanford History Education Group (SHEG), Civic Online Reasoning (COR) aims at helping students discern online information that is credible and to be able to comprehend complexity on the web itself (Wineburg et al., 2016). Using AI algorithms, the modules include information about how to determine credibility on a web site, understand content as it pertains to sponsored advertising and validate news sources. Stripe has its own major AI initiative, as does the News Literacy Project. Real news game, lessons on identifying misinformation, and the role of journalism in a democratic society (News Literacy Project 2021).

Impact of Artificial Intelligence in Media OTT segment

AI, as it develops, helps to build that information terrain by producing the new public opinions and discourses emerging out of this medium turned message machine (Tufekci, 2015). Laying the foundation of an informed and critical citizen with an insight into societal implications due to AI driven media. The AI algorithms, which back the entire social media engine, shape public opinion quite dramatically towards the type of content that one is exposed to. Research has empirically demonstrated that AI-based content recommendations shape skewed perceptions and breed animosity toward social and political topics (Bakshy et al. 2015). Information that is algorithmically magnified can bias public opinion on crucial topics including those related to climate change, vaccination, and electoral integrity (Lewandowsky et al.

2020). Therefore, another method we can ensure students are developing informed digital citizenry is teaching them about how AI influences public opinion. It would help students to understand and recognize that the media they are exposed to is shaped by AI algorithms. That is information that allows them to know when they are lied to, for instance, and when interpretation of information otherwise seems slanted by the one that controls where the information will flow.

The promise and possible pitfalls of teaching AI in media In AI-based tools on the teaching of critical thinking, media literacy, which are especially trying to understand biases in different types of misinformation and its social stereotype, or the information that is closely associated with the AI-driven media. Nevertheless, we must tread with caution in bringing AI into educational practices due to its ethical concerns and dangers. Educators need to communicate with policymakers and stakeholders in media education to develop these kinds of full-fledged programs that would lead the students who are not only trained but have skill and information on how to survive and navigate this digital media age. Through among others, promoting critical thinking and media literacy to give the next generation of citizens healthy doses of scepticism.

While AI offers numerous benefits for media education, concerns are key. The deployment of AI faces serious questions when it comes to Data Privacy, Algorithmic bias and Displacement of human jobs. For example, if a company personalised learning experiences based on data collection from students, that may involve privacy issues unless this is properly managed. Also, AI systems could serve to perpetuate existing, and even exacerbate historical biases that might compromise student success and equity. Therefore, educators have to set a strong ethical framework in using AI technology that leads to fair and equitable application with transparency. This is where technology, the new media education can step in a positive light so long as an atmosphere that encourages responsible AI practices. Over the past few years, AI has redrawn the landscape of several industries including education. However, application of AI in media education gives way to some sort of ethical dither and the practical part comes into play here mostly when it comes to deployment.

The one absolute dilemma that sits in our minds is Data Privacy, when it comes to the ethical use of AI. Rather than such a course, huge datasets are gathered utilising AI-driven systems to refine instructive substance (West et al. 2020). Then there is the potential for AI to monitor how students are engaging with their work or even predict where a pupil may be failing and provide them with a bespoke curriculum. However, again this brings many data privacy risks too. Open or ill- handled data leave data available to be accessed and misused, which leads to Student Granularity Conundrum.(Chun et al. 2021). Organisations in the education sphere have increased 58% over last year through 2022 (IAPP). As a result, these breaches can cause very critical factors such as: identity thefts and other exploitations. Therefore, in order to ensure that AI platforms comply with a plethora of privacy regulations, such as the General Data Protection Regulation (GDPR) and Family Educational Rights and Privacy Act (FERPA) institutions should adopt robust data security measures (ICO, 2021).

One more significant ethical concern in AI is algorithmic bias; an inherent component of AI systems. These biased algorithms are trained on data sets that tend to replicate historical biases and structural inequalities (Noble, 2018). Thus when AI systems are used to make decisions, they can magnify these biases, because algorithms learn what an individual determined to be the "right" plan and decision based on a particular dataset. Another study (Danza et al. 2019) has found that AI grading systems discriminate against students of colour, that can lead to bias. In a global sample of countries, this has also been seen to result in the misidentification of students of colour to predict professional aptitude (Buolamwini et al. 2018), as shown by facial recognition technology used in classrooms. The existence of such inequalities emphasises why AI systems should be transparent and fair. They will have to verify that the datasets used to train AI algorithms are representative and unbiased. Long-term monitoring of the outcomes of AI is also required to detect patterns, and mitigate unjust ones, as they surface in future use.

Job displacement in the education sector is also a concern amplified by AI evolutionary development. McKinsey & Company (2021) reported that more than 14% of global jobs could be automated out of existence by the end of this decade, with both teachers and educational support staff particularly at risk. HR can automates administrative tasks (grading, student monitoring) instead of seeking out human intervention for all cases (Huang, 2019). AI can increase productivity and decrease workload but also the danger of losing a job. Meanwhile, an associated phenomenon, known as the fear displacement, may push educators and staff to resist the adoption of AI (Brynjolfsson et al. 2014). As a result, it is essential for institutions to leverage AI in a way that supports rather than replaces human jobs. Science Fiction has gone a long way from the radical ideas in 1984 to inspire people to climb upon the backs of that nearby hovering beetle, and by investing in professional development and retraining programs we can equip educators with the tools required to begin working alongside AI: shifting their position rather than phasing it out (Autor, 2015).

In order to integrate ethics in the AI application in media education, one must establish a strong foundation of an ethical framework for educational institutions. Consistent with transparency and fairness such a framework would be grounded in these principles of equity. Transparency requires knowing how AI systems work and what data they use. Educational institutions must communicate to students, parents, and teachers the nature of the data that are being collected and for what purposes it is used. Regular reporting and auditing of AI systems can also serve to build trust and ensure accountability (Floridi et al.) Fairness dictates that AI systems should not discriminate and further, the differences in society should be deleted. This calls for the need to remove biases in training datasets and algorithms proactively. Coordinating the actions of technologists, educators and ethicists is essential for producing equitable AI (Dastin, 2018). Equity means that AI functions will provide benefit to all students, regardless of their previous and universally applied across peculiarities. Therefore, representations should also act on ensuring that the access to AI technologies is equitable, and resources are imbued across all. The federal, state and local governments can include AI practices that are fair through equal-policy making. There is co-production of being collaborative and creating partnership which ensures equity in AI for the students (Eubanks, 2018). Despite the huge possibilities for enhancing media education, AI requires very careful ethical considerations. Responsible AI is necessary to ensure data privacy and protections against algorithmic bias, and preserve jobs. Its way forward is as unique as it has been with using an ethical framework built on the pillars of transparency, fairness and equity together which can unlock the potential power of AI in media education without compromising on its ethics.

DISCUSSION

This chapter has explored the historical evolution of AI in media and its growing integration into media education programs. Through a comprehensive review, we have gained valuable insights into the potential of AI to revolutionize the way media knowledge and skills are shared.AI, having gradually become an integral part of various media sectors, has demonstrated its transformative potential through its ability to disrupt traditional media practices. The integration of AI into media education programs is a relatively recent development, but it has already shown promising results. AI-powered tools are being used for a variety of tasks, such as content creation, data analysis, and personalized learning. Educators are also exploring innovative pedagogical approaches to leverage AI to enhance student learning experiences. The potential of AI to transform media education is significant. AI can provide personalized learning experiences, foster creativity, and prepare students for the challenges of the digital age. By automating routine tasks, AI can free up students and educators to focus on more creative and critical thinking activities. Additionally, AI can help bridge the digital divide by providing access to education and resources for students from diverse backgrounds.

While the potential benefits of AI in media education are substantial, it is important to acknowledge the challenges and considerations associated with its implementation. Ethical concerns, such as bias, privacy, and job displacement, must be carefully addressed. Ensuring that AI is used responsibly and ethically is crucial for its successful integration into media education. AI is poised to play a transformative role in media education. By understanding its historical evolution, exploring its integration into media programs, and assessing its potential benefits and challenges, we can harness the power of AI to create a more innovative, equitable, and effective media education landscape. As AI technology continues to advance, it is essential for educators and policymakers to stay informed and adapt their approaches to embrace the opportunities and address the challenges presented by this rapidly evolving field.

CONCLUSION

Some possibilities and repercussions are deep and wide for the media education Industry, contributing new pedagogical prospects. AI could reshape what media education is and how it is taught, through personalization that develops creator mindsets, critical thinking, and media literacy. Further, as media workers will likely work more in environments driven by AI in the near future (Selwyn 2021), it also becomes critical to incorporate these within the educational curriculum. One of the biggest and most obvious cases for how AI can be used in media education is by providing personalised learning. The importance of customisation and personalisation in education has been debated for years but the Covid pandemic really put these into practice. For example, AI can observe how a student learns or the skills they need to strengthen and deliver customised educational content that suits every unique need of each student in real-time (Means et al., 2009). This form fine tune is crucial in higher yields of educational outputs encouraging for smarter way coding of learning. AI may be the key to unlocking media schools' creative potential, as well. AI is a useful tool when it comes to creativity; to construct, deconstruct, and reconstruct which is essential for any media professional (McDougall et al. 2020). For example, AI can generate insights or new creative solutions, and help you in the process of creating art. Through 'processing large datasets in order to discover underlying patterns and trends invisible by human analysts' that spark-up new perspectives, potentials (Manovich, 2019). Media content analysing AI and ML algorithms predict the trend this how they show the different trend to students actually what is going on in the media world. Other AI-powered creative tools could utilise the Generative Adversarial Networks (GANs) to create new media types as well. One of the uses of AI, for instance, is in the creation of music and films (Bhardwaj,

2018). Our need is slightly different in that these tools can serve as an additional resource to spark something new and further a student's creativity.

In an age where the media landscape has become more complex than ever with new technology and methods of distribution, critical thinking is crucial to understand that manipulation can occur on these communication channels. AI can also go a long way to augment these skills (Buckingham, 2019). Educators can also help students uncover AI-driven exploration and content analysis tools which can provide different perspectives, sources, bias detection and a more thorough frame for understanding media content (Mason, 2018). Given the fact that media professionals of the future will work in AI-supported environments, it is therefore important to incorporate AI into educational programs (Castells, 2010). Training students in this way ensures they will develop the technical skills needed to actually utilise AI tools properly once they graduate. Media programs from various educational institutions are already jumping on the AI bandwagon with their curriculum. One example is a "AI for Media" class at the University of Southern California that covers AI's impacts on media industries as well as prepares students by teaching them skills in AI (USC Annenberg School for Communication and Journalism, 2021). Our focus on AI-related tools and initiatives help students learn the skills they need to be a responsible consumer, an informed and ethical user, or even assess whether what we currently have is good enough.

However, with all of these benefits, the AI integration in media education does present significant ethical concerns as well. Similarly, data privacy, algorithmic bias and the digital divide are some examples of issues that need to be dealt with in order for AI to support equitable and responsible learning (Noble, 2018). AI-powered educational tools can also lead to some problems since they collect vast amounts of personal data, raising concerns about privacy and data security (Lupton et al. 2017). Protecting data is important therefore it becomes necessary that schools protect the data they have about their students and be clear in terms of where they are collecting this, how much of it, for what purpose and Where are storing such information. For instance, if the data on which AI preferences are learned are biased, recommendations and decisions made by AI will be biased too, leading to perpetuation of intermediating stereotypes and discrimination (Barocas et al. 2019). In particular, this necessitates making efforts to train AI algorithms on diverse and representative datasets and regularly evaluating, monitoring, and updating such algorithms. In addition, the digital divide is one of the most serious problems wherein not all students have the opportunity to learn with this AI-based tool (Warschauer, 2004). To prevent AI from deepening pre-existing educational inequity, it is vital to guarantee equitable access to ed tech and learning materials. This gap can be bridged with area-wide initiatives like lowering the price to buy AI tools and offering a free of charge training course for educators to learn how to plug in and profit.

In general, the integration of AI in media education offers important possibilities to shape learning processes more individually, to increase creativity and to promote differentiated critical reflection and media literacy. Future media professionals will operate in AI-driven environments, educational programs need to address AI. But such an integration must be carried out thoughtfully and with due reflection on the morality behind to ensure that AI is facilitating fair and responsible learning. AI can help transform media education and train students well to work with AI in the rapidly changing world of media. To teach students to drive with AI, instead of just cruising on autopilot, would help empower human creativity and insight in a world run by AI. Which makes it all the more critical for educators, policymakers and technologists. Together, they have the power to design a world in which AI integration in media education is conducted ethically, equitably, and effectively fuelling a new wave of learning that truly values inclusion and innovation.

REFERENCES

Adobe. (2020). Adobe Sensei. https://www.adobe.com/sensei.html

Ahuja, S. (2019). Creativity and AI: Augmenting human creativity with advanced technologies. *Journal of Innovation and Entrepreneurship*, 8(1), 9. DOI: 10.1186/s13731-019-0101-2

Anderson, T., & Carter, L. (2021). Artificial intelligence and collaborative creativity in the media classroom. *Journal of Medical Education*, 32(4), 147–162.

Autor, D. H. (2015). Why are there still so many jobs? The history and future of workplace automation. *The Journal of Economic Perspectives*, 29(3), 3–30. DOI: 10.1257/jep.29.3.3

Baker, R. S., & Inventado, P. S. (2014). Educational data mining and learning analytics. In Seel, N. M. (Ed.), *Encyclopedia of the sciences of learning* (pp. 1073–1076). Springer., DOI: 10.1007/978-1-4614-3305-7_4

Bakshy, E., Messing, S., & Adamic, L. A. (2015). Exposure to ideologically diverse news and opinion on Facebook. *Science*, 348(6239), 1130–1132. DOI: 10.1126/science.aaa1160 PMID: 25953820

Barocas, S., Hardt, M., & Narayanan, A. (2019). Fairness and machine learning. *fairmlbook.org*. https://fairmlbook.org/

Bhardwaj, J. (2018). AI in the creative industries: The shift from co-creation to autonomous creation. *Journal of Creative Technology*, 5(2), 48–62.

Bolukbasi, T., Chang, K., Zou, J. Y., Saligrama, V., & Kalai, A. (2016). Man is to computer programmer as woman is to homemaker? Debiasing word embeddings. *Proceedings of the 30th Conference on Neural Information Processing Systems (NeurIPS 2016)*, 4356–4364. https://doi.org/DOI: 10.5555/3157382.3157584

Brown, H., & Wilson, M. (2021). Generative AI in media education: Unleashing creative potential. *Computers & Education*, 154, 103919. DOI: 10.1016/j.compedu.2020.103919

Brynjolfsson, E., & McAfee, A. (2014). *The second machine age: Work, progress, and prosperity in a time of brilliant technologies*. W.W. Norton & Company.

Buckingham, D. (2003). *Media education: Literacy, learning and contemporary culture*. Polity Press.

Buckingham, D. (2019). *The media education manifesto*. Polity Press.

Bui, A., Veit, D., & Webster, J. (2015). Gamification: A novel phenomenon or a new wrapping for existing concepts? In *Proceedings of the 36th International Conference on Information Systems* (ICIS 2015). https://doi.org/DOI: 10.13140/RG.2.2.34660.27524

Buolamwini, J., & Gebru, T. (2018). Gender shades: Intersectional accuracy disparities in commercial gender classification. *Proceedings of the 1st Conference on Fairness, Accountability and Transparency (FAT 2018)*, 77–91. https://proceedings.mlr.press/v81/buolamwini18a.html

Castells, M. (2010). *The rise of the network society* (2nd ed.). Wiley-Blackwell.

Chen, E., Gee, L., Mangelsdorf, I., Munina, I., Principe, C., & Saiyed, A. (2020). Personalized learning in AI: The next frontier in education technology. *Journal of Artificial Intelligence in Education*, 31(1), 1–20.

Chen, X., Liu, T., & Zhao, Y. (2021). AI tools for content creation and their implications for media education. *International Journal of Educational Technology in Higher Education*, 18(1), 29. DOI: 10.1186/s41239-021-00264-5

Chun, A., & Warner, J. (2021). AI in education: Today's challenges and tomorrow's promise. *EdTech Magazine*. https://edtechmagazine.com/

Dastin, J. (2018). Amazon scraps secret AI recruiting tool that showed bias against women. *Reuters*. https://www.reuters.com/article/us-amazon-com-jobs-automation-insight/amazon-scraps-secret-ai-recruiting-tool-that-showed-bias-against-women-idUSKCN1MK08G

Diakopoulos, N. (2016). *Algorithmic accountability: Journalistic investigation of computational power structures*. Data & Society.

Diakopoulos, N., Trielli, D., Stanton, A., & Smrž, P. (2019). Automated news: How algorithms impact the news we read. *The AI Now Report*, 1–30.

EdSurge. (2019). Report on the impact of adaptive learning technologies on student outcomes. *EdSurge*. https://www.edsurge.com

Elgammal, A., Liu, B., Elhoseiny, M., & Mazzone, M. (2017). CAN: Creative adversarial networks, generating "art" by learning about styles and deviating from style norms. *arXiv Preprint* arXiv:1706.07068. https://arxiv.org/abs/1706.07068

Eliashberg, J., Hui, S. K., & Zhang, Z. J. (2014). Assessing box office performance using movie scripts: A machine learning approach. *Management Science*, 60(6), 1425–1439. DOI: 10.1287/mnsc.2013.1836

Eubanks, V. E. (2018). *Automating inequality: How high-tech tools profile, police, and punish the poor*. St. Martin's Press.

Factmata. (2017). Factmata: AI-powered fact-checking. *Factmata*. https://www.factmata.com

Ferrucci, D., Levas, A., Bagchi, S., Gondek, D., & Mueller, E. T. (2013). Watson: Beyond Jeopardy! *Artificial Intelligence*, 199, 114–137. DOI: 10.1016/j.artint.2012.06.009

Floridi, L., Cowls, J., Beltrametti, M., Chatila, R., Chazerand, P., Dignum, V., Luetge, C., Madelin, R., Pagallo, U., Rossi, F., Schafer, B., Valcke, P., & Vayena, E. (2018). AI4People—An ethical framework for a good AI society: Opportunities, risks, principles, and recommendations. *Minds and Machines*, 28(4), 689–707. DOI: 10.1007/s11023-018-9482-5 PMID: 30930541

Ford, J., & Martin, R. (2020). The role of AI in media feedback: Enhancing student creativity through data-driven critiques. *Journal of Educational Technology & Society*, 23(3), 56–72.

Freire, P. (1970). Pedagogy of the oppressed. *Continuum : an Interdisciplinary Journal on Continuity of Care*.

Gallup. (2018). The state of student engagement in U.S. schools. *Gallup*. https://www.gallup.com

Graesser, A. C., Conley, M., & Olney, A. (2011). Intelligent tutoring systems. In Seel, N. M. (Ed.), *Encyclopedia of the sciences of learning* (pp. 1709–1711). Springer., DOI: 10.1007/978-1-4419-1428-6_1499

Graves, L. (2018). Understanding the promise and limits of automated fact-checking. *Digital Journalism (Abingdon, England)*, 6(8), 939–954. DOI: 10.1080/21670811.2018.1531688

Green, S., & Thomas, P. (2020). Accessibility of AI-driven tools in media production: A pathway for non-technical students. *Journal of Visual Arts Education*, 35(2), 121–135.

Hamari, J., Koivisto, J., & Sarsa, H. (2014). Does gamification work? A literature review of empirical studies on gamification. In *Proceedings of the 47th Hawaii International Conference on System Sciences* (pp. 3025-3034). IEEE. https://doi.org/DOI: 10.1109/HICSS.2014.377

Hobbs, R. (2010). *Digital and media literacy: Connecting culture and classroom*. Corwin Press.

Huang, T., & Rust, R. T. (2019). Artificial intelligence in service. *Journal of Service Research*, 21(2), 155–172. DOI: 10.1177/1094670517752459

IBM. (2020). IBM Watson: Explore AI for media. Retrieved from https://www.ibm.com/watson/media

International Association of Privacy Professionals (IAPP). (2022). Data breach trends in the education sector. https://iapp.org/

Jenkins, H. (2006). *Convergence culture: Where old and new media collide*. NYU Press.

Jenkins, H., Purushotma, R., Weigel, M., Clinton, K., & Robinson, A. J. (2009). *Confronting the challenges of participatory culture: Media education for the 21st century*. MIT Press. DOI: 10.7551/mitpress/8435.001.0001

Jones, R., & Richardson, K. (2020). AI-assisted storytelling: New frontiers in media education. *Journal of Creative Media*, 28(3), 190–204.

Kahne, J., & Bowyer, B. (2017). Educating for democracy in a partisan age: Confronting the challenges of motivated reasoning and misinformation. *American Educational Research Journal*, 54(1), 3–34. DOI: 10.3102/0002831216679817

Knewton. (2014). Personalized learning for all. Retrieved from https://www.knewton.com

Knewton. (2015). Impact of adaptive learning on student retention rates. *Knewton*. Retrieved from https://www.knewton.com

Kulkarni, S. (2020). The role of AI in education: A comprehensive guide. Retrieved from https://www.techaconsulting.com/ai-in-education-guide

Leeflang, P. S., Verhoef, P. C., Dahlström, P., & Freundt, T. (2014). Challenges and solutions for marketing in a digital era. *European Management Journal*, 32(1), 1–12. DOI: 10.1016/j.emj.2013.12.001

Lewandowsky, S., Ecker, U. K. H., & Cook, J. (2017). Beyond misinformation: Understanding and coping with the "post-truth" era. *Journal of Applied Research in Memory and Cognition*, 6(4), 353–369. DOI: 10.1016/j.jarmac.2017.07.008

Liu, M., & Stewart, G. (2019). AI in visual content production: Implications for media education. *Media Culture & Society*, 41(5), 760–779.

Livingstone, S. (2004). Media literacy and the challenge of new information and communication technologies. *Communication Review*, 7(1), 3–14. DOI: 10.1080/10714420490280152

Luckin, R., Holmes, W., Griffiths, M., & Forcier, L. B. (2016). Intelligence unleashed: An argument for AI in education. Retrieved from https://www.pearson.com/corporate/intelligence-unleashed.html

Lupton, D., & Williamson, B. (2017). The datafied child: The dataveillance of children and implications for their rights. *New Media & Society*, 19(5), 780–794. DOI: 10.1177/1461444816686328

Manovich, L. (2019). AI and new media: New horizons for modern applications. *Digital Creativity*, 22(3), 193–202.

Mason, L. (2018). Media literacy in the age of algorithmic personalization: The role of artificial intelligence in enhancing critical thinking skills. *Journal of Medical Education*, 9(2), 24–33.

Masterman, L. (1985). *Teaching the media*. Comedia Publishing Group.

McCarthy, J., Minsky, M. L., Rochester, N., & Shannon, C. E. (2006). A proposal for the Dartmouth summer research project on artificial intelligence, August 31, 1955. *AI Magazine*, 27(4), 12.

McDougall, J., & Skoog, S. (2020). Creative AI in education: Investigating the implications and potentials. *Learning, Media and Technology*, 45(3), 287–299.

McKinsey & Company. (2021). The future of work after. *COVID*, 19, •••. https://www.mckinsey.com/

McLuhan, M. (1964). *Understanding media: The extensions of man*. McGraw-Hill.

Means, B., Bakia, M., & Murphy, R. (2014). *Learning online: What research tells us about whether, when and how*. Routledge. DOI: 10.4324/9780203095959

Muji, S., Svensson, E., & Faraon, M. (2024). Engaging with artificial intelligence in graphic design education. In *Proceedings of the 2023 IEEE World Artificial Intelligence Education Conference* (pp. 31-37). IEEE. DOI: 10.1109/WAIE60568.2023.00013

National Association for Media Literacy Education (NAMLE). (2007). Core principles of media literacy education in the United States. Retrieved from https://namle.net/publications/core-principles

National Association of Media Educators (NAME). (2021). *Survey on AI-assisted storytelling in media education*. NAME.

News Literacy Project. (2021). Checkology Virtual Classroom. Retrieved from https://www.newslit.org/

Nkambou, R., Bourdeau, J., & Mizoguchi, R. (Eds.). (2010). *Advances in intelligent tutoring systems*. Springer., DOI: 10.1007/978-3-642-14363-2

Noble, S. U. (2018). *Algorithms of oppression: How search engines reinforce racism*. NYU Press. DOI: 10.18574/nyu/9781479833641.001.0001

O'Neil, C. (2016). *Weapons of math destruction: How big data increases inequality and threatens democracy*. Crown Publishing Group.

Pariser, E. (2011). *The filter bubble: How the new personalized web is changing what we read and how we think*. Penguin Press.

Paul, R., & Elder, L. (2005). *Critical thinking: Tools for taking charge of your learning and your life*. Prentice Hall.

Rodriguez, P., & Patel, N. (2022). Bridging the gap: AI in underfunded media programs. *Journal of Educational Enquiry*, 39(1), 47–63.

Rogers, T., & Kim, S. (2020). Experimental media in the age of AI: Opportunities for creative exploration. *Journal of Digital Media Arts*, 27(3), 137–153.

Rumelhart, D. E., Hinton, G. E., & Williams, R. J. (1986). Learning representations by back-propagating errors. *Nature*, 323(6088), 533–536. DOI: 10.1038/323533a0

Selwyn, N. (2021). Should robots replace teachers? AI and the future of education. *Polity*.

Sheerman, L., Marston, H. R., Musselwhite, C., & Morgan, D. (2020). COVID-19 and the secret virtual assistants: The social weapons for a state of emergency. *Emerald Open Research*, 2(2), 19. DOI: 10.1108/EOR-02-2023-0005

Smith, A., Lee, J., & Gonzalez, J. (2019). Bias in AI grading systems: A study on the impact on minority students. *Journal of Education and Technology*, 54(1), 27–38. DOI: 10.1080/21532963.2022.1694378

Smith, J. (2022). Democratizing media creation through AI. In Brown, R. (Ed.), *Advances in media education* (pp. 57–72). Routledge.

Tufekci, Z. (2015). Algorithmic harms beyond Facebook and Google: Emergent challenges of computational agency. *Colorado Technology Law Journal*, 13(2), 203–217.

UNESCO. (2022). *Global education equity report: The role of AI in bridging the educational divide*. UNESCO.

USC Annenberg School for Communication and Journalism. (2021). AI for media [Course description]. Retrieved from https://uscannenberg.com/courses

Vosoughi, S., Roy, D., & Aral, S. (2018). The spread of true and false news online. *Science*, 359(6380), 1146–1151. DOI: 10.1126/science.aap9559 PMID: 29590045

Warschauer, M. (2004). *Technology and social inclusion: Rethinking the digital divide*. MIT Press.

West, D. M. (2019). AI in education: Building ethics into design. Brookings Institution Report. Retrieved from https://www.brookings.edu/wp-content/uploads/2019/04/AI-in-education_Building-ethics-into-design_Updated-cover.pdf

West, S. M., Whittaker, M., & Crawford, K. (2020). Discriminating systems: Gender, race, and power in AI. *AI Now Institute*. https://ainowinstitute.org/discriminatingsystems.html

Wibbitz. (2019). Wibbitz: AI-powered video creation. Retrieved from https://www.wibbitz.com

Wineburg, S., McGrew, S., Breakstone, J., & Ortega, T. (2016). *Evaluating information: The cornerstone of civic online reasoning*. Stanford Digital Repository.

Woolf, B. P. (2009). *Building intelligent interactive tutors: Student-centered strategies for revolutionizing e-learning*. Morgan Kaufmann., DOI: 10.1016/B978-0-12-373594-2.00001-8

Wright, L., & Bell, J. (2019). AI in media production: Enhancing quality and creative freedom. *Technology and Media Education*, 31(2), 203–215.

Xu, Z. (2024). AI in education: Enhancing learning experiences and student outcomes. *Applied and Computational Engineering*, 51(1), 104–111. DOI: 10.54254/2755-2721/51/20241187

ADDITIONAL READING

Holmes, W. (2020). Artificial intelligence in education. In *Encyclopedia of education and information technologies* (pp. 88–103). Springer International Publishing. DOI: 10.1007/978-3-030-10576-1_107

Saputra, I., Astuti, M., Sayuti, M., & Kusumastuti, D. (2023). Integration of Artificial Intelligence in Education: Opportunities, Challenges, Threats and Obstacles. A Literature Review. *The Indonesian Journal of Computer Science*, 12(4). Advance online publication. DOI: 10.33022/ijcs.v12i4.3266

Wu, D., Shen, H., & Lv, Z. (2021). An artificial intelligence and multimedia teaching platform based integration path of IPE and IEE in colleges and universities. *Journal of Intelligent & Fuzzy Systems*, 40(2), 3767–3776. DOI: 10.3233/JIFS-189410

Zhang, R. (2022). Digital media teaching and effectiveness evaluation integrating big data and artificial intelligence. *Computational Intelligence and Neuroscience*, 2022(1), 1217846. DOI: 10.1155/2022/1217846 PMID: 36188689

Zhou, C. (2023). Integration of modern technologies in higher education on the example of artificial intelligence use. *Education and Information Technologies*, 28(4), 3893–3910. DOI: 10.1007/s10639-022-11309-9

KEY TERMS AND DEFINITIONS

Algorithmic Bias: The presence of systematic and unfair discrimination in AI algorithms, often due to biased training data, which can result in unequal treatment of certain groups.

Artificial Intelligence (AI): The field of computer science focused on creating systems that perform tasks typically requiring human intelligence, such as decision-making, language processing, and problem-solving.

Content Creation: The process of generating digital media, such as text, audio, and visual content, often enhanced by AI tools to streamline production and support creativity.

Critical Thinking: The ability to analyze and evaluate information or arguments logically and objectively to form a reasoned judgment.

Digital Media: Media created, distributed, and consumed through digital technology, including social media, streaming platforms, and online publications.

Media Literacy: The skills required to access, analyze, evaluate, and create media in various forms, essential for navigating today's digital information landscape.

Personalized Learning: An educational approach that tailors learning experiences to the unique needs and preferences of each student, often supported by AI technologies.

Quality of Experience (QoE): A measure of user satisfaction with a service, such as an AI-driven learning platform, based on factors like usability, content relevance, and performance.

Real-Time Feedback: Immediate feedback provided by AI tools during the learning or content creation process, enhancing user engagement and improving outcomes.

Virtual Learning Environment (VLE): An online platform that supports various educational activities, including course management, content delivery, and student collaboration, often incorporating AI for personalization.

Chapter 11
Using Risk-Free Artificial Intelligence in the Classroom:
Insights From Higher Education Professors

Ankur Nandi
https://orcid.org/0009-0008-3459-3429
University of Kalyani, India

Tapash Das
https://orcid.org/0000-0003-4619-0009
Kazi Nazrul University, India

Tarini Halder
https://orcid.org/0009-0007-8807-7182
University of Kalyani, India

Santu Karmakar
https://orcid.org/0009-0007-6092-7974
Kazi Nazrul University, India

ABSTRACT

This chapter examines professors' perspectives on using risk-free artificial intelligence (AI) in higher education classrooms, focusing on the perceived benefits, challenges, and ethical considerations surrounding AI implementation. Researchers gathered insights into professors' experiences and viewpoints on integrating AI into educational settings through a qualitative study using a survey method, semi-structured interviews, and questionnaires. The findings reveal that while AI offers substantial

DOI: 10.4018/979-8-3373-1017-6.ch011

opportunities for enhancing teaching and learning, it also brings notable challenges and ethical concerns. Based on these insights, the chapter recommends best practices to ensure the responsible and effective use of AI tools in higher education.

INTRODUCTION

Artificial intelligence (AI) is a transformative technology working in the field of computer science. It emphasizes the creation of intelligent machines that perform functions such as speech recognition, learning, planning and problem-solving, robotics, games, and modeling (Firschein et al., 1973). AI is changing rapidly in various aspects and education is no exception (George & Wooden, 2023) as AI technology becomes more integrated into the classroom. Therefore, it provides tools and methods that have the potential to enhance the teaching and learning experience. From personalized learning paths to automated grading systems, AI has the potential to support educators in meeting the needs of diverse students and managing administrative tasks more efficiently throughout history. Innovation has always been a key mechanism for improving living standards. However, the innovation process can be highly disruptive. As they make traditional technologies obsolete, cloud computing, the Internet of Things (IoT), big data, data science, artificial intelligence (AI), and blockchain are emerging technologies that can create winners and disruptors. Lost all over the world but the situation has changed dramatically in recent years. At present, almost Every sector uses one or more technologies. There are many factors responsible for this, such as the advancement of computer technology (Soni, 2020). However, including AI in education also raises important questions and concerns among teachers (Khosravi et al., 2022). Faculty perspective was extremely valuable this is because it provides insights into the practical implications of AI adoption and its impact on teaching methods and student learning experiences (Al-Zahrani and Alasmari, 2024).

The chapter aims to explore professors' opinions on the use of risk-free artificial intelligence (AI) in the classroom, study professors' views on perceived benefits and challenges of implementing such AI, analyze professors' opinions on the ethical considerations and concerns related to AI technologies in educational settings, and provide some suggestions for best practices for effectively using AI tools in higher education classrooms. The present study followed a qualitative approach and survey method. Researchers applied a semi-structured interview and questionnaire for data collection and data analysis was done qualitatively. This study aims to explore professors' opinions on the use of risk-free AI in the classroom, focusing on their opinions of its benefits and challenges. It seeks to identify how professors view the implementation of AI technologies, particularly in terms of ethical considerations and concerns related to its usage in educational settings. Also, offers practical suggestions for effectively integrating AI tools in higher education classrooms.

BACKGROUND

Understanding Risk-Free AI

Risk-free AI refers to AI applications guided by ethical standards and principles to minimize potential harms while maximizing educational benefits. The concept encompasses safeguarding student data privacy, ensuring transparency in AI decision-making processes, and mitigating biases inherent in AI algorithms (Akgun & Greenhow, 2021). Risk-free AI emphasizes the importance of ethical applications that prioritize minimizing potential harms and maximizing benefits in education including those guided by an ethical standard (Jackson, 2024) transparency in decision-making, and mitigating algorithmic bias (Jackson, 2024; jmu.edu, 2024). The concept encompasses safeguarding student data privacy, ensuring transparency in AI decision-making processes, and mitigating biases inherent in AI algorithms.

Artificial Intelligence in Higher Educational Settings

Integrating AI into higher education should be approached thoughtfully, considering the potential impacts, and ensuring that technology serves as a tool for human advancement rather than a means of control (Popenici & Kerr, 2017). In the context of teaching-learning AI tools facilitate personalized education, allowing instructors to tailor content and assessments to meet individual student needs, improving engagement, and learning outcomes substantially (Lopez-Chila, 2023). Personalization is a key advantage of AI in education, allowing for tailored learning experiences. AI algorithms can analyze students' learning patterns and preferences, adapting content, and pacing to suit individual needs. This concept is discussed by Chen, Chen, and Lin (2020), who highlight AI's role in personalized learning. AI applications enable institutions to analyze data from various sources, leading to more informed decision-making regarding course offerings, resource allocation, and program evaluation, ultimately fostering a more agile administrative framework that responds effectively to changing educational demands (Popenici & Keer, 2017). Machine learning techniques allow for the identification of factors influencing student performance, thus equipping educators and administrators with actionable insights that can inform curriculum design and intervention strategies (Truncgil Technology, 2024). Bill Gates (2023) underscores that the integration of AI can lead to greater efficiency in education, enabling educators to focus on higher-order pedagogical tasks while AI handles administrative and repetitive tasks.

Ethical Concerns of Artificial Intelligence in Higher Educational Settings

AI's integration into higher education presents significant ethical concerns, particularly in data privacy, fairness, accountability, and student autonomy. AI systems often collect and analyze large amounts of student data, raising privacy issues and risks of data misuse (Aiken & Epstein, 2020). Furthermore, biases embedded in AI algorithms may reinforce existing inequalities, impacting marginalized student groups unfairly (Binns, 2018). The "black box" nature of AI complicates accountability, as decisions made by AI systems are often opaque, making it challenging for institutions to explain or rectify issues (Floridi & Cowls, 2019). Additionally, the increasing reliance on AI-driven learning pathways risks diminishing students' critical thinking and independence, as they may become overly dependent on automated feedback and recommendations (Williamson & Eynon, 2020). Addressing these concerns necessitates robust ethical frameworks and interdisciplinary collaboration to ensure AI's responsible use in fostering an equitable, transparent, and supportive educational environment.

Need for Faculty Perspectives on AI Integration

The integration of artificial intelligence (AI) in higher education has received considerable attention in recent years, especially the impact on teaching and learning practices. In addition, the introduction of AI in higher education often involves many ethical considerations and challenges. Faculty frequently express concerns about data privacy, algorithm bias, and the impact of AI on traditional teaching (Richardson et al, 2024). In India, where diverse educational institutions operate under varying degrees of technological sophistication, the disparity in AI adoption among faculty members can be attributed to differences in their preparedness and familiarity with these tools (CINEFORUM, 2024). Moreover, studies consistently point to the need for comprehensive professional development programs that equip educators with the skills necessary to harness AI effectively, which can enhance their willingness to embrace these innovations (Rahiman & Kodikal, 2023). Nevertheless, the successful implementation of artificial intelligence in educational contexts hinges upon various factors, including instructors' perspectives (Parviz, 2024). Understanding faculty perspectives regarding AI integration becomes essential considering these challenges. By exploring educators' experiences, insights, and reservations about adopting AI in the classroom, research can identify pathways for fostering successful implementation strategies.

METHODOLOGY

This section presents the method used for the study. Following the purpose of the study researchers used a qualitative approach followed by a survey method. To explore professors' opinions on using risk-free artificial intelligence (AI) in the classroom researchers conducted semi-structured interviews with 50 university teachers and 50 undergraduate college teachers shown in Table 1. Systematic codes are used followed by the analyses. Here numerical descriptions like percentages of responses are prepared and presented. For analysis software like MS-Word, and Excel are used. The entire coding and scoring procedure is divided into three stages. The first stage is Compilation, the second stage is Analysis, and the final stage is Synthesis. In the "compilation" stage data are refined, eliminating non-essential parts, and put together under exploration question or query. In the analysis stage, common responses for each query are grouped, then percentages of each code are counted. These are presented in Table 1. After considering the percentage a short paragraph is written summarizing the findings for each question. Lastly a general conclusion is drawn. The researcher used a questionnaire to identify the perceived benefits and challenges associated with the implementation of risk-free AI in the classroom. Since it is a point scale, numerical values were assigned. A simple percentage calculation was used for analyzing opinions. It is presented in Tables 2 &3.

RESULTS AND DISCUSSION

To EXPLORE PROFESSORS' OPINIONS on USING RISK-FREE ARTIFICIAL INTELLIGENCE (AI) in the CLASSROOM.

Table 1. Professors' opinions on using risk-free artificial intelligence (AI) in the classroom

Sl. no.	Quarries	Codes of Responses	Respondents							
			Professors of Universities				Professors of Colleges			
			Percentage (%)				Percentage (%)			
			Male	Female	Rural	Urban	Male	Female	Rural	Urban
1	What kind of risks do you think are associated with using AI in the classroom?	Data privacy and security	47	53	59	41	63	37	67	33
		Technical problems	42	48	63	47	56	44	66	34
		Gap in teacher-student interaction	49	51	69	31	41	59	68	32
		Over-dependence on technology	37	63	70	30	47	53	37	63
		Loss of teacher autonomy	35	65	58	42	31	69	35	65
		Bias or discrimination	43	57	71	29	30	70	43	57
		Job displacement	37	63	69	31	44	56	41	59
		Cost related issue	44	56	73	27	35	65	37	63
		Ethical concern	52	48	79	21	43	57	31	69
2	Do you think why AI is relevant to classroom settings?	Personalized learning	47	53	56	44	54	46	30	70
		24/7 availability of educational resources and support	41	59	54	46	37	63	71	29
		Data-driven insights	39	61	67	33	65	35	69	31
		Realtime feedback and assessment	55	45	66	44	57	43	41	59

continued on following page

Table 1. Continued

Sl. no.	Quarries	Codes of Responses	Respondents							
			Professors of Universities				Professors of Colleges			
			Percentage (%)				Percentage (%)			
			Male	Female	Rural	Urban	Male	Female	Rural	Urban
3	In your opinion how can institutions help in ensuring that AI adoption remains risk-free?	Develop Ethical AI Guidelines	63	37	47	53	55	45	57	43
		Establishing an ethics committee	71	29	55	45	64	36	51	49
		offer Comprehensive AI Training for teachers	41	59	71	29	61	39	48	52
		Follow National and International AI using Regulations	66	34	76	24	52	48	64	36
		Create AI Use Guidelines for Student	35	65	35	65	31	69	67	33
		Adopt Accreditation Standards AI Tools	56	44	30	70	44	56	33	67
		Establishment of AI ethics committee	47	53	31	69	39	61	41	59
4	In your opinion what is the future of artificial intelligence and education?	Beneficial of learners	49	51	59	41	63	37	43	57
		Efficiency in administrative task	48	52	46	54	44	56	66	34
		Individualized learning	49	51	58	42	41	59	68	32
		Negativity of teachers-students relationship	37	63	70	30	46	54	37	63
		Joyful learning	43	57	58	42	31	69	35	65
		Emotional deficit	56	44	71	29	30	70	43	57
		Data privacy concern	47	53	59	41	63	37	67	33
		Over-reliance on technology	42	48	63	47	56	44	41	59

The data privacy and security risks associated with AI are perceived significantly by both male and female professors across university and college settings. In universities, 47% of male professors express concern, while a higher percentage of female professors 53% indicate similar apprehensions. This trend is even more pronounced in colleges, where 63% of male professors and only 37% of female professors share these concerns. Interestingly, rural professors demonstrate a greater sense of vulnerability regarding data privacy, with 59% in universities and 67% in colleges, compared to their urban counterparts 41% in universities and 33% in colleges. This indicates that rural professors may be more acutely aware of potential data breaches and security risks, possibly due to a lack of technological infrastructure or support (Catota et al., 2019). Concerns about technical problems related to AI integration are also notable among respondents. University male professors report a 42% concern rate, while female professors show a slightly higher concern at 48%. In colleges, the concern rises, with 56% of male professors versus 44% of females. When broken down by location, rural professors show a significant worry, with 63% of university professors and 66% of college professors highlighting this risk. Urban professors, however, report lower levels of concern 47% in universities and 34% in colleges, suggesting that the technological challenges may be more pronounced in rural areas where access to reliable technology is often limited (Salemink et al., 2015). The potential gap in teacher-student interaction due to AI usage raises different levels of concern among genders and locations. At the university level, 49% of male and 51% of female professors express concern, suggesting a balanced view. However, this balance shifts in colleges, where male professors exhibit a lower concern 41% compared to female professors 59%. The rural-urban divide is striking here, with 69% of rural university professors worried about this gap, compared to only 31% of their urban counterparts.

On the other hand, 68% of college professors are in rural areas, while 32% are in urban areas. This disparity may indicate a deeper investment in personal interactions and relationships in educational settings, particularly among rural professors who may value traditional teaching methods (Christenson et al., 2012). Over-dependence with 63% of female university professors and 70% of rural university respondents expressing worries, compared to 37% of male university professors and 30% of urban ones. In colleges, 47% of male professors and 53% of female professors viewed this as a risk, with urban respondents 63% expressing more concern than rural ones 37%. In urban settings, the numbers drop significantly, indicating that urban professors may feel more confident in managing technology's role in education (Tettegah & Mayo, 2005). The perceived risk of losing teacher autonomy is another area of concern that shows notable gender differences, 65% of female university professors were concerned, as were 58% of rural university respondents, while male university professors and urban respondents were less worried 35% and 42%, respectively. In colleges, 69% of female professors were apprehensive about this issue, compared to only 31% of male professors. Both rural and urban respondents from colleges showed relatively equal concern 35% and 65%, respectively. Concerns regarding bias and discrimination in AI applications reflect significant disparities based on gender and location.

Male university professors show a concern rate of 43%, while female professors report 57%. In college settings, 30% of male professors versus 70% of female professors express concern. The rural-urban dynamic is also relevant here, with rural professors showing greater apprehension 71% in universities and 43% in colleges than their urban counterparts 29% in universities and 57% in colleges. This suggests a greater awareness of ethical implications and the potential for biases to affect teaching and learning environments among female and rural respondents. The worry about job displacement due to AI technologies shows a consistent pattern, with both genders expressing concern. Male professors in universities and colleges report concerns at 37% and 44%, respectively, while female professors express higher concern levels, with 63% in universities and 56% in colleges. The concern levels are particularly notable in rural settings, where 69% of university professors and 41% of college professors fear job displacement, compared to 31% of urban professors in universities and 59% in colleges. This may indicate a stronger belief among rural professors that AI could directly impact their job security (Ahmad et al., 2023). When considering cost-related issues, rural university professors 73% and female university professors 56% identified this as a major concern, while urban university respondents 27% and male professors 44% were less concerned. In colleges, 65% of female professors and 63% of urban respondents highlighted cost issues, with rural respondents 37% and male professors 35% showing less concern. Ethical concerns regarding AI's use in education show a significant disparity, particularly among male university professors, 52% of whom express concern compared to 48% of females.

However, in college settings, female professors show slightly higher concern 57% compared to male professors 43%. The rural-urban divide is pronounced, with 79% of rural university professors indicating concern versus 21% of urban professors and 69% of urban respondents highlighted ethical issues as a risk, while rural professors 31% were less worried. This indicates a strong recognition among rural educators of the moral implications of AI technologies and their potential impact on education (Ali et al., 2023). Among university professors, female respondents 53% showed more support for personalized learning than male respondents 47%. Rural professors 56% were more supportive of this aspect compared to their urban colleagues 44%. In colleges, male professors 54% expressed stronger support than female professors 46%. Urban professors 70% were more inclined to support personalized learning than rural professors 30%. The availability of educational resources and support around the clock was favored by female university professors 59% more than male professors 41%. Rural professors 54% were more supportive of this initiative compared to urban professors 46%. Among college professors, female respondents 63% expressed stronger support for 24/7 resource availability than male professors 37%. Rural professors 71% were far more supportive than their urban counterparts 29%. The use of AI for data-driven insights was backed more by female university professors 61% compared to male professors 39%. Rural professors 67% were significantly more supportive than urban professors 33%. In colleges, male professors 65% showed greater support for data-driven insights than female professors 35%, with rural professors 69% expressing more support than their urban counterparts 31% (Gauthier et al., 2022).

For real-time feedback and assessment, male university professors 55% expressed more support than female professors 45%. Rural university professors 66% were more supportive of this concept than urban professors 44%. Among college professors, males 57% were more supportive of real-time feedback than females 43%, while urban professors 59% showed stronger support compared to rural professors 41% (Hooda et al., 2022). Among university professors, male respondents 63% showed more support for developing ethical AI guidelines compared to female respondents 37%. Rural professors 47% were slightly less supportive than urban professors 53%. A similar pattern was observed among college professors, where males 55% were more inclined than females 45%. Interestingly, rural college professors 57% were more supportive than urban professors 43% (Adams et al., 2023). Establishing ethics committees had strong backing, especially among male university professors 71%, while female university professors 29% were less supportive. Rural university professors 55% expressed more interest in this initiative than their urban peers 45%. In colleges, male professors 64% were more inclined to support this measure compared to female professors 36%. Rural college professors 51% supported it more than their urban counterparts 49% (Fukuda-Parr & Gibbons, 2021). Comprehensive AI training for teachers was supported mostly by female university professors 59% compared to male university professors 41%.

The rural university professors 71% showed much stronger support for this initiative compared to urban professors 29%. Similarly, in colleges, rural professors 61% were more in Favor than urban professors 52% (Zhang & Aslan, 2021). Male university professors 66% were highly supportive of following national and international AI regulations, particularly among rural professors 76%. Female university professors 34% and urban professors 24% were less supportive of this initiative. In colleges, male professors 52% expressed more support than female professors 48%. Rural professors 64% were significantly more supportive than their urban counterparts 36%. Female university professors 65% expressed more support for creating AI use guidelines for students than male professors 35%. Rural university professors 65% were also more inclined to support this measure compared to urban professors

35%. In colleges, female professors 69% and rural professors 67% were stronger advocates of this initiative, while male 31% and urban 33% professors expressed less enthusiasm. Adopting accreditation standards for AI tools was favored more by male university professors 56% compared to female professors 44%. Urban professors 70% showed a stronger preference than rural professors 30%. In colleges, the gender divide was less pronounced, with both male 44% and female 56% professors supporting it equally. However, rural professors 67% were far more supportive of this measure compared to their urban counterparts 33% (Tayan et al., 2023).

Female university professors 53% expressed more support for establishing AI ethics committees than male professors 47%. Among rural university professors, only 31% showed support, compared to 69% of urban professors. In colleges, male professors 39% were less supportive compared to female professors 61%. Rural college professors 41% were also less enthusiastic compared to urban professors 59%. The idea that AI would be beneficial to learners saw almost equal support from male 49% and female 51% university professors. Rural professors 59% were more optimistic than their urban colleagues 41%. In colleges, male professors 63% were more positive than female professors 37%, and urban professors 57% were more optimistic than rural professors 43%. Male university professors 48% and female professors 52% showed balanced views on AI's potential to increase administrative efficiency. Rural professors 46% were slightly less supportive than urban professors 54%. In colleges, female professors 56% were more optimistic about AI improving administrative tasks compared to male professors 44%. Rural professors 66% in colleges were significantly more supportive of this view than their urban counterparts 34%. The prospect of AI enabling individualized learning was favoured equally by male 49% and female 51% university professors.

Rural university professors 58% were more positive about AI's role in individualized learning compared to urban professors 42%. In colleges, rural professors 68% showed stronger support for individualized learning than urban professors 32%. Concerns about AI negatively affecting teacher-student relationships were more prominent among female university professors 63% compared to male professors 37%. Rural professors 70% also expressed greater concern than urban professors 30%. In colleges, female professors 54% were more worried than male professors 46%, and urban professors 63% showed more concern than rural professors 37% (Chiu et al., 2023). Female university professors 57% were more optimistic about AI fostering joyful learning than male professors 43%. Rural professors 58% were more inclined to see the benefits of AI in this regard compared to urban professors 42%. In colleges, male professors 69% were more optimistic than female professors 31%. Urban professors 65% were more supportive than rural professors 35%. Concerns about AI contributing to emotional deficits were more prominent among female university professors 44% compared to male professors 56%. Rural professors 71%

expressed stronger concerns than their urban counterparts 29%. Among college professors, female professors 70% were more concerned than male professors 30%, and urban professors 57% were more worried than rural professors 43% (Thakkar et al., 2024). Data privacy concerns were equally shared by male 47% and female 53% university professors. Rural professors 59% expressed stronger concerns than urban professors 41%. In colleges, male professors 63% were more concerned than female professors 37%, and rural professors 67% were more worried than urban professors 33% (Alier et al., 2021). The concern about over-reliance on technology was shared equally by male 42% and female 48% university professors. Rural professors 63% were more worried than their urban counterparts 47%. In colleges, male professors 56% expressed more concern than female professors 44%, and urban professors 59% showed more concern than rural professors 41% (Zhai et al., 2024).

To IDENTIFY the PERCEIVED BENEFITS and CHALLENGES ASSOCIATED with the IMPLEMENTATION of RISK-FREE AI in the CLASSROOM.

Table 2. Benefits associated with the implementation of AI in the classroom

Benefits associated with the implementation of AI in the classroom				
Sl.no.	**Statements**	**Responses**		
		Agree	**Neutral**	**Disagree**
1	AI is an important asset in many aspects of education	61	20	19
2	Use of artificial intelligence in education makes administrative work easier	58	22	20
3	With the use of AI, students will be able to solve their learning problems independently	53	27	20
4	Assessment of student learning can be done very quickly with various artificial intelligence tools	65	20	15
5	Use of Artificial intelligence makes classroom learning enjoyable	52	28	20
6	Artificial intelligence helps to boost and increase motivation to learn	60	21	19
7	Mixing artificial intelligence with traditional methods will improve the learning process	67	20	13
8	Application of artificial intelligence will increase the rate of digital literacy	71	20	9
9	Using artificial intelligence in the classroom, teachers can teach more in less time	56	24	20
10	The use of AI increases students' interest in learning	61	20	19
11	AI simplifies the work of teachers and improves the quality of education	64	22	14

continued on following page

Table 2. Continued

Benefits associated with the implementation of AI in the classroom				
Sl.no.	**Statements**	**Responses**		
		Agree	**Neutral**	**Disagree**
12	Students will benefit from 24/7 learning materials and support using AI	66	20	14
13	AI fosters inclusivity in the classroom by providing personalized learning for all students	58	22	20
14	AI improves access to education for rural and remote areas	51	25	24
15	AI can reduce teacher burnout by automating repetitive tasks	61	21	18
16	AI systems offer multilingual support, breaking language barriers in the classroom	57	23	20
17	AI allows for real-time feedback on student performance	66	20	14
18	AI-driven data analytics can help teachers improve their teaching strategies	61	20	19
19	AI can suggest students to learn independently	53	27	20
20	AI helps provide specific guidance to students to tackle educational challenges	62	25	13
21	AI makes lesson preparation and presentation more effective for teachers	57	23	20
22	Artificial intelligence makes education much easier	61	20	19
23	The use of artificial intelligence is increasing computer skills among students	67	22	11
24	Artificial intelligence helps to enhance the technological knowledge of students	72	20	8

A significant response of 61% agree that AI is an important asset in education, suggesting strong support for AI's role in education. 20% remain neutral, indicating some uncertainty, while 19% disagree, reflecting skepticism or concern over AI's role (Ocumpaugh et al., 2024). 58% agree that AI helps in making administrative work easier. However, 22% remain neutral, likely indicating that these respondents may not have enough experience with AI in this area, while 20% disagree, possibly doubting AI's effectiveness in administrative work (Ahmad et al., 2022). 53% agree that AI will help students solve learning problems independently (Fitria, 2021), but 27% are neutral, signalling uncertainty about this capability. 20% disagree, suggesting that AI might not be seen as effective in fostering student independence. 5% believe that AI can assess student learning quickly, a strong endorsement of AI's efficiency.

However, 20% remain neutral, possibly reflecting a lack of direct experience with AI tools, and 15% disagree, questioning AI's accuracy or fairness in assessments. 52% of respondents agree that AI makes learning enjoyable, though 28% are neutral, indicating uncertainty about this benefit. 20% disagree, reflecting that for some, AI may not enhance engagement in the classroom. 60% agree that AI can boost motivation to learn, but 21% are neutral, suggesting doubts about AI's consistent impact on motivation (Agestiningrum & Siswanto, 2024). 19% disagree, indicating that some believe AI may not always motivate students effectively. 67% agree that mixing AI with traditional methods improves learning, showing strong support for integrating AI in classrooms (Lin & Chen, 2024). 20% are neutral, reflecting some uncertainty, while 13% disagree, possibly preferring traditional methods over AI. A large majority 71% believe that AI will increase digital literacy among students, though 20% remain neutral, possibly unsure of how much AI will contribute to this skill. Only 9% disagree, showing minimal resistance to this idea. 56% of respondents agree that AI helps teachers teach more in less time, but 24% are neutral, indicating some uncertainty about this potential. 20% disagree, possibly doubting AI's ability to improve teaching efficiency. 61% agree that AI increases students' interest in learning, but 20% are neutral, reflecting mixed feelings. 19% disagree, suggesting AI might not engage all students equally. 64% agree that AI simplifies teachers' work and improves the quality of education, with 22% neutral.

The neutral responses may reflect some uncertainty about how AI impacts day-to-day teaching (Hur, 2024). 14% disagree, showing some resistance to this idea. 66% agree that AI provides 24/7 learning materials and support, but 20% are neutral, likely reflecting concerns about accessibility or the practicality of 24/7 learning (Murtaza et al., 2022). 14% disagree, suggesting that some teachers or students may not fully trust AI-based support systems. 58% of respondents agree that AI fosters inclusivity by providing personalized learning, but 22% are neutral, indicating doubts about AI's inclusivity for all students. 20% disagree, suggesting some skepticism about its ability to address diverse learning needs. 51% agree that AI improves access to education in rural and remote areas (Mutambara & Bayaga, 2020), while 25% are neutral, showing uncertainty about how well AI can be implemented in these areas. 24% disagree, reflecting doubts about infrastructure or access to AI tools in rural regions. 61% of respondents agree that AI can help reduce teacher burnout by automating repetitive tasks. 21% are neutral, possibly unsure about whether AI will truly reduce burnout. 18% disagree, indicating that some feel AI might not have a meaningful impact on workload reduction. 57% agree that AI offers multilingual support, helping to break language barriers in classrooms (Heugh et al., 2022). 23% are neutral, possibly unsure of AI's effectiveness across different languages, and 20% disagree, suggesting that language support might not be adequate. 66% agree that AI provides real-time feedback on student performance, with 20% neutral. This neutrality could stem from concerns about the accuracy or timeliness of the feedback (Hooda et al., 2022).

Only 14% disagree, indicating broad support for AI's use in student assessment (Hooda et al., 2022). 61% believe AI-driven data analytics help teachers improve their teaching strategies, but 20% are neutral, possibly reflecting uncertainty about data-driven instruction. 19% disagree, indicating skepticism about AI's ability to meaningfully enhance teaching. 53% agree that AI encourages students to learn independently, but 27% are neutral, showing hesitation about this benefit. 20% disagree, suggesting doubts about whether AI can truly foster independent learning habits. 62% of respondents agree that AI provides specific guidance to students to tackle challenges, while 25% are neutral, likely reflecting uncertainty about AI's effectiveness in offering personalized guidance. Only 13% disagree. 57% agree that AI makes lesson preparation and presentation more effective (Carbonell, 1970), with 23% neutral, possibly indicating uncertainty about the practicality of AI in lesson design. 20% disagree, showing some reluctance to rely on AI in this aspect. 61% agree that AI makes education easier, though 20% are neutral, reflecting uncertainty about AI's impact on simplifying educational processes (X. Zhai et al., 2021). 19% disagree, suggesting that some find AI either too complex or disruptive. 67% agree that AI increases students' computer skills, but 22% are neutral, indicating that some may not see a direct link between AI use and technical skill improvement. Only 11% disagree, showing broad agreement on AI's role in enhancing digital competencies. 72% agree that AI helps students enhance their technological knowledge (Chen et al., 2020), with 20% neutral, showing some uncertainty.

Only 8% disagree, indicating that most respondents acknowledge AI's contribution to tech knowledge. AI has been instrumental in automating various administrative duties within educational institutions. Tasks such as grading, attendance tracking, and scheduling can be performed more efficiently with AI systems. For example, AI can automatically grade assignments and tests, freeing educators from this time-consuming responsibility, and allowing them to focus more on teaching and engaging with students (Analytikus, 2023; rmontalvo, 2023). Managing student records and data can be a complex and time-consuming endeavor for educational institutions. AI systems facilitate easy handling of data input, retrieval, and organization, allowing educators to access the information they need swiftly (Fredrik Filipsson, 2024; Analytikus, 2023). Now, students living in remote areas can get access to education 24/7. This has only been made possible with artificial intelligence in education (technouser, 2024). AI-driven platforms can generate multilingual learning resources that cater to various linguistic backgrounds. By automatically adapting educational materials into multiple languages, these systems make it possible for students to study in their preferred languages, thus eliminating barriers to understanding and engagement (Stuart Cooke, 2024). The availability of multilingual support through AI fosters a more inclusive classroom environment. By enabling students from diverse backgrounds to participate meaningfully in discussions and activities, AI helps bridge gaps in understanding and encourages collaboration among peers (www.perfectessaywriter.ai/blog/ai-in-multilingual-education)

Table 3. Challenges associated with the implementation of AI in the classroom

Challenges associated with the implementation of AI in the classroom				
Sl.no.	**Statements**	**Responses (%)**		
		Agree	**Neutral**	**Disagree**
1	Artificial intelligence will disable the brain	53	21	26
2	The use of artificial intelligence will wipe out humanity	62	14	24
3	The use of artificial intelligence destroys the ability to think for oneself	57	18	25
4	The use of artificial intelligence hinders the development of creativity in students	33	19	48
5	Use of artificial intelligence destroys culture among students	55	13	32
6	The use of artificial intelligence creates the possibility of students becoming addicted to technology	72	15	13
7	Artificial intelligence is very expensive	58	21	21
8	Due to the use of artificial intelligence, the habit of reading books for a long time is disappearing	51	27	22
9	Students are becoming self-centered with the use of artificial intelligence	56	14	30
10	Use of artificial intelligence destroys the self-effort of students	69	9	22
11	Artificial intelligence destroys student motivation	59	11	30
12	The use of artificial intelligence creates a digital divide in education	52	27	21
13	AI assisted learning is not good for poor students	71	16	13
14	Use of artificial intelligence in education is not good for backward students	62	13	25
15	In education using artificial intelligence, there is less opportunity for interaction between the teacher and the student	76	9	15
16	The application of artificial intelligence in education is of considerable concern in future employment in education	53	19	28
17	Artificial intelligence in education creates a sense of loneliness and isolation among students	64	14	22
18	The application of artificial intelligence in education makes the learner mechanized	46	13	41
19	The effectiveness of artificial intelligence is limited	72	16	12
20	Artificial intelligence will make students lazy	63	15	22

The opinion that "artificial intelligence will disable the brain" is evidenced by a survey among university professors, with 53% agreeing, 21% neutral, and 26% disagreeing, and another opinion that "The use of artificial intelligence destroys the ability to think for oneself" with 57% agreeing, 18% neutral, and 25% disagreeing. Morales-Garcia (2024) highlighted that however, the increasing reliance on AI presents ethical and practical challenges, including the potential loss of cognitive skills and decreased student motivation. Research highlights that reliance on AI can lead to neglect of essential cognitive skills. As tasks become automated, individuals may lose the motivation to engage in challenging mental activities, impairing analytical skills and creativity (Abbound, 2024). However, it is also noted that students must be cautious of becoming overly dependent on AI, which can hinder their ability to think critically and innovate (Darwin et al., 2023). While AI offers significant cognitive benefits, research indicates that an overreliance on AI tools can result in decreased mental stimulation and engagement. For example, the convenience of AI for tasks like data collection and analysis may lead to cognitive atrophy by reducing the need for critical thinking and problem-solving (Daniel Dillu, 2023). Additionally, a study reported that 68.9% of students felt that their reliance on AI resulted in laziness and a decline in decision-making skills, showing a direct correlation between AI usage and diminishing cognitive capabilities (Leanne Fan, 2024).

"Artificial intelligence destroys student motivation with 59% agreeing, 11% neutral, and 30% disagreeing by university professors. Ahmad et al. (2023) noted that reliance on AI could lead to the loss of cognitive skills and a decline in student motivation. "The use of artificial intelligence will wipe out humanity with 62% agreeing, 14% neutral, and 24% disagreeing, and another opinion that "Use of artificial intelligence destroys culture among students" with 55% agreeing, 13% neutral, and 32% disagreeing. AI's integration into daily life may contribute to dehumanization and social isolation. Studies suggest that increased reliance on AI systems, such as virtual assistants and chatbots, can diminish face-to-face interactions, leading to a lack of empathy and social skills among individuals (infinitivehost, 2023). "The use of artificial intelligence hinders the development of creativity in students" with 33% agreeing, 19% neutral, and 48% disagreeing opined by university professors. AI, in particular generative intelligence, and large language models, can impact human creativity, and possibly increase human creativity (Habib et al, 2024). The use of artificial intelligence creates the possibility of students becoming addicted to technology with 72% agreeing, 15% neutral, and 13% disagreeing opined by university professors. However, in the AI era, dependence has extended to behavioral addictions, like pathological gambling and internet addiction disorder, sharing similarities in their neurobiological and behavioral processes (Fu et al., 2010; Weinstein & Lejoyeux, 2010; Van Rooij et al., 2011; Sairitupa-Sanchez et al., 2023).

Due to the use of artificial intelligence, the habit of reading books for a long time is disappearing with 51% agreeing, 27% neutral, and 22% disagreeing opined by university professors. However, the online nature of digital devices sometimes includes the ability to interrupt any other activity - such as reading. As a result, people generally read shorter texts in a digital media environment (Baron, 2015; Mangen & Van der Weel, 2016). In education using artificial intelligence, there is less opportunity for interaction between the teacher and the student with 76% agreeing, 9% neutral, and 15% disagreeing opined by university professors. For example, frequent use of intelligent electronic devices has a negative impact on adolescents' interpersonal relationships (Halpern & Katz, 2017) and social adaptability (Jin et al., 2017). AI-assisted learning is not good for poor and backward students opined by university professors. Students from varying socioeconomic backgrounds may not have equal access to AI tools and resources, which can result in unequal opportunities for engagement and learning outcomes (Bakhtawar Amjad, 2024).

To ANALYZE PROFESSORS' OPINIONS on ETHICAL CONSIDERATIONS and CONCERNS of USING AI TECHNOLOGIES in EDUCATIONAL ENVIRONMENTS.

Table 4. Opinions on ethical considerations and concerns of using AI

Opinions on ethical considerations and concerns of using AI				
Sl.no.	**Statements**	**Responses**		
		Agree	**Neutral**	**Disagree**
1	Developing clear ethical guidelines to ensure the responsible use of AI in the classroom	64	22	14
2	Ethical guidelines for AI usage should prioritize protecting student privacy and data security	70	20	10
3	Equip teachers with the knowledge and skills to understand, manage, and supervise AI technologies used in the classroom	61	23	16
4	AI tools used in educational institutions should meet recognized accreditation standards to ensure quality and safety	68	24	8
5	Conduct regular reviews of AI systems to identify and mitigate any biases	60	25	15
6	Involve AI educators in critical decision-making processes to counterbalance any potential biases in AI outputs	66	20	14
7	Use AI as a supplementary tool rather than the sole method of assessment	72	20	8
8	Educate students on the ethical use of AI, making them aware of how their data is used and empowering them to protect their digital rights	75	15	10
9	Focus on maintaining and promoting human attributes such as empathy, critical thinking, and creativity, which AI cannot fully replicate	78	18	4
10	Establish clear ethical guidelines for AI use in education, co-created with input from teachers, students, ethicists, and policymakers	74	20	6
11	Ensure that AI tools are accessible to all students, including those with disabilities or from disadvantaged backgrounds	70	22	8
12	Periodically evaluate AI systems to ensure they remain aligned with educational goals and ethical standards over time	68	20	12

continued on following page

Table 4. Continued

Opinions on ethical considerations and concerns of using AI				
Sl.no.	**Statements**	**Responses**		
		Agree	**Neutral**	**Disagree**
13	Create channels for students and teachers to report any ethical concerns or issues with AI systems	73	19	8
14	Adopt international ethical guidelines for AI use in education developed by UNESCO	76	16	8
15	The curriculum should include the ethical principles of artificial intelligence and its use	71	20	9

A significant 64% of respondents agree that developing clear ethical guidelines for AI use in the classroom is essential, highlighting a strong recognition of the need for structured policies (Shneiderman, 2020). 22% are neutral, possibly indicating uncertainty about what such guidelines should entail, while 14% disagree, suggesting some skepticism about the necessity of these guidelines. A robust 70% agree that ethical guidelines for AI usage should prioritize protecting student privacy and data security (Adams et al., 2023). The 20% neutral responses reflect varying levels of awareness about privacy issues, and 10% disagree, indicating that some may not see privacy as a pressing concern. 61% agree that it is crucial to equip teachers with the knowledge and skills to manage and supervise AI technologies.

However, 23% are neutral, suggesting that not all educators feel confident in their ability to handle AI tools, while 16% disagree, possibly due to a lack of belief in the effectiveness of training programs (Ottenbreit-Leftwich et al., 2022). 68% believe that AI tools used in education should meet recognized accreditation standards for quality and safety. This strong agreement indicates a collective desire for assurance regarding the reliability of AI systems. 24% remain neutral, potentially due to a lack of familiarity with accreditation processes, while 8% disagree, perhaps questioning the relevance of accreditation in this context. 60% agree on the importance of conducting regular reviews of AI systems to identify and mitigate biases. The 25% neutral responses show some uncertainty about the effectiveness of these reviews, while 15% disagree, suggesting a belief that existing oversight mechanisms are sufficient. 66% agree that involving AI educators in critical decision-making processes can help counterbalance potential biases in AI outputs. The 20% neutral responses reflect varying levels of confidence in this approach, while 14% disagree, indicating skepticism about the effectiveness of this involvement.

A substantial 72% believe that AI should be used as a supplementary tool rather than the sole method of assessment, showing a preference for maintaining traditional assessment methods alongside AI. 20% are neutral, perhaps unsure about the practicality of integrating AI into assessments, while 8% disagree, indicating some support for exclusive AI use in assessment. 75% agree on the necessity of educating students about the ethical use of AI, empowering them to understand data usage and protect their rights (Akgun & Greenhow, 2021). The 15% neutral responses might reflect uncertainty about the best ways to implement such education, while 10% disagree, suggesting some belief that students may not need this education. A strong 78% agree on the importance of focusing on human attributes such as empathy and critical thinking, which AI cannot replicate. Only 18% are neutral, while a small 4% disagree, emphasizing widespread recognition of the limitations of AI. 74% agree that establishing clear ethical guidelines for AI use in education should involve input from teachers, students, ethicists, and policymakers. 20% remain neutral, reflecting uncertainty about stakeholder involvement, and 6% disagree, indicating a belief that guidelines could be developed without broad collaboration. 70% agree that AI tools should be accessible to all students, including those with disabilities or from disadvantaged backgrounds (Osorio et al., 2024). 22% are neutral, indicating some uncertainty about the accessibility of AI tools, while 8% disagree, suggesting concerns about equitable access. 68% agree that AI systems should be periodically evaluated to ensure alignment with educational goals and ethical standards.

20% neutral responses reflect uncertainty, and 12% disagree, indicating that some believe periodic evaluations may not be necessary. 73% agree that creating channels for students and teachers to report any ethical concerns with AI systems is essential. 19% are neutral, while 8% disagree, possibly feeling that existing reporting mechanisms are sufficient. 76% agree on the importance of adopting international ethical guidelines for AI use in education, developed by organizations like UNESCO (Pedro et al., 2019). 16% are neutral, reflecting uncertainty about the relevance of international standards, while 8% disagree, indicating that some may question the applicability of such guidelines. A strong 71% agree that the curriculum should include ethical principles related to AI use, with 20% neutral responses showing some uncertainty. Only 9% disagree, indicating broad support for integrating ethics into education.

To OFFER SUGGESTIONS for BEST PRACTICES for USING AI TOOLS EFFECTIVELY in HIGHER EDUCATION CLASSROOMS.

Effectively using AI tools in higher education classrooms requires a thoughtful approach that balances innovation with ethical considerations (Saaida, 2023). One of the primary steps institutions should take is to establish clear ethical guidelines for AI use. These guidelines must prioritize student data privacy, ensure transparency in AI decision-making processes, and address biases within algorithms. Forming an ethics committee can help oversee the implementation of these guidelines, ensuring that AI is used in a manner that complies with both national and international regulations (Nguyen et al., 2022). Ethical AI use is crucial in maintaining trust between students, faculty, and the institution (Nguyen et al., 2022).

Professional development of teachers plays a key role in AI integration (Al-Zyoud, 2020). Educators need comprehensive training on how to effectively use AI tools in their teaching practices (Lameras & Arnab, 2021). This training should cover both the technical and ethical aspects of AI, allowing educators to confidently integrate these tools into their classrooms. Continuous learning and adaptation are essential, as AI technologies evolve rapidly, and educators must stay informed to maximize their potential benefits (Kinshuk et al., 2016). AI's ability to personalize learning is one of its greatest strengths in education. By analyzing individual student data, AI can tailor learning materials and assessments to meet the unique needs of each student, thus enhancing engagement and improving learning outcomes. This also allows for differentiated instruction, where students can learn at their own pace and in ways that suit their learning styles. Implementing AI in this manner can make learning more inclusive and effective, especially in diverse classrooms with varied student needs. Another significant advantage of AI is its ability to enhance data-driven decision-making. By collecting and analyzing data on student performance and learning patterns, AI provides educators with valuable insights that can inform curriculum design and instructional strategies (Ejjami, 2024). AI tools also offer real-time feedback, enabling students to monitor their progress and identify areas for improvement. This immediate feedback loop helps foster a more responsive and dynamic learning environment. Collaboration between students and AI should be encouraged. Educators can design activities that foster collaboration between students and AI, turning the technology into a learning partner rather than just a tool (Lee et al., 2021). Peer learning experiences, where students share how they use AI tools, can also create a supportive community that encourages exploration and creativity in AI use (Lee et al., 2021).

Despite AI's potential, it is essential to maintain human oversight in the teaching and learning process (Chaudhry & Kazim, 2021). AI can support many administrative tasks and provide data-driven insights, but it should not replace the critical human elements of education, such as mentorship, emotional support, and nuanced decision-making (Ghamrawi et al., 2023). Teachers must remain central to the educational process, ensuring that AI is used to enhance, rather than replace, their roles. This includes setting limits on AI's role in assessments to preserve the integrity of personalized feedback and evaluations (Swiecki et al., 2022) Monitoring and evaluating the effectiveness of AI tools is an ongoing process. Regular assessments should be conducted to determine whether AI tools are meeting educational goals and ethical standards. Feedback from both students and educators is vital in this process, as it provides insights into the impact of AI on teaching and learning (Zhai et al., 2021). If certain tools are not effective or present ethical concerns, they should be adapted or replaced. This iterative process ensures that AI continues to serve its intended purpose without compromising educational values.

Inclusivity must also be a priority in AI integration. Institutions need to ensure that AI tools are accessible to all students, including those with different learning abilities or backgrounds (Ayala-Pazmiño, 2023). This can involve selecting tools that accommodate diverse learning styles and making resources available to support underrepresented groups. Furthermore, educators should be vigilant about potential biases in AI algorithms and take steps to minimize their effects on student assessments and experiences (Wang, 2020). Engaging stakeholders' faculty, students, and administrative staff in discussions about AI integration is another best practice. These conversations provide a platform for sharing experiences, concerns, and solutions, which can inform better AI implementation strategies. Hosting workshops or forums where educators and students can exchange their experiences with AI tools can help build a collective understanding of best practices and common challenges. It is essential for educators and institutions to stay informed about advancements in AI. As AI technologies continue to evolve, staying updated on the latest trends and research will enable educators to use these tools more effectively. Sharing findings from the broader educational community can foster innovation and improve AI integration in higher education settings.

CONCLUSION

To conclude the research on the use of risk-free artificial intelligence (AI) in the classroom based on insights from professors of higher education institutions, several key findings emerge. AI's integration into educational settings presents both profound opportunities and significant challenges. The technology offers vast potential to revolutionize teaching and learning, enabling personalized education, streamlining administrative processes, and providing real-time feedback, which enhances learning outcomes and institutional efficiency. However, adopting AI also raises concerns about data privacy, ethical considerations, teacher autonomy, and the potential to exacerbate inequalities, especially in rural and disadvantaged areas. The study emphasizes that AI can facilitate personalized learning by tailoring educational experiences to meet individual student needs, thus improving engagement, and learning outcomes. Professors highlighted AI's ability to analyze learning patterns, allowing for more customized instruction, which is particularly beneficial in diverse classrooms. Additionally, AI supports educators by handling administrative tasks such as grading and attendance, freeing teachers to focus on more complex pedagogical duties. Despite these benefits, the research highlights concern about AI's overuse, particularly its potential to undermine teacher-student interaction and increase dependence on technology. There is significant apprehension about AI diminishing teachers' roles, leading to a loss of autonomy, and potentially reducing the human aspect of teaching. Professors from rural settings and those working with underrepresented student populations also expressed concerns that AI could deepen educational inequalities due to uneven access to technological infrastructure. Ethical concerns surrounding AI were a focal point of the study. Professors stressed the importance of developing clear ethical guidelines to safeguard student privacy, ensure transparency, and mitigate algorithmic biases. Many respondents recommended the establishment of ethics committees and regular reviews of AI systems to ensure their alignment with educational goals and ethical standards. Moreover, professors underscored the need for comprehensive training for educators to equip them with the skills to use AI responsibly and effectively. The study also highlights the importance of maintaining human oversight in AI-assisted education. While AI can significantly enhance efficiency, it should not replace the critical human elements of education, such as emotional support and mentorship. The success of AI in education ultimately depends on the collaboration between AI technologies and educators, where AI is used as a supplementary tool rather than a substitute for traditional teaching methods.

REFERENCES

Abbound, M. (2024). OPINION: AI's effect on cognitive development: A future of success or a public detriment? The Red & Black. https://www.edandblack.com/opinion/opinion-ai-s-effect-on-cognitive-development-a-future-of-success-or-a-public-detriment/article_685f3fbe-5e9a-11ef-a088-77a0bace301c.html

Adams, C., Pente, P., Lemermeyer, G., & Rockwell, G. (2023). Ethical principles for artificial intelligence in K-12 education. *Computers and Education Artificial Intelligence*, 4, 100131. DOI: 10.1016/j.caeai.2023.100131

Agestiningrum, R., & Siswanto, S. (2024). The effect of AI learning system on student learning outcomes and motivation. *An-Nuha Jurnal Kajian Islam Pendidikan Budaya Dan Sosial*, 11(1), 1–10. DOI: 10.36835/annuha.v11i1.582

Ahmad, S. F., Alam, M. M., Rahmat, M. K., Mubarik, M. S., & Hyder, S. I. (2022). Academic and administrative role of artificial intelligence in education. *Sustainability (Basel)*, 14(3), 1101. DOI: 10.3390/su14031101

Ahmad, S. F., Han, H., Alam, M. M., Rehmat, M. K., Irshad, M., Arrano-Munoz, M., & Ariza-Montes, A. (2023). Impact of artificial intelligence on human loss in decision making, laziness and safety in education. *Humanities & Social Sciences Communications*, 10(1), 1–14. DOI: 10.1057/s41599-023-01787-8 PMID: 37325188

Ahmad, S. F., Han, H., Alam, M. M., Rehmat, M. K., Irshad, M., Arrano-Munoz, M., & Ariza-Montes, A. (2023). Impact of artificial intelligence on human loss in decision making, laziness and safety in education. *Humanities & Social Sciences Communications*, 10(1), 311. Advance online publication. DOI: 10.1057/s41599-023-01787-8 PMID: 37325188

Aiken, R., & Epstein, R. (2000). Ethical guidelines for AI in education: Starting a conversation. *International Journal of Artificial Intelligence in Education*, 11, 163–176. https://www.researchgate.net/publication/228600407_Ethical_guidelines_for_AI_in_education_Starting_a_conversation

Akgun, S., & Greenhow, C. (2021). Artificial intelligence in education: Addressing ethical challenges in K-12 settings. *AI and Ethics*, 2(3), 431–440. DOI: 10.1007/s43681-021-00096-7 PMID: 34790956

Al-Zahrani, A. M., & Alasmari, T. M. (2024). Exploring the impact of artificial intelligence on higher education: The dynamics of ethical, social, and educational implications. *Humanities & Social Sciences Communications*, 11(1), 912. Advance online publication. DOI: 10.1057/s41599-024-03432-4

Al-Zyoud, H. M. M. (2020). The role of artificial intelligence in teacher professional development. *Universal Journal of Educational Research*, 8(11B), 6263–6272. DOI: 10.13189/ujer.2020.082265

Ali, O., Murray, P. A., Momin, M., Dwivedi, Y. K., & Malik, T. (2023). The effects of artificial intelligence applications in educational settings: Challenges and strategies. *Technological Forecasting and Social Change*, 199, 123076. DOI: 10.1016/j.techfore.2023.123076

Alier, M., Guerrero, M. J. C., Amo, D., Severance, C., & Fonseca, D. (2021). Privacy and E-Learning: A pending task. *Sustainability (Basel)*, 13(16), 9206. DOI: 10.3390/su13169206

Amjad, B. (2024). Over-Reliance of Students on Artificial Intelligence. Medium. https://bakhtawaramjad0786.medium.com/over-reliance-of-students-on-artificial-intelligence-709a931bdc79

Analytikus. (2023). AI in Education: Streamlining Administrative Tasks for a Brighter Future. analytikus. https://www.analytikus.com/post/ai-in-education-streamlining-administrative-tasks-for-a-brighter-futureeducation-is-a-sector-that

Artificial Intelligence Influencing Higher Education in India. CINEFORUM. (2024). revistadecineforum.com. https://revistadecineforum.com/index.php/cf/article/view/62

Ayala-Pazmino, M. (2023). Artificial intelligence in Education: Exploring the potential benefits and risks. 593 *Digital Publisher CEIT, 8* (3), 892-899. DOI: 10.33386/593dp.2023.3.1827

Baron, N. S. (2015). *Words Onscreen: The Fate of Reading in a Digital World.* Oxford University Press.

Binns, R. (2017). Fairness in Machine Learning: Lessons from Political Philosophy. *arXiv (Cornell University)*. https://doi.org//arxiv.1712.03586DOI: 10.48550

Carbonell, J. (1970). AI in CAI: An Artificial-Intelligence Approach to Computer-Assisted Instruction. *IEEE Transactions on Man-Machine Systems*, 11(4), 190–202. DOI: 10.1109/TMMS.1970.299942

Catota, F. E., Morgan, M. G., & Sicker, D. C. (2019). Cybersecurity education in a developing nation: The Ecuadorian environment. *Journal of Cybersecurity*, 5(1). Advance online publication. DOI: 10.1093/cybsec/tyz001

Chaudhry, M. A., & Kazim, E. (2021). Artificial Intelligence in Education (AIEd): A high-level academic and industry note 2021. *AI and Ethics*, 2(1), 157–165. DOI: 10.1007/s43681-021-00074-z PMID: 34790953

Chen, L., Chen, P., & Lin, Z. (2020). Artificial Intelligence in Education: A review. *IEEE Access : Practical Innovations, Open Solutions*, 8, 75264–75278. DOI: 10.1109/ACCESS.2020.2988510

Chiu, T. K., Moorhouse, B. L., Chai, C. S., & Ismailov, M. (2023). Teacher support and student motivation to learn with Artificial Intelligence (AI) based chatbot. *Interactive Learning Environments*, •••, 1–17. DOI: 10.1080/10494820.2023.2172044

Christenson, S. L., Reschly, A. L., & Wylie, C. (2012). Handbook of Research on Student Engagement. In *Springer eBooks*. DOI: 10.1007/978-1-4614-2018-7

Cooke, S. (2024). Language Support with AI: Breaking Barriers for International Students - Techstrong.ai. Techstrong.ai. https://techstrong.ai/articles/language-support-with-ai-breaking-barriers-for-international-students/

Darwin, R., Rusdin, D., Mukminatien, N., Suryati, N., Laksmi, E. D., & Marzuki, . (2024, December 31). D., Mukminatien, N., Suryati, N., Laksmi, E. D., & Marzuki. (2023). Critical thinking in the AI era: An exploration of EFL students' perceptions, benefits, and limitations. *Cogent Education*, 11(1), 2290342. Advance online publication. DOI: 10.1080/2331186X.2023.2290342

Dillu, D. (2023). How Over-Reliance on AI Could Lead to Cognitive Atrophy. NeuraNest. https://medium.com/neuranest/how-over-reliance-on-ai-could-lead-to-cognitive-atrophy-d04d214c7e75

Ejjami, R. (2024). The Future of Learning: AI-Based Curriculum development. *International Journal for Multidisciplinary Research*, 6(4), 24441. Advance online publication. DOI: 10.36948/ijfmr.2024.v06i04.24441

Fan, L. (2024). AI reduces critical thinking. The Nexus. https://wvnexus.org/opinions/ai-reduces-critical-thinking/

Filipsson, F. (2024). AI in Educational Administration: Transforming School Operations. Redress Compliance - Just another WordPress site. https://redresscompliance.com/ai-educational-adminisitration/

Firschein, O., Fischler, M. A., Coles, S., & Tenenbaum, J. M. (1973). Forecasting and Assessing the Impact of Artificial Intelligence on Society. International Joint Conference on Artificial Intelligence, 105-120. https://www.semanticscholar.org/paper/Forecasting-and-Assessing-the-Impact-of-Artificial-Firschein-Fischler/489d1e39812f298622323b7c32a73fe403f7c45e

Fitria, T. N. (2021). ARTIFICIAL INTELLIGENCE (AI) IN EDUCATION: USING AI TOOLS FOR TEACHING AND LEARNING PROCESS. *Prosiding Seminar Nasional & Call for Paper STIE AAS, 4* (1), 134-147. Retrieved from https://prosiding.stie-aas.ac.id/index.php/prosenas/article/view/106

Floridi, L., & Cowls, J. (2019). A unified framework of five principles for AI in society. *Harvard Data Science Review*. Advance online publication. DOI: 10.1162/99608f92.8cd550d1

Fu, K. W., Chan, W. S. C., Wong, P. W. C., & Yip, P. S. F. (2010). Internet addiction: Prevalence, discriminant validity and correlates among adolescents in Hong Kong. *The British Journal of Psychiatry*, 196(6), 486–492. DOI: 10.1192/bjp.bp.109.075002 PMID: 20513862

Fukuda-Parr, S., & Gibbons, E. (2021). Emerging consensus on 'Ethical AI': Human rights critique of stakeholder guidelines. *Global Policy*, 12(S6), 32–44. DOI: 10.1111/1758-5899.12965

Gates, B. (2023). The Age of AI Has Begun, gatesnotes.com, https://www.gatesnotes.com/The-Age-of-AI-Has-Begun (accessed September 2, 2024)

Gauthier, A., Rizvi, S., Cukurova, M., & Mavrikis, M. (2022). Is it time we get real? A systematic review of the potential of data-driven technologies to address teachers' implicit biases. *Frontiers in Artificial Intelligence*, 5, 994967. Advance online publication. DOI: 10.3389/frai.2022.994967 PMID: 36304958

George, B., & Wooden, O. (2023). Managing the Strategic Transformation of Higher Education through Artificial Intelligence. *Administrative Sciences*, 13(9), 196. DOI: 10.3390/admsci13090196

Ghamrawi, N., Shal, T., & Ghamrawi, N. A. (2023). Exploring the impact of AI on teacher leadership: Regressing or expanding? *Education and Information Technologies*, 29(7), 8415–8433. DOI: 10.1007/s10639-023-12174-w

Habib, S., Vogel, T., Anli, X., & Thorne, E. (2024). How does generative artificial intelligence impact student creativity? *Journal of Creativity*, 34(1), 100072. Advance online publication. DOI: 10.1016/j.yjoc.2023.100072

Halpern, D., & Katz, J. E. (2017). Texting's consequences for romantic relationships: A cross-lagged analysis highlights its risks. *Computers in Human Behavior*, 71(11), 386–394. DOI: 10.1016/j.chb.2017.01.051

Heugh, K., French, M., Arya, V., Pham, M., Tudini, V., Billinghurst, N., Tippett, N., Chang, L., Nichols, J., & Viljoen, J. (2022). Multilingualism, translanguaging and transknowledging. *AILA Review*, 35(1), 89–127. DOI: 10.1075/aila.22011.heu

Hooda, M., Rana, C., Dahiya, O., Rizwan, A., & Hossain, M. S. (2022). Artificial intelligence for assessment and feedback to enhance student success in higher education. *Mathematical Problems in Engineering*, 2022, 1–19. DOI: 10.1155/2022/5215722

Hur, J. W. (2024). Fostering AI literacy: Overcoming concerns and nurturing confidence among preservice teachers. *Information and Learning Science*. Advance online publication. DOI: 10.1108/ILS-11-2023-0170

infinitivehost. (2023). The Negative Impacts of Artificial Intelligence on Humanity. infinitivehost. https://www.infinitivehost.com/blog/the-negative-impacts-of-artificial-intelligence-on-humanity/

Jackson, N. (2024). How can educators approach AI-based learning in ethical ways? https://www.vktr.com/ai-ethics-law-risk/practicing-ai-ethics-in-education/

Jin, M. G., Luo, X. M., & Zhang, G. H. (2017). The Development and Relationship between Freshmen's Mobile Phone Dependence and Social Adaptation: A Cross Lagged Regression Analysis. Psychology. *Techniques and Application.*, 5(8), 449–454. DOI: 10.16842/j.cnki.issn2095–5588.2017.08.001

Khosravi, H., Shum, S. B., Chen, G., Conati, C., Tsai, Y.-S., Kay, J., Knight, S., Martinez-Maldonado, R., Sadiq, S., & Gasevic, D. (2022). Explainable Artificial Intelligence in Education. Computers and Education. *Artificial Intelligence*, 3, 100074. Advance online publication. DOI: 10.1016/j.caeai.2022.100074

Kinshuk, N., Chen, N., Cheng, I., & Chew, S. W. (2016). Evolution Is not enough: Revolutionizing Current Learning Environments to Smart Learning Environments. *International Journal of Artificial Intelligence in Education*, 26(2), 561–581. DOI: 10.1007/s40593-016-0108-x

Lameras, P., & Arnab, S. (2021). Power to the Teachers: An Exploratory review on Artificial intelligence in education. *Information (Basel)*, 13(1), 14. DOI: 10.3390/info13010014

Lee, S., Mott, B., Ottenbreit-Leftwich, A., Scribner, A., Taylor, S., Park, K., Rowe, J., Glazewski, K., Hmelo-Silver, C. E., & Lester, J. (2021). AI-Infused Collaborative Inquiry in Upper Elementary School: A Game-Based Learning approach. *Proceedings of the AAAI Conference on Artificial Intelligence*, 35(17), 15591–15599. DOI: 10.1609/aaai.v35i17.17836

Lin, H., & Chen, Q. (2024). Artificial intelligence (AI) -integrated educational applications and college students' creativity and academic emotions: Students and teachers' perceptions and attitudes. *BMC Psychology*, 12(1), 487. Advance online publication. DOI: 10.1186/s40359-024-01979-0 PMID: 39285268

Lopez-Chila, R., Llerena-Izquierdo, J., Sumba-Nacipucha, N., & Cueva-Estrada, J. (2023). Artificial Intelligence in Higher Education: An Analysis of Existing Bibliometrics. *Education Sciences*, 14(1), 47. Advance online publication. DOI: 10.3390/educsci14010047

Morales-Garcia, W. C., Sairitupa-Sanchez, L. Z., Morales-Garcia, S. B., & Morales-Garcia, M. (2024). Development and validation of a scale for dependence on artificial intelligence in university students. *Frontiers in Education*, 9, 1323898. DOI: 10.3389/feduc.2024.1323898

Multilingual Education. AI's Language Barrier Solutions. (2024). perfectessaywriter.ai. https://www.perfectessaywriter.ai/blog/ai-in-multilingual-education

Murtaza, M., Ahmed, Y., Shamsi, J. A., Sherwani, F., & Usman, M. (2022). AI-Based Personalized E-Learning Systems: Issues, challenges, and solutions. *IEEE Access : Practical Innovations, Open Solutions*, 10, 81323–81342. DOI: 10.1109/ACCESS.2022.3193938

Mutambara, D., & Bayaga, A. (2020). Determinants of mobile learning acceptance for STEM education in rural areas. *Computers & Education*, 160, 104010. DOI: 10.1016/j.compedu.2020.104010

Nguyen, A., Ngo, H. N., Hong, Y., Dang, B., & Nguyen, B. T. (2022). Ethical principles for artificial intelligence in education. *Education and Information Technologies*, 28(4), 4221–4241. DOI: 10.1007/s10639-022-11316-w PMID: 36254344

Ocumpaugh, J., Roscoe, R. D., Baker, R. S., Hutt, S., & Aguilar, S. J. (2024). Toward asset-based instruction and assessment in artificial intelligence in education. *International Journal of Artificial Intelligence in Education*. Advance online publication. DOI: 10.1007/s40593-023-00382-x

Osorio, C., Fuster, N., Chen, W., Men, Y., & Juan, A. A. (2024). Enhancing Accessibility to Analytics Courses in Higher Education through AI, Simulation, and e-Collaborative Tools. *Information (Basel)*, 15(8), 430. DOI: 10.3390/info15080430

Ottenbreit-Leftwich, A., Glazewski, K., Jeon, M., Jantaraweragul, K., Hmelo-Silver, C. E., Scribner, A., Lee, S., Mott, B., & Lester, J. (2022). Lessons Learned for AI Education with Elementary Students and Teachers. *International Journal of Artificial Intelligence in Education*, 33(2), 267–289. DOI: 10.1007/s40593-022-00304-3

Parviz, M. (2024). AI in education: Comparative perspectives from STEM and Non-STEM instructors. *Computers and Education Open*, 6, 100190. Advance online publication. DOI: 10.1016/j.caeo.2024.100190

Pedro, F., Subosa, M., Rivas, A., & Valverde, P. (2019). *Artificial intelligence in education : challenges and opportunities for sustainable development*. https://hdl.handle.net/20.500.12799/6533

Popenici, S. A. D., & Kerr, S. (2017). Exploring the impact of artificial intelligence on teaching and learning in higher education. *Research and Practice in Technology Enhanced Learning*, 12(1), 22. Advance online publication. DOI: 10.1186/s41039-017-0062-8 PMID: 30595727

Rahiman, H. U., & Kodikal, R. (2023). Revolutionizing education: Artificial intelligence empowered learning in higher education. *Cogent Education*. Advance online publication. DOI: 10.1080/2331186X.2023.2293431

Research Guides. Artificial Intelligence (AI) in Education: AI and ethics. (2024). jmu.edu. https://guides.lib.jmu.edu/AI-in-education/ethics

Richardson, E., Gordon, J., Conklin, S., Barreto, D., & Ginnetti, R. (2024). Artificial Intelligence in Higher Education: Faculty Perceptions of Integration and Other Considerations. UNC System *Learning and Technology Journal, 2* (1), 1-39. https://journals.charlotte.edu/ltj/article/view/1776/1505

rmontalvo. (2023). The Benefits of AI in Education - CIS University. CIS University - EN. https://www.cis-spain.com/en/blog/the-benefits-of-ai-in-education/

Saaida, M. B. E. (2023). AI-Driven transformations in higher education: Opportunities and challenges. Zenodo (CERN European Organization for Nuclear Research). DOI: 10.5281/zenodo.8164415

Sairitupa-Sanchez, L. Z., Collantes-Vargas, A., Rivera-Lozada, O., & Morales-Garcia, W. C. (2023). Development and validation of a scale for streaming dependence (SDS) of online games in a Peruvian population. *Frontiers in Psychology*, 14, 647. DOI: 10.3389/fpsyg.2023.1184647 PMID: 37691786

Salemink, K., Strijker, D., & Bosworth, G. (2015). Rural development in the digital age: A systematic literature review on unequal ICT availability, adoption, and use in rural areas. *Journal of Rural Studies*, 54, 360–371. DOI: 10.1016/j.jrurstud.2015.09.001

Shneiderman, B. (2020). Bridging the gap between ethics and practice. *ACM Transactions on Interactive Intelligent Systems*, 10(4), 1–31. DOI: 10.1145/3419764

Soni, N., Sharma, E. K., Singh, N., & Kapoor, A. (2020). Artificial intelligence in business: From research and innovation to market deployment. *Procedia Computer Science*, 167, 2200–2210. DOI: 10.1016/j.procs.2020.03.272

Swiecki, Z., Khosravi, H., Chen, G., Martinez-Maldonado, R., Lodge, J. M., Milligan, S., Selwyn, N., & Gasevic, D. (2022). Assessment in the age of artificial intelligence. Computers and Education. *Artificial Intelligence*, 3, 100075. DOI: 10.1016/j.caeai.2022.100075

Tayan, O., Hassan, A., Khankan, K., & Askool, S. (2023). Considerations for adapting higher education technology courses for AI large language models: A critical review of the impact of ChatGPT. *Machine Learning with Applications*, 15, 100513. DOI: 10.1016/j.mlwa.2023.100513

Technology, T. (2024). Unveiling the Potential: Experts' Perspectives on Artificial Intelligence Integration in Higher Education. eu-jer.com. https://www.eu-jer.com/unveiling-the-potential-experts-perspectives-on-artificial-intelligence-integration-in-higher-education

technouser. (2024). AI in Education: 24/7 Learning Access for Students. Technocrats Horizons. https://technocratshorizons.com/how-ai-in-education-can-provide-24-7-access-to-learning-for-students/

Tettegah, S. Y., & Mayo, C. (2005). Urban education and technology in the digital age. *Urban Education*, 40(4), 363–367. DOI: 10.1177/0042085905276374

Thakkar, A., Gupta, A., & De Sousa, A. (2024). Artificial intelligence in positive mental health: A narrative review. *Frontiers in Digital Health*, 6, 1280235. Advance online publication. DOI: 10.3389/fdgth.2024.1280235 PMID: 38562663

Van Rooij, A. J., Schoenmakers, T. M., Vermulst, A. A., Van Den Eijnden, R. J. J. M., & Van De Mheen, D. (2011). Online video game addiction: Identification of addicted adolescent gamers. *Addiction (Abingdon, England)*, 106(1), 205–212. DOI: 10.1111/j.1360-0443.2010.03104.x PMID: 20840209

Vanden Abeele, M. M. P., Halfmann, A., & Lee, E. W. J. (2022). Drug, demon, or donut? Theorizing the relationship between social media use, digital well-being, and digital disconnection. *Current Opinion in Psychology*, 45, 101295. DOI: 10.1016/j.copsyc.2021.12.007 PMID: 35123383

Wang, Y. (2020). When artificial intelligence meets educational leaders' data-informed decision-making: A cautionary tale. *Studies in Educational Evaluation*, 69, 100872. DOI: 10.1016/j.stueduc.2020.100872

Weinstein, A., & Lejoyeux, M. (2010). Internet addiction or excessive internet use. *The American Journal of Drug and Alcohol Abuse*, 36(5), 277–283. DOI: 10.3109/00952990.2010.491880 PMID: 20545603

Williamson, B., & Eynon, R. (2020). Historical threads, missing links, and future directions in AI in education. *Learning, Media and Technology*, 45(3), 223–235. DOI: 10.1080/17439884.2020.1798995

Zhai, C., Wibowo, S., & Li, L. D. (2024). The effects of over-reliance on AI dialogue systems on students' cognitive abilities: A systematic review. *Smart Learning Environments*, 11(1), 28. Advance online publication. DOI: 10.1186/s40561-024-00316-7

Zhai, X., Chu, X., Chai, C. S., Jong, M. S. Y., Istenic, A., Spector, M., Liu, J., Yuan, J., & Li, Y. (2021). A Review of Artificial Intelligence (AI) in Education from 2010 to 2020. *Complexity*, 2021(1), 1–18. DOI: 10.1155/2021/8812542

Zhang, K., & Aslan, A. B. (2021). AI technologies for education: Recent research & future directions. *Computers and Education Artificial Intelligence*, 2, 100025. DOI: 10.1016/j.caeai.2021.100025

ADDITIONAL READING

Alzubaidi, L., Al-Sabaawi, A., Bai, J., Dukhan, A., Alkenani, A. H., Al-Asadi, A., Alwzwazy, H. A., Manoufali, M., Fadhel, M. A., Albahri, A. S., Moreira, C., Ouyang, C., Zhang, J., Santamaría, J., Salhi, A., Hollman, F., Gupta, A., Duan, Y., Rabczuk, T., & Gu, Y. (2023). Towards Risk-Free Trustworthy Artificial Intelligence: Significance and Requirements. *International Journal of Intelligent Systems*, 2023(1), 4459198. DOI: 10.1155/2023/4459198

Ding, Y. (2021). Performance analysis of public management teaching practice training based on artificial intelligence technology. *Journal of Intelligent & Fuzzy Systems*, 40(2), 3787–3800. DOI: 10.3233/JIFS-189412

Schofield, J. W., Evans-Rhodes, D., & Huber, B. R. (1990). Artificial intelligence in the classroom: The impact of a computer-based tutor on teachers and students. *Social Science Computer Review*, 8(1), 24–41. DOI: 10.1177/089443939000800104

Zakharova, I., & Jarke, J. (2024). Do predictive analytics dream of risk-free education? The politics of risk mitigation. *Postdigital Science and Education*, 6(1), 32–51. DOI: 10.1007/s42438-023-00411-x

KEY TERMS AND DEFINITIONS

Adaptive Learning: A method of personalized education that uses AI to tailor the learning experience based on the student's progress, strengths, and areas for improvement.

Artificial Intelligence (AI): A branch of computer science focused on creating machines capable of performing tasks that typically require human intelligence, such as learning, reasoning, and problem-solving.

Communication Skills: Abilities that enable individuals to convey, receive, and interpret messages effectively, including verbal, nonverbal, and written communication methods.

Generative AI (Gen AI): A subset of AI focused on generating new content based on training data, such as text, images, or videos, to support various applications, including education and content creation.

Hybrid Learning: An instructional approach that combines in-person and digital learning activities to offer a flexible, blended educational experience.

Role-Based Interaction: A structured form of communication where participants interact according to defined roles and responsibilities to achieve specific learning or service objectives.

Service-Learning: A teaching method that integrates community service with academic instruction, emphasizing real-world application of knowledge, civic responsibility, and social engagement.

Skill Communication: The structured process of teaching, transferring, or demonstrating skills within educational or training contexts, focusing on effective collaboration and knowledge sharing.

Soft Gen AI: A human-centered approach to AI that prioritizes adaptive, flexible interactions between technology and users, particularly in fields requiring creativity, ethics, and social considerations.

Structured Design Approach: A systematic methodology for planning and executing projects that align with specific objectives, ensuring consistent and effective outcomes tailored to educational or service-based applications.

Chapter 12
Fostering Inclusivity and Empowerment:
Crafting Culturally Responsive Literacy Ecosystems

Goh Ying Yingsoon
https://orcid.org/0000-0002-6654-2887
University Teknoligi MARA, Malaysia

Zhang Suyan
https://orcid.org/0009-0003-4518-1650
Shandong Jianzhu University, China

Nurul Ain Chua
https://orcid.org/0000-0003-2915-1577
University Terengganu Malaysia, Malaysia

Yiming Chen
https://orcid.org/0009-0002-8906-2736
Shenzhen University, China

ABSTRACT

In today's increasingly diverse educational landscape, culturally responsive literacy practices are not just beneficial—they are essential. This chapter examines strategies for creating literacy ecosystems that honor and reflect learners' cultural, experiential, and linguistic diversity. We argue that adopting a culturally responsive approach strengthens literacy skills, validates students' identities, and promotes social equity. The chapter begins with exploring the theoretical foundations of culturally responsive literacy, emphasizing the importance of recognizing and valuing students' cultural wealth. Following this, a comprehensive framework is provided

DOI: 10.4018/979-8-3373-1017-6.ch012

for building a culturally responsive literacy ecosystem, covering curriculum design, instructional methods, assessment strategies, and classroom management. Ultimately, we demonstrate how these practices foster inclusive environments that empower all learners and encourage active, meaningful engagement with literacy.

INTRODUCTION

In an educational landscape that grows increasingly diverse with each passing year, fostering inclusivity and empowerment has become a paramount concern for educators and administrators. As classrooms fill with students from a myriad of cultural, linguistic, and socio-economic backgrounds, the need for culturally responsive pedagogies becomes more critical. Culturally responsive literacy ecosystems are designed to acknowledge and honor the unique identities and experiences of each student, creating an environment where every child feels valued and understood. By weaving the cultural tapestries of their students into the fabric of instruction, educators can build bridges of empathy and mutual respect that are essential for academic success and personal growth (Nichols, & LeBlanc, 2021). Crafting these ecosystems involves a multifaceted approach that extends beyond the mere inclusion of diverse literature in the curriculum. It requires a deep commitment to understanding the cultural contexts of students and integrating their backgrounds into all aspects of teaching and learning. This means not only selecting texts that reflect the diversity of experiences but also employing instructional strategies that resonate with different learning styles and cultural norms. In doing so, culturally responsive literacy ecosystems empower students to see themselves as capable and important contributors to the educational process, thereby enhancing their engagement, motivation, and ultimately, their achievement in the classroom (Häggström, & Schmidt, 2021).

In Malaysia, the educational landscape mirrors this global trend towards diversity, with higher education institutions becoming melting pots for students from a variety of ethnic, religious, and socio-economic backgrounds. This situation necessitates the application of culturally responsive pedagogies within Malaysian universities to cater to this increasingly diverse student body. The discussion of culturally responsive literacy ecosystems can be made more pragmatic and attractive to Malaysian readers by incorporating country-specific examples and comparative insights. For instance, within the context of Malaysian higher education, the incorporation of culturally responsive practices might involve addressing the linguistic diversity, where English is used as the medium of instruction alongside Malay and other vernacular languages. Educators in Malaysia can draw upon the rich cultural narratives of the country's multi-ethnic population, which includes Malay, Chinese, Indian, and indigenous groups, to create inclusive learning environments. For example, literature and case studies from the various ethnic groups can be integrated into the curriculum to ensure that all students see their heritage and experiences reflected in their studies.

By discussing how culturally responsive literacy ecosystems can be tailored to the unique cultural mosaic of Malaysia, the chapter can resonate more deeply with Malaysian educators and administrators. For example, it can explore how universities in Malaysia are adapting their teaching methods to cater to the diverse learning styles of students from different cultural backgrounds, or how they are using culturally relevant examples and materials in their teaching to enhance student engagement and academic performance. Crafting these ecosystems within the Malaysian higher education context involves a particularly nuanced approach due to the nation's multiracial and multicultural society. Educators must not only be sensitive to the different ethnicities and languages spoken but also to the religious practices that inform the daily lives of Malaysian students. This means that in addition to selecting literature that represents the breadth of Malaysian experiences, instructional strategies must be adaptable to the varying degrees of formality and communication styles inherent in different cultural groups. For example, incorporating elements of storytelling and oral traditions from indigenous cultures can help to bridge the gap between classroom material and the lived experiences of students from these communities. As such, culturally responsive literacy ecosystems in Malaysia serve not only to empower students but also to foster a greater sense of national identity and unity within diversity.

Culturally responsive literacy practices are an educational approach that recognizes and validates the cultural identities, backgrounds, and experiences of all students. This method involves intentionally designing literacy instruction that incorporates a variety of cultural perspectives, languages, and experiences into the curriculum. It goes beyond merely adding diverse books to the reading list; it encompasses using teaching strategies that are sensitive to students' cultural contexts, engaging in dialogue that respects their voices, and creating learning environments that reflect the diversity of the student body. By doing so, culturally responsive literacy practices aim to make learning more accessible, meaningful, and relevant to each student (Minor 2023).

The critical need for culturally responsive literacy practices arises from the reality that traditional educational models often fail to meet the needs of students from diverse backgrounds. These students may feel marginalized or disengaged when their cultures and experiences are not reflected in the curriculum, leading to a lack of motivation and lower academic performance. By implementing culturally responsive practices, educators can create a more inclusive and equitable learning environment that supports all students in achieving their full potential. It helps to close achievement gaps, fosters a sense of belonging, and prepares students to participate in a multicultural society where understanding and appreciation for different cultures are essential skills. In essence, culturally responsive literacy practices are not just a teaching strategy but a necessary step towards educational justice and social equity (Akiva, et al, 2023).

In the context of Malaysia's higher education, the framework of cultural responsiveness can be exemplified by the initiatives taken at a leading public university with a diverse student body, including a significant number of Indigenous students from various ethnic groups. The university developed a culturally responsive curriculum by first establishing a task force comprising educators, cultural experts, and student representatives to map out the cultural and linguistic diversity within the student population. This task force then worked to infuse the curriculum with modules that drew upon the histories, languages, and knowledge systems of Malaysia's ethnic groups, such as incorporating traditional storytelling techniques into communication courses and using local case studies in business and law classes. Furthermore, the university fostered a supportive learning environment by organizing cultural exchange programs, providing language support services, and encouraging faculty to adopt inclusive teaching methods that recognized and valued the different cultural perspectives brought by their students. These efforts not only enhanced the educational experience for all students but also contributed to a more harmonious and inclusive campus atmosphere, aligning with the national goal of promoting unity in diversity.

This chapter's focus is on the development and implementation of culturally responsive literacy ecosystems within the context of an increasingly diverse educational landscape. Its objectives are to explore the theoretical underpinnings of culturally responsive literacy, provide a comprehensive framework for creating inclusive and empowering literacy environments, and offer practical strategies for educators to engage with families and communities. Ultimately, the chapter aims to equip readers with the insights and tools necessary to validate students' cultural backgrounds, enhance literacy skills, and promote social justice through literacy education.

THEORETICAL FOUNDATIONS OF CULTURALLY RESPONSIVE LITERACY

Definition and Core Principles of Culturally Responsive Literacy

Culturally responsive literacy is an educational framework that acknowledges the importance of culture in the teaching and learning of literacy skills. It is defined as an approach to literacy education that is grounded in the belief that students' cultural backgrounds significantly influence their learning experiences. This framework emphasizes the integration of students' cultural references, experiences, and linguistic resources into literacy instruction to create an educational environment that is inclusive, respectful, and effective for all learners (Harrison, & Skrebneva, 2020).

The core principles of culturally responsive literacy are centered around several key concepts that guide its implementation in the classroom. First, it acknowledges the legitimacy of students' home languages and cultures, promoting bilingualism and biculturalism as strengths rather than barriers to learning. Second, it advocates for a social justice orientation, where educators work to dismantle systemic biases and inequalities that affect students' educational outcomes. Third, it emphasizes the importance of developing cultural competence among educators, ensuring they have the knowledge and skills to understand and appreciate the diverse backgrounds of their students. Fourth, it calls for the use of culturally relevant materials and resources that reflect the lives and experiences of all students. Finally, it involves fostering a community of learners where students' voices are heard and valued, and where they are encouraged to connect their personal experiences with the content they are learning. These principles collectively aim to create a literacy ecosystem that is both equitable and empowering for every student (Tanase, 2020).

Recognizing and Valuing Cultural Assets in the Classroom

Recognizing cultural assets in the classroom involves a deep and intentional observation of the diverse backgrounds, experiences, and talents that students bring with them. Educators must be attuned to the various cultural markers that shape students' identities, including their languages, traditions, beliefs, and family practices. This recognition is not just about noticing surface-level diversity but about understanding the nuanced ways in which culture influences students' interactions, learning styles, and perspectives. By being alert to these cultural assets, teachers can identify the unique strengths and resources that each student contributes to the educational environment (Lähdesmäki, et al, 2022). Valuing cultural assets in the classroom is about affirming and leveraging these unique qualities to enhance the learning experience for all students. When educators value cultural assets, they create an atmosphere where diversity is celebrated and where students feel their backgrounds are not only accepted but also integral to their education. This approach involves integrating students' cultural knowledge into the curriculum, allowing them to draw on their personal experiences to make connections with the material. By valuing cultural assets, teachers send a powerful message of inclusion and respect, which can boost students' self-esteem, motivation, and academic engagement. It also prepares students to appreciate and navigate the multicultural world they live in, fostering a more inclusive and empathetic society (Watts-Taffe, 2022).

The Intersection of Literacy and Social Justice

Literacy ecosystems encompass the complex network of individuals, institutions, policies, and practices that influence the development and application of literacy skills within a community. At the intersection of literacy and social justice, these ecosystems are particularly crucial as they highlight the inequalities and power dynamics that shape access to educational resources and opportunities. Literacy is not just about reading and writing; it is a tool for empowerment, critical thinking, and civic engagement. In a social justice context, literacy ecosystems must address the systemic barriers that prevent certain groups from achieving full literacy, thereby perpetuating cycles of disadvantage and marginalization (Kellogg, 2021). To promote a literacy ecosystem that aligns with social justice principles, it is essential to adopt an inclusive and equitable approach. This begins with recognizing and confronting the biases and discrimination that affect literacy education. Actions include advocating for diverse and culturally relevant curriculum, providing resources and support to underserved communities, and fostering partnerships between schools, libraries, and community organizations. Additionally, policymakers and educators must work collaboratively to implement policies that ensure equitable access to quality education, while also engaging in continuous professional development to understand and address the diverse needs of learners. By doing so, we can create a literacy ecosystem that not only builds skills but also empowers individuals to advocate for their rights and contribute to a more just society (De Abreu, 2022).

DESIGNING A CULTURALLY RESPONSIVE LITERACY ECOSYSTEM

Understanding Literacy Ecosystems

Designing a culturally responsive literacy ecosystem involves creating an educational environment that acknowledges, respects, and incorporates the cultural backgrounds, experiences, and languages of all learners. This approach recognizes that literacy development is deeply influenced by one's cultural context and that traditional, one-size-fits-all methods may not be effective for all students. A culturally responsive literacy ecosystem is one that not only teaches reading and writing skills but also validates students' identities, encourages critical consciousness, and prepares them to navigate and contribute to a multicultural society (Chong 2021). To increase understanding of literacy ecosystems, particularly those that are culturally responsive, it is important to engage in ongoing professional development and community outreach. Educators, policymakers, and community members must educate themselves about the diverse cultural and linguistic assets that students bring to the classroom. This can be achieved through workshops, cultural exchange programs, and the integration of multicultural literature and resources into the curriculum. Additionally, fostering open dialogue and collaboration between schools, families, and community organizations can help stakeholders develop a deeper appreciation for the complexity of literacy ecosystems and the role culture plays in shaping literacy practices. By enhancing this understanding, stakeholders can better support the creation and maintenance of literacy ecosystems that are inclusive, equitable, and reflective of the communities they serve (Pahl, & Rowsell, 2020).

Framework for Culturally Responsive Literacy Ecosystems

The framework for culturally responsive literacy ecosystems is structured around four integral components: curriculum design, instructional strategies, assessment practices, and classroom management techniques. Each part of this framework is crucial in ensuring that the literacy ecosystem is not only academically sound but also culturally affirming and inclusive, thereby promoting a more equitable and effective educational experience for all students (Jackson, et al, 2021).

Curriculum Design

Curriculum design in the context of culturally responsive literacy ecosystems refers to the deliberate and intentional process of creating a curriculum that is reflective of the diverse cultural, linguistic, and experiential backgrounds of students. It involves selecting and organizing content, materials, and learning activities that are relevant to students' lives, while also aligning with educational standards and goals. This type of curriculum goes beyond a surface-level inclusion of multicultural texts; it integrates deep cultural knowledge, perspectives, and practices that honor the heritage and experiences of all learners, making the educational process more meaningful and engaging (Atenas, et al, 2021).

To effectively design a culturally responsive curriculum, educators must first engage in self-reflection to understand their own cultural biases and assumptions. They should then collaborate with students, families, and community members to co-create a curriculum that resonates with the cultural contexts of the learners. This process includes identifying themes and topics that are relevant to the students' lives, incorporating a variety of culturally diverse texts and resources, and ensuring that the curriculum allows for multiple perspectives and voices. Additionally, educators should provide professional development opportunities to enhance their cultural competence and should regularly assess and adjust the curriculum based on student feedback and outcomes, thereby creating a dynamic and responsive educational experience (Haagen-Schützenhöfer, & Hopf, 2021). Refer table 1 for vital steps involved.

Table 1. Vital steps involved

Number	Step	Elaboration
1	Self-Reflection and Bias Awareness	Educators must engage in introspection to recognize and address their own cultural biases and assumptions. This step is crucial for developing an open mindset and ensuring that the curriculum is designed from an inclusive perspective.
2	Collaborative Curriculum Development	Teachers should actively involve students, families, and community members in the curriculum design process. This collaborative approach helps to ensure that the curriculum is culturally relevant, incorporates diverse perspectives, and addresses the interests and needs of the learners.
3	Ongoing Assessment and Adaptation	Educators must continuously assess the effectiveness of the curriculum through student feedback, learning outcomes, and reflection on their teaching practices. This feedback loop allows for necessary adjustments to be made, ensuring the curriculum remains dynamic, responsive, and culturally inclusive.

Instructional Strategies

Instructional strategies in culturally responsive literacy ecosystems are the methods and techniques that teachers use to deliver content in a way that is inclusive, engaging, and respectful of students' cultural identities. These strategies are designed to build upon the strengths and experiences that students bring to the classroom, fostering a learning environment where all students feel valued and empowered. Effective instructional strategies in this context often involve collaborative learning, project-based activities, storytelling, and the use of culturally relevant materials, which collectively aim to enhance literacy skills while promoting critical thinking and cultural competence (Minor, 2023).

To implement culturally responsive instructional strategies, educators must first establish a classroom climate that encourages open communication and respect for diversity. This involves getting to know students individually, learning about their cultural backgrounds, and incorporating their experiences into the teaching process. Teachers can then select or develop instructional methods that are interactive and allow for multiple modes of expression, such as group discussions, peer teaching, and multimedia projects. It is also essential to provide ongoing support and professional development to help teachers refine their skills in using these strategies effectively. By continuously reflecting on their practice, seeking feedback from students and colleagues, and adapting their approach based on student needs, educators can create a dynamic and culturally responsive instructional environment that enhances literacy learning for all (DeVries, 2023). Refer table 2 for vital strategies with examples.

Table 2. Vital strategies with examples

Number	Strategy	Example
1	Fostering Individualized Learning Experiences	Educators should tailor instruction to accommodate students' unique cultural backgrounds and learning styles. For example, a teacher might incorporate students' native languages into literacy activities or use family stories and traditions as the basis for writing assignments, allowing students to draw on their personal experiences and cultural knowledge.
2	Utilizing Interactive and Multimodal Teaching Methods	Teachers can implement instructional strategies that engage students in active learning and allow for diverse forms of expression. For instance, organizing a group discussion where students explore themes from a multicultural novel, engaging in peer teaching where students teach each other about a topic from their cultural perspective, or creating a multimedia project where students can combine visual, oral, and written communication to convey their understanding of a subject.
3	Providing Culturally Informed Professional Development	Ongoing professional development should focus on enhancing teachers' cultural competence and ability to implement responsive strategies. An example of this could be workshops on culturally sustaining pedagogies, where educators learn to integrate community resources, such as local artists or elders, into their teaching to provide authentic cultural insights and experiences for their students.

Assessment Practices

Assessment practices within culturally responsive literacy ecosystems refer to the methods and tools used to evaluate student learning in ways that are fair, equitable, and reflective of diverse cultural contexts. These practices go beyond traditional testing to include a variety of formative and summative assessments that value students' cultural knowledge, language diversity, and different ways of demonstrating understanding. Culturally responsive assessments are designed to identify and celebrate students' strengths, provide meaningful feedback for improvement, and ensure that all students can showcase their literacy skills in a manner that is authentic to their experiences (Chan & Luo, 2022).

To implement culturally responsive assessment practices, educators must first recognize and address the cultural biases that may exist in traditional assessment methods. This involves creating assessments that are inclusive of different languages and cultural references, and that allow for a range of responses beyond standardized answers. Teachers can incorporate performance-based assessments, projects, portfolios, and peer and self-assessments to provide a more comprehensive view of a student's literacy abilities. Additionally, educators should use assessment data to inform instruction, adapting their teaching strategies to better meet the needs of diverse learners. It is also crucial to involve students and their families in the assessment process, ensuring that assessments are culturally sensitive, and that feedback is constructive, supportive, and aimed at promoting student growth and confidence (Morton, 2020). Refer table 3 for vital practices with examples.

Table 3. Vital practices with examples

Number	Practice	Example
1	Inclusive and Multilingual Assessments	Educators should design assessments that are accessible to all students, including those who are English language learners or come from non-dominant cultural backgrounds. For example, providing reading passages or writing prompts that incorporate students' native languages or offering translation services during assessments can ensure that language is not a barrier to demonstrating literacy skills.
2	Performance-Based and Authentic Assessments	Incorporating performance-based assessments allows students to demonstrate their literacy abilities through real-world applications. An example of this could be asking students to create a presentation on a topic of cultural importance to them, which assesses their research, writing, and speaking skills in a context that is personally meaningful.
3	Student and Family Involvement in Assessment	Engaging students and their families in the assessment process not only makes it more culturally sensitive but also empowers students in their learning journey. For instance, teachers could involve families in developing criteria for a portfolio assessment or use student-led conferences where learners reflect on their work and set goals for improvement, with the support and input of their families.

Classroom Management Techniques

Classroom management techniques in culturally responsive literacy ecosystems refer to the strategies and approaches that teachers use to create a positive, inclusive, and productive learning environment. These techniques are designed to support the academic and social development of students from diverse cultural backgrounds by establishing clear expectations, promoting respectful interactions, and maintaining a classroom culture that values and celebrates each student's unique identity and contributions. Effective classroom management in this context is not just about discipline; it's about fostering a sense of community and belonging that enables all students to engage fully in literacy activities (Burden, 2020).

To employ culturally responsive classroom management techniques, educators must begin by building strong, trust-based relationships with their students. This involves taking the time to learn about students' cultural backgrounds, interests, and learning styles, and using this knowledge to shape the classroom environment. Teachers should develop clear, fair rules and routines that are communicated and understood by all, while also being flexible enough to accommodate the cultural needs of individual students. Additionally, incorporating restorative practices and conflict resolution strategies that are sensitive to cultural differences can help maintain a harmonious classroom. Educators should also provide consistent positive reinforcement, use culturally relevant examples and materials, and encourage student voice and leadership. By consistently reflecting on their management practices and seeking feedback from students and colleagues, teachers can refine their techniques to better support a culturally responsive literacy ecosystem (Caldera, et al, 2020). Refer table 4 for vital techniques with examples.

Table 4. Vital techniques with examples.

Number	Technique	Example
1	Culturally Informed Relationship-Building	Teachers can foster strong, trust-based relationships by integrating activities that celebrate and explore students' cultural backgrounds. For example, starting each day with a "circle time" where students share personal stories or cultural traditions can help build a sense of community and understanding among classmates.
2	Flexible and Culturally Sensitive Routines	Classroom rules and routines should be adaptable to the cultural contexts of the students. An example of this is allowing for flexible seating arrangements that respect cultural norms around personal space or modifying group work guidelines to accommodate different cultural expectations of collaboration and communication.
3	Restorative and Culturally Aware Conflict Resolution	When conflicts arise, using restorative practices that are mindful of cultural differences can help maintain a respectful classroom environment. For instance, a teacher might facilitate a restorative circle where students discuss a conflict, with an emphasis on understanding each other's perspectives and making amends, which respects the cultural values of reconciliation and community harmony.

INCLUSIVITY AND EMPOWERMENT IN CULTURALLY RESPONSIVE LITERACY

Strategies for Fostering Inclusivity

Inclusivity and empowerment in culturally responsive literacy refer to an educational approach that acknowledges, respects, and incorporates students' cultural backgrounds, experiences, and languages into literacy instruction. This method recognizes the diversity of learners and seeks to create an inclusive learning environment where all students feel valued and understood. By integrating students' cultural heritages into literacy activities, educators can foster a sense of belonging and relevance, which in turn enhances students' engagement and motivation to learn. Inclusivity and empowerment in culturally responsive literacy aim to dismantle barriers that may hinder students' academic success, promoting a more equitable and just educational system (Emery, et al, 2021).

To foster inclusivity and empowerment in culturally responsive literacy, educators must take several steps to ensure that their teaching practices are attuned to the needs of their diverse student population. Firstly, teachers should engage in ongoing self-reflection to examine their own biases and assumptions about culture and literacy. Secondly, they should build strong relationships with students and their families, learning about their cultural backgrounds, interests, and experiences. This information can then be used to select and adapt literacy materials that reflect and honor students' cultures. Additionally, educators can incorporate multicultural literature, diverse authors, and culturally relevant texts into their curriculum, allowing students to see themselves and their communities positively represented in the materials they study. Furthermore, teachers should use inclusive teaching strategies, such as cooperative learning, student-led discussions, and project-based learning, which empower students to share their knowledge and perspectives. By implementing these strategies, educators can create a culturally responsive and inclusive literacy environment that empowers all students to achieve academic success (Cerna, et al, 2021). Refer table 5 for vital strategies with examples.

Table 5. Vital strategies with examples

Number	Strategy	Example
1	Incorporating Multicultural Literature and Diverse Authors	One key strategy for fostering inclusivity and empowerment in culturally responsive literacy is to integrate a wide range of multicultural literature and texts by diverse authors into the curriculum. This approach not only exposes students to different cultures and perspectives but also validates their own experiences. For example, a teacher might include readings in al language arts class to provide insight into the experiences of foreign migrant workers. Another example could be using readings in a language class to discuss identity and belonging through the lens of a different cultural group teenager.
2	Utilizing Student-Centered Teaching Methods	Another essential strategy is to employ student-centered teaching methods that empower students to take an active role in their learning. Cooperative learning is a prime example of this strategy. In a cooperative learning activity, students might work in small groups to create a culturally themed book club where they select and discuss a novel that relates to their cultural heritage or a culture they are interested in exploring. For instance, students could read cultural based readings and engage in a fishbowl discussion to share their thoughts on the racial tensions and social justice issues presented in the book.
3	Adapting Literacy Materials to Reflect Student Cultures	The third vital strategy involves adapting literacy materials to reflect the cultures of the students in the classroom. This can be done by incorporating students' cultural references into reading and writing assignments. For example, a teacher might ask students to write a narrative based on a family tradition or a significant cultural event, such as the cultural festival or Chinese New Year. Additionally, teachers can create culturally themed writing prompts or reading comprehension questions that connect to students' lives. An example would be using news articles about events in students' home countries as the basis for a lesson on informational text analysis, allowing students to apply their background knowledge to understand and engage with the material more deeply.

Empowering Students Through Literacy

Empowering students through literacy involves providing them with the skills, knowledge, and confidence necessary to navigate the world effectively using reading, writing, speaking, and listening abilities. Literacy is not just about decoding words on a page; it is about comprehension, critical thinking, and the ability to communicate ideas persuasively. When students are empowered through literacy, they gain a sense of agency and control over their learning and their lives. This empowerment enables them to express their thoughts and emotions, to advocate for themselves and others, and to engage with and contribute to society in meaningful ways (Lutnæs, 2020).

To empower students through literacy, educators must adopt a holistic approach that addresses the diverse needs and interests of all learners. Firstly, teachers should create a literacy-rich environment that promotes reading and writing as joyful and purposeful activities. This can be achieved by filling the classroom with a variety of books, providing opportunities for students to write for authentic purposes, and encouraging regular reading both inside and outside of school. Secondly, teachers should differentiate their instruction to meet students at their individual reading and writing levels, offering support and challenges as needed. This might involve using flexible grouping, providing targeted interventions, and incorporating technology to personalize learning experiences. Additionally, educators can empower students by giving them choice in their reading and writing topics, allowing them to explore their passions and interests. By fostering a supportive and inclusive classroom community where students feel safe to take risks and share their work, teachers can help students develop the confidence and skills necessary to become lifelong learners and active participants in their education and beyond (Shapiro, et al, 2021). Refer table 6 for vital ways with examples.

Table 6. Vital ways with examples

Number	Way	Example
1	Offering Choice and Autonomy in Literacy Activities	One vital way to empower students through literacy is by offering them choice and autonomy in their reading and writing activities. This allows students to pursue their interests and strengths, which can significantly increase their engagement and motivation. For example, during independent reading time, a teacher might implement a "Reading Workshop" model where students can select books from a classroom library that align with their personal interests and reading levels. Similarly, in writing, a teacher could provide a menu of writing prompts or projects and allow students to choose the one that resonates most with them, such as writing a personal narrative, a persuasive essay on a topic they are passionate about, or even creating a short story in their preferred genre.
2	Facilitating Peer Collaboration and Support	Another key method for empowering students through literacy is to facilitate peer collaboration and support. When students work together, they can share their strengths, learn from one another, and build confidence in their literacy skills. An example of this is peer editing, where students in a writing class exchange drafts and provide constructive feedback to help each other improve their work. Another example is book clubs or literature circles, where students discuss a shared text, taking on different roles such as summarizer, connector, and questioner, which enhances their comprehension and critical thinking skills while also fostering a sense of community and shared purpose.
3	Integrating Real-World Applications and Authentic Audiences	The third vital way to empower students through literacy is by integrating real-world applications and authentic audiences into literacy activities. When students understand the relevance of their literacy skills beyond the classroom, they are more likely to be engaged and see the value in their learning. For instance, a teacher might organize a "Poetry Event" where students perform their original poems for an audience of their peers, teachers, and even community members. Another example is having students write letters to local officials or op-eds for a school newspaper on issues that matter to them, which not only develops their literacy skills but also gives them a voice and the opportunity to make a real impact.

Validating Students' Identities and Experiences

Validating students' identities and experiences is a critical aspect of creating an inclusive and supportive educational environment. It involves recognizing and affirming the unique cultural, social, and personal backgrounds that students bring to the classroom. This validation helps students feel seen, heard, and valued, which is essential for their emotional well-being and academic success. By acknowledging their identities and experiences, educators can build trust and rapport with students, encouraging them to engage more fully in their learning and to explore their own perspectives and the perspectives of others (Kitchen, et al, 2021).

To validate students' identities and experiences, educators must take deliberate and thoughtful actions both inside and outside the classroom. One approach is to incorporate diverse and representative materials into the curriculum that reflect the lives and experiences of all students. For example, teachers can include literature, history, and resources that feature characters and narratives from a wide range of backgrounds, including those that are often underrepresented in traditional educational materials. Additionally, teachers can create opportunities for students to share their personal stories and experiences through discussions, presentations, and projects. This might involve inviting students to bring in family artifacts for a "show and tell" session or to lead a lesson on a topic related to their cultural heritage. Furthermore, educators should actively listen to students, offering empathy and understanding when discussing sensitive or personal topics. By using inclusive language, celebrating cultural holidays and events, and addressing students by their preferred names and pronouns, teachers can send a clear message that every student's identity and experience is respected and valued in the classroom (Cross, et al, 2022).

THE ROLE OF FAMILIES AND COMMUNITIES

Engaging Families in Literacy Practices

Engaging families in literacy practices refers to the active involvement of parents, guardians, and other family members in the literacy development of children. This collaboration between educators and families recognizes that literacy learning extends beyond the school walls and that family support can significantly enhance a child's reading and writing skills. By engaging families, educators can create a continuity of learning that bridges the gap between home and school, reinforcing the importance of literacy as a fundamental part of daily life and a key to future success (Hannon, et al, 2020).

To effectively engage families in literacy practices, educators must establish open lines of communication and provide opportunities for family involvement that are accessible and meaningful. One strategy is to host regular family literacy events at the school, such as reading nights or book fairs, where families can participate in literacy activities together and receive resources to support reading at home. Another approach is to provide families with information and guidance on how to support their child's literacy development, including tips for reading aloud, discussing books, and incorporating writing into everyday activities. Teachers can also assign homework that encourages family participation, such as reading together and sharing responses to a book or creating a family story. Additionally, educators can use technology to connect with families, whether through a classroom blog, a messaging app, or a shared digital platform where families can track their child's progress and find resources. By making an effort to understand families' cultural backgrounds and priorities, educators can tailor their engagement strategies to better meet the needs and interests of the entire family, thereby strengthening the support network for a child's literacy journey (Kelty, & Wakabayashi, 2020).

Building Authentic Partnerships with Communities

Building authentic partnerships with communities involves creating and maintaining mutually beneficial relationships between schools and the various community groups, organizations, and individuals that surround them. These partnerships are based on trust, respect, and a shared commitment to the educational success and well-being of students. By engaging with the community, schools can tap into additional resources, expertise, and perspectives that enrich the educational experience and better prepare students for life beyond the classroom (Shah, 2020).

To build authentic partnerships with communities, schools must adopt a proactive and inclusive approach that values the contributions of all stakeholders. Firstly, educators and school leaders should identify community assets and needs through dialogue and collaboration with community members. This could involve conducting surveys, hosting community forums, or participating in local events to understand what the community has to offer and what it hopes to gain from the partnership. Secondly, schools should develop clear goals and objectives for the partnership that align with both the educational mission and the community's interests. For example, a school might partner with a local business to provide students with internship opportunities or with a cultural center to offer workshops on heritage and history. Additionally, schools should ensure that the partnership is dynamic and ongoing, with regular communication and opportunities for feedback. This might include creating joint committees, organizing community service projects, or involving community members in school decision-making processes. By fostering these authentic partnerships, schools can create a supportive and interconnected environment that not only benefits students but also strengthens the community (Hanell, 2020).

CASE STUDIES: SUCCESSFUL COLLABORATIONS BETWEEN SCHOOLS AND COMMUNITIES

Case studies of successful collaborations between schools and communities are detailed examinations of instances where partnerships have led to positive outcomes for both educational institutions and the broader community. These case studies often highlight the strategies, processes, and impact of collaborative efforts, providing a blueprint for other schools and communities looking to establish similar partnerships. They showcase a range of initiatives, from community service projects to shared educational programs, and demonstrate how these collaborations can enhance student learning, promote community engagement, and address local needs (O'neil, et al, 2020).

To document and learn from successful collaborations between schools and communities, researchers and educators can follow a structured approach to gather and analyze data. Firstly, they should identify and select case studies that exhibit strong partnership elements and measurable outcomes. This involves conducting interviews with key stakeholders, including school administrators, teachers, students, community leaders, and parents, to understand the motivations, processes, and results of the collaboration. Secondly, the case study should detail the context in which the partnership was formed, the activities undertaken, and the challenges and successes encountered. It is also important to collect quantitative and qualitative data to assess the impact of collaboration on student achievement, community well-being, and other relevant metrics. Once documented, these case studies can be shared through publications, conferences, and professional development workshops to disseminate best practices and inspire others to engage in similar partnerships. By learning from these examples, schools and communities can replicate successful models, adapt them to their unique circumstances, and contribute to a growing body of knowledge on effective school-community collaborations (Wu & Lin, 2020).

This case study of O'neil, et al, (2020) explores how urban harbors, specifically those of New York and Chesapeake Bay, are utilized to enhance experiential and environmental literacy among students. By integrating field trips, hands-on research, and stewardship projects into the curriculum, schools in these regions are transforming the harbors into living classrooms. Students engage directly with the ecological systems of the harbors, learning about marine life, water quality, and the impact of human activities on these environments. Relating this to a literary ecosystem, the case study illustrates how the physical environment of the harbors serves as a textual landscape, where students "read" the natural world to interpret ecological narratives, much like they would analyze characters and themes in a novel. This approach not only deepens their understanding of environmental issues but also fosters a sense of responsibility and connection to their local literary ecosystem, where the stories of the natural world are as rich and complex as those found in traditional literature.

This case study of Wu & Lin, (2020) examines the integration of innovation and entrepreneurship within Taiwan's educational ecosystem, highlighting how schools and universities are fostering a culture of creativity and entrepreneurial thinking among students. Through initiatives such as startup incubators, interdisciplinary projects, and mentorship programs, educational institutions in Taiwan are nurturing a generation equipped to address complex challenges with innovative solutions. Relating this to a literary ecosystem, the case study suggests that the educational environment is akin to a rich narrative where students are not just characters but also authors of their own stories. Just as a literary ecosystem thrives on diverse voices and perspectives, the educational ecosystem in Taiwan is enriched by the varied and dynamic experiences of students who are encouraged to write their own plots of success, failure, and learning, thereby contributing to a collective story of innovation and growth.

IMPLEMENTATION OF CULTURALLY RESPONSIVE LITERACY ECOSYSTEMS

Challenges and Considerations for Educators

The implementation of culturally responsive literacy ecosystems refers to the process of creating and maintaining educational environments where literacy instruction is deeply rooted in the cultural contexts of students. This approach requires a comprehensive overhaul of traditional literacy practices to ensure that they are inclusive, relevant, and empowering for all learners. Challenges arise as educators must navigate the complexities of diverse student backgrounds, language proficiencies, and learning styles, while also addressing systemic biases and gaps in resources and support (Akiva, et al, 2023).

To effectively implement culturally responsive literacy ecosystems, educators must undertake a multifaceted approach that addresses both the structural and interpersonal aspects of education. Firstly, educators need to engage in continuous professional development to build their cultural competence and understanding of responsive teaching strategies. This includes learning about the histories, traditions, and languages of the students they teach. Secondly, schools must commit to curriculum reform, ensuring that literacy materials reflect a wide range of cultural perspectives and that instruction is adaptable to the unique needs of each student. Additionally, educators should foster strong home-school connections by involving families in the literacy process and recognizing their cultural wealth as a valuable resource. To overcome challenges, schools may also need to allocate resources for additional staffing, professional development, and the acquisition of culturally relevant materials. By taking these steps, educators can create a literacy ecosystem that not only respects and values the cultural diversity of their students but also promotes academic success and personal growth (Alim, et al, 2020).

Practical Advice for Implementation

Practical advice for the implementation of culturally responsive literacy ecosystems encompasses the actionable steps and strategies that educators can employ to transform their classrooms and schools into inclusive environments that support the literacy development of all students. This advice is grounded in the realities of classroom instruction and school dynamics, offering tangible ways to integrate cultural responsiveness into everyday teaching practices. To follow practical advice for implementing culturally responsive literacy ecosystems, educators should start by assessing their current practices and identifying areas for growth. This involves reflecting on their own cultural awareness and biases, as well as the cultural make-up of their student body. Refer to table 7 on practical advice on what educators can do. By following these steps, educators can translate the theoretical framework of culturally responsive literacy ecosystems into concrete actions that make a meaningful difference in the lives of their students.

Table 7. Practical advice on what educators can do.

Number	Advice	Elaboration
1	Develop a Culturally Responsive Curriculum	Integrate literature and resources that reflect the diverse backgrounds of students, ensuring that all students see themselves and their cultures represented in the curriculum.
2	Foster Inclusive Classrooms	Create a welcoming environment where students feel safe to express their cultural identities and share their experiences. This can be achieved through classroom discussions, cultural celebrations, and the display of student work.
3	Engage in Ongoing Professional Learning	Participate in professional development that focuses on culturally responsive teaching strategies, including how to differentiate instruction to meet the needs of English language learners and students with diverse learning styles.

continued on following page

Table 7. Continued

Number	Advice	Elaboration
4	Build Partnerships with Families and Communities	Establish strong relationships with families and community members to better understand students' cultural contexts and to involve them in the educational process.
5	Use Data to Inform Practice	Collect and analyze data on student performance and progress to identify gaps and adjust instruction accordingly.

Tools and Resources for Educators

Tools and resources for educators in culturally responsive literacy encompass a wide range of materials, technologies, and supports designed to assist teachers in creating and sustaining inclusive literacy environments. These may include diverse literature collections, professional development programs, classroom management strategies, and digital platforms that facilitate culturally responsive teaching. These tools and resources are essential for educators to effectively address the diverse needs of their students and to promote literacy development that is both equitable and engaging (Nichols, & LeBlanc, 2021). To utilize tools and resources for culturally responsive literacy effectively, educators should first identify their specific needs and the needs of their students. Table 8 shows what educators can about the tools and resources. By thoughtfully selecting and integrating these tools and resources into their teaching, educators can create a more inclusive and responsive literacy environment that celebrates diversity and supports all students in their literacy journey.

Table 8. What the educators can about the tools and resources

Number	What to do	Elaboration
1	Access Diverse Literature	Seek out and incorporate a variety of literature that represents the cultural, linguistic, and racial diversity of the classroom. This can be done through school libraries, online databases, and recommendations from professional organizations.
2	Engage with Professional Development	Participate in workshops, webinars, and courses that focus on culturally responsive practices. These opportunities can provide educators with new strategies and a deeper understanding of cultural responsiveness.
3	Leverage Technology	Use educational technology to enhance literacy instruction. This might involve using apps that support language learning, digital storytelling tools, or online platforms that provide culturally relevant content.
4	Collaborate with Colleagues	Work together with fellow educators to share resources, co-plan lessons, and support each other in implementing culturally responsive practices.
5	Incorporate Student Voices	Involve students in the selection of resources and materials, ensuring that the curriculum resonates with their experiences and interests.

CASE STUDIES AND EXAMPLES

Transformative Outcomes of Culturally Responsive Literacy Ecosystems

Case studies and examples of transformative outcomes of culturally responsive literacy ecosystems are detailed narratives and instances that illustrate the significant and positive impacts of such ecosystems on students, educators, and the broader school community. These case studies often highlight the strategies, implementations, and results of culturally responsive literacy practices, providing concrete evidence of how these approaches can lead to improved academic achievement, increased student engagement, and a more inclusive and equitable educational environment (Akiva, et al, 2023). To document and learn from case studies and examples of transformative outcomes of culturally responsive literacy ecosystems, researchers and educators can follow a systematic approach as shown in table 9. By carefully studying and disseminating these case studies and examples, the educational community can continue to refine and expand the implementation of culturally responsive literacy ecosystems, ultimately leading to more transformative outcomes for all students.

Table 9. Systematic approach in documenting and learning from case studies and examples of transformative outcomes of culturally responsive literacy ecosystems

Number	Step	Elaboration
1	Identify Successful Models	Look for schools or districts that have implemented culturally responsive literacy ecosystems and have seen measurable success in terms of student outcomes and community engagement.
2	Gather Data	Collect qualitative and quantitative data through interviews, observations, student work, and standardized test scores to understand the implementation process and the outcomes achieved.
3	Analyze and Reflect	Analyze the data to identify key factors that contributed to the success of the culturally responsive literacy ecosystem. Reflect on how these factors might be replicated or adapted in other contexts.
4	Share and Disseminate	Publish the case studies and examples in educational journals, at conferences, and through professional networks to share best practices and inspire others to adopt similar approaches.
5	Implement and Adapt	Use the insights gained from these case studies to inform and guide the development of culturally responsive literacy ecosystems in other schools or districts, adjusting practices based on the specific needs and contexts of the new setting.

LESSONS LEARNED FROM REAL-WORLD APPLICATIONS

Lessons learned from real-world applications of culturally responsive literacy ecosystems refer to the insights and knowledge gained through the practical implementation of these ecosystems in various educational settings. These lessons encompass the successes, challenges, and effective practices that emerge from the experiences of educators, students, and communities as they work to create inclusive and culturally affirming literacy environments. They provide a valuable repository of wisdom that can inform future efforts to enhance educational equity and student achievement (Elberzhager, et al, 2021). To extract and apply lessons learned from real-world applications of culturally responsive literacy ecosystems, stakeholders can undertake the following steps as shown in table 10. By systematically extracting and applying these lessons, educators and policymakers can better equip themselves to create and sustain literacy ecosystems that are truly responsive to the cultural diversity of their students, leading to more equitable and effective educational experiences.

Table 10. Steps to extract and apply lessons learned from real-world applications of culturally responsive literacy ecosystems

Number	Step	Elaboration
1	Review and Reflect	Conduct thorough reviews of existing case studies, research, and reports to identify key takeaways and reflect on their relevance to the local educational context.
2	Engage in Dialogue	Foster discussions with educators, students, and community members who have direct experience with culturally responsive practices to gain firsthand insights and perspectives.
3	Identify Best Practices	Isolate the strategies and approaches that have consistently led to positive outcomes across different settings and consider how these can be adapted to fit local needs.
4	Iterate and Improve	Use the lessons learned to refine and improve current practices, recognizing that the process of cultural responsiveness is ongoing and requires continuous adaptation.
5	Disseminate Findings	Share the lessons learned with a broader audience through professional development, workshops, and publications to promote a wider understanding and application of culturally responsive literacy ecosystems.

How to Apply These Insights in Diverse Educational Settings

Applying insights from culturally responsive literacy ecosystems in diverse educational settings involves leveraging the knowledge and strategies gained from successful implementations to inform and improve literacy instruction across a variety of school environments. This process recognizes the heterogeneity of educational contexts and aims to adapt best practices to meet the unique needs of different student populations, whether they are urban, rural, suburban, or international (Mirra, & Garcia, 2021). To apply these insights effectively in diverse educational settings, educators and administrators should follow suggestions as proposed in table 11. By taking these steps, educators can ensure that the insights from culturally responsive literacy ecosystems are applied in a way that respects and empowers the diverse students they serve, leading to more inclusive and effective educational outcomes.

Table 11. Suggestions on applying insights effectively in diverse educational settings

Number	Suggestion	Elaboration
1	Assess the Specific Context	Begin by understanding the cultural, linguistic, and socioeconomic characteristics of the student body and the community. This assessment will guide the selection and adaptation of culturally responsive strategies.
2	Customize Implementation Plans	Tailor the implementation of culturally responsive literacy practices to the specific context. This may involve modifying curriculum, adjusting teaching methods, and selecting resources that resonate with the local culture and student experiences.
3	Provide Ongoing Professional Development	Offer continuous training for educators to build their capacity to implement culturally responsive practices. This should include both foundational knowledge and practical skills.
4	Foster Collaborative Relationships	Encourage collaboration among teachers, students, families, and community members to create a supportive network that values and integrates diverse cultural perspectives into the educational process.
5	Monitor and Evaluate Progress	Regularly assess the impact of culturally responsive practices on student learning and engagement. Use this data to make informed adjustments and to celebrate successes.

CONCLUSION

This chapter underscores the imperative of culturally responsive literacy practices in today's diverse educational landscape, advocating for the design and implementation of literacy ecosystems that respect and reflect all learners' cultural backgrounds. It outlines a comprehensive framework for creating such ecosystems, emphasizing the integration of curriculum, instruction, assessment, and classroom management strategies that honor students' identities and promote social justice. The chapter also underscores the collaborative role of families and communities and provides practical advice and case studies to guide educators in fostering authentic partnerships and implementing transformative culturally responsive literacy practices in their schools. The future of culturally responsive literacy lies in an educational landscape where diverse voices and experiences are not only included but celebrated, fostering inclusive classrooms that honor the backgrounds and identities of all students. By integrating a wide array of literature that reflects the multiplicity of cultures, histories, and languages, educators will better equip learners with the critical thinking skills needed to navigate and contribute to our increasingly globalized world. This approach will not only enhance comprehension and engagement but also empower students to see themselves and others with greater empathy and respect, ultimately bridging societal divides and nurturing a generation of informed, compassionate, and culturally literate individuals (Bang, 2020).

The importance of inclusivity and empowerment in literacy education cannot be overstated; it is the cornerstone of creating a just and equitable society. By embracing a pedagogy that recognizes and values the unique perspectives of every student, we ensure that literacy is not just a tool for academic success but a transformative force that builds confidence, validates cultural narratives, and empowers marginalized communities. This commitment to inclusivity not only enriches the educational experience for all but also paves the way for a future where every voice is heard and every individual is equipped to participate fully in the social, economic, and cultural fabric of our world (Tariq, 2024). In Malaysia's higher education sector, this commitment to cultural responsiveness in literacy ecosystems is exemplified by the establishment of dedicated centers for Indigenous knowledge and the integration of multicultural content across various disciplines. These efforts underscore the nation's dedication to ensuring that its diverse ethnic groups are not only represented but also empowered through education, thereby strengthening the foundation for a more inclusive and equitable society.

REFERENCES

Akiva, T., Delale-O'Connor, L., & Pittman, K. J. (2023). The promise of building equitable ecosystems for learning. *Urban Education*, 58(6), 1271–1297. DOI: 10.1177/0042085920926230

Alim, H. S., Paris, D., & Wong, C. P. (2020). Culturally sustaining pedagogy: A critical framework for centering communities. In *Handbook of the cultural foundations of learning* (pp. 261–276). Routledge. DOI: 10.4324/9780203774977-18

Atenas, J., Havemann, L., & Timmermann, C. (2020). Critical literacies for a datafied society: Academic development and curriculum design in higher education.

Bang, M. (2020). Learning on the move toward just, sustainable, and culturally thriving futures. *Cognition and Instruction*, 38(3), 434–444. DOI: 10.1080/07370008.2020.1777999

Burden, P. R. (2020). *Classroom management: Creating a successful K-12 learning community*. John Wiley & Sons.

Caldera, A., Whitaker, M. C., & Conrad Popova, D. A. (2020). Classroom management in urban schools: Proposing a course framework. *Teaching Education*, 31(3), 343–361. DOI: 10.1080/10476210.2018.1561663

Cerna, L., Mezzanotte, C., Rutigliano, A., Brussino, O., Santiago, P., Borgonovi, F., & Guthrie, C. (2021). Promoting inclusive education for diverse societies: A conceptual framework.

Chan, C. K. Y., & Luo, J. (2022). Exploring teacher perceptions of different types of 'feedback practices' in higher education: Implications for teacher feedback literacy. *Assessment & Evaluation in Higher Education*, 47(1), 61–76. DOI: 10.1080/02602938.2021.1888074

Chong, S. W. (2021). Reconsidering student feedback literacy from an ecological perspective. *Assessment & Evaluation in Higher Education*, 46(1), 92–104. DOI: 10.1080/02602938.2020.1730765

Cross, R., D'warte, J., & Slaughter, Y. (2022). Plurilingualism and language and literacy education. *Australian Journal of Language and Literacy*, 45(3), 341–357. DOI: 10.1007/s44020-022-00023-1

De Abreu, B. S. (Ed.). (2022). *Media literacy, equity, and justice*. Routledge. DOI: 10.4324/9781003175599

DeVries, B. A. (2023). *Literacy assessment and intervention for classroom teachers.* Routledge. DOI: 10.4324/9781003230397

Elberzhager, F., Mennig, P., Polst, S., Scherr, S., & Stüpfert, P. (2021). Towards a digital ecosystem for a smart city district: Procedure, results, and lessons learned. *Smart Cities*, 4(2), 686–716. DOI: 10.3390/smartcities4020035

Emery, N. C., Bledsoe, E. K., Hasley, A. O., & Eaton, C. D. (2021). Cultivating inclusive instructional and research environments in ecology and evolutionary science. *Ecology and Evolution*, 11(4), 1480–1491. DOI: 10.1002/ece3.7062 PMID: 33613983

Haagen-Schützenhöfer, C., & Hopf, M. (2020). Design-based research as a model for systematic curriculum development: The example of a curriculum for introductory optics. *Physical Review. Physics Education Research*, 16(2), 020152. DOI: 10.1103/PhysRevPhysEducRes.16.020152

Häggström, M., & Schmidt, C. (2021). Futures literacy–to belong, participate and act!: An educational perspective. *Futures*, 132, 102813. DOI: 10.1016/j.futures.2021.102813

Hanell, F. (2020). Co-learning in a digital community: information literacy and views on learning in pre-school teacher education. In Sustainable Digital Communities: 15th International Conference, iConference 2020, Boras, Sweden, March 23–26, 2020 [Springer International Publishing.]. *Proceedings*, 15, 327–342.

Hannon, P., Nutbrown, C., & Morgan, A. (2020). Effects of extending disadvantaged families' teaching of emergent literacy. *Research Papers in Education*, 35(3), 310–336. DOI: 10.1080/02671522.2019.1568531

Harrison, N., & Skrebneva, I. (2020). Country as pedagogical: Enacting an Australian foundation for culturally responsive pedagogy. *Journal of Curriculum Studies*, 52(1), 15–26. DOI: 10.1080/00220272.2019.1641843

Jackson, C., Mohr-Schroeder, M. J., Bush, S. B., Maiorca, C., Roberts, T., Yost, C., & Fowler, A. (2021). Equity-oriented conceptual framework for K-12 STEM literacy. *International Journal of STEM Education*, 8(1), 1–16. DOI: 10.1186/s40594-021-00294-z

Kellogg, S. (2021). *Urban ecosystem justice: Strategies for equitable sustainability and ecological literacy in the city*. Routledge. DOI: 10.4324/9780367858711

Kelty, N. E., & Wakabayashi, T. (2020). Family engagement in schools: Parent, educator, and community perspectives. *SAGE Open*, 10(4), 2158244020973024. DOI: 10.1177/2158244020973024

Kitchen, J. A., Perez, R., Hallett, R., Kezar, A., & Reason, R. (2021). Ecological validation model of student success: A new student support model for promoting college success among low-income, first-generation, and racially minoritized students. *Journal of College Student Development*, 62(6), 627–642. DOI: 10.1353/csd.2021.0062

Lähdesmäki, T., Baranova, J., Ylönen, S. C., Koistinen, A. K., Mäkinen, K., Juškiene, V., & Zaleskiene, I. (2022). *Learning cultural literacy through creative practices in schools: Cultural and multimodal approaches to meaning-making*. Springer Nature. DOI: 10.1007/978-3-030-89236-4

Lutnæs, E. (2020). Empowering responsible design literacy: Identifying narratives in a new curriculum.

Minor, C. (2023). *Best practices in literacy instruction*. Guilford Publications.

Mirra, N., & Garcia, A. (2021). In search of the meaning and purpose of 21st-century literacy learning: A critical review of research and practice. *Reading Research Quarterly*, 56(3), 463–496. DOI: 10.1002/rrq.313

Morton, T. (2020). Cognitive discourse functions: A bridge between content, literacy and language for teaching and assessment in CLIL. *CLIL Journal of Innovation and Research in Plurilingual and Pluricultural Education*, 3(1), 7–17. DOI: 10.5565/rev/clil.33

Nichols, T. P., & LeBlanc, R. J. (2021). Media education and the limits of "literacy": Ecological orientations to performative platforms. *Curriculum Inquiry*, 51(4), 389–412. DOI: 10.1080/03626784.2020.1865104

O'neil, J. M., Newton, R. J., Bone, E. K., Birney, L. B., Green, A. E., Merrick, B., Goodwin-Segal, T., Moore, G., & Fraioli, A. (2020). Using urban harbors for experiential, environmental literacy: Case studies of New York and Chesapeake Bay. *Regional Studies in Marine Science*, 33, 100886. DOI: 10.1016/j.rsma.2019.100886

Pahl, K., & Rowsell, J. (2020). *Living literacies: Literacy for social change*. MiT Press. DOI: 10.7551/mitpress/11375.001.0001

Shah, R. W. (2020). *Rewriting partnerships: Community perspectives on community-based learning*. University Press of Colorado.

Shapiro, S., Beninger, S., Domegan, C., Reppel, A., Stanton, J., & Watson, F. (2021). Macromarketing pedagogy: Empowering students to achieve a sustainable world. *Journal of Macromarketing*, 41(1), 104–115. DOI: 10.1177/0276146720949637

Tanase, M. (2020). Is good teaching culturally responsive? *Journal of Pedagogical Research*, 4(3), 187–202. DOI: 10.33902/JPR.2020063333

Tariq, M. U. (2024). Equity and Inclusion in Learning Ecosystems. In Preparing Students for the Future Educational Paradigm (pp. 155-176). IGI Global. DOI: 10.4018/979-8-3693-1536-1.ch007

Watts-Taffe, S. (2022). Multimodal literacies: Fertile ground for equity, inclusion, and connection. *The Reading Teacher*, 75(5), 603–609. DOI: 10.1002/trtr.2080

Wu, S., & Lin, C. Y. Y. (2020). *Innovation and entrepreneurship in an educational ecosystem: Cases from Taiwan*. Springer Nature.

ADDITIONAL READINGS

Almufareh, M. F., Kausar, S., Humayun, M., & Tehsin, S. (2024). A conceptual model for inclusive technology: Advancing disability inclusion through artificial intelligence. *Journal of Disability Research*, 3(1), 20230060. DOI: 10.57197/JDR-2023-0060

Becken, S., & Coghlan, A. (2024). Knowledge alone won't "fix it": Building regenerative literacy. *Journal of Sustainable Tourism*, 32(2), 385–401. DOI: 10.1080/09669582.2022.2150860

Häggström, M., & Schmidt, C. (2021). Futures literacy–to belong, participate and act!: An educational perspective. *Futures*, 132, 102813. DOI: 10.1016/j.futures.2021.102813

Heck, T., Kullmann, S., Hiebl, J., Schröder, N., Otto, D., & Sander, P. (2020). Designing open informational ecosystems on the concept of open educational resources. *Open Education Studies*, 2(1), 252–264. DOI: 10.1515/edu-2020-0130

Judijanto, L., Aini, M. A., Asfahani, A., Sain, Z. H., & Vandika, A. Y. (2022). Utilization AI for Socially Responsive Education as a Path to Inclusive Development. *Journal of Artificial Intelligence and Development*, 1(2), 69–78.

Persson, K., Andrée, M., & Caiman, C. (2022). Down-to-earth ecological literacy through human and nonhuman encounters in fieldwork. *The Journal of Environmental Education*, 53(2), 99–116. DOI: 10.1080/00958964.2022.2046534

Roshanaei, M., Olivares, H., & Lopez, R. R. (2023). Harnessing AI to foster equity in education: Opportunities, challenges, and emerging strategies. *Journal of Intelligent Learning Systems and Applications*, 15(04), 123–143. DOI: 10.4236/jilsa.2023.154009

Saborío-Taylor, S., & Rojas-Ramírez, F. (2024). Universal design for learning and artificial intelligence in the digital era: Fostering inclusion and autonomous learning. *International Journal of Professional Development, Learners and Learning, 62.*

Tariq, M. U. (2024a). Equity and Inclusion in Learning Ecosystems. In Preparing Students for the Future Educational Paradigm (pp. 155-176). IGI Global. DOI: 10.4018/979-8-3693-1536-1.ch007

Tariq, M. U. (2024b). Empowering Educators in the Learning Ecosystem. In Preparing Students for the Future Educational Paradigm (pp. 232-255). IGI Global. DOI: 10.4018/979-8-3693-1536-1.ch010

KEY TERMS AND DEFINITIONS

Cultural responsiveness: The ability of educational practices to recognize, include, and affirm the cultural assets and backgrounds of all students, ensuring that teaching is respectful of and relevant to diverse cultural experiences.

Diverse perspectives: A range of viewpoints and experiences that arise from differences in race, ethnicity, gender, age, religion, ability, sexual orientation, socioeconomic status, and other human dimensions.

Empowerment: The process by which individuals and groups gain control over their own lives and circumstances, often through the acquisition of knowledge, skills, and resources, leading to increased autonomy and self-determination.

Equitable education: An approach to education that ensures all students have access to the resources and educational opportunities they need to succeed, regardless of their background or circumstances, thereby aiming to reduce and ultimately eliminate achievement gaps.

Inclusivity: The state of being inclusive, where diversity is valued, and all individuals feel respected, accepted, and have equal opportunities to participate and succeed.

Literacy ecosystems: A comprehensive framework that encompasses all the interconnected elements—such as educational institutions, community resources, and policy environments—that contribute to the development of literacy skills within a community.

Chapter 13
Integrating Artificial Intelligence to Foster Inclusivity in Social Work and Community Development Education:
A Transatlantic Online Collaboration

Jennifer Lanham
Campbellsville University, USA

Garreth Smith
https://orcid.org/0009-0001-3725-5299
Technological University Dublin, Ireland

ABSTRACT

This chapter explores the integration of artificial intelligence (AI) into social work and community work education to foster an inclusive learning environment. By aligning with both the Council on Social Work Education's mandates, and the All-Ireland Standards for Community Work Education, educators leverage AI tools to design competency-based educational frameworks that emphasize anti-racism, diversity, equity, and inclusion. Incorporating AI elevates education quality, empowering a diverse student body to flourish in nurturing learning communities. Through a transatlantic collaboration between Campbellsville University in the United States and Technological University Dublin in Ireland, this chapter examines the practical application of these technologies and their impact on social work and community

DOI: 10.4018/979-8-3373-1017-6.ch013

work education.

INTRODUCTION

In an era when social work and community work education seeks to center anti-racism, diversity, equity, and inclusion (ADEI), artificial intelligence (AI) emerges as a transformative tool. This chapter delves into how educators leverage AI to tailor teaching and learning experiences, ensuring adherence to the Council on Social Work Education's (CSWE's) core competencies, the National Association of Social Work's ethical standards, and All-Ireland Standards for Community Work Education (AIEB). Integrating AI into social work and community work realms demands an ethical, intentional approach that personalizes education across diverse student landscapes. The survey research project described in this chapter aims to investigate how AI and collaborative platforms contribute to the creation of inclusive teaching and learning environments in both social work and community work education. The project will focus on evaluating the impact of the technologies on student engagement, diversity, and inclusion, with specific reference to the CSWE Educational Policy and Accreditation Standards (EPAS) and the (AIEB) requirements.

CHAPTER OBJECTIVES

- Explore the influence of AI on social work and community work education.
- Evaluate the effectiveness of AI in enhancing personalized and inclusive teaching and learning experiences.
- Examine the ethical considerations associated with AI integration.
- Illustrate AI's role in tailoring learning experiences to diverse student needs.
- Assess the role of collaborative platforms in promoting diversity, inclusivity, and student interaction.
- Gather perceptions of social work and community work students and faculty regarding the use of AI and collaborative platforms in their educational experiences.
- Examine the alignment of these technological tools with CSWE's ADEI principles, and AIEB's principles of Human Rights, Equality, Anti-Discrimination, Social Justice, Sustainable Development, Participation, Collectivity and Community Engagement (CSWE, 2021; AIEB, 2016).

BACKGROUND

The Importance of Creating Diverse Learning Environments

What Does "Inclusivity" Mean in Education? Imagine a classroom that ensures that all students, no matter who they are or where they come from, have the tools and help they need to achieve. This creates a welcoming environment that fosters personal and academic growth. The benefits of such a setting are immense, leading to improved academic performance and a more positive learning environment. Traditional teaching methods may not adequately prepare students for a diverse world with varying needs. These programs often do not make it easy for students with different learning styles to access them, which can make some students feel alone or uninterested. These obstacles, whether practical, such as not having enough accessible features, or educational, such as not having diverse curricula, can stop students from reaching their best potential. Students who feel like they fit in are more likely to put effort into their schoolwork, and their grades show they are doing well. This is also true for students from underrepresented groups (Walton & Cohen, 2011). Recognizing and understanding inclusivity is not just a "nice-to-have"—it is significant for success. For example, even if a classroom seems welcoming, students may not feel appreciated or supported if inclusivity works only on surface-level diversity projects and does not deal with deeper systemic issues of bias and discrimination. This lack of inclusion can hurt students' performance instead of helping them. Educators, administrators, and policymakers play a crucial role in addressing these systemic issues, empowering them to make a positive change.

How Has Technology Improved Educational Settings?

Platforms that use AI are changing how we teach and how students learn. Technology is not just a tool in social and community work schooling; it is a way to connect theory with practice in the real world. What can AI do to help? For one thing, it helps students learn to think critically and solve problems in ways that traditional methods might not be able to. It offers flexible learning experiences adapted to different learning styles. It is not enough to make school easier; we must also make it fair. AI levels the playing field by giving each student individualized help, fair tests, and valuable feedback that helps guide them on their unique path through school (Zharova et al., 2021). AI can make personalized quizzes and engaging models for people who learn best by seeing, and it can offer audio recordings and text-to-speech choices for people who learn best by hearing. This makes the classroom a better place for everyone to learn by letting students with different learning styles interact with the information in a way that works best for them.

MAIN FOCUS OF THE CHAPTER

Exploring the Use of AI and Collaborative Platforms in Teaching Social Work and Community Work

AI in education is both good and bad. On the one hand, it offers the opportunity to take enormous steps forward; on the other hand, it raises important moral questions. How can we ensure that AI tools do not violate privacy, are not biased, and stay open to communication and innovative ideas? One big worry is that AI could replace human educators, which many of us find unsettling. However, here is the thing: AI is not meant to replace instructors; it is meant to help them. Balancing AI and human interaction are crucial. Also, all students, regardless of their family income, should have equal access to AI technology so that they can all gain from what it can do. AI can help educators in essential ways, but it can only partially replace the human link and one-on-one care instructors give. This emphasizes the integral role of human educators in the age of AI, making the students feel valued. AI should not replace educators in the classroom; it should work with them.

If AI is going to change how we teach, we need to ensure that instructors are ready for it. The consequences of educators lacking the necessary tools for AI integration in the classroom must be considered. To ensure that instructors can use these tools to improve learning, they must keep learning and growing as professionals. There have also been discussions about whether AI can help students understand other cultures. We should be careful with this. Are we ready to trust AI to make choices that need careful, human-centered ethical thought? Aside from knowing how AI works technically, instructors also need to know what it means in terms of ethics. For instance, educators might be able to use AI tools well in the classroom only if they are adequately trained in how to do so. This could make it hard for them to incorporate the tools into their lessons and help students benefit and may cause students to miss chances to learn, making it harder for them to build important skills for the future.

One of the most exciting, and scary, things about AI in education is how it changes students' decisions. Does AI give students the power to choose how they learn, or does it gently lead them down paths that have already been planned? It is essential to make sure that AI helps students be independent instead of getting in the way of that. Education approaches should evolve alongside advancements in AI technology. Educators must adapt to ensure that AI enhances learning environments without worsening bias or unfairness. AI can help students be more independent and provide unique learning experiences; however, it may also limit their ability to think critically and be creative by leading them down set paths. AI should help students think for themselves and solve problems, but instructors must carefully watch and control how it is used in the classroom. Imagine a school where students do not just sit and take in information; they also make it the setting where they learn. That is what AI can do. Recent studies showed that AI can personalize educational experiences and simplify routine tasks, allowing more time for students to connect fully with the material (Mollick & Mollick, 2023). What would that look like if we could use this ability to create learning places with students? When students help make these places, especially in social and community work, they feel more like they own, and are responsible for, their learning.

Practical Challenges and Ethical Concerns in AI Adoption for Educational Institutions

As artificial intelligence in the modern world continues to transform and change how industries operate and perform, it's use within educational settings requires a particular focus. Although AI has the potential to enhance both teaching and learning within universities, it's use within these settings brings practical challenges such as digital infrastructure, resource constraints, and ethical considerations. One of the primary challenges for AI adoption within educational settings is the practical challenge of resources which may include access to reliable technologies that support the implementation of AI driven systems. Educational institutions often face resource constraints, particularly in terms of funding and technical expertise, which can hinder the successful adoption of AI (Bulut et al., 2024; Saputra et al., 2023). Furthermore, students may not have equal access to the latest technologies to support their learning, and may also have different levels of digital literacy, creating the potential for a digital divide and educational inequalities.

While AI offers promising opportunities to enhance learning outcomes, personalize educational experiences, and streamline administrative tasks, its adoption also raises critical ethical concerns that must be carefully addressed (Karpouzis, 2024). Integrating AI into university education brings several ethical challenges, ranging from concerns about data privacy to issues of fairness and accountability. Both the United States Department of Education and the European Commission have both published guidelines to support AI use and it's ethical integration in education, highlighting the potential benefits for both teaching and learning. These ethical guidelines on AI and data usage in teaching and learning are designed to help educators understand the potential that the applications of AI and data usage can have in education and to raise awareness of the possible risks so that they are able to engage positively, critically and ethically with AI systems and exploit their full potential (European Commission, 2022).

Discover the Power of Diverse Learning Environments

In education, inclusivity goes beyond mere acceptance; it involves providing all students with the necessary tools to succeed. What can we do to make spaces that accept differences and enjoy them? The first step is to understand that every student can learn, but they do so in diverse ways. Inclusive education acknowledges this fundamental truth by providing all students with the support they require to excel. One crucial part of modern education is inclusive education, which shows a dedication to ensuring all students can receive and benefit from education (Brusilovsky, 2024; Srivastava, 2023). People who advocate inclusive education believe that everyone can learn and needs help (Makoelle, 2014). Even though inclusive education is important for understanding and supporting diverse ways of learning, it may not always be possible or necessary to celebrate differences in the classroom. Ensuring that all students have the same chances of success is more important than the celebration of differences between people (Chen, Kinshuk, Wei, & Liu, 2011).

Embracing Technology in Teaching

Teaching social work and community work can be challenging for everyone. If our teaching methods need to be updated, how can we prepare students for the varied and challenging fields of social work and community work? Traditional lessons do not always reflect the variety of students we are supposed to teach. Educators can close these gaps by using technology to make classrooms more welcoming, accommodating different learning styles and encouraging more participation (Dillenbourg, 1999). For instance, using virtual reality simulations in social work and community work classes can help students improve their skills at working with people from diverse backgrounds by giving them more experience. Online groups and discussion boards allow students to interact with people with different ideas and share their own outside the classroom.

Fostering Inclusion for Student Success

There is no doubt that students do better in school when they feel supported and honored; however, how can we make sure that every student feels this way? Inclusion is the key to helping all students reach their full potential. By making students feel like they belong, we help them do better in school and improve their general health and happiness, especially those who have felt left out (Walton & Cohen, 2011; D'Mello & Graesser, 2012). Being open to everyone is essential for school progress, but it is not the only thing that makes a difference. A student's outcomes are also affected by their access to tools, teaching quality, and their level of drive.

Leveraging Technology for Inclusive Education

Technology is changing how we teach, especially in social work, community work, and other related areas. Collaborative platforms driven by AI make learning more flexible so that all learning styles can be met, and critical thinking can be improved. How can technology make ideas come to life? By modeling real-life social work and community work situations, technology helps students close the gap between what they learn in school and what they do for a living (Zawacki-Richter et al., 2019; Nguyen, Javela, & Hadwin, 2020). For instance, virtual reality games can put students in situations where they must make moral choices and deal with clients, giving them practical, real-life experiences. Online groups and videoconferencing tools also let students work with experts and peers across the world, broadening their views and knowledge.

Technology can make learning engaging by simulating real-life situations and letting students work together. However, it may also make students less connected to the human side of social work and community work because they may rely too much on virtual interactions instead of developing valuable social skills through real-life experiences. Also, not all students may have access to the technology or internet connections needed for these intensive learning experiences, potentially making it more evident who can afford the most up-to-date technology and who cannot.

Teaching Ways to Promote Diversity, Inclusivity, and Global Citizenship

Educators today must meet the needs of a broad group of students and teach them how to be good global citizens. How can we teach students to be part of a society with many kinds of people? Instructors can use AI and virtual learning to bring together students from all over the world so they can learn about different points of view. This helps students learn the skills they need to be active global citizens (Shulman, 2005; Tichnor-Wagner et al., 2016). UNESCO member countries approved the 2030 Agenda for Sustainable Development in September 2015 (Shulla, K et al, 2020). The agenda asks global citizens, such as many multilateral partners, UN agencies, civil society groups, researchers, and scientists, to help take the long-term steps needed to protect the planet's climate and environment and the well-being of all its people (Bergman, Z. et al, 2018). Sustainable Development Goal 4, to ensure everyone has access to high-quality education and learning, is central to this global effort. This includes early childhood education; primary and secondary education; and technical, vocational, tertiary, and adult education (including adult literacy, numeracy, and work-related skills). Implementing the 2030 Agenda for Sustainable Development project requires a focus on ensuring safe and up-to-date learning environments and supporting regular student attendance. AI can significantly support Sustainable Development Goal 4 by creating inclusive learning environments tailored to students' needs and fostering global citizenship. For instance, AI can ensure that all students get a good education by creating unique learning paths that are based on their needs and skills. AI can also help students work together across borders by putting them in touch with classmates from other countries. This can encourage cultural sharing and foster a sense of being a good global citizen.

USING AI TO ADVANCE INCLUSIVITY

Tailoring Learning with AI

How can we use AI to make schools more welcoming for everyone? AI-powered systems can tailor learning to each student, make managerial chores more manageable, and show the real-time progress of each student (Luckin et al., 2016; Kamalov, Calonge & Gurrib, 2023). This not only lightens the load for educators but also ensures that every student's unique learning needs are met. AI can look at student data to find out how they learn best and what they like, which lets instructors make their lessons more relevant (Graesser et al., 2018). AI can also help break down language barriers by translating for students from various language backgrounds in real time. When students in a school speak different languages, an AI-powered system can provide real-time translations for those who may have trouble understanding what is being said in the primary teaching language. This level of support ensures that all students can fully access the material and take part in all classroom activities and discussions, making schools more welcoming and accessible to all students (Kim, Lee, & Choo, 2022).

Personalized Learning

With AI, students can learn in ways that suit their needs, making personalized learning a reality. AI can look at data about how well students are doing to suggest tools, change challenging tasks, and give each student individual feedback. Individualized care like this helps everyone feel welcome by giving every student the help they need to do well. AI could make learning more personalized, but it also raises worries about data protection and the morality of making decisions about students' education based on algorithms (Ouyang, Wu, Zheng, Zhang, & Jiao, 2023). Also, depending too much on AI could mean that students do not have the chance to connect with real people or get personalized help from their instructors.

Enhanced Cultural Sensitivity and Importance of Inclusion

AI can help people become more culturally competent. It helps students learn how to connect with people from diverse backgrounds by giving them access to different points of view and interactive material. AI-powered scenarios and case studies push students to use what they have learned in ways that are sensitive to other cultures. This makes them more aware and empathic (Ouyang, Xu, & Cukurova, 2023). AI can create situations where students must work with clients from diverse cultures. This gives them a safe way to practice talking to people and fixing problems. Furthermore, AI can look at students' answers and tell them where they need to improve their cultural skills, successfully guiding their learning process (Nguyen, Jarvela, & Hadwin, 2021). Inclusion in education is not optional; it is essential. We are supposed to create a space to learn where every student can do well and add to society, regardless of their background, skills, or experiences. The National Association of Social Work (2023) highlights the critical role of education in social work practice. A welcoming attitude makes this process easier. We should give people who want to become social workers and community workers the tools they need to fight for societal fairness and justice. Nevertheless, even though social work and community work stresses being open to everyone, there are still times when views that need to be heard are not represented or appropriately supported (Singer, Baez, & Rios, 2023).

Collaborative Learning Tools

The changing landscape of education, driven by AI and collaborative learning tools, supports this inclusivity. AI's ability to analyze large datasets and provide personalized feedback is invaluable in education. For example, AI can create models that help students understand diverse cultural contexts (Roscoe et al., 2019). Concurrently, collaborative learning tools enable students worldwide to work together on shared learning experiences (Jarvela et al.,2016). This encourages peer collaboration and aligns with the CSWE EPAS's call for innovative teaching methods that prepare students for the complexities of social work practice (Jones, Smith, & Lee, 2022).

By leveraging AI and interactive learning tools, we can advance inclusivity in education, preparing students to engage with a diverse and interconnected world. These technologies not only support personalized and culturally competent learning but also ensure that every student has the opportunity to succeed.

BUILDING COMMUNITIES AND EMPHASIZING COLLABORATIVE LEARNING

The Power of Collaborative Learning Tools

Regarding contemporary higher education, educators and students working together go far beyond a typical classroom or Zoom call. Collaborative learning tools allow students to interact with their peers in ways that push them to expand learning and improve their understanding of global issues from diverse perspectives. Students now can collaborate and learn together even if they live in various places, have different routines, or are in diverse time zones because collaborative learning platforms allow for real-time and asynchronous contact (Laal & Ghodsi, 2012; Lin & Wang, 2024). Collaborative platforms in education support socially shared regulation of learning, fostering individual and group-level collaboration (Jarvela et al., 2016). However, it is essential to recognize that these platforms also present challenges, including technical and accessibility issues and the necessity for effective communication skills.

Real-World Applications of Collaborative Platforms

Consider an example of a group of students working on a global issue project about homelessness in a social and community work context. Students could share resources and papers using a shared workspace and talk in real time through videoconferencing. They could also have in-depth conversations about policy, ethics, and solutions without meeting in person. For instance, they could discuss the best strategies for supporting homeless individuals in their community. These community platforms mirror standard classrooms and allow for a more fluid and adaptable experience to support active participation and critical thinking (Graesser et al., 2018). Educators play a crucial role in guiding students to work together to discuss and solve problems, just like they will in the workplace, whether this learning takes place on public whiteboards, with project management tools, or when editing documents together. Students learn through platforms like the ones used in real-world practice. Educators are there to guide, navigate, facilitate, and support this learning process. These tools empower students to take charge of their learning, fostering a sense of community and belonging (Kim, Lee & Cho, 2022). This empowerment is crucial in social work and community work, in which teamwork and collaboration are paramount.

TECHNOLOGY-BASED WAYS TO ENCOURAGE COMMUNITY INVOLVEMENT

Collaboration in social work and community work education is not new, but technology has changed how we create and keep up with learning groups (De Weger et al., 2018). It is essential to do this when teaching social work and community work skills because we base everything we do on kindness, support, and understanding. However, how can we encourage these traits in a modern setting?

Virtual Support Systems

Support systems exist for students in virtual learning groups, especially those who might feel alone in real-life settings. Think about a student living in a rural area or balancing family responsibilities with their studies. For these students, being able to connect with others online can mean the difference between feeling alone and being linked to others (Purdy et al., 2023). Discussion boards, group talks, and peer mentoring programs can help students share their experiences, give help, and have deep conversations about their work and studies.

Amplifying Voices Through Technology

In addition, collaborative platforms give students who need more support a special place to find their voice. Some students may feel unsafe speaking up in a real classroom but feel free to do so online. This makes conversations more interesting and fuller of different ideas that show how big the area of social work and community work is. Technology brings us together and amplifies the voices of those who may not otherwise be heard, promoting a sense of inclusivity and value among students (Hartman, Townsend, & Jackson, 2019).

Building Lasting Connections

Virtual groups offer benefits that go beyond the classroom. They help establish connections that can be crucial for students' future careers. These networks provide a platform for seeking advice, collaborating, and fostering professional growth even after graduation, instilling a sense of hope and optimism about the future. Although the platforms may be virtual, the relationships formed are real and enduring (Radovan & Radovan, 2024).

INVESTIGATING THE ROLE OF AI AND COLLABORATIVE PLATFORMS IN ENHANCING INCLUSIVITY IN SOCIAL WORK AND COMMUNITY DEVELOPMENT EDUCATION

The Importance of a Global Mindset

In a rapidly globalizing world, social and community work students need more than just a local perspective—they need a global mindset. Enter the transatlantic online collaboration between Campbellsville University and Technological University Dublin. This innovative partnership breaks down geographical boundaries, allowing students worldwide to unite in one virtual space. The program exemplifies how AI-powered collaborative platforms can bridge international borders, fostering co-regulation in learning (Hardwin, Jarvela, & Miller, 2018; Popenici & Kerr, 2017).

Cultural Exchange and Professional Development

The integration of both cultural exchange and professional development makes this collaboration genuinely unique. Students are not just learning about the social issues in their own country; they are gaining insights into global practices and challenges. Whether discussing immigration policies in Europe or child welfare systems in the United States, students are exposed to diverse perspectives that enrich their understanding of the field. For example, imagine a joint project in which students analyze homelessness in Dublin and Kentucky. They could compare the cultural, economic, and political factors contributing to homelessness in both regions and propose solutions that draw from the strengths of each system (Gallagher, Cook, Tebb, & Berg-Weger, 2003). Through these exchanges, students gain a more nuanced understanding of global social work and community work practices, which is critical in preparing them for an increasingly interconnected world.

The Transatlantic Online Collaboration Program: The Proposed Study

At its core, this program is about much more than academic advancement. It is about fostering personal growth, cultural competence, and a global outlook that will serve students long after graduation. Through AI tools and collaborative platforms, students will be equipped to navigate the complexities of social work and community work in a global context (Singer, Baez, & Rios, 2021).

Measuring Success: A Mixed-Methods Approach

How do we measure the success of such an innovative program? The proposed research project will take a mixed-methods approach, gathering quantitative and qualitative data to assess student performance and engagement. For example, we might look at a metric like academic achievement. However, we will also focus on students' reflections on their experiences and how these have shaped their understanding of global social and community work. This comprehensive assessment approach ensures that we will produce skilled social workers, community workers and global citizens who can tackle complex, cross-cultural issues (Seo et al., 2021; Xu & Ouyang, 2022). In an increasingly interconnected world, where borders blur and communities transcend geographical boundaries, the fields of social work and community work face exciting opportunities and unique challenges. This research project aims to explore how the integration of AI and collaborative platforms can enhance inclusivity in educational settings; specifically, we will focus on the trans-atlantic context, where students and educators from diverse backgrounds engage in online collaboration (Nguyen, Jarvela & Hadwin, 2021). By evaluating the impact of these technologies on student engagement, diversity, and inclusion, we seek to inform pedagogical practices aligned with accreditation standards.

RESEARCH OBJECTIVES AND METHODOLOGY

The central research question driving this project is this: How can AI and collaborative platforms contribute to the creation of inclusive teaching and learning environments in social work and community work education? Our survey research project is designed to investigate this very question, focusing on how AI and collaborative platforms can shape more inclusive learning environments. We will evaluate these technologies' impact on student engagement, diversity, and inclusion, particularly reference to CSWE's EPAS and the AIEB requirements. These standards emphasize inclusivity and diversity, making them crucial benchmarks for assessing the effectiveness of AI in fostering an equitable learning experience (Singer, Baez, & Rios, 2023; National Association of Social Workers, 2023). To achieve this, we have set several objectives. First, we aim to explore the seamless integration of AI tools and collaborative platforms into existing curricula. By examining how these technologies are incorporated we can assess their potential to enhance student experiences (Popenici & Kerr, 2017; Kamalov, Calonge, & Gurrib, 2023). In addition, we seek to evaluate the impact of these technologies on student engagement, diversity, and inclusion—key factors in creating a sense of belonging and cultural competence in educational environments (Nguyen, Jarvela, & Hadwin, 2021). Finally, we will look at how our findings can inform accreditation processes, specifically, how they align with CSWE's EPAS and AIEB requirements, ensuring that social work and community work education remains adaptable and relevant.

Mixed-Methods Approach for Comprehensive Insights

Our research method will have a mixed-methods approach, with a focus on survey research to gather data from a diverse group of participants, including students, educators, and practitioners from both the United States and Ireland. In the quantitative phase, we will distribute surveys to measure student perceptions of AI-integrated learning environments. These surveys will assess engagement levels, satisfaction, and perceived inclusivity while also quantifying the impact on diversity representation (Xu & Ouyang, 2022; Seo et al., 2021). In the qualitative phase, we will conduct interviews with educators and practitioners to explore their nuanced experiences with AI and collaborative platforms. Through these interviews, we aim to uncover challenges, success stories, and best practices for fostering inclusivity in social work and community work education.

Expected Outcomes and Policy Implications

The outcomes of this study are expected to provide evidence-based insights into whether AI and collaborative platforms are truly effective in promoting inclusivity. Our findings will offer practical guidelines for educators on how to integrate AI tools while maintaining a human-centered pedagogy (Nguyen, Jarvela, & Hadwin, 2020). Moreover, the results will have policy implications, informing accreditation bodies, such as CSWE and AIEB, about the evolving educational landscape. By aligning our research with these accreditation standards, we hope to contribute to a more inclusive, adaptive future for social work and community development education.

AI INTEGRATION

AI will be pivotal in shaping the virtual classroom experience. But this is not just about using technology for its own sake; AI is carefully integrated to enhance the learning journey.

Learning Analytics Dashboard

For instance, the Learning Analytics Dashboard provides real-time feedback to students and educators, allowing tailored learning experiences. A Learning Analytics Dashboard (LAD) is a visual tool designed to provide educators and students with actionable insights into learners' performance, behaviors, and progress in educational environments. The dashboard collects and presents data such as engagement, achievement, and participation metrics, helping instructors monitor learning processes and identify areas where students might need support. This tool aids in decision-making and enhances learning outcomes by offering real-time feedback and enabling personalized interventions (Verbert et al., 2013; Graesser et al., 2018). If a student struggles with a particular concept, the AI system can suggest resources or adapt the difficulty level to meet the student's needs.

AI-Powered Discussion Facilitator

The most exciting aspect of AI in this program is its ability to facilitate dialogue across cultures. The AI-Powered Discussion Facilitator ensures that every student's voice is heard, even in large, diverse groups. This tool can highlight key points from discussions, suggest follow-up questions, and even detect when certain voices might be missing from the conversation. An AI-powered discussion facilitator is an artificial intelligence system designed to guide and enhance discussions in educational, professional, or collaborative settings. It uses natural language processing and machine learning to analyze conversation dynamics, suggest relevant questions or topics, and ensure that discussions remain productive and inclusive (Chaudhuri et al., 2020). These facilitators can moderate discussions, encourage participation from quieter members, and help keep the conversation focused on key objectives. By adapting in real-time, AI-powered facilitators can provide tailored feedback, enabling more meaningful and efficient dialogue among participants. In this way, AI does not replace human interaction; it augments it, ensuring that every student feels valued and included.

Philosophy of Co-Creation

What sets this program apart is its philosophy of co-creation. Students are not just passive consumers of knowledge but active participants in shaping the curriculum (Hadwin, Jarvela, & Miller, 2018). This could mean anything from suggesting new topics for discussion to co-designing assessment methods. This sense of ownership is critical in fostering engagement and motivation (Johnson & Johnson, 2009).

Participatory Approach and Benefits

This participatory approach benefits students and enriches the program. When students bring their own experiences, backgrounds, and perspectives into the learning process, the result is a dynamic, inclusive curriculum relevant to the challenges social and community workers face today (Popenici & Kerr, 2017). The benefits of this program are clear: Students will gain academic knowledge and develop a global mindset that is essential for navigating the complexities of social and community work in the 21st century. From virtual field trips that provide real-world context, to cross-cultural group projects that foster collaboration, students will leave this program with a well-rounded, global perspective on the field (Purdy et al., 2023). Moreover, by taking part in this collaborative program, students will develop a deep understanding of their role as change agents. They will learn to work across borders, cultures, and systems to effect change in an interconnected world (Jarvela et al., 2023). That is what social work and community work are all about.

Commitment to Cultural Competence

One of this program's most significant strengths is its commitment to cultural competence. Navigating the ethical and cultural complexities of global social work and community work practice requires sensitivity, respect, and a willingness to learn (Graesser et al., 2018). The project's dedicated module on cultural competence is designed to provide students with the tools to critically reflect on their biases, assumptions, and practices (Gallagher et al., 2003). Through case studies, role-playing scenarios, and reflective discussions, students will confront the cultural implications of their actions and decisions globally. For example, they will consider how one navigates issues like consent or confidentiality when working with communities that have diverse cultural norms. Students will grapple with these kinds of real-world issues in the program (Kamalov, Calonge, & Gurrib, 2023).

Addressing Ethical Dilemmas

Of course, a discussion of AI in education would not be complete if it does not address the ethical dilemmas it raises. Privacy, consent, and bias are just a few of the critical issues that will be explored in the program. Students will be encouraged to think critically about AI's potential risks and benefits, particularly in fields as sensitive as social and community work (Hodgson et al., 2022). By engaging with these dilemmas, students will leave the program not only technologically proficient but also ethically conscious (Singer et al.,2021).

Commitment to Ethical Considerations

This program's commitment to ethical considerations sets it apart. Integrating AI into the classroom is not enough; we must do so in a way that respects the core values of social work: integrity, respect, and social justice (National Association of Social Workers, 2023). The program's commitment to inclusivity, respect, and diversity is not just theoretical; it is woven into the very fabric of the learning environment (Richardson et al., 2017). The program charter, coauthored by students and faculty, will reflect the learning community's collective values and ethos. This will ensure that every student feels safe, valued, and respected in the classroom and online interactions.

TRANSFORMATIVE USES OF AI AND COLLABORATIVE PLATFORMS

Learning Analytics Dashboards (LAD)

At Georgia State University, the use of Learning Analytics Dashboards (LAD) has transformed the virtual classroom experience. These dashboards collect and present data on student engagement, achievement, and participation metrics, providing real-time feedback to both students and educators. This system has allowed for the early identification of at-risk students and the implementation of tailored interventions, which have notably improved retention and graduation rates (Verbert et al., 2013; Graesser et al., 2018).

AI-Powered Discussion Facilitators

At the University of California, Irvine, an AI-powered discussion facilitator is used in online courses to ensure active student participation. This tool analyzes conversation dynamics in discussion forums, highlights key points, suggests follow-up questions, and ensures that every student's voice is heard. It encourages quieter students to participate, fostering a more inclusive and dynamic class environment (Chaudhuri et al., 2020).

Co-Creation in Curriculum Design

The University of Helsinki provides an exemplary model of co-creation in curriculum design. By involving students in the curriculum design process, the university has created a more engaging and relevant educational experience. Students contribute by suggesting new topics and co-designing assessment methods, which increases their motivation and ownership of their learning process. This participatory approach not only benefits students but also enriches the overall program (Hadwin, Jarvela, & Miller, 2018).

Virtual Field Trips and Cross-Cultural Projects

In the context of global social work education, the University of Sydney has integrated virtual field trips and cross-cultural group projects into their curriculum. These activities provide students with real-world context and foster collaboration across cultures. Students report enhanced understanding of cultural competence and a more inclusive learning experience, demonstrating the ability of AI-facilitated programs to bridge cultural divides and prepare students for global social work (Purdy et al., 2023).

Learning Outcomes

These examples illustrate the potential of AI and collaborative platforms to create inclusive, engaging, and ethically sound learning environments. They provide evidence-based insights and practical guidelines that align with your research objectives, demonstrating how these technologies can shape the future of social work and community work education. By examining these implementations, we can develop strategies to effectively integrate these technologies into our curricula, ensuring that social work education remains adaptive, relevant, and inclusive, ultimately contributing to a more equitable learning experience.

Assessment and Evaluation

The program's framework is designed with well-articulated learning outcomes, such as enhanced engagement in ADEI practices, ability to make ethical decisions, and adaptability to technological advancements (Jones et al., 2022). These outcomes will ensure that each educational encounter is purposeful and synergistic with the broader pedagogical goals. The program will also include robust student participation through dynamic activities and introspective exercises, bridging the gap between theoretical knowledge and practical application.

Formative and Summative Assessments

Students will be assessed through formative and summative assessments, including reflective journals, group projects, and presentations. These assessments will encourage critical thinking and self-reflection, helping students develop a deeper understanding of the material and its relevance to their future practice. The program will also include peer feedback and self-assessment opportunities, allowing students to take an active part in learning and development (Xu & Ouyang, 2022).

Research Project Insights

The research project predicts significant enhancements in student involvement and a profound comprehension of cultural intricacies, fostering a diverse and inclusive educational milieu (Dillenbourg, 1999). This study will explore the complexities of incorporating AI into social and community work education, addressing critical issues such as ethical dilemmas, data privacy concerns, and the imperative for digital ability among students and educators.

Proactive strategies will be delineated to navigate these challenges effectively, ensuring that integrating technological advancements enriches the educational experience while upholding the core values of social work and community work education (Zhang et al., 2022). The insights gleaned from this study are expected to have a transformative impact on how technology shapes the evolution of social and community work education and practice.

Mode for Integration

The program will serve as a model for other institutions looking to integrate AI and collaborative platforms into their social work and community work curricula. By sharing the findings and best practices from this study, the program will contribute to the broader discourse on the role of technology in education and help shape the future of social work and community work education on a global scale.

FOCUS ON SELF-REFLECTION AND CULTURAL HUMILITY

This program will go beyond academic development at its essence; it also will focus on encouraging self-reflection with a touch of cultural humility and an anti-racist and anti-oppressive mindset that will help students even after they graduate (Radovan & Radovan, 2024). By using AI tools and working together on platforms, students can effectively engage globally with the intricate aspects of social work and community involvement (Wang et al., 2023).

The Study We Are Planning

The study we are planning will combine methods to collect descriptive data to evaluate how well students are doing and how engaged they are in their studies. For instance, we could examine measures such as success; however, we will also pay attention to what students think about their experiences and how those experiences have influenced their ideas about international social work and community work. This thorough evaluation approach is designed to help us educate professionals who can tackle various complex cross-cultural challenges effectively (Xu & Ouyang, 2022; Hartman Townsend & Jackson, 2019).

Enhancing Learning Experiences Through AI Integration

AI will play a crucial role in positively transforming the virtual classroom environment by thoughtfully integrating technology to enrich the learning process instead of merely for the sake of using it alone. One example is the Learning Analytics Dashboard mentioned earlier, which offers instant feedback to students and teachers to create a personalized and dynamic learning environment through collaborative efforts. When a student meets challenges with a topic or problem area, the Learning Analytics Dashboard tool recommends relevant resources or adjusts the difficulty level to effectively match the student's requirements (Verbert et al., 2013; Graesser et al., 2018).

Facilitating Cross-Cultural Communication

One of the exciting things about AI in this educational program is how it helps people from diverse cultures communicate better with each other. The AI-Powered Discussion Facilitator mentioned earlier ensures that students can speak up and share their thoughts in large and diverse groups. This tool can pick out points from discussions, suggest new questions to keep the conversation going, and even notice when some voices are not being heard (Chaudhuri et al., 2020). By doing this, AI does not take over interaction; instead, it enhances it by ensuring every student is included and appreciated (Nguyen, Jarvela, & Hadwin, 2020).

WHAT SETS THIS PROJECT APART

What sets this project apart is its philosophy of co-creation. Students play an active role in shaping the curriculum rather than passively receiving knowledge. This could include students suggesting new topics for discussion and helping with co-designing assessment methods. A student's sense of ownership is critical in fostering engagement and motivation (Johnson & Johnson, 2009). After all, who is more invested in their learning than the students themselves? When students bring their lived experiences, backgrounds, and perspectives into the learning process, the result is a dynamic, inclusive curriculum relevant to the challenges social workers and community workers face today (Hadwin, Jarvela, & Miller, 2018).

Enhancing a Global Perspective

The advantages of this program are clear and essential. Students can acquire expertise while fostering a worldly outlook crucial for tackling the intricacies of social and community endeavors in this modern era. They can also broaden their understanding by taking part in virtual excursions and engaging in cross-cultural initiatives to deepen their insight into the field (Purdy et al., 2023).

Developing Change Agents

Furthermore, engaging in this initiative will give students a profound insight into their responsibility as catalysts for change. They will acquire the skills to collaborate across boundaries, be they cultural, geographical, or institutional, and drive transformation in a globally interconnected society (Kim, Lee, & Cho, 2022). Does this not encapsulate the essence of social work and community work?

COMMITMENT TO CULTURAL COMPETENCE AND HUMILITY

One of this program's most significant strengths is its commitment to cultural competence and humility. To navigate the ethical and cultural challenges inherent to global social work and community work, one needs self-awareness, reflection, and an appreciation of diversity (Gallagher et al., 2023; Hodgson et al., 2022). This project's curriculum will include dedicated modules on cultural competence designed to provide students with the tools to reflect critically and with humility on their biases, assumptions, and practices.

Educational Considerations and the Role of Instructors in Harmonizing the Integration of Technology and Teaching Methods

In a rapidly changing education system, the best teaching approach is to combine technology with traditional methods. However, we must consider how AI can assist educators without undermining the essential human connections in schools. Striking the right balance is crucial, and teachers must exercise caution in integrating AI into the classroom. We should leverage technology to enhance student learning rather than allowing technology to dictate our actions (Kim, Lee & Cho, 2022, Jarvela et al., 2023).

Curriculum Planning with AI Integration

Planning the curriculum is essential here. If you want to use technology in the classroom, it must fit the learning results and goals. Educators need to think about how AI tools can help with the main goals of their classes instead of getting in the way of them (Chen et al., 2011). For example, AI can help students with different learning styles by changing material to meet their individual needs. In addition, instructors need to keep their own learning to feel confident in their abilities to use AI tools correctly, fix problems, and constantly change their lessons to keep up with technological changes (Brusilovsky, 2024).

THE ROLE OF EDUCATORS IN GUIDING INTERACTIONS WITH AI

Facilitating Critical Thinking

What should instructors do in a school where AI is used? At first glance, there is a chance that AI could teach many things; however, AI is only as valuable as the information given by the teacher (Roscoe et al., 2019). Educators need to help students understand and make sense of insights created by AI and guide them to think critically about the knowledge AI gives them. Students need to learn how to ask the right questions, such as "How reliable are these data?" "What kinds of flaws could exist in AI algorithms?" and "How could this knowledge help me choose as a future social worker or community worker?" (Graesser & D'Mello, 2012; Gallagher et al., 2003).

Encouraging Deep Thinking

Educators play a pivotal role in managing AI-driven inclusivity. They must ensure that AI tools are used to complement, rather than replace, human interaction. Instructors should guide students in critically assessing AI-generated insights and help them understand the ethical implications of AI (Singer et al., 2023). By fostering a human-centered approach to AI integration, educators can mitigate the risk of reinforcing inequalities. Instructors can help students learn how to use AI tools by creating a setting that encourages questioning and deep thinking. Technology should add to the learning experience instead of taking away from it (Kim, Lee, & Cho, 2022). After all, technology is only as useful as the critical eye we use to look at it.

BALANCING AI IN EDUCATION AND HUMAN INTERACTIONS

Striking a Balanced Perspective

AI has the capacity to revolutionize education by providing personalized learning experiences, automating administrative tasks, and facilitating inclusive learning environments. Tools such as AI-powered learning analytics dashboards can offer real-time feedback, helping educators tailor their teaching strategies to meet individual student needs (Verbert et al., 2013; Graesser et al., 2018). Despite these advantages, AI is not without its limitations. Over-reliance on AI can lead to a depersonalized learning experience, where human interaction is diminished. Moreover, AI algorithms can perpetuate existing biases if not carefully managed. For instance, an AI system trained on biased data can reinforce stereotypes and inequalities, rather than alleviating them (Nguyen, Jarvela, & Hadwin, 2020). Educators play a pivotal role in managing AI-driven inclusivity. They must ensure that AI tools are used to complement, rather than replace, human interaction. Instructors should guide students in critically assessing AI-generated insights and help them understand the ethical implications of AI (Singer et al., 2023). By fostering a human-centered approach to AI integration, educators can mitigate the risk of reinforcing inequalities.

Maintaining Human Connections

Educators who are already busy will appreciate that AI can help with routine tasks but let us be clear: AI should never replace human contact in the classroom. Connecting personally with the instructor, getting advice and mental support, and giving thoughtful feedback cannot be programmed into a computer (Singer et al., 2023). Can AI cheer students on when they are having a challenging time, or help them see the bigger picture when they have too many details? Not really. That is where educators of people shine.

Prioritizing Human Aspects

When you use AI, educators should allocate more time and space for these human aspects. AI can free up instructors to do what they do best—building relationships with students, giving them advice, and encouraging them to think critically—by automating boring jobs such as marking papers or keeping track of attendance (Chen et al., 2011). This means using AI to give real-time comments, keep track of each student's progress, and make custom lesson plans. It also means that instructors must be extra careful that AI does not replace the social parts of teaching that are important for building trust and intellectual growth (Jarvela et al., 2023; Johnson & Johnson, 2009).

USING AI FOR DATA ANALYSIS AND EVIDENCE-BASED SUGGESTIONS

Benefits of Data-Driven Insights

One of the most exciting things about AI is that it can look at big data sets and make suggestions that are based on proof. Imagine finding students who are about to fall behind and helping them before it is too late. Alternatively, think about how AI could help educators determine which parts of the program work well and which need to be reviewed (Graesser et al., 2018). Instructors can make better choices about teaching when they have this kind of data-driven knowledge (Dillenbourg, 1999; Ouyang et al., 2023).

Enhancing Social Work and Community Work Education

AI's ability to analyze social data significantly affects how social work and community work are taught. For example, AI can predict how policy changes will impact at-risk populations. This demonstrates to students how data can improve social and community work practices. In this way, AI not only enhances learning but also prepares students for a future where data analysis will be an essential part of their jobs (Goldkind, 2021; Singer et al., 2021).

FUTURE RESEARCH DIRECTIONS

Evolving Paradigms and Models

As AI continues to evolve, so will social work and community work education paradigms and models. How will the classroom of the future look? Will traditional lecture halls give way to immersive, AI-driven environments? Although these changes may seem distant now, the rapid pace of technological advancement suggests that the future of education is closer than we think. AI-driven adaptive learning systems will likely refine the delivery of social work and community work curricula, making education more responsive and tailored to individual student needs.

Ethical Considerations and Professional Development

With these exciting opportunities come significant challenges. How do we ensure that AI tools are used ethically? Data privacy, bias, and transparency are all concerns that must be addressed as we move forward with AI integration. Moreover, continuous professional development for educators will be essential to ensure that they remain competent and confident in using AI tools. Without these safeguards, the potential for AI to augment human interaction will be lost, and we risk losing the humanistic essence of social and community work education.

Enhancing Cultural Competence and Inclusivity

AI and collaborative platforms offer unique opportunities to enhance cultural competence and inclusivity. By providing exposure to diverse perspectives through AI-driven simulations, we can help students better understand cultural dynamics in social work and community work practice. These technologies can simulate real-world scenarios, helping students develop empathy and an awareness of cultural differences in ways that traditional textbooks cannot. This approach aligns perfectly with the ADEI principles that are foundational to social work and community work education.

Practical Implementation Issues

Is integrating AI into social work and community work education viable on a large scale? The answer depends on several factors, including institutional investment in infrastructure, continuous improvement of AI tools, and educators' commitment to ethical practices. For AI integration to succeed, it must be adaptable, meeting the unique needs of social work and community work education while enhancing, rather than undermining, the humanistic values central to the field.

Implementing AI in Resource-Limited Educational Settings: Practical Insights and Recommendations

AI has the potential to transform education by offering personalized learning experiences and improving administrative efficiency. However, implementing AI in resource-limited educational settings presents unique challenges. This section provides practical guidance on how educators can successfully integrate AI, including examples of low-cost AI tools and public-private partnerships.

Challenges of AI Implementation in Resource-Limited Settings

Resource-limited educational settings often face challenges such as inadequate funding, lack of technical expertise, and insufficient infrastructure. These challenges can hinder the successful integration of AI tools, making it difficult to leverage their full potential (Saputra et al., 2023).

Low-Cost AI Tools and Public-Private Partnerships

Despite these challenges, there are several low-cost AI tools available that can enhance the learning experience without requiring significant investment. Tools such as Google's TensorFlow and Microsoft's Azure Machine Learning offer free tiers and educational discounts, making them accessible to schools with limited budgets. Additionally, public-private partnerships can provide the necessary support and resources for AI implementation. For instance, collaborations between educational institutions and tech companies can facilitate access to advanced technologies and training programs (Karpouzis, 2024).

Actionable Recommendations for Educators

1. **Leverage Open-Source AI Tools:** Utilize open-source AI tools that offer robust functionalities without the associated costs. Platforms like TensorFlow and Scikit-learn provide extensive resources and community support.
2. **Foster Public-Private Partnerships:** Engage in partnerships with tech companies to access their expertise, training programs, and resources. These collaborations can help bridge the gap between technological capabilities and educational needs.

3. **Invest in Professional Development:** Provide ongoing training for educators to ensure they are proficient in using AI tools. This will enable teachers to integrate AI effectively into their teaching strategies and enhance student learning outcomes.
4. **Focus on Inclusivity:** Ensure that AI tools are used to promote inclusivity by addressing the diverse needs of students. AI can help identify and support students who may require additional assistance, thereby fostering a more equitable learning environment (Chen et al., 2011).

Practical Challenges of Implementing AI and Collaborative Platforms

The practical challenges of implementing AI and collaborative platforms cannot be underestimated. Students need access to high-speed internet, compatible devices, and technical support—resources that are not always equally distributed. Ongoing training for educators is also critical to ensure they can effectively incorporate AI tools into their teaching. Finally, curricula must be designed to leverage AI's strengths while focusing on the humanistic aspects of social and community work education.

Areas Ripe for Further Research

As AI and collaborative platforms become more integral to education, several areas are ripe for further research. The following areas highlight where future research can focus:

- **Impact Assessment:** Conducting longitudinal studies to evaluate the long-term effects of AI on student engagement, academic performance, and preparedness for professional practice.
- **Bias Mitigation:** Researching ways to identify and mitigate biases in AI systems to ensure equitable learning opportunities for all students.
- **AI in Field Education:** Exploring AI's potential in supporting field education, such as through virtual field experiences or real-time feedback, to enhance practical training.
- **Cross-Cultural Collaboration:** Evaluating the effectiveness of international collaborative platforms in fostering global perspectives and cultural competence in social and community work education.

CONCLUSION

The future of social work and community work education is at a crossroads. The integration of AI and collaborative platforms presents a tremendous opportunity to create more inclusive, dynamic, and effective learning environments. The road ahead is not without its challenges, though. Ethical concerns, equitable access, and continuous professional development for educators will ensure that AI enhances—rather than diminishes—the core values of social and community work. As educators, we have a responsibility to mindfully embrace these technological advancements. AI should be viewed not as a replacement for human connection but as a tool that can tremendously empower educators and students to succeed. When used thoughtfully, AI can create personalized learning paths, increase access to global perspectives, and foster collaboration across cultural and geographical boundaries. Implementing AI in resource-limited educational settings is challenging but feasible. By leveraging low-cost AI tools, fostering public-private partnerships, and investing in professional development, educators can harness the benefits of AI to create a more inclusive and effective learning experience. We must keep asking ourselves this: How can we use AI to elevate education without losing sight of the human elements that make learning meaningful? By embracing this challenge, we can ensure that the future of social work and community work education is not only technologically advanced but also deeply rooted in the empathy, equity, and justice that define the professions. The future is bright, and together we can build an educational landscape that truly reflects every student's diversity, complexity, and potential.

REFERENCES

Bergman, Z., Bergman, M. M., Fernandes, K., Grossrieder, D., & Schneider, L. (2018). The contribution of UNESCO chairs toward achieving the UN sustainable development goals. *Sustainability (Basel)*, 10(12), 4471. DOI: 10.3390/su10124471

Body, A. I. E. (2018). *All Ireland standards for community work*. Community Work Ireland.

Brusilovsky, P. (2024). AI in education, learner control, and human–AI collaboration. *International Journal of Artificial Intelligence in Education*, 34(1), 122–135. DOI: 10.1007/s40593-023-00356-z

Chaudhuri, S., Kumar, R., & Kalyan, A. (2020). AI in facilitating collaborative online discussions. *IEEE Transactions on Learning Technologies*, 13(3), 476–486. DOI: 10.1109/TLT.2020.3012835

Chen, N.-S., Kinshuk, , Wei, C.-W., & Liu, C.-C. (2011). Effects of matching teaching strategy to thinking style on learner's quality of reflection in an online learning environment. *Computers & Education*, 56(1), 53–64. DOI: 10.1016/j.compedu.2010.08.021

D'Mello, S., & Graesser, A. (2012). Dynamics of affective states during complex learning. *Learning and Instruction*, 22(2), 145–1573. DOI: 10.1016/j.learninstruc.2011.10.001

De Weger, E., Van Vooren, N., Luijkx, K. G., Baan, C. A., & Drewes, H. W. (2018). Achieving successful community engagement: A rapid realist review. *BMC Health Services Research*, 18(1), 285. Advance online publication. DOI: 10.1186/s12913-018-3090-1 PMID: 29653537

Dillenbourg, P. (1999). What do you mean by collaborative learning? In Dillenbourg, P. (Ed.), *Collaborative-learning: Cognitive and computational approaches* (pp. 1–19). Elsevier.

European Commission. Directorate-General for Education, Youth, Sport and Culture. (2022). Ethical guidelines on the use of artificial intelligence (AI) and data in teaching and learning for educators. Publications Office of the European Union. https://data.europa.eu/doi/10.2766/153756

Gallagher, M. B., Cook, C. A. L., Tebb, S., & Berg-Weger, M. (2003). Practicing social justice: Community-based research, education, and practice. In Wilson, J., Burkemper, E., Hutchison, W. J., & Stretch, J. J. (Eds.), *Practicing social justice* (pp. 27–39). Routledge.

Goldkind, L. (2021). Social work and artificial intelligence: Into the Matrix. *Social Work*, 66(4), 372–374. DOI: 10.1093/sw/swab028 PMID: 34279661

Graesser, A. C., Hu, X., Nye, B. D., VanLehn, K., Kumar, R., Heffernan, N., Woolf, B., Olney, A. M., Rus, V., Andrasik, F., Pavlik, P., Cai, Z., Wetzel, J., Morgan, B., Hampton, A. J., Lippert, A. M., Wang, L., Chen, Q., & Baer, W. (2018). ElectronixTutor: An intelligent tutoring system with multiple learning resources for electronics. In *International Journal of STEM Education, 5*, Article 15. DOI: 10.1186/s40594-018-0110-y

Hadwin, A. F., Järvelä, S., & Miller, M. (2018). Self-regulation, co-regulation, and shared regulation in collaborative learning environments. In Schunk, D. H., & Greene, J. A. (Eds.), *Handbook of self-regulation of learning and performance* (2nd ed., pp. 83–106). Routledge.

Hartman, R. J., Townsend, M. B., & Jackson, M. (2019). Educators' perceptions of technology integration into the classroom: A descriptive case study. *Journal of Research in Innovative Teaching & Learning*, 12(3), 236–249. DOI: 10.1108/JRIT-03-2019-0044

Hodgson, D., Goldingay, S., Boddy, J., Nipperess, S., & Watts, L. (2022). Problematizing artificial intelligence in social work education: Challenges, issues and possibilities. *British Journal of Social Work*, 52(4), 1878–1895. DOI: 10.1093/bjsw/bcab168

Järvelä, S., Kirschner, P. A., Hadwin, A., Järvenoja, H., Malmberg, J., Miller, M., & Laru, J. (2016). Socially shared regulation of learning in CSCL: Understanding and prompting individual- and group-level shared regulatory activities. *International Journal of Computer-Supported Collaborative Learning*, 11(3), 263–280. DOI: 10.1007/s11412-016-9238-2

Järvelä, S., Nguyen, A., & Hadwin, A. (2023). Human and artificial intelligence collaboration for socially shared regulation in learning. *British Journal of Educational Technology*, 54(4), 1057–1076. DOI: 10.1111/bjet.13325

Johnson, D. W., & Johnson, R. T. (2009). An educational psychology success story: Social interdependence theory and cooperative learning. *Educational Researcher*, 38(5), 365–379. DOI: 10.3102/0013189X09339057

Jones, L., Smith, M., & Lee, J. (2022). Using AI to enhance social work education: A case study of an adaptive learning platform. *Journal of Technology in Human Services*, 40(1), 23–45.

Kamalov, F., Calonge, D. S., & Gurrib, I. (2023). New era of artificial intelligence in education: Towards a sustainable multifaceted revolution. *Sustainability (Basel)*, 15(16), 12451. DOI: 10.3390/su151612451

Karpouzis, K. (2024). Artificial intelligence in education: Ethical considerations and insights from ancient Greek philosophy. https://doi.org//arXiv.2409.15296DOI: 10.48550

Kim, J., Lee, H., & Cho, Y. H. (2022). Learning design to support student–AI collaboration: Perspectives of leading teachers for AI in education. *Education and Information Technologies*, 27(5), 6069–6104. DOI: 10.1007/s10639-021-10831-6

Laal, M., & Ghodsi, S. M. (2012). Benefits of collaborative learning. *Procedia: Social and Behavioral Sciences*, 31, 486–490. DOI: 10.1016/j.sbspro.2011.12.091

Lin, Y.-L., & Wang, W.-T. (2024). Enhancing students' online collaborative PBL learning performance in the context of coauthoring-based technologies: A case of wiki technologies. *Education and Information Technologies*, 29(2), 2303–2328. DOI: 10.1007/s10639-023-11907-1 PMID: 37361760

Luckin, R., Holmes, W., Griffiths, M., & Forcier, L. B. (2016). *Intelligence unleashed: An argument for AI in education*. Pearson. https://discovery.ucl.ac.uk/id/eprint/1475756/

Makoelle, T. M. (2014). Inclusive education: Are we there? Some global challenges, contradictions and anomalies. *Journal of Sociology and Social Anthropology*, 5(3), 303–309. DOI: 10.1080/09766634.2014.11885634

Mollick, E. R., & Mollick, L. (2023, September 23). *Assigning AI: Seven approaches for students, with prompts*. The Wharton School Research Paper. https://doi.org/ DOI: 10.2139/ssrn.4475995

National Association of Social Workers. (2021). Social work education: A comprehensive guide to education and careers in social work. NASW Press. https://www.socialworkers.org

National Association of Social Workers. (2023). *AI and social work*. https://www.socialworkers.org/About/Ethics/AI-and-Social-Work

Nguyen, A., Järvelä, S., & Hadwin, A. (2020). Human and artificial intelligence collaboration for learning: A scoping review. *Educational Research Review*, 30, 100326.

Nguyen, A., Järvelä, S., & Hadwin, A. (2021). AI roles for supporting socially shared regulation in learning. In Rosé, C., Martínez-Maldonado, R., Hoppe, H. U., Luckin, R., Mavrikis, M., Porayska-Pomsta, K., McLaren, B., & du Boulay, B. (Eds.), *Artificial intelligence in education* (pp. 387–401). Springer.

Ouyang, F., Wu, M., Zheng, L., Zhang, L., & Jiao, P. (2023). Integration of artificial intelligence performance prediction and learning analytics to improve student learning in online engineering courses. *International Journal of Educational Technology in Higher Education*, 20(1), 4. Advance online publication. DOI: 10.1186/s41239-022-00372-4 PMID: 36683653

Ouyang, F., Xu, W., & Cukurova, M. (2023). An artificial intelligence–driven learning analytics method to examine the collaborative problem-solving process from the complex adaptive systems perspective. *International Journal of Computer-Supported Collaborative Learning*, 18(1), 39–66. DOI: 10.1007/s11412-023-09387-z

Potency, S. A. D., & Kerr, S. (2017). Exploring the impact of artificial intelligence on teaching and learning in higher education. *Research and Practice in Technology Enhanced Learning*, 12(1), 22. Advance online publication. DOI: 10.1186/s41039-017-0062-8 PMID: 30595727

Purdy, N., Hall, K., Khanolainen, D., & Galvin, C. (2023). Reframing teacher education around inclusion, equity, and social justice: Towards an authentically value-centered approach to teacher education in Europe. *European Journal of Teacher Education*, 46(5), 755–771. DOI: 10.1080/02619768.2023.2288556

Radovan, M., & Radovan, D. M. (2024). Harmonizing pedagogy and technology: Insights into teaching approaches that foster sustainable motivation and efficiency in blended learning. *Sustainability (Basel)*, 16(7), 2704. DOI: 10.3390/su16072704

Richardson, J. C., Besser, E., Koehler, A., Lim, J., & Strait, M. (2017). Instructors' perceptions of instructor presence in online learning environments. *The International Review of Research in Open and Distributed Learning*, 18(6), 233–251.

Roscoe, R. D., Allen, L. K., Weston, J. L., Crossley, S. A., & McNamara, D. S. (2019). The Writing Pal intelligent tutoring system: Usability testing and development. *Computers and Composition*, 53, 70–85.

Rovai, A. P. (2002). Sense of community-perceived cognitive learning and persistence in asynchronous learning networks. *The Internet and Higher Education*, 5(4), 319–332. DOI: 10.1016/S1096-7516(02)00130-6

Samadi, M. A. JaQuay, S., Gu, J., & Nixon, N. (2024). The AI Collaborator: Bridging human–AI interaction in educational and professional settings. arXiv:2405.10460v1. https://arxiv.org/html/2405.10460v1

Saputra, I., Astuti, M., Sayuti, M., & Kusumastuti, D. (2023). Integration of artificial intelligence in education: Opportunities, challenges, threats and obstacles. *Indonesian Journal of Computer Science*, 12(4). Advance online publication. DOI: 10.33022/ijcs.v12i4.3266

Seo, K., Tang, J., Roll, I., Fels, S., & Yoon, D. (2021). The impact of artificial intelligence on learner–instructor interaction in online learning. *International Journal of Educational Technology in Higher Education*, 18(1), 54. Advance online publication. DOI: 10.1186/s41239-021-00292-9 PMID: 34778540

Shulla, K., Filho, W. L., Lardjane, S., Sommer, J. H., & Borgemeister, C. (2020). Sustainable development education in the context of the 2030 Agenda for sustainable development. *International Journal of Sustainable Development and World Ecology*, 27(5), 458–468. DOI: 10.1080/13504509.2020.1721378

Shulman, L. S. (2005). Signature pedagogies in the professions. *Daedalus*, 134(3), 52–59. DOI: 10.1162/0011526054622015

Singer, J., Báez, J., & Rios, R. (2023). Artificial intelligence and natural language processing in social work: Opportunities and challenges. *Journal of Social Work Education*, 59(2), 201–215.

Singer, J. B., Báez, J. C., & Rios, R. (2021). Artificial intelligence and natural language processing in social work: A scoping review. *Journal of Technology in Human Services*, 39(1), 1–27. DOI: 10.1080/15228835.2020.1862401

Srivastava, S.Ms Sanchana Srivastava. (2023). The evolution of education: Navigating 21st-century challenges. *International Journal for Multidisciplinary Research*, 5(5), 6314. Advance online publication. DOI: 10.36948/ijfmr.2023.v05i05.6314

Tichnor-Wagner, A., Parkhouse, H., Glazier, J., & Cain, J. M. (2016). Expanding approaches to teaching for diversity and social justice in K–12 education: Fostering global citizenship across the content areas. *Education Policy Analysis Archives*, 24, 59. DOI: 10.14507/epaa.24.2138

Verbert, K., Duval, E., Klerkx, J., Govaerts, S., & Santos, J. L. (2013). Learning analytics dashboard applications. *The American Behavioral Scientist*, 57(10), 1500–1509. DOI: 10.1177/0002764213479363

Walton, G. M., & Cohen, G. L. (2011). A brief social-belonging intervention improves academic and health outcomes of minority students. *Science*, 331(6023), 1447–1451. DOI: 10.1126/science.1198364 PMID: 21415354

Wang, T., Lund, B. D., Marengo, A., Pagano, A., Mannuru, R. N., Teel, Z. A., & Pange, J. (2023). Exploring the potential impact of artificial intelligence (AI) on international students in higher education: Generative AI, chatbots, analytics, and international student success. *Applied Sciences (Basel, Switzerland)*, 13(11), 6716. DOI: 10.3390/app13116716

Xu, W., & Ouyang, F. (2022). The application of AI technologies in STEM education: A systematic review from 2011 to 2021. *International Journal of STEM Education*, 9(1), 59. Advance online publication. DOI: 10.1186/s40594-022-00377-5

Zawacki-Richter, O., Marín, V. I., Bond, M., & Gouverneur, F. (2019). Systematic review of research on artificial intelligence applications in higher education—Where are the educators? *International Journal of Educational Technology in Higher Education*, 16(1), 39. Advance online publication. DOI: 10.1186/s41239-019-0171-0

Zhang, Y., Chen, X., & Liu, H. (2022). The impact of artificial intelligence on social work educators' well-being and job satisfaction: A mixed-methods study. *Computers in Human Behavior*, 118, 106–714.

Zharova, M. V., Trapitsin, S. Y., & Timchenko, V. V. (2021). Prospects for the use of artificial intelligence technologies in education. 2021 International Conference on Quality Management, Transport and Information Security, Information Technologies (IT&QM&IS), Yaroslavl, Russian Federation, 2021, pp. 754–759. IEEE. https://doi.org/DOI: 10.1109/ITQMIS53292.2021.9642866

Zimmerman, B. J. (2002). Becoming a self-regulated learner: An overview. *Theory into Practice*, 41(2), 64–70. DOI: 10.1207/s15430421tip4102_2

ADDITIONAL READING

Abulibdeh, A., Zaidan, E., & Abulibdeh, R. (2024). Navigating the confluence of artificial intelligence and education for sustainable development in the era of industry 4.0: Challenges, opportunities, and ethical dimensions. *Journal of Cleaner Production*, 437, 140527. DOI: 10.1016/j.jclepro.2023.140527

Akintayo, O. T., Eden, C. A., Ayeni, O. O., & Onyebuchi, N. C.Olateju Temitope AkintayoChima Abimbola EdenOyebola Olusola AyeniNneamaka Chisom Onyebuchi. (2024). Integrating AI with emotional and social learning in primary education: Developing a holistic adaptive learning ecosystem. *Computer Science & IT Research Journal*, 5(5), 1076–1089. DOI: 10.51594/csitrj.v5i5.1116

Islam, M. M. (2024). Utilizing AI for Social Good: Tackling Global Issues and Fostering Inclusive Solutions. *Journal of Artificial Intelligence General science (JAIGS) ISSN: 3006-4023, 3*(1), 341-362.

Judijanto, L., Aini, M. A., Asfahani, A., Sain, Z. H., & Vandika, A. Y. (2022). Utilization AI for Socially Responsive Education as a Path to Inclusive Development. *Journal of Artificial Intelligence and Development*, 1(2), 69–78.

KEY TERMS AND DEFINITIONS

Anti-Racism: A proactive stance against racism that actively challenges discriminatory practices, policies, and beliefs. Anti-racism seeks to dismantle systemic inequalities and promote equity.

Artificial Intelligence (AI): A field of computer science that focuses on creating intelligent machines capable of performing tasks that typically require human intelligence, such as problem solving, learning, and decision making.

Association for Innovation and Enterprise in Community-Based Education (AIEB) Principles and Values of Community Work: The principles and values advocated by AIEB in the context of community work. These may include empowerment, social justice, and community engagement.

Collaborative Platforms: Digital tools or software that facilitate communication, cooperation, and joint work among individuals or groups. Examples include project management software, shared document platforms, and virtual meeting spaces.

Community Work: Community Work is a developmental activity comprised of both a task and a process. The task is social change to achieve equality, social justice and human rights, and the process is the application of principles of participation, empowerment and collective decision making in a structured and coordinated way.

Council on Social Work Education (CSWE) Core Competencies: CSWE's established standards that define the essential knowledge, skills, and values expected of social work graduates. These competencies guide social work education and practice.

Diversity, Equity, and Inclusion Principles: Guiding concepts that emphasize valuing differences, ensuring fairness, and creating environments in which everyone feels respected and included.

Inclusive Learning: An educational approach that ensures that all learners, regardless of their backgrounds, abilities, or identities, have equitable access to learning opportunities. It promotes diversity, removes barriers, and fosters a supportive environment.

Learning Communities: Collaborative and interactive groups of learners who engage in shared activities, discussions, and reflection. Learning communities promote peer support, knowledge exchange, and a sense of belonging.

National Association of Social Workers' (NASW's) Ethical Standards: NASW's code of ethics, which outlines professional responsibilities, ethical principles, and standards of conduct for social workers.

Nurturing Learning: Creating an environment that supports and encourages continuous learning, growth, and development. It involves fostering curiosity, critical thinking, and a love of learning.

Social Work Education: The formal training and preparation of individuals to become professional social workers. This includes academic coursework, field placements, and skill development related to social work practice.

Compilation of References

Abbas, N., Whitfield, J., Atwell, E., Bowman, H., Pickard, T., & Walker, A. (2022). Online chat and chatbots to enhance mature student engagement in higher education. *International Journal of Lifelong Education*, 41(3), 308–326. DOI: 10.1080/02601370.2022.2066213

Abbound, M. (2024). OPINION: AI's effect on cognitive development: A future of success or a public detriment? The Red & Black. https://www.edandblack.com/opinion/opinion-ai-s-effect-on-cognitive-development-a-future-of-success-or-a-public-detriment/article_685f3fbe-5e9a-11ef-a088-77a0bace301c.html

Abele, E., Chryssolouris, G., Sihn, W., Metternich, J., ElMaraghy, H., Seliger, G., Sivard, G., ElMaraghy, W., Hummel, V., Tisch, M., & Seifermann, S. (2017, January 1). Learning factories for future oriented research and education in manufacturing. Elsevier BV, 66(2), 803-826. DOI: 10.1016/j.cirp.2017.05.005

Acar, O. (2020). *Yapay zeka fırsat mı yoksa tehdit mi?* Kriter Yayınevi.

Acar, O. A. (2024). Commentary: Reimagining marketing education in the age of generative AI. *International Journal of Research in Marketing*, 41(3), 489–495. DOI: 10.1016/j.ijresmar.2024.06.004

Adams, C., Pente, P., Lemermeyer, G., & Rockwell, G. (2023). Ethical principles for artificial intelligence in K-12 education. *Computers and Education: Artificial Intelligence*, 4, 100131. DOI: 10.1016/j.caeai.2023.100131

Adams, D., Joo, M. T. H., Sumintono, B., & Oh, S. P. (2020). Blended Learning Engagement in Higher Education Institutions: A Differential Item Functioning Analysis of Students' Backgrounds. *Malaysian Journal of Learning and Instruction*, 17(1), 133–158. DOI: 10.32890/mjli2020.17.1.6

Adeshola, I., & Adepoju, A. P. (2023). The opportunities and challenges of ChatGPT in education. *Interactive Learning Environments*, •••, 1–14. DOI: 10.1080/10494820.2023.2253858

Adiguzel, T., Kaya, M. H., & Cansu, F. K. (2023). Revolutionizing education with AI: Exploring the transformative potential of ChatGPT. *Contemporary Educational Technology*, 15(3), ep429. DOI: 10.30935/cedtech/13152

Adnan, M., Habib, A., Ashraf, J., Mussadiq, S., Raza, A. A., Abid, M., Bashir, M., & Khan, S. U. (2021). Predicting at-risk students at different percentages of course length for early intervention using machine learning models. *IEEE Access : Practical Innovations, Open Solutions*, 9, 7519–7539. DOI: 10.1109/ACCESS.2021.3049446

Adobe. (2020). Adobe Sensei. https://www.adobe.com/sensei.html

Aflalo, E. (2014, May 14). The Invisible Barrier to Integrating Computer Technology in Education. *Canadian Center of Science and Education*, 3(2). Advance online publication. DOI: 10.5539/jel.v3n2p120

Agestiningrum, R., & Siswanto, S. (2024). The effect of AI learning system on student learning outcomes and motivation. *An-Nuha Jurnal Kajian Islam Pendidikan Budaya Dan Sosial*, 11(1), 1–10. DOI: 10.36835/annuha.v11i1.582

Aghaziarati, A., Nejatifar, S., & Abedi, A. (2023). Artificial intelligence in education: Investigating teacher attitudes. *AI and Tech in Behavioral and Social Sciences*, 1(1), 35–42. DOI: 10.61838/kman.aitech.1.1.6

Agjencia e Sigurimit të Cilësisë së Arsimit Parauniversitar. (n.d.). Udhëzues. https://www.ascap.edu.al/category/udhezues/

Agus, M., Purnomo, W., Fatkhurohman, A., Marifah, M., Mardliyah, S., & Supratikta, H. (2023, July 13). The Impact of Implementation of the 2013 Curriculum Transition to the Independent Learning Curriculum on Learning Interests of SMA Negeri 9 Students in South Tangerang., 06(07). DOI: 10.47191/jefms/v6-i7-16

Ahmad, S. F., Alam, M. M., Rahmat, M. K., Mubarik, M. S., & Hyder, S. I. (2022). Academic and administrative role of artificial intelligence in education. *Sustainability (Basel)*, 14(3), 1101. DOI: 10.3390/su14031101

Ahmad, S. F., Han, H., Alam, M. M., Rehmat, M. K., Irshad, M., Arrano-Munoz, M., & Ariza-Montes, A. (2023). Impact of artificial intelligence on human loss in decision making, laziness and safety in education. *Humanities & Social Sciences Communications*, 10(1), 1–14. DOI: 10.1057/s41599-023-01787-8 PMID: 37325188

Ahmad, S. F., Rahmat, M. K., Mubarik, M. S., Alam, M. M., & Hyder, S. I. (2021). Artificial intelligence and its role in education. *Sustainability (Basel)*, 13(22), 12902. DOI: 10.3390/su132212902

Ahuja, S. (2019). Creativity and AI: Augmenting human creativity with advanced technologies. *Journal of Innovation and Entrepreneurship*, 8(1), 9. DOI: 10.1186/s13731-019-0101-2

Aiken, R., & Epstein, R. (2000). Ethical guidelines for AI in education: Starting a conversation. *International Journal of Artificial Intelligence in Education*, 11, 163–176. https://www.researchgate.net/publication/228600407_Ethical_guidelines_for_AI_in_education_Starting_a_conversation

Akgun, S., & Greenhow, C. (2022). Artificial intelligence in education: Addressing ethical challenges in K-12 settings. *AI and Ethics*, 2(3), 431–440. DOI: 10.1007/s43681-021-00096-7 PMID: 34790956

Akiva, T., Delale-O'Connor, L., & Pittman, K. J. (2023). The promise of building equitable ecosystems for learning. *Urban Education*, 58(6), 1271–1297. DOI: 10.1177/0042085920926230

Akyürek, H. A. (2013). *Yapay zekâ teknikleri kullanarak akıllı iş gücü yönetimi (Yayımlanmamış yüksek lisans tezi)*. Mevlana Üniversitesi.

Alahmari, F., Naim, A., & Alqahtani, H. (2023). E-learning modeling technique and convolution neural networks in online education. In *IoT-Enabled Convolutional Neural Networks: Techniques and Applications* (pp. 261-295). River Publishers. DOI: 10.1201/9781003393030-10

Alasadi, E. A., & Baiz, C. R. (2023). Generative AI in Education and Research: Opportunities, concerns, and solutions. *Journal of Chemical Education*, 100(8), 2965–2971. DOI: 10.1021/acs.jchemed.3c00323

Alavi, M., & Leidner, D. E. (2021). Knowledge management and knowledge management systems: Conceptual foundations and research issues. *Management Information Systems Quarterly*, 25(1), 107–136. DOI: 10.2307/3250961

Alebaikan, R. (2011, February). A blended learning framework for Saudi higher education. In *A paper Presented at the Second International Conference of E-Learning and Distance Learning, Riyadh: National Center for E-Learning and Distance Learning*.

Alenezi, M. (2023). Digital learning and digital institution in higher education. *Education Sciences*, 13(1), 88. Advance online publication. DOI: 10.3390/educsci13010088

Alexandron, G., Wiltrout, M. E., Berg, A., Gershon, S. K., & Ruipérez-Valiente, J. A. (2023). The effects of assessment design on academic dishonesty, learner engagement, and certification rates in MOOCs. *Journal of Computer Assisted Learning*, 39(1), 141–153. DOI: 10.1111/jcal.12733

Ali, M. F., Joyes, G., & Ellison, L. (2015). Proposing the third generation of an aligned activity system as a theoretical framework in blended learning research. *Jurnal Teknologi, 75*(3). Alshahrani, K., & Qureshi, R. J. Review the Prospects and Obstacles of AI-Enhanced Learning Environments: The Role of ChatGPT in Education.

Aliabadi, R., Singh, A., & Wilson, J E. (2023, January 1). Transdisciplinary AI Education: The Confluence of Curricular and Community Needs in the Instruction of Artificial Intelligence. Springer International Publishing, 137-151. DOI: 10.1007/978-981-99-7947-9_11

Alier, M., Casañ Guerrero, M. J., Amo, D., Severance, C., & Fonseca, D. (2021). Privacy and e-learning: A pending task. *Sustainability (Basel)*, 13(16), 9206. DOI: 10.3390/su13169206

Alim, H. S., Paris, D., & Wong, C. P. (2020). Culturally sustaining pedagogy: A critical framework for centering communities. In *Handbook of the cultural foundations of learning* (pp. 261–276). Routledge. DOI: 10.4324/9780203774977-18

Ali, O., Murray, P. A., Momin, M., Dwivedi, Y. K., & Malik, T. (2023). The effects of artificial intelligence applications in educational settings: Challenges and strategies. *Technological Forecasting and Social Change*, 199, 123076. DOI: 10.1016/j.techfore.2023.123076

Alismail, H. A. (2015). Integrate digital storytelling in education. *Journal of Education and Practice*, 6(9), 126–129.

Allam, H., Dempere, J., Akre, V., & Flores, P. (2023, January 1). Artificial Intelligence in Education (AIED): Implications and Challenges. Atlantis Press, 126-140. DOI: 10.2991/978-94-6463-286-6_10

Almeda, M. V., Zuech, J., Utz, C., Higgins, G., Reynolds, R., & Baker, R. S. (2018). Comparing the factors that predict completion and grades among for-credit and open/MOOC students in online learning. *Online Learning : the Official Journal of the Online Learning Consortium*, 22(1), 1–18. DOI: 10.24059/olj.v22i1.1060

Almusaed, A., Almssad, A., Yitmen, I., & Homod, R. Z. (2023). Enhancing student engagement: Harnessing "AIED"'s power in hybrid education—A review analysis. *Education Sciences*, 13(7), 632. DOI: 10.3390/educsci13070632

Alsawaier, R S. (2017, November 14). The effect of gamification on motivation and engagement. Emerald Publishing Limited, 35(1), 56-79. DOI: 10.1108/IJILT-02-2017-0009

Aluthman, E. S. (2016). The effect of using automated essay evaluation on ESL undergraduate students' writing skill. *International Journal of English Linguistics*, 6(5), 54. DOI: 10.5539/ijel.v6n5p54

Alwabel, R. (2024). *The Future of AI in Education: Important Cautions to Consider.*

Alyammahi, A. (2020). *Investigating the Impact of AI-Powered Digital Educational Platforms on Students' Learning and Teachers' Practice in Abu Dhabi Schools* (Doctoral dissertation, The British University in Dubai).

Al-Zahrani, A. M., & Alasmari, T. M. (2024). Exploring the impact of artificial intelligence on higher education: The dynamics of ethical, social, and educational implications. *Humanities & Social Sciences Communications*, 11(1), 912. Advance online publication. DOI: 10.1057/s41599-024-03432-4

al-Zyoud, H. M. M. (2020). The role of artificial intelligence in teacher professional development. *Universal Journal of Educational Research*, 8(11B), 6263–6272. DOI: 10.13189/ujer.2020.082265

Amdan, M. A. B., Janius, N., Jasman, M. N. B., & Kasdiah, M. A. H. B. (2024a). Advancement of ai-tools in learning for technical vocational education and training (TVET) in Malaysia (empowering students and tutor). *International Journal of Science and Research Archive*, 12(1), 2061–2068. DOI: 10.30574/ijsra.2024.12.1.0971

Amdan, M. A. B., Janius, N., & Kasdiah, M. A. H. B. (2024b). Concept paper: Efficiency of Artificial Intelligence (AI) tools For STEM Education In Malaysia. *International Journal of Science and Research Archive*, 12(2), 553–559. DOI: 10.30574/ijsra.2024.12.2.1273

Amjad, B. (2024). Over-Reliance of Students on Artificial Intelligence. Medium. https://bakhtawaramjad0786.medium.com/over-reliance-of-students-on-artificial-intelligence-709a931bdc79

Analytikus. (2023). AI in Education: Streamlining Administrative Tasks for a Brighter Future. analytikus. https://www.analytikus.com/post/ai-in-education-streamlining-administrative-tasks-for-a-brighter-futureeducation-is-a-sector-that

Anderson, T., & Carter, L. (2021). Artificial intelligence and collaborative creativity in the media classroom. *Journal of Medical Education*, 32(4), 147–162.

Andrejevic, M., & Selwyn, N. (n.d.). *Facial recognition technology in schools: Critical questions and concerns*. Learning., DOI: 10.1080/1469662121

Ang, S. M. O., & Aragon, M. J. D. (2020). *Development of AI-Enhanced Information Technology Program: Preparing Today's Students in AI Era* (No. 4049). EasyChair.

Aparicio, M., Bacao, F., & Oliveira, T. (2016). An e-learning theoretical framework. *An e-learning theoretical framework*, (1), 292-307.

Araújo, J. L., & Saúde, I. (2024). Can ChatGPT enhance chemistry laboratory teaching? Using prompt engineering to enable AI in generating laboratory activities. *Journal of Chemical Education*, 101(5), 1858–1864. DOI: 10.1021/acs.jchemed.3c00745

Argyris, C., & Schön, D. A. (1978). *Organizational learning: A theory of action perspective*. Addison-Wesley.

Arslan, K. (2020). Eğitimde yapay zeka ve uygulamaları. [Derleme Makale Western Anatolia Journal of Educational Sciences.]. *Batı Anadolu Eğitim Bilimleri Dergisi*, 11(1), 71–88.

Artificial Intelligence and the Future of Teaching and Learning. (2023, December 4). https://tech.ed.gov/files/2023/05/ai-future-of-teaching-and-learning-report.pdf

Artificial Intelligence Influencing Higher Education in India. CINEFORUM. (2024). revistadecineforum.com. https://revistadecineforum.com/index.php/cf/article/view/62

Aşık, F., Yıldız, A., Kılınç, S., Aytekin, N., Adalı, R., & Kurnaz, K. (2023). Yapay Zekânın Eğitime Etkileri. [JSHSR]. *International Journal of Social and Humanities Sciences Research*, 10(98), 2100–2107. DOI: 10.5281/zenodo.8307107

Atenas, J., Havemann, L., & Timmermann, C. (2020). Critical literacies for a datafied society: Academic development and curriculum design in higher education.

Athanassopoulos, S., Manoli, P., Gouvi, M., Lavidas, K., & Komis, V. (2023). The use of ChatGPT as a learning tool to improve foreign language writing in a multilingual and multicultural classroom. *Advances in Mobile Learning Educational Research*, 3(2), 818–824. DOI: 10.25082/AMLER.2023.02.009

Atlas, S. (2023). ChatGPT for higher education and professional development: A guide to conversational AI. https://digitalcommons.uri.edu/cba_facpubs/548

Autor, D. H. (2015). Why are there still so many jobs? The history and future of workplace automation. *The Journal of Economic Perspectives*, 29(3), 3–30. DOI: 10.1257/jep.29.3.3

Ayala-Pazmino, M. (2023). Artificial intelligence in Education: Exploring the potential benefits and risks. 593 *Digital Publisher CEIT, 8* (3), 892-899. DOI: 10.33386/593dp.2023.3.1827

Babameto, E., & Pano, D.Dr. Etleva Babameto, Dr. Doriana Pano. (2024). The Future Higher Education in Albania in the Digital Era–Challenges and Opportunities. [Baig, M. A. A. The Future of AI in Higher Education: Opportunities & Challenges Ahead: AI and Higher Education.]. *Journal of Electrical Systems*, 20(4s), 1809–1820. DOI: 10.52783/jes.2244

Baker, R. S., & Inventado, P. S. (2014). Educational data mining and learning analytics. In Seel, N. M. (Ed.), *Encyclopedia of the sciences of learning* (pp. 1073–1076). Springer., DOI: 10.1007/978-1-4614-3305-7_4

Bakshy, E., Messing, S., & Adamic, L. A. (2015). Exposure to ideologically diverse news and opinion on Facebook. *Science*, 348(6239), 1130–1132. DOI: 10.1126/science.aaa1160 PMID: 25953820

Bang, M. (2020). Learning on the move toward just, sustainable, and culturally thriving futures. *Cognition and Instruction*, 38(3), 434–444. DOI: 10.1080/07370008.2020.1777999

Bao, Y., & Li, B. (2023). A preliminary study on graduate student instructors' exploration, perception, and use of ChatGPT. *International Journal of Computer-Assisted Language Learning and Teaching*, 13(1), 1–23. DOI: 10.4018/IJCALLT.332873

Barocas, S., Hardt, M., & Narayanan, A. (2019). Fairness and machine learning. *fairmlbook.org*. https://fairmlbook.org/

Baron, N. S. (2015). *Words Onscreen: The Fate of Reading in a Digital World.* Oxford University Press.

Basogain, X., Olabe, M. Á., Olabe, J. C., & Rico, M. J. (2018). Computational thinking in pre-university blended learning classrooms. *Computers in Human Behavior*, 80, 412–419. DOI: 10.1016/j.chb.2017.04.058

Baule. S. M. & Carter, E. (2024, September 24). Four tips for designing AI-resistant assessments. *Tech & Learning.*

Bayerlein, L. (2014, January 9). Students' feedback preferences: how do students react to timely and automatically generated assessment feedback?. Taylor & Francis, 39(8), 916-931. DOI: 10.1080/02602938.2013.870531

Bazelais, P. (2022). *Investigating the Impact of Blended Learning on Academic Performance in Higher Education*. McGill University.

Bearman, M., Ryan, J., & Ajjawi, R. (2023). Discourses of artificial intelligence in higher education: A critical literature review. *Higher Education*, 86(2), 369–385. DOI: 10.1007/s10734-022-00937-2

Becher Araujo Moraes, S. (2023). Blended learning in higher education: an approach, a model, and two theoretical frameworks. In *Journal of Teaching and Learning in Higher Education* (Vol. 4, No. 1). Malmö universitet. DOI: 10.24834/jotl.4.1.820

Belfer, R., Kochmar, E., & Serban, I V. (2022, January 1). Raising Student Completion Rates with Adaptive Curriculum and Contextual Bandits. Springer Science+Business Media, 724-730. DOI: 10.1007/978-3-031-11644-5_74

Bendou, I. (2021). *Automatic Arabic Translation of English Educational Content Online using Neural Machine Translation: the Case of Khan Academy.*

Berendt, B., Littlejohn, A., & Blakemore, M. (2020). AI in education: Learner choice and fundamental rights. *Learning, Media and Technology*, 45(3), 312–324. ucl.ac.uk. DOI: 10.1080/17439884.2020.1786399

Bergman, Z., Bergman, M. M., Fernandes, K., Grossrieder, D., & Schneider, L. (2018). The contribution of UNESCO chairs toward achieving the UN sustainable development goals. *Sustainability (Basel)*, 10(12), 4471. DOI: 10.3390/su10124471

Bervell, B., Nyagorme, P., & Arkorful, V. (2020). LMS-enabled blended learning use intentions among distance education tutors: Examining the mediation role of attitude based on technology-related stimulus-response theoretical framework. *Contemporary Educational Technology*, 12(2), ep273. DOI: 10.30935/cedtech/8317

Bhagat, K K., Rodrigo, M M T., & Chang, C. (2018, May 11). Current status, challenges, and opportunities of the Intelligent Tutoring System (ITS) in developing countries in Asia. Informa, 382-395. DOI: 10.4324/9781315694382-36

Bhardwaj, J. (2018). AI in the creative industries: The shift from co-creation to autonomous creation. *Journal of Creative Technology*, 5(2), 48–62.

Bhutoria, A. (2022). Personalized education and artificial intelligence in the United States, China, and India: A systematic review using a human-in-the-loop model. *Computers and Education: Artificial Intelligence*, 3, 100068. DOI: 10.1016/j.caeai.2022.100068

Biagini, G., Cuomo, S., & Ranieri, M. (2024). Developing and validating a multidimensional AI literacy questionnaire: Operationalizing AI literacy for higher education. In Schicchi, D., Taibi, D., & Temperini, M. (Eds.), *Proceedings of the first international workshop on high-performance artificial intelligence systems in education* (p. 1), 0.

Bilkis, M., Kohler, J. M., & Vilariño, F. (2024). Challenge-device-synthesis: A multi-disciplinary approach for the development of social innovation competences for students of artificial intelligence. *arXiv preprint arXiv:2405.19243*. DOI: 10.21125/edulearn.2024.1501

Binns, R. (2017). Fairness in Machine Learning: Lessons from Political Philosophy. *arXiv (Cornell University)*. https://doi.org//arxiv.1712.03586DOI: 10.48550

Binns, R. (2018). Fairness in Machine Learning: Lessons from Political Philosophy. *Proceedings of the 2018 Conference on Fairness, Accountability, and Transparency*.

Bliuc, A. M., Casey, G., Bachfischer, A., Goodyear, P., & Ellis, R. A. (2012). Blended learning in vocational education: Teachers' conceptions of blended learning and their approaches to teaching and design. *Australian Educational Researcher*, 39(2), 237–257. DOI: 10.1007/s13384-012-0053-0

Boddington, P. (2017, January 1). Towards a Code of Ethics for Artificial Intelligence. Springer International Publishing. DOI: 10.1007/978-3-319-60648-4

Body, A. I. E. (2018). *All Ireland standards for community work*. Community Work Ireland.

Bogina, V., Hartman, A., Kuflik, T., & Shulner-Tal, A. (2022). Educating software and AI stakeholders about algorithmic fairness, accountability, transparency and ethics. *International Journal of Artificial Intelligence in Education*, 32(3), 1–26. DOI: 10.1007/s40593-021-00248-0

Boles, C. (2024, April 17). The impact of Generative AI In manufacturing. *Forbes*. https://www.forbes.com/councils/forbestechcouncil/2024/04/17/the-impact-of-generative-ai-in-manufacturing/

Bolukbasi, T., Chang, K., Zou, J. Y., Saligrama, V., & Kalai, A. (2016). Man is to computer programmer as woman is to homemaker? Debiasing word embeddings. *Proceedings of the 30th Conference on Neural Information Processing Systems (NeurIPS 2016)*, 4356–4364. https://doi.org/DOI: 10.5555/3157382.3157584

Bozkurt, A. (2023). Generative artificial intelligence (AI) powered conversational educational agents: The inevitable paradigm shift. *Asian Journal of Distance Education*, 18(1), 198–204.

Bragg, L. A., Walsh, C., & Heyeres, M. (2021). Successful design and delivery of online professional development for teachers: A systematic review of the literature. *Computers & Education*, 166, 104158. Advance online publication. DOI: 10.1016/j.compedu.2021.104158

Brinson, J R. (2015, July 10). Learning outcome achievement in non-traditional (virtual and remote) versus traditional (hands-on) laboratories: A review of the empirical research. Elsevier BV, 87, 218-237. DOI: 10.1016/j.compedu.2015.07.003

Brown, H., & Wilson, M. (2021). Generative AI in media education: Unleashing creative potential. *Computers & Education*, 154, 103919. DOI: 10.1016/j.compedu.2020.103919

Bruner, J. (2003). *Making stories: Law, literature, life*. Harvard University Press.

Brusilovsky, P. (2024). AI in education, learner control, and human–AI collaboration. *International Journal of Artificial Intelligence in Education*, 34(1), 122–135. DOI: 10.1007/s40593-023-00356-z

Brynjolfsson, E., & McAfee, A. (2014). *The second machine age: Work, progress, and prosperity in a time of brilliant technologies*. W.W. Norton & Company.

Buckingham, D. (2003). *Media education: Literacy, learning and contemporary culture*. Polity Press.

Buckingham, D. (2019). *The media education manifesto*. Polity Press.

Bui, A., Veit, D., & Webster, J. (2015). Gamification: A novel phenomenon or a new wrapping for existing concepts? In *Proceedings of the 36th International Conference on Information Systems* (ICIS 2015). https://doi.org/DOI: 10.13140/RG.2.2.34660.27524

Buolamwini, J., & Gebru, T. (2018). Gender shades: Intersectional accuracy disparities in commercial gender classification. *Proceedings of the 1st Conference on Fairness, Accountability and Transparency (FAT 2018)*, 77–91. https://proceedings.mlr.press/v81/buolamwini18a.html

Burden, P. R. (2020). *Classroom management: Creating a successful K-12 learning community*. John Wiley & Sons.

Burton, C. (2023, June 26). 25+ best ChatGPT prompts for instructional designers. https://www.thinkific.com/blog/best-chatgpt-prompts-for-instructional-designers/

Buzhardt, J., Greenwood, C. R., Jia, F., Walker, D., Schneider, N., Larson, A. L., Valdovinos, M., & McConnell, S. R. (2020). Technology to guide data-driven intervention decisions: Effects on language growth of young children at risk for language delay. *Exceptional Children*, 87(1), 74–91. DOI: 10.1177/0014402920938003

Byrd, D., & Polychroniadou, A. (2020, October). Differentially private secure multi-party computation for federated learning in financial applications. In *Proceedings of the First ACM International Conference on AI in Finance* (pp. 1-9). DOI: 10.1145/3383455.3422562

Cai, Q., Lin, Y., & Yu, Z. (2023). Factors influencing learner attitudes towards ChatGPT-assisted language learning in higher education. *International Journal of Human-Computer Interaction*, •••, 1–15. DOI: 10.1080/10447318.2023.2291616

Caldera, A., Whitaker, M. C., & Conrad Popova, D. A. (2020). Classroom management in urban schools: Proposing a course framework. *Teaching Education*, 31(3), 343–361. DOI: 10.1080/10476210.2018.1561663

Çam, M. B., Çelik, N. C., Turan Güntepe, E., & Durukan, Ü. G. (2021). Öğretmen adaylarının yapay zekâ teknolojileri ile ilgili farkındalıklarının belirlenmesi. *Hatay Mustafa Kemal Üniversitesi Sosyal Bilimler Enstitüsü Dergisi*, 18(48), 263–285.

Campus Technology. (2024, August). *Streamlining instructional design with generative AI* [Podcast]. https://campustechnology.com/Podcasts/2024/08/Streamlining-Instructional-Design-with-Generative-AI.aspx?admgarea=podcast

Carbonell, J. (1970). AI in CAI: An Artificial-Intelligence Approach to Computer-Assisted Instruction. *IEEE Transactions on Man-Machine Systems*, 11(4), 190–202. DOI: 10.1109/TMMS.1970.299942

Carvalho, L., Martinez-Maldonado, R., Tsai, Y. S., Markauskaite, L., & De Laat, M. (2022). How can we design for learning in an AI world? *Computers and Education: Artificial Intelligence*, 3, 100053. DOI: 10.1016/j.caeai.2022.100053

Cassidy, C. (2023, January 10). Australian universities to return to 'pen and paper' exams after students caught using AI to write essays. *The Guardian*. https://www.theguardian.com/australianews/2023/jan/10/universities-to-return-to-pen-and-paper-exams-after-students-caught-using-ai-to-write-essays

Castells, M. (2010). *The rise of the network society* (2nd ed.). Wiley-Blackwell.

Catota, F. E., Morgan, M. G., & Sicker, D. C. (2019). Cybersecurity education in a developing nation: The Ecuadorian environment. *Journal of Cybersecurity*, 5(1). Advance online publication. DOI: 10.1093/cybsec/tyz001

Cekrezi, A. (2021, June). How Fair is Education Policy in Albania? In *London International Conference, June 2021: PROCEEDINGS 2021-3* (Vol. 3). UKEY Publishing. DOI: 10.31039/ljss.2021.1.42

Celik, I. (2023). Towards Intelligent-TPACK: An empirical study on teachers' professional knowledge to ethically integrate artificial intelligence (AI)-based tools into education. *Computers in Human Behavior*, 138, 107468. DOI: 10.1016/j.chb.2022.107468

Celik, I., Dindar, M., Muukkonen, H., & Järvelä, S. (2022). The promises and challenges of artificial intelligence for teachers: A systematic review of research. *TechTrends*, 66(4), 616–630. DOI: 10.1007/s11528-022-00715-y

Cerna, L., Mezzanotte, C., Rutigliano, A., Brussino, O., Santiago, P., Borgonovi, F., & Guthrie, C. (2021). Promoting inclusive education for diverse societies: A conceptual framework.

Chan, C. K. Y., & Hu, W. (2023). Students' voices on generative AI: Perceptions, benefits, and challenges in higher education. *International Journal of Educational Technology in Higher Education*, 20(43), 1–18. DOI: 10.1186/s41239-023-00411-8

Chan, C. K. Y., & Luo, J. (2022). Exploring teacher perceptions of different types of 'feedback practices' in higher education: Implications for teacher feedback literacy. *Assessment & Evaluation in Higher Education*, 47(1), 61–76. DOI: 10.1080/02602938.2021.1888074

Chapman, J. (2024, August 1). Lumi Pro for Brightspace idea generation for assignments overview. https://community.d2l.com/brightspace/kb/articles/26143

Chassignol, M., Khoroshavin, A., Klimova, A., & Bilyatdinova, A. (2018). Artificial Intelligence trends in education: A narrative overview. *Procedia Computer Science*, 136, 16–24. DOI: 10.1016/j.procs.2018.08.233

Chaudhry, M. A., & Kazim, E. (2021). Artificial Intelligence in Education (AIEd): A high-level academic and industry note 2021. *AI and Ethics*, 2(1), 157–165. DOI: 10.1007/s43681-021-00074-z PMID: 34790953

Chaudhry, M. A., & Kazim, E. (2021, July 7). Artificial Intelligence in Education (AIEd): A high-level academic and industry note 2021. *SSRN*, 2(1), 157–165. DOI: 10.2139/ssrn.3833583 PMID: 34790953

Chaudhuri, S., Kumar, R., & Kalyan, A. (2020). AI in facilitating collaborative online discussions. *IEEE Transactions on Learning Technologies*, 13(3), 476–486. DOI: 10.1109/TLT.2020.3012835

Chavez, H., Chavez-Arias, B., Contreras-Rosas, S., Alvarez-Rodríguez, J. M., & Raymundo, C. (2023). Artificial neural network model to predict student performance using nonpersonal information. *Frontiers in Education*, 8, 1106679. DOI: 10.3389/feduc.2023.1106679

Chen, X., Xie, H., & Hwang, G. (2020, January 1). A multi-perspective study on Artificial Intelligence in Education: grants, conferences, journals, software tools, institutions, and researchers. Elsevier BV, 1, 100005-100005. DOI: 10.1016/j.caeai.2020.100005

Chen, Y., Chen, Y., & Heffernan, N. (2020). Personalized math tutoring with a conversational agent. arXiv preprint arXiv:2012.12121.

Chena, Y., Liub, M., & Cheng, Y. (2023). Discovering Scientific Creativity with Digital Storytelling. *Journal of Creativity*, ISSN: 2713-3745, 33 (1), 100041, DOI: 10.1016/j.yjoc.2022.100041

Chen, B., Wu, Z., & Zhao, R. (2023a). From fiction to fact: The growing role of generative AI in business and finance. *Journal of Chinese Economic and Business Studies*, 21(4), 471–496. DOI: 10.1080/14765284.2023.2245279

Chen, E., Gee, L., Mangelsdorf, I., Munina, I., Principe, C., & Saiyed, A. (2020). Personalized learning in AI: The next frontier in education technology. *Journal of Artificial Intelligence in Education*, 31(1), 1–20.

Chen, L., Chen, P., & Lin, Z. (2020). Artificial intelligence in education: A review. *IEEE Access : Practical Innovations, Open Solutions*, 8, 75264–75278. DOI: 10.1109/ACCESS.2020.2988510

Chen, N.-S., Kinshuk, , Wei, C.-W., & Liu, C.-C. (2011). Effects of matching teaching strategy to thinking style on learner's quality of reflection in an online learning environment. *Computers & Education*, 56(1), 53–64. DOI: 10.1016/j.compedu.2010.08.021

Chen, X., Liu, T., & Zhao, Y. (2021). AI tools for content creation and their implications for media education. *International Journal of Educational Technology in Higher Education*, 18(1), 29. DOI: 10.1186/s41239-021-00264-5

Chen, X., Xie, H., Zou, D., & Hwang, G.-J. (2020). Application and theory gaps during the rise of artificial intelligence in education. *Computers and Education: Artificial Intelligence*, 1, 100002. DOI: 10.1016/j.caeai.2020.100002

Chen, Y., Clayton, E. W., Novak, L. L., Anders, S., & Malin, B. (2023, March 24). Human-Centered Design to Address Biases in Artificial Intelligence. *Journal of Medical Internet Research*, 25, e43251–e43251. DOI: 10.2196/43251 PMID: 36961506

Chen, Y., & Esmaeilzadeh, P. (2024). Generative AI in medical practice: In-depth exploration of privacy and security challenges. *Journal of Medical Internet Research*, 26, e53008. Advance online publication. DOI: 10.2196/53008 PMID: 38457208

Chen, Y., Jensen, S., Albert, L. J., Gupta, S., & Lee, T. (2022). Artificial intelligence (AI) student assistants in the classroom: Designing chatbots to support student success. *Information Systems Frontiers*, 25(1), 161–182. DOI: 10.1007/s10796-022-10291-4

Chen, Y., Xu, Z., & Gong, B. (2023b). Generative design for product innovation: A comprehensive review. *Artificial Intelligence for Engineering Design, Analysis and Manufacturing*, 37(1), 1–35.

Chesbrough, H. (2003). *Open innovation: The new imperative for creating and profiting from technology*. Harvard Business School Press.

Cheung, S. K. S., Kwok, L. F., Phusavat, K., & Yang, H. H. (2021). Shaping the future learning environments with smart elements: Challenges and opportunities. *International Journal of Educational Technology in Higher Education, 18*(1), 16, s41239-021-00254-1. DOI: 10.1186/s41239-021-00254-1

Chiu, T. K., Moorhouse, B. L., Chai, C. S., & Ismailov, M. (2023). Teacher support and student motivation to learn with artificial intelligence (AI) based chatbot. *Interactive Learning Environments*, •••, 1–17. DOI: 10.1080/10494820.2023.2172044

Choi, E. P. H., Lee, J. J., Ho, M. H., Kwok, J. Y. Y., & Lok, K. Y. W. (2023). Chatting or cheating? The impacts of ChatGPT and other artificial intelligence language models on nurse education. *Nurse Education Today*, 125, 105796. DOI: 10.1016/j.nedt.2023.105796 PMID: 36934624

Chong, S. W. (2021). Reconsidering student feedback literacy from an ecological perspective. *Assessment & Evaluation in Higher Education*, 46(1), 92–104. DOI: 10.1080/02602938.2020.1730765

Christenson, S. L., Reschly, A. L., & Wylie, C. (2012). Handbook of Research on Student Engagement. In *Springer eBooks*. DOI: 10.1007/978-1-4614-2018-7

Christudas, B. C. L., Kirubakaran, E., & Thangaiah, P. R. J. (2018). An evolutionary approach for personalization of content delivery in e-learning systems based on learner behavior forcing compatibility of learning materials. *Telematics and Informatics*, 35(3), 520–533. DOI: 10.1016/j.tele.2017.02.004

Chun, A., & Warner, J. (2021). AI in education: Today's challenges and tomorrow's promise. *EdTech Magazine*. https://edtechmagazine.com/

Clark, T. M. (2023). Investigating the use of an artificial intelligence chatbot with general chemistry exam questions. *Journal of Chemical Education*, 100(5), 1905–1916. DOI: 10.1021/acs.jchemed.3c00027

Cleveland-Innes, M., & Wilton, D. (2018). Guide to blended learning.

Coeckelbergh, M. (2023, March 29). Chatbots can kill. *Medium*. https://coeckelbergh.medium.com/chatbots-can-kill-d82fde5cf6ca

Çolak, A. F. (2022). Okullarda yapay zeka öğretimi için geliştirilen kurs planı ve içeriklerin öğrencilerin üstbilişsel davranışlarına etkisi / The effect of course plan and contents developed for artificial intelligence teaching in secondary schools on students' metacognitive behaviors, Trabzon Üniversitesi / Lisansüstü Eğitim Enstitüsü, Yüksek lisans tezi

Colchester, K., Hagras, H., Alghazzawi, D., & Aldabbagh, G. (2016, December 17). A Survey of Artificial Intelligence Techniques Employed for Adaptive Educational Systems within E-Learning Platforms. Polish Neural Network Society, the University of Social Sciences in Lodz & Czestochowa University of Technology, 7(1), 47-64. DOI: 10.1515/jaiscr-2017-0004

Comas-Quinn, A. (2011). Learning to teach online or learning to become an online teacher: An exploration of teachers' experiences in a blended learning course. *Re-CALL*, 23(3), 218–232. DOI: 10.1017/S0958344011000152

Conway, T. (2024, September 13). Adaptive learning: A practical guide to personalized paths and future-ready teaching. *Linkedin*. https://www.linkedin.com/pulse/adaptive-learning-practical-guide-personalized-paths-conway-ph-d--ixqce

Cooke, S. (2024). Language Support with AI: Breaking Barriers for International Students - Techstrong.ai. Techstrong.ai. https://techstrong.ai/articles/language-support-with-ai-breaking-barriers-for-international-students/

Cooper, G. (2023). Examining science education in ChatGPT: An exploratory study of generative artificial intelligence. *Journal of Science Education and Technology*, 32(3), 444–452. DOI: 10.1007/s10956-023-10039-y

Correlation One. (2023, June 23). Five barriers to AI readiness. https://www.correlation-one.com/blog/5-barriers-to-ai-readiness

Coşkun, F., & Gülleroğlu, H. D. (2021). Yapay zekanın tarih içindeki gelişimi ve eğitimde kullanılması. *Ankara Üniversitesi Eğitim Bilimleri Fakültesi Dergisi, 54*(3), 947-966. DOI: , E-ISSN: 2458-8342, P-ISSN: 1301-3718.DOI: 10.30964/auebfd.916220

CoSN and Teach AI. (2023). AI guidance for schools toolkit: Principles for AI in education. https://www.teachai.org/toolkit-principles

Coulton, P., Jacobs, N., Lindley, J., Richards, D., Stockton, G., & Whitham, R. (2023). Design pedagogy and generative AI. DPxGenAI Working Group, Lancaster University School of Design.

Crawford, J., Cowling, M., & Allen, K. A. (2023). Leadership is needed for ethical ChatGPT: Character, assessment, and learning using artificial intelligence (AI). *Journal of University Teaching & Learning Practice*, 20(3). Advance online publication. DOI: 10.53761/1.20.3.02

Creswell, J. W., & Creswell, J. D. (2018). *Research design: Qualitative, quantitative, and mixed methods approaches* (5th ed.). SAGE Publications.

Crisostomo, M., Bernarte, P., & Ambag, S. (2022). Cross-cultural translation studies in the context of artificial intelligence: Challenges and response. *European Online Journal of Natural and Social Sciences: Proceedings*, 11(4 (s)), 187–199. DOI: 10.18690/978-961-286-555-8.7

Cronje, J. (2020). Towards a new definition of blended learning. *Electronic Journal of e-Learning*, 18(2), 114–121. DOI: 10.34190/EJEL.20.18.2.001

Cross, R., D'warte, J., & Slaughter, Y. (2022). Plurilingualism and language and literacy education. *Australian Journal of Language and Literacy*, 45(3), 341–357. DOI: 10.1007/s44020-022-00023-1

D'Mello, S., & Graesser, A. (2012). Dynamics of affective states during complex learning. *Learning and Instruction*, 22(2), 145–1573. DOI: 10.1016/j.learninstruc.2011.10.001

Dangwal, K. L. (2017). Blended learning: An innovative approach. *Universal Journal of Educational Research*, 5(1), 129–136. DOI: 10.13189/ujer.2017.050116

Darwin, R., Rusdin, D., Mukminatien, N., Suryati, N., Laksmi, E. D., & Marzuki, . (2024, December 31). D., Mukminatien, N., Suryati, N., Laksmi, E. D., & Marzuki. (2023). Critical thinking in the AI era: An exploration of EFL students' perceptions, benefits, and limitations. *Cogent Education*, 11(1), 2290342. Advance online publication. DOI: 10.1080/2331186X.2023.2290342

Dastin, J. (2018). Amazon scraps secret AI recruiting tool that showed bias against women. *Reuters*. https://www.reuters.com/article/us-amazon-com-jobs-automation-insight/amazon-scraps-secret-ai-recruiting-tool-that-showed-bias-against-women-idUSKCN1MK08G

Davenport, T. H. (2005). *Thinking for a living: How to get better performances and results from knowledge workers*. Harvard Business School Press.

Davenport, T. H., & Prusak, L. (1998). *Working knowledge: How organizations manage what they know*. Harvard Business Press.

Davis, R. O., & Lee, Y. J. (2023). Prompt: ChatGPT, create my course, please! *Education Sciences*, 14(1), 24. DOI: 10.3390/educsci14010024

De Abreu, B. S. (Ed.). (2022). *Media literacy, equity, and justice*. Routledge. DOI: 10.4324/9781003175599

De Weger, E., Van Vooren, N., Luijkx, K. G., Baan, C. A., & Drewes, H. W. (2018). Achieving successful community engagement: A rapid realist review. *BMC Health Services Research*, 18(1), 285. Advance online publication. DOI: 10.1186/s12913-018-3090-1 PMID: 29653537

Deeva, G., Bogdanova, D., Serral, E., Snoeck, M., & De Weerdt, J. (2021). A review of automated feedback systems for learners: Classification framework, challenges and opportunities. *Computers & Education*, 162, 104094. DOI: 10.1016/j.compedu.2020.104094

Deiana, G., Dettori, M., Arghittu, A., Azara, A., Gabutti, G., & Castiglia, P. (2023). Artificial intelligence and public health: Evaluating ChatGPT responses to vaccination myths and misconceptions. *Vaccines*, 11(7), 1217. DOI: 10.3390/vaccines11071217 PMID: 37515033

Dellarocas, C. (2023, December 8). How genAI could accelerate employee learning and development. *Harvard Business Review*, https://hbr.org/2023/12/how-genai-could-accelerate-employee-learning-and-development

Deloitte. (2023). *Proactive risk management in generative AI*. Deloitte AI Institute.

Dempere, J., Modugu, K., Hesham, A., & Ramasamy, L. K. (2023). The impact of ChatGPT on higher education. *Frontiers in Education*, 8, 1206936. Advance online publication. DOI: 10.3389/feduc.2023.1206936

DeVries, B. A. (2023). *Literacy assessment and intervention for classroom teachers*. Routledge. DOI: 10.4324/9781003230397

Diakopoulos, N., Trielli, D., Stanton, A., & Smrž, P. (2019). Automated news: How algorithms impact the news we read. *The AI Now Report*, 1–30.

Diakopoulos, N. (2016). *Algorithmic accountability: Journalistic investigation of computational power structures*. Data & Society.

Dillenbourg, P. (1999). What do you mean by collaborative learning? In Dillenbourg, P. (Ed.), *Collaborative-learning: Cognitive and computational approaches* (pp. 1–19). Elsevier.

Dillu, D. (2023). How Over-Reliance on AI Could Lead to Cognitive Atrophy. NeuraNest. https://medium.com/neuranest/how-over-reliance-on-ai-could-lead-to-cognitive-atrophy-d04d214c7e75

Ding, A. E., Shie, L., Yang, H., & Choi, I. (2024, June). Enhancing teacher AI literacy and integration through different types of cases in teacher professional development. *Computers and Education Open*, 6, 100178–1000191. DOI: 10.1016/j.caeo.2024.100178

Drucker, P. F. (2019). *The effective executive: The definitive guide to getting the right things done*. Routledge., DOI: 10.4324/9780367330752

Du, Y. (2022, January 4). Application of the Data-Driven Educational Decision-Making System to Curriculum Optimization of Higher Education. Wiley, 2022, 1-8. DOI: 10.1155/2022/5823515

Dutta, S., Ranjan, S., Mishra, S., Sharma, V., Hewage, P., & Iwendi, C. (2024, February). Enhancing Educational Adaptability: A Review and Analysis of AI-Driven Adaptive Learning Platforms. In *2024 4th International Conference on Innovative Practices in Technology and Management (ICIPTM)* (pp. 1-5). IEEE. DOI: 10.1109/ICIPTM59628.2024.10563448

Dziuban, C. D., & Picciano, A. G. (2021). Education and Blended Learning: Some Possible Futures. In *Blended Learning* (pp. 365-402). Routledge.

Eacott, S. (2021). AI and Decision-Making in Australian Educational Leadership. *Educational Management Administration & Leadership*, 49(3), 399–415.

Edeni, C. A., Adeleye, O. O., & Adeniyi, I. S.Chima Abimbola EdeniOlabisi Oluwakemi AdeleyeIdowu Sulaimon Adeniyi. (2024). The role of AI-enhanced tools in overcoming socioeconomic barriers in education: A conceptual analysis. *World Journal of Advanced Research and Reviews*, 21(3), 944–951. DOI: 10.30574/wjarr.2024.21.3.0780

Edgley, R. (2006, July 9). Education for Industry. https://www.tandfonline.com/doi/full/10.1080/0013188770200104

EdSurge. (2019). Report on the impact of adaptive learning technologies on student outcomes. *EdSurge*. https://www.edsurge.com

Ejjami, R. (2024). The Future of Learning: AI-Based Curriculum development. *International Journal for Multidisciplinary Research*, 6(4), 24441. Advance online publication. DOI: 10.36948/ijfmr.2024.v06i04.24441

Elberzhager, F., Mennig, P., Polst, S., Scherr, S., & Stüpfert, P. (2021). Towards a digital ecosystem for a smart city district: Procedure, results, and lessons learned. *Smart Cities*, 4(2), 686–716. DOI: 10.3390/smartcities4020035

Elgammal, A., Liu, B., Elhoseiny, M., & Mazzone, M. (2017). CAN: Creative adversarial networks, generating "art" by learning about styles and deviating from style norms. *arXiv Preprint* arXiv:1706.07068. https://arxiv.org/abs/1706.07068

Eliashberg, J., Hui, S. K., & Zhang, Z. J. (2014). Assessing box office performance using movie scripts: A machine learning approach. *Management Science*, 60(6), 1425–1439. DOI: 10.1287/mnsc.2013.1836

Elimadi, I., Chafiq, N., & Ghazouani, M. (2024). Artificial Intelligence in the Context of Digital Learning Environments (DLEs): Towards Adaptive Learning. In *Engineering Applications of Artificial Intelligence* (pp. 95–111). Springer Nature Switzerland. DOI: 10.1007/978-3-031-50300-9_6

Elmas, Ç. (2018). *Yapay zeka uygulamaları*. Seçkin Yayıncılık.

Emery, N. C., Bledsoe, E. K., Hasley, A. O., & Eaton, C. D. (2021). Cultivating inclusive instructional and research environments in ecology and evolutionary science. *Ecology and Evolution*, 11(4), 1480–1491. DOI: 10.1002/ece3.7062 PMID: 33613983

Emmanuel, J. S., Bhandigadi, P., & Ch'ng, L. K. (2019). Student Engagement and Its Impact on Achievement in a Blended Learning Environment in Malaysia. *Asian Journal of Distance Education*, 14(1), 56–67.

Erickson, J. A., Botelho, A. F., McAteer, S., Varatharaj, A., & Heffernan, N. T. (2020, March). The automated grading of student open responses in mathematics. In *Proceedings of the tenth international conference on learning analytics & knowledge* (pp. 615-624). DOI: 10.1145/3375462.3375523

Eubanks, V. E. (2018). *Automating inequality: How high-tech tools profile, police, and punish the poor*. St. Martin's Press.

European Commission. (2019). *Ethics guidelines for trustworthy AI*. European Commission.

European Commission. Directorate-General for Education, Youth, Sport and Culture. (2022). Ethical guidelines on the use of artificial intelligence (AI) and data in teaching and learning for educators. Publications Office of the European Union. https://data.europa.eu/doi/10.2766/153756

Factmata. (2017). Factmata: AI-powered fact-checking. *Factmata.* https://www.factmata.com

Fahri, L M. (2022, August 31). The Effect of Problem-Based Learning Strategies and Direct Learning Strategies on Students' Fiqh Learning Outcomes. Altezoro s.r.o. (Slovak Republic) and Publishing Center "Dialog" (Ukraine), 8(8), 2025-2031. DOI: 10.22178/pos.84-5

Familoni, B. T. (2024). *Cybersecurity challenges in the age of AI: Theoretical approaches and practical solutions.* Computer Science & IT Research Journal., DOI: 10.1007/s40593-021-00147-2

Fan, L. (2024). AI reduces critical thinking. The Nexus. https://wvnexus.org/opinions/ai-reduces-critical-thinking/

Felix, C. (2020). In Sengupta, E., Blessinger, P., & Makhanya, M. S. (Eds.), *"The role of the teacher and AI in education" in International perspectives on the role of Technology in Humanizing Higher Education Innovations in higher education teaching and learning* (Vol. 33, pp. 33–48). Emerald Publishing Limited.

Ferikoğlu, D., & Akgün, E. (2022). An investigation of teachers' artificial intelligence awareness: A scale development study. *Malaysian Online Journal of Educational Technology*, 10(3), 215–231. DOI: 10.52380/mojet.2022.10.3.407

Fernández-Batanero, J. M., Montenegro-Rueda, M., Fernández-Cerero, J., & García-Martínez, I. (2022). Digital competences for teacher professional development: Systematic review. *European Journal of Teacher Education*, 45(4), 513–531. DOI: 10.1080/02619768.2020.1827389

Ferrucci, D., Levas, A., Bagchi, S., Gondek, D., & Mueller, E. T. (2013). Watson: Beyond Jeopardy! *Artificial Intelligence*, 199, 114–137. DOI: 10.1016/j.artint.2012.06.009

Feuerriegel, S., Dolata, M., & Schwabe, G. (2020, May 11). Fair AI. *Business & Information Systems Engineering*, 62(4), 379–384. DOI: 10.1007/s12599-020-00650-3

Filipsson, F. (2024). AI in Educational Administration: Transforming School Operations. Redress Compliance - Just another WordPress site. https://redresscompliance.com/ai-educational-adminisitration/

Firschein, O., Fischler, M. A., Coles, S., & Tenenbaum, J. M. (1973). Forecasting and Assessing the Impact of Artificial Intelligence on Society. International Joint Conference on Artificial Intelligence, 105-120. https://www.semanticscholar.org/paper/Forecasting-and-Assessing-the-Impact-of-Artificial-Firschein-Fischler/489d1e39812f298622323b7c32a73fe403f7c45e

Fitria, H., & Suminah, S. (2020). Role of teachers in digital instructional era. *Journal of social work and science education, 1*(1), 70-77.

Fitria, T. N. (2021). ARTIFICIAL INTELLIGENCE (AI) IN EDUCATION: USING AI TOOLS FOR TEACHING AND LEARNING PROCESS. *Prosiding Seminar Nasional & Call for Paper STIE AAS, 4* (1), 134-147. Retrieved from https://prosiding .stie-aas.ac.id/index.php/prosenas/article/view/106

Floridi, L., & Cowls, J. (2019). A unified framework of five principles for AI in society. *Harvard Data Science Review*. Advance online publication. DOI: 10.1162/99608f92.8cd550d1

Floridi, L., Cowls, J., Beltrametti, M., Chatila, R., Chazerand, P., Dignum, V., Luetge, C., Madelin, R., Pagallo, U., Rossi, F., Schafer, B., Valcke, P., & Vayena, E. (2018). AI4People—An ethical framework for a good AI society: Opportunities, risks, principles, and recommendations. *Minds and Machines*, 28(4), 689–707. DOI: 10.1007/s11023-018-9482-5 PMID: 30930541

Ford, J., & Martin, R. (2020). The role of AI in media feedback: Enhancing student creativity through data-driven critiques. *Journal of Educational Technology & Society*, 23(3), 56–72.

Frank, M., Kurtz, G., & Levin, N. (2002). Implications of presenting pre-university courses using the blended e-learning approach. *Journal of Educational Technology & Society*, 5(4), 137–147.

Freire, P. (1970). Pedagogy of the oppressed. *Continuum : an Interdisciplinary Journal on Continuity of Care*.

Fu, K. W., Chan, W. S. C., Wong, P. W. C., & Yip, P. S. F. (2010). Internet addiction: Prevalence, discriminant validity and correlates among adolescents in Hong Kong. *The British Journal of Psychiatry*, 196(6), 486–492. DOI: 10.1192/bjp.bp.109.075002 PMID: 20513862

Fukuda-Parr, S., & Gibbons, E. (2021). Emerging consensus on 'Ethical AI': Human rights critique of stakeholder guidelines. *Global Policy*, 12(S6), 32–44. DOI: 10.1111/1758-5899.12965

G¨ottel, T. (2011). Reviewing children's collaboration practices in storytelling environments. In *Proceedings of the 10th international conference on interaction design and children* (Vol. 11, pp. 153–156). IDC. https://doi.org/DOI: 10.1145/1999030.1999049

Gallagher, M. B., Cook, C. A. L., Tebb, S., & Berg-Weger, M. (2003). Practicing social justice: Community-based research, education, and practice. In Wilson, J., Burkemper, E., Hutchison, W. J., & Stretch, J. J. (Eds.), *Practicing social justice* (pp. 27–39). Routledge.

Gallup. (2018). The state of student engagement in U.S. schools. *Gallup*. https://www.gallup.com

García-Martínez, I., Batanero, J. M. F., Cerero, J. F., & León, S. P. (2023, January 1). Analysing the Impact of Artificial Intelligence and Computational Sciences on Student Performance: Systematic Review and Meta-analysis. *University of Alicante*, 12(1), 171–171. DOI: 10.7821/naer.2023.1.1240

García-Peñalvo, F. J. (2023). The perception of artificial intelligence in educational contexts after the launch of ChatGPT: Disruption or Panic? *Education in the Knowledge Society*, 24, e31279.

Gates, B. (2023). The Age of AI Has Begun, gatesnotes.com, https://www.gatesnotes.com/The-Age-of-AI-Has-Begun (accessed September 2, 2024)

Gauthier, A., Rizvi, S., Cukurova, M., & Mavrikis, M. (2022). Is it time we get real? A systematic review of the potential of data-driven technologies to address teachers' implicit biases. *Frontiers in Artificial Intelligence*, 5, 994967. Advance online publication. DOI: 10.3389/frai.2022.994967 PMID: 36304958

Geerling, W., Mateer, G. D., Wooten, J., & Damodaran, N. (2023). Is ChatGPT smarter than a student in principles of economics? SSRN *Electronic Journal,* 1-24. https://doi.org/DOI: 10.2139/ssrn.4356034

George, B., & Wooden, O. (2023). Managing the Strategic Transformation of Higher Education through Artificial Intelligence. *Administrative Sciences*, 13(9), 196. DOI: 10.3390/admsci13090196

Getz, I., & Carney, B. (2009). *Freedom, Inc.: Free your employees and let them lead your business to higher productivity, profits, and growth.* Crown Business.

Ghaffar Nia, N., Kaplanoglu, E., & Nasab, A. (2023). Evaluation of artificial intelligence techniques in disease diagnosis and prediction. *Discover Artificial Intelligence*, 3(1), 5. DOI: 10.1007/s44163-023-00049-5

Ghamrawi, N., Shal, T., & Ghamrawi, N. A. (2023). Exploring the impact of AI on teacher leadership: Regressing or expanding? *Education and Information Technologies*, 29(7), 8415–8433. DOI: 10.1007/s10639-023-12174-w

Gilardi, F., Alizadeh, M., & Kubli, M. (2023). ChatGPT outperforms crowd workers for text-annotation tasks. *Proceedings of the National Academy of Sciences of the United States of America*, 120(30), E2305016120. DOI: 10.1073/pnas.2305016120 PMID: 37463210

Gillani, N., Eynon, R., Chiabaut, C., & Finkel, K. (2023). Unpacking the "Black Box" of AI. *Education.Journal of Educational Technology & Society*, 26(1), 99–111. DOI: 10.30191/ETS.202301_26(1).0008

Giraud, L., & Autissier, D. (2020). *Nouveaux modes de management organisationnel: Enjeux et pratiques*. Dunod.

Gison, C. (2024, April 7). Overcoming the limitations of AI in creative content generation. *Medium*. https://medium.com/@chasegison/overcoming-the-limitations-of-ai-in-creative-content-generation-7e0e08f31207

Goldkind, L. (2021). Social work and artificial intelligence: Into the Matrix. *Social Work*, 66(4), 372–374. DOI: 10.1093/sw/swab028 PMID: 34279661

Goodfellow, I., Pouget-Abadie, J., Mirza, M., Xu, B., Warde-Farley, D., Ozair, S., Courville, A., & Bengio, Y. (2020). Generative adversarial networks. *Communications of the ACM*, 63(11), 139–144. DOI: 10.1145/3422622

Graesser, A. C., Hu, X., Nye, B. D., VanLehn, K., Kumar, R., Heffernan, N., Woolf, B., Olney, A. M., Rus, V., Andrasik, F., Pavlik, P., Cai, Z., Wetzel, J., Morgan, B., Hampton, A. J., Lippert, A. M., Wang, L., Chen, Q., & Baer, W. (2018). ElectronixTutor: An intelligent tutoring system with multiple learning resources for electronics. In *International Journal of STEM Education, 5*, Article 15. DOI: 10.1186/s40594-018-0110-y

Graf, S., & Kinshuk, K. (2013, May 22). Adaptive Technologies. Springer Nature, 771-779. DOI: 10.1007/978-1-4614-3185-5_62

Graham, C. R. (2021). Exploring definitions, models, frameworks, and theory for blended learning research. In *Blended Learning* (pp. 10–29). Routledge. DOI: 10.4324/9781003037736-3

Graham, C. R., Henrie, C. R., & Gibbons, A. S. (2013). Developing models and theory for blended learning research. In *Blended learning* (pp. 13–33). Routledge.

Graves, L. (2018). Understanding the promise and limits of automated fact-checking. *Digital Journalism (Abingdon, England)*, 6(8), 939–954. DOI: 10.1080/21670811.2018.1531688

Green, S., & Thomas, P. (2020). Accessibility of AI-driven tools in media production: A pathway for non-technical students. *Journal of Visual Arts Education*, 35(2), 121–135.

Guan, C., Mou, J., & Jiang, Z. (2020). Artificial intelligence innovation in education: A twenty-year data-driven historical analysis. *International Journal of Innovation Studies*, 4(4), 134–147. DOI: 10.1016/j.ijis.2020.09.001

Guilherme, A. (2017, February 4). AI and education: The importance of teacher and student relations. *AI & Society*, 34(1), 47–54. DOI: 10.1007/s00146-017-0693-8

Gunasena, U., Kumara, S., & Soyster, A L. (1989, January 1). A KNOWLEDGE-BASED SYSTEM FOR COURSE SCHEDULING. Taylor & Francis, 3(4), 463-482. DOI: 10.1080/08839518908949938

Guo, K., & Wang, D. (2024). To resist it or to embrace it? Examining ChatGPT's potential to support teacher feedback in EFL writing. *Education and Information Technologies*, 29(7), 8435–8463. DOI: 10.1007/s10639-023-12146-0

Gupta, M., Akiri, C., Aryal, K., Parker, E., & Praharaj, L. (2023). From ChatGPT to threatGPT: Impact of generative AI in cybersecurity and privacy. *IEEE Access : Practical Innovations, Open Solutions*, 11, 80218–80245. DOI: 10.1109/ACCESS.2023.3300381

Guskey, T. R., & Link, L. J. (2022). Feedback for teachers: What evidence do teachers find most useful? *AASA Journal of Scholarship & Practice*, 4(4), 9–20.

Gutiérrez-Caneda, B., Vázquez-Herrero, J., & López-García, X. (2023). AI application in journalism: ChatGPT and the uses and risks of an emergent technology. *El Profesional de la Información*, 32(5), e320514. Advance online publication. DOI: 10.3145/epi.2023.sep.14

Haagen-Schützenhöfer, C., & Hopf, M. (2020). Design-based research as a model for systematic curriculum development: The example of a curriculum for introductory optics. *Physical Review. Physics Education Research*, 16(2), 020152. DOI: 10.1103/PhysRevPhysEducRes.16.020152

Habib, S., Vogel, T., Anli, X., & Thorne, E. (2024). How does generative artificial intelligence impact student creativity? *Journal of Creativity*, 34(1), 100072. Advance online publication. DOI: 10.1016/j.yjoc.2023.100072

Hadjerrouit, S. (2010). A theoretical framework to Foster digital literacy: The case of digital learning resources. In Reynolds, N., & Turcsányi-Szabó, M. (Eds.), *Key competencies in the knowledge society* (pp. 144–154). Springer., DOI: 10.1007/978-3-642-15378-5_14

Hadwin, A. F., Järvelä, S., & Miller, M. (2018). Self-regulation, co-regulation, and shared regulation in collaborative learning environments. In Schunk, D. H., & Greene, J. A. (Eds.), *Handbook of self-regulation of learning and performance* (2nd ed., pp. 83–106). Routledge.

Haenlein, M., & Kaplan, A. (2021). Artificial intelligence and robotics: Shaking up the business world and society at large. *Journal of Business Research*, 124, 405–407. DOI: 10.1016/j.jbusres.2020.10.042

Häggström, M., & Schmidt, C. (2021). Futures literacy–to belong, participate and act!: An educational perspective. *Futures*, 132, 102813. DOI: 10.1016/j.futures.2021.102813

Hagiu, A., & Wright, J. (2023). To get better customer data, build feedback loops into your products. *Harvard Business Review*. https://hbr.org/2023/07/to-get-better-customer-data-build-feedback-loops-into-your-products

Haider, S. (2022). *Digital transformation and innovation: Leveraging digital technologies for business success*. Springer.

Haines, S. G. (1998). *The managers guide to systems thinking & learning*. HRD Press.

Hakak, S., Noor, N F M., Ayub, M. N., Affal, H., Hussin, N., Ahmed, E., & Imran, M. (2019, March 5). Cloud-assisted gamification for education and learning. https://www.sciencedirect.com/science/article/pii/S0045790618304968

Halaweh, M. (2023). ChatGPT in education: Strategies for responsible implementation. *Contemporary Educational Technology*, 15(2), ep421. DOI: 10.30935/cedtech/13036

Halim, L., Ramli, M., & Ali, M. N. (Eds.). (2022). *Culturally Responsive Science Pedagogy in Asia: Status and Challenges for Malaysia, Indonesia and Japan*. DOI: 10.4324/9781003168706

Halpern, D., & Katz, J. E. (2017). Texting's consequences for romantic relationships: A cross-lagged analysis highlights its risks. *Computers in Human Behavior*, 71(11), 386–394. DOI: 10.1016/j.chb.2017.01.051

Halverson, L. R., & Graham, C. R. (2019). Learner engagement in blended learning environments: A conceptual framework. *Online Learning : the Official Journal of the Online Learning Consortium*, 23(2), 145–178. DOI: 10.24059/olj.v23i2.1481

Hamari, J., Koivisto, J., & Sarsa, H. (2014). Does gamification work? A literature review of empirical studies on gamification. In *Proceedings of the 47th Hawaii International Conference on System Sciences* (pp. 3025-3034). IEEE. https://doi.org/DOI: 10.1109/HICSS.2014.377

Hamel, G. (2007). *The future of management*. Harvard Business School Press.

Hamza, M., Siemon, D., Akbar, M. A., & Rahman, T. (2024, April). Human-AI Collaboration in Software Engineering: Lessons Learned from a Hands-On Workshop. In *Proceedings of the 7th ACM/IEEE International Workshop on Software-intensive Business* (pp. 7-14).

Hanell, F. (2020). Co-learning in a digital community: information literacy and views on learning in pre-school teacher education. In Sustainable Digital Communities: 15th International Conference, iConference 2020, Boras, Sweden, March 23–26, 2020 [Springer International Publishing.]. *Proceedings*, 15, 327–342.

Hannon, P., Nutbrown, C., & Morgan, A. (2020). Effects of extending disadvantaged families' teaching of emergent literacy. *Research Papers in Education*, 35(3), 310–336. DOI: 10.1080/02671522.2019.1568531

Harkness, L., Robinson, K., Stein, E., & Wu, W. (2023). *How generative AI can boost consumer marketing*. McKinsey & Company.

Harris, A., & Jones, M. (2020). Artificial Intelligence and Educational Leadership in the UK. *Educational Management Administration & Leadership*, 48(4), 578–598.

Harrison, N., & Skrebneva, I. (2020). Country as pedagogical: Enacting an Australian foundation for culturally responsive pedagogy. *Journal of Curriculum Studies*, 52(1), 15–26. DOI: 10.1080/00220272.2019.1641843

Harry, A., & Sayudin, S. (2023). Role of AI in Education. [INJURITY]. *Interdiciplinary Journal and Hummanity*, 2(3), 260–268.

Hartman, R. J., Townsend, M. B., & Jackson, M. (2019). Educators' perceptions of technology integration into the classroom: A descriptive case study. *Journal of Research in Innovative Teaching & Learning*, 12(3), 236–249. DOI: 10.1108/JRIT-03-2019-0044

Hashem, R., Ali, N., El Zein, F., Fidalgo, P., & Khurma, O. A. (2024). AI to the rescue: Exploring the potential of ChatGPT as a teacher ally for workload relief and burnout prevention. *Research and Practice in Technology Enhanced Learning*, 19, 104701. Advance online publication. DOI: 10.1186/s41039-023-00180-8

Hashim, S., Omar, M. K., Ab Jalil, H., & Sharef, N. M. (2022). Trends on technologies and artificial intelligence in education for personalized learning: Systematic literature. *Journal of Academic Research in Progressive Education and Development*, 12(1), 884–903. DOI: 10.6007/IJARPED/v11-i1/12230

Heinze, A., & Procter, C. T. (2004). Reflections on the use of blended learning.

Hemachandran, K., Verma, P., Pareek, P., Arora, N., Kumar, K. V. R., Ahanger, T. A., & Ratna, R. (2022). Artificial intelligence: A universal virtual tool to augment tutoring in higher education. *Computational Intelligence and Neuroscience*, 2022, 1–8. Advance online publication. DOI: 10.1155/2022/1410448 PMID: 35586099

Henrickson, L., & Meroño-Peñuela, A. (2023). Prompting meaning: A hermeneutic approach to optimising prompt engineering with ChatGPT. *AI & Society*. https://link.springer.com/article/10.1007/s00146-023-01752-8

Heugh, K., French, M., Arya, V., Pham, M., Tudini, V., Billinghurst, N., Tippett, N., Chang, L., Nichols, J., & Viljoen, J. (2022). Multilingualism, translanguaging and transknowledging. *AILA Review*, 35(1), 89–127. DOI: 10.1075/aila.22011.heu

Hobbs, R. (2010). *Digital and media literacy: Connecting culture and classroom*. Corwin Press.

Hodgson, D., Goldingay, S., Boddy, J., Nipperess, S., & Watts, L. (2022). Problematizing artificial intelligence in social work education: Challenges, issues and possibilities. *British Journal of Social Work*, 52(4), 1878–1895. DOI: 10.1093/bjsw/bcab168

Holmes, W., & Porayska-Pomsta, K. (2022). The ethics of artificial intelligence in education: Practices, challenges, and debates. *srce.hr*. https://doi.org/DOI: 10.1007/s11528-022-00660-5

Holmes, W., Bialik, M., & Fadel, C. (2019). *Artificial Intelligence in Education: Promises and Implications for Teaching and Learning*. Center for Curriculum Redesign.

Holmes, W., Porayska-Pomsta, K., Holstein, K., Sutherland, E., Baker, T., Shum, S. B., Santos, O. C., Rodrigo, M. T., Cukurova, M., Bittencourt, I. I., & Koedinger, K. R. (2022). Ethics of AI in education: Towards a community-wide framework. *International Journal of Artificial Intelligence in Education*, 32(3), 1–23. DOI: 10.1007/s40593-021-00239-1

Holstein, K., Aleven, V., & Rummel, N. (2020, January 1). A Conceptual Framework for Human–AI Hybrid Adaptivity in Education. Springer Science+Business Media, 240-254. DOI: 10.1007/978-3-030-52237-7_20

Holstein, K., McLaren, B M., & Aleven, V. (2019, January 1). Designing for Complementarity: Teacher and Student Needs for Orchestration Support in AI-Enhanced Classrooms. Springer Science+Business Media, 157-171. DOI: 10.1007/978-3-030-23204-7_14

Holstein, K., Wortman, J., Daumé, H.III, & Dudik, M. (2019). Improving Fairness in Machine Learning Systems: What Do Industry Practitioners Need? *Proceedings of the 2019 CHI Conference on Human Factors in Computing Systems*. DOI: 10.1145/3290605.3300830

Hooda, M., Rana, C., Dahiya, O., Rizwan, A., & Hossain, M. S. (2022). Artificial intelligence for assessment and feedback to enhance student success in higher education. *Mathematical Problems in Engineering*, 2022(1), 5215722. DOI: 10.1155/2022/5215722

Horn, E. (2023, July 27). Prompts for lesson planning with ChatGPT. https://blog.tcea.org/prompts-for-lesson-planning-with-chatgpt/

Horn, M. B., & Staker, H. (2016). *Blended leaning: 21st century learning revolution.*

Hu, L. (2023). Generative AI and future. Last accessed 2024/05/01 from https://pub.towardsai.net/generative-ai-and-future-c3b1695876f2

Huang, L. (2023, June 30). Ethics of Artificial Intelligence in Education. *Student Privacy and Data Protection.*, 16(2), 2577–2587. DOI: 10.15354/sief.23.re202

Huang, T., & Rust, R. T. (2019). Artificial intelligence in service. *Journal of Service Research*, 21(2), 155–172. DOI: 10.1177/1094670517752459

Huang, W., & Looi, C. K. (2021). A critical review of literature on "unplugged" pedagogies in K-12 computer science and computational thinking education. *Computer Science Education*, 31(1), 83–111. Advance online publication. DOI: 10.1080/08993408.2020.1789411

Hubackova, S., & Semradova, I. (2016). Evaluation of blended learning. *Procedia: Social and Behavioral Sciences*, 217, 551–557. DOI: 10.1016/j.sbspro.2016.02.044

Humphry, T., & Fuller, A. L. (2023). Potential ChatGPT use in undergraduate chemistry laboratories. *Journal of Chemical Education*, 100(4), 1434–1436. DOI: 10.1021/acs.jchemed.3c00006

Hur, J. W. (2024). Fostering AI literacy: Overcoming concerns and nurturing confidence among preservice teachers. *Information and Learning Science*. Advance online publication. DOI: 10.1108/ILS-11-2023-0170

Hwang, G. J., Xie, H., Wah, B. W., & Gašević, D. (2020). Vision, challenges, roles and research issues of artificial intelligence in education. *Computers and Education: Artificial Intelligence*, 1, 100001. DOI: 10.1016/j.caeai.2020.100001

IBM. (2020). IBM Watson: Explore AI for media. Retrieved from https://www.ibm.com/watson/media

Idowu, J. A., Koshiyama, A. S., & Treleaven, P. (2024). Investigating algorithmic bias in student progress monitoring. *Computers and Education: Artificial Intelligence*, 7, 100267. Advance online publication. DOI: 10.1016/j.caeai.2024.100267

Idrees, H. (2024, July 10). The evolution of transformers: From 'attention is all you need' to GPT-4. *Medium.*https://medium.com/@hassaanidrees7/the-evolution-of-transformers-from-attention-is-all-you-need-to-gpt-4-1baac3c038cd

Imchen, A., & Ndem, F. (2020). Addressing the learning crisis: An urgent need to better finance education for the poorest children. *UNICEF*. https://ed.gov

infinitivehost. (2023). The Negative Impacts of Artificial Intelligence on Humanity. infinitivehost. https://www.infinitivehost.com/blog/the-negative-impacts-of-artificial-intelligence-on-humanity/

International Association of Privacy Professionals (IAPP). (2022). Data breach trends in the education sector. https://iapp.org/

Iskender, A. (2023). Holy or unholy? Interview with Open AI's ChatGPT. *European Journal of Tourism Research*, 34, 3414. DOI: 10.54055/ejtr.v34i.3169

Islam, A., Ali, R., Singh, G., Islam, B., Islam, A., & Hossain, S. (2024, May). An Evaluation of AI-Enhanced Collaborative Learning Platforms. In *2024 International Conference on Communication, Computer Sciences and Engineering (IC3SE)* (pp. 207-211). IEEE. DOI: 10.1109/IC3SE62002.2024.10593320

İşler, B., & Kılıç, M. (2021). Eğitimde yapay zekâ kullanimi ve gelişimi. *Yeni Medya Elektronik Dergisi*, 5(1), 1–11.

Jackson, N. (2024). How can educators approach AI-based learning in ethical ways? https://www.vktr.com/ai-ethics-law-risk/practicing-ai-ethics-in-education/

Jackson, C., Mohr-Schroeder, M. J., Bush, S. B., Maiorca, C., Roberts, T., Yost, C., & Fowler, A. (2021). Equity-oriented conceptual framework for K-12 STEM literacy. *International Journal of STEM Education*, 8(1), 1–16. DOI: 10.1186/s40594-021-00294-z

Järvelä, S., Kirschner, P. A., Hadwin, A., Järvenoja, H., Malmberg, J., Miller, M., & Laru, J. (2016). Socially shared regulation of learning in CSCL: Understanding and prompting individual- and group-level shared regulatory activities. *International Journal of Computer-Supported Collaborative Learning*, 11(3), 263–280. DOI: 10.1007/s11412-016-9238-2

Järvelä, S., Nguyen, A., & Hadwin, A. (2023). Human and artificial intelligence collaboration for socially shared regulation in learning. *British Journal of Educational Technology*, 54(4), 1057–1076. DOI: 10.1111/bjet.13325

Jenkins, H. (2006). *Convergence culture: Where old and new media collide*. NYU Press.

Jenkins, H., Purushotma, R., Weigel, M., Clinton, K., & Robinson, A. J. (2009). *Confronting the challenges of participatory culture: Media education for the 21st century*. MIT Press. DOI: 10.7551/mitpress/8435.001.0001

Jeon, J., & Lee, S. (2023). Large language models in education: A focus on the complementary relationship between human teachers and ChatGPT. *Education and Information Technologies*, 28(12), 15873–15892. DOI: 10.1007/s10639-023-11834-1

Jia, X. H., & Tu, J. C. (2024). Towards a New Conceptual Model of AI-Enhanced Learning for College Students: The Roles of Artificial Intelligence Capabilities, General Self-Efficacy, Learning Motivation, and Critical Thinking Awareness. *Systems*, 12(3), 74. DOI: 10.3390/systems12030074

Jin, C. (2023). MOOC student dropout prediction model based on learning behavior features and parameter optimization. *Interactive Learning Environments*, 31(2), 714–732. DOI: 10.1080/10494820.2020.1802300

Jin, M. G., Luo, X. M., & Zhang, G. H. (2017). The Development and Relationship between Freshmen's Mobile Phone Dependence and Social Adaptation: A Cross Lagged Regression Analysis. Psychology. *Techniques and Application.*, 5(8), 449–454. DOI: 10.16842/j.cnki.issn2095–5588.2017.08.001

Johnson, M., Schuster, M., Le, Q., Krikun, M., Wu, Y., Chen, Z., ... & Chen, Y. (2016). Google's neural machine translation system: Bridging the gap between human and machine translation. arXiv pre.

Johnson, D. W., & Johnson, R. T. (2009). An educational psychology success story: Social interdependence theory and cooperative learning. *Educational Researcher*, 38(5), 365–379. DOI: 10.3102/0013189X09339057

Johnson, D., Alsharid, M., El-Bouri, R., Mehdi, N., Shamout, F. E., Szenicer, A., Toman, D., & Binghalib, S. (2022, June 28). An Experience Report of Executive-Level Artificial Intelligence Education in the United Arab Emirates. *Association for the Advancement of Artificial Intelligence*, 36(11), 12766–12773. DOI: 10.1609/aaai.v36i11.21555

Johnson, L. F., & Levine, A. H. (2008, April 16). Virtual Worlds: Inherently Immersive. *Theory into Practice*, 47(2), 161–170. DOI: 10.1080/00405840801992397

Jokinen, P., & Mikkonen, I. (2013). Teachers' experiences of teaching in a blended learning environment. *Nurse Education in Practice*, 13(6), 524–528. DOI: 10.1016/j.nepr.2013.03.014 PMID: 23608218

Joksimovíc, S., Poquet, O., Kovanović, V., Dowell, N., Mills, C., Gašević, D., Dawson, S., Graesser, A. C., & Brooks, C. (2017, November 14). How Do We Model Learning at Scale? A Systematic Review of Research on MOOCs. *Review of Educational Research*, 88(1), 43–86. DOI: 10.3102/0034654317740335

Jones, K. M., Asher, A., Goben, A., Perry, M. R., Salo, D., Briney, K. A., & Robertshaw, M. B. (2020). "We're being tracked at all times": Student perspectives of their privacy in relation to learning analytics in higher education. *Journal of the Association for Information Science and Technology*, 71(9), 1044–1059. DOI: 10.1002/asi.24358

Jones, L., Smith, M., & Lee, J. (2022). Using AI to enhance social work education: A case study of an adaptive learning platform. *Journal of Technology in Human Services*, 40(1), 23–45.

Jones, R., & Richardson, K. (2020). AI-assisted storytelling: New frontiers in media education. *Journal of Creative Media*, 28(3), 190–204.

Joshi, S., Rambola, R. K., & Churi, P. (2021). Evaluating artificial intelligence in education for next generation. *Journal of Physics: Conference Series*, 1714(1), 012039. DOI: 10.1088/1742-6596/1714/1/012039

Ka Yuk Chan, C. (2023). Is AI changing the rules of academic misconduct? An in-depth look at students' perceptions of 'AI-giarism.' The University of Hong Kong. https://www.researchgate.net/publication/371347082_Is_AI_Changing_the_Rules_of_Academic_Misconduct_An_In-depth_Look_at_Students'_Perceptions_of_'AI-giarism'

Kabudi, T., Pappas, I., & Olsen, D. H. (2021). AI-enabled adaptive learning systems: A systematic mapping of the literature. *Computers and Education: Artificial Intelligence*, 2, 100017. DOI: 10.1016/j.caeai.2021.100017

Kadaruddin, K. (2023, August 2). Empowering Education through Generative AI. *Innovative Instructional Strategies for Tomorrow's Learners.*, 4(2), 618–625. DOI: 10.56442/ijble.v4i2.215

Kahne, J., & Bowyer, B. (2017). Educating for democracy in a partisan age: Confronting the challenges of motivated reasoning and misinformation. *American Educational Research Journal*, 54(1), 3–34. DOI: 10.3102/0002831216679817

Kajiwara, Y., & Kawabata, K. (2024). AI literacy for ethical use of chatbot: Will students accept AI ethics? *Computers and Education: Artificial Intelligence*, 6, 100251. DOI: 10.1016/j.caeai.2024.100251

Kakhkharova, M., & Tuychieva, S. (2024, April). AI-Enhanced Pedagogy in Higher Education: Redefining Teaching-Learning Paradigms. In 2024 *International Conference on Knowledge Engineering and Communication Systems (ICKECS) (Vol. 1*, pp. 1-6). IEEE.

Kalantari, S., Rubegni, E., Benton, L., & Vasalou, A. (2023). "When I'm writing a story, I am really good" Exploring the use of digital storytelling technology at home. *International Journal of Child-Computer Interaction*, 38, 100613, ISSN 2212-8689, DOI: 10.1016/j.ijcci.2023.100613

Kamalov, F., Calonge, D. S., & Gurrib, I. (2023, August 16). New Era of Artificial Intelligence in Education: Towards a Sustainable Multifaceted Revolution. *Sustainability (Basel)*, 15(16), 12451–12451. DOI: 10.3390/su151612451

Karakoyun, F., & Kuzu, A. (2016). The investigation of preservice teachers' and primary school students' views about online digital storytelling. *European Journal of Contemporary Education*, 15(1), 51–64.

Karasavvidis, I. (2009, January). Activity Theory as a theoretical framework for the study of blended learning: a case study. In *Proceedings of the 6th International Conference on Networked Learning* (pp. 195-202).

Kateryna, A., Oleksandr, R., Mariia, T., Iryna, S., Evgen, K., & Anastasiia, L. (2020). Digital literacy development trends in the professional environment. *International Journal of Learning. Teaching and Educational Research*, 19(7), 55–79.

Kaur, M. (2013). Blended learning-its challenges and future. *Procedia: Social and Behavioral Sciences*, 93, 612–617. DOI: 10.1016/j.sbspro.2013.09.248

Kaya, İ. (2024). *Eğitim yönetiminde yapay zekâ kullanımına ilişkin okul yöneticileri ve öğretmenlerin görüşleri / School administrators and teachers' views on the use of artificial intelligence in education administration. İstanbul Aydın Üniversitesi / Lisansüstü Eğitim Enstitüsü / Eğitim Bilimleri Ana Bilim Dalı*. Yüksek Lisans Tezi.

Kayode-Ajala, O. (2023). Establishing cyber resilience in developing countries: An exploratory investigation into institutional, legal, financial, and social challenges. *International Journal of Sustainable Infrastructure for Cities and Societies*, 8(9), 1–10. https://vectoral.org

Kayyali, M. (2024). Future possibilities and challenges of AI in education. In *Transforming education with generative AI: Prompt engineering and synthetic content creation* (pp. 118–137). IGI Global. DOI: 10.4018/979-8-3693-1351-0.ch006

Keiper, M. C., Fried, G., Lupinek, J., & Nordstrom, H. (2023). Artificial intelligence in sport management education: Playing the AI game with ChatGPT. Journal of Hospitality, Leisure, Sport & Tourism Education, 33, 100456, ISSN 1473-8376, https://doi.org/DOI: 10.1016/j.jhlste.2023.100456

Kellogg, S. (2021). *Urban ecosystem justice: Strategies for equitable sustainability and ecological literacy in the city*. Routledge. DOI: 10.4324/9780367858711

Kelsky, K. (2015). *The professor is in: The essential guide to turning your Ph.D. into a job*. Three Rivers Press.

Kelty, N. E., & Wakabayashi, T. (2020). Family engagement in schools: Parent, educator, and community perspectives. *SAGE Open*, 10(4), 2158244020973024. DOI: 10.1177/2158244020973024

Kem, D. (2022). Personalised and adaptive learning: Emerging learning platforms in the era of digital and smart learning. *International Journal of Social Science and Human Research*, 5(2), 385–391. DOI: 10.47191/ijsshr/v5-i2-02

Kharb, P., & Samanta, P. P. (2016). Blended learning approach for teaching and learning anatomy: Students' and teachers' perspective. *Journal of the Anatomical Society of India*, 65(1), 43–47. DOI: 10.1016/j.jasi.2016.06.001

Kharchenko, Y. V., & Babenko, O. M. (2024). Advantages and limitations of large language models in chemistry education: A comparative analysis of ChatGPT, Gemini and Copilot. *IX International Workshop on Professional Retraining and Life-Long Learning using ICT: Person-oriented Approach, co-located with the 19th International Conference on ICT in Education, Research, and Industrial Applications (ICTERI 2024) September 23, 2024, Lviv, Ukraine*

Khosravi, H., Shum, S. B., Chen, G., Conati, C., Tsai, Y.-S., Kay, J., Knight, S., Martinez-Maldonado, R., Sadiq, S., & Gasevic, D. (2022). Explainable Artificial Intelligence in Education. Computers and Education. *Artificial Intelligence*, 3, 100074. Advance online publication. DOI: 10.1016/j.caeai.2022.100074

Khreisat, M. N., Khilani, D., Rusho, M. A., Karkkulainen, E. A., Tabuena, A. C., & Uberas, A. D. (2024). Ethical Implications Of AI Integration In Educational Decision Making: Systematic Review. *Educational Administration: Theory and Practice*, 30(5), 8521–8527.

Kim, J. (2024). Leading teachers' perspective on teacher-AI collaboration in education. *Education and Information Technologies*, 29(7), 8693–8724. DOI: 10.1007/s10639-023-12109-5

Kim, J., Lee, H., & Cho, Y. H. (2022). Learning design to support student-AI collaboration: Perspectives of leading teachers for AI in education. *Education and Information Technologies*, 27(5), 6069–6104. DOI: 10.1007/s10639-021-10831-6

Kimmel, S. (2024). AI Facilitated Critical Thinking in an Undergraduate Project Based Service-Learning Course. *Journal of Behavioral and Applied Management*, 24(2), 123–130. DOI: 10.21818/001c.122149

Kimsesiz, F. (2023). An examination of digitalized self-directed language learning practices of tertiary level EFL learners in Türkiye. *Journal of Educational Technology and Online Learning*, 6(3), 683–701. DOI: 10.31681/jetol.1276105

Kinshuk, N., Chen, N., Cheng, I., & Chew, S. W. (2016). Evolution Is not enough: Revolutionizing Current Learning Environments to Smart Learning Environments. *International Journal of Artificial Intelligence in Education*, 26(2), 561–581. DOI: 10.1007/s40593-016-0108-x

Kitcharoen, P., Howimanporn, S., & Chookaew, S. (2024). Enhancing teachers' AI competencies through artificial intelligence of things professional development training. *International Journal of Interactive Mobile Technologies*, 18(2), 4–15. DOI: 10.3991/ijim.v18i02.46613

Kitchen, J. A., Perez, R., Hallett, R., Kezar, A., & Reason, R. (2021). Ecological validation model of student success: A new student support model for promoting college success among low-income, first-generation, and racially minoritized students. *Journal of College Student Development*, 62(6), 627–642. DOI: 10.1353/csd.2021.0062

Kleinheksel, A. (2014, May 17). Transformative Learning through Virtual Patient Simulations. *Clinical Simulation in Nursing*, 10(6), e301–e308. DOI: 10.1016/j.ecns.2014.02.001

Knewton. (2014). Personalized learning for all. Retrieved from https://www.knewton.com

Knewton. (2015). Impact of adaptive learning on student retention rates. *Knewton*. Retrieved from https://www.knewton.com

Knight, S., Wise, A. F., & Chen, B. (2017). Time for change: Why learning analytics needs temporal analysis. *Journal of Learning Analytics*, 4(3), 7–17. DOI: 10.18608/jla.2017.43.2

Kohnke, L., Moorhouse, B. L., & Zou, D. (2023). Exploring generative artificial intelligence preparedness among university language instructors: A case study. *Computers and Education: Artificial Intelligence*, 5, 100156. DOI: 10.1016/j.caeai.2023.100156

Kraja, P. (2023). Report on Smart Education in Albania. In *Smart Education in China and Central & Eastern European Countries* (pp. 51–79). Springer Nature Singapore. DOI: 10.1007/978-981-19-7319-2_3

Kuleto, V., Ilić, M., Dumangiu, M., Ranković, M., Martins, O. M., Păun, D., & Mihoreanu, L. (2021). Exploring opportunities and challenges of artificial intelligence and machine learning in higher education institutions. *Sustainability (Basel)*, 13(18), 10424. DOI: 10.3390/su131810424

Kulkarni, S. (2020). The role of AI in education: A comprehensive guide. Retrieved from https://www.techaconsulting.com/ai-in-education-guide

Kumar, A., Krishnamurthi, R., Bhatia, S., Kaushik, K., Ahuja, N. J., Nayyar, A., & Masud, M. (2021). Blended learning tools and practices: A comprehensive analysis. *IEEE Access : Practical Innovations, Open Solutions*, 9, 85151–85197. DOI: 10.1109/ACCESS.2021.3085844

Kung, T. H., Cheatham, M., Medenilla, A., Sillos, C., De Leon, L., Elepaño, C., Madriaga, M., Aggabao, R., Diaz-Candido, G., Maningo, J., & Tseng, V. (2023). Performance of ChatGPT on USMLE: Potential for AI-assisted medical education using large language models. *PLOS Digital Health*, 2(2), e0000198. DOI: 10.1371/journal.pdig.0000198 PMID: 36812645

Kunjumuhammed, S. K. (2024). Artificial Intelligence in Addressing Educational Inequality Dimensions in Higher Education Institutions (HEIs): A Critical Review. Risks and Challenges of AI-Driven Finance: Bias, Ethics, and Security, 146-164. [HTML]

Kurilovas, E. (2020). On data-driven decision-making for quality education. *Computers in Human Behavior*, 107, 105774. DOI: 10.1016/j.chb.2018.11.003

Kurni, M., Mohammed, M. S., & Srinivasa, K. S. (2023). *A beginner's guide to introduce artificial intelligence in teaching and learning*. Springer.

Kurzweil, R. (2005). *The Singularity Is Near: When Humans Transcend Biology*. Penguin Books.

Laal, M., & Ghodsi, S. M. (2012). Benefits of collaborative learning. *Procedia: Social and Behavioral Sciences*, 31, 486–490. DOI: 10.1016/j.sbspro.2011.12.091

Labadze, L., Grigolia, M., & Machaidze, L. (2023). Role of AI chatbots in education: Systematic literature review. *International Journal of Educational Technology in Higher Education*, 20(1), 1–17. DOI: 10.1186/s41239-023-00426-1

Lähdesmäki, T., Baranova, J., Ylönen, S. C., Koistinen, A. K., Mäkinen, K., Juškiene, V., & Zaleskiene, I. (2022). *Learning cultural literacy through creative practices in schools: Cultural and multimodal approaches to meaning-making*. Springer Nature. DOI: 10.1007/978-3-030-89236-4

Laloux, F. (2014). *Reinventing organizations: A guide to creating organizations inspired by the next stage in human consciousness*. Nelson Parker.

Lameras, P., & Arnab, S. (2021). Power to the Teachers: An Exploratory review on Artificial intelligence in education. *Information (Basel)*, 13(1), 14. DOI: 10.3390/info13010014

Laupichler, M. C., Aster, A., Schirch, J., & Raupach, T. (2022). Artificial intelligence literacy in higher and adult education: A scoping literature review. *Computers and Education: Artificial Intelligence*, 3, 100101. DOI: 10.1016/j.caeai.2022.100101

Lean, J., Moizer, J., Derham, C., Strachan, L., & Bhuiyan, Z. (2020, November 5). Real World Learning: Simulation and Gaming. Springer Nature, 187-214. DOI: 10.1007/978-3-030-46951-1_9

Lee, D., Arnold, M., Srivastava, A., Plastow, K., Strelan, P., Ploeckl, F., Lekkas, D., & Palmer, E. (2024). The impact of generative AI on higher education learning and teaching: A study of educators' perspectives. *Computers and Education: Artificial Intelligence*, 6, 100221. DOI: 10.1016/j.caeai.2024.100221

Leeflang, P. S., Verhoef, P. C., Dahlström, P., & Freundt, T. (2014). Challenges and solutions for marketing in a digital era. *European Management Journal*, 32(1), 1–12. DOI: 10.1016/j.emj.2013.12.001

Lee, M. Y., & Edmondson, A. C. (2017). Self-managing organizations: Exploring the limits of less-hierarchical organizing. *Research in Organizational Behavior*, 37, 35–58. DOI: 10.1016/j.riob.2017.10.002

Lee, S., Mott, B., Ottenbreit-Leftwich, A., Scribner, A., Taylor, S., Park, K., Rowe, J., Glazewski, K., Hmelo-Silver, C. E., & Lester, J. (2021). AI-Infused Collaborative Inquiry in Upper Elementary School: A Game-Based Learning approach. *Proceedings of the AAAI Conference on Artificial Intelligence*, 35(17), 15591–15599. DOI: 10.1609/aaai.v35i17.17836

Lee, Y.-J., Davis, R. O., & Ryu, J. (2024). Korean in-service teachers' perceptions of implementing artificial intelligence (AI) education for teaching in schools and their AI teacher training programs. *International Journal of Information and Education Technology (IJIET)*, 14(2), 214–219. Advance online publication. DOI: 10.18178/ijiet.2024.14.2.2042

Lei, L., Li, J., & Li, W. (2023, April 4). Assessing the role of artificial intelligence in the mental healthcare of teachers and students. Springer Science+Business Media. DOI: 10.1007/s00500-023-08072-5

Leon, A. J., & Vidhani, D. (2023). ChatGPT needs a chemistry tutor too. *Journal of Chemical Education*, 100(10), 3859–3865. DOI: 10.1021/acs.jchemed.3c00288

Lewandowsky, S., Ecker, U. K. H., & Cook, J. (2017). Beyond misinformation: Understanding and coping with the "post-truth" era. *Journal of Applied Research in Memory and Cognition*, 6(4), 353–369. DOI: 10.1016/j.jarmac.2017.07.008

Li, E Y., Yen, H J R., & Cheng, C J. (2008, January 9). A fit-gap analysis of e-business curricula and job demand in Taiwan and the US. Elsevier BV, 51(3), 969-987. DOI: 10.1016/j.compedu.2007.09.013

Liang, J., Wang, L., Luo, J., Yan, Y., & Fan, C. (2023, December 22). The relationship between student interaction with generative artificial intelligence and learning achievement: Serial mediating roles of self-efficacy and cognitive engagement. *Frontiers of Medicine*, 14, 1285392. Advance online publication. DOI: 10.3389/fpsyg.2023.1285392 PMID: 38187430

Li, B., Lowell, V. L., Wang, C., & Li, X. N. (2024). A systematic review of the first year of publications on ChatGPT and language education: Examining research on ChatGPT's use in language learning and teaching. *Computers and Education: Artificial Intelligence*, 7, 100266. DOI: 10.1016/j.caeai.2024.100266

Liebowitz, J. (2016). *Knowledge management handbook: Collaboration and social networking*. CRC Press., DOI: 10.1201/9781315279740

Lin, H., & Chen, Q. (2024). Artificial intelligence (AI) -integrated educational applications and college students' creativity and academic emotions: Students and teachers' perceptions and attitudes. *BMC Psychology*, 12(1), 487. Advance online publication. DOI: 10.1186/s40359-024-01979-0 PMID: 39285268

Lin, Y.-L., & Wang, W.-T. (2024). Enhancing students' online collaborative PBL learning performance in the context of coauthoring-based technologies: A case of wiki technologies. *Education and Information Technologies*, 29(2), 2303–2328. DOI: 10.1007/s10639-023-11907-1 PMID: 37361760

Li, S., Du, J., & Sun, J. (2022). Unfolding the learning behaviour patterns of MOOC learners with different levels of achievement. *International Journal of Educational Technology in Higher Education*, 19(1), 22. DOI: 10.1186/s41239-022-00328-8

Littlejohn, A., Beetham, H., & McGill, L. (2012). Learning at the digital frontier: A review of digital literacies in theory and practice. *Journal of Computer Assisted Learning*, 28(6), 547–556. DOI: 10.1111/j.1365-2729.2011.00474.x

Liu, C.-C., Liao, M.-G., Chang, C.-H., & Lin, H.-M. (2022). An analysis of children's interaction with an AI chatbot and its impact on their interest in reading. *Computers & Education*, 189, 104576. Advance online publication. DOI: 10.1016/j.compedu.2022.104576

Liu, G., & Ma, C. (2023). Measuring EFL learners' use of ChatGPT in informal digital learning of English based on the technology acceptance model. *Innovation in Language Learning and Teaching*, •••, 1–14.

Liu, M., & Stewart, G. (2019). AI in visual content production: Implications for media education. *Media Culture & Society*, 41(5), 760–779.

Livingstone, S. (2004). Media literacy and the challenge of new information and communication technologies. *Communication Review*, 7(1), 3–14. DOI: 10.1080/10714420490280152

Lo, C. K. (2023). What is the impact of ChatGPT on education? A rapid review of the literature. *Education Sciences*, 13(4), 410–455. DOI: 10.3390/educsci13040410

Lo, L. S. (2023). The art and science of prompt engineering: A new literacy in the Information Age. *Internet Reference Services Quarterly*, 27(4), 203–210. DOI: 10.1080/10875301.2023.2227621

Long, D., & Magerko, B. (2020). What is AI Literacy? Competencies and Design Considerations. *Proceedings of the 2020 CHI Conference on Human Factors in Computing Systems*, 1–16. https://doi.org/DOI: 10.1145/3313831.3376727

Loots, S., Strydom, F., & Posthumus, H. (2023). Learning from students: Factors that support student engagement in blended learning environments within and beyond classrooms. *Journal of Student Affairs in Africa*, 11(2), 73–88. DOI: 10.24085/jsaa.v11i2.4897

Lopez-Chila, R., Llerena-Izquierdo, J., Sumba-Nacipucha, N., & Cueva-Estrada, J. (2023). Artificial Intelligence in Higher Education: An Analysis of Existing Bibliometrics. *Education Sciences*, 14(1), 47. Advance online publication. DOI: 10.3390/educsci14010047

Lowry, O., Rosebrough, N., Farr, A., & Randall, R. (1951, November 1). PROTEIN MEASUREMENT WITH THE FOLIN PHENOL REAGENT. Elsevier BV, 193(1), 265-275. DOI: 10.1016/S0021-9258(19)52451-6

Luan, H., Geczy, P., Lai, H., Gobert, J., Yang, S. J., Ogata, H., & Tsai, C. C. (2020). Challenges and future directions of big data and artificial intelligence in education. *Frontiers in Psychology*, 11, 580820. DOI: 10.3389/fpsyg.2020.580820 PMID: 33192896

Luckin, R., Holmes, W., Griffiths, M., & Forcier, L. B. (2016). *Intelligence unleashed: An argument for AI in education*. Pearson. https://discovery.ucl.ac.uk/id/eprint/1475756/

Luckin, R., Holmes, W., Griffiths, M., & Forcier, L. B. (2016). Intelligence unleashed: An argument for AI in education. Retrieved from https://www.pearson.com/corporate/intelligence-unleashed.html

Luo, Q. Z., & Hsiao-Chin, L. Y. (2023). The influence of AI-powered adaptive learning platforms on student performance in Chinese classrooms. *Journal of Education*, 6(3), 1–12. DOI: 10.53819/81018102t4181

Lupton, D., & Williamson, B. (2017). The datafied child: The dataveillance of children and implications for their rights. *New Media & Society*, 19(5), 780–794. DOI: 10.1177/1461444816686328

Lutnæs, E. (2020). Empowering responsible design literacy: Identifying narratives in a new curriculum.

Ma, X., & Jiang, C. (2023, May 30). On the Ethical Risks of Artificial Intelligence Applications in Education and Its Avoidance Strategies., 14, 354-359. DOI: 10.54097/ehss.v14i.8868

Magomadov, V. S. (2020, November 1). The application of artificial intelligence and Big Data analytics in personalized learning. *Journal of Physics: Conference Series*, 1691(1), 012169–012169. DOI: 10.1088/1742-6596/1691/1/012169

Makoelle, T. M. (2014). Inclusive education: Are we there? Some global challenges, contradictions and anomalies. *Journal of Sociology and Social Anthropology*, 5(3), 303–309. DOI: 10.1080/09766634.2014.11885634

Mallik, S., & Gangopadhyay, A. (2023, May 5). Proactive and reactive engagement of artificial intelligence methods for education: A review. *Frontiers of Medicine*, 6, 1151391. Advance online publication. DOI: 10.3389/frai.2023.1151391 PMID: 37215064

Manovich, L. (2019). AI and new media: New horizons for modern applications. *Digital Creativity*, 22(3), 193–202.

Marín, V., & Castañeda, L. (2023). Developing Digital. *Literacy, Teaching and Learning*, •••, 1089–1108. DOI: 10.1007/978-981-19-2080-6_64

Markauskaite, L., Marrone, R., Poquet, O., Knight, S., Martinez-Maldonado, R., Howard, S., Tondeur, J., De Laat, M., Buckingham Shum, S., Gašević, D., & Siemens, G. (2022). Rethinking the entwinement between artificial intelligence and human learning: What capabilities do learners need for a world with AI? *Computers and Education: Artificial Intelligence*, 3, 100056. DOI: 10.1016/j.caeai.2022.100056

Martin, F., Chen, Y., Moore, R L., & Westine, C D. (2020, June 15). Systematic review of adaptive learning research designs, context, strategies, and technologies from 2009 to 2018. Springer Science+Business Media, 68(4), 1903-1929. DOI: 10.1007/s11423-020-09793-2

Mason, L. (2018). Media literacy in the age of algorithmic personalization: The role of artificial intelligence in enhancing critical thinking skills. *Journal of Medical Education*, 9(2), 24–33.

Masterman, L. (1985). *Teaching the media*. Comedia Publishing Group.

McAfee, A. (2009). *Enterprise 2.0: New collaborative tools for your organization's toughest challenges*. Harvard Business Press.

McCarthy, J., Minsky, M. L., Rochester, N., & Shannon, C. E. (1955). A proposal for the Dartmouth summer research project on artificial intelligence. *AI Magazine*, 27(4), 12–14.

McCarthy, J., Minsky, M. L., Rochester, N., & Shannon, C. E. (2006). A proposal for the Dartmouth summer research project on artificial intelligence, August 31, 1955. *AI Magazine*, 27(4), 12.

McDougall, J., & Skoog, S. (2020). Creative AI in education: Investigating the implications and potentials. *Learning, Media and Technology*, 45(3), 287–299.

McGrath, C., Pargman, T. C., Juth, N., & Palmgren, P. J. (2023). University teachers' perceptions of responsibility and artificial intelligence in higher education: An experimental philosophical study. *Computers and Education: Artificial Intelligence*, 4, 100139. DOI: 10.1016/j.caeai.2023.100139

McKinsey & Company. (2021). The future of work after. *COVID*, 19, •••. https://www.mckinsey.com/

McKinsey. (2023). *What's the future of generative AI? An early view in 15 charts.* McKinsey & Company.

McLuhan, M. (1964). *Understanding media: The extensions of man.* McGraw-Hill.

Meadows, D. (2003). Digital storytelling: Research-based practice in new media. *Visual Communication*, 2(2), 189–193. DOI: 10.1177/1470357203002002004

Means, B., Bakia, M., & Murphy, R. (2014). *Learning online: What research tells us about whether, when and how*. Routledge. DOI: 10.4324/9780203095959

Meccawy, M. (2018, July 29). The Brilliant Scheduler: Automated Scheduling System for Video Conferencing Courses. *Canadian Center of Science and Education*, 11(3), 82–82. DOI: 10.5539/cis.v11n3p82

Meng, N., Dhimolea, T. K., & Ali, Z. (2022). AI-enhanced education: Teaching and learning reimagined. In *Bridging human intelligence and artificial intelligence* (pp. 107–124). Springer International Publishing. DOI: 10.1007/978-3-030-84729-6_7

Mentoring Complete. (2024, January 29). The future of AI in mentorship. https://www.mentoringcomplete.com/the-future-of-ai-in-mentorship/

Mhlanga, D. (2021). Artificial intelligence in the industry 4.0, and its impact on poverty, innovation, infrastructure development, and the sustainable development goals: Lessons from Africa. *Sustainability (Basel)*, 13(18), 10424. DOI: 10.3390/su13115788

Miço, H., & Cungu, J. (2022). The Need for Digital Education in the Teaching Profession: A Path toward Using the European Digital Competence Framework in Albania. *IAFOR Journal of Education*, 10(2), 29–50. DOI: 10.22492/ije.10.2.02

Minor, C. (2023). *Best practices in literacy instruction.* Guilford Publications.

Mintzberg, H. (2009). *Managing*. Berrett-Koehler Publishers.

Mirra, N., & Garcia, A. (2021). In search of the meaning and purpose of 21st-century literacy learning: A critical review of research and practice. *Reading Research Quarterly*, 56(3), 463–496. DOI: 10.1002/rrq.313

Miterianifa, M., Ashadi, A., Saputro, S., & Suciati, S. (2021, January). Higher order thinking skills in the 21st century: Critical thinking. In *Proceedings of the 1st International Conference on Social Science, Humanities, Education and Society Development*, ICONS 2020, 30 November, Tegal, Indonesia. DOI: 10.4108/eai.30-11-2020.2303766

Mohamed, A. M. (2024). Exploring the potential of an AI-based Chatbot (ChatGPT) in enhancing English as a Foreign Language (EFL) teaching: Perceptions of EFL Faculty Members. *Education and Information Technologies*, 29(3), 3195–3217. DOI: 10.1007/s10639-023-11917-z

Mohammed, P., & Watson, E. (2019, January 1). Towards Inclusive Education in the Age of Artificial Intelligence: Perspectives, Challenges, and Opportunities. Springer Nature, 17-37. DOI: 10.1007/978-981-13-8161-4_2

Mohd Rahim, N. I., & Iahad, A., N., Yusof, A. F., & A. Al-Sharafi, M. (. (2022). AI-based chatbots adoption model for higher-education institutions: A hybrid PLS-SEM-neural network modelling approach. *Sustainability*, 14(19), 12726. DOI: 10.3390/su141912726

Mollick, E. R., & Mollick, L. (2023, September 23). *Assigning AI: Seven approaches for students, with prompts*. The Wharton School Research Paper. https://doi.org/ DOI: 10.2139/ssrn.4475995

Moorhouse, B. L., Yeo, M. A., & Wan, Y. W. (2023). Generative AI tools and assessment: Guidelines of the world's top-ranking universities. *Computers & Education*, 5, 100151.

Morales-Garcia, W. C., Sairitupa-Sanchez, L. Z., Morales-Garcia, S. B., & Morales-Garcia, M. (2024). Development and validation of a scale for dependence on artificial intelligence in university students. *Frontiers in Education*, 9, 1323898. DOI: 10.3389/feduc.2024.1323898

Moreale, R. (2024, September 27). NextGen Med and data at scale. Presentation to Rochester (MN) Chamber of Commerce. The Mayo Clinic.

Moreno-Marcos, P. M., Alario-Hoyos, C., Munoz-Merino, P. J., & Kloos, C. D. (2019). Prediction in MOOCs: A Review and Future Research Directions. *IEEE Transactions on Learning Technologies*, 12(3), 384–401. DOI: 10.1109/TLT.2018.2856808

Morton, T. (2020). Cognitive discourse functions: A bridge between content, literacy and language for teaching and assessment in CLIL. *CLIL Journal of Innovation and Research in Plurilingual and Pluricultural Education*, 3(1), 7–17. DOI: 10.5565/rev/clil.33

Moskal, P. D., Dziuban, C. D., & Picciano, A. G. (2023). Data Analytics and Adaptive Learning: Research Perspectives. [HTML]

Mozer, M C., Wiseheart, M., & Novikoff, T P. (2019, February 19). Artificial intelligence to support human instruction. National Academy of Sciences, 116(10), 3953-3955. DOI: 10.1073/pnas.1900370116

M-powering teachers (2024). About. https://www.mpoweringteachers.com/

Muji, S., Svensson, E., & Faraon, M. (2024). Engaging with artificial intelligence in graphic design education. In *Proceedings of the 2023 IEEE World Artificial Intelligence Education Conference* (pp. 31-37). IEEE. DOI: 10.1109/WAIE60568.2023.00013

Multilingual Education. AI's Language Barrier Solutions. (2024). perfectessaywriter.ai. https://www.perfectessaywriter.ai/blog/ai-in-multilingual-education

Muñoz, J. L. R., Ojeda, F. M., Jurado, D. L. A., Peña, P. F. P., Carranza, C. P. M., Berríos, H. Q., & Vasquez-Pauca, M. J. (2022). Systematic review of adaptive learning technology for learning in higher education. *Eurasian Journal of Educational Research*, 98(98), 221–233.

Murtarellia, G., Gregory, A., & Romentia, S. (2021). A conversation-based perspective for shaping ethical human–machine interactions: The particular challenge of chatbots. *Journal of Business Research*, 129, 927–935. DOI: 10.1016/j.jbusres.2020.09.018

Murtaza, M., Ahmed, Y., Shamsi, J. A., Sherwani, F., & Usman, M. (2022). AI-Based Personalized E-Learning Systems: Issues, challenges, and solutions. *IEEE Access : Practical Innovations, Open Solutions*, 10, 81323–81342. DOI: 10.1109/ACCESS.2022.3193938

Mutambara, D., & Bayaga, A. (2020). Determinants of mobile learning acceptance for STEM education in rural areas. *Computers & Education*, 160, 104010. DOI: 10.1016/j.compedu.2020.104010

Mutambik, I. (2024). The Use of AI-Driven Automation to Enhance Student Learning Experiences in the KSA: An Alternative Pathway to Sustainable Education. *Sustainability (Basel)*, 16(14), 5970. DOI: 10.3390/su16145970

Nabiyev, V. V. (2012). Yapay Zekâ: İnsan-Bilgisayar Etkileşimi. Baski Yeri: Seçkin Yayıncılık.

Nam, B. H., & Bai, Q. (2023). ChatGPT and its ethical implications for STEM research and higher education: A media discourse analysis. *International Journal of STEM Education*, 10(1), 66. Advance online publication. DOI: 10.1186/s40594-023-00452-5

National Association for Media Literacy Education (NAMLE). (2007). Core principles of media literacy education in the United States. Retrieved from https://namle.net/publications/core-principles

National Association of Media Educators (NAME). (2021). *Survey on AI-assisted storytelling in media education*. NAME.

National Association of Social Workers. (2021). Social work education: A comprehensive guide to education and careers in social work. NASW Press. https://www.socialworkers.org

National Association of Social Workers. (2023). *AI and social work*. https://www.socialworkers.org/About/Ethics/AI-and-Social-Work

Nazaretsky, T., Ariely, M., Cukurova, M., & Alexandron, G. (2022). Teachers' trust in AI-powered educational technology and a professional development program to improve it. *British Journal of Educational Technology*, 53(4), 914–931. DOI: 10.1111/bjet.13232

Nazir, A., & Wang, Z. (2023). A comprehensive survey of ChatGPT: Advancements, applications, prospects, and challenges. *Meta-Radiology*, 1(2), 100022. DOI: 10.1016/j.metrad.2023.100022 PMID: 37901715

Neumeier, P. (2005). A closer look at blended learning—Parameters for designing a blended learning environment for language teaching and learning. *ReCALL*, 17(2), 163–178. DOI: 10.1017/S0958344005000224

News Literacy Project. (2021). Checkology Virtual Classroom. Retrieved from https://www.newslit.org/

Ng, D. T. K., Leung, J. K. L., Chu, S. K. W., & Qiao, M. S. (2021). Conceptualizing AI literacy: An exploratory review. *Computers and Education: Artificial Intelligence*, 2, 100041. DOI: 10.1016/j.caeai.2021.100041

Ng, D. T. K., Leung, J. K. L., Su, J., Ng, R. C. W., & Chu, S. K. W. (2023). Teachers' AI digital competencies and twenty-first century skills in the post-pandemic world. *Educational Technology Research and Development*, 71(1), 137–161. DOI: 10.1007/s11423-023-10203-6 PMID: 36844361

Nguyen, H. (2014, November 29). Grounded in Practice: Designing & Implementing Relevant and Student-Centered Curriculum. Emerald Publishing Limited, 161-181. DOI: 10.1108/S1479-366020140000021019

Nguyen, T. (n.d.) Generative AI in education: Benefits, barriers, and use cases. Neurond. https://www.neurond.com/blog/generative-ai-in-education

Nguyen, T., & Sirichokcharoenkun. (2023). The limitations and potential of chatgpt in chemistry education. Available online: https://www.researchgate.net/publication/374087925_The_Limitations_and_Potential_of_ChatGPT_in_Chemistry_Education

Nguyen, A., Järvelä, S., & Hadwin, A. (2020). Human and artificial intelligence collaboration for learning: A scoping review. *Educational Research Review*, 30, 100326.

Nguyen, A., Järvelä, S., & Hadwin, A. (2021). AI roles for supporting socially shared regulation in learning. In Rosé, C., Martínez-Maldonado, R., Hoppe, H. U., Luckin, R., Mavrikis, M., Porayska-Pomsta, K., McLaren, B., & du Boulay, B. (Eds.), *Artificial intelligence in education* (pp. 387–401). Springer.

Nguyen, A., Ngo, H. N., Hong, Y., Dang, B., & Nguyen, B. P. T. (2023). Ethical principles for artificial intelligence in education. *Education and Information Technologies*, 28(4), 4221–4241. DOI: 10.1007/s10639-022-11316-w PMID: 36254344

Nichols, T. P., & LeBlanc, R. J. (2021). Media education and the limits of "literacy": Ecological orientations to performative platforms. *Curriculum Inquiry*, 51(4), 389–412. DOI: 10.1080/03626784.2020.1865104

Niemi, H., Niu, S., Vivitsou, M., & Li, B. (2018). Digital storytelling for twenty-first-century competencies with math literacy and student engagement in China and Finland. *Contemporary Educational Technology*, 9(4), 331–353. DOI: 10.30935/cet.470999

Nkambou, R., Bourdeau, J., & Mizoguchi, R. (Eds.). (2010). *Advances in intelligent tutoring systems*. Springer., DOI: 10.1007/978-3-642-14363-2

Noble, S. U. (2018). *Algorithms of oppression: How search engines reinforce racism*. New York University Press. DOI: 10.18574/nyu/9781479833641.001.0001

Nonaka, I. (1994). A dynamic theory of organizational knowledge creation. *Organization Science*, 5(1), 14–37. DOI: 10.1287/orsc.5.1.14

Nonaka, I., & Takeuchi, H. (1995). *The knowledge-creating company: How Japanese companies create the dynamics of innovation*. Oxford University Press., DOI: 10.1093/oso/9780195092691.001.0001

Nonaka, I., & Takeuchi, H. (2019). *The wise company: How companies create continuous innovation*. Oxford University Press.

Nonaka, I., & von Krogh, G. (2009). Tacit knowledge and knowledge conversion: Controversy and advancement in organizational knowledge creation theory. *Organization Science*, 20(3), 635–652. DOI: 10.1287/orsc.1080.0412

Novawan, A., Walker, S. A., & Ikeda, O. (2024). The new face of technology-enhanced language learning (TELL) with artificial intelligence (AI): Teacher perspectives, practices, and challenges. *Journal of English in Academic and Professional Communication*, 10(1), 1–18. DOI: 10.25047/jeapco.v9i1.3754

Núñez, J L M., Harris, P., Fernández, R P., Abbas, A., & Radovanović, D. (2023, January 1). Does intrinsic motivation mediate perceived artificial intelligence (AI) learning and computational thinking of students during the COVID-19 pandemic?. Elsevier BV, 4, 100128-100128. DOI: 10.1016/j.caeai.2023.100128

Nye, B D. (2014, October 7). Intelligent Tutoring Systems by and for the Developing World: A Review of Trends and Approaches for Educational Technology in a Global Context. Springer Science+Business Media, 25(2), 177-203. DOI: 10.1007/s40593-014-0028-6

O'Neil, C. (2016). *Weapons of math destruction: How big data increases inequality and threatens democracy*. Crown Publishing Group.

O'Neil, C. (2016). *Weapons of Math Destruction: How Big Data Increases Inequality and Threatens Democracy*. Crown Publishing Group.

O'neil, J. M., Newton, R. J., Bone, E. K., Birney, L. B., Green, A. E., Merrick, B., Goodwin-Segal, T., Moore, G., & Fraioli, A. (2020). Using urban harbors for experiential, environmental literacy: Case studies of New York and Chesapeake Bay. *Regional Studies in Marine Science*, 33, 100886. DOI: 10.1016/j.rsma.2019.100886

Obari, H., & Lambacher, S. (2019). Improving the English Skills of Native Japanese Using Artificial Intelligence in a Blended Learning Program. Retrieved from: https://files.eric.ed.gov/fulltext/ED600973.pdf

Ocumpaugh, J., Roscoe, R. D., Baker, R. S., Hutt, S., & Aguilar, S. J. (2024). Toward asset-based instruction and assessment in artificial intelligence in education. *International Journal of Artificial Intelligence in Education*. Advance online publication. DOI: 10.1007/s40593-023-00382-x

Ogwu, E N., Emelogu, N U., Azor, R O., & Okwo, F A. (2022, July 16). Educational Technology Adoption in Instructional Delivery in the New Global reality. Springer Science+Business Media, 28(1), 1065-1080. DOI: 10.1007/s10639-022-11203-4

Open Society Foundation for Albania. (n.d.). Home. https://www.osfa.al/

Open, A. I. (2022, November 30). Introducing ChatGPT. OpenAI. https://openai.com/blog/chatgpt

Oprescu, C. M. (2020). Exploring the potential of the blended learning method in the romanian pre-university educational system. In *Conference proceedings of» eLearning and Software for Education «(eLSE)* (Vol. 16, No. 02, pp. 610-619). Carol I National Defence University Publishing House. DOI: 10.12753/2066-026X-20-166

Ordax, E. (2024, January 16). Fine tuning vs. pre-training. *Medium*. https://medium.com/@eordaxd/fine-tuning-vs-pre-training-651d05186faf

Osipovskaya, E., & Dmitrieva, S. (2022). The Issue of Adaptive Learning as Educational Innovation. In *Technology, Innovation and Creativity in Digital Society: XXI Professional Culture of the Specialist of the Future* (pp. 606-617). Springer International Publishing. DOI: 10.1007/978-3-030-89708-6_50

Osorio, C., Fuster, N., Chen, W., Men, Y., & Juan, A. A. (2024). Enhancing Accessibility to Analytics Courses in Higher Education through AI, Simulation, and e-Collaborative Tools. *Information (Basel)*, 15(8), 430. DOI: 10.3390/info15080430

Ottenbreit-Leftwich, A., Glazewski, K., Jeon, M., Jantaraweragul, K., Hmelo-Silver, C. E., Scribner, A., Lee, S., Mott, B., & Lester, J. (2022). Lessons Learned for AI Education with Elementary Students and Teachers. *International Journal of Artificial Intelligence in Education*, 33(2), 267–289. DOI: 10.1007/s40593-022-00304-3

Ouyang, F., Wu, M., Zheng, L., Zhang, L., & Jiao, P. (2023). Integration of artificial intelligence performance prediction and learning analytics to improve student learning in online engineering course. *International Journal of Educational Technology in Higher Education*, 20(1), 4. DOI: 10.1186/s41239-022-00372-4 PMID: 36683653

Ouyang, F., Xu, W., & Cukurova, M. (2023). An artificial intelligence–driven learning analytics method to examine the collaborative problem-solving process from the complex adaptive systems perspective. *International Journal of Computer-Supported Collaborative Learning*, 18(1), 39–66. DOI: 10.1007/s11412-023-09387-z

Ouyang, F., Zheng, L., & Jiao, P. (2022). Artificial intelligence in online higher education: A systematic review of empirical research from 2011 to 2020. *Education and Information Technologies*, 27(6), 7893–7925. DOI: 10.1007/s10639-022-10925-9

Pabba, C., & Kumar, P. (2022). An intelligent system for monitoring students' engagement in large classroom teaching through facial expression recognition. *Expert Systems: International Journal of Knowledge Engineering and Neural Networks*, 39(1), e12839. DOI: 10.1111/exsy.12839

Pahl, K. (2011). My family, my story: Representing identities in time and space through digital storytelling. *Teachers College Record*, 113(13), 17–39. DOI: 10.1177/016146811111301302

Pahl, K., & Rowsell, J. (2020). *Living literacies: Literacy for social change*. MiT Press. DOI: 10.7551/mitpress/11375.001.0001

Paquet, G., Schooten, V., & Simon, S. (2020). *Digital governance: Navigating the new technological epoch*. Routledge.

Pariser, E. (2011). *The filter bubble: How the new personalized web is changing what we read and how we think*. Penguin Press.

Park, J., & Lim, H. (2022). Privacy-preserving federated learning using homomorphic encryption. *Applied Sciences (Basel, Switzerland)*, 12(9), 1240. DOI: 10.3390/app12091240

Parviz, M. (2024). AI in education: Comparative perspectives from STEM and Non-STEM instructors. *Computers and Education Open*, 6, 100190. Advance online publication. DOI: 10.1016/j.caeo.2024.100190

Patil, V. (2024). *The Potential of AI in Enhancing Education Access and Quality*.

Patronov, A., Papadopoulos, K., & Engkvist, O. (2022). Has artificial intelligence impacted drug discovery? *Methods in Molecular Biology (Clifton, N.J.)*, 2390, 153–176. DOI: 10.1007/978-1-0716-1787-8_6 PMID: 34731468

Paul, R., & Elder, L. (2005). *Critical thinking: Tools for taking charge of your learning and your life*. Prentice Hall.

Pavlik, J. V. (2023). Collaborating With ChatGPT: Considering the Implications of Generative Artificial Intelligence for Journalism and Media Education. *Journalism & Mass Communication Educator*, 78(1), 84–93. DOI: 10.1177/10776958221149577

Pedro, F., Subosa, M., Rivas, A., & Valverde, P. (2019). *Artificial intelligence in education : challenges and opportunities for sustainable development*. https://hdl.handle.net/20.500.12799/6533

Perkins, M., Furze, L., Roe, J., & MacVaugh, J. (2024). The Artificial Intelligence Assessment Scale (AIAS): A framework for ethical integration of generative AI in educational assessment. *Journal of University Teaching & Learning Practice*, 21(6). Advance online publication. DOI: 10.53761/q3azde36

Pfoertsch, W., & Sulaj, K. (2023, December). Integrating Artificial Intelligence with Customer Experience in Banking: An Empirical Study on how Chatbots and Virtual Assistants Enhance Empathy. In *2023 International Conference on Computing, Networking, Telecommunications & Engineering Sciences Applications (CoNTESA)* (pp. 69-74). IEEE. DOI: 10.1109/CoNTESA61248.2023.10384979

Phillips, A., Pane, J F., Reumann-Moore, R., & Shenbanjo, O. (2020, February 27). Implementing an adaptive intelligent tutoring system as an instructional supplement. Springer Science+Business Media, 68(3), 1409-1437. DOI: 10.1007/s11423-020-09745-w

Polanyi, M. (1966). *The tacit dimension.* University of Chicago Press.

Polaris Learning. (2018, April 3). The three stages of training, development and competence. https://polaris-learning.com/three-stages-training-development-competence/

Popenici, S. A. D., & Kerr, S. (2017). Exploring the impact of artificial intelligence on teaching and learning in higher education. *Research and Practice in Technology Enhanced Learning*, 12(1), 22. Advance online publication. DOI: 10.1186/s41039-017-0062-8 PMID: 30595727

Poth, R. D. (2023, November 9). Effective professional development on AI. Edutopia. https://www.edutopia.org/article/ai-professional-development-helps-teachers-tech-integration/

Prabhakar, R. R. C. (2024). Barriers to AI adoption for non-technical educators in the digital age. *Journal of Scientific and Engineering Research*, 11(8), 211–214.

Pranathi Software. (2023, December 6). NLP text summarization for 5 best APIs, AI models. *Medium.* https://medium.com/@pranathisoftwareservices/nlp-text-summarization-for-5-best-apis-ai-models-5b61534483a2

Praveen, S. V., Gajjar, P., Ray, R. K., & Dutt, A. (2024). Crafting clarity: Leveraging large language models to decode consumer reviews. *Journal of Retailing and Consumer Services*, 81, 103975. DOI: 10.1016/j.jretconser.2024.103975

Prifti, R. (2020). Implementation of blended learning in a higher education institution in Albania: An analysis of factors that affect students' learning experience. *International Journal of Innovation and Learning*, 27(3), 233–253. DOI: 10.1504/IJIL.2020.106809

Purdy, N., Hall, K., Khanolainen, D., & Galvin, C. (2023). Reframing teacher education around inclusion, equity, and social justice: Towards an authentically value-centered approach to teacher education in Europe. *European Journal of Teacher Education*, 46(5), 755–771. DOI: 10.1080/02619768.2023.2288556

Putri, A. A. (2021). The effectiveness of khan academy as a science learning support to improve student's mastery of skills: Literature review. *Journal of Environmental and Science Education*, 1(2), 52–56. DOI: 10.15294/jese.v1i2.50370

Qafzezi, E. (2023). Online Collaborative Learning in Higher Education in Albania: Some Necessary Innovations. *International Journal of Management. Knowledge and Learning*, 12(1), 2–11.

Quivy, R., & Van Campenhoudt, L. (1995). *Manuel de recherche en sciences sociales*. Dunod.

Radovan, M., & Radovan, D. M. (2024). Harmonizing pedagogy and technology: Insights into teaching approaches that foster sustainable motivation and efficiency in blended learning. *Sustainability (Basel)*, 16(7), 2704. DOI: 10.3390/su16072704

Rahiman, H. U., & Kodikal, R. (2023). Revolutionizing education: Artificial intelligence empowered learning in higher education. *Cogent Education*. Advance online publication. DOI: 10.1080/2331186X.2023.2293431

Rajkoomar, M., & Raju, J. (2016). A framework using blended learning for innovative teaching and learning. *Res Rev J Educ Stud*, 2, 1–9.

Ramachandra Rao, V., & Heng, N. M. (2018). Teaching basic programming to pre-university students through blended learning pedagogy: A descriptive study.

Ramakrisnan, P., Yahya, Y. B., Hasrol, M. N. H., & Aziz, A. A. (2012). Blended learning: A suitable framework for e-learning in higher education. *Procedia: Social and Behavioral Sciences*, 67, 513–526. DOI: 10.1016/j.sbspro.2012.11.356

Ratten, V., & Jones, F. (2023). Generative artificial intelligence (ChatGPT): Implications for management educators. *International Journal of Management Education*, 21(3), 100857. DOI: 10.1016/j.ijme.2023.100857

Ray, A., & Pani, P. (2021, January 1). Learning Continuum in a Blended Mode: A Case of a Skill-based Course. DOI: 10.2991/assehr.k.211224.020

Regan, P. M., & Jesse, J. (2019). *Data Privacy Law: A Practical Guide to the GDPR and Other International Regulations*. Routledge.

Renz, A., & Hilbig, R. (2020). Prerequisites for artificial intelligence in further education: Identification of drivers, barriers, and business models of educational technology companies. *International Journal of Educational Technology in Higher Education*, 17(1), 14. DOI: 10.1186/s41239-020-00193-3

Renz, A., & Vladova, G. (2021). Reinvigorating the discourse on human-centered artificial intelligence in educational technologies. *Technology Innovation Management Review*, 11(5), 5–16. DOI: 10.22215/timreview/1438

Resce, G., Zinilli, A., & Cerulli, G. (2022). Machine learning prediction of academic collaboration networks. *Scientific Reports*, 12(1), 1–16. DOI: 10.1038/s41598-022-26531-1 PMID: 36539469

Research Guides. Artificial Intelligence (AI) in Education: AI and ethics. (2024). jmu.edu. https://guides.lib.jmu.edu/AI-in-education/ethics

Richardson, E., Gordon, J., Conklin, S., Barreto, D., & Ginnetti, R. (2024). Artificial Intelligence in Higher Education: Faculty Perceptions of Integration and Other Considerations. UNC System *Learning and Technology Journal, 2* (1), 1-39. https://journals.charlotte.edu/ltj/article/view/1776/1505

Richardson, J. C., Besser, E., Koehler, A., Lim, J., & Strait, M. (2017). Instructors' perceptions of instructor presence in online learning environments. *The International Review of Research in Open and Distributed Learning*, 18(6), 233–251.

Riemann, C., Ostendorf, S., & Umphres, B. (2024). *Generative AI in transportation management: AI's impact on supply chain logistics*. Deloitte.

Rigby, D. K., Sutherland, J., & Takeuchi, H. (2016). Embracing agile. *Harvard Business Review*. Advance online publication. DOI: 10.1177/0008125616635597

rmontalvo. (2023). The Benefits of AI in Education - CIS University. CIS University - EN. https://www.cis-spain.com/en/blog/the-benefits-of-ai-in-education/

Robertson, B. J. (2015). *Holacracy: The new management system for a rapidly changing world*. Henry Holt and Company.

Rodriguez, P., & Patel, N. (2022). Bridging the gap: AI in underfunded media programs. *Journal of Educational Enquiry*, 39(1), 47–63.

Roeper., Pace, S., & Marshall, S P. (2014, October 5). Re-Imagining Specialized STEM Academies: Igniting and Nurturing Decidedly Different Minds, by Design. https://www.tandfonline.com/doi/abs/10.1080/02783190903386884

Rogers, T., & Kim, S. (2020). Experimental media in the age of AI: Opportunities for creative exploration. *Journal of Digital Media Arts*, 27(3), 137–153.

Rong, Q., Lian, Q., & Tang, T. (2022). Research on the influence of AI and VR technology for students' concentration and creativity. *Frontiers in Psychology*, 13, 767689. Advance online publication. DOI: 10.3389/fpsyg.2022.767689 PMID: 35401322

Roscoe, R. D., Allen, L. K., Weston, J. L., Crossley, S. A., & McNamara, D. S. (2019). The Writing Pal intelligent tutoring system: Usability testing and development. *Computers and Composition*, 53, 70–85.

Ross, E. M. (2024, October 2). How generative AI can support professional learning for teachers. Harvard Graduate School of Education. https://www.gse.harvard.edu/ideas/usable-knowledge/24/10/how-generative-ai-can-support-professional-learning-teachers

Routley, N. (2023). *What is generative AI? An AI explains*. World Economic Forum.

Rovai, A. P. (2002). Sense of community-perceived cognitive learning and persistence in asynchronous learning networks. *The Internet and Higher Education*, 5(4), 319–332. DOI: 10.1016/S1096-7516(02)00130-6

Rožman, M., Tominc, P., & Vrečko, I. (2023, August 29). Building skills for the future of work: Students' perspectives on emerging jobs in the Data and AI Cluster through artificial intelligence in education., 8(2). DOI: 10.54517/esp.v8i2.1670

Rudolph, J., Tan, S., & Tan, S. (2023). ChatGPT: Bullshit Spewer or the end of traditional assessments in higher education? *Journal of Applied Learning and Teaching*, 6(1), 342–363. DOI: 10.37074/jalt.2023.6.1.9

Rumelhart, D. E., Hinton, G. E., & Williams, R. J. (1986). Learning representations by back-propagating errors. *Nature*, 323(6088), 533–536. DOI: 10.1038/323533a0

Rusmiyanto, R., Huriati, N., Fitriani, N., Tyas, N. K., Rofi'I, A., & Sari, M. N. (2023). The role of artificial intelligence (AI) in developing English language learner's communication skills. *Journal of Education*, 6(1), 750–757.

Saaida, M. B. E. (2023). AI-Driven transformations in higher education: Opportunities and challenges. Zenodo (CERN European Organization for Nuclear Research). DOI: 10.5281/zenodo.8164415

Saaida, M. B. (2023). AI-Driven transformations in higher education: Opportunities and challenges. *International Journal of Educational Research and Studies*, 5(1), 29–36.

Sahlberg, P., & Hargreaves, A. (2020). Leadership transformation through AI in Finnish schools. *International Journal of Leadership in Education*, 23(5), 594–610.

Sairitupa-Sanchez, L. Z., Collantes-Vargas, A., Rivera-Lozada, O., & Morales-Garcia, W. C. (2023). Development and validation of a scale for streaming dependence (SDS) of online games in a Peruvian population. *Frontiers in Psychology*, 14, 647. DOI: 10.3389/fpsyg.2023.1184647 PMID: 37691786

Sak, U., & Ayas, M. (2013). Creative scientific ability test (C-SAT): A new measure of scientific creativity. *Psychological Test and Assessment Modeling*, 55, 316–329.

Salemink, K., Strijker, D., & Bosworth, G. (2015). Rural development in the digital age: A systematic literature review on unequal ICT availability, adoption, and use in rural areas. *Journal of Rural Studies*, 54, 360–371. DOI: 10.1016/j.jrurstud.2015.09.001

Salman, A., & Alexandron, G. (2024). The digital fingerprint of learner behavior: Empirical evidence for individuality in learning using deep learning. *Computers and Education: Artificial Intelligence*, 100322.

Samadi, M. A. JaQuay, S., Gu, J., & Nixon, N. (2024). The AI Collaborator: Bridging human–AI interaction in educational and professional settings. arXiv:2405.10460v1. https://arxiv.org/html/2405.10460v1

Sánchez-Caballé, A., Esteve-Mon, F. M., & González-Martínez, J. (2020, January 5). What to Expect When You Are Simulating?: About Digital Simulation Potentialities in Teacher Training. https://www.igi-global.com/gateway/article/241256

Sanders, D. A., & Mukhari, S. S. (2024). Lecturers' perceptions of the influence of AI on a blended learning approach in a South African higher education institution. *Discover Education*, 3(1), 135. DOI: 10.1007/s44217-024-00235-2

Sanderson, K. (2023, March 16). GPT-4 is here: what scientists think. *Nature*. https://www.nature.com/articles/d41586-023-00816-5

Saputra, I., Astuti, M., Sayuti, M., & Kusumastuti, D. (2023). Integration of artificial intelligence in education: Opportunities, challenges, threats and obstacles. *Indonesian Journal of Computer Science*, 12(4). Advance online publication. DOI: 10.33022/ijcs.v12i4.3266

Sargiotis, D. (2024). Integrating AI and Big Data in Virtual Infrastructures: Transforming Educational Landscapes for the Future. *Available atSSRN* 4789850. DOI: 10.2139/ssrn.4789850

Sarnovska, N., Rybinska, J., & Mykhailichenko, Y. (2024). Enhancing university remote language learning through innovative applications of artificial intelligence technologies amidst global challenges. *Teaching Languages at Higher Educational Establishments at the Present Stage.Intersubject Relations*, (44), 151–165.

Schiff, D. (2022). Education for AI, not AI for education: The role of education and ethics in national AI policy strategies. *International Journal of Artificial Intelligence in Education*, 32(3), 527–563. DOI: 10.1007/s40593-021-00270-2

Schultz, D. P. ve Ellen-Schultz, S. (2007). *Modern psikoloji tarihi* (Y. Aslay, çev.). İstanbul: Kaknüs Yayınları.

Schulze, S. (2024, April 2). Adaptive learning: What it is & how AI supports it. *Medium.*https://masterplan.com/en-blog/adaptive-learning

Schwendicke, F. A., Samek, W., & Krois, J. (2020). Artificial intelligence in dentistry: Chances and challenges. *Journal of Dental Research*, 99(7), 769–774. DOI: 10.1177/0022034520915714 PMID: 32315260

Sedkaoui, S., & Benaichouba, R. (2024). Generative AI as a transformative force for innovation: A review of opportunities, applications and challenges. *European Journal of Innovation Management*. Advance online publication. DOI: 10.1108/EJIM-02-2024-0129

Selwyn, N. (2021). Should robots replace teachers? AI and the future of education. *Polity*.

Sen, S., & Banerjee, S. (2022). How Sport-for-Development Initiatives Influence Quality of Life in Post Pandemic Era? *Jharkhand Journal of Development and Management Studies*, 20 (4). 9535-9548, https://www.xiss.ac.in/JJDMS/archives

Sengupta, S. (2023, April 1). A deep dive into GPT's transformer architecture: Understanding self-attention mechanisms. *GPTFrontier*. https://www.gptfrontier.com/a-deep-dive-into-gpts-transformer-architecture-understanding-self-attention-mechanisms/

Sen, S., & Banerjee, S. (2023). Adverse Effects of Online Education on Student Engagement during Covid-19: Review, Synthesis and Research Agenda. CARDIOMETRY. 293-301. https://doi.org/DOI: 10.18137/cardiometry.2023.26.293301

Seo, K., Tang, J., Roll, I., Fels, S., & Yoon, D. (2021). The impact of artificial intelligence on learner–instructor interaction in online learning. *International Journal of Educational Technology in Higher Education*, 18(1), 54. Advance online publication. DOI: 10.1186/s41239-021-00292-9 PMID: 34778540

Seufert, S., Guggemos, J., & Sailer, M. (2021). Technology-related knowledge, skills, and attitudes of pre-and in-service teachers: The current situation and emerging trends. *Computers in Human Behavior,* 115, Article 106552. https://doi.org/.chb.2020.106552DOI: 10.1016/j

Sevli, O. (2023). ChatGPT'nin Eğitim Alanında Kullanımı (Using ChatGPT in Education). Conference: 4th International Black Sea Modern Scientific Research Congress (4. Uluslararası Karadeniz Modern Bilimsel Araştırmalar Kongresi) June 2023 At: Rize, Turkey

Shadbolt, N. (2020). Ethics and AI: The Issues. *AI & Society*, 35(4), 767–776.

Shahat Osman, A. M., & Elragal, A. (2021). Smart cities and big data analytics: A data-driven decision-making use case. *Smart Cities*, 4(1), 286–313. DOI: 10.3390/smartcities4010018

Shah, P. (2023). *AI and the Future of Education: Teaching in the Age of Artificial Intelligence*. John Wiley & Sons.

Shah, R. W. (2020). *Rewriting partnerships: Community perspectives on community-based learning*. University Press of Colorado.

Shaji, S., & Nagaraj, P. (2020, December 22). Integration of Technology in English Language Classrooms: A Research Review., 9(S1-Dec2020), 26-29. DOI: 10.34293/english.v9iS1-Dec2020.3608

Sha, L., Raković, M., Das, A., Gašević, D., & Chen, G. (2022). Leveraging class balancing techniques to alleviate algorithmic bias for predictive tasks in education. *IEEE Transactions on Learning Technologies*, 15(4), 481–492. DOI: 10.1109/TLT.2022.3196278

Shapiro, S., Beninger, S., Domegan, C., Reppel, A., Stanton, J., & Watson, F. (2021). Macromarketing pedagogy: Empowering students to achieve a sustainable world. *Journal of Macromarketing*, 41(1), 104–115. DOI: 10.1177/0276146720949637

Sharma, S., Das, A., Birari, A., & Agrawal, S. (2024). *Customer experience unleashed: Harnessing Gen AI and tech innovations for next-level customer engagement*. Everest Group.

Sharma, S., & Kumar, N. (2024). Navigating the ethical landscape of ai-based resources in education: Implications for learning, proper usage, and course design enhancement. *The Online Journal of Distance Education and e-Learning : TOJDEL*, 12(2), 92.

Sharma, S., & Kumar, N. (2024). NAVIGATING THE ETHICAL LANDSCAPE OF AI-BASED RESOURCES IN EDUCATION: IMPLICATIONS FOR LEARNING, PROPER USAGE, AND COURSE DESIGN ENHANCEMENT. *The Online Journal of Distance Education and e-Learning : TOJDEL*, 12(2), 92.

Sheerman, L., Marston, H. R., Musselwhite, C., & Morgan, D. (2020). COVID-19 and the secret virtual assistants: The social weapons for a state of emergency. *Emerald Open Research*, 2(2), 19. DOI: 10.1108/EOR-02-2023-0005

Shen, Y. Q., Heacock, L., Elias, J., Hentel, K. D., Reig, B., Shih, G., & Moy, L. (2023). ChatGPT and other large language models are double-edged swords. *Radiology*, 307(2), e230163. DOI: 10.1148/radiol.230163 PMID: 36700838

Shivam, R., & Singh, S. (2015). Implementation of Blended Learning in Classroom: A review paper. *International Journal of Scientific and Research Publications*, 5(11), 369–372.

Shneiderman, B. (2020). Bridging the gap between ethics and practice. *ACM Transactions on Interactive Intelligent Systems*, 10(4), 1–31. DOI: 10.1145/3419764

Shulla, K., Filho, W. L., Lardjane, S., Sommer, J. H., & Borgemeister, C. (2020). Sustainable development education in the context of the 2030 Agenda for sustainable development. *International Journal of Sustainable Development and World Ecology*, 27(5), 458–468. DOI: 10.1080/13504509.2020.1721378

Shulman, L. S. (2005). Signature pedagogies in the professions. *Daedalus*, 134(3), 52–59. DOI: 10.1162/0011526054622015

Si, S., & Chen, H. (2020). A literature review of disruptive innovation: What it is, how it works and where it goes. *Journal of Engineering and Technology Management*, 56, 101568, ISSN 0923-4748, https://doi.org/DOI: 10.1016/j.jengtecman.2020.101568

Siegel, J. (n.d.). *The art of the prompt: How to get the best out of generative AI.* Microsoft. https://news.microsoft.com/source/features/ai/the-art-of-the-prompt-how-to-get-the-best-out-of-generative-ai/

Simonton, D. K. (2013). Scientific creativity as combinatorial process. In Carayannis, E. G. (Ed.), *Encyclopedia of creativity, invention, innovation and entrepreneurship* (pp. 1592–1595). Springer., DOI: 10.1007/978-1-4614-3858-8_388

Singer, J. B., Báez, J. C., & Rios, R. (2021). Artificial intelligence and natural language processing in social work: A scoping review. *Journal of Technology in Human Services*, 39(1), 1–27. DOI: 10.1080/15228835.2020.1862401

Singer, J., Báez, J., & Rios, R. (2023). Artificial intelligence and natural language processing in social work: Opportunities and challenges. *Journal of Social Work Education*, 59(2), 201–215.

Smith, A., Lee, J., & Gonzalez, J. (2019). Bias in AI grading systems: A study on the impact on minority students. *Journal of Education and Technology*, 54(1), 27–38. DOI: 10.1080/21532963.2022.1694378

Smith, J. (2022). Democratizing media creation through AI. In Brown, R. (Ed.), *Advances in media education* (pp. 57–72). Routledge.

Smith, S. U., Hayes, S., & Shea, P. (2017). A Critical Review of the Use of Wenger's Community of Practice (CoP) Theoretical Framework in Online and Blended Learning Research, 2000-2014. *Online Learning : the Official Journal of the Online Learning Consortium*, 21(1), 209–237. DOI: 10.24059/olj.v21i1.963

Soltis, N. A., McNeal, K. S., Atkins, R. M., & Maudlin, L. C. (2020). A novel approach to measuring student engagement while using an augmented reality sandbox. *Journal of Geography in Higher Education*, 44(4), 512–531. DOI: 10.1080/03098265.2020.1771547

Soni, N., Sharma, E. K., Singh, N., & Kapoor, A. (2020). Artificial intelligence in business: From research and innovation to market deployment. *Procedia Computer Science*, 167, 2200–2210. DOI: 10.1016/j.procs.2020.03.272

Srinivasan, V., & Murthy, H. (2021, January 1). Improving reading and comprehension in K-12: Evidence from a large-scale AI technology intervention in India. Elsevier BV, 2, 100019-100019. DOI: 10.1016/j.caeai.2021.100019

Srivastava, S.Ms Sanchana Srivastava. (2023). The evolution of education: Navigating 21st-century challenges. *International Journal for Multidisciplinary Research*, 5(5), 6314. Advance online publication. DOI: 10.36948/ijfmr.2023.v05i05.6314

Sriwastwa, A., Ravi, P., Emmert, A., Chokshi, S., Kondor, S., Dhal, K., ... & Gupta, R. (2023). Generative AI for medical 3D printing: A comparison of ChatGPT outputs to reference standard education. *3D Printing in Medicine, 9*(1), 21. https://doi.org/DOI: 10.1186/s41205-023-00152-6

Stackpole, B. (2023). *Why generative AI needs a creative human touch*. MIT Sloan School of Management.

Stahl, B. C., Andreou, A., Brey, P., Hatzakis, T., Kirichenko, A., Macnish, K., Laulh'e Shaelou, S., Patel, A., Ryan, M., & Wright, D. (2021). Artificial intelligence for human flourishing – Beyond principles for machine learning. *Journal of Business Research*, 124, 374–388. DOI: 10.1016/j.jbusres.2020.11.030

Stokes, J. M., Yang, K., & Adams, J. H. (2023). Generative AI for drug discovery. *Science*, 382(6642), 1001–1010.

Strielkowski, W., Grebennikova, V., Lisovskiy, A., Rakhimova, G., & Vasileva, T. (2024). AI-driven adaptive learning for sustainable educational transformation. Sustainable Development. wiley.com

Su, J., Zhong, Y., & Ng, D. T. K. (2022). A meta-review of literature on educational approaches for teaching AI at the K-12 levels in the Asia-Pacific region. *Computers and Education: Artificial Intelligence*, 3, 100053. DOI: 10.1016/j.caeai.2022.100065

Sullivan, M., Kelly, A., & McLaughlan, P. (2023). ChatGPT in higher education: Considerations for academic integrity and student learning. *Journal of Applied Learning and Teaching*, 6(1), 31–40.

Sundari, M. S., Penthala, H. R., & Nayyar, A. Transforming Education through AI-Enhanced Content Creation and Personalized Learning Experiences. In *Impact of Artificial Intelligence on Society* (pp. 98–118). Chapman and Hall/CRC.

Swiecki, Z., Khosravi, H., Chen, G., Martínez-Maldonado, R., Lodge, J M., Milligan, S., Selwyn, N., & Gašević, D. (2022, January 1). Assessment in the age of artificial intelligence. Elsevier BV, 3, 100075-100075. DOI: 10.1016/j.caeai.2022.100075

Syahrizal, S., Yasmi, F., & Mary, T. (2024). AI-enhanced teaching materials for education: A shift towards digitalization. *International Journal of Religion*, 5(1), 203–217. DOI: 10.61707/j6sa1w36

Tanase, M. (2020). Is good teaching culturally responsive? *Journal of Pedagogical Research*, 4(3), 187–202. DOI: 10.33902/JPR.2020063333

Tan, C., & Gopinathan, S. (2019). AI in Educational Leadership in Singapore. *Educational Management Administration & Leadership*, 47(1), 87–104.

Tariq, M. U. (2024). Equity and Inclusion in Learning Ecosystems. In Preparing Students for the Future Educational Paradigm (pp. 155-176). IGI Global. DOI: 10.4018/979-8-3693-1536-1.ch007

Tayan, O., Hassan, A., Khankan, K., & Askool, S. (2023). Considerations for adapting higher education technology courses for AI large language models: A critical review of the impact of ChatGPT. *Machine Learning with Applications*, 15, 100513. DOI: 10.1016/j.mlwa.2023.100513

Taylor, D. L., Yeung, M., & Bashet, A. Z. (2021). Personalized and adaptive learning. *Innovative learning environments in STEM higher education: Opportunities, Challenges, and Looking Forward*, 17-34.

Taylor, D., Yeung, M., & Bashet, A Z. (2021, January 1). Personalized and Adaptive Learning. Springer International Publishing, 17-34. DOI: 10.1007/978-3-030-58948-6_2

Teach, F. X. (2024a). About TeachFX. https://teachfx.com/

Teach, F. X. (2024b). Research. https://teachfx.com/research

Technology, T. (2024). Unveiling the Potential: Experts' Perspectives on Artificial Intelligence Integration in Higher Education. eu-jer.com. https://www.eu-jer.com/unveiling-the-potential-experts-perspectives-on-artificial-intelligence-integration-in-higher-education

technouser. (2024). AI in Education: 24/7 Learning Access for Students. Technocrats Horizons. https://technocratshorizons.com/how-ai-in-education-can-provide-24-7-access-to-learning-for-students/

Teece, D. J. (2018). Dynamic capabilities: Routines versus entrepreneurial action. *Journal of Management Studies*, 55(7), 1248–1260. DOI: 10.1111/joms.12311

Teece, D. J., Pisano, G., & Shuen, A. (1997). Dynamic capabilities and strategic management. *Strategic Management Journal*, 18(7), 509–533. DOI: 10.1002/(SICI)1097-0266(199708)18:7<509::AID-SMJ882>3.0.CO;2-Z

Teng, Y., Zhang, J., & Sun, T. (2023). Data-driven decision-making model based on artificial intelligence in higher education system of colleges and universities. *Expert Systems: International Journal of Knowledge Engineering and Neural Networks*, 40(4), e12820. DOI: 10.1111/exsy.12820

Tenório, M M., Reinaldo, F., Góis, L A D., Lopes, R P., & Santos, G D. (2018, January 1). Elements of Gamification in Virtual Learning Environments. Springer Nature, 86-96. DOI: 10.1007/978-3-319-73204-6_12

Tettegah, S. Y., & Mayo, C. (2005). Urban education and technology in the digital age. *Urban Education*, 40(4), 363–367. DOI: 10.1177/0042085905276374

Thakkar, A., Gupta, A., & De Sousa, A. (2024). Artificial intelligence in positive mental health: A narrative review. *Frontiers in Digital Health*, 6, 1280235. Advance online publication. DOI: 10.3389/fdgth.2024.1280235 PMID: 38562663

Thanasi, T., & Mema, O. (2024). Enhancing Mathematics Education with Artificial Intelligence. *EIRP Proceedings, 19*(1), 518-523.

Thorp, H. H. (2023). ChatGPT is fun, but not an author. *Science*, 379(6630), 313. DOI: 10.1126/science.adg7879 PMID: 36701446

Tichnor-Wagner, A., Parkhouse, H., Glazier, J., & Cain, J. M. (2016). Expanding approaches to teaching for diversity and social justice in K–12 education: Fostering global citizenship across the content areas. *Education Policy Analysis Archives*, 24, 59. DOI: 10.14507/epaa.24.2138

Tidd, J., & Bessant, J. (2021). *Managing innovation: Integrating technological, market and organizational change* (7th ed.). John Wiley & Sons., DOI: 10.1002/9781119741686

Ting, K. Y. (2014). Blended Learning as a Theoretical Framework for the Application of Podcasting. *English Language Teaching*, 7(5), 128–135. DOI: 10.5539/elt.v7n5p128

Tlili, A., Shehata, B., Adarkwah, M. A., Bozkurt, A., Hickey, D. T., Huang, R., & Agyemang, B. (2023). What if the devil is my guardian angel: ChatGPT as a case study of using Chatbots in education. *Smart Learning Environments*, 10(1), 15. DOI: 10.1186/s40561-023-00237-x

Toksha, B., Kulkarni, T., & Gupta, P. (2022). Impact of AI on teaching pedagogy and its integration for enhancing teaching-learning. In *Artificial Intelligence in Higher Education* (pp. 137–152). CRC Press. DOI: 10.1201/9781003184157-7

Tomasik, M. J., Berger, S., & Moser, U. (2018, November 20). On the Development of a Computer-Based Tool for Formative Student Assessment: Epistemological, Methodological, and Practical Issues. *Frontiers of Medicine*, 9, 2245. Advance online publication. DOI: 10.3389/fpsyg.2018.02245 PMID: 30515119

Tong, M. S., Zheng, H. Q., & Wan, G. C. (2019). Improvement of education method by using artificial intelligence technology. In *2019 IEEE international conference on engineering, technology and education* (TALE) (pp. 1–5). IEEE. DOI: 10.1109/TALE48000.2019.9225891

Topinka, R. (2024, February 13). The software says my student cheated using AI. They say they're innocent. Who do I believe? *The Guardian*. https://www.theguardian.com/commentisfree/2024/feb/13/software-student-cheated-combat-ai

Trust, T., Whalen, J., & Mouza, C. (2023). Editorial: ChatGPT: Challenges, opportunities, and implications for teacher education. *Contemporary Issues in Technology & Teacher Education*, 23(1), 1–23.

Tsai, Y., Whitelock-Wainwright, A., & Gašević, D. (2020, March 13). The privacy paradox and its implications for learning analytics. DOI: 10.1145/3375462.3375536

Tseng, Y. C., & Lin, Y. H. (2024). Enhancing English as a Foreign Language (EFL) Learners' Writing with ChatGPT: A University-Level Course Design. *Electronic Journal of e-Learning*, 22(2), 78–97. DOI: 10.34190/ejel.21.5.3329

Tufekci, Z. (2015). Algorithmic harms beyond Facebook and Google: Emergent challenges of computational agency. *Colorado Technology Law Journal*, 13(2), 203–217.

Turmuzi, M. (2024). Perceptions of primary school teacher education students to the use of ChatGPT to support learning in the Digital Era. *International Journal of Information and Education Technology (IJIET)*, 14(5), 721–732. DOI: 10.18178/ijiet.2024.14.5.2097

Tzimas, D., & Demetriadis, S. (2021). Ethical issues in learning analytics: A review of the field. *Educational Technology Research and Development*, 69(2), 1101–1133. DOI: 10.1007/s11423-021-09977-4

Ulla, M. B., Perales, W. F., & Busbus, S. O. (2023). To generate or stop generating response: Exploring EFL teachers' perspectives on ChatGPT in English language teaching in Thailand. *Learning: Research and Practice*, 9(2), 168–182. DOI: 10.1080/23735082.2023.2257252

UNESCO, & IRCAI (2024). *Challenging systematic prejudices: An investigation into gender bias in large language models.* The United Nations Educational, Scientific and Cultural Organization (UNESCO) and International Research Centre on Artificial Intelligence (IRCAI). https://www.unesco.org/en/articles/generative-ai-unesco-study-reveals-alarming-evidence-regressive-gender-stereotypes

UNESCO. (2021). *AI and education: Guidance for policymakers.* United Nations Educational, Scientific and Cultural Organization. https://unesdoc.unesco.org/ark:/48223/pf0000376709

UNESCO. (2021). *Global perspective on AI-driven educational leadership.* United Nations Educational, Scientific and Cultural Organization.

UNESCO. (2022). *Global education equity report: The role of AI in bridging the educational divide.* UNESCO.

USC Annenberg School for Communication and Journalism. (2021). AI for media [Course description]. Retrieved from https://uscannenberg.com/courses

Van de Cruys, S., Bervoets, J., & Moors, A. (2022). Preferences need inferences: Learning, valuation, and curiosity in aesthetic experience. In *The Routledge international handbook of neuroaesthetics* (pp. 475-506). Routledge. 45- Wang, T., & Park, J. (2021). Design and implementation of intelligent sports training system for college students' mental health education. *Frontiers in Psychology, 12*, Article 634978. https://doi.org/DOI: 10.3389/fpsyg.2021.634978

van den Berg, G., & du Plessis, E. (2023). ChatGPT and Generative AI: Possibilities for İts contribution to lesson planning, critical thinking and openness in teacher education. *Education Sciences*, 13(10), 998. DOI: 10.3390/educsci13100998

Van Rooij, A. J., Schoenmakers, T. M., Vermulst, A. A., Van Den Eijnden, R. J. J. M., & Van De Mheen, D. (2011). Online video game addiction: Identification of addicted adolescent gamers. *Addiction (Abingdon, England)*, 106(1), 205–212. DOI: 10.1111/j.1360-0443.2010.03104.x PMID: 20840209

Vanden Abeele, M. M. P., Halfmann, A., & Lee, E. W. J. (2022). Drug, demon, or donut? Theorizing the relationship between social media use, digital well-being, and digital disconnection. *Current Opinion in Psychology*, 45, 101295. DOI: 10.1016/j.copsyc.2021.12.007 PMID: 35123383

Venkatraman, S., Benli, F., Wei, Y., & Wahr, F. (2022). Smart classroom teaching strategy to enhance higher order thinking skills (HOTS)—An agile approach for education 4.0. *Future Internet*, 14(9), 255. DOI: 10.3390/fi14090255

Verbert, K., Duval, E., Klerkx, J., Govaerts, S., & Santos, J. L. (2013). Learning analytics dashboard applications. *The American Behavioral Scientist*, 57(10), 1500–1509. DOI: 10.1177/0002764213479363

Vermare, E. G. (2023). *Student-Centred Blended Learning in a Flipped Classroom for a Pre-University Masterclass* (Master's thesis, University of Twente).

Vosoughi, S., Roy, D., & Aral, S. (2018). The spread of true and false news online. *Science*, 359(6380), 1146–1151. DOI: 10.1126/science.aap9559 PMID: 29590045

Vrenozi, B., Harasani, K., Memeti, A., & Dukaj, E. (2020). Evaluation of the online learning process during the Covid-19 pandemic period towards better future approaches of higher education perspectives on the Balkans.

Walker, E., Rummel, N., & Koedinger, K R. (2013, October 17). Adaptive Intelligent Support to Improve Peer Tutoring in Algebra. Springer Science+Business Media, 24(1), 33-61. DOI: 10.1007/s40593-013-0001-9

Walkington, C., & Bernacki, M. L. (2019). Personalizing algebra to students' individual interests in an intelligent tutoring system: Moderators of impact. *International Journal of Artificial Intelligence in Education*, 29(1), 58–88. DOI: 10.1007/s40593-018-0168-1

Walton, G. M., & Cohen, G. L. (2011). A brief social-belonging intervention improves academic and health outcomes of minority students. *Science*, 331(6023), 1447–1451. DOI: 10.1126/science.1198364 PMID: 21415354

Wang, N., & Lester, J C. (2023, June 1). K-12 Education in the Age of AI: A Call to Action for K-12 AI Literacy. Springer Science+Business Media, 33(2), 228-232. DOI: 10.1007/s40593-023-00358-x

Wang, F., Wang, Z., & Hwang, G. J. (2019). Integrating AI into Education: The Role of Teachers. *Journal of Educational Technology & Society*, 22(1), 80–92.

Wang, Q., & Rao, Y. (2024, May). Research on the Enhancement of Digital Capabilities in AI-based Blended Teaching Processes. In *Proceedings of the 2024 International Conference on Computer and Multimedia Technology* (pp. 330-336). DOI: 10.1145/3675249.3675308

Wang, T., Lund, B. D., Marengo, A., Pagano, A., Mannuru, R. N., Teel, Z. A., & Pange, J. (2023). Exploring the potential impact of artificial intelligence (AI) on international students in higher education: Generative AI, chatbots, analytics, and international student success. *Applied Sciences (Basel, Switzerland)*, 13(11), 6716. DOI: 10.3390/app13116716

Wang, X., Li, L., Tan, S. C., Yang, L., & Lei, J. (2023). Preparing for AI-enhanced education: Conceptualizing and empirically examining teachers' AI readiness. *Computers in Human Behavior*, 146, 107798. DOI: 10.1016/j.chb.2023.107798

Wang, Y. (2020). When artificial intelligence meets educational leaders' data-informed decision-making: A cautionary tale. *Studies in Educational Evaluation*, 69, 100872. DOI: 10.1016/j.stueduc.2020.100872

Wang, Y., Liu, C., & Tu, Y. F. (2021). Factors affecting the adoption of AI-based applications in higher education. *Journal of Educational Technology & Society*, 24(3), 116–129.

Warschauer, M. (2004). *Technology and social inclusion: Rethinking the digital divide*. MIT Press.

Warschauer, M., Tseng, W., Yim, S., Webster, T., Jacob, S., Du, Q., & Tate, T. (2023). The affordances and contradictions of AI-generated text for writers of English as a second or foreign language. *Journal of Second Language Writing*, 62, 101071. DOI: 10.1016/j.jslw.2023.101071

Watkins, R. (2022, December 19). Update your course syllabus for chatGPT. *Medium*. https://medium.com/@rwatkins_7167/updating-your-course-syllabus-for-chatgpt-965f4b57b003

Watts-Taffe, S. (2022). Multimodal literacies: Fertile ground for equity, inclusion, and connection. *The Reading Teacher*, 75(5), 603–609. DOI: 10.1002/trtr.2080

Weinstein, A., & Lejoyeux, M. (2010). Internet addiction or excessive internet use. *The American Journal of Drug and Alcohol Abuse*, 36(5), 277–283. DOI: 10.3109/00952990.2010.491880 PMID: 20545603

Wenger, E. (2000). Communities of practice and social learning systems. *Organization*, 7(2), 225–246. DOI: 10.1177/135050840072002

West, D. M. (2019). AI in education: Building ethics into design. Brookings Institution Report. Retrieved from https://www.brookings.edu/wp-content/uploads/2019/04/AI-in-education_Building-ethics-into-design_Updated-cover.pdf

West, S. M., Whittaker, M., & Crawford, K. (2020). Discriminating systems: Gender, race, and power in AI. *AI Now Institute*. https://ainowinstitute.org/discriminatingsystems.html

Wibbitz. (2019). Wibbitz: AI-powered video creation. Retrieved from https://www.wibbitz.com

Wieman, C., Adams, W. K., & Perkins, K. K. (2008, October 30). PhET: Simulations That Enhance Learning. *Science*, 322(5902), 682–683. DOI: 10.1126/science.1161948 PMID: 18974334

Wilkens, U., Langholf, V., Ontrup, G., & Kluge, A. (2021). Towards a maturity model of human-centered AI–A reference for AI implementation at the workplace. *Competence development and learning assistance systems for the data-driven future*, 179-197.

Williamson, B. (2024). The social life of AI in education. *International Journal of Artificial Intelligence in Education*, 34(1), 97–104. DOI: 10.1007/s40593-023-00342-5

Williamson, B., & Eynon, R. (2020). Historical threads, missing links, and future directions in AI in education. *Learning, Media and Technology*, 45(3), 223–235. DOI: 10.1080/17439884.2020.1798995

Wilson, J., Huang, Y., Palermo, C., Beard, G., & MacArthur, C. A. (2021). Automated feedback and automated scoring in the elementary grades: Usage, attitudes, and associations with writing outcomes in a districtwide implementation of MI Write. *International Journal of Artificial Intelligence in Education*, 31(2), 234–276. DOI: 10.1007/s40593-020-00236-w

Wineburg, S., McGrew, S., Breakstone, J., & Ortega, T. (2016). *Evaluating information: The cornerstone of civic online reasoning*. Stanford Digital Repository.

Witts, J. (2024, August 20). [AI code generation solutions for developers. *Expert Insights*. https://expertinsights.com/insights/the-top-ai-code-generation-solutions-for-programmers/]. *Top (Madrid)*, 5, •••.

Wollny, S., Schneider, J., Mitri, D. D., Weidlich, J., Rittberger, M., & Drachsler, H. (2021, July 15). Are We There Yet? - A Systematic Literature Review on Chatbots in Education. *Frontiers of Medicine*, 4, 654924. Advance online publication. DOI: 10.3389/frai.2021.654924 PMID: 34337392

Wong, K. K. (2024, June). Blended Learning and AI: Enhancing Teaching and Learning in Higher Education. In *International Conference on Blended Learning* (pp. 39-61). Singapore: Springer Nature Singapore. DOI: 10.1007/978-981-97-4442-8_4

Wong, L., Tatnall, A., & Burgess, S. (2014). A framework for investigating blended learning effectiveness. *Education + Training*, 56(2/3), 233–251. DOI: 10.1108/ET-04-2013-0049

Woodward, D., Booth, S., Allen, E., Forbes, A., & Morton, C. (2023, November). Reflective practice for educators and learners, and the benefits of being a reflective practitioner. *Scope: Contemporary Research Topics (Learning & Teaching)*, 12, 96–103.

Woo, H., LeTendre, G. K., Pham-Shouse, T., & Xiong, Y. (2021). The use of social robots in classrooms: A review of field-based studies. *Educational Research Review*, 33, 100388. DOI: 10.1016/j.edurev.2021.100388

Woolf, B. P. (2009). *Building intelligent interactive tutors: Student-centered strategies for revolutionizing e-learning*. Morgan Kaufmann., DOI: 10.1016/B978-0-12-373594-2.00001-8

Wright, L., & Bell, J. (2019). AI in media production: Enhancing quality and creative freedom. *Technology and Media Education*, 31(2), 203–215.

Wu, S., & Lin, C. Y. Y. (2020). *Innovation and entrepreneurship in an educational ecosystem: Cases from Taiwan*. Springer Nature.

Wu, W., Burdina, G., & Gura, A. (2023). Use of Artificial Intelligence in Teacher Training. *International Journal of Web-Based Learning and Teaching Technologies*, 18(1), 1–15. DOI: 10.4018/IJWLTT.331692

Xhakaj, F., Aleven, V., & McLaren, B M. (2016, January 1). How Teachers Use Data to Help Students Learn: Contextual Inquiry for the Design of a Dashboard. Springer Science+Business Media, 340-354. https://doi.org/DOI: 10.1007/978-3-319-45153-4_26

Xie, H., Chu, H., Hwang, G., & Wang, C. (2019, June 6). Trends and development in technology-enhanced adaptive/personalized learning: A systematic review of journal publications from 2007 to 2017. Elsevier BV, 140, 103599-103599. https://doi.org/DOI: 10.1016/j.compedu.2019.103599

Xie, B., Liu, H., Alghofaili, R., Zhang, Y., Jiang, Y., Lobo, F. D., Li, C., Li, W., Huang, H., Akdere, M., Mousas, C., & Yu, L. F. (2021). A review on virtual reality skill training applications. *Frontiers in Virtual Reality*, 2, 645153. DOI: 10.3389/frvir.2021.645153

Xu, W., & Ouyang, F. (2022). The application of AI technologies in STEM education: A systematic review from 2011 to 2021. *International Journal of STEM Education*, 9(1), 59. Advance online publication. DOI: 10.1186/s40594-022-00377-5

Xu, Z. (2024). AI in education: Enhancing learning experiences and student outcomes. *Applied and Computational Engineering*, 51(1), 104–111. DOI: 10.54254/2755-2721/51/20241187

Yadav, U., & Shrawankar, U. (2025). Artificial Intelligence Across Industries: A Comprehensive Review With a Focus on Education. AI Applications and Strategies in Teacher Education, 275-320. [HTML]

Yalçın-Çelik, A. & K.Çoban, Ö. (2023). Kimya sorularının cevaplanmasında yapay zekâ tabanlı sohbet robotlarının performansının incelenmesi. *TEBD, 21*(3), 1540-1561. https://doi.org/DOI: 10.37217/tebd.1361401

Yang, H. (2021, February 1). Explore How Artificial Intelligence and VR Technology will Change the Development of Future Education. *Journal of Physics: Conference Series*, 1744(4), 042146–042146. DOI: 10.1088/1742-6596/1744/4/042146

Yang, S. J., Ogata, H., Matsui, T., & Chen, N. S. (2021). Human-centered artificial intelligence in education: Seeing the invisible through the visible. *Computers and Education: Artificial Intelligence*, 2, 100008. DOI: 10.1016/j.caeai.2021.100008

Yang, Y., Sun, W., Sun, D., & Salas-Pilco, S. Z. (2024). Navigating the AI-Enhanced STEM education landscape: A decade of insights, trends, and opportunities. *Research in Science & Technological Education*, •••, 1–25. DOI: 10.1080/02635143.2024.2370764

Yannier, N., Hudson, S E., & Koedinger, K R. (2020, February 3). Active Learning is About More Than Hands-On: A Mixed-Reality AI System to Support STEM Education. Springer Science+Business Media, 30(1), 74-96. https://doi.org/DOI: 10.1007/s40593-020-00194-3

Yao, Y. (2021, November 2). Deep Integration of AI and TPACK: Reconstruction of Teachers'. *Knowledge Structure in the Post-pandemic Era.*, 3, 150–154. DOI: 10.54691/bcpep.v3i.28

Yarger, L., Payton, F C., & Neupane, B. (2019, December 17). Algorithmic equity in the hiring of underrepresented IT job candidates. Emerald Publishing Limited, 44(2), 383-395. https://doi.org/DOI: 10.1108/OIR-10-2018-0334

Yıldırım, A., & Şimşek, H. (2013). *Sosyal bilimlerde nitel araştırma yöntemleri*. Seçkin Yayıncılık.

Yılmaz, A. ve Kaya, U. (2021). *Derin öğrenme* (3. Baskı). İstanbul: Kodlab.

Yim, I. H. Y. (2024). A critical review of teaching and learning artificial intelligence (AI) literacy: Developing an intelligence-based AI literacy framework for primary school education. *Computers and Education: Artificial Intelligence*, 7, 100319. DOI: 10.1016/j.caeai.2024.100319

Yin, R. K. (2009). *Case study research design and methods* (4th ed.). Sage.

Ysseldyke, J., & Tardrew, S. (2007, September 25). Use of a Progress Monitoring System to Enable Teachers to Differentiate Mathematics Instruction. Taylor & Francis, 24(1), 1-28. https://doi.org/DOI: 10.1300/J370v24n01_01

Yuce, A., Abubakar, A M., & İlkan, M. (2019, July 25). Intelligent tutoring systems and learning performance. Emerald Publishing Limited, 43(4), 600-616. https://doi.org/DOI: 10.1108/OIR-11-2017-0340

Yu, H. (2023). Reflection on whether Chat GPT should be banned by academia from the perspective of education and teaching. *Frontiers in Psychology*, 14, 1181712. Advance online publication. DOI: 10.3389/fpsyg.2023.1181712 PMID: 37325766

Yu, R., Li, Q., Fischer, C., Doroudi, S., & Xu, D. (2020). Towards accurate and fair prediction of college success: Evaluating different sources of student data. *Proceedings of the 13th international conference on educational data mining,* 292-301.

Zahra, S. A., & George, G. (2002). Absorptive capacity: A review, reconceptualization, and extension. *Academy of Management Review*, 27(2), 185–203. DOI: 10.2307/4134351

Zawacki-Richter, O., Marín, V. I., Bond, M., & Gouverneur, F. (2019). Systematic Review of Research on Artificial Intelligence in Higher Education – Where Are the Educators? *International Journal of Educational Technology in Higher Education*, 16(1), 39. DOI: 10.1186/s41239-019-0171-0

Zekaj, R. (2023). AI language models as educational allies: Enhancing instructional support in higher education. *International Journal of Learning. Teaching and Educational Research*, 22(8), 120–134.

Zhai, C., Wibowo, S., & Li, L. D. (2024). The effects of over-reliance on AI dialogue systems on students' cognitive abilities: A systematic review. *Smart Learning Environments*, 11(1), 28. Advance online publication. DOI: 10.1186/s40561-024-00316-7

Zhai, X., Chu, X., Chai, C. S., Jong, M. S. Y., Istenic, A., Spector, M., Liu, J.-B., Yuan, J., & Li, Y. (2021). A Review of Artificial Intelligence (AI) in Education from 2010 to 2020. *Complexity*, 2021(1), 8812542. DOI: 10.1155/2021/8812542

Zhang, K., & Aslan, A. B. (2021, January 1). AI technologies for education: Recent research & future directions. https://www.sciencedirect.com/science/article/pii/S2666920X21000199

Zhang, H., Lee, I., Ali, S., DiPaola, D., Cheng, Y., & Breazeal, C. (2023). Integrating ethics and career futures with technical learning to promote AI literacy for middle school students: An exploratory study. *International Journal of Artificial Intelligence in Education*, 33(2), 290–324. DOI: 10.1007/s40593-022-00293-3 PMID: 35573722

Zhang, K., & Aslan, A. B. (2021). AI technologies for education: Recent research & future directions. *Computers and Education: Artificial Intelligence*, 2, 100025. DOI: 10.1016/j.caeai.2021.100025

Zhang, K., & Aslan, A. B. (2021). AI technologies for education: Recent research and future directions. *Computers & Education*, 2, 100025.

Zhang, W., & Liu, J. (2020). AI in Leadership Development in Chinese Higher Education. *Journal of Higher Education Policy and Management*, 42(2), 131–144.

Zhang, X., Li, H., Liu, Z., Chen, Z., Zhou, H., Rong, W., & Ouyang, Y. (2024, March 1). A Review of Data Mining in Personalized Education. *Current Trends and Future Prospects.*, 1(1), 26–50. DOI: 10.1007/s44366-024-0019-6

Zhang, Y., Chen, X., & Liu, H. (2022). The impact of artificial intelligence on social work educators' well-being and job satisfaction: A mixed-methods study. *Computers in Human Behavior*, 118, 106–714.

Zharova, M. V., Trapitsin, S. Y., & Timchenko, V. V. (2021). Prospects for the use of artificial intelligence technologies in education. 2021 International Conference on Quality Management, Transport and Information Security, Information Technologies (IT&QM&IS), Yaroslavl, Russian Federation, 2021, pp. 754–759. IEEE. https://doi.org/DOI: 10.1109/ITQMIS53292.2021.9642866

Zharovskikh, A. (2024, April 23). Bias in generative AI: Types, examples, solutions. *InData Labs*. https://indatalabs.com/blog/generative-ai-bias

Zhou, Y., & Chen, L. ve Xu, Y. (2021). Impact of AI-based language learning tools on students' motivation and engagement. *Educational Technology Research and Development*, 69(5), 1201–1219.

Zimmerman, B. J. (2002). Becoming a self-regulated learner: An overview. *Theory into Practice*, 41(2), 64–70. DOI: 10.1207/s15430421tip4102_2

About the Contributors

Eriona Cela is a distinguished academic and expert in European integration and negotiation, renowned for her contributions to education and public administration in Albania and beyond. Holding prominent positions within multiple institutions, she serves as a key figure at the Academy of European Integration and Negotiations (AIEN), the Albanian School of Public Administration (ASPA), and the Business Academy College. Dr. Cela's expertise is further recognized through her active involvement in various roles related to European Union policies and enlargement strategies. As a Jean Monnet Chair holder at the Institute of European Studies, University of Tirana, Dr. Cela has spearheaded significant projects such as the European Integration School 2023's eighth edition. Her work frequently appears in prestigious publications, including the European Journal of Arts, Humanities and Social Sciences, the European Journal of Contemporary Education, and the International Journal of Balkan Studies. She is also an Associate Editor for the International Journal of Risk and Contingency Management (IJRCM), an IGI Journal. She has also been engaged with the OSCE Academy in Bishkek, Vytautas Magnus University, and the Università degli Studi di Bari Aldo Moro, Dipartimento di Studi Umanistici, where she has furthered research and collaboration on a European scale. Dr. Cela's commitment to educational leadership is demonstrated through her involvement with Shkolla e Drejtorëve (CSL) and the AADF, where she focuses on developing future leaders and administrators. In recognition of her ongoing contributions to education and public administration, Dr. Cela has received numerous accolades and is frequently invited as a keynote speaker at various academic and policy-making webinars. Her work continues to influence the strategic development of education systems in Albania and serves as a benchmark for integrating European educational standards and practices in the region.

Narasimha Rao Vajjhala is working as the Dean of the Faculty of Engineering and Architecture at the University of New York Tirana, Albania. He had previously worked as the Chair of Computer Science and Software Engineering programs at the American University of Nigeria. He is a senior member of ACM and IEEE. He is the Editor-in-Chief (EiC) of the International Journal of Risk and Contingency Management (IJRCM). He is also a member of the Risk Management Society (RIMS), and the Project Management Institute (PMI). He has over 23 years of experience teaching programming and database-related courses at both graduate and undergraduate levels in Europe and Africa. He has also worked as a consultant in technology firms in Europe and has experience participating in EU-funded projects. He has completed a Doctorate in Information Systems and Technology (United States); holds a Master of Science in Computer Science and Applications (India), and a Master of Business Administration with a specialization in Information.

Mathias Mbu Fonkam is a distinguished Associate Professor at the Penn State College of Information Sciences and Technology. With a rich background in computer science and systems engineering, Dr. Fonkam's academic and professional journey is marked by significant contributions to both academia and the software industry. Dr. Fonkam earned his Ph.D. in Computer Science from Cardiff University, where he also completed his Master of Science in Systems Engineering and Bachelor of Science with Honors in Computer Engineering. His scholarly work is complemented by industry certifications, including Sun Certified Programmer on the Java II Platform and multiple certifications from IBM's Cognitivelabs.ai in areas such as Data Science, Blockchain Technologies, and Cryptocurrencies. Professionally, Dr. Fonkam has an extensive record of academic leadership and innovation. Before his current role at Penn State University, he served as the Dean and Associate Professor at the American University of Nigeria (AUN). During his tenure, he played a pivotal role in establishing and leading the development of the University's open-source ERP system and its learning management system, CANVAS. His efforts in curriculum development and the implementation of graduate programs significantly advanced AUN's educational offerings. Dr. Fonkam's contributions extend beyond administrative leadership. He has been actively involved in the Nigerian academic community, participating in committees for the National Universities Commission (NUC) to develop new computing degree programs and accreditations. His international experience includes roles at Albany State University, St. Joseph's University, and as a visiting professor in Brazil, enhancing his global perspective on education in computer science and engineering. A prolific researcher and educator, Dr. Fonkam's interests span various aspects of computer science, including open-source software development, AI, data science, machine learning, and blockchain technology. His publications and conference presentations address a wide range of topics from systems dynamics to the application of ICTs in crisis management. Dr. Mathias Mbu Fonkam is a dedicated educator and researcher whose work continues to influence the fields of information technology and computer science education, preparing the next generation of IT professionals and scholars.

* * *

Omid Afsharpour is pursuing a Master of Finance at Iowa State University, where he passionately explores the intersections of corporate finance, entrepreneurship, and artificial intelligence. With a keen interest in innovative financial strategies, Omid aims to leverage AI to enhance decision-making processes within the finance sector. He is also fascinated by the potential of AI in education and entrepreneurship, seeking to explore how technology can drive growth and learning. Outside of his studies, he enjoys collaborating on projects that bridge technology and finance, aspiring to contribute to the future of the industry.

Andi Asrifan, S.Pd, M.Pd, a distinguished figure in the realm of education, particularly in English Language Education, has made significant contributions through his extensive research, teaching, and leadership roles. As the Head of the Institute for Cooperation and International Affairs at Universitas Muhammadiyah Sidenreng Rappang and now a lecturer in Universitas Negeri Makassar (UNM), Dr. Asrifan's academic journey is marked by a rich tapestry of achievements, including a Doctor of Education in English Language Education. His work spans various facets of education, language, and technology, reflecting the diverse topics covered in his publications and research endeavors. These include, but are not limited to, the impact of the COVID-19 pandemic on educational practices, methodologies in English as a Foreign Language (EFL) classrooms, and the integration of technology in teaching and learning processes. Dr. Asrifan's commitment to advancing educational standards and practices is further evidenced by his active participation in international conferences, webinars, and workshops across countries like India, the Philippines, and Pakistan. These events, organized by various institutions and associations, underscore his role as a global educator and thought leader. His dedication to professional development is also highlighted through his involvement in numerous courses and certifications in personal branding, public speaking, and literacy teaching. Moreover, Dr. Asrifan's leadership extends beyond academia into organizational and educational development, where he has served in various capacities, including as an external examiner for Ph.D. dissertations and a reviewer for scientific journals. His accolades, memberships in professional organizations, and roles as an ambassador for international associations speak volumes of his influence and commitment to fostering educational excellence and sustainable development goals globally.

Steven M. Baule is an Associate Professor of Leadership Education at Winona State University, where he also serves as Director of the Education Doctorate Program. He holds a Ph.D. in Leadership and Educational Policy Studies from Loyola University Chicago and an Ed.D. in Instructional Technology from Northern Illinois University. Dr. Baule's extensive academic career includes numerous publications and presentations focusing on educational leadership, instructional technology, and school library development. He has authored several books and articles that delve into topics such as technology planning, leadership, and historical research.

Simon C. H. Chan is a lecturer at Department of Management and Marketing, Faculty of Business,The Hong Kong Polytechnic University. He has published research papers in Academy of Management Journal, Journal of Organizational Behavior, Journal of Education for Business, etc. His main research interests focus mainly on organizational behavior, leadership, and education.

Yiming Chen, with nearly 20 years of experience in innovation and entrepreneurship education, has dedicated his career to empowering students to navigate the rapidly evolving landscape of science and technology. His work emphasizes the integration of emerging technologies and efficiency tools within educational practices, fostering both academic excellence and the development of practical, career-ready skills. Through a blend of research and applied initiatives, Yiming is committed to enhancing student learning experiences by leveraging advanced tools and methodologies that equip them for the demands of the modern workforce.

Nurul Ain Chua Binti Abdullah is a senior lecturer at Universiti Malaysia Terengganu (UMT), specializing in Mandarin as a foreign language for non-native learners. With over 30 years of experience in education, she has taught at all levels, from primary to tertiary, and is deeply engaged in research on Mandarin language acquisition and educational technology in language learning. Dr. Nurul Ain has presented extensively at national and international conferences, sharing insights from her research. Her primary research interests include mobile learning integration in Mandarin education, language pedagogy, and the development of language teaching materials.

Tapash Das is an Assistant Professor of Education at Kazi Nazrul University in Asansol, West Bengal, India, with over five years of teaching experience. He holds an M.A., M.Phil., and Ph.D. in Education and has qualified for the UGC NET/JRF and WB-SET in Education. Dr. Das has contributed numerous chapters to national and international edited volumes and published several articles in reputable peer-reviewed journals with high impact factors. He has also actively participated in various national and international conferences and seminars, where he has presented his research.

Elpisah earned her Doctorate from Makassar State University and currently serves as a faculty member at Patompo University, specializing in Economics and Management Education. As the Director of the Graduate School at Patompo University, she actively advances her professional expertise through participation in various training programs organized by the Directorate of Higher Education of the Republic of Indonesia. Her academic contributions are substantial, with seven educational books to her credit. In recognition of her dedication to community service, the Mayor of Makassar honored her with the title of Economic Facilitator as part of the National Community Empowerment Program. This accolade highlights her influential role in promoting economic development and empowerment initiatives at the community level. Elpisah's academic and community involvement reflects a profound commitment to enhancing educational and economic systems, making meaningful contributions within academia and in the broader community. Her achievements demonstrate a dedication to lifelong learning and community progress, bridging her expertise in economics and management education with impactful applications that support local and national development efforts.

Tarini Halder is working as a Professor in the Department of Education, University of Kalyani, Kalyani, Nadia, West Bengal, India. He obtained an M.A. in History and Education, and a Ph.D. in Education from the University of Kalyani, West Bengal, India. He has qualified for NET and SET in education. He has acted as a resource person in many national and international seminars and conferences and presented many research his research work at many universities, state, national, and international level seminars, and conferences. He has published more than 50 papers in peer-reviewed national and international journals and more than 20 book chapters in edited books. Along with these publications he also published more than 10 textbooks for different higher education level courses. Under his supervision, many scholars were awarded M.Phil. and Ph.D. degrees.

Herlina, M.Pd., stands out as a distinguished academician with a comprehensive background in early childhood education. Her journey in the educational sector is marked by a blend of extensive educational qualifications and a rich tapestry of work experiences that span across various facets of early childhood education. Dr. Herlina's commitment to the field is further underscored by her active participation in numerous organizational activities and research projects, which highlight her dedication to advancing educational practices and policies. Her scholarly contributions are evident in her array of scientific publications, which not only add to the body of knowledge in her field but also serve as a testament to her expertise and scholarly rigor. Beyond her academic and professional endeavors, Dr. Herlina has also proven her mettle in the competitive arena of scientific research and innovation. Her prowess was nationally recognized when she emerged as a winner in a prestigious national scientific work competition. This accolade is not just a personal achievement for Dr. Herlina but also a moment of pride for the academic and educational communities she represents. It underscores her ability to blend theoretical knowledge with practical insights, thereby creating impactful educational solutions and innovations. Dr. Herlina's journey and achievements illuminate the path for future educators and researchers, embodying the essence of dedication, innovation, and excellence in the field of early childhood education.

Amaresh Jha is an experienced media professional: has been a Senior Producer with Zee News, News Express, TV9, India News, and India TV and has also produced news for DD News. Amaresh has previously taught at Amity University (where he led the UG Program at Amity School of Communication) and Galgotias University. Apart from his work as a multimedia professional, Amaresh's previous teaching includes courses on the web journalism, data journalism, multimedia storytelling, television production, digital media production, and communication research- among other things. Amaresh is a reviewer and article editor of reputed journals published by SAGE and CG Network, USA.

Nagihan Kadıoğlu received her master's degree in chemistry education from Hacettepe University in 2021 and is currently a research assistant in the Department of Chemistry Education at the same institution. Since beginning her doctoral studies, she has focused on the impact of contemporary educational philosophies and technologies on learning environments, with particular emphasis on the flipped learning model. Her research interests also include the application of augmented reality—a rapidly advancing technology in the field of education—to enhance chemistry education.

Ashabul Kahfi Susanto is a dedicated full-time lecturer and researcher in English Department at the Faculty of Language and Literature, Universitas Negeri Makassar, Indonesia. He is also a PhD candidate in Linguistics at the University of Aberdeen, UK. In 2015, Ashabul completed his bachelor's degree in English literature at Hasanuddin University, Indonesia. Following this, he earned his MA in Cross-Cultural Communication and Applied Linguistics from Newcastle University, UK, in 2017. This degree was funded by the Indonesia Endowment Fund for Education (LPDP) Scholarship, which is administered by the Ministry of Finance of Indonesia. His research interests encompass a broad range of topics, including applied linguistics, interactional sociolinguistics, intercultural communication, and discourse analysis—specifically traditional discourse analysis, conversation analysis, and multimodal discourse analysis. Additionally, he focuses on language use in society, exploring how language functions within various social contexts. Ashabul has published several journal articles in the field of applied linguistics, contributing to ongoing discussions and research within this discipline.

Santu Karmakar holds a Master of Arts in Education from Kazi Nazrul University and has a keen research interest in areas such as education, artificial intelligence, sustainability, and related fields. He has contributed several book chapters published on national and international platforms, including works with esteemed publishers like Springer Nature and Taylor & Francis.

Stephen Ko is a lecturer at the Department of Management and Marketing of the Hong Kong Polytechnic University. His research interests include innovation, entrepreneurship, and business education. He published dozens of business cases and other scholarly articles. Currently, he is an Associate Editor of the Journal of Education for Business. He is also an Asia Editor for the Journal of Global Business and Technology, and serves on the editorial review boards of SAGE Business Cases and Emerging Markets Case Studies.

Dhurata Lamçja is a lecturer specializing in Academic Writing for Bachelor's Psychology students, as well as Class Management and Media for Preschool Education majors. Until October 2023, she served as Deputy Director and taught Albanian Language and Literature at the upper secondary level. A distinguished educator with a strong academic foundation, Dhurata holds a Doctor of Science degree in Literature, earned through her research on the poetics of 1980s short prose. Her dedication to academic excellence is demonstrated through her evaluations as a Specialist Teacher in 2006, Qualified Teacher in 2011, and Master Teacher in 2021, all with "Very Good" distinctions. Her educational background includes a postdoctoral program in active learning and a scientific master's degree in Organizational Psychology. In her role as Deputy Director, Dhurata combines her expertise in literature, psychology, and pedagogy to foster a holistic approach to student development.

Jennifer Lanham is an academic and practitioner with extensive expertise in psychology, social work, and mental health. She obtained her BA in Psychology and Family Studies and her Master of Social Work from the University of Kentucky and completed her Ph.D. coursework at the University of Denver, focusing on Global Social Work. With over thirty years of experience as a psychotherapist, Dr. Lanham specializes in mental health and substance use disorders. She holds a tenured professorship at Campbellsville University, where she has served for a decade. As the primary professor for the Clinical Area of Focus, she teaches Psychopathology, World Problems, and Advocacy, and guides students in international peacebuilding studies and sectarian conflict in Ireland. Dr. Lanham's contributions to social work include her publication "Transformational Learning Abroad: Social Work Students and NGOs Collaborating to Revitalize Conflict-Affected Communities Through Peacebuilding Initiatives" and her co-creation of a Faculty-to-Faculty Guide for the National Council for Mental Wellbeing, which enhances the education of social work students in opioid and substance use disorders. Her role in the Opioid Crisis Community Needs Assessment demonstrates her dedication to tackling public health challenges. Her scholarly work also features numerous peer-reviewed presentations on the use of artificial intelligence in trauma-informed interventions for conflict-impacted communities and the promotion of inclusive educational settings. Dr. Lanham's efforts to expand the number of professionals of color and her advocacy for culturally sensitive practices highlight her commitment to fostering diversity and excellence in the field of social work education.

Ankur Nandi is currently a Ph.D. scholar and Senior Research Fellow in the Department of Education at the University of Kalyani, Nadia, West Bengal, India. He holds a B.A. (Hons), an M.A., and an M.Phil. in Education and has qualified for both the UGC NET/JRF and WB-SET in Education. With over 25 papers published in peer-reviewed national and international journals and more than 10 book chapters in edited volumes, he has made substantial contributions to the field. Additionally, Mr. Nandi has actively participated in various national and international conferences and seminars, where he has presented his research.

Jordan O'Connell is a community college leader with a passion for using technology to enhance students' learning experiences. He has over 13 years of experience across three community colleges, serving as an instructional designer, associate professor, and student success coach. O'Connell is currently pursuing a Doctor of Education in Education at Winona State University. He holds a Master of Arts in History from the University of Wisconsin-Eau Claire and has completed coursework towards a Master of Arts in Political Science. His teaching experience spans online, hybrid, and face-to-face formats, including courses in both American history and government. O'Connell is a frequent presenter at educational conferences and is a published author, with recent articles appearing in eCampus News and Essays in Education.

Özge Özyalçın Oskay graduated from Hacettepe University's Faculty of Education in 2001. She earned her M.Sc. in science education from Hacettepe University in 2003 and completed her Ph.D. in 2007 in the Department of Mathematics and Science Education. In 2010, she was appointed as an Assistant Professor in the Department of Chemistry Education at Hacettepe University, where she received the title of Associate Professor in 2013. Since 2018, she has served as a Professor in the same department. Her primary research interests include teaching and learning methods, educational technologies, flipped learning, and technological pedagogical content knowledge.

Salvina Pellumbi has been a STEM teacher since 2017. For several years, she served as a curriculum development specialist at the city's Education Office, where she closely monitored advancements in technology within Albanian education. Currently, she is actively involved with local NGOs as an expert in education and the integration of technology in teaching.

Aidin Salamzadeh is the Vice Dean of the College of Management (University of Tehran) and an integrated researcher at CIICESI, Polytechnic of Porto (Portugal). His interests are startups, new venture creation, and entrepreneurship. Aidin serves as an associate editor for the Humanities and Social Sciences Communications (Nature.com); Journal of Enterprising Communities; Revista de Gestão; Innovation Management Review (Emerald), Entrepreneurial Business and Economics Review, Journal of Women's Entrepreneurship and Education, as well as The Bottom Line (Emerald). Besides, he is a reviewer in numerous distinguished international journals. Aidin is a member of the European SPES Forum (Belgium), the Asian Academy of Management (Malaysia), Ondokuz Mayis University (Turkey), and the Institute of Economic Sciences (Serbia). He co-founded the Innovation and Entrepreneurship Research Lab (London). In 2024, Stanford University listed him as the top 2% scientists.

Syamsuardi Saodi was born in Bulu, Lappariaja District, on February 10, 1983. He is the second child of H. Saodi Nuntung and Hj. Haneria Haddaning. He began his elementary education at State Elementary School 146 Bengo and continued to SLTP Negeri 2 Lappariaja and SMA Negeri 1 Lappariaja. He earned his bachelor's degree from the State University of Makassar in Automotive Engineering Education in 2000 and completed his master's degree in Language Studies with a concentration in Early Childhood Education at the same university in 2006. Dr. Syamsuardi completed his Ph.D. in Educational Sciences at the State University of Makassar in 2021. Dr. Syamsuardi is a permanent lecturer in the Early Childhood Teacher Education Study Program at the Faculty of Education, State University of Makassar.

He has held various significant positions, including Head of the Early Childhood Teacher Education Study Program (2014-2018), Coordinator of the Center for Cooperation and Innovation Development in Education (2021-2022), and Head of the Curriculum and Entrepreneurship Module Center at the Institute for Innovation and Entrepreneurship Development (LIPK) from 2021 to 2025.

Karima Sayari is an Associate Professor in the Department of Managerial and Financial Sciences at Al Zahra College for Women. She holds a bachelor's degree in international trade, a master's degree in economics and international finance, and a PhD in Finance and Economic Sciences. Dr. Sayari has over 10 years of teaching experience and has published extensively in reputable international journals indexed in Scopus and Web of Science. Her research focuses on economics, finance, banking, and digital finance. She is an active peer reviewer in various academic journals.

Indrani Sen is a self-employed professional artist specializing in fine arts, with a diploma from the All India Fine Arts Association and over 20 years of experience in painting and teaching. Her areas of expertise include portraiture, landscapes, glass, and mixed media painting. In addition to her art qualifications, she holds a postgraduate degree in library and information science from IGNOU. Her interests include reading, travel, and painting. She has also contributed to the field of knowledge management, authoring and presenting a research paper titled "Knowledge Management Strategies, Processes and Tools in Learning Organizations: A Review" at the IBS Hyderabad International Conference in 2020.

Subhasis Sen holds an MBA from Jadavpur University Kolkata, an M.Phil. from Bharati Vidyapeeth Deemed University Pune, and a Ph.D. in business management from the University of Calcutta. He is currently a professor of marketing at BITM, Sri Balaji University, Pune, with 25 years of experience in both corporate and academic settings. His teaching interests include marketing research, sports management, and digital marketing. Dr. Sen has authored research papers, case studies, and book chapters indexed in Scopus, ABDC, and UGC Care. His research interests span sports analytics, sport-for-development, attendance behavior in sports events, leadership personality traits, social media advertising, digital inclusion, and quality of life. An avid sports enthusiast, Dr. Sen has won multiple awards, including first place in the Fitness for Freedom Half Marathon organized by Symbiosis International University Pune (three times), winner of the inter-collegiate football tournament in Kolkata, and best paper awards in marketing strategy at the SIBM International Conference Pune and Lexicon International Conference Pune. He has also conducted corporate training for prominent public and private sector companies and promoted executive education for SCMHRD Pune.

Sanjeev Singh is an experienced journalist and digital media expert with a deep passion for emerging technologies. With a background in both journalism and AI, Sanjeev has spent more than a decade exploring the nexus of these fields. Sanjeev is now busy preparing the next generation of content creators as Dean, Times School of Media, Bennett University. Having worked as a journalist, author, content producer in senior positions in Digital, TV, Print Media, and academia, Sanjeev is committed to empowering the next generation of journalists with the tools and knowledge they need to succeed in a rapidly changing landscape.

Garreth Smith is a Lecturer extensively qualified in Applied Social Science, Youth Work, and Community Development. He possesses a Master's degree and a Bachelor of Arts (Hons) in Applied Social Science, as well as a Diploma in Community and Youth Work, all from Maynooth University. Additionally, he holds a Higher Diploma in Management for the Community and Voluntary Sector from Dublin City University. Garreth lectures on Youth Work, Community Development, Social Entrepreneurship and Funding, and Facilitation and Group Work. He is a member of the Youth Work Educators Forum and the All-Ireland Endorsement Body for Community Work. An active academic researcher, Garreth focuses on anti-racism, youth work practice, and community development within educational settings. His work includes embedding anti-racism in youth and community work curricula, and he has presented at various conferences on creating supportive pathways for marginalized students and the importance of supervision in youth worker education and professional formation. His significant contributions are evident in the Irish Journal of Academic Practice and at the Universal Design in Higher Education in Transition conference, showcasing his dedication to the progression of community and youth work.

Goh Ying Soon is a senior lecturer at MARA University of Technology, Malaysia, where he teaches Mandarin as a third language to non-native learners. A member of the International Society for Chinese Language Teaching, he brings over 25 years of experience teaching Mandarin at the primary, secondary, and tertiary levels. Dr. Goh is an active contributor to national and international conferences, presenting research on educational technology in Mandarin language teaching, web-based instruction, and translation. His academic profiles can be found on Google Scholar, ResearchGate, and Academia.edu, with his work indexed in CNKI and Scopus (Author ID: 25925392000).

Suyan Zhang is an Associate Professor at Shandong Jianzhu University, Jinan, China, holding a Doctorate in Education. Her research focuses on factors influencing student engagement in task-based learning within blended English learning environments. Dr. Zhang recently co-authored a study with Dr. Yingsoon Goh, titled "Correlational Study of Factors Affecting Students' Perceived Engagement in Task-Based Learning Under Blended English Learning Environment," which was presented at the 2023 International Conference on University Teaching and Learning (InCULT) and published by IEEE.

Mahnaz Zolfaghari is pursuing a Ph.D. in Curriculum and Instruction with a focus on Science Education at Indiana University Bloomington. Her research centers on the application of artificial intelligence in education, aiming to uncover its impact on educational practices and learning outcomes. Approaching her work as an educational entrepreneur, Mahnaz examines how AI can transform the educational landscape by enhancing student engagement and instructional strategies. This research builds on her year-long master's thesis in Educational Administration at the University of Tehran, where she began investigating the role of emerging technologies in education.

Index

A

B

C

T

U

www.ingramcontent.com/pod-product-compliance
Lightning Source LLC
LaVergne TN
LVHW080613300926
849162LV00005B/1142
9798337310176